Twentieth-Century Russian Drama
From Gorky to the Present

TWENTIETH-CENTURY RUSSIAN DRAMA

From Gorky to the Present

HAROLD B. SEGEL

New York   Columbia University Press   *1979*

Library of Congress Cataloging in Publication Data

Segel, Harold B   1930–
Twentieth-century Russian drama.

Bibliography: p.
Includes index.
1. Russian drama—20th century—History and criticism.
I. Title.
PG3086.S44   891.7′2′509   79-11673
ISBN 0-231-04576-X
ISBN 0-231-04577-8 pbk.

Columbia University Press
New York   Guildford, Surrey

For
Aunt Jeanne
*whose love for Russian art accompanied
her to the stage*

Contents

	Preface	*ix*
ONE	In Search of the New Russian: Gorky's Prerevolutionary Plays	*1*
TWO	Gorky's Later Plays: The Soviet Period	*29*
THREE	The Revolt Against Naturalism: Symbolism, Neo-Romanticism, and Theatricalism	*50*
FOUR	The 1920s and Early 1930s: The Revolution and the Civil War in Russian Drama	*147*
FIVE	The 1920s and Early 1930s: Social Comedy, Absurd and Grotesque NEP Satire, Melodrama	*182*
SIX	Out of the Mainstream: Serapions and Oberiuty	*222*
SEVEN	The 1930s: Socialist Construction and Socialist Realism	*239*
EIGHT	The Fantasy World of Yevgeni Shvarts	*281*
NINE	The Gathering Clouds: On the Eve of War	*295*
TEN	The War Years	*305*
ELEVEN	The "Freeze" of 1946 to 1952	*318*
TWELVE	The "Thaw" of 1953 and 1954	*333*
THIRTEEN	From the Twentieth Party Congress to 1959: The "Year of Protest" and Its Aftermath	*342*
FOURTEEN	The New Theatricalism	*360*
FIFTEEN	The Dissidents: Ivanov, Amalrik, Solzhenitsyn	*380*
SIXTEEN	From Dissent to Divertissement: The 1960s and 1970s	*407*
	Appendix: Guide to Pronunciation	*457*
	Notes	*465*
	Bibliography	*475*
	Index	*491*

Preface

———

THE LATE nineteenth and early twentieth centuries were the golden years of the Russian theater. They brought to prominence the Moscow Art Theater, Stanislavsky, the Method, and then the brilliant avant-garde of Meyerhold, Tairov, and Vakhtangov. The memorable première of *The Seagull*, which was immortalized in the curtain emblem of the Moscow Art Theater, thrust onto the stage of world drama a writer named Anton Chekhov.

Chekhov's international fame owed much to the association with the Moscow Art Theater, but the relationship became symbiotic; each enhanced the reputation of the other and for a time each became virtually synonomous with the other. The long popularity of the Method ensured Chekhov's enshrinement. It was, after all, on the basis of the Art Theater's productions of Chekhov's plays that the Method was to be assimilated. And it was from the plays themselves that the new drama of nuance and innuendo, of indirection and understatement, was to be fashioned.

The dissemination of the great achievements of the Russian stage in the age of Stanislavsky and the Moscow Art Theater has done much, certainly, to enhance the general image of Russian culture. With time and the inevitable expansion of horizons a fuller appreciation of the wealth of early twentieth-century Russian art has become possible. Eisenstein is now a revered name in the annals of cinema and the source of much modern film technique. The Russian theatrical avant-garde that set itself in opposition to the "fourth wall" representationalism of the Moscow Art Theater has at last assumed its rightful place in the sun. Meyerhold has never been more admired, and written about, than at present and lest there be any doubts as to the lasting impact of his innovations one need but consider the work of such outstanding contemporary directors as Peter Brook and Jerzy Grotowski.

As odd as it may seem, the admiration for and subsequent romance with the Russian theater has not been paralleled by similar enthusiasm

for Russian drama. By way of partial rationalization, it ought to be said at
the outset that the accomplishments of early twentieth-century Russian
theater as well as of Russian ballet, music, and painting outshine those
of the drama despite the excellence of turn-of-the-century Russian literature in general. The one exception is Chekhov, but as I pointed out
before, the reputation of Chekhov's playwriting in the West is difficult
to dissociate at least in its early phases from the popularity of the Moscow Art Theater. The historical situation must also be taken into account. It was only in the late seventeenth century that the art of the
stage was introduced into Russia and only in the second half of the eighteenth century, in the comedies of Denis Fonvizin (1745–92), that anything plausibly original began appearing. Furthermore, from the nineteenth century to the Revolution of 1917 Russia had few major writers
who directed their talents exclusively or predominantly to the drama
(the only two in the nineteenth century were Aleksandr Ostrovsky,
1823–86, who is now antiquated, and Aleksandr Sukhovo-Kobylin,
1817–1903, who was "rediscovered" in the 1920s and is barely known
outside Russia). For such reasons, Russian drama has long seemed to be
a poorer cousin of Russian poetry and prose fiction. Thus, when Stanislavsky and the Moscow Art Theater, and a Chekhov hoisted high on the
shoulders of the Art Theater, attracted worldwide attention the neglect
of the Russian dramatic past was, if anything, reinforced. Chekhov
seemed to be all or most of what Russian drama had to offer and the tendency has been to treat him in a vacuum. The opera based on Pushkin's
Shakespearean *Boris Godunov*, a popular film version of Gogol's superb
comedy *The Inspector-General*, and occasional productions of Turgenev's drama of gentlefolk frustrations, *A Month in the Country*,
have done little to redress the balance.

Russian drama of the twentieth century is even less well known despite the popularity of Andreev's grim circus play *He Who Gets Slapped*,
the flirtation of the American stage with Soviet drama in the 1920s and
1930s, and the reappearance of Soviet plays (by Arbuzov, Bulgakov,
Roshchin, Vampilov) on American stages in the 1960s and 1970s. A
significant Gorky revival has occurred in England and America in the
past few years but productions of Gorky's plays are still rare in comparison to those of Chekhov. The complex and fascinating neo-Romantic,
Symbolist, and theatricalist currents in Russian drama from 1900 to the
Revolution are still almost completely obscured by the preoccupation
with both Chekhov and the theater. Since the Revolution, the universal
assumption has been that Soviet regimentation of the arts has stifled

creativity and that because of its nature—its immediacy, its direct contact with audiences—drama has fared the worst. Hence, the emergence of fine new talents in the Russian theater in the decades following Stanislavsky and the avant-garde—Nikolai Akimov, Anatoli Efros, Yuri Lyubimov, Nikolai Okhlopkov, Georgi Tovstonogov, Galina Volchok, Oleg Yefremov—once again focuses attention on theatrical achievement and underscores the neglect of drama.

One regrettable consequence of such an uneven distribution of interest has been the inadequate exploration of the entire history of Russian dramatic literature. We can see this, above all, in the absence in the West of books on Russian drama as drama, apart from studies of Chekhov. Anyone curious about the evolution of the drama in Russia has had to consult encyclopedia articles or search out material on drama in general surveys of Russian literature (in which the level of discussion, qualitatively and quantitatively, falls far below that of other literary genres) or in studies of Russian theater where theater history naturally takes precedence over the drama as literature.

In undertaking a book on twentieth-century Russian drama my aim has been to fill a gap that has existed for too long. The original plan called for a survey of Russian drama from its seventeenth-century origins down to the present. In view of the absence of books on the subject and the unfamiliarity with many of the authors and plays in the West, such a study would have had to include much descriptive as well as historical and critical matter if it was to be more than just a catalogue. The material proved to be too vast to fit comfortably into the confines of a medium-sized volume. The decision to opt instead for a survey limited to the twentieth century was motivated by the following considerations.

Although the drama of the "classical age" of Russian literature—the nineteenth century—has so far been negligibly studied in the West, several of the more prominent writers who wrote plays (Pushkin, Lermontov, Gogol, Ostrovsky, Turgenev, Tolstoy) are familiar. Besides, standard surveys of Russian literature do provide information on the drama. For the period from Chekhov to the present, however, the same cannot be said. Almost all the writing on the early twentieth-century Russian theater has emphasized the stage. Studies of Chekhov usually have little or nothing to say about other dramatists of his time. Books on Russian literature since the Revolution have dealt with the drama even more curtly than the general literary histories focused primarily on the nineteenth century. The result is that twentieth-century Russian drama after Chekhov is a virtual *terra incognita*. To be sure, much Soviet Russian drama has been written in response to and in support of the official ideology. But to dismiss all postrevolutionary Russian drama as a wasteland is as simplistic as it is unfair. The 1920s marked one of the most exciting and colorful periods in the history of Russian art and the drama was no exception. Indeed, a study devoted wholly to the drama of the 1920s would be a valid and welcome contribution. There were lively debates on the drama and interesting plays written in the 1930s and early 1940s. The delightful and quite theatrical fairy-tale satires of Yevgeni Shvarts, for example, surely deserve more recognition than they presently enjoy. Since the waning of the Cold War and the death of Stalin in 1953, Russian drama has pursued different directions and shown signs of considerable variety and vitality in a continuing search for the integrity of individual expression. That there is a growing perception of this in the West is evidenced by the announcement reported by the *New York Times* on May 30, 1979, that Joseph Papp of the New York Shakespeare Festival and the Public Theater is negotiating with the Soviet Union for a theatrical exchange that will bring five recent Russian plays to this country. This comes two years after the more theatrically oriented American-Soviet stage initiative of 1977 which resulted in visits to the United States of such prominent Moscow directors as Efros of the Malaya Bronnaya Theater, Golchok of the Sovremennik, Yefremov of the Moscow Art Theater, and productions of two plays by the popular Soviet dramatist Roshchin.

Everything considered, a reasonable argument can be made that even granting the relatively small number of outstanding Soviet plays since the end of World War II, the twentieth century as a whole has seen more notable achievements in Russian drama and theater than the preceding "classical age." The brilliance of the early twentieth-century Russian theater is now universally acknowledged. If we recognize, moreover, that twentieth-century Russian drama begins, in fact, with Chekhov, that a number of fine plays were written in Russia in the decade and a half before the Revolution by writers long dwarfed by Chekhov's immense reputation, such writers as Blok, Kuzmin, Remizov, Sologub, and Yevreinov, in addition to the better-known Gorky and Andreev, that the remarkable era of the twenties produced a rich harvest of drama especially in the field of comedy (Bulgakov, Erdman, Mayakovsky), and that the history of the drama within the context of Soviet literary development is hardly devoid of interest, the argument may not seem so unreasonable or partisan.

Since the purpose of this book is to present the first survey in English

of Russian drama since Chekhov, that is from Gorky, who was the first
contemporary of Chekhov to achieve fame as a dramatist, to the present,
I have included more descriptive material about many of the plays than
one might expect to find in an account of a more familiar dramatic tradition. I have tried, however, to make this material as much a part of the
play analyses as possible. I also want to emphasize that this is a book
about the drama as literature written for the theater. Because I am writing primarily about plays and not about theater, whatever pertains to
stage production is introduced only where there is a particular relevance
to the play or plays being discussed.

To make the book more useful to the reader I have included two ap-
pendixes. For the reader who does not know Russian and may want to
locate available translations there is a list of twentieth-century Russian
drama in English. All information about translations is located here
rather than in chapter notes or in the general bibliography. The second
appendix is just a list of the more important Russian names occurring in
the book with accents marked to facilitate pronunciation for the non-
Russian speaker. Three additional technical points: a) dates after play
titles are those of known composition or revision unless otherwise indicated; b) quotations from plays in English are from available translations;
where such translations seemed inadequate or where none were available, translations are mine; and c) all Russian names are transliterated in
such a way as to make them easy enough to pronounce without making
the Latinized versions look absurd on the page and without straying far
from accepted transliteration formulae. But since there are different
approaches to transliterating from the Cyrillic alphabet used by the Russians to the Latin, discrepancies inevitably appear in citations from other
sources where spellings have not been changed to bring them into conformity with my own practice. Thus, my "Yevreinov" and "Andreev,"
for example, may be someone else's "Evreinov" and "Andreyev." This
will, I hope, not prove distracting in the pages ahead.

Acknowledgments

The author wishes to express his thanks to the following publishers for permission to quote from the sources listed:

Yale/Theatre, where some of the Gorky material first appeared in my article "Gorky's Major Plays."

Columbia University Press: an excerpt from *Letters of Gorky and Andreev 1899–1912*, Peter Yershov, ed. Lydia Weston, tr. Copyright 1958 Columbia University Press.

Simon and Schuster, a Division of Gulf & Western Corporation: excerpts from *Vladimir Mayakovsky, The Bedbug*, and *The Bathhouse*, in *The Complete Plays of Vladimir Mayakovsky*, Guy Daniels, tr. Copyright © 1968 Washington Square Press, Inc.

Harcourt Brace Jovanovich: excerpts from the plays of Amalrik in *Nose! Nose? No-se! and Other Plays*, Daniel Weissbort, tr. Introduction and English translation copyright © 1973 Harcourt Brace Jovanovich, Inc.

University of Minnesota Press: excerpts from Volodin's *Five Evenings*, Ariadne Nicolaeff, tr. Copyright © 1966 University of Minnesota Press.

Cornell University Press: excerpts from the "Oberiu Manifesto," Kharms' *Elizabeth Bam*, and Vvedensky's *Christmas at the Ivanovs* in *Russia's Lost Literature of the Absurd: Selected Works of Daniel Kharms and Aleksandr Vvedensky*, George Gibian, tr., ed. Copyright © 1971 Cornell University Press.

Indiana University Press: excerpts from Bulgakov's *Flight* in *The Early Plays of Mikhail Bulgakov*, Ellendea Proffer, ed. Carl R. Proffer and Ellendea Proffer, tr. Copyright © 1972 Indiana University Press.

Yale University Press: excerpts from *Barbarians, Enemies, Queer People*, and *Vassa Zheleznova* in *Seven Plays of Maxim Gorky*, Alexander Bakshy, tr., in collaboration with Paul S. Nathan. Copyright 1945 Yale University Press.

Hugh McLean: excerpts from Kron's "A Writer's Notes" and Alyoshin's "Alone" in *The Year of Protest, 1956: An Anthology of Soviet Literary Materials*, Hugh McLean and Walter N. Vickery, trs. and eds. Copyright © 1961 Hugh McLean.

Random House: excerpts from Gorky's *The Lower Depths*, Andreev's *He Who Gets Slapped*, and Shvarts' *The Shadow* in *An Anthology of Russian Plays*, vol. 2: *1890–1960*, F. D. Reeve, tr. Copyright © 1963 F. D. Reeve.

Bobbs-Merrill: excerpts from Pogodin's *A Petrarchan Sonnet* and Shvarts' *The Naked King* in *Contemporary Russian Drama*, F. D. Reeve, tr. Copyright © 1968 Bobbs-Merrill Co., Inc.

Farrar, Straus & Giroux: excerpts from Solzhenitsyn's *The Love-Girl and the Innocent*, Nicholas Bethell and David Burg, trs. English translation copyright © 1969 The Bodley Head.

Drama and Theater: an excerpt from Lunts' Afterword to *Bertran de Born*, Gary Kern, tr. Copyright © 1970 Gary Kern.

The Drama Review: excerpts from Sologub's "The Theatre of One Will," Daniel Gerould, tr. Copyright © 1978 Daniel Gerould.

Performing Arts Journal: an excerpt from Bely's *The Jaws of Night*, Daniel Gerould, tr. Copyright © 1978 Daniel Gerould.

Penguin Books: excerpts from Shvarts' *The Dragon*, Max Hayward and Harold Shukman, trs. in *Three Soviet Plays*, Michael Glenny, ed. Translation copyright © 1966 Max Hayward and Harold Shukman.

Andrew R. MacAndrew: excerpts from Olesha's *A List of Assets* and speech to First Congress of Soviet Writers in *Envy and Other Works*, Andrew R. MacAndrew, tr. Copyright © 1967 Andrew R. MacAndrew.

Houghton Mifflin: excerpts from Afinogenov's *Fear*, Glebov's *Inga*, and Kirshon's *Bread* in *Six Soviet Plays*, Eugene Lyons, ed. Copyright 1934 Houghton Mifflin Company.

For permission to print the photographs appearing in the book, many thanks are due the Performing Arts Research Center of the New York Public Library at Lincoln Center; the Harvard Theatre Collection, whose staff made accessible to me the riches of the H.W.L. Dana Collection and was unstinting in their assistance; and the Long Wharf Theatre of New Haven, the Alley Theatre of Houston, and the Arena Stage of Washington, D.C.—all noteworthy for their productions of Russian plays in the United States. Thanks are also in order to the Department of Slavic Languages of Columbia University for a subsidy to defray some of the expense of printing the photographic material in the book.

My greatest debt of gratitude, herewith happily and sincerely acknowledged, is to the students in my Russian drama courses at Columbia and one fine term at the Slavic Institute of the University of Stockholm who first encouraged me to do the book and to friends and colleagues in this country and elsewhere who ask no credit but whose interest, encouragement, and advice made all the difference in the world.

Last, but certainly not least, a special word of thanks to Joan McQuary and William F. Bernhardt of Columbia University Press for their patience and understanding throughout.

Twentieth-Century Russian Drama
From Gorky to the Present

ONE

In Search of the New Russian: Gorky's Prerevolutionary Plays

"I AM SORRY that apparently you have decided against coming to Yalta. The Art Theater will be here from Moscow in May. It will give five performances and then remain for rehearsals. Do come. You'll study the techniques of the stage at the rehearsals, and then be able to write a play in five to eight days, which I would welcome happily with all my heart."[1]

So wrote Chekhov to his devoted younger admirer Aleksei Peshkov (better known throughout the world by his assumed name Maxim Gorky, "Max the Bitter," 1868–1936) from the Crimean city of Yalta on February 15, 1900. Probably neither writer had any premonition of the outcome of the invitation and Chekhov could only have been facetious in suggesting to the impressionable Gorky that, never having written a play before, he—Gorky—would be able to compose one in about a week's time after observing performances of the touring Moscow Art Theater.

Chekhov repeated his invitation on March 6 and this time Gorky accepted. The subsequent visit with Chekhov, attendance at performances of the Art Theater, and personal meetings with Stanislavsky, Nemirovich-Danchenko, and other members of the company which Chekhov arranged, charmed Gorky beyond measure. Already awed by Chekhov's success as a dramatist and the rapid rise to fame of the Art Theater, Gorky soon became convinced that he, too, was destined to make a name for himself in the theater. After all, Chekhov and now the Moscow Art Theater were urging him to turn to the drama and the climate of expectation about his future contributions to the Russian stage that greeted him in Yalta dissipated any doubts which might still have been lingering.

If not within days of his meetings with the Moscow Art Theater in Yalta, then within a few months Gorky was obsessed with the idea of writing a play. How uncertain he still was about dramatic composition was revealed in a letter to Chekhov in early July 1900 when Gorky asked why a play had to have a third act.[2]

From the correspondence between Chekhov and Gorky from September 1900 to September 1901,[3] the evidence mounts that despite claims to the contrary Gorky was, in fact, anxiously struggling with a literary form new to him. Compassionate as ever, aware of Gorky's frustration at not being able to bend the drama to his will as easily as the short story and the novel, Chekhov counselled patience and tenacity:

> Finish the play, my dear, by all means. You feel that it is not turning out as you would like, but don't trust your feeling; it deceives you. One usually dislikes a play when writing it, and even afterward. Let others judge and make decisions. But be sure you give it to no one to read, no one, but send it straight on to Moscow—to Nemirovich or to me to hand over to the Art Theater. Later on, if something isn't just right, it's possible to change it during rehearsals; even on the eve of the première. (p. 82)

Almost within a month to the day of these encouraging words, another letter from Chekhov dated October 22, 1901, confirmed that at last Gorky's travail was at an end (p. 84). He had completed a play and three of its four acts were already in Chekhov's hands. Again, anxious to encourage Gorky and to avoid any dampening of his enthusiasm for the drama, which he had urged him to enter in the first place, Chekhov praised the parts of the play that he had read, cavilling only about its "conservatism" of form.

The play which inaugurated Gorky's career as a dramatist—*Meshchane* (*The Petty Bourgeois*, or *The Philistines*)—was at once a blast at the bourgeoisie, whom Gorky despised, and an attempt to portray at the dawn of a new century the new Russian hero of proletarian origins. The Moscow Art Theater, which had eagerly awaited Gorky's first play, staged its première in St. Petersburg where it was on tour on March 26, 1902. Aware of Gorky's revolutionary political sentiments and fearing possible demonstrations, the tsarist authorities permitted the production of the play only after a number of cuts in the text were made and after taking the extra precaution of replacing the theater's ushers for the première with policemen dressed in mufti.

If *The Petty Bourgeois* enjoyed only a moderate theatrical success, it was more than compensated for by the stunning reception given Gorky's

Gorky (center rear) and actors of the Moscow Art Theater onstage with members of the cast of The Petty Bourgeois. *Chekhov's wife, the actress Olga Knipper, is seated on the floor in front.*
(H. W. L. DANA COLLECTION OF THE HARVARD THEATRE COLLECTION)

second play, *Na dne* (*The Lower Depths;* literally, On the Bottom), which he had actually begun writing before working on *The Petty Bourgeois.* Premièred by the Moscow Art Theater to rousing ovations on December 18, 1902, less than a year after the first production of *The Petty Bourgeois,* the play has since become the only one by Gorky to gain true international distinction. As a measure of his esteem for the work Stanislavsky himself played the major role of Satin in the original production. Bleak and sullen, *The Lower Depths* nevertheless became an overnight sensation and when the distinguished German director Max Reinhardt mounted the play in Berlin on January 23, 1903, Gorky's entry into the hall of theatrical fame was assured.

This rapid, heady success—which Gorky was unable to sustain as a dramatist through the vicissitudes of the next thirty-three years—had come a little over a year after the première of Chekhov's *The Three Sisters* on February 13, 1901, and two years before the first Moscow Art Theater production of *The Cherry Orchard* on January 30, 1904. Gorky was in his early thirties and already an established and indeed exceptionally popular writer on the basis of such robust stories of a different Russia as "Chelkash," "Makar Chudra," "Twenty-six Men and a Girl," and his powerful novel *Foma Gordeev* (which was dedicated to Chekhov), whose theme of social protest he carried over into his first play.[4]

From a gifted writer of short stories, a genre he never abandoned, Chekhov had grown into a major playwright through nearly a dozen dramatic works beginning with *On the Highway* in 1884. Although the "mature" Chekhov of *Uncle Vanya, The Three Sisters,* and *The Cherry Orchard* is glimpsed only occasionally in the earlier plays, the efforts of the 1880s and 1890s acted collectively as a school of dramaturgy through which Chekhov had to pass first for the confirmation of his talent and then for its refinement. Crowded social melodramas such as *Platonov* or his first stage success *Ivanov,* or caricatures in dramatic form, the early plays nevertheless bear far more than a merely tenuous link to the world-renowned dramas of the first years of the twentieth century. Virtually every type of character, dramatic situation, and technique of the later plays can be found—at times, to be sure, only prototypically or embryonically—in the earlier ones. No parallel evolution marks Gorky's transition from the short story (and the novel) to the drama. When they came in the first flush of Gorky's enthusiasm for the theater, *The Petty Bourgeois* and *The Lower Depths* were not preceded by fledgling exercises on the writer's part to learn the art of drama by actually trying to write plays. Gratified, above all, by the astounding success of *The Lower Depths,* Gorky was convinced of the rightness of his decision to enter the field of drama and went on to write another eighteen full-length plays before his death.

With *The Petty Bourgeois* Gorky demonstrated the proximity to Chekhov that was to inform much of his dramatic writing. The mood of the play is somber. In a provincial setting essentially unhappy and self-pitying people lament the dreariness and emptiness of life. No matter where they look they see the same unrelieved landscape of boredom and banality. Escape, therefore, is futile; the geography may change but the human situation remains the same. Even the symbolism of Moscow, the great city as refuge from provincial tedium, as wish fulfillment, has no further sustaining power. We have gone beyond the malaise of *The Three Sisters.*

Even more so than Chekhov, Gorky is at his best with character when portraying a group. This is amply evidenced in *The Lower Depths* in which the total environment of the cellar flophouse lingers longer in the memory than any finely etched individual portrait. The pattern is already figured in *The Petty Bourgeois*. The play is set in the bourgeois home of the coarse and insensitive house painter Vasili Bessemyonov. Conflict, rarely a cornerstone of Gorky's dramatic style, arises from the interrelations of the residents of the Bessemyonov household which includes several rent-paying lodgers in addition to Vasili's wife (Akulina), daughter (Tatyana), son (Pyotr), and foster son (Nil). The estrangement of parents from their own children who find them bereft of understanding and compassion (the "conflict of generations" theme so richly elaborated in Russian literature from Turgenev's *Fathers and Sons* on) is the immediate source of tension. But even here, where the possibility surely existed, Gorky failed to achieve any single outstanding characterization. What does succeed is the collective portrait of the troubled Bessemyonov household—family and lodgers alike—taken as a single entity. Indeed, the parents-children conflict is intensified by the general atmosphere of the Bessemyonov household and registers above all as an extension of it.

The static quality of the drama, such overt Chekhovian characters as the birdcatcher Perchikin and the alcoholic choir singer Teterev, and the nearly grotesque whining of provincials about the dreariness and futility of existence underscore Gorky's indebtedness to Chekhov. This indebtedness extends also to Gorky's use of sound. When the Bessemyonov household disintegrates and at the end of the play Pyotr runs off with a young widow whom his father considers a tramp, Pyotr's sister Tatyana, emotionally exhausted and physically drained, slumps onto the keyboard of the piano in front of her. The discordant sound of many keys striking at once, then gradually dying out, exemplifies Gorky's assimilation of Chekhovian technique. Yet in fundamental respects Gorky was a quite different dramatist.

In Chekhov's plays the world-weariness of so many of his characters afflicts both the landowning gentry and the intelligentsia. For Gorky, it is rooted primarily in the materialism and spiritual vacuity of the bourgeoisie and the merchant class portrayed so vividly in *Foma Gordeev*. This is worked out generationally in Gorky, for the bitter misunderstandings that exist between the Bessemyonovs and their children is presented as a legacy of the past, a historic inevitability. This historical viewpoint is less urgent in Chekhov and so, too, is the "conflict of generations" theme. Whatever the clear perception of a given social milieu in Chekhov, the revelation of psyche is always individual. In Gorky, it is socially generalized and motivated, thereby explaining perhaps his pervasive somberness. *The Petty Bourgeois,* like *The Lower Depths* and virtually all of Gorky's plays—in striking contrast to Chekhov—makes few concessions toward offsetting the overall atmosphere by anything comic or ironic. The splendid subtlety of Chekhovian nuances disappears, the middle tones wash away, and the resultant canvas is stark and emotionally overburdened.

Gorky's vitriolic depiction of the greed and insensitivity of the Russian bourgeois and merchants and of the ineffectuality of the intelligentsia coupled with his socialist revolutionary sympathies, which Soviet criticism ever dotes on, invests his plays with an ideological zeal that often flaws them noticeably. The treatment of work and the worker in *The Petty Bourgeois* is a case in point. Taking his cue from Chekhov, but without Chekhov's more abstract, philosophical conceptualization of the problem, Gorky also extols the virtues of work. But the work of which Gorky approves most and which he knew so well from his own early life experiences, is physical, the toil of the common laborer perceived as something ennobling.

Shortly after the attempted suicide by poison of Tatyana, Pyotr converses with Yelena, with whom he eventually flees. When she affectionately calls him a "dear, darling boy," Pyotr impetuously responds that he is not a boy and that he has done a lot of thinking. Then, with little or no motivation, he asks Yelena's opinion of the activities of Nil and his friends who, among other things, stage plays for workers. Committed to the cause of the worker (Nil himself is one), the people whom Pyotr mentions admiringly are actively engaged in the struggle for the betterment of man. This, implies Gorky, is the way out of the morass of bourgeois misery in which Pyotr and the entire Bessemyonov family are sunk. The ideological orientation of the play is both lucid and consistent; but contrived incidents such as Pyotr's query to Yelena for the purpose of introducing the theme of the "new" Russian, the "new" hero Gorky sought to exemplify in Nil demonstrate a didacticism which intensifies through Gorky's dramatic writing and trips him into ineptitude. In this respect, the gulf between Chekhov and Gorky defies bridging.

The Lower Depths proceeds from the same ideological premises as *The Petty Bourgeois.* The esteem it has enjoyed in Russia and elsewhere cannot be attributed to any marked advance in dramatic technique. The play is static and oppressive in atmosphere. Indeed, the gloom and somberness of *The Petty Bourgeois* have even deepened. The characters who inhabit the twilight world of the cellar flophouse that serves as the play's setting wallow in self-pity and petty bickering. Unlike Nil and eventually Pyotr in *The Petty Bourgeois*, they are beyond breaking the ties that bind them to their wretched existence. Barren of hope, battered by and fearful of life, they inhabit the cellar as they would a communal cell.

In *The Petty Bourgeois* Gorky exposed the malignancy of bourgeois life, its banality and materialistic pettiness. Not content, however, merely to lay bare the spiritual malaise of a given segment of society, in the manner of Chekhov, Gorky went further and proposed a counterbalance represented by the worker figure Nil and Polya, his future wife. It is with such people who refuse to be crushed by the life around them and who willingly accept the challenge to transform that life, that the future of Russia lies—according to Gorky.

In *The Lower Depths* Gorky operates with a different set of characters and explores the problems raised in *The Petty Bourgeois* from a different perspective. Instead of provincial bourgeoisie, Gorky peoples the "lower depths" of his play with the kind of socially marginal characters who tramp through the pages of his short stories and novels: a flophouse keeper (Kostylyov) and his wife (Vasilisa) and sister (Natasha), a policeman (Medvedev), a locksmith (Kleshch) and his wife (Anna), a meat-dumpling hawker (Kvashnya), a hatmaker (Bubnov), a broken-down actor (Actor), a shoemaker (Alyosha), longshoremen (Krivoy Zob and the Tartar), a "Baron" down on his luck, a thief (Pepel), a murderer (Satin), and a "holy" wanderer (Luka). Doubtless much of the interest in and acclaim lavished on *The Lower Depths* can be attributed to the unusual nature of this assemblage of characters whose life agony becomes the subject of Gorky's exercise in dramatic naturalism.

In *The Petty Bourgeois* Gorky leveled an assault on the false values of bourgeois culture, opposing to these the dynamic optimism of the "new man" Nil. In *The Lower Depths* the conflict is again ideological rather than dramatic. Into the midst of the social dregs inhabiting Kostylyov's flophouse comes a mysterious wandering "healer" named Luka (the Russianized form of the biblical Luke). To the wretchedness and hopelessness of the cellar dwellers he offers a faith of stoic acceptance and trust in the life of peace beyond the grave. To Kleshch's dying wife Anna he says, "Be patient yet. Everybody has to be, dear . . . *everybody has to put up with life as he can.*"[5] And a little later: "You just keep trusting . . . You'll die now, I mean, and have real peace . . . There'll be nothing more to be afraid of, nothing at all. Just peace, and quiet . . . Lie still now! Death—it sets everything at rest. . . . it's sweet for us" (p. 114). The Actor, ruined by drink, is comforted by Luka with news of a nonexistent hospital where drunks are cured and with the advice: "Pull youself together, *and have patience* . . . And then later you'll get cured . . . and you'll start living all over." The thief Pepel is urged to flee the cellar and take himself to Siberia, a "golden land! The man who's strong and got his wits about him can make out there like a cucumber in a hothouse" (p. 117). When Pepel accuses him of telling lies and then "tests" him by asking him if he believes that God exists, Luka replies: "If you believe, he does; if you don't, he doesn't" (p. 118). Believe, in other words, what you will, so long as it makes you happy. This is the self-satisfying illusionary truth Luka advocates, advocates, it must be remembered, out of sincere desire to bring goodness to his fellow man and the conviction that not all men can cope with "truth."

The social implications of what Gorky viewed as a prevalent current in Russian thought were pernicious: accept conditions as they are and comfort yourself with the belief that some day things will be better. Through Satin, Gorky defends the motives of Luka (after the old man has left the flophouse following Pepel's killing of Kostylyov) and then refutes them in the most pregnant ideological moment of the play:

> I understand the old man . . . yes! He was lying . . . but out of pity for you, God damn you! There're lots of people who lie out of pity for their neighbors . . . I know! I've read about it! Lie handsomely, inspiredly, excitingly! . . . There's such a thing as a comforting lie, a reconciling lie . . . A lie explains away the weight that has crushed a workingman's hand . . . and indicts people dying of hunger . . . I know what a lie is! Whoever's weak inside . . . and whoever sucks his life from others—they need lies . . . A lic holds some of them up, others screen themselves behind it . . . But whoever's his own master . . . whoever's independent and doesn't live off somebody else, what's he want a lie for? Lying is the religion of slaves and masters . . . Truth's the god of free man! (*p. 152*)

The famous paean to man situated close to the end of the play and completing the ideological circle of the work is also delivered by Satin:

> Man—that's the truth for you! What's man? . . . It's not you, or me, or them . . . no! It's you, me, them, the old man, Napoleon, Mohammed . . . all in one! . . . You get it? It's pretty clever! All the beginnings and ends are in it . . . Everything's in man, everything's for man! Just man exists, and everything else is what he does with his hands and his brains! Ma-an! It's colossal. It sounds . . . majestic! M-a-n! Got to respect man! No feeling sorry . . . no humiliating him with pity . . . got to respect him! Let's drink to man, Baron! (*p. 156*)

Konstantin Stanislavsky in the role of Satin in the original Moscow Art Theater production of Gorky's The Lower Depths *in 1902.*
(H. W. L. DANA COLLECTION OF THE HARVARD THEATRE COLLECTION)

Gorky's sincerity of conviction rings loud and clear in Satin's emotion-charged monologues, but as in *The Petty Bourgeois* artistic integrity and ideology are not necessarily compatible. In the early play, Nil was plainly conceived as the embodiment of the dynamic optimism enthusiastically championed by Gorky. But apart from the fact that Nil is a worker and committed to the workers' movement, his "positive" accomplishments (and those of his circle) are insufficiently dramatized to be theatrically effective. The emphasis of the play falls instead on the dreariness of the bourgeois life style of Bessemyonov, which Gorky presents as a taint of which even his children cannot completely free themselves. Very much the same problem of emphasis, integration, and motivation occurs in *The Lower Depths*. Despite the moving eloquence of Satin's discourses on truth and man, there is nothing in his earlier characterization to prepare him for his didactic role in the last part of the play. Moreover, the discourses, once delivered, lead nowhere. Luka has departed and the flophouse residents go on as before in their petty bickering and self-pitying. When the veil of illusion concerning the hospital where alcoholism can be cured is stripped from his eyes, Actor takes his own life. The suicide, in fact, ends the play on much the same note that Tatyana's collapse on the piano keyboard ends *The Petty Bourgeois*. In both instances, in a manner reminiscent of Chekhov (for example, in *The Seagull*), the ending of the play is somber, melodramatic, and self-consciously poignant through a calculated use of musical sound. In *The Lower Depths* Krivoy Zob and Bubnov are singing the song Gorky appended to the end of Act I, which runs throughout the rest of the play as a leitmotif, when the Baron enters to announce that he has discovered the hanged body of Actor. The song is cut off, all fall silent, and the play closes with Satin's bitterly ironic remark that by his suicide the Actor "spoiled the song . . . Id-iot!"

I suggested earlier that much of the fame of *The Lower Depths* may be attributed to the novelty of its characters. For all his philosophical posturing (not only in *The Lower Depths* but elsewhere), the fact remains that Gorky was far more an ideological didacticist than an original or profound thinker. The conflict of "truth" or "illusion" which provides the intellectual substance of *The Lower Depths* becomes interesting primarily for the social and political inferences that can legitimately be drawn. Moreover, the play itself does not quite clearly establish Gorky's own position. On the basis of *The Petty Bourgeois* and other earlier (and later) works, the case may be argued rather convincingly that Gorky rejects the palliatives freely dispensed by Luka. Textually, however, Luka is presented as operating from essentially virtuous motives, so the character must not be regarded as entirely negative. Then, the later suicide of Actor and the lack of impact of Satin's passionate monologues on the subject of truth and man (and, additionally, the insensitivity of Satin's closing remark on hearing the news of Actor's death) indicate, to be sure, a certain ambivalence on Gorky's part.

In terms of dramatic structure there is nothing particularly striking about *The Lower Depths*. Except for smaller "private dramas" (Vasilisa's scheme to get rid of her husband, the confrontation between her and Pepel over her sister Natasha, Kostylyov's slaying, the deaths of Anna and Actor), the play is static. The direct confrontation that might have taken place between Luka and Satin never occurs, with the result that when Satin's famous monologues are delivered there is a diminution of dramatic impact and a question of logical motivation arises. The characters, then, become the uniqueness, the "originality" of the play. Where previously in Russian drama did one find a cast of characters consisting in the main of tramps, criminals, and has-beens, presented in the setting of a miserable cellar flophouse, all speaking in a language natural to the characterization and setting? This is what startled audiences and won Gorky such great acclaim. And even when much of the vividness of the original language fades in foreign translation, the novelty of characters and setting is still sufficient to carry the play.

The popularity of *The Lower Depths* in the English-speaking world has been considerable and there are several translations available. Moreover, virtually all studies of Gorky lose little time in pointing out that one particularly outstanding response to the play in the West was the American playwright Eugene O'Neill's *The Iceman Cometh* (1940, 1947).

Superficially, the two plays are so much alike that the Russian influence cannot be doubted.[6] *The Iceman Cometh* is set in a tawdry New York bar-hotel which corresponds to the cellar flophouse in *The Lower Depths*. O'Neill's characters, like Gorky's, are down-and-outers, clinging to their illusions (their "pipe dreams") and fearful of leaving their refuge for still another tilt at life's windmills. While a perfect coincidence of character in the American and Russian works does not obtain, the network of personal relationships is distinctly similar. The ideological counterpart of the Russian Luka is Theodore Hickman (Hickey), a hardware salesman, and of the Russian Satin, Larry Slade, a sometime "Syndicalist Anarchist." Where Luka appears as a stranger in Gorky's play, however, Hickey is a well-known old friend of the habitués of Harry Hope's saloon and rooming house.

It is principally with Hickey and his "message" that O'Neill has parted company with Gorky. Until the character appears, an aura of expectation has been created concerning him. The occasion is the upcoming birthday celebration of Harry Hope and everyone looks forward to the arrival of Hickey who has the reputation of being the life of the party. Attention, therefore, is centered on the character some time in advance of his appearance. When he finally comes onstage, Hickey startles all by expounding a new philosophy which appears the polar opposite to that of Gorky's Luka. The Russian held out dream and illusion as a balm;

Hickey urges his listeners to cast off the dreams and illusions with which they dupe themselves against any further participation in life:

> I meant save you from pipe dreams. I know now, from my experience, they're the things that really poison and ruin a guy's life and keep him from finding any peace. If you know how free and contented I feel now, I'm like a new man. And the cure for them is so damned simple, once you have the nerve. Just the old dope of honesty is the best policy—honesty with yourself, I mean. Just stop lying about yourself and kidding yourself about tomorrows.[7]

Arguing that the addressees of Hickey's new message of hope-through-realism are entitled to their illusions and better left as they are, the bitterly disillusioned alcoholic Larry assumes the antithetical role of Satin in *The Lower Depths,* though pleading (for not entirely the same reasons) the same cause as Luka.

The ambiguity with which Gorky's play ends has no parallel in O'Neill. From other works it can be inferred in *The Lower Depths*—despite the apparent ambiguity—that Gorky personally and vehemently opposed the kind of easy succor proffered by the Lukas of the world. *The Iceman Cometh,* however, crystallized from a quite different premise. Far more pessimistic in his outlook than Gorky, O'Neill not only accepts the necessity of illusion and self-delusion but explores in his play the very process by which the integrity of the dream world is preserved.

Reacting to Hickey's incessant urging, most of the residents of Harry's bar finally get up enough courage to leave the bar and take the first unsure steps toward returning to "life." The efforts prove futile and they return bitter and ill at ease over the painful, inescapable glimpse of self-awareness. Hickey's revelation that he killed his wife Evelyn to end finally—out of love—her "pipe dream" (about him) spares them further anguish, for Hickey's murder and his voluntary surrender to the police are seized upon as acts of insanity. By extension then his entire uncustomary behavior in Harry's, above all his attempt to "rehabilitate" his friends through realism, becomes insane and as such is easily dismissed. By introducing the motif of Hickey's murder of his wife (to which Pepel's slaying of Kostylyov in *The Lower Depths* is not analogous), O'Neill establishes the logic of the return of his characters to the world of dream and illusion from which Hickey had temporarily jolted them. Dismissing Hickey as mad, they can also dismiss his appeal to them to abandon the smug refuge of their pipe dreams as nothing more than the raving of a lunatic. *Plus ça change, plus c'est la même chose.* O'Neill's bleaker vision of man places his characters beyond redemption and suggests that perhaps they are better off that way, sustaining themselves in their wretchedness by their dreams and illusions. By contrast, it is these very dreams and illusions which Gorky sees as obstacles in the way of self-realization.

Artistically, both plays have serious shortcomings. If Gorky does not realize the dramatic potential of a confrontation between Luka and Satin and an unmistakable ambiguity obscures conviction at play's end, O'Neill has erred on the side of excess. *The Iceman Cometh* is long beyond need and proportion and overly demanding of an audience's patience. The verbiage is matched by the overelaboration of various plot elements. The Boer War veterans are implausible as characters (though perhaps no more so than Gorky's Baron); Paritt's suicide, analogous to Actor's in *The Lower Depths,* is more extensively motivated but with the result that the entire episode involving Parritt tends to become more central than it should be in the drama. Gorky's play is more compressed, dramatically tighter than O'Neill's, and theatrically sounder. But in the vital area of idea, O'Neill succeeds where Gorky, I believe, fails. Hickey's entire role in *The Iceman Cometh* and the dialectic aspect of the Hickey-Larry relationship are well conceptualized and effectively translated into dramatic terms.

Opposing views of man generate conflict in both *The Lower Depths* and *The Iceman Cometh,* but in the O'Neill play the philosophical issue is the heart of the matter, the core of the play; every important facet of the drama develops out of it and relates to it. Not so in the Russian work. Gorky's intention seems to have been first to achieve a theatrical sensation, which he did, and second, to moralize on the theme of human dignity. This moralization operates through Luka and Satin and makes for a *sense* of conflict in the play. But this conflict lacks the integral and integrating character of conflict in *The Iceman Cometh.* It seems something externally stimulated, superimposed on rather than organically cultivated out of the milieu and character interrelations of the cellar flophouse. Not insignificantly, Luka is an alien projection into this world instead of an existing component of it like Hickey in the equally dreary world of Harry's bar.

Several of Gorky's prerevolutionary plays after *The Lower Depths* relate much more to *The Petty Bourgeois* than to his best-known effort in the drama. The sharp attack on the philistinism of the Russian bourgeoisie and intelligentsia is resumed again in *Dachniki* (*Summer Folk,* 1904). Successfully revived by the Royal Shakespeare Company, *Summer Folk* still exudes an air of déjà vu. The rustic summer vacation setting again serves as the forum for the open-air spiritual and emotional agonizing of an assortment of Russian intelligentsia types. To the more sensitive of the gathering, particularly Varvara, the wife of a boorish lawyer named Basov and her ardent suitor, the philosophically inclined Ryumin, life is petty, unsatisfying, and empty. To varying degrees, and in various ways, the rest of the characters either share this conviction or exemplify it. Basov's unmarried sister Kaleria seeks refuge in a kind of neo-Romantic nature poetry distantly related to Treplyov's playlet in Chekhov's *The Seagull*. Varvara's brother Vlas struggles to find the path to the meaning of life, to break out of the confines of a world he sees stifling him, and comes under the sway of the only truly positive character in the play, the woman doctor Maria Lvovna. Consistent with his practice elsewhere, Gorky uses extended monologues to hammer home his message should any doubt linger in the minds of his audience (which seems quite unlikely, anyway). Ryumin, for example, is made to articulate the common malaise:

> What is life? The word calls up before me the image of a huge formless monster that's always demanding a sacrifice—a human sacrifice. Day after day it gobbles up human brain and brawn and swills human blood. . . . Why, I don't know. I see no meaning in it, but I know that the longer a man lives, the more filth and vulgarity—crude, loathsome vulgarity—he sees, and therefore the more intense grows his longing for the Beautiful and the Pure. He is unable to overcome life's contradictions or to purge life of its filth and evil. Well, then, at least let him close his eyes to all that crushes his spirit! Let him turn his face away from whatever offends him. He wants to rest, to forget. He wants to live in peace and tranquility.[8]

The antithetical response, by Maria Lvovna, comes later:

> We ought to be different—all of us. We're the children of cooks and laundresses, of wholesome working people, and we ought to be different. Never before have the Russians of education been connected with the masses by ties of blood. These blood ties ought to fill us with a desire to improve and brighten and expand the lives of those, our kith and kin, who sweat in darkness and dirt from morning to night. Not for pity of them, nor for charity's sake, should we seek to improve life, but for our own sake, to escape an accursed isolation, to annihilate the yawning precipice out of which our kith and kin gaze up at us on the heights as at their enemies, who live by their labor. They sent us ahead to find a road leading to a better life for all; we went ahead and got lost. And in this isolation of our own creating our lives are filled with alarm and torn by contra-

dictions. That is the real drama of our lives. But we ourselves are to blame for it. We deserve the suffering we have brought on ourselves, and, as you say, Varya, we have no right to poison the air with our groans. (*p. 333*)

Echoes of Turgenev's *A Month in the Country* and Chekhov's *The Seagull* abound, though the milieu is now that of the bourgeois and not the landowning gentry. The settings and the use made of the settings, the relationship of music and mood are strikingly similar. Varvara as the sensitive wife of an insensitive husband is indeed a familiar character. But it is rather Ryumin, her spiritually anguished suitor of philosophical bent, who in his relations with her justifies a parallel with the Islaev–Natalya Petrovna–Rakitin triangle of Turgenev's play. The Chekhovian echoes ring more clearly. Again, a key ideological role is played by a doctor, this time, in *Summer Folk*, a woman (Maria Lvovna). A theatrical company hovers about the landscape in Gorky's play, recalling the outdoor staging of the playlet in *The Seagull*. The stage directions at the beginning of Act II call, in fact, for the appearance of a small platform and benches. Although some background activity (a rehearsal) occurs here, no play is presented and the episode with the actors and musicians is never meaningfully integrated. Attention throughout centers on the audience who are the "summer folk" and the principals of the play proper. The poetry recital given by Basov's sister Kaleria near the end of Act I is closer in spirit to Chekhov's intentions regarding Treplyov's playlet in *The Seagull*. The poetry functions as an aspect of portraiture, very much as the play does in *The Seagull*, but it carries much less weight as a lever of conflict, as in Chekhov. Toward the end of *Summer Folk* Vlas' parody of Kaleria's poems provokes the crisis in relationships used by Gorky as the means to resolve his plot and bring the overly long, sometimes tedious play to conclusion. Vlas' "challenge," as it were, followed by Ryumin's feeble attempt at suicide with a pistol (a melodramatic touch for which Gorky was doubtless indebted to Chekhov), results in the definitive break of the "sensitive" characters (Vlas, Varvara, Maria Lvovna, and her daughter Sonya) with the stifling, oppressive atmosphere of the *Summer Folk*. Kaleria's poems and the response they eventually arouse in Vlas relate to Gorky's plot in a way reminiscent of Treplyov's theatrical exercise in *The Seagull* but have less dramatic intensity and structural significance. The character of Shalimov, the lionized middle-aged writer who is slightly cynical, suffers from spiritual fatigue, and no longer harbors illusions about anything in life, is more patently Chekhovian. The model? Of course, Trigorin in

The Seagull. Shalimov's words, to Suslov, first, and then to Basov, expel any doubt as to his genesis:

> Put yourself in my place: here am I, a writer, a man who goes through all sorts of emotional experiences, and who, in the end, gets worn out by them. I come here to have a rest, to live in complete relaxation and collect my thoughts, and all of a sudden a lady swoops down on me and begins searching my soul: What do you write about that? Your ideas on this are hazy, on that are wrong, on the other are ugly, Good God! Do your own writing, madam, if you know so well how to make everything clear and right and beautiful! Write the finest book that ever was written, but for God's sake leave me in peace! (*p. 258*)
>
> If you must know, I'm not writing at all. Who can write in times like these? There's no making head or tail of what's going on. People are all so hazy and mixed up—you can't put your finger on them. (*p. 259*)

The final lines of the play, spoken also by Shalimov, sum up not only his feelings but the mood of the entire world of *Summer Folk:*

> It's all so unimportant, old fellow. [The allusion is to Ryumin's bungled suicide attempt.—HBS] Everything. People as well as events. Pour me out a glass of wine. So utterly meaningless, old fellow. (*p. 351*)

Sounding a familiar Chekhovian note, the play ends on a musical echo to Shalimov's closing words: the long low whistle of a watchman in the woods.

Unlike Chekhov, Gorky assigns his writer character an ideological function. In his first play, *The Petty Bourgeois*, Gorky hinted, prophetically, at the Russian man of the future, the "new hero" who was just around the corner of history. Nil in *The Petty Bourgeois* and Vlas in *Summer Folk* are signposts along the way. The "new Russian," free of the pettiness of the bourgeois and of the spiritual malaise of *fin-de-siècle* bourgeois and landowner alike, will hold the power (and the future) of the country in his hands. Shalimov is distinctly aware of his presence, though he does not yet perceive him in any crystallized form. He says to Basov:

> A writer ought to see his reader very clearly in his mind's eye. Who is he? What is he like? Five years ago I was sure I knew who he was and what he wanted of me. But all of a sudden I lost sight of him. That's it—lost sight of him. Are you aware of the drama in those words? They say a new sort of reader has been born. Perhaps, but I don't know him. Who is he? (*pp. 259–60*)

Whenever I walk down the street I see people of a new type. There's something special in their faces—and in their eyes. I look at them and think to myself: They won't read me, they're not interested in what I have to say. This winter I read my work at some sort of gathering. I saw them there, too. They kept looking at me—looking at me with all their eyes—attentively, searchingly, but I could see they weren't my sort. They don't like me. They have about as much need of me as of Latin. They found me outworn—and my ideas too. Who could they be? Who do they like? What is it they want? (*p. 260*)

The sense of what he says is echoed later by Varvara who tells Ryumin:

We have estranged ourselves from everything. We don't know how to make ourselves needed. I have a feeling that soon—sooner than we think—a different sort of people—brave, strong people—will take things over and sweep us away like refuse. (*p. 296*)

The lofty social role of the writer in Russia is voiced, at one point, by Maria Lvovna:

But we live in a country where the only person who can voice the truth, the only one who can judge impartially of the vices and virtues of our people and carry on a struggle to improve their condition, is the writer. He alone can do this, and this alone is what he ought to do. (*p. 276*)

In this spirit, Gorky set out in the half dozen pre-Revolution plays that followed *Summer Folk—Varvary* (*Barbarians*, 1905), *Vragi* (*Enemies*, 1906), *Poslednye* (*The Last Ones*, 1908), *Chudaki* (*Queer People*, 1910), *Vassa Zheleznova* (first version, 1910), *Zykovy* (*The Zykovs*, 1913), *Falshivaya moneta* (*The Counterfeit Coin*, 1913), and *Starik* (*The Old Man*, 1915)—to answer Shalimov's questions.

The quest, on the whole, was far from successful. Vague and unconvincing in his conception of the proud bearers of the "new Russia," Gorky settled on the level at which he inwardly felt most comfortable—the depiction of a world incapable of facing the challenges of tomorrow and hence destined to disappear. In *Barbarians*, the long-awaited arrival in a remote provincial town (Verkhopole) of engineers (Tsyganov, Cherkun, Lukin) who will construct a railway there sets the stage for a drama essentially of marital frustration and romantic conflict that aims at exposing the gap between the intelligentsia and the common people and the inability of the intelligentsia to lead Russia to a better day. The title of the play connotes the irony underscoring the work. Haughty and disdainful of the provincial people they have come among, the engineers, above all Cherkun, see them as little more than "barbarians." At one point the engineer Tsyganov refers to them as savages of Tierra del Fuego; to Cherkun, the area is a "land of mortal gloom." By play's end, however, the would-be transformers of rural Russia in their grossness of manner and lack of compassionate understanding are themselves revealed as barbarians of a sort. Yet Gorky's true position is not really so clear and the ambivalence marking the Luka-Satin polemic in *The Lower Depths* reappears here. Although hardly "barbarians" compared to the uncouth Cherkun, the townspeople of Verkhopole are anything but a flattering collective portrait in their conservative attitude toward change and their fondness for small-town gossip. And the engineers, on the other hand, whatever their faults, do possess the skills necessary to move Russia forward.

The potential conflict of mutually antagonistic attitudes remains dramatically unresolved, however, and once established dissolves into a dreary tale of romantic misery with melodramatic touches superficially reminiscent of Chekhov. The engineer Cherkun no longer loves his wife Anna and eventually tells her so. An inclination toward Lidia, an acquaintance of Tsyganov temporarily living in Verkhopole with her aunt, leads nowhere and Cherkun instead discovers that he is loved by Nadezhda, the wife of the local revenue collector Monakhov. An incurable romantic whose view of the world has been shaped by novels of the heart, Nadezhda feels drawn to the manly "strength" of Cherkun and finally "declares herself." Before Cherkun can reply, the local doctor, a jealous admirer of Nadezhda, rushes in and attempts to shoot Cherkun; but the gun jams. With Monakhov pleading for him to "return" to his wife, Cherkun spurns Nadezhda, telling her that he does not love her and that she should go back to her husband. Contemptuous of Cherkun's callousness, Lidia rejects him; Nadezhda, meanwhile, spurns Tsyganov's protestations of love and, at the end of the play, she kills herself, offstage, with the doctor's revolver. Earlier in Act III, Cherkun and Lukin discuss the tasks before them. Lukin declares that they have to "Open the eyes of those born blind—you can do no more!" To Cherkun's reply that, "We have to build new highways—railways—Iron is the force which will destroy this stupid, wooden life," Lukin replies, giving the sense of the play:

> Men themselves must be like iron to be able to destroy this life. This we cannot do. We can't even destroy what has already lived out its time—help the dead matter to decay—it's too close and dear to our hearts. It won't be we, it seems, who will create the new—

not we! And the sooner we realize this the better—it will put every one of us in his right place.[9]

When Lidia, another in a long line of Gorky's "positive" heroines, turns her back on Cherkun after the Nadezhda episode, her words reinforce Lukin's earlier indictment:

> . . . I thought I might find a man who is staunch and firm, who can be respected—I've been seeking a long time—seeking a man I could bow to—with whom I could walk side by side . . .
> CHERKUN: So that you may bow to him?
> LIDIA: And walk by his side. Why, are there no men upon this earth who are heroes—high priests—some to whom life means great creative work? It cannot be! (*pp. 140–41*)

A killing links *Barbarians* with *Enemies,* written a year later (1906). But the killing is murder, not suicide, and the play a lament not for the gap between the intelligentsia and common folk in the provinces but for that between representatives of the factory-owning capitalist class and the workers whose aspirations for a better life they fail to respond to meaningfully. Among the factory owners, Gorky contrasts two types: the despotic capitalist (Mikhail Skrobotov) who is contemptuous of the workers' demands for improved conditions and pushes for a policy of repression, and a more humane "liberal" (Zakhar Burdin) who inclines to petty compromises which are ultimately incapable of bringing far-reaching reform or of satisfying anyone.

The contrasting positions of Skrobotov and Burdin are tested by socialist agitation among the workers at their plant. Where Skrobotov advocates stern measures, Burdin places his trust in education. But the difference is one of method, not attitude, for as Burdin declares at one point in Act II: "Our masses are crude, uncivilized—give them a finger and they'll grab an arm—. . . There's a great deal of animal greed in them, my friend, and what they need is not petting but educating" (p. 169). Skrobotov's way of dealing with the matter is to close the factory briefly to teach the workers "a lesson." No less troubled by the agitation, Burdin seeks a middle way, to avoid shutting the plant, but only exacerbates already existing animosities. Skrobotov's view, however, prevails. The factory is closed and a violent encounter between Skrobotov and a worker results in the former's murder. To avoid further violence, Burdin reopens the factory and accedes to the workers' demands that a despotic foreman be fired. He imposes one condition, however, and that is that the workers voluntarily turn over Skrobotov's murderer.

The workers counsel among themselves and decide that they will surrender to the police not the real murderer, a man named Akimov, but a
younger less valuable member of their organization, Ryabtsov, who
agrees. The deception fails when a former soldier now in the Burdins'
service, Kon, reveals that he saw Ryabtsov elsewhere at the time the
murder was committed. Not long thereafter Akimov comes forward on
his own to confess. In their investigation of the greater conspiracy behind the crime the secret police have also uncovered a cell of socialist
agitators led by a Tolstoyan apostle of nonviolence named Levshin and
at play's end a number of the workers in addition to Akimov are taken
under arrest.

Gorky's ambivalence and the irony of the title in *Barbarians* are not
paralleled in the case of *Enemies*. In the tense period of unrest and agitation in Russia between 1903 and 1905, culminating in the Moscow in-
surrection of December 1905, Gorky's active sympathies were wholly
with the workers and Socialists. Briefly imprisoned, in fact, for his participation in the revolution, he left Russia as soon as possible after the
events and remained a political émigré for the next eight years.

Whatever attempt at fairness marks the characterization of Zakhar
Burdin, Gorky's general treatment of the capitalist factory owners and
their lackeys in *Enemies* leaves no doubt as to whom the title of the play
refers. When not overtly repressive, like Skrobotov, or ultimately disdainful of the workers despite a surface liberalism, like Zakhar Burdin,
the other representatives of capital and the "old order" (like most of
Gorky's bourgeois types and intelligentsia) are portrayed, familiarly, as
weak-willed, spiritually bankrupt, and uncertain and fearful of the future. The only true compassion is reserved for Burdin's eighteen-year-
old niece Nadya, who crosses the bridge of understanding to the workers (as an enlightened young person, of course, she holds out the hope
of an eventual reconciliation of the classes) and Zakhar Burdin's brother
Yakov, a drunk who no longer has any illusions about himself or life.
Yakov even develops a fondness for the workers and tells his actress wife
Tatyana that he likes them. He also assumes an ideological function in
Enemies. Tatyana asks him, in response to his confession of admiration
for the Socialists, "But why are they so simple? Why do they talk so simply, look at things so simply? Is it because they have no passion, no
heroism in them?" (p. 191). Yakov's reply, "They have a calm faith in
their rightness," removes any trace of doubt as to Gorky's intentions.
Levshin's words at the final curtain reinforce the impression:

You can't throw us out, oh, no! No more of that. We've lived long enough in dark lawlessness. We've caught fire now, and you'll never put that light out. No matter what you do you'll never stamp us out with fear—never! (*p. 201*)

The unambivalent political orientation of *Enemies* prohibited any contemporary production of the play. It was banned by the censors and remained unstaged in Russia proper until 1933. Since then it has become a staple of the Soviet repertoire.[10]

Gorky's next play, *The Last Ones*, written the same year (1908) as *Enemies*, met the same fate, again on political grounds. Less cohesive than *Enemies* and didactically overburdened, *The Last Ones* failed to win censorial approbation because of its subject—the attempt by a young terrorist on the life of an unsavory police chief—and its unmistakable ideological undertones.

In *Queer People*, which followed *Enemies* and *The Last Ones* in 1910, Gorky dropped politics for the time being and returned to the theme of the spiritual malaise of the contemporary intelligentsia. His treatment of it now, however, was less strident. Like previous efforts along these lines, the play is diffuse, theatrically unexciting, tendentious, and outwardly Chekhovian in its exploration of personal relationships in a provincial summer vacation setting. Interest centers on the writer Mastakov and his wife Yelena. A middle-aged doctor (Nikolai Potekhin) who is infatuated with Yelena, his senile father, a self-deprecating ex-army and police officer (Samokvassov) who frets constantly about Russia's international position, an adventuress (Olga) who sets her cap for the weak-willed Mastakov, and a young woman (Zina) who is tormented over a waning love for a consumptive youth (Vasya Turitsin) who dies in the course of the play, round out the Chekhovian cast of characters.

Although the morbid subplot involving Zina and Vasya manages to generate some interest, it is the Mastakov-Yelena-Olga triangle that gives *Queer People* its little substance. Succumbing to temptation, Mastakov carries on an affair with Olga. When Yelena learns of it and confronts him with her knowledge, he backs down from a confrontation and elects to remain with his wife. His romantic peccadillos doubtless will continue, but he will never abandon Yelena, whom Gorky perhaps overdraws in his zeal to portray a woman of towering strength and nobility. Harboring no illusions about Mastakov, Yelena draws sustenance from his youthful optimism and zest for life, and this is what doubtless redeems him in Gorky's eyes also. In the last scene of the play, Mastakov confesses self-awareness to Yelena and then declares ecstatically, striking a theme dominant in Gorky's work:

> Life is more interesting and more honest than human beings. There's wonderful beauty in this human life of ours, and it's a joy to be a dewdrop reflecting a ray of light at sunrise! Lena, my friend, my good friend, it seems to me that all the people—that everybody around you and me—are living their second and third lives. They're born old, and are too lazy to live. Yes, they're born old. But I was born only once—I came to this world as a child, and I'm happy to be young—and I live with a boundless love all this—everything that's alive! . . . I'm glad that I'm alive, I'm drunk with the joy of living, and I feel I want to tell everybody born for the first time how happy I am—you understand me, Lena? (*Seven Plays*, pp. 251–52)

Yelena not only understands but agrees also to forget (not forgive, which he does not ask) Mastakov's moral transgressions.

Alone among the contemporary intelligentsia it was the writer, in Gorky's vision, who could merit redemption because it was the writer who, through the power of his art, could instill hope and enthusiasm for the future in others. This was already hinted at in the case of Shalimov in *Summer Folk*. Projecting his love of Russia and the Russian people and his own optimism and zest for life in Mastakov, Gorky presented a character made human by deficiencies of character but redeemed through a love of life capable of inspiring others. That is why Mastakov appears more attractive and more sympathetically portrayed than other representatives of the intelligentsia (for example, the engineers in *Barbarians*) in Gorky's plays and why Gorky equips him with a life companion who, inspired by his love of life, stands by him and in turn shields him with her own strength of character.

At one point in *Queer People* Mastakov praises Russian womanhood in general and the Russian mother in particular. Gorky had already drawn a moving portrait of a Russian mother in his novel on the Revolution of 1905, *Mat* (*Mother*). The portrait was dramatized in the play *Vassa Zheleznova*, written, like *Queer People*, in 1910.

The play revolves around the efforts by Vassa Zheleznova (a "telling name" from the word for "iron," *zhelezny*) to keep the family business and fortune intact as the family patriarch, Zakhar Zheleznov, lies on his deathbed. By an iron will and sheer ruthlessness, Vassa relentlessly pursues—and attains—her goals. Vassa's sons and their wives (Semyon and Natalya, Pavel and Lyudmila), whom Vassa sees as weak-willed and capable only of squandering money, and her brother-in-law Prokhov, an old reprobate who carries on an affair with Lyudmila, are all, one by one, cunningly dispossessed of their shares in the Zheleznov business.

As a character study of a strong woman, a mother capable of doing evil for what she considers the ultimate good of her family, a type Gorky's interest was strongly drawn to, *Vassa Zheleznova* is dramatically more concentrated and more effective than Gorky's other plays of the period 1905 to 1913. Yet the play is also a sordid exercise in Naturalist theater. Pervading it is the same stench of decay and evil that hangs over Saltykov-Shchedrin's powerful novel of a disintegrating provincial landowning family, *Golovlyovy* (*The Golovlyov Family*, 1868), and Tolstoy's Naturalist tragedy on peasant life *Vlast tmy* (*The Power of Darkness*, 1888).

Whatever the private nobility of Vassa's motivation, her ruthless strength of will and singleness of purpose make the greatest impact. Her son Pavel is deformed and crippled, bringing an element of the grotesque into the play. He is married to Lyudmila, the daughter of the Zheleznov firm manager Vassilev, and Gorky strongly hints that before her marriage Lyudmila's reputation was anything but savory. Her father suggests, moreover, that the marriage to Pavel was engineered by Prokhov just so that he could make Lyudmila his mistress, though Lyudmila later confesses to Vassa's daughter Anna that Prokhov arranged her marriage to Pavel because of her affair with another man. After marriage, however, Lyudmila becomes the special object of the dissolute Uncle Prokhov's attention and the evidence that there has been an affair between them is strong. One of the more morbid scenes of the play is the fight between an envy-crazed Pavel and Prokhov in Act III. Learning that Prokhov has a heart condition, Pavel taunts him till he becomes livid with rage and, beside himself, kicks the crippled Pavel to the floor. But the encounter is more than Prokhov's heart can stand and his end comes soon after, hastened apparently by an additional blow or blows by Mikhail Vassilev. Finally realizing the impossibility of forcing Pavel and Lyudmila to remain together and fearing damage to the Zheleznov family name in an investigation of Prokhov's death, Vassa manipulates Pavel's entry into a monastery.

Illegitimate birth and child murder—among the stock subjects of naturalism—also have their place in *Vassa Zheleznova*. Uncle Prokhov, it is revealed, has an illegitimate son in Moscow whom he supports. From her daughter Anna, who most closely resembles her in spirit, Vassa obliquely extracts the information that the healthy children she bore after the death of her first child, a weak creature, were not fathered by her sickly husband. To keep her son Semyon's philandering instincts within family bounds,

Vassa gives him the family servant, Lipa, as a mistress. When she bears a child, it is at Vassa's insistence that she strangles it to death. Privy to the secret, Lyudmila's father, Mikhail Vassilev, uses it to force Lipa to poison Prokhov (the effort is only partially successful) in order to keep him from withdrawing his money from the Zheleznov firm. Unable to carry the burden of what she regards as a second murder, Lipa commits suicide. By a bitter irony, the child Lipa bore Semyon was strong and healthy before its murder; the offspring Semyon produces with his wife, Natalya, are weak and sickly. To cap the irony, Vassa at one point even berates Semyon for his inability to bear her healthy grandchildren! On a few occasions Vassa indulges in a kind of self-pitying self-justification; but in view of the taint of evil that clings to her, her words ring hollow, as in the following remarks to Anna early in Act III:

> All mothers are wonderful. We're all sinners—and martyrs too. The Lord's judgment on us will be terrible, but I'll never go down on my knees before my fellow men. Remember, all human beings live through us. I'll tell all to Our Mother of God—she'll understand. She pities us sinners. Didn't she say to the archangel, "Ask, beseech my dear son to order me to suffer in hell with the great sinners?" That's the sort she is! (Seven Plays, p. 285)

In order to paint a portrait of a woman of towering strength, of a mother prepared to plunge into the most dreadful evil if convinced it is for the good of her family, a character foreshadowed by the writer Mastakov in Queer People, Gorky may have felt it dramatically necessary to surround Vassa Zheleznova with as much moral degradation as he has. Gorky was no doubt fascinated by his mental construct of such a woman, but so much of the evil of the play ultimately proceeds from Vassa herself, if only by indirection, that the character seems hardly able to evoke compassion and borders on the demonic.

The social and ideological dimensions of the play also have to be considered. The corrupting factor in Vassa's life is the ruble, and Gorky may very well have sought to bring together in his titular character both the most dramatically stunning study of the woman of strength he had created to date and an object lesson on the all-pervasive corrupting and demoralizing power of money. As an anticapitalist play, Vassa Zheleznova relates to his earlier Enemies. Whatever Gorky's original intention regarding the work, however, his excessive use of naturalistic sensationalist motifs taxed the proportions of the drama and the play remains the most sordid of Gorky's dramatic works, more so by far than The Lower Depths.

Of Gorky's remaining prerevolutionary plays—*The Zykovs* (1913), *The Counterfeit Coin* (1913), and *The Old Man* (1915)—the closest in spirit to *Vassa Zheleznova* and the best of the three is *The Zykovs*.

Gorky has again concentrated on character study in a "family drama." The central figure this time is the Russian timber merchant Antipa Zykov, of roughly the same lower bourgeois social origins as Vassa Zheleznova. With the heroine of Gorky's earlier play he shares a great strength of will and a disregard for the rights and sensitivities of others. The plot of *The Zykovs* is thinner than that of *Vassa Zheleznova* and freer of the naturalistic elements of the earlier play. Zykov's sickly son Mikhail is due to marry a girl named Pavla, who has been brought up in a convent and has little knowledge of the world. A widower yearning for a new partner in life and the companionship of a woman, Zykov decides that Pavla will be a more fitting wife for him than for his weak son Mikhail, whom he despises (as Vassa Zheleznova despises her own weak sons Pavel and Semyon). Exerting the full weight of his authority, Zykov intimidates Mikhail into relinquishing Pavla. Despite the misgivings of Pavla's domineering mother and Zykov's proud, capable sister, Sofya, a widow and another of Gorky's "positive heroines," Zykov and Pavla wed. But the relationship soon proves unsatisfactory. Zykov himself is overbearing and fatherly, Pavla too immature and incapable as yet of real love. More from boredom than anything else, she slips into a flirtation with Mikhail and petulantly declares her love for him to Zykov. An ugly confrontation ensues and Mikhail in despair tries to kill himself. The attempted suicide of his son shocks Zykov and at the final curtain he and Mikhail are reconciled. Realizing, moreover, that Pavla will never be right for either one of them, Zykov sends her away.

The subplot in *The Zykovs* has two components: first, Sofya's successful management of her brother's business interests during the period when he is preoccupied with Pavla; and second, Sofya's personal relations with two men who want to marry her—the cynical forester Muratov and Zykov's fastidious German partner Hevern who, Sofya discovers, has been cheating her brother. Though yearning for marriage again, Sofya cannot bring herself to marry men incapable of matching her own strength and prefers to remain alone with her brother whose basic nature her own so closely resembles.

From several points of view, *The Zykovs* is one of Gorky's more convincing dramas. The central character, Antipa Zykov, is a lusty and earthy Russian merchant of the old school, a type first brought onto the stage in the 1840s by the playwright Aleksandr Ostrovsky. Despite

Gorky's patent distaste for capital and the world of mercantilism, he found himself magnetically attracted to the rough-hewn old merchants of the Zykov type. Their robust appetite for life, strength of will, and rugged individualism seemed to Gorky to spring from the soil of Russia itself, and like Ostrovsky before him he contrasted their essential humanity and proximity to the folk with the contemptuousness and spiritually bankrupt cynicism of the home-grown Russian capitalist. Zykov's pride, his source of strength, is his immense drive and capacity for work. He makes this clear himself when, talking to Pavla at one point in Act IV, he draws a comparison between his own nature and that of his son Mikhail:

> ANTIPA: Is it my fault I'm in better health? Is it my fault I don't feel sorry for those who are good-for-nothing? I love business. I love work. On whose bones has this world been built? Whose sweat and blood have watered the earth? That hasn't been done by the likes of him and you. Can he take upon himself the work I do?
> SOFYA: That's enough—
> ANTIPA: Hundreds of people live without want, hundreds have come up in the world, thanks to my work and my father's before me. What has he done? I did something wrong, but at least I'm always working toward some end. To listen to you kindhearted people, every kind of work is a sin against something. That's not true. My father used to say, if you don't kill poverty, you don't wash away sin; and that's the truth.
> PAVLA: Nobody speaks well of you.
> ANTIPA: What of it? Out of their envy they accuse me of being rich. I say everybody should be rich, everybody should have power, so no man would have to bow his head before others or wait on them. Let people live in independence, without envy, and they'll be good in themselves. Let them fail to reach this state, and they will be lost in their baseness . . . (Five Plays, pp. 242–43)

The contrast of strength versus weakness that Gorky delineates between Antipa Zykov and Mikhail is paralleled in the two dominant female portraits of Sofya and Pavla. Like Mikhail, Pavla is weak, unsure of herself, lost. There is a rationalization for the weakness in each case; in fact, a kind of reasoning with which Gorky's readers would be familiar. Mikhail suffers from a physical fraility and Pavla from a retarded maturity and an ignorance of the world, stemming from her convent upbringing. Sofya, however, is a pillar of strength and the true "hero" of the play. It is she who protects her brother's interests and keeps the Zykov business running when Antipa's thoughts are distracted. She is the one who discovers Hevern's deceit and has the courage to confront him with it, even though she thereby destroys what hope there might be to achieve a happy marriage between them.

What distinguishes Sofya's strength from Antipa's is her thoughtfulness, her modesty, and her unwillingness to accept banality. For all Antipa's blunt strength, he is a vain man, insensitive to the feelings and needs of others, as revealed in his relationship with his son and in the unhappy marriage of convenience he had arranged years earlier for Sofya. Unlike her brother, however, Sofya values principle above happiness. She refuses to accommodate herself either to the cynicism and vanity of Muratov or to the treachery of Hevern. And in this rejection of the two men who offer her marriage, she demonstrates an undeniable moral superiority over Antipa.

In *The Zykovs*, as in earlier plays, especially *The Lower Depths*, Gorky scorns a passive and submissive acceptance of fate, favoring instead an affirmation of life through self-determination. That is why he draws a sharp contrast between the positive type of personality, such as that of Antipa and Sofya, which faces up to the challenges of life, and the passive type of personality, as represented by Mikhail and Pavla, which cannot take control of his or her life. But in the differences that can be observed between Antipa and Sofya, Gorky leaves no doubt that there is more to admire in the self-sacrificing courage of the latter than in the raw strength of the former.

The antithetical attitudes toward life contrasted in the parallel triangular relationships of Antipa, Mikhail, and Pavla, on one hand, and of Sofya, Muratov, and Hevern, on the other, constitute the core conflict of *The Zykovs*. While the play outwardly resembles a family drama of the *Vassa Zheleznova* type, its genesis must be related also to the kind of philosophical drama in which Gorky was interested as far back as *The Lower Depths*. This is not to denigrate Gorky's achievements in dramatic portraiture in the play; but beyond the conflicts of opposing natures and aims in *The Zykovs* there lies the broader issue of disparate attitudes toward life in general, in which Gorky's own position is clearly revealed. Significantly differing from *Vassa Zheleznova*, the family conflicts in *The Zykovs* are deliberately underdramatized so as not to overshadow the philosophical issues. Thus, Antipa's usurping of Pavla draws no real opposition from Mikhail; recognizing his own weakness, he believes that Antipa will be a better match for Pavla than he. Even Mikhail's later suicide attempt is presented as a low-key, offstage event, creating only slight family ripples. Eventually the father and son are reconciled; and when Antipa, "coming to his senses," finally dismisses Pavla, she accepts her new fate unchallengingly, still too insecure and fearful of life to respond otherwise. Similarly, in the relations between Sofya and Muratov and, even more so, between Sofya and Hevern, potentially violent conflicts are resolved with a minimum of dramatic intensity.

TWO

Gorky's Later Plays:
The Soviet Period

THE OLD MAN (1915; revised 1922 and 1924), which followed *The Zykovs* by two years, was the last play Gorky wrote before the Revolution. Although his interest in drama did not diminish, he turned out no new complete plays during the next fifteen years. His return to active dramatic writing came only in 1930 with the play *Somov i drugie* (*Somov and Others*), on which he labored during most of 1930 and 1931 when he was on the verge of a definitive return to Russia from abroad. *Somov* was published for the first time in 1941 and reached the stage a decade after that. The play has an unfinished quality of which Gorky himself was aware; but while he intended eventually to revise it, no major reworking was ever accomplished.

Even though it is unconvincing *Somov* merits attention for the fact that of the four plays written by Gorky in the 1930s, during the last stage of his career, it is the only one that has been set in and reflects the Soviet period. Exposing once again the spiritual bankruptcy of the Russian bourgeoisie it portrays their inability to halt the spread of Soviet power, their dismay over the "successes" of the new regime, and their final attempts to turn back history by supporting external intervention aimed at crushing the Soviet state. More important than its trite subject matter and its structural deficiencies is what *Somov* tells us about Gorky's resumption of dramatic writing in the 1930s.

After a long period of residence in the West as a political exile, Gorky availed himself of a tsarist amnesty and returned to Russia in 1914. Increasing difficulties with the new Soviet political leadership, however, sent him West again in 1921, ostensibly for reasons of health. By 1928, four years after Lenin's death, Gorky seriously contemplated a final return home and as if by way of "testing the waters" made two immensely successful journeys to the Soviet Union in 1928 and 1929. Three years later, in 1932, he went back to his homeland for good. His return was a triumph; he found himself admired as a man with enormous prestige, respected as the foremost "progressive" writer of prerevolutionary Russia, and looked to as the leader of the new Soviet literature so badly needed. The esteem in which he was, and still is, held enabled him to move easily to the center of the literary stage. This was of great significance for the organizational role he came to play in Soviet literary affairs until his death in 1936. But his success as a literary organizer and as a formulator of Soviet literary policy was unmatched by a similar success as a writer.

Because of his prestige, Soviet studies always evaluate Gorky's literary output of the 1930s with an excessive and erring generosity. Yet the fact is inescapable that his long physical separation from the "new" Russia and the circumstances in which he left there in 1921 seriously hampered Gorky's ability to effectively identify with and assimilate the new themes of Soviet literature in his own writing. The result was generally weaker works than those which he had written before the Revolution. The first post-hiatus play, *Somov*, is a good example. Anxious to demonstrate an ability to deal with Soviet reality (that is, Soviet reality as it was perceived in terms of contemporary Soviet literature), Gorky wrote a play about the internal enemies of the new Soviet state and its eventual triumph over them. The play's major redeeming feature is the strong portrait of the titular character, Somov, a forty-year-old engineer with a Napoleonic complex and a fierce hatred of the Soviet regime.

More successful were Gorky's next two plays, *Yegor Bulychov i drugie* (*Yegor Bulychov and Others*, finished soon after *Somov*, reworked in 1931 and 1932, and completed definitively in 1933) and its sequel *Dostigaev i drugie* (*Dostigaev and Others*, begun in 1931 and finished in 1933). These were followed by Gorky's last play before his death, a new Soviet version of *Vassa Zheleznova*, completed in 1935. As a precondition for a fuller understanding of Gorky's achievement in *Yegor Bulychov* and *Dostigaev*, the best plays of his later period, and their place in Soviet criticism, the writer's fifteen-year absence from drama requires closer scrutiny.

In retrospect, it now seems incontrovertible that behind Gorky's withdrawal from playwriting between 1915 and 1930 lay his failure to accommodate to the major trends of Soviet Russian drama in the first decade and a half following the Revolution. "Failure," of course, implies attempt, and the evidence amply attests to Gorky's attempt to bring his writing into conformity with the new trends. His efforts were more than just half-hearted. He believed in the rightness of the new paths along which the postrevolutionary drama and theater were being directed and

he lent his considerable prestige in support of them. But when he himself tried to assimilate the new idiom, he found that he could not make
the necessary transition and so preferred silence to continued failure.

At the root of the problem was Gorky's uneasiness with the dramatic
forms that came into greatest prominence after the Revolution, romantic
monumentalism and melodrama. In the effort to rebuild Russian theatrical life after the severe dislocations caused by war and internal upheaval,
the idea gained ground that a new *Soviet* Russian drama and theater
should be brought into existence specifically to depict the epic, monumental character of the events of recent history. The new drama and
theater should serve, above all, to enshrine the heroism and romanticism of the class struggle and the Revolution as well as the victory of
the Red Army in the Civil War. Toward these goals, there were early
grandiose attempts at incorporating the revolutionary experience into
mass open-air spectacles. The most famous of these, *The Seizure of the
Winter Palace,* staged by the director Yevreinov in Petrograd in 1920,
involved some 8,000 participants (a number of whom had actually taken
part in the siege) and was performed before an audience which may
have included as many as 75,000 spectators. *Agitkas*—propagandistic
skits based on topical political issues—also found a fleeting success. But
the mass spectacle and the *agitka,* like similar efforts to create a national
folk theater and to fashion it into an instrument of Bolshevik influence,
had obvious inherent limitations and could play no truly productive role
in the evolution of Soviet drama. This is not to deny their impact on
other dramatic and theatrical forms, especially the romantic-monumental drama of the 1920s and 1930s, the grotesque satirical comedy of the
1920s, and the avant-garde productions of such directors as Meyerhold,
Vakhtangov, and Tairov. But as autonomously viable dramatic forms,
their existence was historically limited to the very early revolutionary
period when conditions of theatrical life were chaotic and art was employed either for educative or propagandistic ends.

In order to fill the temporary void of a Soviet repertoire and to
achieve a theatrical stability through a transitional period of tumult, classics of the European theater were staged, including works by the ancient Greeks, Shakespeare, Lope de Vega, Schiller, and Hugo. The
Symbolist poet and dramatist, Aleksandr Blok, who was then in charge
of the repertorial subsection of the Petrograd Theater Section established by the People's Commissariat of Enlightenment, declared in
defense of the classics: "Finally, I would want us to say decisively that
we demand Shakespeare, Goethe, Sophocles and Molière, great tears

Members of a Soviet "Blue Blouse" (Sinyaya Bluza) troupe, photographed in Moscow in 1927. Originally established by the Moscow State Institute as a kind of "living newspaper" for the benefit of workers' clubs, the Blue Blouse became the most numerous and dynamic Soviet agit proletarian theater organizations of the 1920s. Some 5,000 groups of Blue Blouses were represented at the All-Union Congress of Blue Blousemen held in Moscow in October 1926.

(H. W. L. DANA COLLECTION OF THE HARVARD THEATRE COLLECTION)

and great laughter, and not in homeopathic doses but the real thing . . . We must stand firmly for the classics; we must not yield our positions to the modernistic trends knocking at the gates."[1]

The revival of the classics, and especially of tragedy, accorded with the growing demand for an authentic Soviet drama of revolutionary grandeur. What was admired in classical tragedy, Shakespeare, Schiller, and the Romantics was the element of great spectacle, the plays' monumental proportions, their powerful emotions, and their heroic conflict. Here then were the models for the new Soviet drama. The forms had already been refined; all that was required was the introduction of the new thematic material.

Gorky himself favored the revival of the classics and called for the building of a heroic theater in a short article entitled "Trudny vopros" (A Difficult Question), which was published first in the journal *Dela i dni Bolshogo dramaticheskogo teatra* (*Deeds and Days of the Bolshoy Theater*), No. 1, Petrograd, September 1919: "Our times need a heroic theater, a theater the aim of which would be the idealization of the personality, that would revive romanticism, that would poetically color the individual . . . On the stage of the contemporary theater we have to have a hero in the broad, true meaning of the concept. We have to show people an ideal being for whom the entire world has been longing for so many ages."[2]

Gorky's encouragement of tragedy, Romantic drama, and melodrama,[3] the latter appealing to him principally because of its emphasis on emotion and movement as well as its broad popular appeal, was coupled with a contemptuous attitude toward the drama of social and psychological realism. Through the tumult of the Revolution and the Civil War, Gorky envisioned a drama capable of raising the spectator above the wretchedness and chaos around him. Because of this view, he not only encouraged the writing and production of monumental and melodramatic plays but opposed what he now considered to be the drab realism of such bourgeois playwrights as Ostrovsky and Chekhov. To Gorky, the social and aesthetic education of the masses could be advanced far better by the plays of the Greek tragic dramatists, Shakespeare, Hugo, and Rostand, than ever by the plays of Ostrovsky and Chekhov.

Gorky's ideas on drama were shared by many at the time, among them Blok and especially Anatoli Lunacharsky (1876–1933), the first Soviet Commissar of Education, a prolific dramatist and also a critic who wrote extensively on repertory questions between 1919 and 1923.[4] But the problem for Gorky personally was how to translate theory into practice. His honest efforts to write plays in conformity with contemporary concepts of heroic drama and melodrama proved fruitless. A play about the ancient Normans, for example, was left unfinished even before much progress had been made because Gorky became so aware of its formidable problems.[5]

Following this abortive attempt at writing a romantic historical drama, Gorky next tried his hand at a scenario for theatrical improvisation. Utilizing techniques associated with the theatricalism about which there was much interest at the time and which was related, in part, to the various forms of revolutionary popular drama and theater previously mentioned, he wrote *Rabotyaga Slovotyokov* (*Workhorse Gabalot,*

1920), a sharp satire on obstructionist bureaucracy. Reviews of the production in Sergei Radlov's Theater of Popular Comedy in Petrograd were unfavorable and the play was immediately deleted from its repertoire.[6] Although the production included embellishments that may have somewhat altered Gorky's original intention, contemporary critics (including even admirers of Gorky) judged the satire as being one-sided and faulted it for not taking into consideration responsible bureaucrats who were, in fact, trying their best to bring order out of chaos.

The seemingly insoluble problems of *The Normans* followed by the hostile reception given the *Workhorse Gabalot* were enough evidence for Gorky that however noble his intentions perhaps the time had come to rethink his desire to remain a practicing dramatist. The result was a withdrawal from active participation in the life of Soviet drama that lasted until 1930.

Of the four plays Gorky wrote in the 1930s—*Somov, Yegor Bulychov, Dostigaev,* and the revised version of *Vassa Zhelezova*—the second and third are definitely superior. Although their full titles (. . . *and Others*) suggest a continuation of Gorky's concerns in *Somov and Others,* the later plays are really quite different. However, a certain significance of the similar titles should not be overlooked. What Gorky sought to do in these later plays was to define each titular character against the background of a specific milieu made up of recognizable contemporary types. These milieus are the "others" referred to in the titles. The plays also gave evidence that Gorky was thinking in larger patterns of dramatic structure, since *Dostigaev* was conceived as a sequel to *Yegor Bulychov.*

With the failure of *Somov,* Gorky must have concluded that he was incapable of writing an effective drama utilizing a Soviet setting, whatever the reasons might be. Yet there is also no doubt that he was unwilling to return to the prerevolutionary settings of his earlier plays. The result was a compromise of sorts. Gorky renewed a type of drama and characterization with which he had scored earlier successes, namely the family drama revolving around a powerful three-dimensional hero or heroine (for example, *Vassa Zheleznova, The Zykovs*), but he advanced the chronology and located his new plays in the revolutionary period. This new choice of setting is of critical importance in any analysis of *Yegor Bulychov* and *Dostigaev.* The already proven formulas of a family drama and an arresting, central dramatic portrait offered an advantageously familiar terrain. The choice of a revolutionary setting, however, enabled Gorky to give his later plays a chronological and ideological relevance for Soviet times; much of Soviet drama of the 1920s and 30s was located, after all, in the revolutionary period.

Morris Carnovsky as the titular character in Gorky's Yegor Bulychov *in the 1970 production by the Long Wharf Theater, New Haven, Connecticut. Directed by Arvin Brown.*
(LONG WHARF THEATRE)

The revolutionary setting had another advantage as well. It permitted Gorky in his own way to take a reasonable position in the ongoing controversy in Soviet dramatic theory concerning the values of romantic-monumental drama as opposed to those of traditional social and psychological realism. It was plainly obvious that Gorky had no talent for heroic drama and that the realistic and naturalistic drama of the prerevolutionary period was his proper métier. It was hardly a surprise then that it was toward this métier that he moved in *Yegor Bulychov* and *Dostigaev*. But the World War I and revolutionary background of these plays invests them with an epic quality similar to the drama of romantic monumentalism. The result was an effective balancing act that contributed much to the success of the later plays, not only as works of dramatic literature but also as examples of how social and psychological realism and romantic monumentalism might be joined together in a mutually enriching way.

The epic scope of *Yegor Bulychov* makes it by far the most impressive of Gorky's later plays. Beginning at the end of 1916, during the war against Germany, the work also includes as background events the

murder of Rasputin and the abdication of Tsar Nicholas II. The ending is
particularly dramatic for, as the dying Bulychov laments his doom, tumultuous cries from the rebellious crowd below in the streets herald the
imminence of the Revolution. The symbolism of the play's end is obvious; Bulychov's death is the death of Bulychov's Russia, of the old Russia
of tradesmen, property owners, and capital. The death is no less irrevocable than the passing of the cherry orchard into the hands of Lopakhin
in the Chekhov play. In Chekhov's work, the era of Ranevskaya ends
and that of Lopakhin begins; in *Yegor Bulychov*, it is the era of Lopakhin
ending and that of the people's Russia beginning. The nature of the transition at the end of the Gorky play is described in unavoidable terms.
The birth of the Revolution and the enthusiastic sounds of the surging
demonstrators drown out the futile cry of Bulychov against the death
that is about to overtake him.

The transitional upheaval dominating the historical setting of *Yegor
Bulychov* is reflected in the lives of the people surrounding the play's
titular character. These "others" include types ranging from the pro-
Bolshevik revolutionary Yakov Laptev to the uncompromising an-
tirevolutionist, Abbess Melania. But Gorky's extreme characters are
never very convincing, and Laptev and Melania are much less interesting than other characters grouped more in the ideological center around
Bulychov. The most important of these are his illegitimate daughter,
Shura, the maid Glafira, and certain tradesmen and property owners
who temporarily gained power in Russia during the Provisional Government including Bulychov's business partner Dostigaev and the lawyer
Zvontsov. But like Bulychov's sister-in-law Melania and the priest Father Pavlin, characters such as Dostigaev and Zvontsov are conceived of
primarily as negative types meant to represent the reactionary world
doomed by the Revolution. As the play's action reveals their machinations to seize what they can of Bulychov's disintegrating assets, the audience can but perceive them as vultures descending to feed off carrion.

The only characters with real personalities in the play, besides Bulychov, are the women Shura and Glafira. As the sole members of Bulychov's "circle" who offer him unselfish kindness, they may be considered as representatives of the young generation who with yet unformed
political consciousness will eventually be attracted to the Revolution.
This expectation is fulfilled in *Dostigaev* in which both women reappear
as strong supporters of the Bolshevik cause. Glafira's transformation
seems rather commonplace, as may be expected, because of her lower
social origins. Shura's case, however, is more interesting. Although de-

picted as spoiled, selfish, and barely perceptive of the tumultuous events happening around her, she emerges as a distinctly positive figure, in contrast with Bulychov's legitimate daughter, Varvara, and his wife, Ksenia. Significantly, at the end of *Yegor Bulychov* Shura is the first person Bulychov summons when he feels the end approaching. As he sinks closer to death, Shura rushes to a window and opens it admitting, and greeting, the song of the revolutionaries in the street. Shortly before, Bulychov had heard the faint singing and had inquired about it. Shura's opening of the window can be viewed as a delayed answer to Bulychov's query about the noise as well as a symbolic indication of her own growing enthusiasm for the cause of the Revolution. Bulychov, however, "hears" the singing as a grand requiem mass, finally falling limp into Shura's arms. The interaction of the dying Bulychov and his favored Shura and the misinterpretation of the revolutionary song at the end of the play suggest the expectation that though Bulychov must give his life in order to make way for the new Russia, a part of him through Shura will transmit a productive Bulychov energy and zest for life to the new Soviet era and that his spirit will hence live on.

As in *Vassa Zheleznova* and *The Zykovs,* all the dramatis personae of *Yegor Bulychov* are overshadowed by the main character. In fact, Bulychov is one of Gorky's most moving figures, as well as the last in a long line of incisive portraits of merchants created by Gorky in his novels and plays. Much of the interest of Bulychov lies in the relative complexity given the characterization. Already ill at the beginning of the play with what will be a terminal cancer of the liver, Bulychov is a person stripped of illusions about life and man. As a member of a class about to be swept from the stage of Russian history and treated almost wholly in a negative way by Gorky in his later works, Bulychov nevertheless evokes a remarkable degree of compassion. Both Bulychov and Zykov, who resemble each other, have the strengths and weaknesses of their class—the earthiness, appetite for life, and inner power that Gorky so much admired, and the human insensitivity and petty despotism that Gorky so hated.

What tinges the portrait of Bulychov with compassion is not so much his premature death, which is a historical necessity in the play, but his rebelliousness. Surrounded by predators ready to grab their own gain during the coming momentous historical change, Bulychov strikes back at their hypocrisy, greed, and stupidity. He criticizes the Russian conduct of the war against the Germans, is contemptuous of the war profiteering carried on by many of his own class, and rails against the clergy's

A scene from the 1932 production of Gorky's Yegor Bulychov *by the Bolshoy Dramatic Theater in the Name of Gorky, Leningrad.*
(H. W. L. DANA COLLECTION OF THE HARVARD THEATRE COLLECTION)

exploitation of the ignorance and superstition of the people. Yet Bulychov is still a conservative, a traditionalist, and a supporter, although cynically, of tsarist autocracy. He cannot imagine the peasant assuming any role but that of a maker of bread or a buyer of merchandise. Although Bulychov perceives injustice around him, his enlightenment does not extend to any real comprehension of the social events that are moving to transform the lives of everyone. It is this partial enlightenment, this incomplete rebellion that endows the character of Bulychov with both complexity and interest. But this enlightenment and rebellion are ineffectual, and so Bulychov and his social power will be swept away as quickly and irrevocably as his encroaching disease will surely end his physical being.

The revolution and the disease move to their climactic ends at a frenzied pace, heightened by Gorky's concentration of the play's action within a short period of time and a single setting, the Bulychov house.

The characters' helplessness to resist the claustrophobic pressure of a society about to explode is intensely conveyed, though in a roundabout way, by the almost aphoristic dialogue of the play and by the removal of the characters from any direct role in the action of external events. The lives of all onstage are clearly affected by the events occurring outside the Bulychov house but none of these events intrudes directly. Even at the very end of the play, the crowd of demonstrators is not seen; only their revolutionary song is heard.

Although *Dostigaev* is a sequel to *Yegor Bulychov* and superficially resembles it, the later play is different in several respects. It should be observed, first, that while several of the characters from *Yegor Bulychov* reappear in *Dostigaev*, there is no single overwhelming portrait in the later play to equal that of Bulychov. Whether Gorky intended Dostigaev to be of the same scale as Bulychov seems doubtful; a comparison of the two characterizations suggests that he did not, despite the circumstantial similarity of the play's titles. Bulychov is a figure etched with tragic contours; he rebels against a fate he is incapable of changing. Moreover, this tragic figure symbolizes a whole class, an era, a way of life, an old Russia, all of which are doomed to be swept away by the onrushing revolution. None of this can be said, in the same way, for Dostigaev and the "others" around him. On the stage of Russian history they are merely ephemeral and their heyday is only the short, passing period of the Provisional Government, between July and October 1917. There is nothing tragic or symbolic felt with regard to their demise. Unlike Bulychov, they do not represent the end of a culture. Because of this, there is no single character who can match Bulychov's monumental proportions, though Dostigaev is an effectively drawn representative of the manufacturers, businessmen, tradesmen, landowners, and clerics who struggle during the period of the Provisional Government to consolidate power into their own hands.

Gorky specifically attempted to delineate in Dostigaev the self-serving political acrobatics of a clever man who, beginning to read the handwriting of change on the wall of history, schemes for his own survival. At a time when support for the Provisional Government is declining and the power of the Bolsheviks growing, Dostigaev is moved by reading Darwin to believe that in order not to perish he must learn, above all, to adapt. This point of view is revealed clearly in Dostigaev's conversation with the reactionary Nestrashny, who tries to win Dostigaev over completely to his side. Exasperated with his lack of success, Nestrashny speaks disparagingly and mockingly of Dostigaev: "He's a regular Jesuit!

Walks around, sniffs, takes aim! Whom would it be more useful to betray to whom? Ah, there are many such rascals in our circle!" And later in the play, Dostigaev himself succinctly sums up his own attitude: "In my judgment, the basic question is, whom am I with? The answer is easy. With nobody except myself!"[7]

Throughout the play, Dostigaev's skepticism toward the conservative cause faintly recalls that of Bulychov. Yet, whereas the latter rebels even though he does not fully understand the significance and direction of events gathering momentum around him, Dostigaev does not so react although his comprehension of the crisis is greater. Bulychov is an engrossing study in contradictions, Dostigaev is not. Bulychov's blustering skepticism and determined rebellion are removed a long way from Dostigaev's clever adaptiveness and overriding will to survive.

The differences in structure between *Dostigaev* and *Bulychov* are as striking as those that exist in the area of characterization. In the earlier play Gorky used very concentrated means in order to build up the tension to its tragic climax. The play deals conservatively with time and space, and this spare quality is reinforced by the often terse dialogue. The dramatic external events are felt only through their reflected impact on the characters onstage. The overall mood of the play is somber; Bulychov, like old Russia, does not die easily. This somberness, however, is not totally unrelieved. To partially offset it, Gorky introduces some humor toward the end of the play through the figures of the charlatans who attempt to cure Bulychov, the tuba player who treats people by asking them to blow horns several times daily, the witch Zobunova, and the village innocent and exorcist Propotey.

The concentrated style by which Gorky sought to create a sense of claustrophobic intensity in *Yegor Bulychov* was not carried over into *Dostigaev*. In the later play we have a more crowded canvas of characters, settings, and incidents. If *Yegor Bulychov* is tragic, *Dostigaev* is only melodramatic. However, this increased number of characters and settings in *Dostigaev* produces several significant results. It removes *Dostigaev* beyond the pattern of Gorky's other family dramas by placing less emphasis on the activities and attitudes of the Dostigaevs as a family. Of course, this inhibits the full development of Dostigaev himself as a character study comparable to Bulychov. Also, insufficient motivation is given to explain clearly the behavior of other members of Dostigaev's family, particularly his children. The attempted murder of the Communist Ryabinin, apparently by Dostigaev's son Aleksei, is unconvincing; and the suicide of Dostigaev's daughter Antonina, while psychologically plausible, seems contrived. This attempted murder and suicide (both by the same gun, with a rather obvious touch of poetic justice) heighten the melodramatic quality of the play.

This quality must clearly have been Gorky's intention, since the suicide of Antonina, symbolizing perhaps the collapse of Dostigaev's world, occurs just as the play's underlying melodramatic character surfaces. Nestrashny, the local leader of the ultra-reactionary organization known as the Black Hundreds, accompanied by his henchman Gubin, pays a visit to Dostigaev shortly after hearing about the fall of the Kerensky regime. There have been rumors earlier in the play that the Bolsheviks and the workers' councils were plotting to seize power in the town. Nestrashny and Gubin try to prevail on Dostigaev to join with them. And it is while they are deliberating that Antonina commits suicide offstage. Dostigaev cannot believe the insensitive response of Nestrashny and especially of Gubin to the news of her death, and he orders them from his house, more than ever convinced of the futility of their cause. As Nestrashny and Gubin turn to leave, however, Ryabinin, the district Bolshevik leader and Dostigaev's ideological antagonist in the play, arrives with a contingent of soldiers to arrest them. The play ends with Dostigaev being placed under at least a temporary house arrest; the conclusion is thus left open-ended. However, just prior to the end, the truth is revealed that it was Dostigaev's wife, Yelizaveta, who quietly had the Bolshviks summoned during the visit of Nestrashny and Gubin.

As Gorky approached the October Revolution in the transition from *Yegor Bulychov* to *Dostigaev*, his ideology became more solidified and insistent. In *Yegor Bulychov*, Yakov Laptev, the revolutionary, is the only figure ideologically located firmly on the political Left. In *Dostigaev* the number of "progressives" has increased considerably. Laptev has aligned himself completely with the Bolsheviks and Tyatin, Shura Bulychov's suitor, has also joined the Left. The Bulychov servant Glafira has undergone a ripening of political consciousness and works actively to make a convert of Abbess Melania's servant Taisya. Although Bulychov's illegitimate daughter, Shura, has a minimal role in *Dostigaev,* she assumes importance as a contrasting figure to Dostigaev's Antonina. Leaving her aimlessness and self-centeredness behind, Shura becomes a political disciple of the Bolsheviks. Antonina, on the other hand, is a prisoner of her indecision. As Soviet literature makes abundantly clear, Antonina's inability to take a firm stand or to make herself a part of the future, like Shura and Glafira, could only lead to suicide.

Completing the roster of positive types in *Dostigaev* are two posterlike Bolshevik figures. Ryabinin, whom I have already mentioned, was simply appropriated by Gorky from the literary tradition of the Soviet positive hero.[8] And the bearded soldier who stands guard over the Dostigaevs at the end of the play was conceived of as a simple man of the people; his donning of the Bolshevik uniform is meant to suggest the broad popular support held by the faction.

Gorky's one-dimensional positive heroes have their counterparts at the other end of the political spectrum, in the clergy. The anticlericalism of *Yegor Bulychov* is of a humorous and mildly satirical nature. In *Dostigaev,* however, the clerics play a sinister, conspiratorial role, and the satire here becomes venomous.

In his study of Gorky's plays, the Soviet scholar S. Kastorsky characterizes *Dostigaev and Others* as "a kind of dramatized historical epos."[9] Gorky's introduction into *Dostigaev* of more characters, settings, and incidents, and of a more advanced ideology has indeed created a greater sense of movement, as compared to *Yegor Bulychov;* but it is difficult to agree with Kastorsky's view of this movement as dramatic epos. *Dostigaev* simply does not achieve this. Historical events gather momentum through the play and toward the end become integral with the play's action; yet the melodramatic, overt scenes convey much less a sense of great historic change than in *Yegor Bulychov.* Gorky admirably individuates most of his characters in *Dostigaev* and delineates a wide range of conflicts among them, thereby enriching the play's texture. Nevertheless, there is still no outstanding personality on which attention is riveted, as is the case with Bulychov. The lack of a dominant character in *Dostigaev,* the play's diffuseness, lesser subtlety, and more acidic satire, together with Gorky's greater reliance on intrigue and contrivance, make this later work a much less effective drama than *Yegor Bulychov.* Although some Soviet critics have seen the play as a dramatic historical epos, *Dostigaev* has, in fact, been staged much less in the USSR than *Yegor Bulychov.*

Soviet scholarship on twentieth-century Russian drama has been consistently positive, at times plainly to the point of excess, in its evaluation of Gorky's later works. In order to understand this enthusiasm toward a group of plays which, with the exception of *Yegor Bulychov,* fall below the level of his early dramatic writing, it is essential to understand the Soviet perspective and to view Gorky's later plays against the background of the Russian stage of the late 1920s and early 1930s. Naturally, Gorky's final return to Russia in 1932 and his resumption of active playwriting were received warmly by most Soviet circles. More important, however, was the situation in drama and theater at the time Gorky resumed his playwriting. Soviet scholarship holds, with some justification, that his later plays provided a critical contribution to the resolution of serious problems of genre and repertoire.

The artistically brilliant period of the so-called New Economic Policy (NEP, for short; 1921–28) ended with the institution of the first Five-Year Plan. The regimentation which became a regular feature of Soviet life as the campaign of "socialist construction" was launched extended as well into the arts. For literature, the culminating influences were the establishment in 1932 of the Union of Soviet Writers and the promulgation of the doctrine of Socialist Realism at the inaugural congress of the Union two years later. From at least the Fifteenth Congress of the Communist Party in 1927 through 1934, the regimentation and centralization of theatrical life were carried forward at a relentless pace.

As early as January 1918, just two months after the Bolshevik ascendancy, all theaters had been placed under the administrative jurisdiction of the Theater Section of the People's Commissariat of Enlightenment. The final step in the nationalization of theater was Lenin's signing of a decree of the Council of People's Commissars on August 26, 1919, which subordinated the theaters to a Central Theater Committee (Tsentroteatr). Among the tasks of this committee was the aim, through repertorial guidance, to link the theaters "with the popular masses and their socialistic ideal."[10] In practice, however, the established theaters, such as the Moscow Art Theater, the Maly, the Aleksandrinsky, and Tairov's Kamerny continued to maintain a moderate degree of autonomy, while the lesser theaters and especially the new ones created after the Bolshevik assumption of power were expected to work unswervingly toward a realization of the aesthetic ethos of the Revolution. These secondary stages innovated a myriad of experiments in theatrical style. Since stage-worthy new *Soviet* plays were slow in coming into being,[11] the theaters filled their repertoires by using dramatic literature from all over the world. Performances were often as distinguished for their cosmopolitan content as for the brilliance of their stylistic and technical experimentation. With Meyerhold, Tairov, and Vakhtangov, Russian theater reached impressive heights during the 1920s and won renown far beyond the borders of the Soviet Union.

From the late 1920s on, the picture became progressively bleaker. A Central Repertorial Committee (known in Russia by the abbreviated name of Glavrepertkom) began tightening the control over the selection of plays for production; it decided that the artistic policy of every theater should be subject to the authority of a Party-dominated artistic council. What the Party aimed for was no less than a redirection of the entire course of Russian theatrical life. It sought to reduce the number of foreign plays produced, to end the experimentation that had distinguished the Russian theater of the 1920s, to drastically curtail the power of the *régisseurs* or directors, and to halt further production of satirical and grotesque as well as politically ambivalent comedies so characteristic of NEP (several of which were as critical of the new regime as they were of the old). Of greatest priority now was the performance of plays of a more orthodox Soviet character, in other words, plays which extolled the new regime and its accomplishments, strove to educate the masses on the goals of communism, and exhorted the people to fulfill them. The directors therefore faced a real crisis in the choosing of their repertoires, especially in the established theaters which were reluctant to produce Soviet plays (plays written since the Revolution) on the grounds that few met the theaters' artistic standards. Even as late as the 1930–32 seasons, for example, the Moscow Art Theater and Tairov's Kamerny each staged only three Soviet productions. Faced with the paucity of good Soviet plays, the important theaters stayed alive by concentrating on European and Russian classics and contemporary works drawn from an international range of dramatists. As pressure on these theaters to expand their offering of Soviet plays increased, the theaters responded by urging dramatists to produce more plays, to write on contemporary Soviet life, and to seek to create works of lasting artistic value.

Adding to this repertory crisis of 1927 to 1934 were the often heated polemics concerning dramatic style. Reacting violently to what they regarded as the ideological laxity, decadence, formalism, and political neutralism of NEP, writers who were associated primarily with the militant proletarian organization, the Russian Association of Proletarian Writers (RAPP),[12] demanded instead a deeply committed, highly politicized theater prepared to contribute its role to the great program of socialist construction. At a conference on theater organized by the RAPP leadership in 1931 the principle was reconfirmed that drama, as well as other forms of art, must be viewed as a weapon of the working class in their struggle for power.

But a year after the 1931 conference, the Party formally abolished RAPP together with all other proletarian and nonproletarian literary organizations and laid the groundwork for a new single Union of Soviet Writers. It was clear what had gone wrong. The rigid dogmatism of RAPP, its inability to allow a range of ideas and approaches, the abrasive rivalries and factionalism within its ranks, and the schematism and "vulgar sociologism" which came to characterize the new proletarian literature soon left little doubt among all but the most ardent supporters of proletarian art that instead of revitalizing Soviet literature and drama, RAPP was indeed killing them. If additional proof was needed, one could always point to the pitifully small number of genuinely proletarian works of real artistic distinction.

RAPP, it must be remembered, had addressed itself to all Soviet art forms; the theater was but one of its concerns. Of more direct importance for the theater, however, than the RAPP controversy was the polemic concerning monumental as opposed to psychological drama. This debate, which can be traced back to the beginnings of Soviet drama, again became topical with the end of NEP, with the promulgation of the First-Year Plan with its new directions for literary development, with the agitation of RAPP for a truly proletarian literature, and with the repertory crisis in the theaters.

Exponents of the monumental school, principally the playwrights Vsevolod Vishnevsky and Nikolai Pogodin, argued that the revolutionary struggle to create a socialist Russia was so monumental in nature that it could be fittingly expressed only in dramatic terms that effectively conveyed the romance, pathos, heroism, and historical dynamism of the Revolution. The new drama should be a drama of strong emotions, of great affective power. In Vishnevsky's words, "We have to find a new Soviet style, nourished with hot blood, joy, and passion."[13]

The relationship of this new Soviet drama to past dramatic forms was carefully clarified especially by Vishnevsky in such articles as "Kak ya pisal *Pervuyu konnuyu*" (How I Wrote *The First Horse Army*, 1930) and "O tragedii" (On Tragedy, 1934). It soon became obvious that the past forms of drama which Vishnevsky and Pogodin regarded most highly as prototypes for the new drama and from which the most was to be learned were classical tragedy, melodrama, and the drama of the Romantic period. It was by assimilating and adapting techniques from these dramatic traditions that the goals of the new Soviet drama would be best realized. However, in speaking of tragedy in particular Vishnevsky was careful to point out that "The history of our struggle, of our class struggle, has a tragic character, but it is not the tragedy of Russia, that is, of gloomy, terrible, tsarist Russia. The tragic aspect of life exists, but do not confuse the concept of our tragedy with the tragedy of a dying class."[14]

Recognizing that tragic moments would occur in the life of the new

classless society, tragic moments stemming in most cases from its continuing struggle with vestiges of the capitalist order in Russia, Vishnevsky argued that the new content (the socialist content of postrevolutionary Russian life) should permit their positive resolution. Hence, the
new tragedy was to be a "revolutionary tragedy" and an "optimistic tragedy," the latter phrase used by Vishnevsky as the title of his major dramatic work, a romantic-monumental play written in 1933.

The new Soviet romantic-monumental drama stood opposed then to
the old drama of social and psychological realism and naturalism, which
were viewed as having little or no important consequence for the Soviet
revolutionary experience. Discussing old and new forms in "How I
Wrote *The First Horse Army*," Vishnevsky posed the questions:

> Does not the new theater demand a new form? Why do heroes
> keep on turning their insides out in the old way for three, four, or
> five acts? Why is it that they often do not live but philosophize?
> Why is the balance between the "I" and the "collective" broken?
> . . . Dare I use it [the story of *The First Horse Army*] as a back-
> ground for the sexual-philosophical exercises of two or three
> "heroes" and "heroines"? Never! [15]

Not all dramatists shared the opinions of the monumentalists, to be
sure, and acrimonious polemics soon developed. Opposed to the views
of Vishnevsky, Pogodin, and their associates were, above all, Aleksandr
Afinogenov and Vladimir Kirshon. As early as 1929, in his article "Za sotsialno-obosnovanny psikhologizm" (For a Socially-Based Psychological
Drama), Afinogenov claimed that too much Soviet drama remained ideologically under the shadow of the primitive *agitka* of the immediate postrevolutionary period. There was such an emphasis placed in Soviet
plays on external action that the superficial excitement achieved lacked
depth, that characters most of the time tended to be one-dimensional,
and that psychological motivation was often sadly missing. With the vast
majority of Soviet plays:

> . . . the spectator knows already from the first act how the play is
> going to end, with the result that he concentrates all of his attention
> on the play's external background, on the touches of everyday life
> in it, on obvious outlines, and on any clever use of language. The
> chief protagonists, inevitably boring, walk about the stage and de-
> liver themselves of wise pronouncements about the problem posed
> by the author. That is why our plays so resemble one another. That
> is why negative types, freed from the heavy burden of auctorial
> ideology, appear convincing while the positive personages seem
> pale and stilted. [16]

Arguing for greater subtlety, Afinogenov declared that not every action had to be shown on the stage:

> For example, it is not at all necessary to bring a demonstration onto the stage. It can be "distanced" by the introduction of a few characters who watch the demonstration from a window. But this "estrangement" must sound convincing and must make the spectator feel as though he himself were one of the people viewing the demonstration.[17]

On the matter of psychological motivation, which was the cornerstone of his argument, Afinogenov was careful to distinguish between the no-longer-valid "biological psychologism of the Moscow Art Theater 'man-as-he-is' school," and a "social psychology of the relations that form human character."[18]

Vladimir Kirshon, best known for his play *Khleb* (*Bread*, 1930), dealing with the peasantry in rural Russia during the first Five-Year Plan, joined Afinogenov in his plea for a drama with three-dimensional characters and psychological versimilitude. Aiming particularly at more left-wing theorists who advocated the further development of the agitational theater of the Civil War days, he declared:

> They think that in order to portray the collective and to educate the psychology of the collective it is necessary to bring onstage not one person but ten; not ten, but a hundred. They imagine that the only method suitable for showing the masses onstage is the arithmetical method. They do not seem to realize that in order to understand the psychology of a specific social stratum very often one in-depth portrait can offer much more than a crowd of thirty or forty people representing that stratum and invariably appearing as little more than schematic figures.[19]

Defending the individualization of character in drama, Kirshon attempted to explain in his article "Za sotsialistichesky realizm v dramaturgii" (For Socialist Realism in Dramatic Writing, 1934) that the development of individual character by the playwright is neither a "regression to the positions of bourgeois dramaturgy" nor sufficient reason to condemn him as guilty of the twin evils of "psychologism" or "individualism." Kirshon declared further:

> The hero of a play can never be a social type if the char
> mains undeveloped. The schema of a type of characte
> created without the development of character, but a t
> never, since by "type" we understand not only the social ɛ
> the hero, but a complex of features unique to him alone. ʌ

ters of classical drama are distinguished by the fact that the great philosophical ideas embodied in them are revealed in the course of the play's action and in accord with an extraordinarily true and faithful representation of the human, unique attributes of each pro- tagonist.[20]

The polemics argued over new and old drama during the late 1920s and early 1930s were so passionate that both sides tended to think only in terms of absolutes, of an either/or solution of the matter. Either So- viet drama was to pursue the romantic-monumental path championed by Vishnevsky and Pogodin or it was to follow the direction of social and psychological realism indicated by Afinogenov and Kirshon. Neither side seemed able to recognize that there were no reasons why both, as well as other types of drama, could not be cultivated at the same time or that a single play might well incorporate elements of more than one genre. One type of drama or the other had to prevail and become the basis for an official Soviet dramaturgy. Compromise was out of the question.

As expected, the gap between theory and practice was considerable and few dramatists in the late 1920s and the '30s isolated themselves at one end or the other of the dramatic spectrum. Exemplary works of both types of drama appeared, principally Vishnevsky's *The First Horse Army* (1929) and Afinogenov's *Strakh* (*Fear*, 1934), but the majority of Soviet plays of the 1930s gravitated to the center. Attempting to deal with the many problems of Soviet society during the first great thrust of socialist construction, playwrights preferred to focus on the actuality of their own time and place rather than to continue a lingering romance with the epic of the Revolution and the Civil War. The result was a tacit eschewal of the romantic-monumental genre, which was associated with the revolu- tionary epoch, in favor of the social and psychological realism advocated by Afinogenov and Kirshon.

But as if trying to find a compromise, a way of reconciling the two the- oretical extremes, dramatists, including the major protagonists of the polemics themselves, moved back and forth between the styles and oc- casionally did try to combine elements of both in a single play. This is in essence what Kirshon sought to do in *Bread*, though few critics at the time recognized it. Bemoaning the "wasteland" (as the Soviet critics were wont to consider it) of Soviet drama of the period and the havoc wrought by the passionate debate over drama, critics were only too happy to seize upon Gorky's post-hiatus plays of the early 1930s and hail them as not only possibly the best Soviet drama of the time but splendid demonstrations of how "great" Soviet drama could be written not by rigidly adhering to one extreme theoretical position or another but by fusing elements of both in the same work. To Soviet drama critics and theater historians of the early 1930s, *Yegor Bulychov and Others* and *Dostigaev and Others* eminently succeeded in capturing the monumentality of the final epoch of the monarchy and of the period of the Provisional Government. At the same time Gorky managed to create memorable portraits of characters who were highly individuated (like Yegor Bulychov) and who were typologically acceptable as representatives of specific social strata at a particular juncture in history. Compared to the schematism, unconvincing portraiture, and stiltedness of much contemporary Soviet drama, it is hardly surprising that Gorky's later plays, with their occasionally striking characterizations and masterful use of language, would be held up as models to emulate and to point the way out of the impasse of uncompromising theoretical positions.

THREE

The Revolt Against Naturalism: Symbolism, Neo-Romanticism, and Theatricalism

WHILE GORKY was probing the outer limits of naturalism in *Vassa Zheleznova* (1910), naturalism as well as realism were being vigorously challenged by an entirely new current in Russian drama. It is this current that is commonly subsumed under the rubric of symbolism. But symbolism as a catchall for what were, in fact, several movements within the drama in the late nineteenth and early twentieth centuries is too restrictive. To better understand the development of antirepresentational drama it may be helpful to think of it as wearing three different masks which ought to be distinguished as symbolism proper, neo-romanticism, and theatricalism. Although they occasionally overlap and share an avowed purpose of moving the drama far beyond what their enthusiasts viewed as the narrow interests of psychological realism and naturalism, these antithetical dramatic modes approached the common goal in different ways and from different aesthetic and philosophical premises. Reduced to basics, the differences can be summed up as follows:

1. Stimulated by Wagner's music dramas and his vision of a great synthesis of the arts (the *Gesamtkunstwerk*, the "total," integrated work of art) as well as by the Catholic mass, the French Symbolist poet Stéphane Mallarmé had already articulated the concept of antirepresentational drama in the 1880s.[1] Based on symbols and correspondences this new drama would be sacral or liturgical in that it would celebrate the eternal mysteries of the universe and unite actors and spectators in a new form of communion.

The writer Philippe August Villiers de L'Isle Adam (1838–89), a precursor of symbolism, pointed the way to Symbolist drama with the only play for which he is remembered—the ultra-romantic *Axel*. A ponderous yet spellbinding dramatic prose poem redolent of the idealism and mysticism of the *fin-de-siècle, Axel* was actually begun about 1870, possibly under the inspiration of Wagner whose works Villiers had seen in Germany and with whom he spent some time personally in Lucerne in 1869.[2] A complete version of *Axel* was published in five parts in the review *Jeune France* from November 1885 to June 1886. Villiers was still at work on the drama, correcting proofs for a new four-part version, when he died. The play was performed for the first time, privately, at the Théâtre de la Gaîté Lyrique in Paris on February 26, 1894, and publicly on February 27 at the same theater. Another production was mounted on April 6, 1894, at the Théâtre de la Gaîté-Montparnasse. *Axel* was quickly embraced by the Symbolists and their followers as a veritable masterpiece and the beginning of a new tradition of poetic drama whose impact is amply attested by Edmund Wilson in his study *Axel's Castle* (1931).

The contributions of Mallarmé and Villiers de L'Isle Adam notwithstanding, the most influential and most widely imitated dramatist associated with symbolism was the Belgian Maurice Maeterlinck (1862–1949) who was, to be sure, the first dramatist to embody fundamental elements of the Symbolist *Weltanschauung* in not one but in a whole series of theatrically effective plays considered revolutionary when they were first mounted.[3]

Deriving much of their inspiration from Maeterlinck's theory of the drama as formulated primarily in his philosohpical work *Le Trésor des humbles (The Treasure of the Humble,* 1896), the Symbolists opposed what they regarded as the excessive concern of much contemporary dramatic writing with the representation of the external world and the overemphasis of most nineteenth-century drama in general on plot, incident, and movement, in a physical sense. True drama, it was felt, consisted not of the mirrorlike reflection of the world of the senses or in the theatrical working out of an intrigue assembled by the playwright in an often contrived, artificial manner calculated to achieve audience interest, but in the dramatization of man's inner, spiritual existence. With respect to conflict, symbolism sought to shift emphasis from the external to the internal, which was now invested with a far greater and more universal significance. To Maeterlinck, the concern with external action in the drama was not only wrong in that it represented a misplaced emphasis but detrimental because it drew attention away from the only conflict truly deserving the attention of the dramatist, that taking place within man. These excerpts from *The Treasure of the Humble* make Maeterlinck's position quite clear:

Must we indeed roar like the Atrides, before the Eternal God will
reveal Himself in our life?. . .

I have grown to believe that an old man, seated in his armchair,
waiting patiently, with his lamp beside him; giving unconscious ear
to all eternal laws that reign about his house, interpreting, without
comprehending, the silence of doors and windows and the quiver-
ing voice of the light, submitting with bent head to the presence of
his soul and his destiny . . . does yet live in reality a deeper, more
human and more universal life than the lover who strangles his mistress, the captain who conquers in battle. . . .

I admire Othello, but he does not appear to me to live the august
life of a Hamlet, who has time to live, inasmuch as he does not act.[4]

Although man's inner life, the life of the soul—with everything that
implies—was the natural terrain of Symbolist drama, the conflict Maeterlinck sought to dramatize, in practice, was the individual confrontation with the omnipotence and inevitability of death and the awesome
mystery of the void beyond. Since all life culminates in death and since
death is the door to the Infinite, then death, according to Maeterlinck,
becomes the greatest experience of life after birth and hence the moment of highest drama in man's existence. Now how was the concept to
be realized theatrically? Ideally, the point of initiation of the play is the
moment in which the imminence of approaching death grips the consciousness of the principal or principals. The emotional and psychological impact of nearing death can itself constitute the dramatic experience. This is the situation, for example, in Maeterlinck's two archetypal
Symbolist plays L'Intruse (The Intruder, 1890) and Les Aveugles (The
Blind Ones, 1890). Or the dramatic experience can proceed as well from
the telescoped review of a life lived or the agonized metaphysical speculation concerning the "other" life. The three one-act playlets grouped
under the title Den svåra stunden (The Difficult Hour, 1918) by the
Swedish dramatist Pär Lagerkvist (1891–1974) fall more or less into this
category. Whatever the area of focus, however, death remains the pivotal factor.

This intense preoccupation of symbolism with death led to a corresponding deemphasis of man's physical life. Since all created things are
equalized and dissolved by death, the drives and ambitions of the physical life become ultimately inconsequential in the face of death. The pronounced Schopenhauerian orientation of many of the Symbolists contributed greatly to the negativism and fatalism with which much of their
writing is informed. Not only is everything earthly finally destroyed by
death, reducing man's physical life to an irrelevance absurd for its gro-

tesque self-concern, but man appears no more than a helpless marionette manipulated arbitrarily by mysterious forces collectively represented often simply as Fate which his finite intellect is incapable of
knowing. It was not only to make a statement about the actor's art in his
own time that prompted Maeterlinck originally to designate as "plays for
marionettes" his cycle of early dramas to which *The Intruder*, *The Blind*,
and *La Mort de Tintagiles* (*The Death of Tintagiles*) belong.

Given the direction of most Symbolist thought, the repudiation of the
external and the physical in the drama was to be expected. At the core
of the Symbolist *Weltanschauung* lay the life of the spirit; a Symbolist
drama had to reflect this thematically by pointing up the insignificance
of the mundane before the awesome infinitude of the supernatural and
structurally by either eliminating or greatly minimizing external action.
A corresponding dramatic idiom had to be elaborated as well. Recognizing the inappropriateness of a colloquial, concrete style, the Symbolists
inclined instead toward a highly stylized, more abstract, poeticized, and
"incantatory" idiom. The suggestive incantatory effect was produced
principally by the extensive use of pauses, segments of silence, the almost hypnotic repetition of words, phrases, and lines, and the carefully
orchestrated use of sound. Again, Maeterlinck's early plays, including
the well-known *Pelléas et Mélisande*, may be taken as paradigmatic.
Playing time also became a consideration. In view of the programmatic
eschewal by the Symbolists of external action and the relative absence of
movement in a metphysical or "cosmic" Symbolist drama, playwrights
soon discovered that it was difficult, if not at times impossible, to sustain
conventional play length. The result was a work usually of smaller dimensions, a playlet rather than a play, often in fact short enough to run
no more than a quarter of an hour. It is no coincidence that Maeterlinck's exemplary *The Intruder* and *The Blind Ones* are both quite
short.

2. Symbolism, neo-romanticism, modernism, "decadence," and *fin-
de-siècle* have all been used more or less interchangeably to designate
the antirealist and antinaturalist literature of the turn-of-the-century
period. (Theatricalism has been considered a term applicable only to
certain specific innovations *in the theater* and of little relevance to the
study of dramatic literature.)

In view of important affinities between literary concerns and structures in the late nineteenth and early twentieth centuries and the Romantic movement of the first half of the nineteenth century, a case can
be made for the usefulness of the term neo-romanticism to distinguish

the general mode of creative writing from the 1880s to about 1910. Symbolism is then more aptly applied not to the period as a whole—the various literary phenomena of which it is too narrow to embrace—but to what was indeed the single most important current within neo-romanticism.

Bearing in mind Maeterlinck's enormous contemporary prestige and his great impact as a theorist on the European (and Russian) drama of his time, Symbolist drama proper should be thought of primarily as the type of drama for which such works as *The Intruder* and *The Blind Ones* were intended as models. That is, a new mystery play or "neo-mystery" dramatizing man's spiritual fears and longings and characterized especially by a fixation on death.

If symbolism is given this "narrower" reading, neo-romanticism can then encompass a substantially larger body of non-Maeterlinckian plays—by Symbolists and non-Symbolists alike—in which the reaction against realism, naturalism, and the culture of the bourgeoisie expresses itself in a greater divergence of subjects and forms for which the earlier nineteenth-century Romantic movement was the principal precursor tradition.

For the sake of convenience, the Neo-Romantic plays can be typologically subdivided into such categories as: symbolical (as distinct from Symbolist) and/or allegorical plays with occult and supernatural themes demonstrating the power of forces beyond rational comprehension and the illusionary nature of the material world; plays with medieval settings, often of a legendary character but generally lacking Symbolist sacral aspirations, and inspired by the rediscovery of the medieval theater; plays based on classical antique as well as national myths and legends and reflecting the renewed interest in Greek tragic drama and in the origins of the art of drama itself; plays woven out of fairy tales and fokloric elements exemplifying the greater receptivity of contemporary artists toward popular culture; plays of an escapist nature featuring either exotic settings in time and/or space (for example, Byzantium, late eighteenth-century Venice, rococo France) or alternative societies (for example, the circus) within the existing social order; and plays about art and artists (poets, dancers, actors, and actresses) presenting another perspective on the ferment and divisions within the world of art at the time; the artist as a dramatic personage is not, of course, restricted to such plays and can—and does—appear in a number of works not specifically addressed to problems of art and society.

Like the Symbolist drama proper, the Neo-Romantic plays usually, though not always, operate with a stylized, poeticized diction; many indeed are in verse and on occasion serve as vehicles for metric experimentation. But unlike the Maeterlinckian Symbolist play, the Neo-Romantic is generally much less static and more conducive to the Wagnerian incorporation of music, song, dance, and aspects of the visual arts into the drama.

Many of the plays of the German Gerhart Hauptmann (1862–1946), the Austrian Hugo von Hofmannsthal (1874–1929), the Pole Stanisław Wyspiański (1869–1907), and the Irish William Butler Yeats (1865–1939) are representative of such late nineteenth- and early twentieth-century Neo-Romantic drama. Take Yeats, for example. With Maeterlinck, whom he admired and whose influence he acknowledged, Yeats shared the Symbolist proclivity for shorter plays with relatively few characters and the special prominence accorded elderly and blind people whose proximity to death and presumably richer inner life makes them useful as vehicles of the Symbolist view of the cosmos. Such an early play as *On Baile's Strand* (1903; 1905) and such later ones as *The Resurrection* (1931) and *The Words upon the Windowpane* (1934) exemplify the Symbolist dramatists' abiding preference for the shorter form. Old men and women appear in *Cathleen Ni Hoolihan* (1902), *Deirdre* (1907), *The Player Queen* (1922), *The Words upon the Windowpane* (1934), *Purgatory* (1939), and *The Death of Cuchulain* (1939); blind people, in *On Baile's Strand* and *The Death of Cuchulain*. The familiar Maeterlinckian entrance of an unseen, strange, mysterious, and powerful force signaled by the sound of steps that strike fear in those hearing them reappears in a few of Yeats' plays, most notably *The Resurrection*.

The Neo-Romantic aspects of Yeats' plays overshadow, however, the more obvious links with Maeterlinckian drama. Most of Yeats' dramatic works are in verse, not prose, a practice shared with the great majority of Neo-Romantic playwrights. Musical and choreographical interpolations are common: consider, for example, the musicians in *Deirdre*, *The Only Jealousy of Emer* (1919), *Calvary* (1921), *The Resurrection*, and *The Death of Cuchulain*, and such "dance" plays as the four-part *Plays for Dancers* (1921) and *The King of the Great Clock Tower* (1934). The inspiration for a number of Yeats' plays—*The Countess Cathleen* (1892; extensively revised later), *The Pot of Broth* (1904), *On Baile's Strand*, *Deirdre*, *The Golden Helmet* (1908), *The Only Jealousy of Emer*, and *The Death of Cuchulain*—was drawn from the myths, legends, and tales of folklore, a source of much Neo-Romantic drama in general. Yeats' typically Neo-Romantic use of medieval material is manifest in *The*

King's Threshold (1904). The fantastic, supernatural, and fairy-tale–like cast of Gerhart Hauptmann's well-known *Hanneles Himmelfahrt* (*Hannele's Trip to Heaven*, 1892), *Die Versunkene Glocke* (*The Sunken Bell*, 1896), and *Und Pippa Tanzt* (*And Pippa Dances*, 1906) are paralleled in Yeats' *The Dreaming of the Bones* (1919) and *The Player Queen*. If Yeats did not share quite the same degree of enthusiasm for classical literature and mythology of a Hofmannsthal or Wyspiański, both of whom made extensive use of classical subjects in their plays, his interest was still great enough to lead him to translations of Sophocles' *King Oedipus* (1928) and *Oedipus at Colonus* (1934). The mask, which takes on progressively greater aesthetic and philosophical meaning with the evolution of neo-romanticism in the drama, is striking in Yeats. Stage directions call for the old men to wear *grotesque* masks in *The Player Queen*, for *all* the characters to appear masked in *The Only Jealousy of Emer*, and for Jesus to present himself in a "recognisable but stylistic" mask in *The Resurrection*.

3. The Neo-Romantic use of mask in drama, noted in Yeats, is an appropriate device with which to consider the relationship of theatricalism to other currents in late nineteenth- and early twentieth-century dramatic writing. The repudiation of realism and naturalism in the drama had a corollary in the theater. As new forms of drama were sought as more suitable vehicles for the aesthetics and metaphysics of neo-romanticism and symbolism, new attitudes toward theater were also evolving. Those opposed to theatrical realism rejected the "fourth-wall" convention and the meticulous attention to detail of a Stanislavsky on the grounds that the role of art—and this included theater—was not the mimetic representation of external reality but the probing of universal mysteries and the reassertion of eternal verities through new configurations of image and idea. By parading itself as a reflection, an imitation of one reality (the external), the theater of realism and naturalism was guilty of sham, pretense, illusion, declared the exponents of the new. Art could never reproduce reality with perfect fidelity for there was always the subjective selectivity of the artist at work; besides, the mirrorlike representation of reality was not supposed to be the function of art—and there were realities beyond merely the physical, the external to consider. By pretending *not* to be the illusion that it was in fact, the theater of realism and naturalism continued to practice the dreariest sort of deception on audiences.

To those seeking to end the hegemony of the theater of external reality the first order of business was to expose as fully as possible the illusionary nature of the theatrical art—to show audiences that theater *was* art and hence illusion and then to persuade them that its primary purpose indeed was not merely the objective representation of a single reality of the senses. This they did by reviving the mask and mime of ancient theater, by fusing within the same theatrical work dramatic dialogue, song, and dance, by introducing again the figures and improvisations of the Italian commedia dell'arte, by so stylizing gesture that the actor became reduced to a marionettelike creature, by involving the audience in the events onstage through direct address to the audience either by the character as character, or by the actor as actor, author, or director, by making theatrical performance the subject of the play either by means of plot or by the use of the play-within-a-play device, and by "baring" to the audience the mechanical aspects of production usually by eliminating curtains and thereby enabling the spectators to observe the mechanics of scene changes, the removal and introduction of properties, and so on.

This movement to make theater "theatrical" (which is why it is most often referred to as theatricalism or theatricality) scored considerable success in the second and third decades of the twentieth century in the work of the Italian Futurists (for example, Marinetti) and such outstanding and influential directors as the Englishman Gordon Craig and the Russian Vsevolod Meyerhold. In the light of the "living" and "open" theater movements in the United States in the 1960s and 1970s and the attention surrounding the pronouncements and experiments of such contemporary directorial talents as Peter Brook in England and Jerzy Grotowski in Poland, there can be no doubt that theatricalism as a concept of theater continues to be immensely vital.

Sharing the ideals of the theatricalists of the theater a number of dramatists set out to renovate drama in very much the same spirit and by very much the same means, becoming in a sense theatricalists of the drama. Since their methods are often those of the Neo-Romantics and Symbolists, there would seem little if any justification for the positing of a separate theatricalist current in late nineteenth- and early twentieth-century drama paralleling those of neo-romanticism and symbolism. Granted that the techniques are often the same, it *is* possible to find grounds on which to isolate a theatricalist current distinct in some ways from other contemporary movements in the drama. There is, first, the matter of philosophy. *Fin-de-siècle* romanticism and symbolism have philosophical as well as social points of view. The movements are overwhelmingly antibourgeois and aesthetically oriented. Their profound concern is not with man's material existence, but his spiritual one. There is a Schopenhauerian negativism and determinism common to both: in view of the inescapability of death, life on earth is tragic and futile; man, a creature of forces over which he exerts no control and cannot fully know, has only an *illusion* of free will and is, in effect, little more than a puppet; through a spiritualized, mysticized life man can gain some knowledge of the universe and find some meaning in existence.

Such attitudes—philosophical and social—are either absent entirely in theatricalist plays or of minor significance, for theatricalism's first commitment is to *play*. If a landmark more by circumstance and time than by intent, Alfred Jarry's *Ubu Roi* (1896) splendidly embodies this ideal: irreverent, mocking, grotesque almost to an extreme, the work breathes with the very spirit of play. From here to Dada was but a short step.

Symbolism

The ties between French and Russian literary symbolism were quite close. Mallarmé, Rimbaud, and Verlaine were quickly translated into Russian and extensively read in the original. When the three-volume collection *Russkie simvolisti (Russian Symbolists)*, compiled principally by the poet Valeri Bryusov (1873–1924), appeared in 1894 and 1895, a Russian Symbolist movement became a reality. The age of European modernism had come to Russia and in the poetry and prose of Balmont, Bely, Blok, Bryusov, Gippius, Ivanov, Merezhkovsky, Remizov, Sologub, Solovyov, and others achieved a new grandeur for Russian letters. Literary historians, forever fond of labels, most of the time refer to the Russian *fin-de-siècle* as the "silver age," the "golden" being that of Pushkin in the first three decades of the nineteenth century. This is high praise as it is for Russian literature of the late nineteenth and early twentieth centuries. But given the truly remarkable range and quality of the writing of the time, one can readily understand the willingness of some to declare that, Pushkin excepted, the Russian *fin-de-siècle* was far more a golden age than that of romanticism itself.

Although associated primarily with poetry and prose fiction, the Russian Symbolists—like their counterparts in the West—were by no means indifferent to drama and theater and wrote many plays. As metaphysical visions or exercises in modern liturgical drama, more lyrical than dramatic, most of their plays, however, were ill-suited to theatrical production. Few were, in fact, staged; almost all have since been ignored in

Russia—in large measure due to the Soviet hostility toward the literature of the *fin-de-siècle* and symbolism in particular which it regards as
"decadent"—and they remain little known elsewhere. Ironically, the
best-known play associated with the Symbolist movement in Russia,
Blok's *The Fairground Booth,* is mockingly anti-Symbolist. Yet whatever
their shortcomings as theater, the Symbolist plays collectively represent
a serious effort to redirect the course of Russian drama and a body of
writing in some instances of considerable philosophical and artistic appeal which the following account may help illuminate.

The first evidence of a movement away from realism and naturalism in
Russian drama appeared in the 1880s and 1890s. As early as 1880 a
precursor of symbolism and a prolific translator of Maeterlinck, the poet
Nikolai Minsky (pseudonym of N. M. Vilenkin, 1855–1937), wrote a
short verse "neo-mystery" under the title of *Solntse* (*The Sun*) which,
like Villiers de L'Isle Adam's *Axel,* rhapsodized on the theme of non-be-
ing. In 1887, the industrious Symbolist writer and ardent exponent of
mystical Christianity Dmitri Merezhkovsky (1865–1941) wrote a "dramatic fairy tale" called *Vozvrashchenie k prirode* (*Return to Nature*)
based on Calderón's *La Vida es sueño* (*Life Is a Dream*) from which
Hugo von Hofmannsthal similarly drew inspiration for his later *Der
Turm* (*The Tower,* 1925; 1927). Because of the spiritual dimension of his
plays, his depiction of the phenomenal world as illusion, Calderón was
hailed as a kindred soul in turn-of-the-century Europe and much imitated.[5] Two years after *Return to Nature,* Merezhkovsky identified and
welcomed the crystallizing new spirit in European drama in his article
"Neoromantizm v drame" (Neo-Romanticism in the Drama).

Merezhkovsky's wife, Zinaida Gippius (or Hippius, 1869–1945), an
important literary figure in her own right and, like Merezhkovsky, a passionate disseminator of mystical Christian beliefs, also became interested in the drama and wrote three plays.[6] Two of these, *Makov tsvet*
(*The Red Poppy,* 1912, allegedly written together with Merezhkovsky
and their friend D. V. Filosofov) and *Zelyonoe koltso* (*The Green Ring,*
1914), deal with contemporary themes: the first with the impact on an
affluent Russian family of the Revolution of 1905 with which Merezhkovsky and Gippius soon became disenchanted; the second, with young
people (members of the "Green Ring Society," an obvious allusion to
the Merezhkovskys' own "Green Lamp Society") attempting to assert
their independence often in conflict with the older generation.

Gippius' first play, *Svyataya krov* (*Sacred Blood,* 1901), anticipates a
folkloric current in Neo-Romantic drama and at the same time drama-

tizes the transfigurative power of mystical Christianity with which much
Symbolist thought was informed. Distantly echoing Gerhart Hauptmann's famous *The Sunken Bell, Sacred Blood* tells the story of the
water sprite (*rusalka*) who yearns to acquire a human soul. In Gippius'
version, the folk motif assumes a distinctly Christian aspect. The water
sprite has heard of the sacrifice of Christ because of which man thereafter enjoys immortality of the soul and it is the beauty of Christ's Passion
and Resurrection which inspires her. Eventually she learns that she can
acquire a soul only by killing the old monk Pafnuti who has befriended
her and whom she has come to love. When she plunges a knife in him,
it is his blood spurting on her that will endow her with the immortal
soul she fervently desires. Repelled at the thought of having to murder
the monk, the water sprite in the end commits the deed. The murder,
kept as an offstage action in the play, embodies two central concepts of
Gippius' mysticism, namely love and sacrifice. It is only through love
that life acquires meaning, death is vanquished, and man gains true immortality. The water sprite is finally able to kill Father Pafnuti because
her love for Christ transcends her repugnance at the means she must
use to unite with Him. By the same token, it is his love for the water
sprite and his compassionate understanding of the love that motivates
her that enables Father Pafnuti to offer himself in sacrifice. Both characters suffer but can accept their suffering as they perceive the love in
which it is rooted and the spiritual perfection to which it gives rise. Although it has never been produced, *Sacred Blood* is by far the most interesting of Gippius' plays. The prose of the dialogue has the appealing
quality of the *naïf* while the two water sprites' songs in the first and
third acts provided Gippius with an opportunity to engage in novel experimentation with free unrhymed verse.

One year after the appearance of Gippius' *Sacred Blood*—1902—a watershed in the emergence of a distinct Russian Symbolist drama was
reached. This was the publication in the fourth number of Sergei Diagi-
lev's art journal *Mir isskustva* (*The World of Art*) of a programmatic article on the "new drama" by Bryusov. The article was called "*Nenuzhnaya pravda*" ("Unnecessary Truth") and amounted to a repudiation of
the naturalistic exactness of Stanislavsky and the Moscow Art Theater
tradition. "It is time," wrote Bryusov

> for the theater to stop fabricating reality. A cloud in a picture is flat,
> does not move, does not change its form or its light—but there is
> something that gives us the same sensation as a real cloud in the
> sky. The stage should do everything possible to help the spectator

fix in his imagination the situation demanded by the plot of the play. If a battle, for example, is absolutely necessary, it is ridiculous to let loose on the stage tens of extras or even ten companies of them with fake swords; perhaps a musical picture in the orchestra will perform the spectator a better service. If a wind is to be represented, it is not necessary to blow whistles in the wings and pull the curtain by a chord. The actors themselves must depict a storm, conducting themselves as people always do in a strong wind. There is no need to eliminate décor, but it should be consciously conventional (*uslovny*). It should be, so to speak, stylized. . . .

Dramatic authors should renounce the superfluous, the unnecessary, and, above all, the unattainable duplication of life . . . Everything external should be reduced to a minimum. . . . About externals, the drama can give an idea only indirectly, through the souls of the *dramatis personae*. The sculptor cannot chisel souls and feelings, and thus he embodies the spiritual in the corporeal. The dramatist, on the other hand, must give the actor the possibility of expressing the corporeal in the spiritual . . .

Thus, from the unnecessary truth of today's stages I summon you to the conscious conventionality (*uslovnost*) of the antique theater.[7]

The lines of the "new drama" were clearly drawn. It was to shift from the external world of phenomena to the inner world of the spirit, from the "real" world to the ideal; it was to be suggestive rather than expressive, connotative reather than denotative, symbolic rather than concrete; it was to shun naturalistic exactness in favor of stylized abstraction; it was to cease being a mere entertainment but a metaphysical experience for the spectator by means of which he would be drawn from the realm of the finite to the infinite of cosmic mystery; it would be a theater of essence instead of existence and it would find its sources primarily in the great theater of the ancient Greeks and in the medieval theater of Christian mystery.

As if in response to Bryusov's appeal, the young poet Andrei Bely (pseudonym of Boris Bugaev, 1880–1934), who was to become one of the major literary figures of early twentieth-century Russia, appeared in print with an unfinished mystery which he had written, in fact, a few years earlier. It was called *Prishedshy* (*He Who Has Come*), subtitled an "Excerpt from an Unwritten Mystery," and was published in 1903 in the Symbolist literary miscellany *Severnye tsvety* (*Northern Flowers*) in which Gippius' *Sacred Blood* had first appeared. In a setting symbolic of the state of the world at the Second Coming, Bely's play depicts the agonized tensions within a community of mystics immediately preceding the appearance of an apocalyptical figure on the seashore near the Temple of Glory. Pretentious and excruciatingly portentous, its dialogue imitative of Maeterlinck, *He Who Has Come* reads most like a parody of itself. A few years after breaking with Symbolist drama, in his *Zapiski chudaka* (*Notes of an Eccentric,* written in 1912, published 1922), Bely recalled how he came to write his mystery play, which offers some insight into the thought processes of a Symbolist-in-the-making. Once during Holy Week he had a vision while in church and

> it was as if one wall of the church opened into the void. I saw the End (I don't know of what—my life or the world's), but it was as if the road of history rested upon two domes—upon a Temple; and crowds of people thronged toward it. To myself, I called the Temple I saw the "Temple of Glory," and it seemed to me that Antichrist was threatening this Temple. I ran out of the church like a madman. . . . In the evening, in my little room, I drafted the plan for a mystery drama, and I gave it the title "He Who Has Come"; and soon after, I drafted the entire first section (extremely incomplete). I did not finish the drama.[8]

Haunted by dark, fearsome visions of the inevitable collapse of the world into the abyss, the death of the sun, the end of life, and the coming of the Antichrist—which became obsessive anxieties of his later writing—Bely made a further attempt in 1907 to complete the mystery drama begun with *He Who Has Come.* The fragmentary *Past nochi* (*The Jaws of Night*), which postdates Bryusov's full-length apocalyptic drama *Zemlya* (*Earth*) by three years and could very well have been influenced by it, reiterates the pervasive sense of impending doom and frenzied anticipation of the Unknown of *He Who Has Come.*

On a forbidding mountain plateau cut off from the rest of the world by a deep abyss and illuminated by the pale light of the moon, a band of Christians bewail the apparent extinction of the sun and await with dread apprehension and prayer the imminent attack of "black hosts"—which will herald the end of the world. A strange old Prophet tries with frail conviction to bolster their hopes of salvation, but at the end of the fragment all is plunged into total darkness and the only sound heard is that of a "deep, sorrowful voice full of despair" crying "Woe!"

More hypnotically arresting than *He Who Has Come, The Jaws of Night* makes up in an eerie interplay of light and sound what it lacks in dramatic action.[9] In its images and rhythms it also reflects the Symbolist desire to achieve a theatrical synthesis of space, sound, light, color, and—as we know from other Symbolist experiments—even smell. Most of the play's visual effects originate with the Prophet who embodies a truly hallucinatory incandescence, as the following excerpts show:

CHILD: What does he cry out so often for? When I fall asleep at home in my own little bed and hear that cry, I feel like weeping.

PROPHET (*trying to calm him*): That is the nightwatchman. He is on our side. During the night he makes the rounds of the citadel. He peers into the darkness. He does not want anything bad to happen to us under cover of night. . . .

CHILD: Is it really so dangerous here?

PROPHET (*gravely*): Yes, perhaps it is. (*Silence. The Prophet suddenly straightens up his bent frame. His powerful build now becomes striking. Bright beams fly off his body and shafts of light stream forth from his illumined head. A luminous spot spreads around his stooped back. His hair, as though saturated with electricity, stands up all over his head. He jumps up on the railing. Standing erect above the chasm, he cries out in a resounding voice, cupping his hand around his mouth.*) I see and I hear.

CHILD (*grabbing hold of the Prophet's iridescent clothing, he gives a tug and comes running into the circle of light beams, but in his hands there only remain tatters that take on the shape of sweet-smelling flower cups.*) . . .

PROPHET (*coming down from the railing*): There is still time. Our forces are not yet exhausted. Oh, Lord, do not abandon us! (*He goes towards the rocks. His face is uplifted to the heavens. His blue eyes seem like huge sapphires. His clothing, covered with beams of light, undulates behind him. A luminous circle floats around him. Colored lights of various hues dance along the edges of this luminous circle. It is like flowers opening or beetles—golden, pearly, bright, beautiful—dancing.*)[10]

Long interested in theater and the author of a few significant essays on drama, Bely, nevertheless, was unable to achieve more than a fragmentary dramatization of his projected mystery on the Antichrist and eventually repudiated Symbolist drama as a theatrical impossibility. As his talent ripened and a surer sense of medium cohered, he succeeded in embodying his psychic experiences and apocalyptic visions far more felicitously and provocatively in such bold experiments in prose as *The Silver Dove* (1909), *St. Petersburg* (1913), and *Kotik Letaev* (1922) which have secured his place in the history of the twentieth-century novel.

Bryusov's ideas about Greek theater and medieval Christian drama, which might have encouraged Bely to publish *He Who Has Come*, were little more than schematic whatever their inspirational importance at the time. It was left to other Symbolists to flesh them out. One of these was the brilliant and influential Vyacheslav Ivanov (1866–1949)—whose "Tower" apartment was a gathering place of the St. Petersburg Symbol-

ists. In a series of erudite articles—"Nietzsche and Dionysus," "New
Masks," "Wagner and Dionysian Action," and "Presentiments and Por-
tents: The New Organic Epoch and the Theater of the Future"—
published in such leading Symbolist journals as *Vesy* (*The Scales*) and
Zolotoe runo (*The Golden Fleece*) between 1904 and 1909 and in book
form in 1909 under the title *Po zvyozdam* (*Along the Stars*), Ivanov elaborated the concept of a Symbolist liturgical and theurgical drama
through which the poet as priest and the audience as celebrants in a
communal religious rite enter into a corporate creative act.[11] Ivanov's
views on the mythic and religious character of the drama were shaped
by Wagner and Nietzsche, but especially by the latter from whose *Birth
of Tragedy* he derived the basic notions of the dithyrambic, sacrificial,
and ecstatic art of Dionysus out of which the drama issued and the affinities between the ancient cult of Dionysus as slain and resurrected god
and the Christian myth celebrated in the mysteries of medieval Europe.

Another leading exponent of Symbolist drama was the outstanding
poet and prose writer Fyodor Sologub (pseudonym of Fyodor Teternikov, 1863–1927), whose grotesque novel *Melky bes* (*The Petty
Demon*, 1907) was one of the great literary achievements of its time. Informed with the same sense of vision and ecstasy as much Symbolist
writing, Sologub's essay "Teatr odnoy voli" (The Theater of One Will),
published in a collection of Symbolist essays on theater in 1908, further
defines the Symbolist emphasis on mystery and considers additionally
the importance of dance for returning the theater—and man—to their
primitive origins:

> A theatrical spectacle, which people come to watch for amusement
> and for entertainment, will not long remain for us simply a spec-
> tacle. And very quickly the spectator, tired by the change of spec-
> tacles alien to him, will wish to become a participant in the mys-
> tery, as he once was a participant in the playing. Expelled from
> Eden, he will soon knock with a bold hand on the door behind
> which the bridegroom feasts with the wise virgins. He was a partici-
> pant in innocent play when he was still alive, when he still dwelt in
> paradise . . . And now the sole way to resurrection for him lies in
> becoming a participant in the mystery, in joining hands with his
> brother and his sister in the liturgical rite, and in pressing his lips,
> eternally parched from thirst, against the mysteriously filled cup
> where "I shall mix blood with water." To do in a brightly lighted
> temple open to all the people what can only be done now in cata-
> combs. . . .
>   There is no everyday life, and there are no customs and man-
> ners—there is only the playing out of the eternal mystery. There

are no stories and intrigues, and all the plots have long ago been plotted, and all the denouements long ago foretold—and only the eternal liturgy takes place. And what about all the words and dialogue? One eternal dialogue is being conducted, and the questioner himself responds and thirsts for the answer. And what are the themes? Only Love, only Death.

There are no different people—there is only one single man, only one single I in the entire universe, willing, acting, suffering, burning in the inextinguishable fire, and from the fury of a horrible and hideous life finding salvation in the cool and comforting embraces of the eternal consoler—Death. . . .

Whatever the content of future tragedy may be, it will not be able to get along without the dance. . . .

The action of the tragedy will be accompanied by and alternated with the dance. Joyous dancing? Perhaps. In any case, more or less frantic. Because dance is nothing other than the rhythmic frenzy of body and soul, plunging into the tragic element of music. . . .

The rhythm of liberation is the rhythm of the dance. The grandeur of liberation is the joy of the beautiful, bare body.[12]

The first promising attempts to translate Symbolist theory into theatrical reality were made by the future great director Vsevolod Meyerhold (1874–1940). Responding to the new ideas about drama and theater Meyerhold founded a "Fellowship of the New Drama" before the start of his second season (1903–4) in Kherson in south Russia.[13] The literary manager of the Fellowship was the original and eccentric Symbolist poet, prose writer, and dramatist Aleksei Remizov (1877–1957). Writing about the new enterprise and its meaning for the Russian stage in his article "Tovarishchestvo novoy dramy" (The Fellowship of the New Drama) in the fourth issue of *The Scales* for April 1904, Remizov's words echo those of Bryusov, Ivanov, and Sologub:

The "New Drama" has as its task the creation of a theater which . . . seized with unquenchable thirst would go in search of new forms for the expression of eternal mysteries . . .

Fulfilling such a task, the theater will rise to the highest summits—great distances will open before the eyes of man, dark depths will gape beneath his feet—and the holy mystery will begin. . . And the actor and viewer, like one being, gripped by ecstasy, will sink into one action, into one feeling. The voices of the soul are incomprehensible and fearful; the voices of the soul are audible only in terrible moments—they blaze up with the fiery tongue of unknown images. And the earth will light up with the smile of the beauty-martyr. The theater is not a game and entertainment; the theater is not a copy of human infirmity. It is a cult, a mass, in the mysteries of which perhaps the Redemption is concealed . . . It is about such a theater that the "New Drama" dreams. (*Vesy, pp. 36–39*)

Under the aegis of the Fellowship Meyerhold turned more in the direction of nonrepresentational drama in the second Kherson season and in the 1904–5 season in Tiflis, the capital of Georgia, doing plays by Maeterlinck, Ibsen (with whom the Symbolists found much that was compatible), and the *enfant terrible* of Polish *fin-de-siècle* literature Stanislaw Przybyszewski (1868–1927). His greatest opportunity to work more with the "new drama" at this early stage of his career came when he was invited by Stanislavsky to become artistic director of a new experimental studio of the Moscow Art Theater founded primarily to stage nonrepresentational plays after its failure in 1904 with a trilogy of Maeterlinck one-acters. The Revolution of 1905 left the project stillborn, however, but hardly had Meyerhold rejoined his Fellowship in Tiflis when his reputation prompted Vera Komissarzhevskaya to invite him to join her company in St. Petersburg as an actor and director. The two indeed stormy seasons Meyerhold worked with Komissarzhevskaya before being dismissed from her company were the highlight of his involvement with Symbolist and Neo-Romantic drama.

After breaking new ground with a more abstract, stylized, and ultimately unsuccessful production of Ibsen's *Hedda Gabbler* on November 10, 1906, Meyerhold proceeded to striking productions of Maeterlinck's liturgical drama *Sister Beatrice*, Blok's *Balganchik* (*The Fairground Booth*), Andreev's *Zhizn cheloveka* (*The Life of Man*), Wedekind's *Spring's Awakening*, and Sologub's *Pobeda smerti* (*The Triumph of Death*), his last work with Komissarzhevskaya before his dismissal.

The years 1904 to 1909 were the most fertile for the realization of a Russian Symbolist mystery drama corresponding to the theoretical desiderata of Bryusov, Ivanov, Sologub, and Remizov, and to the ideas and theatrical experiences of Meyerhold.

Apart from his articles about the drama, Bryusov also wrote plays, the most ambitious of which was *Zemlya* (*Earth*, 1904). The play is unique for Russian symbolism in that it is the only one with a future time setting. Its theme, however, of the apocalyptic end of civilization was typical of many Symbolist works.

On the last days of the Earth the only people still alive are distributed on different levels of a vast roofed city-building resembling the Star City of Bryusov's thematically similar futuristic story "The Republic of the Southern Cross" (1906). One of their number, Nevatl, rejects the passive acceptance of their fate urged by the Order of Liberators and by the political leader of the city, the Consul Tlakatl, who prefer a progressive and "beautiful" extinction. After exploring the different levels of the city Nevatl ascends its uppermost region and comes upon a window in the great cupola-roof through which he can see the sun and the stars. Sharing his inspired vision with others he expresses the belief that the Earth can be saved if only the roof covering the city were opened and fresh air permitted to enter.

The sage Teopikski, who is revered for his wisdom, is consulted and lends his support to the plan. What he does not reveal, however, is that the roof was originally constructed to keep in the air remaining on the planet since there is no atmosphere beyond it. Once the roof is opened, the air on the inside will rush out and all will die. He agrees to the opening of the roof because he would prefer to see mankind pass into oblivion in a tragic but noble struggle to oppose its fate rather than to behold the horrid spectacle of the last survivors of the planet fighting among themselves like animals for the shrinking supplies of food, water, and air. As he says, "Let the last day of mankind be the proud finish of a powerful hero who has accomplished his deed and not the enraged death of a cornered beast who has lost consciousness and will."[14]

Although Consul Tlakatl and his followers try to prevent the roof from being opened, the mechanism has been set in motion and it is too late to stop it. In the play's last scene, the roof opens with a shattering roar and a sheaf of sunlight breaks in. As one of the hushed throng cries out that it is a "fiery angel sounding a golden trumpet"—in other words, the Apocalypse—the Chairman of the Order of Liberators, Teotl, ecstatically greets Death. Soon the groaning and writhing of the throng of people ceases and the blinding sun illuminates a mass cemetery.

Although *Earth* is scenically intriguing in its design of space and movement and incorporates genuine dramatic tension, it is so much a vehicle for basic Symbolist concepts and images of pretechnological man, naural life, death, transfiguration, and light that it falters rhythmically in torrents of verbosity. For this reason above all Meyerhold advised Bryusov against producing the play.

After a hiatus of several years, Bryusov returned to the drama writing two more original plays before undertaking translations of Molière and Maeterlinck. In 1910 he did the one-act "psychodrama" *Putnik* (*The Wayfarer*), an obvious and unconvincing imitation of the early Maeterlinck about Julia, the forester's daughter, who admits into their home when she is alone a silent stranger to whom she gives the name Robert.

The stranger only nods replies to Julia's questions and after she shares with him her romantic daydreams of a prince charming sent to her by Fate, she offers herself to him. Disturbed by his lack of response, she presses him into her embrace only to discover that he is dead. She thereupon rushes from the house screaming.

The Wayfarer was followed in 1911–12 by an excursion into classical Greek antiquity in the form of the tragedy *Protesilay umershiy* (*Protesilaus Deceased*), yet another treatment of the myth of Laodamia and Protesilaus which held much appeal for the neo-Romantics and was made the subject of several plays by them (as we shall see later in this chapter). Apart from a rather scrupulous adherence to classical Greek dramatic structure—particularly in his use of the Chorus—Bryusov's version of the myth is surprisingly flat, less appealing than those by Annensky and Sologub, and interesting primarily for Bryusov's typically Symbolist theurgical and metaphysical emphases: Protesilaus' brief return to life results from a pact between Laodamia and a witch, and her perception of death as the "sole truth" makes her unafraid to commit suicide with Protesilaus' sword in order to join him in the other world.

Long interested in the theater, Bryusov played an undeniably important role in the development of Russian Symbolist drama, but as a dramatic writer his talent was limited and he never surpassed his first, flawed contribution to the "new drama"—*Earth*.

The cultivation of the "neo-mystery" intensified in the years between Bryusov's *Earth* and *The Wayfarer* and engaged the talents of writers in and outside the Symbolist camp. Among the Symbolists, the lyrico-fantastic *Tri rastsveta* (*Three Blossomings*)[15] by the poet Konstantin Balmont (1867–1943) at least had the distinction of being staged—in January 1906—in one of the small new Petersburg theaters of the time, the Theater of Dionysus.[16] The production, not unexpectedly, was a dismal failure and the weak play about Beauty, Love, and Transfiguration faded with hardly an echo. More successful dramatically, if not theatrically, were two plays conceived in the spirit of the mystery by Aleksei Remizov whom we met earlier as the literary director of Meyerhold's Fellowship of the New Drama.

Remizov was steeped in Old Russian culture, both secular and religious, had a splendid command of the Old Russian language, and mined Russian folklore as a source of myth and style. These various elements combine to inform his theatrical works with a highly personal and unique flavor. In *Besovskoe deystvo* (*The Devil Play*, 1907) and *Tragediya ob Iude, printse Iskariotskom* (*The Tragedy of Judas, Prince of Is-*

cariot, 1909) Remizov fused folk motifs and the medieval mystery for the purpose of conveying the spirit of Russian folk theater in which he was strongly interested. It was this same interest that led him in 1919 to write his own version of the famous Old Russian popular drama *Tsar Maximilian*.

Based on a legend in the medieval Kievo-Pechersk Paterikon (Lives of the Saints of the Monastery of the Caves in Kiev), *The Devil Play* is a macabre yet rollicking free-for-all of devils stalking souls for hell and the eventual salvation of a cave-dwelling ascetic monk who becomes their special target. There are scenes in hell that could just as well have come from the canvases of a Hieronymus Bosch and one stage direction that gives pause for thought—it calls for the onstage separation of a soul from its body and its transport to hell in the maws of a serpent who spews it out onto the hellfires. Of all the plays written by the Russian Symbolists in what they construed to be the spirit of the Middle Ages, none comes closer to the style and color of the popular medieval mystery and morality than Remizov's *Devil Play*.

The Tragedy of Judas, in some ways the more interesting of Remizov's theatrical works, dramatizes an apocryphal legend of Judas of unknown origin found in the Church of the Resurrection in Putivl, in the district of Kursk. Although new interpretations of various biblical events and personages resulted from the Christian revisionism of the *fin-de-siècle*, Remizov's version of Judas is indeed curious. The imminent betrayal of Jesus in Jerusalem comes only as a declared intention by Judas at the very end of the play. Until then, the *Tragedy of Judas* unfolds as a melodrama of dynastic rivalry invoving the princes of the island of Iscariot—Judas and Stratim—and the scheming Unkrada, a distant relation from a far-off northern land, presumably Russia. Complicating the political intrigue is the fact that Judas is also the central figure in an Oedipal prophecy fulfilled in the course of the play. An exile from Iscariot in Jerusalem, Judas becomes the steward of Pilate's manor. While fetching golden apples for his master from an adjacent garden Judas kills the keeper of the miraculous orchard, marries his widow, and then discovers that the gardener was his father and that his wife is his mother who abandoned him at birth out of fear of a dreadful prophecy. Burdened with grief and self-loathing, Judas rushes out to find Jesus in order to expiate his sin by taking upon himself for the whole world—in the spirit of Christ's sacrifice—the "last and heaviest guilt" which Unkrada articulates as the betrayal of Jesus, the bearer of a "new order."

Remizov's play merits attention not only for the merging of the classical Greek myth of Oedipus and the New Testament account of Judas's betrayal of Jesus—which follows a pattern of medieval apocrypha—but also for its extensive use of folk elements. This folk stylization manifests itself especially in the speech of Judas' followers Orif and Zif who, like Pilate and the King of the Apes who appears in the play, wear half-masks throughout in a borrowing from antique theater as well as from the Italian commedia dell'arte. Furthermore, Judas himself is linked by name to ancient Slavic mythology, according to Remizov, since Yuda is a Slavic water divinity and is preserved in the person of the Russian fairy-tale hero Chuda-Yuda. Remizov has one of his characters explain, in fact, that the Slavic Yuda is from the Latin root *und* (as in the English "undine"). Although *The Devil Play* was staged in 1907 to a slightly less hostile and incredulous reception than Balmont's *Three Blossomings*, Remizov's colorful mystery plays must be regarded as among the more fascinating Symbolist contributions to the drama.

At one point in the *Tragedy of Judas* the King of the Apes, attended by a great retinue, presents himself at the court of Pilate. This procession is accompanied by an "ape march" composed by another sometime associate of Meyerhold and one of the more talented though lesser known writers of the period, the post-Symbolist Mikhail Kuzmin (1875–1936).

Long denied the recognition commensurate with his talent because of the notoriety over his unapologetic advocacy of homosexual love, above all in his novel *Krylya* (*Wings*, 1907), Kuzmin would truly be a forgotten figure today were it not for the work of his Western admirers, especially in the United States.[17]

The ease with which Soviet literary scholarship prefers to ignore him is constrained only by the fact that Kuzmin's musical as well as literary abilities were highly valued—and made use of—by Meyerhold. It was Kuzmin, in fact, who wrote the music for Meyerhold's brilliant première production of Blok's *The Fairground Booth* at Vera Komissarzhevskaya's theater on December 30, 1906. Both Kuzmin and Meyerhold were also prominently associated with the small theaters and cabarets from which the artistic life especially of St. Petersburg drew so much vitality and color in the early years of this century.

Sharing Meyerhold's enthusiasm for the traditions of the commedia dell'arte, the plays of Carlo Gozzi, and the whole brilliant rococo ambience of late eighteenth-century Venice, it was Kuzmin who suggested that Meyerhold take the name of Dr. Dapertutto for his "unofficial" theatrical activity in the period of his directorship of the St. Petersburg Imperial theaters from 1908 to 1917. And when Meyerhold's "intimate" cabaret theater, the Dom intermedii (House of Interludes), opened on October 9, 1910, the first item on the program was a "prologue" by Kuzmin.

A native of the world of *fin-de-siècle* Art Nouveau aestheticism and "decadence" exemplified by the drawings of Aubrey Beardsley (whose poems Kuzmin translated for a Russian collection of the Englishman's work in 1912), Kuzmin's tastes inclined to the elegant, the graceful, the stylishly erotic. Inspired by the arts of eighteenth-century rococo France as well as Venice he was keenly interested in the stage and wrote a number of plays, pantomimes, ballets, masquerades, and pastorals. Printed in journals or separate editions in very small quantities and never reprinted in Russia,[18] his works have been difficult to find and have long enjoyed the status of bibliophilic rarities. The sole collections of his plays to have been published appeared in 1907 and 1908.[19] The first volume contains three short works: *Opasnaya predostorozhnost* (*Dangerous Precaution*), a "comedy with singing" with a homosexual theme; *Dva pastukha i nimfa v khizhine* (*Two Shepherds and a Nymph in a Hut*), a "pastoral for a masquerade"; and the "mime ballet" *Vybor nevesty* (*The Choice of a Bride*). The second, more important volume is made up of three short "comedies" in the vein of the Symbolist efforts to create a new liturgical drama through a modernization of the medieval mystery play.

Kuzmin's plays in the collection of 1908—*O Yevdokii iz Geliopolya, ili Obrashchonnaya kurtizanka* (*Eudoxia of Heliopolis, or The Reformed Courtesan*), *O Aleksee cheloveke bozhem, ili Poteryanny i obrashchonny syn* (*Alexis, Man of God, or The Lost and Found Son*), and *O Martiniane* (*Martinianus*)—belong, in one sense, to the mystery genre in that each play celebrates a spiritual triumph over worldly temptation. In *Eudoxia of Heliopolis*, the abiding sense of loneliness experienced by the superbly drawn and patently *fin-de-siècle* courtesan Eudoxia, the "rose of Heliopolis," is overcome at last when she renounces the world and enters a convent. So powerful is her new saintliness that she succeeds in converting Filostrat, who loves her madly. He even expresses a desire to become a monk just to be near her. A similar conversion of the courtesan Zoe takes place in *Martinianus*. One of two women sent by the Devil to seduce the young monk Martinianus, she is so inspired by his self-mortifying holiness that she renounces her past way of life. Torn between love of God and love of his new wife, the saintly Alexis, in the play bearing his name, leaves his bride on their wedding night to follow the path of piety. Returning home out of loneliness after seventeen years away, he is unrecognized by his insensitive wife and by his father, who at least provides him shelter as a pious stranger. Only with his death do they learn that a miracle took place in their midst.

Unlike most Russian efforts of the time to create a new mystery play, Kuzmin's little "comedies" are immensely appealing and lend themselves to the stage. Much of their appeal, which brief synopses in no way can convey, lies in their conciseness, their mixture of prose, verse, and song, their simplicity of diction, and their marvelous blending of humor and irony. If their purpose is solemn, their manner indeed is not, which sets them poles apart from the majority of Symbolist "neo-mysteries." Blok's remarks about *Eudoxia of Heliopolis* in his article "O drame" (On Drama, 1907) are particularly apt for all three plays: "The melody of the mystery rings like a little silver bell in the fresh evening air. This is the most perfect creation in the sphere of *lyrical drama* in Russia, permeated with a kind of charming melancholy and imbued with the most delicate poisons of that irony which is so unique to the art of Kuzmin."[20]

Although Symbolist-inspired mystery plays continued to be written down to the early 1920s (as late as 1922, for example, the prominent Soviet writer Ilya Ehrenburg published a mystery called *Zolotoe serdtse, The Golden Heart,* during his long residence in the West), the years 1907 and 1908 seemed to mark both the outward range of productive cultivation of the genre among writers part of or close to the Symbolist movement and at the same time the appearance of a reaction against the mystery play and Symbolist dramaturgy in general.

In the time that Kuzmin was working on what may ultimately be recognized as the brightest and most theatrically viable plays related to the Symbolist development of the mystery, an institution came into being with the purpose of providing a platform for the exhibition of exemplary mystery plays drawn from the European historical tradition. In view of the absence of a native Russian medieval theater and yet the contemporary enthusiasm for the mystery play emanating from Symbolist quarters, the establishment of the St. Petersburg Starinny teatr (Theater of Antiquity) in 1907 was intended to fill the gap by making available in translation and adaptation representative European medieval plays. The theater was the brainchild of Meyerhold's successor at Vera Komissarzhevskaya's theater and one of the pioneers of theatricalism in early twentieth-century Russia, Nikolai Yevreinov (1879–1953).[21] Collaborating with him in the enterprise were the well-to-do theatrophile Baron N. V. Drizen (Driesen) and several prominent artists of the World of Art group.

A truly extraordinary, multifaceted talent, Yevreinov was a lawyer by profession, a musician by training, and an all-around man of the theater by inclination. He was a prolific dramatist, a theorist and historian of the theater, a director, a producer, and an actor. Although he lived over a quarter of a century in France after exiling himself from Russia in 1925, his most important and far-reaching theater work dates from before his departure.

The Theater of Antiquity, which was to be an important proving ground for Yevreinov's evolving theory of theatricalism, lasted just two seasons. The first, 1907–8, was given over almost entirely to medieval drama; the second, 1911–12, was devoted to productions of the great Spanish Baroque drama of Lope de Vega and Calderón which became a major source of theatricalist inspiration. A third season, for performances of the commedia dell'arte, was planned but never materialized.

Accompanying the first manifestations of a crystallizing Symbolist sensibility in Russia in the late 1880s and the '90s was a new interest in medieval drama and theater, as we have seen. Recognition of the absence of a native tradition led to attempts to assimilate the West European, especially that of France, by means of translations and adaptations such as Merezhkovsky's short and undramatic *Khristos, angely i dusha* (*Christ, the Angels, and the Soul,* 1892) which was based on a work by the Italian medieval religious poet Jacopone da Todi.[22]

As symbolism developed into an important literary movement, more scholarly and popular writing about the medieval stage was disseminated. But when the contemporary Russian theater began to respond to the new impulses, beginning with Meyerhold's Fellowship, the foreign mystery plays staged were not those of the medieval tradition but rather "neo-mysteries" by contemporary European authors, principally Maeterlinck. It was only with the first season of Yevreinov's Theater of Antiquity that a systematic effort was made to bring the authentic medieval drama to the stage.

In the 1907–8 season, the Theater of Antiquity mounted, in the course of two evenings, an eleventh-century Latin language liturgical drama on the three Magi theme for which Yevreinov wrote a special prologue under the title *Tri volkhva* (*The Three Magi*); the twelfth-century *Le Miracle de Théophile* by the French poet Rutebeuf, translated by the poet Blok; the thirteenth-century pastorale *Le Jeu de Robin et Marion* by the French trouvère Adam de la Halle; the fifteenth-century morality play known in Russian as *Dva brata* (*Two Brothers*); and two short sixteenth-century farces. Of equal importance in the productions of the Theater of Antiquity was the care and artistic ingenuity with which the audience of the period of each play was depicted.

Yevreinov's prologue to the *Three Magi* is perhaps the most interesting example of this. In an eleventh-century German locale, the prologue sets the stage for the performance of a mystery play about the Christ child and the visit of the three Magi. The mystery play proper, which will be performed on the steps of and within a church, is presented entirely in Latin. In the Russian prologue Yevreinov dramatizes the preparation of the playing area for the performance, the arrival of the actors, and the increasing and finally explosive involvement of the audience in the performance. Yevreinov had a very definite purpose in mind in his prologue and that was to demonstrate the communion of spectator and actor achieved by the strong emotional appeal of medieval sacral theater. Since this spiritual communion was a goal of the Symbolist writers of "neo-mysteries" and also underlay the contemporary European revival of "festival theater," Yevreinov sought to convey the marvelous theatrical process whereby this communion takes place. The growing agitation and bewilderment of the crowd as the Latin play commences reaches a fever pitch when it becomes apparent that Herod has ordered the killing of the Christ child. Angered, people in the crowd curse, shake their fists, and expectorate at the whispering of Herod and a sword-bearer. But when soldiers appear and make their way toward the interior of the church wherein the image of Christ is kept, the crowd overturns its benches and surges wildly into the church to save the Christ child from certain death. The contrast at this time between the precise movements of the actors, their recitation in Latin, and the singing of a choir within the church, and the frenzied onrush of the crowd is theatrically gripping as this excerpt from the end of the prologue may suggest:

> CHORUS (*Choir singing within the church*): Gloriosi et famosi regis festum celebrantes gaudeamus; cujus ortum vitae portum nobis datum praedicantes habeamus. (*But the crowd no longer hears the choir. As soon as the soldiers appeared, it rushed toward the church with sighs, curses, and a frenzied roar. Almost everyone seated on benches jumped up from their places, knocking over the benches in the process. Burgomasters, bailiff, and guards helplessly wave their*

*hands at the crowd. Darkness. The fading singing of the choir can
be heard.*)[23]

By the time the "medieval" season of the Theater of Antiquity had
drawn to an end and with it the most impressive theatricalization of the
mystery play in *fin-de-siècle* and early twentieth-century Russia, voices
of opposition to symbolism in the drama and theater began to be heard,
the most audible coming eventually from within the Symbolist camp itself. The pattern had already been established as early as 1896 by Chekhov's *The Seagull* in which the unfortunate Treplyov's Symbolist playlet
about the end of the world remains one of the most telling parodies of
the archetypal Symbolist play ever written.

Blok was the first major Symbolist writer to break ranks. Beginning
with *The Fairground Booth* of 1906, which will be discussed more fully
under the rubric of "theatricalism," the lyrical, mystic, apocalyptic, and
thanatomantic tendencies of symbolism became the ever more frequent
targets of parody, satire, and outright ridicule. As polemical as it is
parodical, *The Fairground Booth* mocks not only Maeterlinck, the most
important foreign source of inspiration for Russian Symbolist drama, but
also as patently ludicrous an attempt at Symbolist mystic drama as Bely's
He Who Has Come of 1903. In his intelligent essay "On Drama" of 1907
Blok went so far, in fact, as to dismiss virtually the entire canon of European Symbolist drama:

> The last great dramatist of Europe was Ibsen . . . with the work of
> Hauptmann,   d'Annunzio,   Maeterlinck,   even   Hofmannsthal,
> Przybyszewski, and Schnitzler the sun began to set. Some of these
> writers it befell to rid the drama of a hero, to deprive it of action, to
> surrender dramatic pathos, to lower the metallic voice of tragedy to
> the hoarse whisper of life. But in the West this happened according
> to some immutable laws; Western drama reached its crisis with a
> kind of mathematical precision, by way of cultural evolution.

Blok's sharpest barbs, however, are reserved for Maeterlinck and especially the cult of Maeterlinck in Russia:

> . . . his name alone is already a dogma, one of those dogmas clung
> to by people who violate others. Visitors to Russian productions of
> Maeterlinck are already daring to reprove though only in a whisper.
> (The performances sometimes are hilarious: the actors try their best
> to be subtle, with the result that nothing can be heard, and some-
> times, for the sake of subtlety, nothing can be seen; the audience,

on the other hand, listens attentively and applauds, but frequently neither the actors nor the spectators understand anything.[24]

As if following Blok's example of the auto-parody with which *The Fairground Booth* is also informed, Sologub, whose Symbolist essay on theater, "The Theater of One Will," was quoted earlier, similarly incorporated parodic and satirical elements in his first play to be staged, *The Triumph of Death*. A legendary Neo-Romantic drama with a medieval setting, *The Triumph of Death* was staged by Meyerhold at Vera Komissarzhevskaya's theater on November 6, 1907, and published in 1908. For the production of the play, which came nearly a year after he wrote it, Sologub added a Prologue with a tone entirely different from that of the play proper, which is a tragedy.

In the Prologue, a Poet (played by Meyerhold himself in the original production), clearly intended as a burlesque of a Symbolist incapable of relating to the world around him, and a Lady suddenly appear within the halls of an enchanted royal castle which they take to be a restaurant. Their modern clothing and banal conversation contrast with the fantastic surroundings and invite laughter. At one point, for example, the "living and dead water" of Russian folklore they take to be red and white wine. When they are joined by the poor, plain-looking peasant girl Aldonsa, who is to be transformed into a major personage of the tragedy, it soon becomes evident that the Prologue has been conceived as an ironic commentary on the transfigurative aspirations of the Symbolist mystery. Sologub could also have had in mind his own dramatized ritual *Liturgiya mne* (*A Liturgy to Myself*, 1907). As the Prologue draws to an end Aldonsa, frustrated in her desire to be recognized as the legendary beauty Dulcinea she believes she is and to be celebrated by poets, tells the Poet and his Lady to take seats and behold the play that follows. Then this dialogue occurs:

POET: . . . this strange girl promises us a spectacle.
ALDONSA (DULCINEA): It depends on you whether it is to be only a spectacle or a mystery.
POET: She's speaking about the "intimate theater." Let's have a look.[25]

Shortly thereafter, Aldonsa-Dulcinea closes the Prologue by declaring resignedly that once again "a spectacle will remain a spectacle and not become a mystery." For the Poet and his world at least no transfiguration is possible.

The theme of the ultimate hopelessness of communication between the real and the ideal world is taken up again by Sologub in his play *Noch-nye plyaski* (*Nocturnal Dances*, 1908). When it was staged by Yevreinov at Fyodor Komissarzhevsky's Merry Theater for Grown-up Children (Vesyoly teatr dlya pozhilykh detey) in St. Petersburg, several leading personalities of the contemporary Russian art world (the writer Remizov, the painter Leon Bakst, for example) took part in the production (choreographed by Michel Fokine) and made of it a memorable theatrical event.[26] The play is a delightful dramatization of the Russian fairy tale of the twelve princesses who slip away at night to dance ecstatically in an enchanted underground kingdom. Like the Poet in the Prologue to *The Triumph of Death*, the Young Poet who is sent to spy on the princesses by the king in *Nocturnal Dances* becomes an intruder in a realm of fantasy whose magic he cannot grasp and only defiles. The report he delivers to the king achieves the same discordant juxtaposition of the contemporary and the fantastic, the real and the ideal as the conversation between the Poet and the Lady in the Prologue to *The Triumph of Death*: "The lovely princesses enter the underground kingdom of an enchanted ruler and dance there all night, performing in the style of the famous Isadora Duncan to the music of composers of different times and nations."[27]

Perhaps it was only fitting for the author of one of the most pretentiously silly Symbolist "neo-mystery" plays to repudiate symbolism in the drama in the strongest terms. Five years after the publication of *He Who Has Come* and a year after the equally fragmentary *The Jaws of Night*, in 1908, Andrei Bely dispelled some of his personal demons in his essay "Teatr i sovremennaya drama" (The Theater and Contemporary Drama) which was included in the same important collection of Symbolist essays on theater, *Teatr: Kniga o novom teatre* (*Theater: A Book about the New Theater*), in which Sologub's "Theater of One Will" appeared. Beginning with an assault on the "neo-mystery" play, Bely concludes by emphasizing the nontheatrical nature of Symbolist drama:

> These sweet summonses to mysterion are suspicious in our time; they lull courage to sleep. When we are told now that the stage is a religious rite, the actor a priest, and viewing the play our communion with the mystery, we understand these words in an undefined, almost senseless way. What is a religious rite? Is it a deed of religious action? But of what sort? Before whom is this a religious rite? And to what god must we pray? If so, give us a goat for the sacrifice. The "temple" is still the Mariinsky Theater, and the restaurant a restaurant. We must not flee from life into a theater in order to sing and dance over the tragic dead goat and then, happen-

ing upon life, to be amazed at what we have done. This is how flight from Fate takes place. . . .

Symbolist drama is not drama, but a homily of the great, ever growing drama of mankind. It is a homily of the approach of a fateful denouement. And the best examples of Symbolist drama must be read and not viewed on the stage. The theater is not the place for Symbolist drama.[28]

===== **Neo-Romanticism** =====

Metaphysical Allegory

If theatrical success eluded the Symbolists it came bountifully to one of the best-known Russian writers of the early twentieth century, Leonid Andreev (1871–1919). A Neo-Romantic only marginally related to the Symbolists (who, with the exception of Blok, held him in light regard), Andreev succeeded where the Symbolists failed at devising a theatrically plausible and at times even effective type of allegorical rather than symbolistic "cosmic" drama that demonstrates perhaps better than the plays of any of his contemporaries the impact on Russian drama of Maeterlinck's ideas on static drama and metaphysical tragedy (which Andreev later repudiated).

Remembered now chiefly for such macabre stories as *The Seven Who Were Hanged* and *The Red Laugh* and for his one play to evince any real theatrical durability, *Tot, kto poluchaet poshchochiny (He Who Gets Slapped*, 1915), Andreev was a formidable literary presence in his own time: prolific, admired, debated, and very widely translated especially in the English- and Spanish-speaking worlds. A sometime member of Gorky's *Znanie* (under whose auspices his first published play *Savva* appeared in 1910), Andreev turned markedly conservative after the Revolution of 1905 and severed his connections with the socially activist, prorevolutionary group. The Bolshevik seizure of power in 1917 so exacerbated this conservatism that he felt it was no longer possible for him to remain in Russia. He emigrated to Finland and, bitter and disillusioned, remained there until his death in 1919.

Within a few years after his passing, Andreev's Russian reputation suffered a sharp decline. To the Soviets he was totally unacceptable for his repudiation of the revolutionary cause and his venomous postrevolutionary anti-Bolshevik pamphleteering. Moreover, until recent times the Soviets have tended to dismiss the literature of neo-romanticism as "decadent" except in the cases of writers (like Blok) who embraced the Revolution and sang its praises in their works. Symbolist aesthetics and the marked proclivity of neo-romanticism for the mystic, occult, and erotic ran so counter to the artistic and social views of the Communists that precious little room for accommodation existed.

Among Russian émigrés—and, with changes in style, among most non-Russians as well—Andreev's extreme pessimism and taste for the macabre progressively lost favor, with the result that he came to be looked upon as not much more than a once-popular but basically shallow writer of philosophic pretensions. With little modification, the image has persisted to the present. The qualification is based on the appearance of the first new monographs on Andreev in many years: James B. Woodward's *Leonid Andreev: A Study* (Oxford, 1969), a substantial, well-reasoned, and objective book, and Josephine M. Newcombe's considerably shorter but competent *Leonid Andreyev* (New York, 1973); both of these may initiate a partial rehabilitation of Andreev's reputation, at least in the English-speaking world.

In his own time, Andreev was a productive and varied dramatist. *Savva* (1906), his first published play, is realistic in mode and based on the bombing of the famous holy image in the Znamensky Monastery in Kursk by a self-taught inventor of nihilistic inclinations, A. G. Ufimtsev, and several of his friends. The affair also served as the subject of a play, *V ogne* (*In the Fire*), by F. N. Falkovsky, which was produced in the Korsh Theater in Moscow in 1903. Andreev's original intention was to use the material as the subject for a story, but the Falkovsky play probably opened his eyes to its dramatic potential and resulted in a change of plans.

Andreev never completely abandoned realistic drama, although his name is usually linked to the metaphysics of symbolism. In 1908 he wrote *Dni nashey zhizni* (*The Days of Our Life*), about the life of a poor student reflecting, at least in part, his own experiences as a law student in Petersburg and Moscow. The play proved quite popular and continued to be performed until 1938. *Gaudeamus* (1910) and *Mladost* (*Youth*, 1915) hewed to the same line of traditional realism. More naturalistic in style and dealing with themes common to naturalism such as the disintegration of a bourgeois family, philistine vulgarity, and the "fall" of a woman of passion are: *Anfisa* (1909), *Professor Storitsyn* (1912), *Yekaterina Ivanovna* (1912), and *Nye ubiy* (*Thou Shalt Not Kill*, 1913). Andreev's interest in politics, dating back at least to his *Znanie* days, furnished him material for plays of an essentially realistic character throughout his career. If they began with an attitude of calm sympathy for revolution as in his earliest drama, *K zvyozdam* (*To the Stars*, 1905), they gradually became more conservative in tone and notable for their antibourgeois and antipseudoliberal satire, as in the one-act *Luybov k blizhnemu (Love for One's Neighbor,* 1908), *Prekrasnye Sabinyanki (The Fair Sabine Women,* 1911), the publicistic *Korol, zakon i svoboda (King, Law and Freedom,* 1914), the one-act *Kon v senate (A Horse in the Senate,* 1915), and the one-act *Monument* (1916). Andreev's principal efforts in a symbolic and allegorical vein, derived partly from Maeterlinck, date from 1906 to 1910 and include *Zhizn cheloveka (The Life of Man,* 1906), *Tsar-Golod (King Hunger,* 1907), *Chornye maski (Black Masks,* 1908), and *Anafema* (Anathema) and *Okean (Ocean),* both written in 1910. A few years before his death Andreev wrote the play he is best known for in the West, *He Who Gets Slapped* (1915), a merging of realism and romantic melodrama, the biblical and psychological *Samson v okovakh (Samson in Chains,* 1915), and *Milye prizraki (Pleasant Phantoms,* 1916), a psychological study of the earlier Dostoevsky.

Following the realistic *To the Stars* and *Savva,* Andreev struck out in a new direction—that of philosophical allegory—in his next play, *The Life of Man,* also completed in 1906. A theatrical event when it opened at Komissarzhevskaya's theater on February 22, 1907, it deserves to be considered a high-water mark of Russian dramatic symbolism, although Andreev's detractors have been quick to dismiss it as inflated and pretentious. Andreev, to be sure, is often overblown and pretentious in his "philosophical" plays; but in the case of *The Life of Man* the overly negative assessment is the result, to a great extent, of a common misinterpretation of the play as a derivative Maeterlinckian tragedy in allegorcial style about the universal human condition.

In five acts undivided into scenes, Andreev dramatizes his conception of the five periods of a common—if not necessarily universal—life cycle: birth (I), marriage and the hardships of a beginning career (II), success and fame (III), misfortune and decline (IV), and death (V). The vision of man's earthly sojourn is personal and grim yet consonant with the Neo-Romantic *Weltanschauung:* there is no pleasure that is not accompanied or followed by pain, no attainment without loss. The joy of birth is tempered by the terrible pains of the mother in labor; the happiness of love and marriage is offset by the misery of poverty; success brings fame and riches but also sycophantic fawning and envy; worldly success and material wealth are followed by failure and loss (in *The Life of Man* wealth is dissipated and Man's son is cruelly taken from him by death); death, when it finally comes to Man himself, claims its victim in loneliness and despair. And beyond death, what? Andreev is silent.

Ever present as Man treads the bittersweet path of life is the Someone-in-gray (Death? Fate? God? A projection of Man's own conception of life?), expressionless, a candle in his hand, its length and the
brightness of its flame symbolic of the period of life and the length of the
road yet to be traversed.

Light sets the mood of the play; a chiaroscuro extends from the synop-
tic Prologue to the final curtain. Figures move from darkness or a
grayness into a dim, hazy light, or into the flickering light of a candle or,
conversely, from bright warm light into an ever encroaching darkness.
Apart from the second act, when Man and his wife early in their marriage take refuge from the reality of their poverty in a game- and flower-
filled private world of dreams and illusions, the stiff, jerky, puppetlike
movements of the characters correspond to the artificial, highly stylized
rhythms of the language. This is best seen in Act III when Andreev uses
a ball scene, with music and dance, to convey the sumptuousness of
Man's life style after the attainment of material success and the shallowness and insincerity of personal relationships.

In the original version of the drama, the first part of Act V is played in
a shabby basement peopled with drunkards, a setting reminiscent of
Gorky's *The Lower Depths*. Alone, his wife dead, Man, his own death
close at hand, seeks the companionship of even the grotesque figures of
the basement tavern to relieve the bitterness of his loneliness and isolation. Later, reacting to the adverse judgments of critics (Blok, for example), Andreev wrote a variant of Act V in which the barroom scene is
omitted and the poignancy of Man's lonely suffering is set in bold relief
by the introduction of heirs who surround his deathbed waiting for him
to die. Their thoughts on the anticipated legacy, their conversation is
unfeeling and inane.

The tenor of much of the criticism of *The Life of Man*—the recognition that Andreev had created something new in Russian drama and yet
the inability to grasp fully what Andreev intended with it—is amply
demonstrated in the long letter Gorky wrote him from Capri in October
1906 after reading the play:

> *The Life of Man* is a superb thing as an attempt to create a new
> form of drama. I think that of all the efforts of this kind yours is re-
> ally the most successful. It seems to me that you have taken the
> forms of the old mystery but have discarded the mystery heroes,
> with extremely interesting and original results. In places, as for ex-
> ample in describing the friends and enemies of the man, you in-
> troduce the simplicity and evil naïveté of the cheap religious pic-

ture; that is also your own, and it too is good. The language in this play is the best that you have ever achieved.

But—you hurried. In the life of your man, there is almost no human life, and what there is is too artificial, not real. The man therefore has turned out to be very insignificant, less and weaker than he actually was, less interesting. The man who speaks so splendidly with Someone-in-gray cannot live such an empty life as he lives in your play; his existence is more tragic, the dramas in his life are more frequent. In the life of your man I see one drama only: the death of his son. This is a trifle. When he gets rich, he is completely incomprehensible; is he satisfied with riches? How much? Is he dissatisfied? How much? And riches are also dramatic for a strong spirit. His (your hero's) relations toward his wife are bucolic, not natural. People don't live with their wives all their lives as if they were just friends and that's the way you have shown him; why?

Now I have met an odd fellow, the famous artist Diffenbakh. In one of his pictures he painted himself in this way: he is dragging a heavy cross up a mountain. On the end of the cross his wife is sitting, and a church lashes him with a whip while it upholds his wife. This is of course too coarse as a symbol, but it is reality. You say: I don't want reality! Understand (I am speaking about content, not form); it cannot but be real; I hope this needs no proof.

In general, you have stripped your man down too much, removing him from reality and in this way depriving him of tragedy, flesh, and blood. All this has been written with too much emphasis on the form, and I can't avoid the natural desire to emphasize the insignificance, the incompleteness, the poverty of the life of your man. I also note that the presence of old women in the first acts recalls *L'Intruse* by Maeterlinck. The old women are hard to understand; what are they? You told I. P. that they are lesser fates (*podsudbinki*), but lesser fates, as Afanasev points out, symbolize not only the forces of nature hostile to man but primarily represent those things in life which people think are chance happenings but which result from a chain of causes arising from the relations between people and thus become logically necessary. The last act is beautiful, a picture, but the old women hinder us from understanding it and ruin the tragedy of the end of life. I also cannot understand why you chose a tavern as the place for your man's final downfall. Why not a church? Not the square where he begins his fight with Somone-in-gray before the people's eyes. My certainty of the force of your talent tells me that you might have written this very significant work still better than you wrote it. There. But you hurry. Where to? You haven't anywhere to rush to, believe me. No one values you as I do, and I know that you are not writing just for the present, and I emphasize this. You will not only be read in the future but will be studied.[29]

Behind Gorky's essentially negative appraisal and that of many other critics (including such prominent writers of the Symbolist camp as Bryusov and Gippius) lay the erroneous reading of *The Life of Man* as a universal statement of the human condition; through the character of Man, it was believed, Andreev sought to generalize all human life experience. Not only that, but in view of the somberness and pessimism of the play it was assumed that Andreev intended a repudiation of life itself. By failing to appreciate that in *The Life of Man* Andreev is not repudiating man himself, that is *being*, but a certain quality of life, a life style, the entire ethos, in fact, of bourgeois philistinism, his critics simply missed the point of the work. In a Schopenhauerian sense, Andreev does depict man's life on earth as forever accompanied by pain and misery, forever doomed to frustration in its quest for the fulfillment of all desires. But Andreev's gloom is qualified. Man is capable of rebellion: he can rise up against a universal pattern of life and its values and assert his dignity and even nobility as man through rebellion, whatever the outcome. It is principally through his capacity for and articulation of such rebellion that the Man of *The Life of Man* acquires individuality and refutes the facile charge of mere abstraction. But in the final analysis Man's failure is the failure of the type he represents: the voicing of rebellion remains unsupported by deeds. From the time of his maturity, Man directs his life along the path of conventional bourgeois success. Nothing exists but the gratification of his will and the will manifests itself in the pursuit and attainment of goals held up as ideals by contemporary bourgeois society.

In his long letter to Andreev about *The Life of Man* Gorky mentions the old women of Act I reminding him of Maeterlinck's *The Intruder*. Reacting very adversely to *The Life of Man*, Zinaida Gippius went so far as to dismiss the play as just an inept imitation of Maeterlinck.

The association works up to a point. Andreev was certainly no less susceptible to the Belgian's influence than most of the other dramatists of his time who were inclined to symbolism. But a play such as *The Life of Man*, whatever the Maeterlinckian reminiscences, cannot be defined merely by reference to the type of dramaturgy for which Maeterlinck won greatest renown. Andreev shares with the Belgian a generally pessimistic view of life. Death figures prominently in the plays of both. Language—and often gesture—are stylized, and light, sound, and silence are important in establishing a quality of mood. But Andreev goes beyond the evocation of the mystery and dread of unseen and unknowable forces, beyond the sinister insinuation of the presence of death. *The*

Life of Man is a dramatic symbol of a way of life repugnant to Andreev
for its essential debasement of the inherent dignity of man. The somberness and pervasive mood of Maeterlinckian drama realize Andreev's
point of view, but resemblance vaporizes beyond this level.

In *Anathema*, Andreev's second major excursion into an allegorical
drama of existence, the links to Maeterlinck also hardly range beyond
superficials: characters in close proximity to death, death itself, old and
blind people, and so on. More universal in its philosophical conception
than *The Life of Man* this play too conceals a celebration of man's capacity for nobility beneath a cloak of wretchedness, a point lost on conservative Russian ecclesiastics at the time who regarded *Anathema* as blas-
phemous and fought tooth and nail and finally succeeded in having the
play banned from the stage after twenty-seven performances.[30] Once
again, as in *The Life of Man*, Andreev's vision encompasses both the
metaphysical and the social.

On the metaphysical plane Anathema (a fusion of Satan and Faust)
predicates his demand (of God) for infinite knowledge and wisdom on
the triumph of logic and reason (which he represents) over love (which
God represents). The focus of conflict is a provincial Jewish shopkeeper
named David Leyzer. Anathema appears out of nowhere (and in the
guise of an ordinary mortal) to inform David that he has inherited four
million rubles from a brother who died in America. After finally accepting the money and altering his life style to that of a wealthy man, David
soon discovers that riches and happiness are not necessarily compatible.
As a way out of his growing despair Anathema, now in David's employ
as his private secretary under the name of Nullius, suggests that David
give back what God has given him (the inheritance) and distribute this
wealth among the poor. David agrees. Before long his philanthropy
becomes common knowledge and a steady stream of people begging
money flows to his house. Eventually the funds are exhausted, but the
droves who have come to beseech him for help—even for miracles to
bring the lame back to health and the dead back to life—refuse to accept
the fact and menace him. Out of necessity David, accompanied by Anathema, flees, taking refuge in the wilderness. But the mob pursues him
and catches up with him by the edge of the sea. Realizing finally that
David has nothing more to give them, they accuse him of treachery and
stone him to death.

The moment he has long and carefully prepared has at last come to
pass and Anathema exults in his triumph. Through the Jew, David,
Anathema insists that he has proven, like a theorem, the powerlessness

of love. Herein lies Anathema's challenge to God; by logic and reason he
has, through David, created an evil that can be numbered and weighed
and is greater than God's love. His superiority as ruler thus demonstrated, Anathema approaches the mountain and gates beyond which
resides the Supreme Wisdom of the universe and insists that the Guardian permit him to pass beyond the gates, to the acquisition of infinite
knowledge and wisdom. In the Prologue to the play Anathema had
demanded the Guardian open the gates:

> Open the heavy gates for an instant and allow me to have a glimpse
> of Eternity. . . . But I shall know and become a God, become a
> God, a God! I have so long wanted to become a God—and would I
> be a poor God?[31]

The Guardian, however, spurned him and turned him away.

In his return to the Guardian in the play's Epilogue, Anathema comes
boasting of his triumph and again demands that the gates be opened to
him. But he meets the same rebuff as the Guardian dismisses him with
the words:

> And you will never see, and you will never hear, and you will never
> know, Anathema, unfortunate spirit, deathless in numbers, eter-
> nally alive in measure and in weight, but as yet unborn to life. (p.
> 210)

Anathema thus realizes that his victory of logic and reason is Pyrrhic.
The Guardian tells him that because of his selflessness, his capacity for
love, David has attained immortality in the deathlessness of fire. The
mystery of love and truth, which David exemplifies, is beyond the grasp
of reason and logic, beyond the range of finite intellect. The knowledge
Anathema is willing to crawl serpentlike on his belly to attain cannot be
weighed or counted in numbers.

Defeated, Anathema vows to go to David's grave to spread hate and
dissension:

> And when from the heap of corpses, of filthy, foul-smelling and
> disgusting corpses I shall announce to the people that you are the
> one who killed David and the people,—They will believe me. (p.
> 211)

Just as *Anathema* merges the realistic and supernatural (the Satanlike
Anathema appearing in a Russian village and the pivotal role of the
Christlike Russian Jew, David Leyzer), so also does it bring together the
social and metaphysical, in this latter respect resembling *The Life of
Man*. In the negative, even hostile, treatment of the masses, Andreev's

personal attitude appears unequivocal and the seeds of his later conservatism are sown. The play seems to carry a certain indictment of the futility of altruism, of social philanthropy—David's noble intentions result, ultimately, only in his own disaster. But the Jew's self-abnegation and, in the final analysis, his sacrifice of self in the service of man endow him with an undeniable spiritual nobility. And it is in this that he gains precisely the knowledge denied Anathema.

Anathema's conflict with the Guardian over infinite knowledge and wisdom—the metaphysical dimension of the drama—reaffirms the neo-Romantic repudiation of logic and reason as man's sole means of acquiring universal truth. The realm of the supernatural and the mysteries of the cosmos are beyond the grasp of weights and numbers, beyond logic and reason; for this reason the gates must remain forever closed to Anathema.

Medievalism

Another play by Andreev, *Black Masks* (1908)—dating from the same period as *The Life of Man* and *Anathema*—brings us more within the mainstream of Neo-Romantic drama. Instead of the Maeterlinckian obsession with death in *The Life of Man,* or the abstraction and cosmic monumentalism of *Anathema, Black Masks* is a symbolic drama about illusion, reality, and self-knowledge garbed in the feudal medievalism so extensively used by the Neo-Romantics.

Despite the apparent difficulty of contemporary audiences with the symbolism of *Black Masks,* which accounts for its failure, the sense of the play is hardly abstruse. The Duke Lorenzo of Spadaro, Knight of the Holy Spirit, who is young, gracious, poetic, admired by his people, and loved by his wife (Francesca), decides to hold a masked ball to which everyone will be welcome. On the night of the festivities, he orders the castle brilliantly illuminated. Symbolically, Lorenzo's opening his castle to all who wish to attend the ball can be interpreted as a willingness to peer into his own subconscious existence, into the dark recess of his own soul. There is in his action an element of test, as James B. Woodward points out,[32] in that Lorenzo permits free access to his castle and the illumination of the castle renders concealment virtually impossible.

When the guests come Lorenzo and his family are taken aback, for many wear the grotesque and repulsive masks of the dead, dying, crippled, and deformed. Here Andreev allows his taste for the macabre free reign. When Lorenzo inquires as to the true identity of the masks he is told that they are but projections of his own heart, his own thoughts, and his own falsehoods. The Duke can barely recognize himself in the dreadful masks around him. But the castle continues to fill with new arrivals, the most sinister being a group of Satan-worshiping black maskers. As these creatures of the night surge on toward the lights and fires of the castle, they gradually consume all the light and plunge everything about them into darkness. In doing so, they symbolize the false reality that blinds Lorenzo to the knowledge of the true self.

In the second act Lorenzo recognizes among his guests a figure wearing a mask of himself, an imposter he assumes. It is, in fact, an externalization of the duality of Lorenzo's own personality, the embodiment of a dimension of his psyche. This sole use of the double or *Doppelgänger* motif in Andreev's fiction is another throwback to the romanticism of the first half of the nineteenth century and to the writings of Poe, Gogol, and Dostoevsky which Andreev knew well, admired, and occasionally borrowed from.

Lorenzo challenges his double to a duel the outcome of which is the death of one, presumably the false Lorenzo. As the alter ego lies in a coffin, the victorious Lorenzo—the wound of his slain opponent now also on his own breast—is forced to learn previously unknown truths about himself. A strange procession enacts the illicit love affair of Lorenzo's mother, the Queen, with her own stable groom; a peasant nurse carrying a misshapen infant, half animal, half man, causes Lorenzo to question his own origin; he learns additionally that his participation in the Crusades contributed, in large measure, to the misery of his peasants and that he often satisfied his sexual desires with their daughters. The "demon" within him thus brought into the light for him to perceive clearly for the first time, the true Lorenzo can no longer endure the truths which the strange night has revealed. All illusions stripped away, the false part of himself slain as a result of the duel, he willingly seeks his own death as expiation for his sins in the fire accidentally set by his servant Ecco. The castle is destroyed by the flames and Lorenzo with it; only his wife, Francesca, survives. Her promise to tell the child she is to bear about its father, Duke Lorenzo of Spadaro, brings the play to a close. The following excerpt from the dialogue between the first and second maskers in Act I, scene 1 provides a key to the basic meaning of the play, enabling an audience to chart the symbolism of the castle and the dark events that take place within its walls:

FIRST MASKER: Crazy Lorenzo! He lighted up his castle too brilliantly.
SECOND MASKER: Lights are dangerous in the night

FIRST MASKER: To those who are abroad?
SECOND MASKER: No, to him who lights them.[33]

Some eleven years after the completion of *Black Masks*, in September 1919, Andreev offered a political interpretation of the play which I quote only because of the light it sheds on the writer's postrevolutionary conservatism and the justification for the long Soviet hostility toward Andreev and his works:

> Regarding my *Black Masks*. Only in the days of the Revolution did I understand that this was not only the tragedy of the individual, but the tragedy of the whole revolution, its genuine sad countenance. Behold the Revolution, which has kindled lights amidst the darkness, and is expecting those invited to her feast. Behold her surrounded by the invited . . . or uninvited guests? Who are these maskers? Chernovs? Lenins? But these know at least Satan. While here, lo, are those others, particles of the great human darkness, which extinguish the torches. They creep from everywhere, the light is not bright for them, the fire does not warm them, and even Satin they know not as yet. Black maskers. Then the end of noble Lorenzo. Yes, one may draw a complete analogy, by using quotations. How did it happen that the tragedy of the individual, which my play was intended to express, has become the tragedy of the history of the Revolution?[34]

The ferment of Russian Neo-Romantic drama spanned nearly the first two decades of the twentieth century and far outweighed the more purely Symbolist playwriting inspired by the early Maeterlinck. The common forms and methods of Western Neo-Romantic drama all had their corresponding Russian parallels. Andreev's *Black Masks* (1908) uses a medieval Italian setting, reflecting a widespread preference among the Neo-Romantics who, like their predecessors in the first half of the nineteenth century, felt strong affinities for medieval culture. The result of this preference for late nineteenth- and early twentieth-century drama was not only the assimilation of conventions of the medieval mystery and morality (traces of both of which are easily discovered in Andreev's *The Life of Man* and *Anathema*), but the frequency of medieval settings and characters—in the manner of Maeterlinck's *Pelléas and Mélisande*, several of Yeats's plays, Gabriele D'Annunzio's *Francesca da Rimimi*, Paul Claudel's *L'Annonce faite à Marie* (*The Tidings Brought to Mary*), and Stanisław Wyspiánski's *Bolesław Śmiały* (*Boleslaus the Brave*).

In view of the Russian admiration for Maeterlinck, both as a dramatist and thinker, the vaguely medieval coloration of several of his plays (or specifically medieval in the case of *Sister Beatrice*, 1902, which Meyer-hold staged), and the considerable indebtedness of Russian symbolism to the French, the use by Russian Neo-Romantic dramatists of medieval *French* settings seems understandable. There was also another reason for this. Russian medieval culture was neither rich nor well known because of the relative paucity of source material. Additionally, the Middle Ages in Russia were associated in most minds with the hegemony of the Tatars and hence regarded as an unhappy period of servitude. When Russian dramatists introduced medieval settings, therefore, following the practice of the time, most often the settings took on a French aspect. Probably the most outstanding Russian play in this vein (though hardly the only one) was *Roza i krest* (*The Rose and the Cross*, 1912) by the outstanding poet Aleksandr Blok (1880–1921).

Blok's entry into the drama dates from 1906 when his *Fairground Booth* was first staged.[35] Two years later, this play together with *Korol na ploshchadi* (*The King on the Square*) and *Neznakomka* (*The Unknown Woman*) were published under the common title *Liricheskie dramy* (*Lyrical Dramas*). His next play, which was a distinct failure, was *Pesnya sudby* (*The Song of Fate*), completed also in 1908 and rewritten in 1919. *Ramzes*, set in ancient Egypt and of little value as drama, was written in 1919. *The Rose and the Cross*, Blok's most ambitious and, to my mind, most successful dramatic work, came a year later.

In the Preface to his cycle of *Lyrical Dramas* Blok defines a lyrical play as one which presents the experiences of an individual soul, its doubts, passions, failures, and falls. Ideological, moral, or other inferences have no place in it. The common link of the three-play cycle (and *The Song of Fate* as well) is the search "for a beautiful, free, and luminous life, one capable of removing from weak shoulders the unendurable burden of *lyrical* doubts and contradictions and of dispelling importunate and illusory doubles." These doubts, contradictions, and phantoms are distributed among male characters who represent different aspects of the soul of a single person: the comically unsuccessful Pierrot in *The Fairground Booth*; the morally weak poet in *The King on the Square;* the Poet whose dream eludes him in *The Unknown Woman;* and the vacillating Gherman who attains and then loses his ideal in *The Song of Fate*. These men are variants of what could be called the Masculine figure in Blok. In each case, the search for the beautiful life centers on a woman, representing what Blok himself refers to as the Eternal Feminine. For Pierrot, it is the luminous Columbine; for the Poet in *The King on the Square*, the daughter of the architect; for the Poet in *The Unknown*

Woman, it is the Unknown Woman herself; for Gherman in *The Song of Fate*, it is the singer Faina.

On a first, more immediate level of meaning, these plays dramatize the restless quest of a particular type of personality (a projection of Blok himself?) for an ideal life of beauty and meaningful self-fulfillment and the weaknesses and inadequacies which cause the ideal to be lost even when it is within grasp. But the quest for the beautiful also assumes a transcendent significance. Dissatisfied with the banality and vulgarity of society, the sensitive Masculine figure (a poet or someone of poetic sensibility) yearns for an existence of beauty and meaning necessarily equatable only with the spiritual. The world as he knows it becomes distasteful to him and he seeks a way out of its self-intoxicating clamor and superficial brilliance, suggested by the ball in *The Fairground Booth*, the excitement attending the arrival of the ships in *The King on the Square*, the tavern and intelligentsia party scenes in *The Unknown Woman*, and the International Industrial Fair in *The Song of Fate*. That is why the Feminine figure symbolic of the Ideal not only is presented in all instances as in some way linked to or emergent from "above" or "beyond" or the "other world" but also is dualistic in the sense of combining the life-giving and life-taking. If the Eternal Feminine has to be understood as the spiritual life in the idiom of Gnostic symbolism which Blok makes ample use of in the plays antedating *The Rose and the Cross*,[36] she must also symbolize the leavetaking of the physical, earthly life—death, in other words—which man must first undergo before entering the spiritual.

In his Preface to the *Lyrical Dramas* Blok also mentions the mocking tone of the plays as another element making for a certain unity between them. He associates this tone with the romanticism of the first half of the nineteenth century and, more specifically, with what he refers to as the Romantic "transcendental irony" or what we understand more commonly as Romantic irony. This Romantic irony is often self-ironizing—the dispelling of personal demons through a process of artistic transmutation. There is, to be sure, much of this in Blok's early plays: the *fin de siècle* world-weariness, the exaggerated sense of alienation, the relentless search for an ideal, for an absolute, the self-indulgent fantasizing, the weakness of will when the time for decision making is at hand, the inability to distinguish illusion and reality—all collectively the malaise of the age to which Blok gave expression in the early plays and which he could bring himself to ironize over at a time when he was able to perceive their grip on his own psyche.

But there is also a sociopolitical dimension in the early plays which Blok says nothing about in his Preface and about which it may have been politic, in fact, for him to remain silent. *The King on the Square* and *The Song of Fate* acquire an additional significance from precisely this point of view. In the first play the weaknesses of the Poet are observed against and set into relief by a successful popular revolt against a king. The inhabitants of the kingdom anticipate the arrival of ships symbolizing hope, abundance, and salvation. The long delay in the ships' coming intensifies their sense of frustration and adds fuel to their grievances. When the ships finally arrive, it is already too late. Unable to bear further their frustration, the people rise up against their king, destroying the Poet, the architect's daughter, and a number of their own in the process. When the king is toppled from his pedestal, it is discovered that he is only a *statue;* fearful for the future without a leader, without someone to guide them, the people ask the architect whom can they now turn to for sustenance, both physical and spiritual. He replies in such a way as to suggest that the only master that they need recognize is God. The political sense of the play, coming only a few years after the Revolution of 1905 (which had a profound impact on Blok), seems sufficiently clear. The masses cannot continue to be fed on vain hopes and empty promises (symbolized by the ships) created for them, by and large, by an effete, spiritually crippled intelligentsia and any ruler toppled will prove to be no more than a shattered statue.

Blok's repudiation of the intelligentsia and his crystallizing enthusiasm for the mystique of the great as yet untapped reservoir of national strength represented by the Russian masses—which brings him ideologically (if indeed not aesthetically) close to Gorky—is less obliquely expressed in *The Song of Fate.* Here Gherman's pursuit of the dynamic life force embodied in the character of Faina leads to the Seventy-seventh International Industrial Fair at which he and Faina will finally meet. During the Fair (scene 4) a Man in Spectacles addresses the crowd. He speaks of the gulf between the intelligentsia and the people (who are characterized throughout the play as a slumbering, potentially explosive mass) and the ever increasing irrelevance of the former. Faina appears to him as a symbol of the national spirit and as such he contrasts the weakness of his own voice, as a representative of the intelligentsia, with the strength of hers. When Faina leaves Gherman at the end of the play telling him that the time is not yet ripe for their union, her words extend meaning on several levels.

Blok's three *Lyrical Dramas* together with *The Song of Fate,* which belongs to the cycle in all respects but that of formal link, carry the same problems of stage-worthiness as much essentially poetic neo-Romantic drama. Blok himself was aware of this at least with regard to the *Lyrical Dramas* and in his Preface to them he speaks candidly of their deficiencies and weaknesses from the point of view of stage production. The exception, among the early plays, was *The Fairground Booth,* which the great producer Vsevolod Meyerhold staged with considerable success in 1906—apparently to the surprise even of Blok.

Many of the weaknesses of Blok's early plays disappear, however, in *The Rose and the Cross* (1912), which was originally planned as a scenario for a ballet about Provençal troubadours with music by Glazunov. Set in thirteenth-century Languedoc and Brittany, the play reflects the poet's long-standing interest in medieval French culture. Besides amassing an impressive collection of books and papers on the subject, Blok translated the medieval miracle play, *Le Miracle de Théophile,* by the trouvère Rutebeuf and in 1911 spent most of the summer in Brittany.

The advance in dramaturgy represented by *The Rose and the Cross* relates to both technique and point of view. Prose and verse mingle as in the early plays, but characters (above all, the knight Bertran) become more than poetic symbols and a more lucid and coherently developed plot structure makes for greater dramatic interest.

At the center of the play is the knight Bertran's hopeless love for Isora, the wife of the master of his castle, Count Archimbaut, and her search for the author of a haunting song whose meaning she does not fully comprehend. Song as lyrical interpolation is a recurrent motif in all of Blok's plays. But it is only with *The Rose and the Cross* that song, character, and plot are brought together in an integral relationship of dramatic effectiveness.

The whole sense of the song, which Bertran recites at the beginning of the play, is contained in the words: "Serdtsu zakon neprelozhny—/ Radost—Stradanie odno!" ("The heart's immutable law—/Joy and suffering are one.")[37] Although neither realizes it, the song defines the relationship of Bertran and Isora. Romantically inclined yet callous, Isora is blind to Bertran's love for her. Grateful for the fidelity of his service, she cannot even attribute such feelings to the Knight of Woe, as Bertran is called, because of the contempt in which he is held by all in the castle after a humiliating tournament defeat. But the more futile his love for Isora the more compassion Bertran evokes and the greater the relevance of the mysterious song for his personal dilemma.

On a mission to Burgundy for the Count, Bertran fortuitously comes upon the mysterious author of the song whom Isora has long been seeking, the trouvère Gaetan. The two return to Languedoc and in the guise of a wandering minstrel Gaetan again sings his song for Isora during a festival celebrating the coming of spring. Not long afterward, rebels hostile to Count Archimbaut attack the castle. In the ensuing battle Bertran regains his lost honor by unseating his former victor and saving the castle. The same encounter also reveals the cowardice of the young page Aliscan to whom Isora is attracted.

Bertran's newfound pride is shattered, however, by Isora's request that he stand guard below her window one night during a love tryst with Aliscan. So great is his devotion to Isora that Bertran agrees to play his humiliating role and even assists Aliscan in climbing up to Isora's window. The spell of Gaetan's song at last broken when she dismisses it as a dream after hearing it at the spring celebration and again can neither meet its creator nor fathom its true meaning, Isora equates love with happiness and suffering with unhappiness and in this spirit eagerly pursues her romance with Aliscan. As he zealously keeps his night vigil below Isora's window, Bertran continues to lose blood from a wound received in the earlier combat. Shortly before he dies maintaining his degrading guard he finally grasps the sense of Gaetan's song both personally and in the abstract and performs a last service for his mistress by warning her of the approach of her husband, the Count. Isora's infidelity remains undiscovered and her reaction upon hearing of Bertran's death closes the play. Selfish and insensitive, incapable of perceiving Bertran's love and sacrifice, she can mange to say only: "I feel sorry for him. He was, after all, a loyal servant."

The meaning of Gaetan's song is self-evident: there is no happiness without suffering, in life in general and in love in particular. Bertran suffers because of his hopeless love for Isora, but in this suffering there is also joy in the ability to love fully, without the hope of fulfillment, to love enough to be able to sacrifice oneself so that one's beloved may find what she believes to be her own happiness in the arms of another. Blok's own discovery of this "verity" of life expressed in *The Rose and the Cross* comes as a significant departure from the transcendent Neo-Romantic quest for ideals of truth and beauty dramatized in the early plays. Significantly, the maturation of outlook fitfully revealed through irony in the early plays and now heralded in *The Rose and the Cross* is accompanied by a falling away of the Gnostic imagery characteristic of the *Lyrical Dramas* and *The Song of Fate*. The result is an outward-reaching instead of upward-striving play of richer human understanding and superior design.

Blok's more concentrated and less ambiguous dramatic method in *The Rose and the Cross* still accommodates the symbolic, except that now it is no longer Gnostic. The rose and the cross of the title signify, respectively, happiness and suffering. Throughout the play two types of rose are contrasted: the red, which is associated with Isora and suggests merely fleeting happiness; and the black, which symbolizes the happiness that knows suffering as well and is derived from the dark-red rose tossed by Isora at one point in the play on the sleeping trouvère's breast. It is this rose that Bertran wears into the glory of his victorious defense of the castle and into the ignominy of his night vigil beneath Isora's window. In taking the black rose unto himself Bertran opens his consciousness to the meaning of Gaetan's song. Preferring the red rose which will fade, unlike the black, Isora at once relegates herself to a lower level of awareness.

Medieval France also serves as the setting for two of the most successful plays—*The Triumph of Death* and *Vanka klyuchnik i pazh Zhean* (*Vanka the Valet and the Page Jean*, published 1908)—by the eminent Symbolist poet Fyodor Sologub. Sharing a widespread Neo-Romantic interest in folk culture, Sologub drew heavily on Russian folklore in his plays. He himself points out, for example, that the Russian part of *Vanka* is based on material in the first volume of A. I. Sobolevsky's *Velikorusskie narodnye pesni* (*Great Russian Folk Songs*), which was published in St. Petersburg in 1895. His previously discussed play *Nocturnal Dances*, which is subtitled a "Dramatic Folk Tale in Three Acts," owes its subject to the folk tale of the same name included in the second volume of A. N. Afanasev's famous collection *Narodnye russkie skazki* (*Russian National Folk Tales*, Moscow, 1855–63).

So extensive are the borrowings in *Vanka* that a Russian reader or spectator unfamiliar with the specific folk songs on which the play is based would still have a little trouble recognizing the folkloric origins of the work. But Russian folklore is only a part of the play or, to be more precise, one half of the play. The other half has nothing to do with Russian folklore or Russia, operating instead with French characters in a French locale. That explains the play's subtitle: "A Drama in Thirteen *Double* Scenes" [italics mine—HBS].

The time frame is the same for the two parallel parts of the play: the Middle Ages. But Sologub's interest in the period in *Vanka* is neither metaphysical, nor chivalric, nor historical. The familiar milieu of castles, knights, and ladies is no more than a pretext for a light erotic play about the romantic adventures of servants and their mistresses. The folk songs Sologub drew on for the Russian part of the drama relate the story of the young boy Vanka who was taken into the service of a prince and princess, soon thereafter was embroiled in a romantic liaison with his mistress, inadvertently boasted of his success in a tavern, was betrayed to the prince who spared his life on the intercession of the repentant princess, and was then banished from the castle.

In dramatizing the folk material Sologub retained the story line and recognizable patterns of speech from folk songs and folk tales. But he allowed his imagination license in depicting the love affair between servant and mistress, choosing to present the episode in a distinctly erotic manner (a predilection demonstrated by Sologub in more than one work). Although the problem could have been bypassed by a director, Sologub's stage directions in certain episodes require the shedding of all clothing, raising doubts about any serious intention of production in his own time. The major innovation of the play was not, however, the titillating eroticism, but the development of a parallel plot featuring French equivalents of Vanka and the Russian prince and princess. The story of the page Jean and the French count and countess unfolds along exactly the same lines as that of Vanka, each Russian scene being followed by its parallel French one. This interplay of the Russian and French scenes acquires dramatic interest not only because of the novelty of the device and the comic value of repetition, but also because of certain dissimilarities between the scenes. The most obvious is language. Contrasting with the colorful folk speech of Vanka and the other Russian characters is the more elegant and literary language of the Frenchmen. There are minor differences in the stories themselves, the most important being the behavior of Vanka and Jean when each is brought before his respective master who is already apprised of the illicit conduct of his wife. When asked if the allegations about his affair with the princess are true, Vanka freely confesses. When the prince presses him for the reason for such contemptible behavior, the sauciness of the reply is wholly in keeping with Vanka's robust and brash characterization: "It was by mutual consent, sir. I've served you three whole years and never betrayed you all this time. But am I forbidden to kiss a broad? And she's a broad isn't she, the princess, I mean?"[38] Instead of being forthright about his relationship with the countess, Jean on the other hand dissembles and when he is asked why he boasted of his affair with the countess in the tavern if there never was one, he answers that there is no truth to the gossip and that he invented the whole thing while intoxicated just for the sake of boasting.

The Triumph of Death, a three-act tragedy, has none of the gaiety and eroticism of *Vanka* and reminds one more of Maeterlinck and Blok's *The Rose and the Cross*. As in *Vanka*, Sologub again offers no information on time and place but the names of the characters and the setting make it clear that we are in the Middle Ages. To Maeterlinck, Sologub owes only the general mood of gloom and mystery of *The Triumph of Death*. The similarities with Blok, while still few, are stronger.

The play recounts the cruel deception of King Khlodoveg on his wedding day by Algista, his bride Berta's maidservant, and Malgista, Algista's mother. Berta is unattractive (she has a badly pockmarked face) and is shorter in one leg than the other, but Khlodoveg knows none of this since the marriage is family arranged and he has never seen his bride unveiled. Even on their wedding day Berta keeps her face concealed and wears a special shoe to compensate for the shortness of her leg. Algista's plan is diabolically simple. Since Khlodoveg has never seen his bride or her maidservant, Algista intends to change places with Berta and pretend to be the new queen. Since Berta is unattractive and she herself beautiful, Algista expects no trouble in being accepted as Berta and insisting that Berta is really Algista, her maidservant. Moreover, her ambitious mother (Malgista) will back up everything she says by declaring that Berta is really her daughter. The scheme works perfectly and Berta is even driven out as punishment for stubbornly insisting that she, not Algista, is the real queen.

After ten years of happy marriage between the King and Algista, during which a son (Khilperic) is born to them and their rule over their people proves beneficent, Berta reappears with her brother Etelbert. She also has a young boy with her, the son conceived on her wedding day before Algista's scheme was put into effect. The old wounds are reopened as Berta and her brother accuse Algista of depriving her of her rightful place. Wearied, Algista decides to test Khlodoveg's love by telling him the truth. On hearing her confession, Khlodoveg falls into a rage, deprives her of all rights, restores Berta to the throne, and orders Algista beaten to death and then fed to the dogs. Her son is delivered over to a similar fate. But the dogs only howl over Algista's battered but still live body refusing to harm her, and with Malgista's help she makes her way to Khlodoveg for a final attempt to convince him that she is his one true love regardless of the past. Even though Khlodoveg confesses that he still loves her he refuses to take her back or run away with her. Her impassioned pleas in vain, Algista pronounces the curse on Khlodoveg that he stand like a stone until he is consumed by time and then, together with her son, falls dead at his feet. As Khlodoveg, Berta, and their retinue remain immobile, turned to stone, a voice is heard at the final curtain calling attention to the fleeing of light from the place where the last deeds have occurred and ending the play with the words: "And believe me, Love is conquered by Death; Love and Death are but one."[39]

These closing words, issued like a pronouncement of doom by an unseen voice, express what Sologub no doubt intended as the underlying philosophical theme of the play: the view shared by Romantic and Neo-Romantic alike that romantic love brings sadness and pain and can only result in tragedy. Whatever her guilt, the audience's sympathy is bound to lie with Algista, not only because she is far more attractive than Berta but because of the power of her love for Khlodoveg and her kindness to all as queen. In refusing to be guided by his love for her, which he admits, and either take her back as queen or go away with her to a new life, Khlodoveg becomes a living death and brings death to all about him.

Sologub's love-death equation and Blok's joy-suffering are closely related. In *The Rose and the Cross* true love also ends in death, for Bertran's devoted service to Isora on the occasion of her tryst with Aliscan makes it impossible for him to look after his wound and finally causes his death. Blok's belief that there is no happiness unattended by suffering assumes its proper significance in the context of his total development as a man and a writer when it is related, above all, to the views expressed in the *Lyrical Dramas*. But Isora's insensitivity and the hoplessness of Bertran's love, to which the knight sacrifices his own life, make for an essentially negative image of romantic love that places Blok, like Sologub, within the mainstream of European neo-Romantic art and thought.

There are other affinities between *The Triumph of Death* and *The Rose and the Cross*. Both plays spring from an interest in earlier French history. Blok was very careful about a faithful representation of medieval French culture and left extensive notes on the sources on which he drew for *The Rose and the Cross*. In a note to *The Triumph of Death* Sologub also indicates his sources and his degree of indebtedness. The basic plot of the play, he points out, derives from medieval legends about Charlemagne's mother Berthe aux grands pieds (Berthe of the Big Feet; Berta

in Russian) and indeed in the play Berta's son is named Karl (the Russian form of Charles; Charlemagne in Russian is Karl Veliky). However,
Sologub has changed the name of the king in order to "remove this tragedy from history and even from legend, which unfolds somewhat differently and ends not quite like my play."[40]

Even more than Blok's play, *The Triumph of Death* strives for maximum dramatic concentration, eliminating the semblance of any subplot
such as the uprising of the dissidents in *The Rose and the Cross*. This is
reinforced by Sologub's more cohesive style: poeticized prose (unlike
Blok's mixture of prose and verse) and the avoidance of the lyrical interpolations so often encountered in Blok's plays (though in *The Rose
and the Cross* a song for once is an integral part of the plot).

It was probably, however, from Maeterlinck that Sologub derived the
"atmosphere" for *The Triumph of Death*. In broadest terms, the play is
about death (everyone dies at the end in one way or another) and other
familiar signposts of a Maeterlinckian landscape reappear: the dark, dank
passageways of a medieval castle, tempestuous weather, mysterious
comings and goings, dread-inspiring footsteps, an all-pervading climate
of mystery and gloom thrust upon the audience almost from the outset.

Analogies with Maeterlinck and Blok ought not to be pressed too insistently, however. Apart from evident stylistic differences, Sologub's
play is neither a programmatic exercise in Symbolist drama in the manner of Maeterlinck nor the symbol-oriented dramatization of a new level
of perception in the development of the author's psyche as in *The Rose
and the Cross*. Points of contiguity with Maeterlinck and Blok are
reached, but *The Triumph of Death* is, at its core, a melodrama of lust
and revenge dressed in the fashionable medieval attire of much neo-
Romantic neo-tragedy. In this respect, it has more in common with
D'Annunzio's *Francesca da Rimini* (which is based on the same legend
as *Pelléas and Mélisande*) than with Maeterlinck, Blok, or a more complex play like Andreev's *Black Masks* from which it is even more distantly removed.

Classical Antiquity

The same Neo-Romantic predilection for legend revealed in the new
medievalism of the late nineteenth and early twentieth centuries led
logically to classical mythology as well; not unexpectedly, many plays on
classical themes were written throughout Europe. Other sources also
nourished the interest in classical antiquity: the common *fin-de-siècle*

view of man as a virtually helpless plaything of fate (appropriately realized metaphorically by the figure of the marionette) and, as a corollary,
a renewed interest in tragic drama—another important affinity with the
romanticism of the first half of the nineteenth century (Shelley's *Prometheus Unbound*, Grillparzer's *Sappho*, Kleist's *Penthesilea*, to mention a few).

The number of Russian Neo-Romantic plays on classical subjects was
substantial, but few are remembered any more, let alone performed, a
fate shared by nearly all their European counterparts. Some of these
were written by writers of exceptional classical erudition such as Innokenti Annensky (1856–1909) and Vyacheslav Ivanov (1866–1949), both of
whom produced distinguished scholarly works in the field of classical
civilization, Annensky as a translator of Euripides and Ivanov as a student of Greek mythology and religion, as we saw earlier. Other plays
with classical settings came from poets like the greatly talented Marina
Tsvetaeva (1892–1941), whose interest in the classical past stemmed
most probably from the literary climate—the widespread Neo-Romantic
interest in classical mythology and pagan beliefs, the attempt of dramatists to evolve new dramatic forms, in particular a new tragic drama, by
studying the way that drama evolved among the ancients, the impact of
the Apollonian-Dionysian dichotomy of Nietzsche's *The Birth of Tragedy*, and doubtless the example of the classical plays of such predecessors as Annensky and Ivanov.

These Russian classical tragedies differ in only a few important respects from similar efforts elsewhere in Europe during more or less the
same period. The subjects of the plays are classical myths, usually interpreted freely in that the authors feel no special obligation to adhere
slavishly to all aspects of the particular myth as it has come down from
antiquity. Then, there is a pronounced interest in human psychology.
The principal characters often become plausible psychological portraits
or studies endowing them, despite their antique garb, with a certain
contemporary relevance. At times, they are clearly projections of the author's individual psyche. Structurally, the plays often preserve essential
features of classical tragedies, such as the use of messengers to provide
narrative information, of offstage deaths, and of choruses. But these represent only an outer shell. Within the shell, considerable license prevails. Chroruses are sometimes supplemented by musical and choreographical interludes. The plays, usually in verse, often display dazzling
metric variety. Seldom do the authors aim for an appropriate stylized ar-

chaic idiom but instead freely mix styles and lexical levels, such as the lofty with the coarse, the contemporary with the archaic (Church Slavic mainly, in the case of the Russian).

We can best appreciate this Neo-Romantic approach to classical tragedy by turning to specific works. Annensky wrote four tragic dramas with classical settings: *Melanippa-filosof* (*Melanippe the Philosopher*, 1901), *Tsar Iksion* (*King Ixion*, 1902), *Laodamiya* (*Laodamia*, finished 1902; published 1906), and *Famira-Kifared* (*Thamyras the Cythara Player*, finished 1906, published 1913, and the only play by Annensky ever to be staged, in 1916).[41] Vyacheslav Ivanov wrote two classical tragedies, *Tantal* (*Tantalus*, 1905) and *Prometey* (*Prometheus*, 1919). Tsvetaeva's two classical plays, *Tezey* (*Theseus*) or *Ariadna* (*Ariadne*), as Tsvetaeva later retitled the play, and *Fedra* (*Phaedra*) date from 1924 and 1927, respectively. When *Phaedra* was published, it was designated the second part of a trilogy of which *Theseus-Ariadne* must have been intended as the first. No third part appeared, however, possibly because of the harsh reception given the first two plays by émigré critics (Tsvetaeva lived outside Russia from 1922 until 1939). Probably the most interesting of the Russian Neo-Romantic classical plays are Annensky's *Laodamia* and Tsvetaeva's *Ariadne*.

The myth of Laodamia who committed suicide out of love in order to be reunited after death with her slain husband, Protesilaus, was the subject of Euripides' *Protesilaus*, of which only fragments remain. This source and others in classical antiquity are mentioned by Annensky in the learned introduction which he wrote to preface this play as, indeed, he similarly prefaced all his classical dramas.

The story of Laodamia attracted other Slavic writers in Annensky's time and his introduction to the play takes due note of them: his fellow Russians Sologub and Bryusov whose plays *Dar mudrykh pchol* (*The Gift of the Wise Bees*) and *Protesilay umershy* (*Protesilaus Deceased*), respectively, deal with the same myth; and the major Polish Neo-Romantic dramatist, Stanisław Wyspiański, whose *Protesilas i Laodamia* (*Protesilaus and Laodamia*) is praised by Annensky.

Besides providing valuable information, Annensky's introduction reveals an orientation toward a reading as opposed to a theatergoing public, not only of *Laodamia* but of his other plays and virtually all Neo-Romantic classical tragedy in general. Poetic rather than dramatic and better read than seen performed on a stage, Neo-Romantic tragedy was essentially "closet" drama in the tradition of the serious drama of the Romantics. And as was the case with Romantic tragedy, musical adaptation seemed to be the sole means available for achieving a longer stage life.

Annensky's conception of *Laodamia* primarily as a reading experience can be seen not only in his scholarly preface but also in the poet's descriptive stage directions and the extensive use of color, so generally characteristic of his poetic style. When Laodamia herself first appears on stage she is described as follows: "She is tall and thin, with luxuriant blonde [white, in Russian] tresses and dressed entirely in white. In her lines and movements there is something girlishly shy. Her elbows are pink and her fingers are thin and white and unadorned with rings. Her eyes are hazel with a pinkish reflection."[42]

Although ornamented by musical entr'actes in addition to the regular choruses, the basic plot of *Laodamia* is simple. This simplicity permits Annensky to concentrate more on characterization. And it is chiefly in the area of characterization that the play exercises its greatest appeal, becoming one of the more successful Neo-Romantic plays in the classical tragic idiom.

The drama's theme of the longing of women for their men away at war is established at the very outset by the rapid, nervous rhythms of the chorus of widows lamenting their lost husbands and of wives longing for the safe return of their warriors. This sets the stage for the appearance of Laodamia, who relates to the nurse trying to comfort her (in a more narrative rhymed iambic pentameter) a recurrent dream of foreboding ill. Although not specifically stated in the play, there is at least the subtle insinuation that Protesilaus had to leave Laodamia before the consummation of their marriage. This intensifies Laodamia's pining and, at the same time, imbues it with a certain erotic quality. It may also be why Annensky thrusts into particular prominence the motif of the wax statue of Protesilaus, which is mentioned though not elaborated upon in such classical sources as Ovid. In Annensky's drama, the wax statute is of considerable importance. Laodamia uses it to console herself in her husband's absence, even going so far as to take the full-length statue to bed with her. Moreover, it is the statue that sets in motion a chain of events culminating in Laodamia's suicide.

Laodamia's account to the nurse of her dream is paralleled structurally by the appearance of the messenger who brings the tragic news of Protesilaus' death (he was killed by Hector in the version Annensky follows). In classical Greek tragedy, especially Euripides, the messenger's speeches are often high points of the drama. Annensky adhered to this practice and made the messenger's report of Protesilaus' death, rendered in blank verse, one of the most stirring moments of the play. Laodamia's response, a mixture of disbelief and anger, has an exceptional psychological verisimilitude. In Annensky's skillful hands, Laodamia becomes a wholly plausible portrait of a distraught young woman who has just been informed that the husband she has not even begun to live with has been killed in battle in a faraway land.

Refusing to accept the messenger's evidence and clinging fervently to the hope that Protesilaus somehow may yet still be alive, Laodamia sinks into an obsessive longing. Her sole comforts are the wax statue, sensuous dreams, and what seem very much like mystic revelations in which her intense desire for reunion with her husband is gratified. The merging of classical tragedy and Neo-Romantic sensibility, as evidenced in such a play as *Laodamia,* is a typical fusion in late nineteenth- and early twentieth-century tragic drama. A renewed interest in dreams and mystic experiences, not only as steps to a higher spiritual realm but also as keys capable of unlocking the vaults of the subconscious, is a centrally important element in the Neo-Romantic *Weltanschauung.* The prominence of dream and mystic transport in Annensky's *Laodamia* is best seen in this light.

The tension built up by the intensity and also irrationality of Laodamia's longing requires a certain eventual decrescendo. This comes in the third of the play's four acts when Hermes and the shade of Protesilaus arrive as if in answer to Laodamia's pleas. When Laodamia eagerly conducts Protesilaus into the house, she does not yet realize that it is only with her husband's shade that she is reuniting. Nor does she know that the gods to whom the sufferings of ordinary mortals mean little are allowing her only three hours for this reunion before Hermes must take Protesilaus back whence they came. After the reunion, Laodamia finally learns the truth about her husband and when she asks whether or not she should follow him, he does not reply directly to her question but tells her instead to mourn him. And then he departs with Hermes.

Early in the fourth act, the wax statue, to which Laodamia has returned to console herself once again following the departure of Protesilaus' shade, comes into its sharpest focus as an element in the plot structure. A boy slave attending Laodamia reports that when he came to her in the morning he found her "not alone" in bed. Word of Laodamia's supposed infidelity reaches her stern father, Acastes, who orders her put to the torch for her "betrayal" of Protesilaus. Acastes is also another well-crafted miniature portrait: obstinate, narrow-minded, unyielding, but belatedly repentant. When the slave boy discovers that Laodamia had a wax statue in her bed and not a man and brings the statue to Acastes, the father still does not understand and orders the statue burnt instead of his daughter. To him the statue is something evil. His tone of implacable anger subsides only when Laodamia tells him that she is still a virgin and pleads with him to leave her "the last of her three husbands" (her husbands having been the live Protesilaus, his shade, and the wax statue). Convinced that his daughter is mad, he begs her to sacrifice the statue to the gods and to offend them and the dead no more by her desires gone astray. Shortly thereafter, as the stake that was erected originally for the burning of Laodamia flames up, she hurls herself into the blaze. Immediately the gods seem to "signal" their assent of her sacrifice by sending a gust of wind. Laodamia and Protesilaus are at last united and Acastes is left behind, grief-ridden and conscious-stricken. The play ends with the Chorus singing its praise of Laodamia's "madness," which poets will glorify; and this Neo-Romantic leitmotif capsulizes the lyrical tragedy as a whole:

When thought sits heavy on the shoulders . . .
Thou, O golden needle of dream,
Art dear to the heart, like a moon-filled night—
And poets will glorify madness.

Dream is an antidote for or, perhaps more accurately, an escape from the cares of the world. If it leads to madness, this madness is an expression of true feeling, of ideal love and desire, of primeval motivations which ennoble the person and merit the immortal praise of poets. So it is that the love of Laodamia should be immortalized.

Laodamia was followed by Thamyras the Cythara Player, Annensky's last tragedy and the play usually thought of as his best work in the field of drama. While the play does have several interesting features it is less satisfying as a whole than Laodamia and enjoys its reputation as Annensky's major tragedy in part anyway to the virtue of its having been staged.

The subject of Thamyras, subtitled a "Bacchic drama," is based on the legend of Thamyras' challenge to the Muses. Living only for his art and disinterested in everything else in life, Thamyras' pride grows beyond all normal bounds. He convinces himself that as a musician he has no peers and to prove his claim he challenges the Muses (specifically, the Muse Euterpe). He is defeated, however, and as punishment he is deprived of both his sight and his musical talent.

Annensky has introduced certain significant modifications in his adaptation of the legend. The idea of the contest with the Muse originates in the play with Argiope, Thamyras' mother, who has found him again after a separation of twenty years. Thamyras is indifferent to her, especially when it becones obvious that her sensual love for him is hardly of a motherly character. Fearing a rebuff, Argiope shrewdly appeals to her son's artistic vanity and suggests that she can arrange for him to hear the playing and singing of the Muse Euterpe. But since the Muse will not perform before a mortal, a contest must be held.

At this point Annensky makes a major departure from the legend. Sensing that art and love are becoming confused in Thamyras' mind (he now expects to marry the Muse and produce through her another Orpheus) Argiope jealously asks Zeus to intercede and to deny Thamyras the victory. When the time arrives for the contest, the Muse performs first. Thamyras is so struck by the perfection of her music, completely beyond the realm of human attainment, that he cannot bring himself to perform once the Muse has finished. When Argiope sees what has happened, she realizes that she must be the one to bear the ultimate responsibility for the destruction of Thamyras. Her personal tragedy is made more horrendous when Thamyras blinds himself, burdened with the sorrow of losing his talent and with the guilt of having dared to challenge the Muses. To punish Argiope for her destructive love, the gods turn her into small bird that perches on Thamyras' shoulder. This physical metamorphosis is a personal touch added by Annensky, with no precedent in classical literature.

Stylistically, *Thamyras* contains most of the features already remarked in *Laodamia*. Structurally, however, it is quite different. Instead of being divided into acts, the play contains twenty scenes, each of which has been given a color-associated name such as "pale-cold" (*bledno-kholodnaya*) or "blue-enamel" (*golubaya-emal*). These color names are meant to suggest different times of the day at which various actions occur (Annensky strictly observes the "unities" in *Thamyras*).

Musical interludes and dances abound in the play; the Chorus appears prominently, but unlike the more familiarly classical chorus of *Laodamia* it does not retain the same members throughout the play, varying them instead (Satyrs, Bacchantes, and so on). Like the Romantics before them, the Neo-Romantics sought to eliminate the barriers between the arts in their works. Writing for the theater provided an excellent opportunity to do this because a play could be made to serve as a vehicle for poetry, music, and dance. All of Annensky's dramatic writing reflects this desire to unite the arts within the single work. The poetic texture of

the dialogues and monologues is enriched by considerable metrical variation as well as the alternation of verse and prose (such as we find in
Thamyras). Around the classical Chorus an often elaborate, ancillary
structure of song and dance is built. There is an abundant use of this in
both *Laodamia* and *Thamyras*. There is also an ample use of color in
both tragedies, especially in *Thamyras* with its "color-coded" scenes,
revealing that Annensky thought in terms of painting as well as music
and choreography in his conception of the overall dramatic design.

Although *Thamyras* is striking for its psychological complexities, for
its probing of the tortured relationship between art and love as well as
for its structural properties, the play lacks the concentrated simplicity of
Laodamia. The story of the love triangle of Argiope, Philammon (Thamyras' father), and Zeus sometimes awkwardly intrudes on the main action. This is particularly true of the weakly motivated appearance of the
shade of the dead Philammon. The central characters Argiope and Thamyras are well delineated but the secondary characters, with the exception of the old Silenus, are less individuated than those in *Laodamia*.
While Annensky's effort to merge the arts in the plays often produces
splendid results, *Thamyras* seems overdone in this respect, thereby dif-
fusing the intensity of the dramatic conflict.

Marina Tsvetaeva, although now known almost exclusively for her poetry, had throughout her life a continuing interest in the theater. In her
teens she did a verse translation of Edmund Rostand's *L'Aiglon*, and she
began writing plays herself after the Revolution. The stimulus may have
come from her new friends and associates in the Moscow theater world
at a time when she was separated from her husband. Her earlier plays
were costume dramas set in the eighteenth or early nineteenth centuries; they are discussed later in this chapter in the section on "romantic-escapist" drama. Tsvetaeva's last works for the theater were
tragedies with classical settings, partly inspired by the plays of Ivanov
and Annensky whom Tsvetaeva regarded highly. The first was *Theseus*,
written in 1924 and published in a Paris émigré journal three years
later. Its title was later changed to *Ariadne*. The second was *Phaedra*,
written in 1927 and published in Paris in 1928. Although *Phaedra* was
designated the second part of a trilogy, no third part was ever published
or, as far as is known, was ever written.[43]

Without the classical erudition of Ivanov and Annensky, Tsvetaeva fell
back for source material on popular works, particularly the German
paraphrases of Gustav Schwab (1792–1850) in *Die schönsten Sagen des
klassischen Altertums*.[44] This probably accounts for the idiosyncrasies

marking her treatment of the legends of Theseus, Ariadne, and Phaedra. We can see this in an analysis of the first and the best of her two plays, *Theseus-Ariadne*.

Tsvetaeva's work is divided into the traditional five acts of neo-classical tragedy, unlike Annensky's tragedies where the division is handled more arbitrarily. In *Theseus-Ariadne* Poseidon, disguised as a wanderer, incites the Athenians to demand that King Aegaeus include his son Theseus among the youths and maidens periodically sent to Crete to be sacrificed to the Minotaur as retribution for the death of King Minos' son, a slaying attributed to Aegaeus. Despite his father's objections, the brave Theseus accepts the challenge to go and end the sending of sacrifices to Crete. In the palace of Minos he meets Ariadne and reluctantly accepts her offer to help without knowing who she really is.

With the sword and ball of yarn given him by Ariadne, Theseus slays the Minotaur, finds his way out of the labyrinth, and persuades Ariadne to accompany him to Athens. On their return journey, they stop at the island of Naxos. While Ariadne is asleep, Bacchus, here the god of divine inspiration, appears to Theseus as a beam of light and demands that he relinquish Ariadne to him. Bacchus argues that through union with a god, that is, with *him*, Ariadne will gain immortality, while if she remains with Theseus she will suffer old age and death, as any other mortal. Out of love for Ariadne, Theseus finally agrees. But he is so troubled by the loss of her that as he sails up to Athens he forgets to raise a white sail signaling victory and a safe return and instead flies the black flag of defeat and death. When Aegaeus espies this, he believes that his son is lost and in despair throws himself over a cliff into the sea. At the end of the tragedy, when Theseus learns what has happened, he blames Aphrodite, the goddess of physical love, who wished to punish him for his surrender of Ariadne to Bacchus.

Tsvetaeva's chief departure from the classical legend occurs with Theseus' abandonment of Ariadne on Naxos. Traditionally, the surrender of the sleeping Ariadne, who is not awakened to be asked her own preference, is no more or less than an act of betrayal. As Simon Karlinsky shows in his study of Tsvetaeva, Gustav Schwab "in trying to set up Theseus as an example for German children of the Victorian era skirted the abandonment completely substituting in its place a prophetic dream in which Bacchus claims Ariadne as his own fated bride from a Theseus unwilling to challenge the will of a higher authority, i.e., a god" (pp. 259–60).

Tsvetaeva adds still another personal interpretation to her play. The-

seus' surrender of Ariadne to Bacchus and hence to her divine destiny
becomes an act of the purest love. As a consequence, Theseus becomes
a tragic hero. On the other hand, Ariadne, whatever her personal feelings, is freed to move up to the higher level of existence, so important
not only in Tsvetaeva's personal *Weltanschauung* but in the metaphysics
of the Neo-Romantics in general. However immense the price Theseus
has paid in the loss of the woman he loves and in the death of his father,
and however great Ariadne's unhappiness over Theseus' "betrayal," to
Tsvetaeva's mind the attainment of the "higher realm" made it all worth-
while. As with Annensky, personal factors motivating the reinterpreta-
tion of various aspects of classical legends merge with more generalized
Neo-Romantic attitudes.

Possibly because of her weaker grasp of classical culture than Annensky, Tsvetaeva seems less tempted to experiment with classical
tragic structure. As we have seen, *Theseus-Ariadne* is divided into the
familiar five acts of seventeenth- and eighteenth-century Classicist tragic
drama. Musical and choreographical interludes are avoided, with the exception of a more or less traditional chorus of citizens and, near the
beginning of the play, the choruses of the youths and maidens who are
about to be sent to their doom on Crete. The color that is so striking in
Annensky's *Thamyras* is also absent. But just as Annensky's use of color
in his tragedies is an extension of a technique widely used in his poetry,
so also is the style of Tsvetaeva's *Theseus-Ariadne* (and *Phaedra*) a carryover into the drama of the character of the poetry she was writing at the
time. What we notice almost immediately is an extensive use of ellipsis
(the omission of a word or words, particularly in this case the omission of
verbs), anaphora (repetition of the same word or phrase at the beginning
of a sentence), the parallel arrangement of words and phrases, and the
use of exclamations and dashes. Moreover, there is a preference shown
for the use of shorter lines and for a metric pattern (the choriamb), interwoven with other meters, in which the first and fourth syllables of a
tetrasyllabic unit are stressed while the second and the third remain un-
stressed. While this is a rather rare pattern in Russian metrics, we can
find at least one earlier use of it in Russian Neo-Romantic classical tragedy, by Annensky in a chorus in *Thamyras*. Often this choriamb is
preceded by a stressed syllable and dash, this marking off the choriamb.
The use of this prosodic feature has resulted in an expressive, emotion-
tinged, staccato-like rhythm, characteristic of so much of Tsvetaeva's poetry of the period. There are also echoes here of Russian folk poetry,
with which Tsvetaeva was fascinated over a long period of time and

which strongly influenced one of her major works, the epic poem *Tsar-devitsa* (*The Folk Maiden*) which she wrote in 1920. Here are a few random excerpts from *Theseus-Ariadne* illustrating the distinct style of the play; the first are the opening lines spoken by the messenger:

> Vstavay, kto nye spal!
> Vstavay, kto, kak dukh brodyachiy,
> Ochey nye smykal!
> Vstavayte nastal
> Den placha! [45]

(Arise, whoever has not slept!/ Arise, whoever like a wandering spirit,/ Has not shut his eyes!/ Arise, the day/ Of grief has dawned!)

> Sem utrennykh zvyozd,
> Spes pradeda, radost brata,
> Vstavayte v otezd,
> Kotoromu nest
> Vozvrata!

(Seven morning stars,/ A great-grandfather's pride, a brother's happiness,/ Arise and prepare for the journey/ Of restitution!)

> Tak—rukhayut tsarstva!
> V prakh—brusom na brus!
> Ne-besny potryassya
> Svod,—reki iz rusl!

(So—crumble, empires!/ Unto dust—beam upon beam!/ The heavenly vault has been shaken/ —Rivers change course!)

> Gore! Gore!
> Vostry nozh!
> More, more,
> Chto nesyosh?

(Woe! Woe!/ A sharp dagger!/ O sea, O sea,/ What do you bear?)

The classical tragedies of the Russian Neo-Romantics, despite their dramatic form, do not lend themselves readily to stage production; with the exception of Annensky's *Thamyras*, they were, in fact, not staged. Indeed, they are rarely read. The tragedies were written by writers who were first and foremost poets, such as Annensky and Tsvetaeva. And yet—although their plays are largely unstageable and are extremely difficult to translate—they do command much interest, both for the quality of their poetry and for the psychological motivation which often resulted in a personal interpretation of ancient legends and myths.

The Romantic-Escapist Play

Less well defined as a category or type of drama are Neo-Romantic plays which, for a lack of a more precise definition, may be termed "romantic-escapist." Unlike the "cosmic," medieval, or classical drama of the same period, these plays rarely experiment with the creation of a new dramatic form or even with the revamping of an old one. They are also rarely concerned with the conceptualization of a philosophical or metaphysical point of view. Clearly operating within the general frame-work of the Neo-Romantic *Weltanschauung* and utilizing identifiable motifs common to Neo-Romantic literature, their principal *raison d'être* seems to be a literary escape into times, places, and characters invested with an unmistakable romantic aura. Virtually all the plays are period pieces; and, like other types of Neo-Romantic drama, they were written by writers known primarily as poets.

The two most important romantic-escapist dramatists were Nikolai Gumilyov (1886–1921), who in 1912 founded the post-Symbolist poetic group known as the Acmeists, and the poet Marina Tsvetaeva.

Between 1912 and 1918 Gumilyov wrote six dramatic works of a ro-mantic-escapist character. The first was *Don Zhuan v Egipte* (*Don Juan in Egypt*, published in 1912), a diverting one-act play in verse, influ-enced probably by Pushkin's "little tragedy" *Kamenny gost* (*The Stone Guest*) and by George Bernard Shaw's *Man and Superman*. The second, also a one-act play in verse, was *Akteon* (*Actheon*, published in 1913). *Actheon* appeared the same year as Annensky's larger and more impres-sive *Thamyras*, and both plays share the theme of the mortal artist who attempts to enter the realm of the gods and who is subsequently pun-ished by them for his audacity. *Igra* (*The Game*, written in 1916) is a "dramatic scene" set in a Paris gambling casino in 1813 and plainly in-tended for reading. *Gondla* (which appeared the following year, 1917) is a four-act "dramatic poem" set in ninth-century Iceland; like *The Game* it is also more suitable for reading than for stage performance. In 1918 one of Gumilyov's best works was published, the charming *Ditya Al-lakha* (*A Child of Allah*), an "Arabian Tale in Three Scenes" which Gumilyov wrote originally for the puppet theater.[46] Gumilyov's last romantic-escapist play, *Otravlennaya tunika* (*The Poisoned Tunic*), was also completed in 1918 though it was not printed until 1952 by the Chekhov publishing house of New York in the volume *Neizdanny Gumi-lyov* (*Gumilyov's Unpublished Works*, ed. by G. P. Struve). This five-act tragedy in verse was Gumilyov's most successful dramatic effort.

Long fascinated by the romantic, the heroic, and the exotic, as much of his expressive and robust poetry reflects, Gumilyov was no café or library dreamer but a decorated World War I officer who knew Africa and the Middle East at first hand. The interest in the past and present Middle East was widespread among the Neo-Romantics just as it had been earlier among the Romantics, and for primarily the same reasons. Like the Gypsy, the desert Arab was admired as a type of natural man whose stoic heroism and austere way of life offered a wholesome alternative to the stifling, bourgeois-dominated urban civilization of Europe. Also, in their search for new spiritual values and for alternatives to what they regarded as a corrupted contemporary Christianity, the Neo-Romantics often turned to the religions of the East, to Buddhism, Hinduism, Islam and Islamic (especially Sufi) mysticism. Middle Eastern religious writing as well as imaginative literature (above all, Arabic and Persian) were widely translated and enjoyed a definite vogue, primarily among the artists and writers of the late nineteenth and early twentieth centuries. Cultural interest occasionally led to foreign travel, as had been the case with Byron, Chateaubriand, and Flaubert. Gumilyov's experiences were by no means unique either for his time or for his artistic preferences.

Because of his fondness for and personal knowledge of Africa and the Middle East, it is not unusual that Gumilyov's most successful dramatic works, *A Child of Allah* and *The Poisoned Tunic*, are both set in this part of this world. In both plays prominent roles are assigned to outstanding poets of the region. In *A Child of Allah*, it is the Persian poet Hafiz (1326–90) with whom the heavenly Peri at last finds true love on earth. In *The Poisoned Tunic*, it is the pre-Mohammedan Bedouin poet Imr-ul-Qais who is loved by the Byzantine empress Theodora and by Zoe, her stepdaughter and the daughter of Emperor Justinian.

With direct, concentrated, and unembellished style, characteristic of much of his poetry, Gumilyov constructs the tragedy of *The Poisoned Tunic* around Theodora's unyielding jealousy and hatred of her stepdaughter Zoe. The interpretation of sixth-century Byzantine history is quite personal, for Gumilyov was not interested in historical exactness.

The plot begins in a very direct manner as Imr-ul-Qais appears at the court of Justinian seeking the emperor's help to form a punitive expedition against the Bedouin tribe responsible for the murder of his father. While there, he meets the thirteen-year-old Zoe; and before he discovers her true identity, he makes romantic advances toward her. Like the artists who stand in the foreground of Gumilyov's other plays, Imr-ul-Qais is a great lover. Zoe succumbs to him and eventually allows him to initiate her into love. However, the young girl is supposed to marry the king of Trapezond. Neither Zoe nor her intended know of Justinian's plot to kill the king by means of a poisoned tunic being sewn for him for his wedding. With the king then disposed of, Zoe will be left to rule the throne of Trapezond, and Justinian through her will be able to control a realm he covets with political ambitions. When a delay in the sewing of the tunic occurs, Justinian decides to send the brave and experienced king of Trapezond as leader of the expedition against Imr-ul-Qais' enemies. Then, upon his return, Justinian plans to present him with the tunic.

Justinian's bold plot against the king of Trapezond is paralleled by Theodora's more subtle campaign to destroy Zoe, whose love for Imr-ul-Qais she envies. She tells the king of Trapezond of the couple's love and proceeds to play the rivals off, one against the other. To each, she promises her help to win Zoe. Her scheme bears fruit when Imr-ul-Qais and the king of Trapezond exchange heated words and the latter vows to destroy the former's land once the expedition against Imr-ul-Qais' enemies is successfully concluded.

Now hopelessly in love with the Bedouin poet, Zoe tells the king of Trapezond that she and Imr-ul-Qais are lovers and that she wants to marry him. In despair, the king leaps to his death from the cupola of Hagia Sophia. Meanwhile, playing on Justinian's love for her and his jealousy of other male suitors, Theodora tells him of her own past affair with Imr-ul-Qais and of her present fear of temptation. Instead of killing or imprisoning the Bedouin, however, Justinian is persuaded by Zoe to let him lead the expedition in place of the king of Trapezond. But soon after Imr-ul-Qais has set out for the expedition, Justinian's trusted eunuch comes to report the king's suicide. Struck with remorse, Zoe confesses to her father her relationship with the Bedouin. Enraged at his daughter's affair with a poor and inconsequential nomad, Justinian orders Zoe to become a nun and his servant to take the poisoned tunic to Imr-ul-Qais as a token of esteem and affection. At the end of the play, beside a distraught and despairing Zoe, Theodora gloats in her triumph.

When one compares *The Poisoned Tunic* as a tragic drama with a remote historical setting to the classical tragedies of Annensky and Tsvetaeva the differences in intent and style become immediately apparent. By treating dramatic form as an extension of poetry, both Annensky and Tsvetaeva sought to create a new tragic idiom by freely interpreting classical legends and by enveloping them in complex structures of image and meter. Gumilyov, on the other hand, eschewed experimentation with structure and prosody. *The Poisoned Tunic* is written in a five-foot line, mostly unrhymed iambic verse; the play, furthermore, contains all the traditional conventions: five acts, six characters, and three "unities." Each act is divided into four or five fairly short scenes in which generally only two people appear onstage. There are no lengthy stage directions nor are there any structural embellishments in the form of interpolated interludes (choral, musical, choreographical, or otherwise). Though the play's setting is in "ancient" times, it is not in classical Greece or Rome; and no motifs from classical mythology appear. Of the six characters in the play, only Justinian, Theodora, and Imr-ul-Qais are actual historical figures; the others were invented by the author. The tragedy does not result from an individual's struggle against his fate or against the gods, but from the destructive forces of human ambition.

The plot of *The Poisoned Tunic* unfolds easily and rapidly, with an emphasis on contrast. The characters are sharply etched: the scheming Theodora, driven by jealousy and hate; the young Zoe, enraptured by love for the first time; the brave king of Trapezond, honorable but unromantic; the sly eunuch who knows all yet is utterly loyal to his master; the empire-builder, Justinian, ready to utilize whatever means are necessary to realize his political goals; and finally Imr-ul-Qais, the "romantic" hero, poet, lover, and natural man.

Of course, the simplicity and concentration of *The Poisoned Tunic* indicate that Gumilyov thought in terms of having his play performed on the stage. It is neither an experiment in dramatic form nor the dramatic embodiment of the Neo-Romantic *Weltanschauung*. *The Poisoned Tunic* remains what Gumilyov doubtless intended it to be, a romantic-escapist play, meant to entertain.

Tsvetaeva's romantic-escapist plays were written only a few years after Gumilyov's. The first to be published, *Metel* (*The Snowstorm*), with the subtitle "Dramatic Scenes in Verse," was written in Moscow in 1918 and appeared in print in a Russian émigré journal in Paris in 1923. This was followed by a dramatic cycle about the great lover Casanova: the one-act verse play *Konets Kazanovy* (*Casanova's End*, date of writing uncertain, published in Moscow in 1922); the three-act *Feniks* (*Phoenix*, an expanded version of *Casanova's End*, published in an émigré journal in Prague in 1924); and *Priklyuchenie* (*An Adventure*, a five-act play in verse, published in Prague in 1923). Tsvetaeva's last romantic play to be published (in Paris in 1923) was *Fortuna* (*Fortune*), about another great lover in the Casanova tradition, Armand Louis de Gontaut Biron, duc de Lauzun.

Much of Gumilyov's inspiration for his romantic-escapist drama derived from his interest in and travel among exotic peoples in foreign lands. In Tsvetaeva's plays the exotic influence is negligible, for her greatest stimulus was her affection for French Romantic drama, which was evident even in her youth. Two of her favorite authors were Musset and Rostand. In 1920, she translated Musset's best-known drama, *On ne badine pas avec l'amour*, though her translation was never published and has since been lost.[47] Rostand's famous *Cyrano de Bergerac* delighted her and, as we have seen, while still in her teens she completed a verse translation of the same author's *L'Aiglon*.

Her first published play, *The Snowstorm*, though short, forecasts in several ways her better work in the romantic-escapist vein. The setting, characters, and mood are wholly romantic. On a stormy New Year's Eve in 1830 several travelers are thrown together in an inn in the Bohemian woods. As the other travelers pass the time conversing and drinking, interest quickly focuses on a mysterious Lady (Dama) who remains aloof from the others. Suddenly, a Gentleman (Gospodin) appears and announces that he is the Prince of the Moon, Chevalier of the Rotonde, and Knight of the Rose. Soon the identity of the Lady is revealed; she is the Countess Lanska. That morning, having come to the realization that she no longer loved her husband, she left her home and went out into the storm. As the conversation between her and the Gentleman progresses, the Lady senses that she has met him before. He confides to her his belief that they have known each other in a previous existence and that their present meeting is their last. He then places a dreamlike spell over her, from which she will awaken with no recollection of their meeting. At the end of the play, as the Lady remains motionless in the spell, the Gentleman makes a cryptic statement suggesting that henceforth whenever the moon shines into her room he will come back to her. Then while she is still asleep, he departs. The last sound heard is that of sleigh bells disappearing into the night, never to return.

The Snowstorm is of slight value as drama and ought to be regarded as a fledgling effort by Tsvetaeva in a new medium. The familiar characteristics of Romantic literature are rather easily recognized: the nocturnal setting, the snowstorm, the mysterious stranger, the idea of predestined love, and the contrast between the sublime and otherwordly relationship between the Lady and the Gentleman and the mundaneness of their environment. In his study of the poet, Simon Karlinsky demonstrates Tsvetaeva's dependence in *The Snowstorm* especially on Pushkin and Blok and on the poet Anna Akhmatova. Most obviously is this true of the play's basic situation, the "mysterious bond between an astral being and a chosen unique mortal, depicted against a background of vulgarity and incomprehension," which Karlinsky ascribes to Blok's play *Neznakomka (The Unknown Woman)*.[48]

Tsvetaeva's more original achievements in drama came in her plays about two of history's great lovers and adventurers, Giacomo Casanova de Seingalt (1725–98) and Armand Louis de Gontaut Biron, duc de Lauzun (1747–93). It is not difficult to suggest probable reasons for her interest in these men. Tsvetaeva had a continuing fascination with France and especially with the era that came to an end with the French Revolution. Moreover, there is a strong likelihood that she saw distinct parallels between France of the revolutionary period and Russia of her own time. The lives of Casanova and Lauzun spanned both the pre- and postrevolutionary periods, ending almost with the century itself, and seemed to her to embody much of the brilliance and style of eighteenth-century rococo France. To Tsvetaeva, their memoirs were a remarkable mirror image of the age itself. She must have read them avidly, as well as drawing from them the inspiration for her Casanova and Lauzun plays.

The first was the one-act *Casanova's End*. Although short, the play has an undeniable theatrical quality, an observation that cannot be made about most of Tsvetaeva's dramatic writing. Some of the Romantic motifs of *The Snowstorm* reappear. The action of the play takes place again on New Year's Eve (of 1799, although Casanova died, in fact, in 1798). The setting is again Bohemia, this time at the Castle of Dux, which belonged to Count Waldstein and where Casanova spent the last years of his life as the Count's librarian. Again, a snowstorm is raging. Casanova, now seventy-five, is shown burning old love letters, preparatory to leaving the castle where he has not been happy. He is visited by Francesca, the thirteen-year-old adopted daughter of the forest warden. She is madly in love with the old adventurer and tries to seduce him. Although tempted, Casanova declines to take advantage of the situation. Instead, he begins to tell the girl stories and finally sings her to sleep with a lullaby. As the play ends, he is ready to depart and, as in *The Snowstorm*, sleigh bells can be heard in the distance. He instructs the butler to deliver the young Francesca back to her father.

In the expanded three-act version of the play entitled *Phoenix*, the author uses *Casanova's End*, with slight modifications, as the third act. The first two acts deal with the indignities visited upon Casanova at Dux. The culminating point is a poetry contest between Casanova and the court poet Viderol that leads to a quarrel. To appease the disgruntled Casanova after this episode, the aristocratic ladies present prevail upon him to recount his adventures. As he does so, however, the assembled guests find the amorous details distasteful and gradually leave. After this further indignity, Casanova resolves to leave Dux and wins the approval of the Prince de Ligne, Count Waldstein's uncle, the only one of the guests who has been kind to him. Later, Casanova is visited by Francesca and the story of *Casanova's End* is repeated intact. As Karlinsky shows in his study of Tsvetaeva, *Phoenix* is less successful as drama than *Casanova's End.* In the longer work there are too many minor roles, a structural feature possibly assimilated from Rostand's plays. The contrast that Tsvetaeva apparently sought to unfold in the first two acts between Casanova and the assembled guests never becomes a dynamic one. With the exception of the sympathetic Prince de Ligne, the other guests are boors who either bait Casanova or treat him condescendingly. In view of the number of characters, the contrast becomes overdrawn; the contest between Casanova and the guests never coheres theatrically.

More successful is the five-act *An Adventure,* the last of the Casanova plays and the only one based directly on Casanova's memoirs.[49] The particular episode Tsvetaeva used was the famous one about the young Casanova and the mysterious Frenchwoman known as Henriette. In the memoirs, Casanova first encountered the shy and mysterious Henriette when she was traveling in Italy, disguised as a man and accompanied by an older Hungarian army officer who insisted on speaking only Latin with everyone. Finally, Casanova prevailed upon the Hungarian to give him Henriette as his mistress. They lived happily together for several months, though her identity continued to remain a mystery to Casanova. Then, at a private concert, Henriette, without advance rehearsal, replaced the soloist and performed a difficult violoncello concerto with amazing skill. Rumors of the performance eventually reached her aristocratic parents from whom she had run away. Henriette was subsequently traced to Casanova; and when she received a mysterious letter one day through the local French ambassador, she left Casanova for good. Her farewell to her lover was, "Vous oublierez aussi Henriette," scratched with her diamond on the windowpane of their hotel room.

In her dramatization of the episode, Tsvetaeva made several important changes, the most striking involving the character of Henriette. In the memoirs, she is shy and retiring and dresses as a male out of necessity. In the play, Henriette becomes not only more brilliant and dynamic but also more ambiguous. At the beginning of *An Adventure* she appears dressed as a hussar named Henri (she is identified in the cast of characters as Henri-Henriette). Unlike the memoirs version, she takes the initiative to come to Casanova's quarters and to force herself upon him. There is an echo here of the Francesca of *Casanova's End,* and it is possible that in the conception of *An Adventure* a certain coalescence of the characters of Francesca and Henriette occurred.

The ambiguity of Henri-Henriette is established from the beginning. Answering Casanova's question regarding her identity, she replies, "I am a moonbeam, free to go wherever I chose." Her reply to his question why she came to his room is another question, "Why does this moonbeam descend onto the couch here?" As the dialogue continues, she declares that to the public she is the hussar Henri, but to Casanova she will be an eternal satellite, just as the moon is the satellite of the earth. The character of Tsvetaeva's Henriette is also established early as being more forceful, aggressive, and provocative, as she tauntingly pretends to bargain with Casanova before agreeing to go with him to Parma as his mistress. When the bargain is finally sealed with a kiss on Casanova's forehead, the great lover asks when he can expect to be kissed on the lips. Reverting to her ambiguity, Henriette taunts the love-mad Casanova: "God created his marvelous world in a week./ A woman is a hundred worlds. With one breath,/ How can I become a woman in just one day?/ Yesterday a hussar—in spurs and sword./ Today, a lace and satin angel./ And tomorrow, perhaps, who knows?"[50]

The important concert episode that ultimately leads to Henriette's discovery by her parents is also treated quite differently in Tsvetaeva's play. In the memoirs Casanova has to persuade the girl to go to the concert. In *An Adventure,* the audience is plunged *in medias res.* The concert takes on more the nature of a ball attended by many people and there is no suggestion of Henriette's reluctance to appear at a social function together with Casanova. On the contrary, in keeping with Tsvetaeva's view of the character, she is the star of the evening, beautiful, witty, and admired by all. Karlinsky is quite right in regarding the ball scene, which comprises the whole of Act III, as a serious weakness in the play. In *Phoenix,* Tsvetaeva has Casanova surrounded by a pack of unsympathetic boors. Henriette, as the central character of *An Adventure,* is almost worshiped by everyone she meets and Casanova is admired and envied for his success with her. In both plays, the treatment is lopsided and somewhat simplistic.

Doubtless for heightened dramatic effect, Tsvetaeva condenses the events in the memoirs by having the fateful letter come to Henriette at the ball after she has started playing the violoncello. As soon as she sees the envelope, she knows what the seals mean; without opening it, she immediately informs Casavnova that they must leave the ball.

The fourth act of the play is given over entirely to the final moments together of Henriette and Casanova. Reminiscent of *The Snowstorm*, lunar imagery appears in the dialogue of the lovers and may be a conscious carryover from the earlier play. Finally, at the moment of departure, Henriette disappears in a beam of moonlight.

The fifth act is a radical departure from the events in the memoirs. In Casanova's version, he discovers the farewell message Henriette has scratched with a diamond on the windowpane as he returns to their hotel room after her departure. In Tsvetaeva's version, the discovery comes thirteen years later when Casanova returns to the hotel accompanied by a young woman whom Tsvetaeva refers to in the stage directions as his "thousand and first female companion." The belated discovery of Henriette's message is made first by Casanova's slut. Interestingly, her discovery immediately follows her looking through the window at the moon, which she describes as bluish in color. When the girl reads the message to him, Casanova flies into a rage and smashes the pane of glass. Then he orders the girl out of the room with insults. But as she is about to leave, the old Casanova reasserts himself and with a change of heart he asks her to remain. When the girl asks him about the message in the glass, he tells her that it was just connected with an adventure he once had but not an amorous one. The girl teases Casanova about it, asks if the door to the room is locked, and then as the last action of the play covers up the statue of the Virgin Mary nearby before giving herself to Casanova's waiting arms.

In contrast to the extensive linguistic and metric innovations that add so much interest to Tsvetaeva's later classical tragedies, *Theseus-Ariadne* and *Phaedra*, a conservatism characterizes the earlier romantic-escapist plays. In fact, these early plays are considerably more conservative than her lyric poetry of the same period. This timidity, which Tsvetaeva seems to begin to overcome only in the last of her plays, *Fortune*, must have stemmed from an inhibiting self-consciousness which she felt toward the new medium of drama. Probably for the same reason, the poet leaned heavily on the works of others, especially Blok in the case of *The Snowstorm* and Rostand, whom she admired so much, in her later plays. Even metrically, the Casanova plays adhere to the iambic tetrameter and pentameter made famous by Aleksandr Griboedov in his satire *Gore ot uma* (*Woe from Wit* 1822–24) and used by Lermontov in his Romantic drama *Maskarad* (*Masquerade,* 1835).

Tsvetaeva wanted her plays thought of primarily as poems, though given a dramatic form. As poetic works to be read, the romantic-escapist and even classical tragedies have much to recommend them. They contain many sensitive moments and engaging images. But as plays they lack the quality to come alive, and the sharp, plausible characterization and dramatic conflict of strong theater. It is in the latter area that Tsetaeva fails most notably. Even when we sense her desire to create a conflict, as in *Phoenix,* her overstatement produces an unsatisfying result. *An Adventure* and *Fortune* do have charm at times, but this is no adequate substitute for a theatrical viability which the plays lack. Only *Fortune,* which has a more elaborate plot structure than the other Romantic plays (recounting various adventures from the life of Lauzun, from his birth to death), shows some promise in this direction. Gumilyov may have been only slightly less a poet than Tsvetaeva, but in *A Child of Allah* and *The Poisoned Tunic* he showed that poetry and drama could be combined to produce romantic-escapist fare that read well as poetry and yet could also be presented on the stage.

Romantic Escapism in a Contemporary Vein:
Leonid Andreev's *He Who Gets Slapped*

Generally speaking, the Neo-Romantics disdained subjects drawn from contemporary life. They were either hostile or indifferent to the society around them and they preferred to look to the classical past, to the Middle Ages, to the Romantic era, to distant, exotic cultures, or to their own dreams and fantasies, rather than at the real, everyday world. Their repudiation of realism and naturalism and their quest for new forms of dramatic expression tended to militate against plays with contemporary settings.

There were exceptions, of course, and Neo-Romantic plays set in the late nineteenth and early twentieth centuries did appear from time to time. Such plays were of two types. Some, in the spirit of social criticism, sought to expose various vulgar and coarse aspects of bourgeois life and often contained heroes and heroines in conflict with it. Other plays focused on the artist and the privileged sanctuary of art.

One Russian Neo-Romantic dramatist whose *œuvre* includes several plays with contemporary settings was Leonid Andreev. The most important of these were *To the Stars* (1905), *Savva* (1906), *Days of Our Lives*

(1908), *Anfisa* (1909), *Gaudeamus* (1910), *Yekaterina Ivanovna* (1912), *Professor Storitsyn* (1912), and *He Who Gets Slapped* (1915). While all of these plays have caused misunderstanding and controversy, the one which has endured and has become something of an international classic is *He Who Gets Slapped*. It is the only play of Andreev's many that a reader may sometime actually have a chance to see on a stage. It was made into a film in Russia as early as 1916 and in 1956 its plot was used by the American, Robert Ward, as the framework for his opera *Pantaloon*. [51]

Much of the appeal of *He Who Gets Slapped* is related to its circus milieu and characters. But Andreev's choice of a circus setting was by no means unique. As we shall see later in the discussion of theatricalism in drama, the figure of the clown developed as one of the more important tools in the antirepresentational concept of theater and drama. The appeal of the clown was complex. Antirepresentational writers rediscovered and made ample use of elements from earlier types of masked theater, particularly the Italian commedia dell'arte of the sixteenth and seventeenth centuries and classical Oriental theater. With his costume and makeup, the clown could be regarded as a kind of masked performer. Also, to the contemporary exponents of tragicomic drama, the clown seemed to have a symbolic value. Who knows what private wretchedness and misery lay beneath the outward mask of gaiety?

From the clown to the circus itself was a short step. Yet the appeal of the circus did not arise solely from the fact that it was the clown's natural habitat. To the Neo-Romantic mind, the circus was a sort of contemporary refuge from the ugly reality of the bourgeois world. The circus performers were artists in their own right and they had succeeded in creating a special world of their own, within the borders of society, yet at the same time distinctly apart from it and openly contemptuous of it. The circus as an environment exerted an irresistible charm on the Neo-Romantics. It was a part of their own reality, yet it offered a romantic escapism similar to the settings of the Middle Ages, the late eighteenth and early nineteenth centuries, and the distant exotic lands of the Middle and Far East.

Andreev may have shared the general interest of the Neo-Romantics in the circus, but this did not result in any idealization of the circus world in *He Who Gets Slapped*. On the contrary, the final portrait is anything but flattering and most probably should be regarded as a reflection of Andreev's state of mind at the time.

The He of the play is a mysterious gentleman from the "other world,"

A scene from the 1922 Theatre Guild production of Leonid Andreev's He Who
Gets Slapped *with Richard Bennett in the role of He.*

the world outside the circus. Although almost nothing is revealed of his
past or of his reasons for wanting to join the circus, he is obviously a person of culture and refinement. The job he seeks in the circus of Papa
Briquet (the play is set in an unspecified large French city) is that of a
clown. When asked to choose a character for himself, the stranger immediately offers to play the role of He Who Gets Slapped, the clown
who will entertain the public by being slapped by the other clowns.

Only in Act III is the audience given more information about He.
Andreev introduces another man from the other world, someone out of
He's past who, driven by his conscience, has been searching for He for

some time and only discovers him by chance in Briquet's circus. From the conversation between the two, the audience finally discovers that He was formerly an intellectual of some stature. However, his ideas were taken by the other man, were popularized, and brought success to the second man which should have come to He. Frustrated and irate over his "friend's" hypocrisy and deceit, He disappeared, leaving everyone to come to the conclusion that he had somehow mysteriously died. After his "death," the friend and He's wife marry. The friend thus appropriated not only He's professional career but his personal life as well.

We have here a familiar Neo-Romantic situation involving a sensitive person who is infringed upon and finally overwhelmed by a less sensitive and less scrupulous person, someone, in short, whom the author uses to represent the hypocrisy and venality of bourgeois society. He is dispossessed by his friend just as Chekhov's three sisters were dispossessed some fourteen years earlier by the crass and vulgar Solyony and Natasha Prozorov. Both Chekhov and Andreev effectively deny their sensitive characters any successful escape. For the sisters, their only haven is a Moscow that lies beyond their grasp. He seeks only a temporary and imperfect refuge in the circus, where for the moment he can strike back at the society he has fled through the character he has assumed, the clown who is slapped. The slaps he receives represent a grotesque reenactment of the real plunder of his personal dignity. However, by his reaction to the slaps in the arena, he returns the humiliation to the public itself. Symbolically, the public, here representing the other world, is connected with the ultimate responsibility for He's dispossession, flight, and self-abasement. But the satisfaction this provides He is brief; the refuge of the circus is illusory and finally He takes his own life.

From the beginning of *He Who Gets Slapped* Andreev's pessimism is inescapable. The world depicted is one in which there is no escape from the crass, the vulgar, and the hypocritical. Actually, the circus in which He seeks a haven is a microcosm of the society beyond; both are filled with pettiness, materialism, banality, and squabbling. The only exception is the lovely bareback rider, Consuella, the adopted daughter of "Count" Mancini. Although He falls in love with her as an ideal of beauty, he is still aware of the impossibility of any real communication between them. When He learns that Mancini will not be dissuaded from his intention to improve his own status by arranging a marriage of convenience between Consuella and the wealthy Baron Regnart (from the other world), the die is cast and the play moves inexorably toward its melodramatic climax.

To He, the loss of Consuella to the Baron repeats the dispossession he had earlier experienced in the other world. That he can be robbed of something dear to him even within the circus, his refuge from the other world, seems intolerable to He, and he sets about to thwart it. Since Consuella has refused to take seriously his own declarations of love, He tries at least to block her marriage to the Baron by promoting her relationship with the young jockey Bezano, whom Consuella likes. But Bezano does not understand what He is trying to do for him; besides, Consuella enjoys the prospect of being wealthy and will not oppose Mancini in his plan. And so, finally, rather than permit the object of his idealization to be prostituted by being sold to a person from the other world, He poisons Consuella and then drinks from the same glass himself. In a final melodramatic moment, the Baron also kills himself (offstage) with a gun, presumably from remorse. When told of this, the dying He expresses merely disbelief that the Baron's love for Consuella was so strong. Then, in a more defiant mood, He vows that in the world beyond the grave he will contest the Baron for eternal possession of Consuella, as fiercely as he did on earth.

The highly melodramatic ending of *He Who Gets Slapped* is more important in understanding the conception of the drama than may appear at first glance. As the relationship between He and Consuella intensifies throughout the play, it assumes a mythic character. He speaks to Consuella about himself, her, and Bezano as being "gods." By this he infers that they are not like the gray masses of the other world that can only torment and repress them; rather they are exceptional beings, beings of physical and/or spiritual beauty; they are gods. To dissuade her from marrying the Baron, He tells Consuella that she must heed the words of Jupiter who warns her against belonging to any earthling. More germane to the play's mythic element, He tries to convince her that she is Venus; almost hypnotically He draws her into a recollection of her birth from the ocean's foam:

> HE: Sleep and again awaken, Consuella! And once you have awakened, recall that time when you emerged from the azure sea! Recall that sky, and the gentle wind from the east, and the bubbling of the foam around your marble legs.
>
> CONSUELLA (*shutting her eyes*): The weather . . . Yes, I seem to remember something. Remind me of more. (*Inclining over Consuella and raising his hands,* HE *speaks softly but authoritatively in an almost incantatory manner.*)
>
> HE: Do you see how the waves are playing? Recall that the sirens were then singing. Recall their griefless joy, their white bodies,

half-blue in the blue of the water. Or is it the sun singing? Golden
rays extending themselves, like the strings of a heavenly harp. Do
you not see the hands of the god bestowing harmony, light and love
on the world? Do not the mountains give off a bluish incense of celebration? Recall the prayer of the mountains, recall the prayer of
the sea, Consuella![52]

The conclusion of *He Who Gets Slapped* can be seen then as consistent
with the play's mythic substructure. He's last words, the dying challenge flung the dead Baron, move the action of the drama to the metaphysical plane, where their rivalry for possession of Consuella-Venus
will become a contest of gods.

Although myth and circus combine in *He Who Gets Slapped* to produce a theatrically appealing work and one of the most durable plays of
the Russian Neo-Romantics as a whole, the pervasive pessimism of the
work must be noted. Although outwardly escapist, *He Who Gets
Slapped* should perhaps best be regarded as a refutation of the notion
of escape, as a dramatization of the futility of escape. He comes to the
circus in flight from a society no longer bearable to him. But even inside
the world of the circus, he discovers much the same pettiness, greed,
and lack of understanding from which he fled. Finally, the other world,
represented by his former friend and especially the Baron, intrudes on
the terrain of the circus, ultimately to destroy it as a refuge for He and
furthermore to destroy both He himself and the new ideal of beauty discovered by him beneath its tents.

In his theatricalist play *The Fairground Booth,* Aleksandr Blok breaks
with his earlier mystic symbolism in a reaffirmation of life. With *He Who
Gets Slapped,* Andreev appears to oppose the romantic-escapist trend
within neo-romanticism by showing the futility of flight. What makes the
pessimism of the play so striking is not simply that its subject is the
death of nobility and beauty, but that the theme of inescapability from
society is etched with such venom. That nobility and beauty perish by
poison in *He Who Gets Slapped* is no mere coincidence; to Andreev the
other world acts on whatever comes within its grasp like a poison
spreading throughout the whole system.

Theatricalism

In their desire to move drama and theater away from the representationalism (the "illusionism," as they saw it) of realism and naturalism as
well as from the metaphysicality of symbolism, the theatricalists often

fell back on "older" theatricalist techniques. These included, as we have seen, the device of the play-within-a-play, the masks of the commedia dell'arte, pantomime, motifs borrowed from marionette performances, prologues and epilogues, direct addresses of onstage characters to the audience, the inclusion of figures representing the author and/or director among the dramatis personae, and stage directions calling for the absence of curtains and/or set changes in full view of the public.

In making use of several of these techniques within the limited space of a play no longer than a traditional one-acter, Aleksandr Blok's first dramatic work, *The Fairground Booth,* broke new ground, becoming thereby the first important manifestation of theatricalism in early twentieth-century Russian drama.

The Fairground Booth originated as an "occasional piece." In 1905, Vyacheslav Ivanov and other Petersburg Symbolists conceived the idea for a theatrical and journalistic enterprise to be called *Fakely (The Torches).* To launch the new theater Blok was prevailed upon to dramatize his poem "Balaganchik" ("The Fairground Booth") which tells the story of a boy and a girl at a puppet show who become alarmed when instead of the queen they expect to see a procession of devils appears onstage. Blok wrote a rough draft of the play in less than a month. In the meantime, the plan for the Torches theater fell through; the journal, actually an almanac, did become a reality, however, and it was on its pages in April 1906 that Blok's little play first appeared. Eight months later, on December 30, *The Fairground Booth* was staged by Meyerhold at Komissarzhevskaya's theater and immediately found itself the subject of heated controversy and debate.

The innovative character of *The Fairground Booth* is established virtually from the outset by what seems to be a double-edged parody of Maeterlinckian symbolism and St. Petersburgian mysticism. I say "double-edged" because Blok appears to be both parodying and satirizing not only Symbolist drama itself but the mystic symbolism of his own earlier writing as well. With *The Fairground Booth* Blok is declaring, in effect, his liberation from the mystic orientation of his previous writing and, on the launching of his career as a playwright, from the style of Maeterlinckian dramaturgy. Abandoning "Maeterlinckianism" Blok seems to suggest that henceforth the direction he intends to follow is that of theatricalist drama, a promise unfulfilled in his later plays.

The first characters onstage are Maeterlinckian "mystics" who at once establish an air of mystery and dread about an unknown something that is about to happen, much like the people awaiting the Second Coming in Andrei Bely's Symbolist "neo-mystery" *He Who Has Come*. Hardly do the mystics appear when Blok sets down the first plank in his theatricalist platform. Pierrot, a derivative of one of the traditional commedia dell'arte masks, arrives singing a sad song about his beloved but unfaithful Columbine. When his song is ended, another theatricalist plank falls into position: the author as dramatis persona emerges protesting that his play was not written as a puppet show and that the actor who plays Pierrot is mocking his rights as an author.

As soon as the author disappears in comes Columbine, whom the mystics, in true Maeterlinckian fashion, assume to be oncoming Death. Because they insist on seeing her only as the fulfillment of their mystico-visionary expectations, the mystics refuse to be persuaded by Pierrot that Columbine is his fiancée. The next character to enter is a handsome youth, Harlequin—presumably modeled on Bely—thereby completing the trio of classic commedia dell'arte figures. As Pierrot falls prostrate, Harlequin leads Columbine away.

The author reappears to protest still more vigorously that the actors are not playing their parts as he wrote them suggesting, in a foreshadowing of Pirandellian drama, that the created beings assume an autonomous existence independent of the purpose and wishes of their creator. Objecting strenuously to the commedia dell'arte clowns acting out some old legend, he declares that his intention was to write a traditional romantic comedy about lovers who overcome obstacles and are eventually united. But before he can finish a hand protrudes from the curtain and yanks him behind it by the neck.

When the curtain reopens Pierrot further recounts in verse his triangular relationship with Harlequin and Columbine amidst masked dancers at a ball. When Pierrot finishes his plaint, he is followed onstage by two different sets of vividly costumed lovers from the ball. The verse dialogue of the first pair expresses the joy of love while that of the second relates the seduction of a lover from his fiancée by another woman whom he finds irresistible.

What Blok appears to be doing now is restoring the Pierrot-Columbine-Harlequin relationship to the original lofty purpose of the intrusive author—not a fully developed play-within-a-play but the contours of one. The Pierrot-Columbine-Harlequin triangle thus becomes a kind of clownish parody of the "original" drama.

A clown is introduced, in fact, after a very brief comic scene of clear parodic intent on the theme of the Eternal Female. After the second pair of lovers quits the stage, a third appears, the man wearing a cardboard helmet. In every line he proclaims his happiness with his beloved who divines his soul. She responds, however, only by repeating the last word of each of his lines. When the clown appears, he sticks out his tongue and is beaten by the cardboard-helmeted lover wielding a wooden sword. This kind of buffoonery from the traditions of medieval drama, the commedia dell'arte, and the marionette theater, and the figure of the clown himself, underscore the frivolous "play" element of *The Fairground Booth* and proceed wholly from Blok's theatricalist conception of the drama. The degree of Blok's commitment to theatricalism—at least at this point in his career—is obvious from his treatment of the encounter between the clown and the lover. The distinct puppet theater character of the episode is striking. The lover, in his cardboard helmet, hits the clown with a wooden sword and the clown, after receiving the blow, crumbles and hangs over the footlights of the stage, a stream of cranberry juice spurting from his head. The partial eradication of barriers between audience and players by actors leaving the stage and moving among the audience again is not fully realized in *The Fairground Booth,* only hinted at. The age of Piscator, Brecht, and "epic theater" has not yet been reached, but the path to it has been revealed.

The end of *The Fairground Booth* is heralded by the reappearance of Harlequin soon after the clown episode. Embedded in his verse monologue is the intellectual kernel of the play—the expressed desire to rediscover true love not by a romantic mystic withdrawal from life but by a reunion with it, with its joys and sorrows. "Greetings, world!," declares Harlequin at the close of his speech, "You're with me again!/ Your soul has long been close to mine! I go to breathe the spring/ Through your golden window frame!"[53]

His part over, Harlequin leaves the stage not by a conventional wing exit but via a marvelous concoction of theatricalist inventiveness: he jumps through a window painted on paper which he bursts with his leap. Through the hole the rising dawn becomes visible and against this background the figure of Death bearing a scythe appears. As all the other characters onstage scatter in terror, Pierrot approaches Death, who at his approach becomes Columbine. Just as Pierrot is about to touch her, the author reappears to come between them. This time he is happy, however, since the plot seems to be working out as he originally conceived it. Harlequin is out of the picture and the lovers, Pierrot and Columbine, are at last uniting. But when the author moves to join their hands the scenery rolls up and Pierrot is left lying on the bare stage. Again, Blok shatters the fantasy world of idealized, romanticized love and thrusts reality upon the audience. At the end of the play, Pierrot is alone onstage bemoaning his fate and the loss of Columbine, whom he now dismisses as a cardboard fiancée. In typical theatricalist fashion, his last words are addressed to the audience to whom he declares his sadness and asks, "Is it funny to you?"

Short as it is, *The Fairground Booth* has several layers of meaning. With one, involving the mystics, Blok proclaims his repudiation of mystical otherworldliness and, in terms of dramatic tradition, of the Maeterlinckian "static" theater of death. Through the "inner drama" of Pierrot, Columbine, Harlequin, and the author, and the scenes with the masked lovers he projects the desire to accept life realistically rather than to make it palatable and hence "unreal" by spiritualizing and romanticizing both life and love. The failure of Pierrot and Columbine to unite and the frustration of the author's original scheme mark the abandonment of idealization and the acceptance of the unpredictability of human experience. The author's plan for a conventional "happy ending" play of romantic love is constantly thwarted and *The Fairground Booth* ends with Pierrot's loss of Columbine.

The third layer of meaning of Blok's play—and perhaps the most important in view of the form of the work—is its patent theatricalism, a conscious planned assault of a very specific sort on the illusionistic drama of realism and naturalism and on the mystico-metaphysical drama of symbolism. It was to point up the underlying theatricalist premise of the play that Blok introduced the figure of the author, masked actors and actresses in costume ball attire, traditional figures of the commedia dell'arte, the physical buffoonery of the Italian improvised theater, the partial extension of an actor (the clown) beyond the proscenium into the audience, and the baring of the stage by the rolling up of the scenery near the end of the play.

The use of the "Harlequinade" with its commedia dell'arte and marionette theater associations to further the cause of theatricalism also characterized some of Yevreinov's more interesting writing. In between his two seasons (1907–8; 1911–12) with the Theater of Antiquity Yevreinov in 1910 assumed the directorship of the famous St. Petersburg cabaret theater the Crooked Mirror (*Krivoe zerkalo*, 1908–18), founded by Zinaida Kholmsky and A. R. Kugel; he held the position until 1917. With the cabaret, Yevreinov had at his disposal a theater of "small forms" in which he could freely experiment with a variety of short comic plays generally oriented toward the ironic and grotesque and with a form of monodrama in which everything onstage is presented as subjective projections of a central character. The best example of such monodrama is the one-act play *V kulisakh dushi* (*Behind the Curtains of the Soul,* or *The Theater of the Soul*). By inviting the spectator to enter into the main protagonist's inner world and then perceive reality in the subjective terms of the protagonist, Yevreinov hoped to eliminate all remaining barriers between audience and actor and to weld both into a single emotional and spiritual entity.

At this early stage of his career, in which elements of Symbolist theatrical theory (extreme subjectivity and the "communion" of spectator and player) reveal themselves, Yevreinov regarded the intimacy and dramatic style of the Crooked Mirror as a goal of all theater, a view developed in his treatise *Vvedenie v monodramu* (*An Introduction to Monodrama,* 1909).

Long enthusiastic about theatrical improvisation and the traditions of the commedia dell'arte, with which he also experimented at the Crooked Mirror, Yevreinov wrote several Harlequinades designed not only to propagate the theatricalist concept of theater but even more importantly to illustrate by means of the drama the theatricalist philosophy of life expounded by him in such collections of essays as *Teatr kak takovoy* (*The Theater as Such,* 1913) and especially the three-volume *Teatr dlya sebya* (*Theater for Onseself,* 1914–16). These ideas are most lucidly expressed in the best of Yevreinov's Harlequin plays, *Vesyolaya smert* (*A Merry Death,* 1908), the dramatist's personal favorite among his one-act plays, and *Samoe glavnoe* (*The Chief Thing,* 1919), Yevreinov's best-known and most frequently performed play both in Russia and abroad.

In *A Merry Death* Harlequin is told by a fortuneteller that he will not live another day because the time has come when he sleeps more hours than he devotes to merriment. These sad tidings are borne by Pierrot, who divulges them in the direct address to the audience with which the play opens. To trick both Death and Harlequin, Pierrot moves the latter's clock back two hours, from eight to six, Harlequin being scheduled to die at the stroke of midnight. However, when Columbine appears and she and Harlequin taunt him by openly flirting before him, Pierrot changes his mind and advances the clock again in order to be rid of Harlequin all the sooner.

As midnight approaches and Harlequin is unable to continue his merriment with Columbine, Death appears. Showing his old vivacity and his readiness to die, Harlequin bids Death do her dance. She obliges him and after dancing claims Harlequin as her own. The last words of the play, addressed to the audience, are spoken by Pierrot. He tells the public that their approval or disapproval of the play is of no concern to the author, "who preaches that nothing in life is worth taking seriously."[54]

This, in brief, is the general idea Yevreinov intended *A Merry Death* to convey. The little comedy is an affirmation of life which, Yevreinov advises through Harlequin, should be lived as fully and happily as possible each day with no thought of the following. By living as though there were no tomorrow life can be lived fully and when death finally comes it can be met as cheerfully as it is by Harlequin. This is the prescription for a good life Harlequin at one point gives the doctor who pays a visit during his illness. Harlequin tells him that the man who lives wisely always desires his death. When the doctor fails to understand the sense of his words, Harlequin prophesies and then acts out the deathbed behavior of people like the doctor:

> HARLEQUIN (*lies on his bed and shivers with all his body, then groans*): Oh! Ah! Ugh! I'm still so young. I haven't been able to live yet as I ought. Why have I been so abstinent all my life? I've still got all sorts of things I want to do. Turn me to the window. I'm not tired yet of looking at the world. Help! I've not been able to do half I wanted. I was never in a hurry to live because I always forgot about death. Help, help! I haven't been able to enjoy myself yet; I've always kept my health, my strength, and my money for the morrow. I filled it with beautiful hopes, and it rolled on like a snowball, growing bigger and bigger. Has that morrow rolled for ever beyond the bounds of the possible? It has rolled down the slope of my mortal wisdom. Oh! Ah! Ugh! (*Twists for the last time, extends, and dies. The Doctor weeps. Harlequin, with a laugh, gets up and applauds himself.*) No! Not so dies Harlequin![55]

The affirmation of life as joy expressed through the Harlequin figure in *A Merry Death* assumes a distinct theatricalist aspect in the more substantial and complex *The Chief Thing*, the only Yevreinov play as far as I know to have been staged commercially in the United States.[56] To Yevreinov, it is not only the theater that must be revitalized by theatricality, but life itself. Through the true, nonrepresentational illusionism of theatrical art, life must be made as happy as possible for as many people as possible. And how is this to be accomplished? By supplying people, by whatever agency, with the dreams, fantasies, illusions they require to face life optimistically. Philosophically, we are back to the central issue of Gorky's *The Lower Depths*, with the scales tipped this time in favor of Luka.

The most unequivocal exposition of Yevreinov's concept of the theatricalization of life comes late in the first act of *The Chief Thing*, in a speech to a group of actors by the main character of the play, Paraclete, who appears in several guises (a fortuneteller, Doctor Fregoli, Schmidt, a monk, and Harlequin):

Ladies and gentlemen, I have come to the theater not to "explain the law, but to execute it." I regard what is known as the theater only as a laboratory of illusions, and I would have a greater theater which will be a marketplace for these illusions—a theater still more in need of reform, because it is the theater of Life itself! Life, where illusion is needed not less than on this stage, and where, since we are powerless to make everybody happy, we should give at least the illusion of happiness. That is the chief thing. I am an actor myself! But the place where I play—is not the ordinary theater, but the stage of Life, to which I call you, too, friends, to play roles which will create the illusions of happiness! I believe with all my heart in the mission of the actor descending from the light of the stage into the absolute darkness of life with all the weapons of his art! For it is my sincere conviction that the world will be regenerated through the actor and his magic art.[57]

As if to compensate for the "abstractness" of Paraclete's words on the mission of theater as art in life, the theater manager appears immediately thereafter to "interpret" his speech:

MANAGER (*to* DOCTOR FREGOLI): Allow me! I'll explain your idea simply. Now for instance.
DOCTOR FREGOLI (*smiling*): Please do!
MANAGER: I'll take your own examples . . . Ladies and gentlemen . . . This is what Doctor Fregoli has in mind. There are certain unfortunates who are deprived of that which is dearer than all material things: talent, beauty, spiritual strength, health, youth, and so forth. There lives, let us imagine, an old man alone, wretched, no one to care for him. He doesn't want to go to the poorhouse yet, that is, "to become a name in a register,"—but to live as he does, without friends, without relatives, is also, God knows, not very sweet. And so Doctor Fregoli invites you, as experienced actors, to become acquainted with an unfortunate like that, to pretend to be his friend, and brighten his last days. (*To* DOCTOR FREGOLI): That's what you meant, isn't it?
DOCTOR FREGOLI: Quite! (*p. 84*)

The dramatization of Paraclete's theory forms the plot of Yevreinov's play. To demonstrate the validity of his ideas, Paraclete first engages three actors from a provincial theater—an actor who plays the Lover, his wife (the Dancer), and the Comedian. When Paraclete first encounters the actors they are in the midst of a hilarious rearsal of a play based on the Polish novelist Henryk Sienkiewicz's famous *Quo Vadis?* The play-within-a-play device which we observe Yevreinov using here is as notable a feature of his dramatic style as it is of Pirandello's. It appears prominently, for example, in the two plays Yevreinov declared formed the rest of a trilogy begun with *The Chief Thing: Korabl pravednykh* (*The Ship of the Righteous*, 1924), about the failure of a nautical utopian society, and the still more pessimistic *Teatr vechnoy voyny* (*The Theater of Eternal War*, 1927), in which the "eternal war" is life itself and the theatrical metaphor an allusion to the "arts" of cynicism, deceit, and hypocrisy needed to survive in it.

Paraclete orders the actors to take up lodging in a rooming house and there translate his ideas into reality by bringing happiness through their talent as actors to certain specific residents of the rooming house whom Paraclete has encountered previously (in Act I) in his guise as a fortune-teller. They are the plain daughter of the landlady, a stenographer who fears that she will die without having ever known love, the son of a retired government clerk who is bent on committing suicide because life seems meaningless to him, and a prim spinster schoolteacher in need of romance. The Dancer is assigned to the student; the actor who plays the Lover to the stenographer; and the Comedian to the schoolteacher. The common denominator in all three cases is the need for love and love indeed is the prescription Paraclete favors for most human unhappiness.

Despite the disappointment caused in each case by the imminent leavetaking of the actors (with the expiration of the contracts they sign with Paraclete), their performances prove eminently successful and the transformation of life through illusion sought by Paraclete is effected. The stenographer comes to know love at last, even though she is temporarily saddened by the departure of the Lover, who uses as the reason for his leaving the existence of a wife to whom he has to return. Through love for the Dancer the student overcomes desires to commit suicide and confesses, moreover, that the reason he wanted to take his own life was not personal despair but his inability to go on pretending, for the sake of his father, that his brother Volodya, whom his father believes to be still alive, died at sea the year before. Without being aware of it, the student himself has been propagating Paraclete's belief that happiness must be created through illusion. In baring his soul to the Dancer, the student compares himself to an actor:

> I was playing a part, you see . . . like an actor. Do you know what an actor is? Have you ever been in a theater? I want to grieve for my brother, but I must smile and be hopeful.
>
> DANCER (*touched, her voice sympathetic*): My God!
>
> STUDENT: It's a hard part to play. God save anybody else from it. Not everybody can bear it . . . Well, and so, in the beginning—I wanted to . . .
>
> DANCER (*after a pause*): We all have our troubles.
>
> STUDENT: That's true! And blessed be those who help us bear them. (*Takes the DANCER's hands in his.*) Thank you for your kindness to me, for the courage which I get from just watching you work without complaining . . . we are all actors before the Lord God . . . Who knows, Anyuta, perhaps in the other world we are to be rewarded with better parts, both of us, but meanwhile, Anyuta, we'll endure our trials here; we'll help one another to endure them! (*p. 185*)

The student's own role-playing and his words to the Dancer further demonstrate the rightness of Paraclete's views. But there is also another lesson contained in the student-Dancer relationship, the lesson hinted at earlier by Paraclete that in transforming life through the art of the theater even the actors themselves can be transformed. In the first act of the play, when Paraclete appeared in the guise of a fortuneteller, he was visited by the Dancer who feared that her husband (the actor who plays the Lover) was losing interest in her romantically. The fortuneteller's advice? Win back his love by making him jealous. After the student makes his confession, the Dancer kisses him warmly, which her husband sees on entering the room. Jealous, he realizes that he not only loves his wife but appreciates her perhaps for the first time. He declares his love for her and they fall into an embrace. By bringing love to others they again discover it themselves and so are transformed by art no less than the people whose lives they set out to change.

The resolution of the Comedian-schoolteacher relationship deviates somewhat from the others. In her exaggerated sense of propriety, the teacher is a difficult case for the Comedian's gay company. But his insistent charm eventually melts her frigid façade. While scolding him for his "lasciviousness," she encourages his flirtation and enjoys every minute of it. The Comedian, however, is not content just to play the part as-

signed in the contract with Paraclete. He takes advantage of the
teacher's fondness for him to try to extract money from her. Paraclete
learns about it and berates him. Without realizing that the schoolteacher
is eavesdropping on their conversation, the Comedian curses and
mimics her, then swears to tell everyone the truth about the playacting
in the rooming house. Paraclete dismisses his threat by saying that so
expert were the actors in their illusion-making that nobody would believe the Comedian—which is just what happens. But aware of the truth
and disillusioned by the Comedian, the schoolteacher attempts suicide
near the end of the play (a reported offstage action). Just before the
student discovers what he thinks is her dead body (the teacher eventually is brought around) and after Paraclete has taken leave of him, the
Comedian sees—in a fantastic, flickering light—a shrouded figure with a
mask of death emerging from the teacher's room. Thinking that it is the
teacher in costume, the Comedian resumes his usual flirtation and tries
to embrace her around the waist. Feeling nothing there, however, he
panics and flees, unaware that the "phantom" is nothing more than a
skull mask atop a shroud-covered pole. Indulging in some make-believe
of her own, the schoolteacher has taken her revenge.

To redirect *The Chief Thing* from the sphere of philosophical theatricalism to that of a *theater*-oriented theatricalism after the role-playing of
Paraclete (as fortuneteller), the rehearsal of *Quo Vadis*, and the
roominghouse acting of the Dancer, Lover, and Comedian, Yevreinov
locates the final act on the evening of the last day of Shrovetide. This
permits the introduction of costumes and masks connected with the
Shrovetide carnival and in a way recalls Blok's use of a costume ball and
masked dancers in *The Fairground Booth*.

The principal masks and decorations with which the roominghouse
setting is adorned are drawn from a single familiar source: the commedia
dell'arte. The Lover thus becomes the lover of the commedia—Pierrot;
the Dancer, appropriately, is now Columbine; the Comedian continues
his roominghouse guise of a doctor (the Dottore of the commedia); and
Paraclete himself is none other than the master manipulator—Harlequin
(Paraclete actually assumes two guises in the last act: that of Harlequin
and that of a Capuchin monk whose habit he wears beneath his Harlequin costume).

Invited to the Shrovetide festivities at the rooming house are not only
the other actors from the provincial theater but also the three wives of a
polygamist for whom a detective (Svetozarov—actually the actor who
plays the Lover's part) has been looking. As the central mystification of

McKay Morris as Paraclete-Harlequin and Estelle Winwood as the Dancer-Colombine in a scene from the production of Nikolai Yevreinov's The Chief Thing *by the Theatre Guild at the Guild Theater, New York, in 1926. Directed by Philip Moeller and Nikolai Yevreinov; settings and costumes by Sergei Sudeykin.*

(PERFORMING ARTS RESEARCH CENTER OF THE NEW YORK PUBLIC LIBRARY) the play is finally explicated, Paraclete, costumed at the moment as a Capuchin monk, reveals himself as the fortuneteller of whom the wives and the detective earlier sought advice and the polygamist himself!

Paraclete's "defense" is that he *is* Paraclete—an adviser, a helper, a consoler—and that his mission is to bring solace to as many people as he can. That is why besides his first wife he wed a deaf-mute and a street-walker without faith or hope and why, needing freedom to continue his work, he had to leave them and assume other identities. When the detective, costumed as Pierrot, prepares to seize Paraclete as the polyga-mist he has been searching for, Paraclete, wearing his monk's costume and still a mystery to the detective, disarms him by speaking to him of the traditional attributes of the commedia Pierrot:

> MONK: Who I am you must guess for yourself; as to who you are, there is no need to guess.
> PIERROT: Who am I, do you think?
> MONK: You are a ridiculous Pierrot.
> PIERROT: Ridiculous?
> MONK: Why, yes. That is your duty, since you are Pierrot; that is, a simpleton who often gets into scrapes by doing what is not his business.
> PIERROT: Well, what is *my* business, do you think?
> MONK: Love. That is taught by hundreds of comedies dell'arte, hun-dreds of harlequinades . . .
> PIERROT: But if I am Pierrot, only Harlequin can make me ridicu-lous. That also is taught by hundreds of comedies dell'arte, hundreds of harlequinades! (*pp. 222–23*)

Stripping off his monk's habit, Paraclete reveals himself as Harlequin to a dumbfounded Svetozarov-Pierrot. They are joined by Columbine and the Doctor, and in the style of ancient comedies approach the footlights and address the audience directly on the sense of the play. Harlequin is the speaker.

> We are all here! . . . count: Harlequin, Pierrot, Columbine, and the Doctor from Bologna—the beloved characters of the merry harlequin-ade . . . We have been resurrected, my friends . . . We are risen anew! And not for the theater alone, but for life itself, which is un-savory without our pepper and salt and sugar! We have entered into the pie of life as a seasoning, without which it would be tasteless, and we have painted its fire with our love, like a holiday tart! Glory to us—eternal masks of the sunny south! Glory to the genuine artists who with their art save the pitiful comedy of unfortunate dilettantes!

. . . Glory to you, people, if you carry away in your hearts the memory of the *chief* thing, not only spoken here, but also demonstrated! The play is finished, and if you have nothing against a curtain, we will lower it with fitting ceremony. But if the Chief Thing for you is not that which was shown here, but the disentanglement of the dramatic plot, which everybody has the right to expect from a play in the theater, where the repertoire is supervised by able persons of experience, who adjust themselves to the public taste, then . . . "do us the kindness people, please, it will cost you nothing to end the play in any way you wish!" (*pp. 223–24*)

The end is a typical theatricalist flourish. Yevreinov has Paraclete suggest to the audience different conclusions to the play from which to choose. In the same vein, the manager of the provincial theater then appears to suggest that the chief thing is to end a play by eleven o'clock for several practical reasons. He is followed by the director, who advises that the chief thing is to end a play effectively. To achieve this, he produces a tube of Bengal fire which he lights and gives to Harlequin, who holds it to illuminate the gaiety of the actors onstage as they waltz to the lowering of the final curtain.

The stylishness so apparent in Mikhail Kuzmin's polished little comedy-mysteries of 1908 bore the promise of a riper theatricalist stylization fulfilled in his major play *Venetsianskie bezumtsy* (*The Venetian Madcaps*, 1912). An exemplification, in part, of thoughts on stylized or theatricalized art eventually collected in book form and published in 1923 under the title *Uslovnosti* (*Conventions*), *The Venetian Madcaps* gracefully intertwines traditional masks of the commedia dell'arte, now restored to their natural habitat of Venetian Italy, and such pervasive Kuzminian motifs as homosexual love and woman as demonic temptress.

The play may well have been inspired by Meyerhold's magnificent production of Lermontov's *Masquerade* at the Aleksandrinsky Theater in St. Petersburg on the eve of the February Revolution of 1917. A culmination of his fascination with the commedia dell'arte, late eighteenth-century Venice, and the plays of Gozzi and Goldoni, Meyerhold began work on the production in 1911. Kuzmin wrote his own Venetian Harlequinade in 1912 and the work was performed two years later, on February 23, 1914, at the Moscow mansion of E. P. and V. V. Nosov, two wealthy patrons of the arts.[58] With music composed by Kuzmin himself and sets and costumes by the fine artist Sudeykin, the production, though amateur, had a characteristic Kuzminian elegance.

In a setting of candle-lit and costume-filled pleasure-seeking eight-

eenth-century Venice, *The Venetian Madcaps* explores the tragic implications of a male relationship destroyed by a female seductress. The two
men are Count Stello, the embodiment of a *fin-de-siècle* aesthete, and
his lover Narcisetto. Finette, an actress in a commedia dell'arte troupe
of players engaged for a fete at the estate of Marquise Marcobruno, is
fascinated by the Count's apparent indifference to women and determines to seduce him. She fails and then maliciously shifts her attention
to Narcisetto, with whom she is more successful. Before the tragic finale, Count Stello proposes to Harlequin that he and Narcisetto, both of
whom are good dancers, should participate, in disguise, in the pantomime Harlequin is staging at the fete. The Count will play Finette
(Columbine) and Narcisetto Harlequin. Pantomime, commedia masks,
and the play-within-a-play were among the foremost conventions of
early twentieth-century theatricalism. The opulent Venetian setting and
recurrent Kuzminian patterns of interchangeable sexual roles and ma-
leficent female seductiveness add a new dimension to this theatricalism.

The gay mood of the play turns sinister when Narcisetto, driven to
frenzy by his love for Finette, stabs the Count to death and throws his
body over a bridge during the procession of the commedia troupe on
their way to the performance. After the murder, Narcisetto rushes to
Finette but hardly confesses his crime when he repulses her telling her
that he hates her and never loved anyone but Stello. Apprised of the
grim turn of events, Harlequin cancels the performance and announces
his intention to conduct his troupe posthaste to Verona.

Finette brings the play to an end by singing a song (one of several in
the work) addressed to the audience. The song reiterates the theatricalist philosophy of life as a stage and includes a refrain of *fin-de-siècle*
metaphysical determinism that all men are actors playing roles preor-
dained by a mysterious power or powers:

> Let not our deeds discomfort you or daunt,
> You honest burghers, pups and poppinjays.
> What is our life if not a merry jaunt?
> Actors all of us in plays . . .
> Stand not amazed at altered circumstances,
> In life we all play parts, some well, some ill,
> But in the giddy whirl of change and chance
> We serve Another's will.[59]

After Yevreinov and Kuzmin, theatricalism appears most strikingly in
the plays of the great Russian poet associated, above all, with the

emergence of Russian futurism, Vladimir Mayakovsky (1893–1930).[60]
Vladimir Mayakovsky, subtitled a "tragedy" and written in 1913, was
the poet's first attempt at playwriting. It came at a time when Mayakovsky was keenly interested in the advances in cinematography and in
the revolutionary theater work of Yevreinov and especially of Meyerhold, with whom the twenty-year-old poet developed a close relationship. Several essays also from 1913 on theater and film (and the interrelations between them) clearly indicate the expansion of
Mayakovsky's interest in the visual arts and his avant-garde orientation.[61] The essays are only a few pages in length but should be considered in conjunction with *Vladimir Mayakovsky* in order to form a better
idea of the writer's thinking at the time of his first venture into the field
of drama.

Taking his cue from the theatricalists, Mayakovsky asserts in a typical
essay, "Teatr, kinematograf, futurizm" ("Theater, Cinematography, Futurism"), that in his own time theater no longer exists as an autonomous
art form. However, Shakespearean theater and the Passion play tradition of Oberammergau suggest that this was not always the case. By
studying the lessons of the past as well as the new possibilities of artistic
expression opened up by the development of cinema, Mayakovsky in-
timates that ways might be found to revitalize the theater and turn it
away from the sterile path of realism and naturalism. The decline of theater in his own age Mayakovsky attributes to the attempts to present life
in a photographically representational manner. But since this is something the camera can do still more effectively than the stage, theater
should surrender its patrimony to cinematography. Freed thus from the
burden of attempting to depict life representationally, the theater will
be able to release the actor from the strait-jacket of illusionism and
hence regain the status of an autonomous art.

It was in this spirit then of theatrical innovation and renovation that
Vladimir Mayakovsky: A Tragedy was written. The title is well chosen,
for the play is wholly a projection of Mayakovsky himself. Not only did
Mayakovsky stage it, play the lead role, and assign himself the declaration of both Prologue and Epilogue, but he made himself—his poetic
uniqueness, genius, and destiny—the subject of the work. The Epilogue
concludes with words "But at other times, what pleases me more than
anything is my own name: Vladimir Mayakovsky."[62]

The Prologue and Epilogue, devices later to be used more effectively
in the two versions of *Misteriya-Buff* (*Mystery-Bouffe*, 1918, 1921), establish an unmistakable theatricalist presence. The radical departure

from illusionistic drama is still more pronounced in the case of characters. Apart from Mayakovsky himself we find such items as The Enormous Woman who does not speak and is fifteen to twenty feet tall; an
Old Man with Scrawny Black Cats, who is "several thousand years old";
a Man with a Long Drawn-Out Face; a Man with Two Kisses; a Woman
with a Tiny Tear, and others. Whimsy, obviously, and theatrically realiz-
able only by virtue of a director's imagination. The imagery of the dialogue sustains the fantasy of the characters. Exuberant, novel, at times
brilliant, often excruciatingly obscure, it impresses ultimately as dazzling and narcissistic verbal showmanship. The following excerpt from
the Prologue is representative:

> Can you understand
> why I,
> quite calmly,
> through a hailstorm of jeers,
> carry my soul on a platter
> to be dined on by future years?
> On the unshaven cheek of the plazas,
> trickling down like a useless tear,
> I
> may well be the last poet there is.
> Have you noticed dangling
> above the pebbled paths
> the striped face of boredom—hanged?
> And on lathery necks
> of rushing rivers,
> bridges wringing their iron hands?
> The sky is weeping—
> uncontrollably,
> loudly;
> a cloud,
> its little mouth twisted, is looking wry,
> like a woman expecting a baby,
> to whom God has tossed an idiot blind in one eye.
> With swollen fingers sprouting reddish hairs,
> the sun has caressed you with a Gadfly's persistence:
> in your souls, a slave has been kissed to death. (*p. 21*)

Analyzing *Vladimir Mayakovsky* for sense is as speculative as trying to
invest an abstract painting with a specific meaning. Reacting impres-
sionistically, the viewer, or reader, grasps the exaltation of poetic self-
celebration. Mayakovsky projects himself as the embodiment of the

spirit of poetry, of creative energy, as the dawning of a new era of poetic expression. But the dawning of the new must be preceded by the destruction of the old, and so the appeal to destroy resounds loudly through the two short acts of which *Vladimir Mayakovsky* consists. In subtitling his play "a tragedy" perhaps the poet intended more than whimsy or the response of disbelieving laughter. Extended throughout the play is the insinuation of spiritual anguish masked by the outward gaiety of the creative artist as jester. Endowed with a transcending, immortalizing power the poet nonetheless cleaves to a solitary path. Perceiving beyond the finite capacity of ordinary mortals, he knows the true pain of existence. The sorrows of others represented by the tears offered him in Act II only repel him; he is weighted down by his own burden. But in the end the poet cannot turn away. Self-fulfillment must be more than withdrawn self-adulation and a public mask of joy. And so, reluctantly, the poet accepts the tears:

I,
with my heavy load,
will walk on;
I'll stumble and fall;
I'll crawl
further
northward,
to where,
in the vise of infinite anguish,
the fanatic sea
with the fingers of waves
tears at its breast
eternally.
I'll drag myself there
exhausted;
and in my last ravings
I'll throw your tears
to the dark god of storms,
at the source of bestial faiths. (*p. 37*)

The acceptance of the anguish of mankind becomes the ultimate self-realization of the poet whose creative power alone holds the possibility of a reordering of existence.

As unlikely as it may seem, *Vladimir Mayakovsky: A Tragedy* was brought to the stage. A still little-known poet, Mayakovsky directed the production and played himself when the work was first presented by art-

ists of the Union of Youth (*Soyuz molodyozhi*) society on the stage of the
Luna Park Theater in St. Petersburg. Public reaction was anything but
encouraging and only two performances were given (December 2 and 4,
1913). Undaunted, Mayakovsky took the play on a brief provincial tour
where he encountered the same boos, catcalls, and bad press as in St.
Petersburg.

Apart from the use of prologue and epilogue and the appearance of
such fantastic characters as the Enormous Woman and the Old Man
with Scrawny Black Cats, Mayakovsky's first play is considerably less
noteworthy as an exercise in theatricalism than *The Fairground Booth*.
That Mayakovsky was thinking along theatricalist lines when he wrote
his "tragedy" is evident from the film and theater essays written in the
same year. But *Vladimir Mayakovsky* is an immature work as drama, a
platform from which a beginning author convinced of the magnitude of
his poetic genius could publicly proclaim his own advent as a poet. This
he sought to do by astounding, shocking, and mystifying, but the posturing and self-glorifying of the playlet relate more to Mayakovsky's own artistic development at the time than to the expansion of a Russian theatricalist art.

Vladimir Mayakovsky: A Tragedy closes with the poet repudiating an
art of the self and proclaiming his willingness to accept the burden of
commitment. The anguish of the people will henceforth become his
own; through his art—in poetry and now in drama—their mute voices of
despair will be able to speak.

The Revolution of 1917 brought the fulfillment of the vision of *Vladimir Mayakovsky*. The poet embraced it ardently and until a later disenchantment and his suicide in 1930 he placed his talent at its disposal and
became its poet laureate.

The burden the poet declares his willingness to accept, finally, in
Vladimir Mayakovsky is borne positively, even rapturously in May-
kovsky's first postrevolutionary dramatic work, *Mystery-Bouffe*. Finished in 1918 and later revised in 1921, *Mystery-Bouffe* is a political play
hailing the ultimate triumph of the workers of the world. Structured like
a medieval mystery with the biblical account of Noah's Ark as its point of
departure, it presents the boarding of a new ark by seven pairs of Clean
(capitalists, imperialists, rulers, and their henchmen) and seven pairs of
Unclean (workers) after the Flood inundates the earth's surface. When
the Clean attempt to impose their will on the Unclean during the
voyage, they are unceremoniously tossed overboard. The Unclean then
sail off themselves to discover that Hell holds no terror for them for they

knew a worse hell on earth, that Paradise offers nothing but empty hopes and vain illusions, and that self-seekers, idlers, and speculators fill the ranks of the army of Chaos. With the defeat of Chaos, who came to rule over the land they left with the receding of the Flood's waters, the Unclean enter the promised land where worker and machine are now united not for the enslavement of man but for the betterment of man, where a new society—a true paradise on earth—will be created.

The obvious ideology of the play, reinforced especially in the later version by an epilogue consisting of the singing in chorus by the Unclean of an adaptation of the Communist *Internationale,* may suggest a tedious exercise in tendentious drama, but this is by no means the case. The posturing and Futurist-Surrealist mannerisms of *Vladimir Mayakovsky* behind him, Mayakovsky created in *Mystery-Bouffe* a true revolutionary drama but at the same time a more impressively theatricalist play striking for its farcical action and humor.

The choice of form was no literary accident. Structuring a revolutionary political drama along the lines of a medieval mystery with all its traditional religious associations is an irreverence rich in mocking irony. *Mystery-Bouffe* is a repudiation of Christianity, of Christian concepts of Heaven and Hell. That this repudiation assumes the form of a mystery play only sets the mockery in bolder relief.

Other factors besides the satiric may have influenced Mayakovsky in his choice of dramatic structure. One, certainly, was the theatrical. Mayakovsky had a good knowledge of European drama and theater and was well aware that medieval religious drama accommodated laugh-provoking scenes of sheer buffoonery. There is much of this in *Mystery-Bouffe,* particularly in the journey of the Unclean through Heaven and Hell.

Medieval drama and such early manifestations of European domestic secular comedy as the fourteenth- and fifteenth-century German Shrovetide comedies (*Fastnachtsspiele*) also made extensive use of prologues and epilogues. The prologue was used to attract the attention of the public and to say something about the nature of the work to be presented. In the epilogue, the players generally expressed their hope that their performance pleased the audience which would demonstrate its pleasure by monetary means. The direct communication with the audience on the part of the author himself or through a character or characters which prologues and epilogues made possible appealed to Mayakovsky's sense of the theatrical and confirmed his interest in medieval drama.

In the better-known 1921 version of *Mystery-Bouffe* the Epilogue consists of the choral singing of the *Internationale* and is of slight significance dramatically save for the chorus itself, another theatricalist signpost. The Prologue, however, is of far greater importance. Spoken by one of the Unclean it not only introduces the play but assumes the character of a typical theatricalist manifesto. The point is made unequivocally in the third line where Mayakovsky stresses the "newness" of his play:

> But first I must say a few words.
> This play is something new. [63]

He then declares his break with "fourth-wall" illusionism by announcing his intention of carrying the action of his play beyond the confines of the stage:

> First, let me ask you:
> Why is this playhouse in such a mess?
> To right-thinking people
> it's a scandal, no less!
> But then what makes you go to see a show?
> You do it for pleasure—
> isn't that so?
> But is the pleasure really so great, after all,
> if you're looking just at the stage?
> The stage, you know, is only one-third of the hall.
> Therefore,
> at an interesting show,
> if things are set up properly,
> your pleasure is multiplied by three.

This is followed by a swipe at Chekhovian realism:

> For other theatrical companies the spectacle doesn't matter:
> for them
> the stage
> is a keyhole without a key.
> "Just sit there quietly," they say to you,
> "either straight or sidewise,
> and look at a slice of life of other folk's lives."
> You look—and what do you see?
> Uncle Vanya
> and Auntie Manya
> parked on a sofa as they chatter.

But we don't care
about uncles or aunts:
you can find them at home—or anywhere!

In the next few lines Mayakovsky's approach to theatricalism echoes
Yevreinov's:

We, too, will show life that's real—
Very!
But life transformed by the theater into a spectacle most
extraordinary!

Such demonstrative, programmatic theatricalism is virtually absent
from the Prologue to the original 1918 version of *Mystery-Bouffe*, leading one to presume that in the few intervening years between the first
and second versions Mayakovsky's interest in and knowledge of theatricalism deepened. The influence here of the writings and productions of
both Yevreinov and Meyerhold should not be discounted.

Mystery-Bouffe was not Mayakovsky's last theatricalist play. Elements
of theatricalism reappear in his two later satirical comedies *Klop* (*The
Bedbug*, 1928) and *Banya* (*The Bathhouse*, 1929). These works will be
treated at greater length in the discussion of the drama of the NEP (New
Economic Policy) period, 1921–28. At this point, I should just like to
consider the theatrical motifs in *The Bathhouse*, an absurd and grotesque comedy about the early Soviet bureaucracy to which Mayakovsky
gave the typical theatricalist subtitle, "A Drama in Six Acts, with a
Circus and Fireworks."

Much of the play's third act is given over to what really ought to be
considered an apologia by Mayakovsky in the face of imminent reaction
to his overt ridicule of the new Communist bureaucracy. Far less ambivalent in its mockery than *The Bedbug, The Bathhouse* did, to be
sure, provoke vehement official protest and was hastily withdrawn from
the stage.

As dramatized in Act III, Mayakovsky's point is that a Soviet artist
should be permitted to satirize aspects of his own society, including officialdom, as freely as Western decadence and the bourgeoisie. The
plea, as we know only too well, fell on deaf ears. But my concern here,
however, is not so much the nature of Mayakovsky's argument as the
theatricalist frame in which it is presented.

At the beginning of Act III, a stage direction calls for the extension of
the audience onto the stage. Actually, part of the downstage area has
been equipped with seats and actors playing spectators in order to

suggest the incorporation of the audience itself into the polemic that is
to ensue. The stage—literally and figuratively—is now set for the familiar theatricalist introduction of the director as a character, recalling the
appearance of the author in Blok's *The Fairground Booth* and the director in Yevreinov's *The Chief Thing.*

A slightly longer than usual time lag is assumed between Acts II and
III of *The Bathhouse,* both in order to prepare the audience for the
exchange of views on drama and satire in Act III and the stage for the
theater-within-a-play setting with which the third act opens. The actors
playing spectators in the stage extension of the orchestra stamp their
feet to protest the delay in the opening of the act. This functions as the
motivation for the appearance of the director who steps forward to calm
them. The director is soon followed by the bureaucrat Pobedonosikov[64]
and others who address the stage and theater audience directly as they
discuss their *own* roles and the pros and cons of the play as a whole.
This is a page out of the theatricalist handbook—whatever other issues
the third act treats—and easily brings to mind the play- and theater-
within-a-play motifs of Pirandello's *Six Characters in Search of an Author* and *Tonight We Improvise!*

When Pobedonosikov, Mezalyansova, and others are through arguing
their cases, the director agrees to consider their proposals and immediately rehearses a symbolic and pantomimic tableau on revolutionary
themes which Pobedonosikov and his followers find much more to their
liking than topical satire. But as if to suggest that the urgencies of life
cannot be barred from the theater, Mayakovsky introduces at this point
the harried inventor Chudakov's friend, Velosipedkin,[65] who tries to get
into the first row of seats in the onstage theater extension from farther
back in the rear. His purpose is to present Chudakov's case (he is peti-
tioning for government support for the time machine he has invented)
directly to Pobedonosikov. The director scolds Velosipedkin for almost
wrecking the whole show and calls on the rest of the cast to continue the
play, thus ending Act III and Mayakovsky's theatricalist appeal not only
for a fair reception for his own play but for the rights of citizenship of
topical satire in the postrevolutionary Russian theater.

With the withdrawal of *The Bathhouse* from the stage and the tragic
end of Mayakovsky himself in 1930, the freewheeling era of NEP and its
splendid achievements in the arts was definitively at an end. An aesthetic system (Socialist Realism) compatible with Bolshevik ideology was
soon to be formulated and made the only permissible technique of artistic expression. The theatricalism which appears so striking a component

of the dramatic style of Blok, Yevreinov, Kuzmin, and Mayakovsky, and which parallels the magnificent work of the contemporary avant-garde *régisseurs,* above all Meyerhold, was not a creature of NEP in the way that the absurd and grotesque satire of the prose writer Mikhail Zoshchenko (1895–1958) or of Mayakovsky was. Its emergence as an approach to drama and theater antedates the Revolution itself by nearly a decade. But it flourished in the climate of artistic innovation and experimentation engendered by the conditions of the NEP period, and when the climate changed and NEP withered, no future growth for theatricalism was really possible. Ironically, in Mayakovsky's *The Bathhouse* theatricalist technique becomes the means by which the author pleads for the survival of theater itself.

FOUR

The 1920s and Early 1930s

The Revolution and the Civil War
in Russian Drama

W ITH THE restoration of peace following the calamitous years of World War I, the Revolution, and the Civil War, Russian literature in the time of the New Economic Policy entered a relatively short period of remarkable accomplishment. Poetry and prose fiction sought new directions in an enthusiastic climate of experimentation and achieved stunning results in works of enduring merit by Babel, Bulgakov, Mayakovsky, Olesha, Pilnyak, Zoshchenko, and many others. In the theater and film the same audacity and brilliance brought international recognition to such producers and directors as Meyerhold, Vakhtangov, Tairov, Eisenstein, Dovzhenko, and Pudovkin, whose theories continue to attract admirers and adherents. Dramatists during the NEP era also responded to the search for new directions and brought forth a large number of plays in different dramatic genres. Many of these plays, especially in the field of comedy, are among the best dramatic works written in Russian since the Revolution.

The serious drama in the 1920s and early 1930s was of two types, principally. The first, set in the period of the Revolution and the Civil War and dealing with various aspects of the revolutionary experience, lends itself to further subdivision along thematic and stylistic lines. Before Russian dramatists found appropriate ways—in the second half of the 1920s—of translating events of the Bolshevik seizure of power and the ensuing fraternal war between Reds and Whites into the stuff of drama, they circumvented the problem by first writing plays about analogous social and political upheavals in other countries, real or imaginary. Both types of revolutionary plays—those with foreign settings and those with Russian settings—were written in a variety of styles. Plays with non-Russian settings such as Tretyakov's *Are You Listening, Moscow?!* (1923) and Faiko's *Bubus the Teacher* (1924) often dramatize the contemporary revolutionary movements in Germany and reveal the influence of German expressionism which, despite its avant-garde Western origin, was acceptable to Soviet ideologues—with some modifications—because of its strident anticapital and proleft sentiments. The most famous of this group of plays, however, Tretyakov's *Roar, China!* (1924), is set in China and has few Expressionist elements. Strongly influenced by the *agitka*, Bill-Belotserkovsky's crowded, crude yet energetic *Echo* (1922) and *Levo rulya* (*Port the Helm*, 1923) concentrate instead on reverberations of the Russian Revolution in America and the efforts of prorevolutionary seamen and dock workers to halt the shipment of arms to anti-Bolshevik forces in Russia. The plays about the Russian Revolution, the most numerous and by and large the most interesting of those dealing with revolution, generally conform to either one of two dominant styles: an "old-fashioned" realistic style deemed suitable to the nature of the material such as we find, for example, in Bulgakov's famous *Days of the Turbins* (1926), and an epic style greatly indebted to European, particularly German, Romantic drama, and referred to variously as "romantic-revolutionary," "romantic-monumental," "romantic-heroic," or "romantic-epic." The best examples of this latter style are Vishnevsky's *The First Horse Army* and *An Optimistic Tragedy*.

Melodrama comprises the second type of "serious" drama to come into prominence during the 1920s. Like the romantic-monumental play about the Revolution and the Civil War, the cultivation of this genre came as a response to the call by some early Soviet theorists (Lunacharsky and V. Volkenshteyn, whose *Dramaturgiya* was probably the most esteemed theoretical study of the drama in the USSR in the 1920s) for a drama of action, excitement, and strong emotions. Most Soviet plays of the 1920s about the Revolution and the Civil War rely heavily on classical melodramatic techniques. But in the second half of the decade a distinct Soviet melodrama came into existence. It drew its subject material chiefly from the machinations of swindlers and speculators associated with the NEP era. Later, however, with the end of NEP, it was used as a means of exposing what were regarded as still "unassimilated" elements in Soviet society ranging from the "internal émigré," *antiobshchestvennik* (literally, "antisocial person"), or "wrecker" (*diversant*) implacably opposed to the Soviet regime and intent on destroying it from within to artists and intellectuals unable to find productive outlets for their talents inside the confines of the new Soviet social order.

Comedy was even more variegated than serious drama. As the vehicle best suited, in their opinion, to dramatize the drastically altered conditions of Russian life after the Revolution, some playwrights revived the comedy of manners. Kataev's *Squaring the Circle* is perhaps the best example. Other dramatists, focusing instead on the zanier aspects of life in the early period of the new Soviet state, inclined toward a satirical comedy of the absurd and grotesque. Mayakovsky's comedies *The Bedbug* and *The Bathhouse* are the most familiar examples of the type. But the NEP itself gave rise to a very special set of circumstances—economic, social, and cultural—best reflected in the phenomenon of the "NEP-man," a home-grown con artist and rogue with bourgeois tastes and aspirations. Several of the most hilarious Russian comedies of the 1920s, by Bulgakov, Erdman, and Romashov especially, base their humor on the antics of the NEP-man and should be thought of collectively as a subgenre of the absurd and grotesque comedy of satire.

In order to deal more systematically with Russian drama of the 1920s and early 1930s, that is NEP drama as well as post-NEP plays still conceived in the spirit of relatively free expression and experimentation associated with the art of the NEP period, I have divided the material into two chapters. The first (the present chapter) is devoted to both the realistic and the romantic drama of the Revolution and the Civil War; the second, to comedy, which is further broken down typologically into social comedy and NEP absurd and grotesque satire. Because of its links with the satire of the period, melodrama is discussed in the last part of the chapter on comedy.

Of the Russian plays of the 1920s on the theme of international revolution, none has achieved the eminence of *Rychi, Kitay!* (*Roar, China!*, 1924) by Sergei Tretyakov (1892–1939). Although known in the West for just this one play, which was staged widely outside of Russia, Tretyakov had a remarkably varied literary career and deserves greater recognition.[1] He was a poet, a prose writer, a journalist of some distinction, an author of film scenarios, a collaborator in theater and film of Meyerhold and Eisenstein, and a close friend and co-worker of Mayakovsky on the journal *Lef* (the organ of the Left Front group which Mayakovsky edited from 1923 to 1925) and later on *Novy Lef* (*New Lef*, 1927–28). His first dramatic work was *Slyshish, Moskva?!* (*Are you Listening, Moscow?!*, first staged in 1923), a play about contemporary revolutionary events in Germany in which grotesque elements of the *guignol* tradition—inspired by Meyerhold's theatrical experiments—freely mix with the shrill propagandistic style of the early Soviet *agitka;* appropriately, the play was subtitled an "agit-guignol." It was followed by the expressionistic melodrama *Protivogazy* (*Gas Masks*), which attracted considerable attention at its première and following two performances in February 1924 when it was staged not in a theater but in a shop of the Moscow gas plant located near the Kursk railway station. Tretyakov's most famous play, *Roar, China!*, premièred at the Meyerhold Theater in January 1926. The same year he wrote his last full-length drama *Khochu rebyonka* (*I Want a Baby*), a play that aroused great controversy—and was denied permission for production—because of its frank treatment of female sexuality, childbearing, and eugenics.

The reflection of personal experiences in China, which Tretyakov visited in 1924–25 as a lecturer on Russian literature at Peking University, *Roar, China!* also points up the international tenor of Bolshevik missionary zeal in the early 1920s. When we recall the intense Russian interest in China at this time and the close cooperation between Russian agents and Chiang's newly created Kuomintang Party, we can easily appreciate the ideology of such a play as *Roar, China!* as well as the appearance of heroic Chinese Red partisans in other Russian plays of the period.

Roar, China! is based on a true episode and reflects the reportagelike "factographic" style of some Soviet literature in the 1920s.[2] It was a style with which Tretyakov became personally identified. On June 22, 1924, not long after Tretyakov's arrival in Peking a dispute between the British Navy and local Chinese at Wan-Hsien on the Yangtze River resulted in the execution of two Chinese boatmen on order of the commander of the British gunboat *Cockchafer*, Captain Whitehorn.

Impressed by the senseless cruelty of the incident and convinced of the imminence of a great upheaval of the Chinese people against foreign interests in China (feelings to which he had given voice in the Futurist poem *Roar, China!*, which antedates the play), Tretyakov seized upon the affair as the subject for a theatrical broadside against Western imperialism in general. In the Russian play (which was originally titled *The Cockchafer* but was given the name of Tretyakov's earlier poem on the occasion of its production at the Meyerhold Theater in Moscow on January 23, 1926) the execution of the two Chinese boatmen comes as retribution for the accidental drowning of the agent, Ashlay, of the American business concern of Robert Dollar and Co. Portrayed as harsh, arrogant, and pinch-penny in his treatment of the Chinese, Ashlay haggles over the price of his passage in a small boat on the way ashore from a visit to the *Cockchafer*. Losing his balance as he lunges out to strike the boatman Chee a second time, he tumbles into the river and drowns. Intent on exacting retribution for what he considers an affront to the dignity of all whites in China, the *Cockchafer*'s Captain demands the execution of two members of the boatman's union in the absence of Chee who has since taken flight. If the demand is not met, the Captain threatens to lay waste the entire town of Wan-Hsien. Superstitious, cowardly, and easily intimidated by the whites, the Chinese are thrown into confusion but at last choose straws and send two boatmen to their death by strangulation. The Captain's gratification that "justice" has been done and the enthusiasm of a Western journalist about photographing the bodies are offset by the threats of an aroused China at last ridding itself of foreign parasites hurled at the whites heading back to the *Cockchafer* by a Chinese character identified in the play as the Stoker.

The simplicity of the plot of *Roar, China!* is paralleled by its economy of structure and language. The play is divided into nine scenes set either on the deck of the *Cockchafer* or on the Wan-Hsien wharf and concentrated, for greater dramatic impact, into a period of twenty-four hours. Only in the time-lag device used in the second scene (which enables the audience to view the events on shore leading up to Ashlay's death) and the lengthy descriptive prefaces to a few of the scenes does Tretyakov depart from the overall pattern of simplicity. Among the characters, virtually all of whom are stereotypes, only two command any attention. The first is the Stoker who agitates the Chinese coolies, urging them to take arms against their oppressors. Throughout the play he holds before the incredulous coolies the example of a land where the slaves have overthrown their masters, meaning, of course, Soviet Russia, and in the final scene briefly appears in the dress of a member of the left-wing Canton Workers' Militia. The only other character of any interest is Cordelia, the haughty, vain, pleasure-seeking, and "decadent" daughter of a French family whose interests have kept them in China for twenty-five years. Although French, not Russian, and presented in a Chinese setting, Cordelia nevertheless has analogues elsewhere in Russian drama of the 1920s—young women of well-to-do and/or aristocratic families, living in almost a fantasy world detached from and oblivious to the society around them, functioning even more than their parents as symbols of the old order doomed to perish for its inability to move with the times. But Cordelia's indifference to human misery and suffering has a macabre quality to it. When a young Chinese boy commits suicide (in scene 7) on board the *Cockchafer* in such a way that his body is suspended over the door to the Captain's quarters, Cordelia insists on photographing it ("It would make a marvelous photograph") and later is peeved when she is not permitted to witness the execution of the two Chinese boatmen.

Meyerhold's clever production of *Roar, China!* in 1926 did much to

A scene from the original 1927 production of Sergei Tretyakov's Roar, China!
by Meyerhold's Theater, Moscow.

(H. W. L. DANA COLLECTION OF THE HARVARD THEATRE COLLECTION)

make the play a success and to attract international attention to it. Like
several other Soviet plays of the 1920s and '30s it also found its way to
America. The New York Theatre Guild presented it on October 22,
1930, with striking sets designed by Lee Simonson and with Chinese
actors brought in from the city's Chinatown.

Tretyakov's *Roar, China!* was not the only Soviet play of the 1920s
and early 1930s with a Far Eastern setting. *Kompromiss Naib-Khana*

A scene from the 1930 production of Sergei Tretyakov's Roar, China!
at the Martin Beck Theater, New York, by the Theatre Guild.
Directed by Herbert J. Biberman; settings and costumes by Lee Simonson.
(PERFORMING ARTS RESEARCH CENTER OF THE NEW YORK PUBLIC LIBRARY)

(*The Compromise of Naib-Khan,* 1931) by Vsevolod Ivanov (1895–1963) is located in Afghanistan. But the work never established itself in the repertoires of major Soviet theaters, despite the fact that the critic Yuri Yuzovsky described it once as the best play staged by the Central Theater of the Red Army, where it premièred in 1931.

Besides *The Compromise of Naib-Khan,* Ivanov was the author of another five plays— *Bronepoezd 14–69* (*Armored Train No. 14–69,* written 1927, published 1931), *Blokada* (*Blockade,* 1929), *Pole i doroga* (*Field and Road,* 1934), *Dvenadtsat molodtsev iz tabakerki* (*Twelve Young Men from a Snuffbox,* 1936), set in 1801 during the reign of Paul I, and *Vdokhnovenie* (*Inspiration,* 1940), set in the seventeenth century in the time of Dmitri the Pretender. The best-known and most successful of all, *Armored Train No. 14–69,* based on Ivanov's novel of the same name, uses an eastern locale, like Tretyakov's *Roar, China!;* but this time it is Siberia, not China, and the play's subject is the Russian Civil War.

The setting of *Armored Train No. 14–69* is the area around the Siberian city of Khabarovsk. The story is straightforward. After initial hesitation, Captain Nezelasov, an able White officer, finally agrees to take his armored train (No. 14–69) loaded with White refugees out of the Khabarovsk war zone. The danger of harassment by Red partisan groups is great but American and Japanese "interventionist" armies are nearby and are counted on to insure the train's safe passage to a port from which the refugees will be able to emigrate from war-torn Russia. The plan is foiled when the train is seized by a partisan force headed by a recent peasant convert to the Bolshevik cause, Vershinin. Nezelasov's lack of enthusiasm for the enterprise is paralleled by Vershinin's initial reluctance to become involved in the fighting between Whites, Reds, and "interventionists."

To the peasant Vershinin, the Civil War has no direct relevance to the situation of "simple" people like himself, despite the fact that his children were slain by "interventionist" soldiers. His position shifts, however, under the influence of the zealous (and eventually martyred) Communist organizer Peklevanov, who is sprung from prison for the purpose of bringing about the revolutionary seizure of the city (presumably Khabarovsk). The transformation of Vershinin is indeed remarkable. Once the initial reluctance to participate in the war is overcome, he goes on not only to become a valiant partisan leader but an almost legendary hero. His greatest feat, of course, is the nighttime seizure of the armored train commanded by Nezelasov after a previous plan to halt its movement by blowing up a key bridge fails. The train thus captured, Vershinin is set to accomplish the revolution in the city, thereby fulfilling the task of the slain Peklevanov whose body, like a combat standard, is borne off triumphantly on armored train No. 14–69 at the end of the play.

Despite the esteemed position it holds in Soviet theater as a classic Civil War drama, *Armored Train No. 14–69* is structurally flawed. The taut economy of Tretyakov's *Roar, China!* eludes Ivanov as political exigency leads him to overweight the subplot concerning Peklevanov and the revolution in the city which has to be preceded by the seizure of both a fortress used by American expeditionary troops as a prison and the port of the city itself. The dramatic focus of the play is the imminent confrontation of the antagonists Nezelasov and Vershinin: the Whites led by Nezelasov must attempt to run the train through and Vershinin and his partisans must attempt to stop them and seize the train. The partisans' efforts are crowned with success and the plot in effect culminates

A scene from the original production of Vsevolod Ivanov's Armored Train No.
14–69 *by the Moscow Art Theater in 1927.*
(H. W. L. DANA COLLECTION OF THE HARVARD THEATRE COLLECTION)

in the rousing finale to Act III where the play should have ended. But
this is where the matter of political expediency intrudes. Ivanov assigns
a key ideological role in the play to the idealized Bolshevik Peklevanov.
It is directly owing to Peklevanov's influence that Vershinin's "conversion" takes place. Without the support of the broad masses of the people, Ivanov suggests, the Revolution cannot succeed, and it is the Revolution in the widest possible terms to which Peklevanov is committed.
Whatever excitement and drama attach to the episode of armored train
No. 14–69, it is the Revolution itself that is at stake and of which the adventure with the train is but an infinitesimally small part. Peklevanov is
there to provide the proper perspective and to demonstrate by his example that the activation and support of the masses of peasants and
workers represented by Vershinin *is* necessary and possible, and to be

effected above all by just such dedicated and inspiring Bolshevik leaders as Peklevanov.

To reconcile both his political and dramatic truths, Ivanov unwisely extends the play beyond the third act. The fourth and last act returns the audience's attention to the greater issue of the uprising in the city. After a clumsy opening which establishes the idealized relationship between Peklevanov (as a zealous Bolshevik) and his wife (as the devoted wife of a zealous Bolshevik who has seen Lenin, an experience she can never forget), the tempo quickens, reaching a climax in the murder of Peklevanov by a Japanese "interventionist" soldier. Peklevanov's death balances that of Nezelasov during the seizure of the armored train, but it acquires a symbolic utility as well. The realization of the revolt in the city is then left to Vershinin, the true hero of the play. When the body of the slain Peklevanov is hoisted aboard the armored train at the end of the play, the episode of the train's seizure is thus properly related to the greater political drama of the Revolution itself. By leaving Peklevanov's task to be realized by Vershinin, Ivanov is stating, in effect, his belief that once the masses are activated the collective will must prevail. Peklevanov fulfills his assigned role by drawing Vershinin into the great struggle; this done, Vershinin, as a revolutionary instrument, so to speak, becomes self-operative and Peklevanov's role is reduced to avoid detracting excessively from that of the more plausible and artistically "weightier" character Vershinin.

The obvious structural deficiencies of Armored Train No. 14–69 are somewhat compensated for by the earthy, colorful language of the "plain folk" of the drama, including Vershinin himself, and the linguistic humor that attends the appearance of Vershinin's loyal Chinese supporter, Sin Bin-u. The humor of word and situation come together no more effectively in the play than in Act II when the Russian Red partisan peasants try to establish some communication with a non-Russian-speaking captured American who, it turns out, is a former Detroit automobile factory worker. The scene, which includes also an amusing political interpretation of an icon depicting Abraham's sacrifice of Isaac, is one of the play's brighter moments and in its earthiness and humor typical of early Soviet drama on the Revolution and the Civil War.

The tense confrontation between Reds and Whites in the major dramatic work, Razlom (Breakup, 1927–44), by Boris Lavrenyov (1891–1959) is relieved by similar humor. The time is the summer and fall of 1917—the months preceding the Bolshevik seizure of power; the place—Kronstadt, the great naval base on the Baltic. No subplot detracts from Lavrenyov's drama of the White scheme to blow up the cruiser *Zarya* (*Dawn;* modeled on the historic vessel *Aurora*) before its crew of Red mutineers and its commandant Bersenev, who has thrown in his lot with the Reds, can sail up the Neva River and use it to force the capitulation of Petrograd. The crystallization of the conspiracy and its defeat generates some excitement, but the interplay of disparate personalities commands greater interest. Bersenev quickly calls to mind Ivanov's Nezelasov in *Armored Train No. 14–69;* their positions are roughly analogous. The courage of both men is above reproach but their deeds proceed from quite different convictions. Promise of power enables Nezelasov to accept an originally distasteful assignment, while Bersenev's "conversion" to the Red cause springs from the belief that the Bolsheviks represent the future of Russia. Ivanov's Vershinin also has a counterpart in *Breakup*—the head of the revolutionary committee of mutinous sailors aboard the *Zarya*, Artyom Godum, a rough-hewn seaman, though Godum's acceptance of the Red cause occurs before the action of the play begins. A large number of sailors bring a quality of salty earthiness and some levity to *Breakup;* their role collectively can be compared to that of the partisans in *Armored Train No. 14–69.* Their language, peppered with a rich variety of nautical terms, strikes very much the same note of authenticity as the peasant idiom of the partisans in Ivanov's play. Considering the fact that Lavrenyov never served in the navy the achievement is the more noteworthy.

But the seamen are less important secondary characters than other members of Bersenev's family. His daughters Tatyana and Ksenia are psychologically plausible yet at the same time representative feminine types in Russian Revolution and Civil War plays of the 1920s. In a slightly different guise, we have already met Ksenia as Cordelia in Tretyakov's *Roar, China!*—the young girl of "good" family who is untouched by the cataclysmic events swirling about her and lives in a curiously unreal world of her own making. None of Cordelia's sadistic proclivities mars the portrait of Ksenia; but in her commitment to the interests and tastes of the "Decadence" (she speaks French and quotes the poetry of Zinaida Gippius whom the Soviets long ago dismissed as a representative of the "decadent" trend in Russian literature and as a White émigré) she is no less blithely untouched by the human drama being played out before her eyes. When she casually learns from her friend Polevoy, a young White officer, about the conspiracy to dynamite the *Zarya*, her only thought is to rush to the embankment to watch the thrilling spectacle of a ship being blown up. She is utterly unmindful of the fact that her father who will be on board as commander will also be destroyed. Unwittingly, however, Ksenia becomes the means by which the conspiracy is revealed. When she casually tells Tatyana what is to happen—still unaware of the danger to her father—Tatyana relays the information to the sailors who take appropriate action to foil the plot.

Tatyana is contrasted to Ksenia by her greater seriousness and her ability to relate to the events around her. The ramifications of the Revolution for her marriage to the young officer, Shtube, who serves under her father, reverberate through much early Soviet drama. In other words, the human, psychological aspect of the conflict is dramatized often in terms of the strain on a marriage as husband and wife find themselves on opposite sides of the political fence. The best example of this in the drama of the 1920s is Trenyov's *Lyubov Yarovaya* (1925), about which more later.

In Lavrenyov's play the title *Breakup* is meant to suggest not only the collapse of an order but the disintegration also of family life (among representatives by and large of the upper classes) under the weight of the Revolution and the Civil War. The marriage that "breaks up" in Lavrenyov's work is that of Bersenev's daughter Tatyana and her husband Leopold Shtube. The fact of the breakup is less important than the distinct pattern it represents for Revolution and Civil War plays of the 1920s and early '30s. Tatyana is the daughter of a White officer who has joined the Reds. Shtube, on the other hand, is portrayed as a die-hard White conservative bitterly opposed to the Reds. His arrogance and unrelenting manner alienate Tatyana, whose political sympathies have already begun shifting toward the Reds both because of her father's attitude and because of the attraction she is vaguely aware of exerted by Godum. The sharp contrast drawn between Shtube and Godum and the appeal the latter is made to radiate are politically and dramatically motivated, and expected. But there is another element in the characterization of Shtube which should not escape notice. That is the character's name. While not precisely a "telling name" in the context of the play, it is easily identified as German. This is entirely by design on Lavrenyov's part for two reasons. First, he implies that the arrogance, haughtiness, and intransigence of Shtube, above all in his attitude to and treatment of the Red sailors of the *Zarya*, are attributable to a partly German origin. The inference is plausible, then, that were Shtube wholly Russian his personality would admit of greater compassion and, more important politically, greater flexibility. The second reason is that in making Shtube partly German Lavrenyov was simply accommodating a widespread Russian view of the time that one explanation the Russian artistocracy had lost touch so profoundly with the rest of the nation and was so stubbornly resistant to change was that through generations of intermarriage, especially with Germans, it had become an essentially alien body. Many of the highest ranking officers in the Imperial Russian armed forces bore foreign, primarily Germanic, names and to many Russians represented not only an extreme form of aristocratic arrogance but also the most conservative segment of White society determined to protect and preserve its vested interests at all costs. The White officer of foreign extraction inevitably comes off badly in the Revolution and Civil War drama of the 1920s and early 1930s. Shtube, in Lavrenyov's *Breakup*, suffers the disaffection of his wife Tatyana, and is eventually slain for his part in the conspiracy against the *Zarya*. In Mikhail Bulgakov's better-known *Dni Turbinykh (The Days of the Turbins*, 1925), the analogous character is Vladimir Talberg, a colonel on the General Staff of the White army, whose personality reveals traits of haughtiness and cowardice. If he does not suffer the fate of Shtube, he shares with Lavrenyov's character the loss of the affection of his wife, Yelena.

Another parallel, this time of more obvious political nature, enables us to relate *Breakup* to *Armored Train No. 14–69:* the meeting with or personal recollection of Lenin, now an ideological commonplace in Soviet drama. In Ivanov's *Armored Train No. 14–69* the "Lenin scene" occurs very early in the last act when the Communist organizer Peklevanov appears together with his wife for the first and only time in the play. In the conversation between them Peklevanov is swift to correct any dilution of ideological purity that results from the interjection of the personal and the self-glorifying. When the wife says that Vershinin's successes with the partisans were due to his having fulfilled the dictates of Peklevanov, her husband corrects her, saying that the dictates Vershinin fulfilled were those of Lenin. What follows is the wife's almost mystical account of the time she beheld Lenin with her own eyes. The interpolation, needless to say, is contrived and mechanical.

The parallel scene in Lavrenyov's *Breakup* involves Tatyana Bersenev and Godum. At one point during a political conversation Tatyana asks Godum if he ever saw Lenin. In this case, his recollection of a chance meeting during which Godum in fact failed to recognize Lenin is told in Godum's plain, earthy style and contrasts with that of Peklevanov's wife in *Armored Train No. 14–69*. However chance the meeting, though, the memory of it is sufficiently vivid to enable Godum to recall the way Lenin pronounced the letter *r*.

A scene from the original production of Konstantin Trenyov's Lyubov Yarovaya
by the Maly Theater, Moscow, in 1926.
(H. W. L. DANA COLLECTION OF THE HARVARD THEATRE COLLECTION)

The pressures brought to bear by the Revolution and the Civil War on
family life and marital relations in particular—effectively mined as a
source of dramatic conflict in *Breakup*—stand out vividly in one of the
real classics of early Soviet drama: the five-act *Lyubov Yarovaya* (1925)
by Konstantin Trenyov (1876–1945).

The titular character, a schoolteacher, is a model wartime Bolshevik
heroine and the forerunner of several similar types in later Soviet drama
(for example, the woman commissar in Vsevolod Vishnevsky's *An Optimistic Tragedy*, 1933). Lyubov's devotion to the Communist cause is
put to the acid test when she is faced with the decision either of surrendering to the Reds her husband, Mikhail Yarovoy, who she believed
died in the war a few years earlier but who has reappeared as a White
officer, or of helping him to elude his pursuers. In terms of the character
portrayal, the choice is a foregone conclusion. Despite the obvious emotional dilemma posed by her reunion with a husband she believed dead
and whom she still loves, the strength of Lyubov's ideological convictions keeps her from wavering or weakening at the crucial moment. Her
attitude is decisive, heroic, unambivalent. Lyubov reveals her husband's
identity, causing not only his arrest, but in all probability his death.

Out of a desire to make her act more reasonable morally and yet at
the same time to heighten her sense of commitment to a political cause,
Trenyov adds another dimension to the revelation of Mikhail Yarovoy's
true identity by introducing a transformation motif. Knowing of Lyubov's affection for her husband Kolosov, an engineer in the Red corps,
first pleads with Lyubov to spare Mikhail by hiding him and, failing in

his effort, surreptitiously changes clothes with Mikhail, thereafter presenting himself to the Red patrol seeking the White officer as the man for whom they are searching. To Lyubov, Mikhail's willingness to accept Kolosov's sacrifice makes it all the more imperative for her to bring about his arrest, and after Kolosov declares that he is Mikhail and the latter is about to make good his escape, she reveals the deception to the patrol.

The incident occurs nearly at the end of *Lyubov Yarovaya* as the Reds jubilantly celebrate the defeat of a White force and the recapture of the town that serves as the principal setting. Preceding what has to be considered the most emotionally intense scene of the play is a briskly paced and competently structured melodrama of military conflict, diverting in its humor and the variety of characters represented.

In composing *Lyubov Yarovaya*, Trenyov followed a pattern used often in Russian plays depicting events of the Revolution and the Civil War: the clash of opposing armies and the rapid shifting of military and political fortunes collectively function through much of the work as a sort of epic background against which a wide range of lesser human dramas is played out. Among those sympathetic to the White cause are members of the tsarist aristocracy, the Baron and Baroness, who think only of personal comfort and flight from their war-ravaged country with as many personal belongings as possible; a high-ranking member of the Orthodox clergy, Archbishop Zakatov, an implacable foe of "godless" bolshevism; a champion of constitutional monarchy (Folgin); and a typist-clerk (Pavla Panova), who works with the Reds but remains loyal to the White cause out of "class" feelings. Lyubov Yarovaya herself and the heroic, resourceful commissar Koshkin dominate the substantial number of characters representing the Red camp; but balancing the idealism of their portraiture is the hypocrisy and cynicism of Groznoy whose "telling name"—Fearsome—signals the grotesque letter-of-the-law interpretation of bolshevism represented by the character who is eventually shot to death by his fellow Reds for petty thievery. Other well-etched miniature portraits among the Reds include those of the naïve but coarse and earthy Shvandya, another in a long line of seamen in early Soviet drama; the servant (later adventuress) Dunka; a young girl named Makhova; and a peasant woman whose sons are on opposite sides of the political struggle.

To capture the diversity of the revolutionary pageant and achieve thereby a certain verisimilitude despite the implausibility (Yarovoy's return) on which the dramatic conflict turns, Trenyov painted a canvas

A scene from the original production of Mikhail Bulgakov's Days of the Turbins
by the Moscow Art Theater in 1926.
(H. W. L. DANA COLLECTION OF THE HARVARD THEATRE COLLECTION)

broad enough to encompass a whole spectrum of representative types in
both camps, Red and White. Aside from the expected political bias, a
balanced symmetry of situation and character results. The town in which
the action takes place is held now by Reds, now by Whites, now by
Reds again; a number of Red character types are contrasted with an almost equal number of Whites, running the gamut from human nobility
to human baseness; the idealized central character on the Red side,
Lyubov, is paralleled by the idealized central character on the White
side, her husband Mikhail, who until his deception of her by falsely
promising to release a certain group of Red prisoners and his willingness
to accept Kolosov's sacrifice, matches his wife's sense of honor, sincerity
of conviction, and dedication to a cause. But this symmetry of composition and the poignancy of the conflict between a husband and wife torn
apart by mutually incompatible political beliefs are not the reasons Trenyov's *Lyubov Yarovaya* came to enjoy such a preeminent position in the
Soviet theater. The strengths of the play, particularly from an audience's
point of view, lie instead in its melodramatic excitement, its lively
tempo, and its range of secondary characters whose identification as recognizable political types detracts little from the life with which they
have been infused.

The romantic-monumental style on which such great hopes for the future of Soviet drama were placed in some quarters appeared only fitfully

in most plays of the 1920s about the Revolution and the Civil War. Brisk
tempo, rapid changes of scene, episodic structure, melodrama, much
onstage physical action, primarily of a military character, crowd scenes,
and the focus on a hero representing the collective were the usual devices employed by dramatists to create an aura of the romantic and
monumental. Although essentially exercises in realistic drama, Tretyakov's *Roar, China!*, Ivanov's *Armored Train No. 14–69*, Trenyov's
Lyubov Yarovaya, and another classic Soviet Civil War play, *Shtorm*
(*Storm*, 1924), by Vladimir Bill-Belotserkovsky (1884–1970), all demonstrate some use of these techniques. Conceived, however, wholly in the
romantic-monumental style—and patently intended as a demonstration
of the direction the "new" style was to take—was Vsevolod Vishnevsky's
first major play, *Pervaya konnaya* (*The First Horse Army*), completed in
November 1929 on the tenth anniversary of the Rostov campaign of the
Civil War. In view of Vishnevsky's prominent role in the polemics over
dramatic style and genre in the late 1920s and early '30s, *The First
Horse Army* should be regarded as a key position in the development of
Soviet dramatic theory.

The conception of *The First Horse Army* is that of an epic in dramatic
form. In broad terms, the epic dramatized is that of the Civil War; more
particularly, the campaigns of the famous Red cavalry leader, Marshal
Semyon Budyonny. Although Budyonny's army figures prominently in
the play, Budyonny himself does not. He is rather a figure of mythic
stature; a presence felt but not seen.

Of the many characters who fill Vishnevsky's crowded canvas of war,
the simple recruit Sysoev stands out more clearly than the others. His
role in the play has structural and ideological functions. Structurally, he
represents the same kind of unifying element as the *picaro* in the Spanish picaresque novel, the episodic form of which is paralleled in Vishnevsky's play. Without the unity of such a central character, the loose
composition of the episodic pattern with its setting and character vari-
ables would be unfocused and diffuse. Aware of the problems of such
structure in the formulation of his epic drama, Vishnevsky singled out
one character to serve as the play's unifying agent.

The choice of the simple recruit Sysoev was also motivated by ideological considerations. Through Sysoev, whose career in the army is
traced from tsarist times through the successful conclusion of the Civil
War, Vishnevsky seeks to depict the political maturation of the masses of
whom Sysoev can be seen as a projection. Sysoev's coming-of-age under
the impress of the tumultuous history through which Russia passed in

the first two decades of the twentieth century becomes that of the collective.

The episodic structure of *The First Horse Army* is achieved through a division of the play into four larger units and thirty-six smaller ones. The first larger unit, titled "The Russian Imperial Army," consists of seven episodes; its purpose is to show the brutality and arrogance of the officers' treatment of recruits in the tsarist army on the eve of World War I. The second and third larger units (or "cycles," as they are termed in the original) are titled "The German War" and consist of a total of eleven scenes. In them, the vitriolic portrayal of tsarist military style of the first segment is expanded against the landscape of the Russo-German conflict of World War I. After incurring the displeasure of a superior officer in one of the play's more effective episodes Sysoev, as punishment, is made to mount the breastworks of a trench in full view of the German guns. What saves him and at the same time hastens the process of his political and social awareness is the reluctance of the German troops to fire on another simple recruit such as themselves. Thus, Sysoev's life is spared as he learns firsthand of the camaraderie of the trenches that cuts across the lines of conflict. The fourth larger unit (cycle three), comprising seventeen scenes, bears the title "The Civil War." Packed with the play's greatest concentration of external action the cycle, as its name indicates, shifts the scene from World War I to the Civil War. The focus now is on the exploits of Budyonny's cavalry, viewed from the perspective of Sysoev who has found his way into the ranks of the Red Army as much by accident as by inclination. The rousing singing of the Communist Internationale by victorious Red Army men and their prisoners (White officers excluded, of course) brings the third cycle and the main body of the play to an end.

Following an old dramatic tradition, Vishnevsky encloses the drama proper within a prologue and epilogue. Using letters as a narrative device the epilogue simply brings the play down to the present, that is 1929, the year in which *The First Horse Army* was written. The epilogue is titled "The Front Is Here Too," meaning that even though the military antagonists of the Bolshevik regime have been defeated in the Civil War, the vigil cannot be relaxed for there are enemies within, no longer in uniform but no less fervently devoted to the destruction of the Soviet state. The dramatization of this message follows familiar melodramatic lines. The evildoer in this case, a former tsarist officer guilty of extreme brutality toward his men, masquerades as a veteran of Budyonny's cavalry. He is recognized, however, by Sysoev and is taken into custody after Sysoev magnanimously blocks his summary execution.

Obviously, Vishnevsky's *The First Horse Army* is of no great interest for its ideology. What does attract attention is the variety of devices employed by the playwright to create a romantic-heroic dramatic form. Some of these devices are borrowed from earlier traditions: the play's episodic structure, the use of prologue and epilogue, the appearance throughout of a narrator (the *vedushchy* or "chief"), crowd scenes, on-stage physical conflict, patently melodramatic episodes, the use as narrative devices of extended monologues (such as that of the soldier in the eleventh episode of the third cycle) and letters (those of the men who served under him to the commander at the beginning of the epilogue), and so on. Much of the rousing impact of the play is achieved through sound. Anthems (the French, the Internationale) are sung together with a variety of soldiers' songs (White as well as Red). The song of Budyonny's cavalry becomes a leitmotif of the play occurring usually whenever elements of the cavalry make an appearance. The sound of drums also reverberates throughout the play. When a soldier is sentenced to death for desertion at the end of the second episode of the second cycle, the beating of drums and the simultaneous darkening of the stage signify the execution. At times drums are used to suggest the hoofbeats of Budyonny's cavalry when a reference is made to the Horse Army in the narrator's addresses. When dead heroes of past campaigns are recalled by the narrator near the end of the second episode of the epilogue, a stage direction calls for the playing of a mournful and bitter tune. This, together with a direct appeal of the narrator to the audience to rise up and revere the memory of those who fell in battle, is calculated for emotional appeal and the involvement of the spectators in the spirit of the play.

Some of the techniques employed by Vishnevsky in the elaboration of his epic style derive not from dramatic tradition but from contemporary theatrical and cinematographic practice, particularly of the avant-garde. Consider the use of screens, for example. In a manner reminiscent of German epic theater productions (Piscator, Brecht) texts—usually war communiqués—are flashed on screens. Stage directions are sparse, but the probable arrangement was a huge screen lowered from above with the messages flashed onto it by a projector. The usual stage direction in Russian is *vspykhivaet tekst*, "the message blazes up." This doubtless indicates some type of projection. In one important and effective use of the projected communiqué technique in the sixteenth episode of the third cycle, Lenin's orders to Budyonny's cavalry that they turn against the Whites under Wrangel are prefaced by the narrator who says, "Now, Comrade Lenin has the floor." This is immediately followed by the appearance on screen of Lenin's thirty-four-word communiqué.

The on-screen flashing of communiqués is also accompanied at times by the clicking of a telegraphic apparatus; in one instance, at the end of the tenth episode of the third cycle, a series of communiqués about Budyonny's army is flashed onto the screen in a cavalry rhythm suggestive of the movement of men on horses. The most imaginative use of mechanical devices comes in the fifth episode of the third cycle in which Budyonny's men capture a White armored train by means of a ruse involving telegraphs. The stage is divided into three parts. The setting of the middle area puts before the audience a misty winter night with telegraph poles receding into the distance. The opposing Red and White forces are on opposite sides of the stage. Pretending to be Whites, the Reds exchange telegraph messages with the Whites and dupe them into sending their armored train right into the hands of Budyonny's waiting army. Telegraph relay equipment is set up within each camp. As messages are sent back and forth not only is the clicking of the apparatus heard but telegraphic tape flows out of the machine on the opposite side of the stage. Virtually the entire fifth episode is built around this device.

Prior to Vishnevsky's *The First Horse Army*, Budyonny's Civil War campaigns had been made the subject most prominently of Isaak Babel's collection of stories known under the title *Konarmiya* (usually translated into English as *Red Cavalry*). Babel himself saw action with Budyonny's cavalry, especially in the Polish campaign of 1920–21, and drew on personal experience for his stories. The image of the campaigns that emerges from the pages of *Red Cavalry* is the polar opposite of Vishnevsky's epic and romantic treatment. Babel's world is one of insensate, irrational cruelty; outright acts of savagery are tinged with the cynical and grotesque. This almost obsessive preoccupation with sordid and horrible aspects of the Red campaigns makes for engrossing reading but hardly endeared Babel to many contemporary readers and critics who were disturbed by what they regarded as a highly personal and distorted treatment of the Budyonny campaigns. They expected romanticized portraits of brave Red cavalrymen at war and found instead twisted grimaces of vulgarity and brutality.

Long a faithful worshiper at the altar of Soviet military glory, Vishnevsky took issue with Babel's depiction of Budyonny and his army in

Red Cavalry and determined to write a corrective. This was the genesis of the play *The First Horse Army*. In the light of it, we can see that Vishnevsky intended the work to fulfill a twofold purpose. It was to undo the wrong Babel had done in *Red Cavalry* and it was to serve as a paradigm of the style of drama favored by Vishnevsky as suitable to the treatment of the epic and romance of the Revolution and the Civil War. In the final analysis, it is primarily as a structure that the play evokes the greatest interest.

Unconventionality, but of an entirely different sort than that of Vishnevsky's play, marked the theatrical debut of one of the most brilliant twentieth-century Russian writers, Mikhail Bulgakov (1891–1940). Highly esteemed as the author of the widely translated novel *Master and Margarita* and such collections of satirical tales as *Heart of a Dog* and *The Fatal Eggs*, Bulgakov first turned to drama in response to encouragement that he prepare a stage version of his Civil War novel, *Belaya gvardiya* (*The White Guard*, 1925). Dealing with the intricate web of political intrigue and military conflict in the Ukraine in the winter of 1918 and early 1919, the novel became the focus of considerable controversy and presaged Bulgakov's future difficulties with the Party's theatrical overseers.

Bulgakov's real interest in *The White Guard* is the impact of World War I, the Revolution, and the Civil War on a White family (the Turbins) living near Bulgakov's native Kiev, in the Ukraine. Although set in the time of the Civil War the *White Guard* does not, however, depict any direct conflict between Whites and Reds. Instead, Bulgakov traces the failure of the efforts by the German military command in south Russia to install a Ukrainian hetmanate subordinate to German interests and aligned with the supporters of Russian tsarism, that is, the Whites. The members of the Turbin family in uniform are in the White army and fight with the forces of the German-backed hetmanate not against the Reds but against the Cossacks of Petlura whose goal is an independent Ukrainian state. It is only near the end of the work that allusions, understandably within the context of political approbation, are made to the advancing Reds who will eventually crush Petlura and so prevent the truncation from Russia of the vast territory of the Ukraine.

Bulgakov's dominant and by no means wholly negative concern with a White Guardist family, the negligible role accorded the Reds, and the minimal ideological posturing quickly brought down upon the *White Guard* the wrath of the Party's literary watchdogs. The result was hardly surprising: after the first two parts of the novel appeared serially in the magazine *Rossiya* (*Russia*) in April and May of 1925, further publication was halted. The complete edition of the book appeared for the first time only in 1966.

Bulgakov's dramatic writing experienced the same fate. *The White Guard* was dramatized by its author for the theater in 1926 under the title *Dni Turbinykh* (*The Days of the Turbins*) and staged the same year by the Moscow Art Theater. Despite an enthusiastic reception by the public, the official reaction was hostile and the play became the target of considerable harassment. This resulted in a ban that lasted until 1932 when staging was again permitted—with some minor revisions—presumably after Bulgakov's personal appeal. The bone of contention was Bulgakov's too sympathetic depiction of a White family.

The sequel to *The Days of the Turbins*, *Beg* (*Flight*), was written between 1926 and 1928 and was accepted by the Moscow Art Theater, the only theater, incidentally, which received permission to stage it. When it had already gone into rehearsal, however, some two weeks later, it was ordered withdrawn by the state body entrusted with policy decisions in all theatrical matters, the so-called Glavrepertkom. Such prominent personalities as Stanislavsky and Gorky made a concerted effort to get the Glavrepertkom to rescind its order, but to no avail. The play was thus effectively kept from the boards until 1957 when it was finally permitted to premiere at the Gorky Theater in Volgograd. Its Leningrad debut came in the summer of 1958, in the Pushkin State Academic Theater.

By 1929, a year after the completion of *Flight*, Bulgakov chafed under an official prohibition that made it virtually impossible for him to have anything published or staged. But instead of submitting timidly, recanting, and writing something designed to please Soviet officialdom, he wrote a letter to the Glavrepertkom in March 1930 accusing it of stifling originality and creative individuality and of impeding the further development of Soviet drama. The daring letter concluded with the request that Bulgakov either be given permission to emigrate from the Soviet Union, since he could not continue to exist in a situation where he was denied the possibility of writing, or that at the very least he be permitted to work in the theater in some capacity, however menial. The latter course prevailed. Bulgakov was assigned to the Moscow Art Theater as an assistant director, a post he held for the last ten years of his life.

Aware that there was little if any possibility of gaining the approval of the censors for works on contemporary themes unless he made compromises he could not live with as a creative artist, Bulgakov continued to stay alive as a writer mostly by dramatizing the works of other writers, the most notable being Gogol's novel *Dead Souls.* In an original play entitled *Kabala svyatosh* (*A Cabal of Hypocrites*) or *Molière* (1930), which had a run of just seven performances in February and March 1936, Bulgakov alluded to his personal problems with censorship under the familiar protective cover of history and Aesopian language. His unfinished novel *Teatralny roman* (*A Theatrical Novel,* translated into English under the title *Black Snow;* written in all probability between 1936 and 1939 but discovered and published only in 1965) is a thinly fictionalized account of his theatrical experiences, encounters, and conflicts.

The Days of the Turbins, Bulgakov's first outing as a playwright, is a successful dramatization of his novel *The White Guard.* The historical situation remains unchanged: the political drama unfolding in the Ukraine is the campaign of Petlura and his Cossacks to crush a German-supported "puppet" Ukraine headed by a hetman favorable to the Russian imperial cause. The Whites in the play (the Turbins, Talberg, Mishlaevsky, Shervinsky, and Studzinsky) are aware of the danger posed by the Bolsheviks and the inevitability of a future confrontation with them. But their immediate concern is Petlura, especially in view of the withdrawal of German support for the hetman when their mutual cause appears lost.

For all the background of politics and military action, however, *The Days of the Turbins* is essentially a play about family life and the profound changes it undergoes in consequence of war and revolution. The play is something unique for its time, place, and genre. What makes it so is the understanding and compassion Bulgakov brings to a society which the Russian literature of the period was unable to deal with except in the most hostile and negative terms. This is nowhere more apparent than in the splendid first act, where the musically accentuated aura of the imminent, irrevocable passing of a way of life is as unmistakable as in Chekhov's *The Cherry Orchard.* The hypocritical flight of Talberg to Berlin to save his own skin, leaving behind his wife Yelena (née Turbin) because the German military train refuses to carry women; the drinking and singing following Talberg's departure; Shervinsky's declaration of love and proposal of marriage to Yelena shortly after Talberg leaves; their intoxication and Shervinsky's efforts to force his attentions; the "delicateness" of the Turbins' poetic cousin, Lariosik—these are all building blocks from which the wobbly edifice of social and moral decay is constructed.

The second act is swiftly paced, the first part presenting the collapse of the hetman-White Guardist campaign as, with German collusion, the hetman slips away disguised as a German officer, and the second part— the brisk activity in Petlura's camp as the Cossacks move onto the offensive to take Kiev. The third act shifts to a beleaguered schoolhouse defended by Whites under the command of Colonel Aleksei Turbin. No sooner does Turbin tell his cadets to give up the fight as lost and return to their homes when Petlura's Cossacks burst into the building. Nikolai (Nikolka), Turbin's younger brother, is injured in the retreat but makes his way back to the Turbin's apartment with the news that Aleksei has been killed. On this note, the third act ends. Two months later (Act IV), the tide of battle has again turned and it is Petlura's forces that now face the loss of Kiev to the Bolsheviks.

The family drama again becomes prominent in the last act. Yelena agrees to marry Shervinsky, who has decided to devote full time to his singing career in opera. Now in mufti, Myshlaevsky and Studzinsky arrive and argue over whether or not to remain in Kiev or leave to join Denikin's White army and fight the Bolsheviks. Shervinsky and Yelena inform them of their plans to marry when, without warning, Talberg arrives, also attired as a civilian, with the idea of taking Yelena away to join the White forces of General Krassnov in the Don area. Myshlaevsky forcibly ejects him after Yelena tells him she is divorcing him to marry Shervinsky. As the play ends, with the distant band music of the Internationale getting ever closer, the characters onstage, with the exception of Studzinsky, take some comfort in still being alive and able to look ahead perhaps to a peaceful future. To Nikolai Turbin's optimistic remark (and Bulgakov's only patent if low-key concession to ideology) that the evening marks a "great prologue to a new historical drama," Studzinsky replies soberly: "For some, the prologue; for others, the epilogue," reinforcing the underlying motivation of the play to depict neither the struggle between the old order and the new nor the triumph of the new, but the irrevocable passing of the old.

It is that epilogue of tsarist Russia and the self-exile of its most zealous supporters (the Talbergs and Studzinskys) to which Bulgakov addressed his second play, *Flight*, a sequel to *The Days of the Turbins*. The flight specifically of Serafima Korzukhina, a young Petersburg matron, and Sergei Golubkov, a Petersburg professor's son, assumes a dreamlike quality as Golubkov himself characterizes it shortly after the play begins. The unreality of their detachment, and that of the émigré Whites in general, from Russia serves Bulgakov as the rationale for the division of the four-act drama into eight "dreams."

In the first "dream" the setting is southern Russia in October 1920. After Red Guards leave the monastery church in which Serafima and Golubkov, together with other émigrés, have taken refuge a White hussar regiment arrives—to discover that a pregnant woman named Barabanchikova is none other than the White general Charnota in disguise and that a chemist named Makhrov proves to be the disguised Archbishop Africanus, the spiritual leader of the White armies.

In the second "dream," set in a railway station in the northern Crimea, a White army led by General Khludov is busy drawing up plans to evacuate to Sebastopol and thence overseas in the face of an imminent Red victory. The demoralization in the White camp, manifest in the cruelty of Khludov's behavior, becomes more sinister in the third "dream" when Serafima is accused by White counterintelligence officers of being a Red agent and a confession to this effect is wrung out of Golubkov on threat of torture. The intelligence officers, Tikhy and Slunsky, intend to use the confession to blackmail Mr. Korzukhin who earlier, perhaps out of fear, had denied knowing his wife and is now in Sebastopol preparing to leave Russia.

The brief interrogation of the ill Serafima, grotesque in its cruelty, faintly echoes the nightmarish grilling of the petty clerk Tarelkin, who is accused of vampirism in the almost surrealistic antibureaucracy and antipolice satire *Smert Tarelkina* (*Tarelkin's Death,* 1869), the final part of the *Trilogy* by Aleksandr Sukhovo-Kobylin (1813–1906) and one of the more unusual Russian dramatic works of the later nineteenth century.[3] Before the interrogation goes too far, however, General Charnota enters to save Serafima, who soon thereafter leaves for Constantinople by boat. When Golubkov, who in the interim has become separated from her, learns of her destination he resolves to join her in Turkey.

The fifth and sixth "dreams" are set in Constantinople where the life of the expatriate Russians takes on all the aura of grotesque fantasy becoming thus closer in spirit to Bulgakov's *Master and Margarita* than to *The Days of the Turbins.* Charnota, his common-law wife Lyuska, and Serafima are living together, in difficult straits, in the Turkish capital. In a tenuous link with Mayakovsky's *The Bedbug* and the "entomological" literature of the early twentieth century (Kafka, Karel Čapek, Lorca) Bulgakov seizes on the cockroach to suggest the loathsome wretchedness of the emigration. Cockroach races, described as "Russian gambling" and now the new sensation of Constantinople, not only fill the time of the expatriate colony but also hold out the possibility of welcome financial gain. At least it does to the men. For the women, there is always

prostitution, as in the case first of Lyuska and then of Serafima herself.
"I'm not a fool," the latter says of herself at one point, "but I really *was* a
fool! And does it make any difference what one sells? It's all such nonsense!"[4]

If Charnota stakes his last coin on winning at cockroach races, Golubkov, attired mostly in Turkish dress, has become a street hurdy-gurdy
player and this way, by chance, comes across Charnota and through
him, of course, Serafima. When Lyuska runs away to Paris, unable to
bear their life in Constantinople any longer, Charnota and the others
(including now the clearly mad General Khludov as well), follow her.
The seventh "dream" shifts thus to Paris, and the eighth back to Constantinople. Golubkov and Charnota, the latter fantastically dressed in a
Circassian coat minus silver belt and dagger and only lemon-yellow
shorts on underneath, come to Mr. Korzukhin's apartment in search of
money to help Serafima. With most of his money abroad at the time of
his departure from Russia, Korzukhin has had an easy time establishing
a new life in Paris. He has taken out French citizenship and displays a
hostile attitude toward things Russian. When his Russian valet seems to
be slow in acquiring French, Korzukhin tells him:

> Antoine, you are a Russian lazybones. Remember, a person who lives
> in Paris should know that Russian is good only for swearing in
> unprintable words or, what is still worse, for promulgating some kind
> of destructive slogans. Neither the former nor the other are accept-
> able in Paris. (*p. 223*)

Korzukhin at first refuses to help his former wife but Charnota entices
him into an all night game of chemin de fer and wins the equivalent of
$20,000. When Korzukhin balks at paying and Charnota threatens him
with a gun, his cries for help arouse not only his valet but also Lyuska
(Luci, he calls her) who, it appears, has been living with him as his
mistress since coming to Paris.

Upon returning to Constantinople, where Serafima in the meantime
has been caring for the now deranged Khludov, Charnota and Golubkov
learn that in order to end the agony of the memories that continue to
haunt him, Khludov has made up his mind to return to Russia. Golubkov and Serafima also resolve to return. The rationale for their decision,
and the sense of *Flight* as a whole, is implicit in Serafima's words to
Golubkov at the end:

> What was it this past year and a half, Seryozha? Dreams? Explain it to
> me! Where, why did we flee? Street lamps on the platform, black

bags . . . and then the heat! I want to be on Karavan Street again, I want to see snow again! I want to forget everything, as if it hadn't happened. (*p. 239*)

In reply, Golubkov strikes the same chord:

None of it happened—it was all delirium! Forget it, forget! A month will pass, we'll make it, we'll return, and then the snow will fall and efface our footprints . . . Let's go! Let's go! (*p. 239*)

When they leave Constantinople, only Charnota remains—and the cockroach races.

Bulgakov's conception of the play as a sequence of dreams is handsomely worked out scenically. Each dream opens in either darkness or pale light, gradually becomes illuminated for the duration of the "dream," and closes in darkness again. Throughout *Flight*, Bulgakov operates with a kind of Baroque chiaroscuro, setting the mood of dream and unreality.

In the first "dream," the flickering light of dim candles before icons gradually illumines the darkness; together with the muffled sound of a choir of monks the effect produced is splendidly theatrical. In the second "dream," the darkness recedes before the light of a railway station waiting room with blue electric moons visible through the rear windows. Frosty from the cold, the windows catch the snakelike fiery reflections of passing trains, creating dynamic patterns of light that complement the dizzying, unreal events transpiring on stage. For the third "dream," the melancholy light of autumn twilight again casts an eerie glow. Like the first "dream" the fifth opens with the sound of music, this time Turkish melodies intermingled with strains of a sentimental Russian song played on a hurdy-gurdy. As the stage is illumined, the evening sun casts its reddish glow over minaret-topped Constantinople. This same setting reappears in the eighth "dream," while in the sixth it is a courtyard with cypresses and a two-story house with terrace at evening when the first shadows appear, and in the seventh—the sunset of a Paris autumn glowing faintly beyond the windows of the study of Korzukhin's residence. As the game of chemin de fer grows in length and intensity sunset gives way to night, the lights of Paris flicker in the distance, and the action onstage is lighted by candles burning on the card table beneath little pink shades.

Bulgakov's vision of Russian post-Civil War émigré life as a nightmarish unreality corresponds, despite its grotesque character, to the disposition of early Soviet drama toward emigration in general. The atti-

tude is summed up in Bersenev's words to Shtube in Act III of Lavrenyov's *Breakup*. Shtube tells Bersenev that he cannot remain in Russia
any longer, that he cannot adjust to a society which, in his opinion, is
disintegrating before his very eyes. Bersenev, who has cast his lot with
the Reds, recognizing them as the bearers of the new Russia, replies:

> Go on, look for a place for yourself somewhere else . . . But re-
> member what I'm going to tell you now: Russia will never return to
> the old path. Perhaps not one of us will live to see a better future, but
> it will surely come; and then our new motherland will shower good
> only on those who stood by her during the difficult years, but will for-
> ever curse those who abandoned her like the prodigal son going off in
> search of a warm cozy place in another land. From the day you cross
> the borders of that land, you'll become an eternal wanderer, without a
> country, without a name, without honor. And you will have no way of
> returning . . . Now—do as you think best.[5]

Whatever the opposition to the Bolshevik seizure of power, whatever
the problems of adjustment in the postrevolutionary era, to take flight
from the country, above all, in the "difficult years," was regarded by the
new regime as morally indefensible for a Russian, irrespective of background, and a despicable act tantamount to treachery. The extreme hostility with which émigré and emigration are usually portrayed in Russian
drama of the 1920s and early 1930s and the aura of enthusiastic approbation surrounding the decision of a representative of the old regime to
remain in or, if he has left, to return to Russia no matter how grudgingly
he accepts the irrevocability of the past order abundantly attest to the
degree of emotion aroused by such behavior. When Khludov, Serafima,
and Golubkov determine to return to Russia at the end of Bulgakov's
Flight they are making, in effect, an act of self-redemption; the way to
salvation is open to them. But choosing to remain in emigration, Charnota condemns himself to eternal damnation; the cockroach that figures
so prominently in the play functions as an appropriate symbol for him
and for those like him.

Although Bulgakov parts company with most Russian drama of his
time in *Days of the Turbins* by bringing a family of White Guardists to
the fore of his dramatic canvas, he is ideologically careful, at the conclusion of his play, to grant the most important characters the ability to perceive that their former way of life is beyond recall and that they can and
indeed must stay in Russia and somehow adjust to the new society in
order to remain alive—in more than just one sense. Significantly, it is
only Talberg, the bearer of an odious Germanic name that at once marks

him as a member of that most intransigent, "alien" sector of the tsarist aristocracy, who chooses flight in adversity. Studzinsky's decision to continue fighting the White cause, even though he gives evidence of an awareness of probable disaster, admits of less facile explanation. Like Nezelasov, in Ivanov's *Armored Train No. 14–69*, he may just be another professional soldier whose honor *as an officer* demands that he remain steadfast in his loyalty to his given cause even if his convictions begin to falter or he sees nothing but defeat looming up on the horizon before him. Another possibility also has to be considered, and that is that by giving his character the Polish sounding name of Studzinsky, Bulgakov is hinting that Studzinsky's desire to continue the struggle and his unwillingness to yield or compromise proceed from the "nocturnal" Polish side of his nature: this expresses itself in a love of fighting and a senseless, futile kind of romanticism which Russians have long regarded as characteristically Polish.

Naturally, White officers whose political consciousness evolves to the point where they are willing to fight under the Red banner (like Lavrenyov's Bersenev) are dealt with more sympathetically than those who either continue to fight out of conviction (Ivanov's Nezelasov; Bulgakov's Studzinsky) or give up further struggle and more passively try to reach a *modus vivendi* with the new Russia. As we saw previously, the White officer drawn in the most venomous and negative terms is the aristocrat with a Germanic name (Talberg, Shtube). But even here, some hope was still possible; or at least it became possible in the drama of the early 1930s.

Consider, for example, Vsevolod Vishnevsky's most important though less flamboyant exercise in romantic-epic drama after *The First Horse Army, Optimisticheskaya tragediya* (*An Optimistic Tragedy*, 1933). Like Lavrenyov's *Breakup*, it deals with the exploits of Russian seamen during the Civil War. Resonant with martial clamor and distinguished structurally by an episodic form interspersed with choruses of a patently ideological nature recited by two seamen who were participants in the events dramatized, *An Optimistic Tragedy* chronicles the iron-willed determination and heroism of a less than believable woman commissar who brings order, discipline, and finally honor to an unruly unit of sailors long dominated by an anti-Bolshevik anarchist faction. The commissar's antagonists include, in addition to the anarchist seamen, a naval officer named Behring who vainly attempts to assert his own authority. Now at first meeting Behring would seem to be another member of the Russo-German aristocracy like Talberg or Shtube. Indeed he is, but with an

A scene from the production of Vsevolod Vishnevsky's Optimistic Tragedy *by the Kamerny Theater, Moscow, in 1934. Directed by Aleksandr Tairov. The distinguished actress Alice Koonen appears in the role of the lady commissar.*
(H. W. L. DANA COLLECTION OF THE HARVARD THEATRE COLLECTION)

important distinction. Behring loses no time in informing the lady commissar that the men in his family have served in the Imperial Russian Navy from the time of Peter the Great (when, in fact, Germans, Dutchmen, and Scandinavians were invited to Russia and were granted numerous privileges in order to aid the Russians in the construction of a modern fleet). But so proud is Behring of his family's long history of naval service that he places his career above all other considerations. His disdain for the Bolsheviks is only barely concealed, but in the collapse of the White cause he must either elect to go under with them or serve the Reds if he is to serve any more in a Russian navy. In his choice of the latter course, Vishnevsky establishes beyond any doubt that even an officer of Behring's background can be redeemed if his sense of service to Russia is strong enough. The growth of political consciousness can come later. That it is Behring's patriotism (he must serve in a *Russian* navy, even if it is a *Red* Russian navy) that brings him within the pale of respectability, despite the associations his Germanic name conjures up, is evident from the fact that the military action which the sailors, Behring, and the lady commissar see is against a *foreign* enemy, indeed against Germans.

One of the most withering assaults on Russians who incline toward a life in emigration in preference to remaining in Russia and taking a hand in the building of a postrevolutionary socialist society appears in one of two major plays written by an outstanding literary personality of the late '20s and early '30s the satirist and devoted disciple of Dr. Freud, Yuri Olesha (1899–1960).[6]

Olesha is best remembered for his satirical psychoanalytical novel *Zavist* (*Envy*, 1927), which has been translated into many languages, including English.[7] The less successful dramatization of the novel, under the title *Zagovor chuvstv* (*The Conspiracy of Feelings*, 1929), marked Olesha's first entry into the theater in which he soon became strongly enough interested to write both a second original play and several essays. The play, which he completed in 1931, was titled *Spisok blagodeyanniy* (*A List of Assets*). Marred by an excess of melodrama, the work still has to be considered one of the more interesting Soviet plays of the early 1930s.

The too neatly contrived plot revolves around the visit to Paris of a vain actress, her adventures, and, ultimately, her death there. Proud of being Russian but ambivalent toward the Bolshevik regime because the putative egalitarianism of the new Soviet society seems to deny creative artists sufficient recognition, esteem, and reward, in terms above all of spiritual sustenance, Yelena (Lyolya) Goncharova sees her trip to Paris as the fulfillment of her dreams. In her mind, the French capital, which becomes synonymous with the West in general, has become a highly romanticized and idealized entity. *There* the genius of the creative artist must be properly valued and given its just deserts. That there is the strong likelihood that Lyolya will choose to remain in the West, becoming thus an émigré, is obvious to her closest friends and, on a subconscious level, to Lyolya herself. But her experiences in the West prove a shocking disappointment. Artistically, she discovers to her profound chagrin, the commercial interests of Western entrepreneurs strip the creative artist of far more dignity and self-esteem than do performances before unsophisticated audiences of workers in the Soviet Union. In the fifth scene (of the eight into which *A List of Assets* is divided), Lyolya appears dressed in her favorite role of Hamlet (recalling the prominence of Shakespeare and Hamlet, in particular, in Olesha's *Envy* and *The Conspiracy of Feelings*) for an audition at a music hall run by a Monsieur Margeret. She recites to the blasé Frenchman the dialogue with Guildenstern about the playing of a recorder. M. Margeret is not particularly interested in Shakespeare, but sees a real possibility for something theatrically novel (and hence commercially successful). His suggestions to

Lyolya, and the sociocultural implications with which Olesha invests them, speak for themselves:

> MARGERET: So you can see I'm busy and don't even have time to drink a glass of milk, and still you waste my time. Let's make it short. In order to make this act a success, it should go something like this: first you'd have to play the recorder, some minuet or something, just to put the audience into a melancholy mood. Then you could, for instance, swallow the recorder . . . that would make the audience gasp. The mood would change to one of astonishment, then of alarm. At that point you'd turn your back to the audience and there would be a recorder sticking out of a part of your anatomy from which the recorders don't usually stick out. That would be quite titillating in view of the fact that you're a woman. Now we have something. I've hit on a wonderful idea here! You'll start blowing into the recorder from what we might call your reverse end. But this time it won't be a minuet, but something more cheerful, something like "Oh, Joseph, Joseph, Can't You Make Your Mind Up." . . . Do you see what I mean? That'll bring the house down. (*pp. 258–59*)

The grotesque scene with Margeret shatters Lyolya's romanticized preconceptions about the life of the artist in the West. Her encounters with Russian émigrés shortly thereafter strip away the last shreds of the actress' ambivalence concerning life in the Soviet Union and her return there.

Olesha's image of émigré life in *A List of Assets* lacks the fantasy quality of Bulgakov's *Flight* but surpasses it in satirical venom. Occupying the foreground of his canvas is a nest of sinister émigrés dominated by the figure of Tatarov (a "telling" name in Russian suggesting a Tatar), the pathologically anti-Soviet publisher of a Russian émigré newspaper in Paris. Because of her vanity Lyolya becomes an unsuspecting accomplice in their scheme to exploit her visit to embarrass the Soviet regime. The nature of the scheme is manifest in Tatarov's words:

> The Soviet regime has treated her as its pet. But despite that, I maintain that her desire all along has been to defect and stay here. The very fact that such a highly successful person escapes at the first opportunity will prove once again that life in Russia today is worse than slavery. The whole world is repeating it. But what does the world actually hear? It hears the complaints of woodcutters, the vague mooing of slaves who can neither think nor shout. But now I'll extract a protest from a highly gifted person that will intensify the horror the world

The Shakespeare recital scene from Yuri Olesha's A List of Assets *in the 1931 production of the play by Meyerhold's Theater, Moscow.*
(H. W. L. DANA COLLECTION OF THE HARVARD THEATRE COLLECTION)

feels at the very mention of Soviet Russia. The famous actress from the land of slavery will shout to the world: Do not believe! Do not believe my glory! It has been conferred upon me for my willingness not to think . . . Don't believe that I was free—I was a slave despite everything. (*p. 246*)

Despite warnings by a sympathetically portrayed Soviet trade delegation which Lyolya encounters in Paris, she cannot resist the temptation to attend a politically suspect actors' ball. To put in a proper appearance at the affair she orders a gown from Tregubova, a Russian seamstress in Paris and an intimate of Tatarov. Since she lacks the cash to pay for the gown, she offers an I.O.U. which Tararov shrewdly gets her to write out on a piece of notepaper bearing the letterhead of his newspaper. His intention is to print it in the next day's issue in order to create the impression that Lyolya received the gown from the Russian émigré paper and hence supports not only the ball but, in a sense, the émigré association as well.

The net of intrigue surrounding Lyolya is drawn still tighter when Olesha at last actualizes the play's title. Lyolya, it seems, has been keeping a notebook which includes a list of the positive and negative features of life in Soviet Russia. When she inadvertently leaves it behind in the seamstress' apartment after her fitting, Tatarov loses no time in exploiting the unexpected windfall. In addition to the I.O.U., he prints only the "debit" column of Lyolya's notebook. Moreover, he also sends the Soviet embassy in Paris the I.O.U. and the notebook with the list of assets torn out, accompanied by an insolent letter. Almost beside herself when she learns what has happened, Lyolya rushes to Tatarov's apartment and confronts him with a gun. Tatarov grapples with Lyolya; the gun is knocked from her hand and retrieved by the unemployed epileptic son of a Russian émigré, Dmitri Kizevetter, who has been staying in Tatarov's apartment. Before anyone is killed, French police arrive and promise not to press charges if Kizevetter agrees to fire into a crowd of unemployed workers holding a protest march that night. This will provide them the pretext they need to crush the demonstration. On the cruder level of ideology, the march becomes another element in Olesha's indictment of the West. The episode with Margeret points up the plight of the artist, and culture generally, under capitalism; the march exposes the plight of downtrodden labor whose legitimate grievances are stifled by a police functioning as the "System's" coercive arm. Symbolically, Lyolya's death and martyrdom in the context of the march mark the defeat of her doubt, her ambivalence, her vacillation.

When the fatal moment comes, Kizevetter fires at the leader of the march, the Communist Santillant, but Lyolya, who has fled from Tatarov's apartment after an ugly scene with Tregubova, steps between them and receives the bullet. In death, Loylya is reunited with her own people and her own country. This dramatic resolution of her personal ambivalence recalls that of the intellectual Ivan Kavalerov in *The Conspiracy of Feelings.* Though filled with envy for the Soviet sausage-maker Andrei Babichev and intent on killing him at the urging of Andrei's brother Ivan who represents the "feelings" of the old Russia now doomed to extinction by the impersonal machinelike culture of the Soviet regime, Kavalerov at the last moment changes his mind and kills Ivan instead, thus symbolically completing the destruction of the old order and casting his lost with the new. Before expressing her dying wish that her body be covered with a Red flag, the symbol thus of her "reunion," Lyolya gives voice to the "prophetic truth" her sordid experiences in the decaying West have at last enabled her to perceive:

> I can see: they're coming. . . . The Soviet armies are coming, carrying tattered Red banners, their feet battered by the long, stony marches. . . . The walls of Europe are crumbling. . . . Comrades, tell them I understand everything in the end and that I'm

sorry. . . . (She stands up.) Paris! This, then, is your glory, Paris! (*p. 288*).

Olesha's *A List of Assets* is the last truly interesting Soviet play dealing with the post-Civil War emigration. Apart from its ideological obviousness and contrived, heavily melodramatic character, the play is noteworthy for the sensitivity with which Olesha dramatizes the plausible psychological anxieties experienced by an artist attempting to adjust to the new realities of Russian postrevolutionary life. Perhaps it was these very qualities the significance of which could not effectively be outweighed by the play's ideological "correctness" that eventually brought it under official ban, along with the rest of Olesha's works. The temptation to recognize in the theme the projection of a personal concern, which may not have escaped the notice of more perceptive Soviet literary censors, is hard to resist, particularly in the light of the following words from Olesha's celebrated *apologia* delivered to the First Congress of Soviet Writers on August 22, 1934:

> But then creative imagination came into play. Under its warming breath, the barren concept of social uselessness gradually turned into an idea and I decided to write a story about a beggar. . . .
>
> I never wrote the story about the beggar. At the time I could not understand why I couldn't write it, what was stopping me. Later I understood: it dawned on me that the trouble was not myself but my surroundings. My youth is still in me because I am an artist. And an artist can only write about things that are in him.
>
> While I was thinking about the story of my beggar, our country was building factories. It was the time of the first Five Year Plan, the very time when the socialist national economy was being created.
>
> But this was not a subject for me. Certainly, I could have gone out on a construction site, lived in a factory among the workers and described them in an article or even in a novel. But that was not my theme. The theme in my blood, in my breath. I couldn't handle that subject matter as a true artist. I would have been forced to contrive, to lie. I wouldn't have had what is known as inspiration. It is difficult for me to conceive the type of a worker, a revolutionary hero. Because I cannot be him.
>
> It is beyond my strength, beyond my understanding. And this is why I do not write about him. (*pp. 215, 216–17*)

FIVE

The 1920s and Early 1930s

Social Comedy, Absurd and Grotesque NEP
Satire, Melodrama

W̲HEN NOT reliving the tumultuous moments of the Revolution and the Civil War, Russian drama of the 1920s and early '30s addressed itself to the many problems of social readjustment created by the great national upheaval. The incongruities, anomalies, and even illogicalities related to these problems as the new Soviet state struggled to get on its feet created a fertile field for the rebirth of comedy. Two types of comic drama enjoyed a particular appeal at the time: light social comedy, or what could be regarded as a kind of Soviet comedy of manners, and satirical comedy permeated with the absurd and grotesque.

Social Comedy

Long the most popular social comedy in the Soviet repertoire and an excellent specimen of the genre, *Kvadratura kruga* (*Squaring the Circle*, 1927–28) also had a fair success abroad. It was written by Valentin Kataev (1897–   ), whose literary reputation rests no less on such novels as *Rastrachiki* (*The Embezzlers*, 1927) and *Vremya, vperyod!* (*Time, Forward!*, 1932).

The engaging vaudeville (as Kataev designated his comedy) derives its humor from the romantic antics of four young people: Vasya, a serious worker and a member of the League of Communist Youth; Abram, also a member of the League and Vasya's closest friend and roommate; Lyudmila, Vasya's girl friend, who does not belong to the League and thoroughly enjoys her bourgeois tastes; and Tonya, a League member and an earnest Communist, who disdains what she considers the bourgeois frivolities of life.

For all the sunny humor in the relations of these four young people Kataev's point of departure in *Squaring the Circle*—the harsh living conditions in Russia in the first decade after the chaos and devastation of the Civil War—is anything but comic. Because of the acute housing shortage, the subject of a number of works of early Soviet literature, Vasya and Abram share a room. Unbeknownst to Abram, Vasya marries Lyudmila—which in those days in Russia involved little more than registration at a government bureau—and brings his bride back to the quarters he shares with his friend. Lyudmila is dismayed at discovering that Vasya has a roommate, but quickly resigns herself and sets about organizing a household.

With two romantic couples as its principle characters, the parallel-repetitive structure of *Squaring the Circle* is virtually a foregone conclusion. No sooner does Vasya introduce Lyudmila into his shared room as his wife when attention shifts to Abram who has also married without advising Vasya of his intentions. Like Vasya, he brings his new wife, Tonya, into what is rapidly becoming a very crowded one-room apartment. Neither Vasya nor Abram can bring himself to tell the other that he is married and the hemming and hawing, the attempts to dodge the inevitable produce most of the humor in the first part of Act I. Once the two boys realize what has happened, the next step is to break the news to the girls. For maximum humor this is done piecemeal: Tonya is the first to be told and then Lyudmila. The reactions are obvious.

When tempers are calmed, the couples agree to divide the room in two, Vasya and Lyudmila occupying one half and Abram and Tonya the other. The cacophonous blaring of a malfunctioning radio, the recitation of idiotic poetry by an atheletic versifier named Yemilyan, and the singing of student songs by both couples bring the first act to a close on a note of sheer merriment.

When the curtain opens on Act II, the setting immediately establishes the differences in the living habits of the couples. The half of the room occupied by Vasya and Lyudmila reflects the latter's bourgeois tastes. In their side of the room, Abram and Tonya rule out all "bourgeois frivolities" and a Spartan simplicity deemed appropriate to the living quarters of a pair of earnest Communists prevails.

Before much time elapses the play's intrigue begins to take shape. Lyudmila's bourgeois tastes and childish romantic behavior not only are not shared by Vasya—though he goes along with them in the beginning—but gradually come to irk him. Conversely, in the relationship between Abram and Tonya, it appears that the ship of love is also having rough sailing. Again it is a matter of a surfacing incompatibility of interests and tastes. With Vasya and Lyudmila, the girl is bourgeois and giddy while the boy is serious. It is just the opposite with Abram and Tonya. Despite their earlier vows to maintain an ideal Communist marriage, Abram reveals marked bourgeois tastes: he appreciates a good meal and having his clothes mended by his wife.

What follows is predictable yet well executed by Kataev. Abram begins to draw closer to Lyudmila, whose tastes he basically shares even though she is non-Party. Vasya, on the other hand, gradually finds himself more and more attracted to Tonya, whose Communist earnestness and Spartan style of living correspond to his own seriousness and taste for simplicity.

Duplication continues as the fundamental structural formula of the play as the new romantic relationships crystallize. Using a dream as a pretext, Lyudmila maneuvers Abram into kissing her and declaring his feelings. A similar dream is used by Tonya to bring Vasya to the same point.

The final resolution of the intrigue is delayed by the reluctance of each spouse to tell the other about the romantic realignment. The problem is further complicated by the appearance, about three quarters of the way through Act II, of friends of both couples—fellow members of the League of Communist Youth and Comrade Flavius, an older Bolshevik. Vasya and Tonya are discovered kissing and out of embarrassment they let their friends think that they are married and that Abram and Lyudmila are the other married couple living in the room. By the end of the act, however, the truth is revealed and the couples pretend that the mixup was a deliberate joke.

The hesitancy of the young people to break with their respective mates continues into Act III and links the action here with the level it had reached in the preceding act before the intrusion of Flavius and the others. The issue comes to a head, and the denouement prepared, when each wife leaves her husband out of disgust. Anticipating a clear field now with their newfound loves, the boys are beside themselves with joy. But soon the mood changes to anger as they berate each other for driving away one another's wife. Yemilyan is present during their angry exchange, introduced at this point just to increase the humor of the situation by acting as an echo chamber for the questions and answers Vasya and Abram bounce off him. As the boys rush out for swords to duel with, Flavius enters and Yemilyan brings him up to date on everything that has happened. Very soon after Flavius' entrance, Tonya reappears to gather her remaining belongings. Flavius gets her to acknowledge that she truly loves Vasya and would marry him except for her reluctance to hurt Lyudmila. Her words are overheard by Lyudmila, who has also returned for some things before going her separate way. The girls are reconciled and when Vasya and Abram return dueling with rusty and broken old swords, Flavius takes command of the situation and restores peace. He has the girls declare whom they love, showing thereby that nobody need fear hurting anyone else, and gives his blessings to the new marriages. The play ends with the singing of cheerful couplets in the traditional manner of the vaudeville.

Squaring the Circle is good theatrical entertainment and free of any intrusive political didacticism. If bourgeois attitudes come in for their share of satire, the deadly earnestness of Abram and Tonya in their desire to live together as man and wife in what they conceive to be a true Communist spirit is no less productive a source of comic laughter. A wise old Bolshevik figure, Flavius, brings about the final reconciliation, but he is a character of secondary importance in the comedy and the bearer of no message other than the fact that love and revolution are not incompatible.

In composing his farce, Kataev relied on proven comic formulae: duplication (two couples, parallel incompatibility in both instances, the mutual attraction of the spouses, the dream device used by both girls to further their romantic desires, the inability of each husband to break the news of his new love to his wife, the departure of the girls, and so on); repetition, especially verbal, in the last act when Vasya and Abram turn Yemilyan into the echo chamber I spoke of before; a central misunderstanding—in Act I when each boy thinks that the other knows about his as yet unannounced marriage; mistaken identity, when Flavius and other friends of the two couples are led to believe that Vasya and Tonya and Abram and Lyudmila are married to each other; comic situation— the love play between Vasya and Lyudmila, the frequent restatement of Communist marriage ideals by Abram and Tonya before their break, the hand-kissing scene between Lyudmila and Abram after she mends his trousers, the "meowing" scene between them witnessed from a darkened room by Vasya, Tonya, Flavius, and the other boys and girls of the League (Act II); and extensive use of props and body movement for comic effect—the partitioning of the room, the crossings of the partition back and forth, particularly by Abram in search of food, and the brawling and dueling of Vasya and Abram in the last act.

The introduction of Flavius was probably politically motivated though the character has no direct ideological function in the play. Yemilyan is more of a superfluous element, added primarily for comic effect as a somewhat absurd figure. This absurdity is buttressed by the disjointed almost nonsensical radio broadcasts introduced in Act I and again at the end of the play. But in comparison with Yemilyan, the broadcasts are more germane to the play's comic purpose. As the radio picks up several stations at once, the fragmented bits and pieces of official broadcasts—political exhortations, slogans, songs—assume a comic quality that renders them not only appropriate accompaniment to the general spirit of mirth onstage but invests them with an absurdity of their own. The resultant deflation of the pomposity and self-righteousness of official propaganda handsomely parallels the debunking of the kind of extreme early Communist idealism and high-mindedness represented by the marriage of Abram and Tonya. In *Squaring the Circle* this is no less a goal than the exposure of the shallowness of bourgeois values. Where Kataev scores his greatest success is in bringing the whole thing off with such warmth and good cheer that the comic spirit of his jest is in no way crowded with ideology. Kataev wrote plays before and after *Squaring the Circle,* but it is for this comedy that his place in the history of twentieth-century Russian drama is secure.

══════ Absurd and Grotesque NEP Satire ══════

Russia in the aftermath of the Civil War was economically crippled; famine was widespread, housing critical, thousands of individuals hostile to or incompatible with the new regime had gone into exile, and the Bolsheviks were faced with the necessity of consolidating their power and at the same time launching a program of national reconstruction. If the danger of external enemies was now considerably minimized and would remain so until the late 1930s, there were still—from the Bolshevik point of view—internal enemies, potential "wreckers" of one sort or another to be ferretted out.

Efforts to implement a full-scale socialist economy proved inadequate to cope with the enormous problems legacied by the years of war, and disaster was often the reward of ideological zeal and haste. Retrenchment was in order, the Bolsheviks, with Lenin at their head, reluctantly admitted. In the name of exigency and for the sake of a surer socialist future, limited free enterprise was permitted to exist temporarily. To many for whom the Bolshevik *coup d'état* marked the end of a way of life, the institution in 1921 of what was known as the New Economic Policy (NEP) came like the dawn of a new day. Man's natural instinct for enterprise was rekindled and cultivated with a ferocity and tenacity to win the envy of any die-hard exponent of capital. The immediate goals of NEP were realized and when the strife-wracked country was ready for the first big step in the direction of a socialist economy—industrialization—the New Economic Policy was no longer considered necessary or

A scene from the production of Vladimir Bill-Belotserkovsky's anti-NEP play
Shtil (Calm) *by the State Academic Theater of Drama, Leningrad, in 1927.*
(H. W. L. DANA COLLECTION OF THE HARVARD THEATRE COLLECTION)

desirable and in 1928 was dismantled. Where once existed the relative freedom of NEP, there now stood the iron discipline of the first Five-Year Plan.

Uncertain about the future, about the duration of the New Economic Policy or even the viability of the Soviet regime itself, many who rushed to climb aboard the NEP bandwagon in the early 1920s were out to line their pockets as abundantly and as quickly as possible, by legal means or otherwise. The limits to personal enrichment were seen to be only those imposed by enterprise and ingenuity. Financial intrigue and specula-tion, on a small scale and a big one, swindling and chiseling of a truly dazzling variety ran rampant. Ostentation and "high living"—a sort of Soviet hedonism—gripped many in society.

The relaxation of revolutionary zeal and discipline in the economic sphere had its parallel in the arts, with the result that brilliant achieve-

ments—in the novel, short story, poetry, drama, theater, and film—
were realized. For the arts it was a period as yet unequalled in Soviet
culture. If experimentation later became suspect and condemned as
"formalistic" it was avidly and fruitfully cultivated during NEP. Cultural
contacts with the West, temporarily cut off by revolution and civil war,
were again revived. They were still cramped in some ways, to be sure,
but hardly to the extent that they were to become restrained and even
repressed from the mid-1930s on. What better proof, if proof need be,
of the receptivity to and acceptance of ideas emanating from the West in
Russia in the 1920s than the extensive assimilation of Freudian thought
and psychoanalysis, a cultural fact reflected even in the more orthodox
Soviet writing of the period.

The NEP era was an exciting, colorful, and paradoxical episode in
twentieth-century Russian history, and the literature of the 'twenties is a
vivid record of it.

Drama, like other literary forms, followed two routes. On one, it
sought to immortalize the glory and heroism of the Revolution and the
Civil War, as we have already seen; on another, in a distinctly less
romantic vein, it sought to capture the rhythms, accents, and masks of
NEP. The reemergence of types and habits thought suppressed for all
time by the Revolution, everything connoted by the full deprecatory
weight of the term *burzhuy* (bourgeois) in the Russian linguistic culture
of the age, created a favorable climate for the satire, in all genres, that
blossomed so ebulliently. We have had a taste of this already in Kataev's
Squaring the Circle. But the special target of the satire of the time was
the so-called NEP-man—a home-grown kind of Russian "wheeler-
dealer," an almost fantastic combination of Gogol's Khlestakov in *The
Inspector-General* and Ostrovsky's merchants. Contemporary satire
sought to hold up to ridicule the more ludicrous, grotesque, and even
downright absurd attitudes and behavior of the NEP-men. But in doing
so, it also caught the vivacity and individualism of these new anti-heroes
of Russian literature. The result was not wholly unexpected: the NEP
"types" exert a peculiar fascination of their own and while negative,
while conceived as objects of satirical derision, they come to dominate
the stage on which they appear to such an extent that the "positive" figures conventionally introduced for counterbalance pale by comparison.
Even the barbs of satire are outdistanced by the reach of an almost irresistible comic appeal.

Consider a play such as *Vozdushny pirog* (*The Sweet Soufflé*, 1924–25;
first produced on February 19, 1925, in the Moscow Theater of the Rev-

olution), the best comedy by Boris Romashov (1895–1958), a moderately successful dramatist whose post-World War II play *Velikaya sila* (*The Great Power*, 1946–47) was awarded a Stalin Prize, First Degree, in 1947. It is by all standards one of the outstanding satirical comedies of the 1920s with a specific NEP theme.

The villain of the piece is Semyon Rak (the last name, in Russian, means "crab," "lobster," or "cancer"). Out to make a fortune for himself with the private enterprise mandate of the NEP, his nimble, enterprising mind directs the operations of an organization named TIK (standing for the Society of Industrial Counteragents), whose coffers fill with the profits of a variety of shady dealings. Hard upon the success of TIK, Rak formulates an even more impressive undertaking—ARPA, the American-Russian Industrial Society, which he envisions as a gigantic export and import company specializing in trade with the United States.

Connected with Rak in his ventures are the legal adviser of TIK, Ivan Mordaev (a "telling name": *morda*, in Russian, means "muzzle" or "mug"), and several employees of a bank headed by Ilya Koromyslov (also a "telling name": *koromyslo*, in Russian, means "yoke" or "beam"). These include Koromyslov's brother Fyodor, Adam Plyukhov (a "telling name" suggesting "flopping"), Nartsiss ("Narcissus") Lobzin (a "telling name" meaning "kissing" or "kisser"), and Oskar Brunk. In Russia to cement the ARPA deal with Rak is an American named Mister Puls, characterized as the representative of an American shareholding company named "Broadway and Sons" and a previous visitor to Russia in connection with the affairs of another American shareholding company more fancifully named "Johnny Gangster."

The ARPA enterprise is to be Rak's crowning achievement and to celebrate its successful launching he orders from a pastry shop a gigantic soufflé which will be the main attraction of a banquet. The play opens, in fact, with his visit to the pastry shop and the ordering of the soufflé. Before Romashov reveals more of Rak's financial machinations, he first fills in the picture of the milieu of NEP profiteering by showing the corruption within the bank headed by Koromyslov (a car ordered for the bank, for example, is really intended for the use of Koromyslov's girl friend, an aspiring actress named Rita Kern) and by introducing the figure of Sergei Obrydlov (a "telling name," probably from the Ukrainian or Polish, suggesting someone loathsome), a currency speculator from Odessa.

As an NEP profiteer, Obrydlov is surpassed only by Rak. The relationship between the two produces some of the best comic moments of the play. Obrydlov is not only a fine satirical portrait in himself; he is also used to shed more light on the character of Rak and to thicken the intrigue of *The Sweet Soufflé*. Rak meets Obrydlov by chance and their conversation widens the audience's scope of Rak's activities by disclosing past intrigues in collusion. Obrydlov's value to the elaboration of the play's intrigue becomes apparent when he mentions that he has promissory notes of Rak on which he would like to collect. The tug of war between the two over the money continues through much of the play, now in the foreground, now in the background. Rak's conniving nature and his lack of scruples about cheating even a fellow NEP-man like Obrydlov is best revealed in his attempts to get out of making good on the promissory notes, to the extent not only of giving Obrydlov a bad check but even of causing his detention temporarily by the CHEKA (Soviet internal security police). But Obrydlov matches Rak's cunning and persistence. He manages to escape the clutches of the police and then vents his anger at Rak by throwing him out of a window of his fourth-story apartment. Rak's survival of the fall may be meant to suggest the toughness and resilience of the type.

I spoke before of Romashov's use of Obrydlov both for satirical purposes as a means of viewing Rak from another perspective and to add body to the intrigue of the comedy. Properly speaking, intrigue as such is a relatively insignificant part of Romashov's play. It is made up, for the most part, of (a) the financial machinations of Rak and his cohorts at the bank in connection with the TIK and ARPA organizations; (b) the matter of Rak's promissory notes to Obrydlov, and (c) the bank director Koromyslov's romance with the actress Rita Kern. These components are all related and complement one another. But Romashov is not strongly interested in plot and takes no great pains to construct an exciting and suspenseful comedy of intrigue dealing with high finance in the manner, let's say, of French "well-made" plays of the 1840s and 1850s or, to a lesser extent, of Ostrovsky's plays about speculators and swindlers from the 1860s and 1870s. His primary purpose, which he achieves admirably, is to show something of the NEP life style by filling his canvas with a variety of characters whom he sees as representative of the new NEP bourgeoisie. Given this emphasis on the mores of a very specific social milieu, *The Sweet Soufflé* ought not to be considered so much a comedy of intrigue in the tradition of Gogol's *Revizor* (*The Inspector-General*, 1835) or the "well-made" *Svadba Krechinskogo* (*The Wedding of Krechinsky*, 1854), the first part of the *Trilogy* of Aleksandr Sukhovo-Kobylin, but a comedy of manners.

The Sweet Soufflé often seems like a comedy of intrigue because of the brisk pace Romashov achieves by subdividing his five acts into fifteen scenes and then further dividing the scenes into smaller units on the basis of entrances and exits. These tertiary units are brief and tend to give the play as a whole a rapid tempo; this tempo suggests action often where there is little or none and conveys—and this was doubtless Romashov's intention—the rhythm of life itself during NEP. The many comings and goings and the frequent changes of place also serve another purpose: they enable the dramatist to introduce a variety of characters and settings and thereby construct something of a panorama of NEP society. Thus, the familiar episodic structure of the romantic-heroic plays of the 1920s and the lively tempo of farce are made to work in behalf of a comedy of manners.

Apart from the speculators and swindlers, the most interesting group of characters brought before the audience in The Sweet Soufflé comes from the contemporary world of arts and letters. In several scenes featuring the actress Rita Kern, Romashov introduces friends of hers—Oppel (a ballet master), Gudzonov (an actor), Yasha Mindal (a pianist), Strumiliyan (a theatrical hair stylist), Fitilev (a stage producer's assistant), and Miron Zont (the editor of the theater journal Red Curtains)— who represent both another dimension of NEP society and a commentary, as it were, on the relations between NEP and art. The outspoken, casual, and hedonistic behavior of the artists reflects the more relaxed moral standards of NEP, while their dependence for the funding of a new theater on NEP-men such as Koromyslov and Rak reflects instead the prostitution of the arts by money in a private enterprise economy (something Olesha deals with in A List of Assets).

The outcome of the multifarious financial machinations in The Sweet Soufflé evokes little surprise. Rak, Koromyslov, and the rest of their breed, as negative social elements, must be exposed and then punished. The affair with the bank automobile, Koromyslov's nepotism (his brother, Fyodor, is also on the board of trustees of TIK), and his firing of less "cooperative" bank employees arouse suspicion and lead to the revelation of the crooked connections between Koromyslov's bank and Rak's TIK and ARPA organizations. When it becomes apparent that his position is in jeopardy, it is suggested to Rak that he flee abroad. Ever the optimist, sure that his cunning and skill at maneuvering will yet triumph, Rak refuses and goes ahead planning the banquet for which the great soufflé was ordered at the beginning of the play. But no sooner does the banquet get under way and the huge pyramid-shaped soufflé is brought in, than a group of Red Army men headed by a member of the security police enters to arrest all those present. To add insult to injury, it is also revealed that the greatest swindler of all is—no, not Rak, or Obrydlov, or Koromyslov, or Kizyakovsky, or Morzhinsky (two other speculators who appear in the play)—but the American, Mister Puls. The companies he claims to represent are discovered to be nonexistent (for all his shrewdness Rak never took it into his head to check the American's credentials) and when he slips out of Russia he takes with him a sizable sum of money fleeced from his Russian "business associates." It is almost as though Romashov is saying that when it comes to the financial skullduggery of capitalism even the shrewdest NEP-men are babes-in-the-woods compared to Americans.

The ending of *The Sweet Soufflé* is worth a closer look for what it tells us about Romashov's literary orientation. The banquet has just started, an orchestra is playing, the monumental soufflé is mounted on a pedestal, illuminated and the center of attraction as all of Rak's guests crowd around it. Then in come the security agent and the Red Army soldiers. The last words of the play are spoken by the agent who tells Rak and his guests that they are all under arrest. A stage direction follows calling for a "dumb scene" (that is, pantomime) before the final curtain.

The inspiration for this dumb scene (*nemaya kartina,* in Russian) was most probably the ending of Gogol's *The Inspector-General.* In the Gogol play, the Mayor and his flunkies are all assembled as they pass around the intercepted letter of Khlestakov to his friend in St. Petersburg in which he ridicules the townspeople whom he left not long ago and gleefully describes how he pulled the wool over their eyes. Barely do they finish making their way through the letter when a messenger enters to announce that the inspector-general (the real one from St. Petersburg) has arrived. Gogol's stage directions then call for a dumb scene in which the actors onstage freeze in grotesque positions conveying amazement and fright, which they are to maintain for a minute and a half. Rak's banquet and the soufflé motif, with its several metaphoric connotations in the context of the play, have no parallels in *The Inspector-General,* but the similarity of ending and, above all, the dumb scene (though Romashov specifies no time length) are too similar to Gogol to be only coincidental. Moreover, if *The Sweet Soufflé* and *The Inspector-General* are more closely compared, other parallels can be found despite the many dissimilarities between the two comedies. In very broad terms, the central situation of the comedies is similar: a conniver who is assumed to be something he is not is welcomed by a group of corrupt people whom he eventually succeeds in fleecing. The mistaken identity involving Khlestakov and his swindle of the townspeople are of paramount importance in the development of *the Inspector-General;* Mister Puls' fraud, in *The Sweet Soufflé,* is not. Furthermore, it is circumstance that makes a swindler of Khlestakov; Mister Puls comes to Russia as one already for the express purpose of making a killing during the restoration of a partial free enterprise system there. Given these essential differences, both Khlestakov and Puls ultimately misrepresent themselves and take advantage of the gullibility and naïveté of the people who welcome them in order to cheat them. Also, those cheated are themselves anything but savory and here Romashov completely follows the pattern of *The Inspector-General.* In Gogol's comedy, the townspeople, headed by the Mayor, are all corrupt in one way or another (which is why, of course, they fear the arrival of a government inspector from St. Petersburg). In Romashov's play, who is cheated? A group of NPE "wheeler-dealers," speculators, and connivers headed by Rak.

The absurdity of Gogolian humor and the Gogolian conception of comic characters as grotesque caricatures also left their mark on Romashov's comedy. Since this goes to the heart of the comic laughter of *The Sweet Soufflé,* it was by far the major area of Gogolian influence. There is no better place to observe this than in the characterization of Semyon Rak himself. *The Sweet Soufflé* has several first-rate comic portraits but none more effective and consistently entertaining than that of Rak.

As a speculator and financial manipulator, Rak is expectedly bustling, brash, crafty, and conniving. The frenetic pace he maintains throughout the entire play is established at the very outset when he flies (Romashov uses the verb *vletaet,* which means just that) into a confectionary, briefcase in hand, hurls himself into the first chair he stumbles across, heaves a sigh of exhaustion, calls for sugar, bangs his cane, and yells for pistachio ice cream. When the waitress answers "right away," he says, "Time's money." Rak's comic portrait is rounded by the addition of traits and tastes associated with the petty bourgeois. As Romashov sketches them, they are often as absurd as they are grotesque. When the cashier of the confectionary at the beginning of the play laughs at one point, Rak looks into her mouth and says:

Where'd you pick up those teeth of yours, madame? Blue porcelain. Call on my relative—Third Bourgeois forty-five, second floor from the courtyard—he works as a mechanic in a dental laboratory. You can't imagine what a set you've got there! Take mine, for example (shows her his teeth)—milk. Pearls! And you can remove them as easily as a pair of pince-nez. (Makes a movement.) I can take them out and show them to you.[1]

The deeper Rak goes with his schemes the more grandiose they become and the more inflated his image of himself (resembling in this respect Khlestakov at the height of his masquerade). This is dazzlingly in evidence in the range he envisions of ARPA's operations, his plans for the banquet, the stupendous soufflé he orders, and the observations he makes about himself to his wife in Act IV, scene 14, episode 2. This is one of the most hilarious moments of the comedy; the part of the dialogue between Rak and his wife Raisa (Raya) which follows exemplifies the Gogolian nature of Romashov's comic characterization:

RAK: . . . Semyon Rak will enter history, Raya, that I'm telling you. I can already feel how I'm entering history . . .

RAISA: What are you going to do now?

RAK: My head's splitting from projects! What dreams come into my head! As if I were born a poet. (Grinning.) But what attracts me most of all is the creation of a soufflé.

RAISA: Of what soufflé?

RAK: That's the inventor's secret! You'll see for yourself on Sunday. In that soufflé there'll be the ideal of our work. In that soufflé there'll be our future, as we can conceive of it now. I myself thought up the project. Semyon Rak gets ideas of genius. Splendid, damn it all!

RAISA: Doesn't your head ache, Semyon? Go to sleep. The way you're going, you can completely lose your mind.

RAK: Isn't my head on my shoulders? Sometimes it seems to me that it's an electric power station with a thousand currents leading to the four corners of the globe. "Semyon Rak!"—they call from America, and I answer what I have to. "Semyon Rak!"—they summon from Japan, and I give advice. In a word, the Eiffel Tower!

RAISA: Get undressed, Semyon; your projects are beginning to make me sick.

RAK: Drink a little soda, Venus. (*Takes off his jacket and waistcoat.*) Some kind of a special expression has even come to appear in my face. I've just made up my mind to take pictures of myself every day.

RAISA: And what are you going to do with so many pictures, may I ask?

RAK: We can put them up all over the apartment.

RAISA: You've gone out of your mind, Semyon!

RAK (*looking at himself in the mirror*): When a person creates, his whole figure changes. I never had such a slender waist before. And these hands? Isn't it true, Raya, that there's something bold about my bearing?

RAISA: Idiot!

RAK: Of course, you won't admit it. But Rita Leonova [Rita Kern] noticed it. At the rehearsal yesterday she said to me: "You have the face of Prometheus." Raya, do you know who Prometheus was?

RAISA: All I know is that if you don't go to bed this instant . . .

RAK: Why get mad? You're my Venus, my goddess . . .

RAISA: Do goddesses really come so fat?

RAK: Sometimes they do. But I am—Prometheus. A man feels strength in himself only when he has thoughts. (pp. 152–53)

Romashov wrote more than a half dozen plays after *The Sweet Soufflé* one of which—the satirical melodrama *Konets Krivorylska* (*The End of Krivorylsk*, 1925–26)—also deals with speculation and "retrogressive" elements in the new Soviet society, but never again did he find quite the combination of vivacity, absurdity, and grotesqueness that make *The Sweet Soufflé* one of the brighter moments in the history of postrevolutionary Russian comedy.

Another interesting example of how NEP social conditions were transmogrified into absurd and grotesque comedy is Bulgakov's *Zoykina kvartira* (*Zoya's Apartment*, 1926; substantially revised, 1935). Focusing on the same housing shortage used by Kataev as the basis of the plot of *Squaring the Circle*, Bulgakov's play, however, is a more typical NEP satire, more closely related in spirit and style to *The Sweet Soufflé* than to *Squaring the Circle*.

When *Zoya's Apartment* premiered at the Vakhtangov Theater in Moscow on October 28, 1926, just three weeks after the opening of the controversial *Days of the Turbins*, it immediately received a divided response—enthusiasm from the public and hostility from the critics. The primary objection leveled at the play concerned its risqué content, though this feature was one it shared with many other NEP literary works. Furthermore, the critics pointed out that no positive or redeeming characters appear among the hustlers, hookers, and dope addicts who crowd Zoya's apartment. Because of mounting pressure the production was temporarily banned following the première and several revised performances. But the comedy soon returned to the stage and toured other Russian cities before it was subjected to a final ban, as was also imposed on *Days of the Turbins*, in early 1929.

Although no one character in *Zoya's Apartment* stands out with the sharp prominence of Romashov's Rak, interest eventually centers on Aleksandr Ametistov, Bulgakov's contribution to the gallery of NEP entrepreneurs. Ametistov is an old friend of Zoya who introduces himself around as her cousin upon arriving in Moscow from Baku. It is revealed that his past has included all sorts of shady adventures in which he engaged after receiving amnesty as a political prisoner. With no place to stay, he invites himself into Zoya's apartment, which with six rooms is extraordinarily large for the time. Zoya has managed to hold onto her spacious apartment only by giving in to such subterfuges as graft and blackmail. Her latest ploy is a fake certificate attesting that she is using her apartment to operate a demonstration sewing shop and school which produces work clothes for the wives of workers and civil servants.

As the second act opens, it readily becomes apparent that there is more to the enterprise than first meets the eye. When one of Zoya's customers, Alla Vadimovna, pleads that she is unable to repay a loan, Zoya offers Alla a chance to work off her debt by becoming a mannequin in the shop. The employment arrangements are indeed curious. Besides canceling out her debt, Zoya also agrees to pay Alla the astronomical salary of 1,000 rubles a month, for work in which she will be engaged only in the evenings, every other day. By this point, the true nature of the enterprise is obvious; the sewing shop by day is a bordello by night, with the girls doubling as mannequins and whores.

When the scene with Alla ends and Zoya and Ametistov come together onstage, the conversation between the two makes it clear that the idea for extending the activities of the sewing shop and school in a more profitable direction originated with Ametistov. His scheme for making money may be less grandiose than that of Rak and of other NEP wheeler-dealers, but its shadiness and boldness are rooted in the same ethos.

As usual in plays dealing with NEP characters of low morality, success is short-lived. Toward the end of Act III, two strangers arrive, dressed in civilian clothes and carrying briefcases. They announce that they are officials who have been sent to inspect the workshop. The second stranger mysteriously produces a key which opens a wardrobe wherein he discovers one of the play's two Chinese characters supplying Zoya's useless husband, Obolyaninov, with narcotics. It takes little imagination at this point to guess that the strangers are members of the secret police.

Before its final resolution the comedy undergoes a sudden and significant change of pace. Through the first three acts, the mode is wholly that of an NEP satire. But midway through Act IV, the action clearly

A scene from the production of Mikhail Bulgakov's Zoya's Apartment
by the Vakhtangov Theater, Moscow, in 1927.
(H. W. L. DANA COLLECTION OF THE HARVARD THEATRE COLLECTION)

shifts into melodrama. Seeking respite from his troubled romance with Alla, a character named Goose joins other admirers at one of Zoya's after-hour "fashion shows." Not knowing that Alla has become one of the mannequins, Goose is horrified to see her in the show's lineup. A raucous scene ensues, after which Alla is rushed from the apartment. The grieving Goose is soon joined by the Chinese dope peddler Cherubim, who also bemoans his unhappy romance with Zoya's maid, Manyushka. At one point, Goose carelessly displays a large handful of money. With little ado, Cherubim stabs Goose to death, believing that with his money he will be able to persuade Manyushka to go away with him to Shanghai. Though shortly thereafter Ametistov discovers the corpse, with the finely hewn instinct of a professional con man, he makes a hasty retreat from the premises just before the two strangers return with two other men and with warrants. Zoya, Obolyaninov, and Portupeya, the representative of the House Committee, are all arrested. Only Ametistov, like Gogol's Khlestakov and Sukhovo-Kobylin's Krechinsky and Varravin long before him, eludes arrest.

At the very end of the play, in the dialogue between Obolyaninov and the strangers, Bulgakov restores the play's earlier mood of NEP comic absurdity, parenthesizing the preceding melodramatic outburst. Obolyaninov asks the second stranger why he and the first stranger are wearing tuxedos. The stranger replies, "We intended to come to your place as guests." Obolyaninov answers, "Excuse me please, but one must never wear yellow shoes with a tuxedo." In the last line of the play, the second stranger turns to the first and says, "Didn't I tell you so?!"[2]

Given the subject matter of NEP satire and the common figure of the shady NEP-man, the intrusion of melodrama in such a grotesque comedy should not be considered unusual. There is also in this inclusion a reflection of the prominence in early Soviet dramatic theory of intrigue, suspense, and "strong effects." During the 1920s, based on these devices, a distinct subgenre of Soviet satiric melodrama came into existence. Ellendea Proffer points out in her introduction to the English translation of Zoya's Apartment (p. 99) that this subgenre of satiric melodrama or melodramatic satire sprang from specific conditions present during the NEP period. Romashov's The End of Krivorylsk (1926) is usually credited as the first of the species, although a few earlier comedies such as Romashov's The Sweet Soufflé (1924–25) and Nikolai Erdman's Mandat (The Warrant, 1925) include enough melodramatic elements to justify their being considered within the same general framework. The difference, however, is that in the Romashov and Erdman plays the melodramatic intrigue is secondary to the main thrust of the comedy. The murder of Goose in Zoya's Apartment introduces a sinister element into the plot, but the play would have been a successful NEP farce without it. On the other hand, a work such as Aleksei Faiko's Evgraf, iskatel priklyucheniy (Yevgraf, Seeker of Adventures, 1926), which also includes a stabbing, is so heavily melodramatic and minimally comic in character that it has more in common with such "pure" Soviet melodramas of the 1920s as Faiko's Chelovek s portfelem (The Man with a Briefcase, 1929) than with the Romashov, Erdman, or Bulgakov plays.

Zoya's Apartment not only admixes absurd, grotesque, satirical, farcical, and melodramatic elements, but it also uses devices drawn from the tradition of vaudeville. It can be related in this respect to The Sweet Soufflé and other similar works, including comedies by Mayakovsky. Songs and dances appear frequently in these plays and action often culminates in a celebration, faintly derivative of the wedding party in Chekhov's one-act comedy Svadba (The Wedding). There is an important banquet in Romashov's The Sweet Soufflé, and in Faiko's Yevgraf there is a scene set in a pub, with music, a floor show, dancing, and drinking, much like the entertainment we find in the last act of Zoya's Apartment. The NEP phase of Prisypkin's life in Mayakovsky's The Bed-

bug (1928) also will close with a rowdy party, this time given to celebrate a wedding as in the Chekhov farce.

As a NEP satirical comedy woven together of farce, melodrama, and vaudeville, *Zoya's Apartment* breaks no new ground. It is neither as absurdly humorous as the comedies of Romashov, Erdman, or Mayakovsky nor as serious and melodramatic as some of Faiko's plays. It also develops no intriguing NEP type; Bulgakov's Ametistov is not nearly as splendidly entertaining as Romashov's Rak or Mayakovsky's Prisypkin. The melodramatic element of *Zoya's Apartment* pivots primarily on the murder of Goose and this act of violence comes as a surprising and even discordant note in the play. And yet *Zoya's Apartment* is interesting. Bulgakov was an able dramatist and he managed in *Zoya's Apartment* to compose a reasonably effective satire, avoiding the large dramatis personae, complicated plot structures, and dizzying scene changes so characteristic of many NEP comedies. The play moves along briskly and entertains. But perhaps what comes through most strikingly in *Zoya's Apartment*, when compared to other NEP comedies, is Bulgakov's success in picturing so well the amorality, decadence, and *carpe diem* philosophy of NEP. Although NEP satirical comedies are crowded with get-rich-quick schemes of every hue and shade, *Zoya's Apartment* carries the corruption further, bringing together a heady combination of financial adventurism, prostitution, narcotics, and murder, all of which find their place on a single stage setting.

The compatibility of some NEP satirical comedy and the modern concept of "black" or "dark" comedy may be judged from consideration of a play such as Nikolai Erdman's (1902–70) *Samoubiytsa* (*The Suicide*, 1928 or 1929). Erdman first attracted attention as a dramatist with *The Warrant*, which Meyerhold produced in Moscow in 1925. The work is a riotous farce about unregenerated prerevolutionary types trying to cling to their old way of life under the Soviets and the scheme, in particular, of one tsarist family to secure an "in" with the new regime by insisting that their son's prospective bourgeois bride include in her dowry at least one relative with Communist Party affiliation. Getting *The Suicide* onstage, however, was quite another matter. Although the standards of official censorship may have seemed fairly flexible during the NEP period, there were certain limits that could not be transgressed.

In *The Suicide*, the main protagonist, Semyon Podsekalnikov, looks to suicide as an act of protest against the Soviet regime. Such an idea was apparently too much for even the relaxed standards of the time. Meyerhold planned to stage the play in 1929 and managed to proceed as far as a dress rehearsal. But then the Central Committee of the Party intervened and the production was halted. When the Soviet Union entered the paroxysm of the great purges of the 1930s, Erdman, like Meyerhold and so many other artists, fell victim. He was arrested and sentenced to a twenty-year term in a labor camp. After he was finally released in 1956, at the age of fifty-four, he occupied himself mostly with film work, an interest dating back to the 1920s. He lived to see brief revivals of both *The Warrant* and *The Suicide* in the early 1960s, prior to his death in 1970.

Of the many writers who were popular in Russia during the heyday of NEP, only Babel, Bulgakov, Kataev, Mayakovsky, Zamyatin, and Zoshchenko have been sufficiently translated and written about to have achieved international reputations. Most NEP drama is still unknown outside the Soviet Union; apart from Kataev's *Squaring the Circle*, the only comedies of the 1920s that have made any notable impact abroad are those of Mayakovsky. It may be some time before Erdman's plays become as well known, but *The Warrant* and *The Suicide* do have the distinction of being the only NEP satires besides Bulgakov's, Kataev's, and Mayakovsky's to have been produced in the West. Influenced by a brief Soviet revival of Erdman's work in the early 1960s, foreign producers mounted both *The Warrant* and *The Suicide*. *The Suicide* was staged in Göteborg, Sweden, in March 1969, and later in Austria, Germany, and Switzerland. In a slightly altered version, *The Warrant* was staged at the Royal Dramatic Theater in Stockholm in the fall of 1972.

The Suicide has the same absurd, grotesque, and farcical atmosphere of other NEP satirical comedies. But what distinguishes this play from those of Romashov, Faiko, Bulgakov, and Mayakovsky, is the fact that Erdman is not concerned here merely with a humorous depiction of the absurdities or decadence of NEP or with the problems of adjustment and consolidation faced by the new regime in its early years. Conceived in a darker, more profoundly grotesque spirit than perhaps any other NEP satire, *The Suicide* concentrates instead on the dissatisfaction of an ordinary Soviet citizen with the inadequacies, above all economic, of the new regime and his resolve to commit suicide as the only way out of his troubles.

Unable to make ends meet and thus mirroring in his life the economic hardships of Russia during the 1920s, Podsekalnikov contemplates how he might take his own life. The problem is that he is a coward; and even after he acquires a gun, he cannot bring himself actually to pull the trigger. The first act and a half move with a fast, farcical pace as Podsekalnikov's wife and mother-in-law try in a frenzied way to block his threats of suicide. The despair, lying just beneath the surface of this farce, is relieved at several points by certain intrusions of absurd humor. For example, when Podsekalnikov's wife, Maria, pounds on a neighbor's door, seeking help to get Podsekalnikov out of the bathroom where he has locked himself presumably to do himself in, the following fractured conversation ensues:

> MARIA (*knocking*): Aleksandr Petrovich . . . Comrade Kalabushkin. Comrade Kalabushkin . . .
> ALEKSANDR (*behind the door*): What is it?
> MARIA: It's me, Mrs. Podsekalnikov.
> ALEKSANDR (*behind the door*): Who?
> MARIA: Podsekalnikov, Maria Lukyanovna. Hello!
> ALEKSANDR (*behind the door*): What do you want?
> MARIA: I need you badly, Comrade Kalabushkin.
> ALEKSANDR (*behind the door*): What do you mean, need me?
> MARIA: As a man.
> ALEKSANDR (*behind the door*): What are you saying, Maria Lukyanovna? Shhh, not so loud. People will hear you!
> MARIA: Your mind's on other things, Comrade Kalabushkin. Just think, please, I'm all alone, completely alone. What am I to do, Comrade Kalabushkin?
> ALEKSANDR (*behind the door*): Take a cold shower, Maria Lukyanovna.[3]

Finally deciding against suicide Podsekalnikov takes up the bass tuba, with the plan of making a living by playing concerts with it. The scenes in which he attempts to learn to play the horn are among the funniest in the comedy. Despair soon returns, however, when the instruction book he is following recommends, for preliminary scale practice, a piano which he cannot afford. Again, his thoughts turn to suicide. As he is about to try to kill himself, however, he is interrupted by a character named Goloshchapov who claims to be a representative of the intelligentsia. Goloshchapov has heard of Podsekalnikov's suicide plan (from Kalabushkin, no less, who has been selling the information). Goloshchapov begs Podsekalnikov to identify himself with the intelligentsia so that his suicide may become a socially meaningful act of protest made by a member of an aggrieved but generally mute faction of society. In a black, grotesque tone, which Erdman handles so well, Goloshchapov argues: "At the present time, Comrade Podsekalnikov, only a dead man can exclaim what a live man thinks. I have come to you, therefore, as to a dead man, Comrade Podsekalnikov. I have come to you in the name of the Russian intelligentsia . . ."

Goloshchapov is then followed by representatives of other groups who have heard of Podsekalnikov's desire and who also try to persuade him to commit suicide in the name of each of their particular causes. The height of absurdity is reached when a woman enters and pleads with Podsekalnikov not to kill himself for her rival's sake, as she believes he is doing. She cries:

> To whom did you promise [to commit suicide]? Raisa Fillipovna? Oh, but why her? What were you thinking of, Mr. Podsekalnikov? If you shot yourself on account of that hag, Oleg Leonidovich would drop me. Better to shoot yourself for me. That way Oleg Leonidovich will drop her. Because Oleg Leonidovich is an aesthete but Raisa Fillipovna is nothing but a bitch in heat. I'm telling you all this as a romantic. Why, she even chews on drinking glasses out of passion. She wants him to kiss her body, and she wants to kiss his body. Just body, body, body! While I, on the contrary, want to embrace his soul. And I want him to embrace my soul, just my soul, my soul, my soul. Shoot yourself, Mr. Podsekalnikov; shoot yourself for me. Restore love! Restore romanticism!

Shortly after this, Erdman introduces, at the beginning of Act III, the now familiar motif of the banquet. Two hours before his scheduled suicide, Podsekalnikov is given a farewell celebration by his new-found friends. It is held in a summer garden restaurant and includes singing, dancing, and Gypsy music. This banquet scene gives the playwright occasion to include more absurd humor, some of it clearly bound to set Erdman at odds with the censors. One of the guests arises to toast the assembly, saying: "Esteemed gathering! We are here now to conduct Semyon Semyonovich to a better world, as it were. To a world from which people do not come back." Then another guest muses, "Abroad, no doubt!"

Drunk and imbued with a sense of importance and power, Podsekalnikov decides during the banquet to make a personal call to the Kremlin to inform the authorities of his suicide. He tells the group:

> Dear comrades, I am going to put a call through to the Kremlin right now. Straight to the red heart of the Soviet republic. I'm going to call . . . and give a real piece of my mind to somebody there. What do you say to that, eh?

The call goes through and Podsekalnikov speaks into the phone:

> Somebody there? Kremlin? Podsekalnikov speaking. Pod-se-kal-ni-kov. An individual. In-di-vi-du-al. Get hold of one of the higher-ups. Not in? In that case, tell him for me that I read Karl Marx and I didn't like him. How's that? Don't interrupt me! And tell him, furthermore, that . . . Are you listening? My God. He's hung up.

Following the banquet, Podsekalnikov is expected to kill himself and on the way home he gets drunk to strengthen his resolve. He would like to go through with the suicide but he still cannot. Somewhat later when a coffin is brought in for the "corpse" and people are on their way to pay their last respects to the deceased, he climbs into the coffin. This action recalls, though perhaps coincidentally, the coffin deception and reversal of roles of Tarelkin in *Smert Tarelkina (Tarelkin's Death)*, the third play of Sukhovo-Kobylin's *Trilogy*. *Tarelkin's Death* was given a stunning revival by Meyerhold in 1922, and this coincided with a renewed interest in absurd and grotesque satirical comedy in Russian literature and theater of the time. This revival explains, I believe, certain echoes we find in some NEP plays of Sukhovo-Kobylin's *Trilogy*.

As the guests crowd around the coffin to sing the praises of the "deceased," Podsekalnikov's wife frantically tries to tell them that he is not dead but only drunk. Believing that she has been made irrational by her grief, they ignore her while a priest proceeds with the funeral ceremony. In a wonderfully absurdist touch, Podsekalnikov himself is overcome with emotion, starts to weep, and pulls out a handkerchief to wipe away the tears. A deaf and dumb man kneeling beside the bier at the time sees him and falls into a dead faint, which the other guests attribute to his immense sorrow. The act ends as the coffin is hurriedly borne away to the cemetery.

The fifth and last act takes place in the cemetery and opens in the same vein of absurdist humor. The offering of a eulogy in verse is followed by a fracas that erupts between the two women who earlier had wanted Podsekalnikov to commit suicide for them. Now each woman insists that Podsekalnikov killed himself because he wanted her body but was denied it. When one of the mourners bestows a parting kiss on Podsekalnikov's brow, before the coffin is sealed and lowered into the ground, Podsekalnikov suddenly embraces him in return. The mourner recoils, rushes back into the crowd and pandemonium breaks loose. Finally Podsekalnikov climbs out of the coffin, asking for something to eat. Possessed of new insights because of his experience, he answers the crowd's questions by declaring that he no longer wants to die. His words poignantly sum up the point of the entire play:

> Are we really doing anything against the Revolution? From the first day of the Revolution we haven't done anything. We only visit each other and tell each other that it's hard to live. Because it's easier to live if we say that it's hard to live. For heaven's sake, don't deprive us of the last means of existence; permit us to say that it's hard for us to live. Even if we just whisper that it's hard to live.

Although the crowd is upset and voices are raised demanding the death of Podsekalnikov, no one steps forward to do anything. In a final grotesque twist, a character runs in to announce that a Fedya Petunin has just killed himself with a gun, leaving behind a note which declares that Podsekalnikov was right, that life is not really worth living! For all the play's absurd humor, it betrays an underlying bitterness toward the severe hardships of Russian life during the NEP period. This grimness is made even more touching by the surrounding grotesqueness, brought to full flower with the play's ending. No wonder that the anguished protest sounded by *The Suicide* should lead to the ultimate suppression of the play and to the later harassment of its author.

Comedies such as those by Romashov, Bulgakov, and Erdman, and other more or less typical NEP satires on the NEP-man phenomenon by Aleksandr Popovsky (*Tovarishch Tsatkin i Ko* [*Comrade Tsatkin and Co.*], 1926) and by Vasili Shkvarkin (*Vredny element* [*A Harmful Element*], 1927; and *Shuler* [*The Cardsharp*], 1929) provide an appropriate frame in which to examine Mayakovsky's major contributions to the drama after *Vladimir Mayakovsky* and *Mystery-Bouffe*—the comedies *The Bedbug* (1928) and *The Bathhouse* (1929), both of which were written within two years of his suicide.

To the absurdity and grotesqueness of such a representative NEP comedy as *The Sweet Soufflé*, Mayakovsky brings still another component—fantasy, or, more precisely, scientific fantasy. *The Bedbug*, in fact, is subtitled "A Fantastic Comedy in Nine Scenes" (there is no division into acts). The fantasy begins with the fifth scene; until then, in a little less than half the work, the play is a satirical comedy of manners spiced by elements of the absurd and grotesque.

As the play opens to the cacophonous cries of typical NEP peddlers hawking everything from herring to fur-lined bras, interest rapidly centers on the comic hero of *The Bedbug*, Ivan Prisypkin, whom the dramatis personae identify as a former worker and Party member but now a fiancé. Although he piously mouths Party platitudes and sneers at anything to do with the petty bourgeoisie, it is obvious that Prisypkin himself has picked up something of the hedonism of NEP and its new bourgeois tastes. Grotesquely vulgar and ignorant (he buys a fur-lined bra in the belief that it is an aristocratic bonnet for the future twins he may have), Prisypkin decides to live in a style appropriate to the exaggerated sense he has of his position in Soviet society. As he sets out to "better himself," what he is doing, in effect, is acquiring the same petty bourgeois attitudes and tastes he deprecates. Because his own name seems too common, he prefers what he considers the more aristocratic Frenchified form, Pierre Skripkin; under the tutelage of the real estate owner Oleg Bayan (the name assumed by another "socially advanced" worker named Bochkin) he takes instruction in the social graces; and he drops his old girl friend, Zoya Beryozkina, a worker, in favor of his new fiancée, a beauty parlor manicurist named Elzevira Renaissance. The nuptials between Prisypkin and Elzevira are a hilarious exercise in absurdity, again somewhat reminiscent of the antic humor in Chekhov's *The Wedding*. The tone is set by Bayan:

> We have succeeded in harmonizing and coordinating the class contradictions and other conflicts between the bride and groom. And he who is armed with the Marxist view cannot fail to see in this fact, as in a drop of water, so to speak, the future happiness of mankind—that which the common people call socialism . . . When we were groaning under the yoke of autocracy, could even our great teachers, Marx and Engels, have conjecturally dreamed—or even dreamily conjectured—that someday we would join together by the bonds of Hymen these two: Labor, humble but great; and Capital, dethroned yet still enchanting.[4]

The wedding celebration dissolves into chaos; a stove is overturned, the house catches fire and collapses, burying all the celebrants.

With the fifth scene, Mayakovsky moves the comedy onto the level of science-fiction fantasy. The time is fifty years later and the Institute of Human Resurrection learns that a human being was found frozen in an ice-filled cellar on the site of the former city of Tambov. It is, of course, Prisypkin, the only survivor, of sorts, of the fire. The decision is taken to resurrect him and the experiment succeeds.

The "resurrection" of Prisypkin, apart from the intrinsic humor of the situation, directly relates to Mayakovsky's satirical intentions in the play. The society in which Prisypkin is brought back to life is remarkably advanced technologically. It is automated and dehumanized; the emotional responses of earlier days are nonexistent—no more than terms of historical significance. It is, in effect, Mayakovsky's projection of a future machine-dominated Soviet society bereft of any trace of human compassion. In the broader context, it is the anxiety-ridden vision of European expressionism which beholds a future in which man, wholly subordinate to the machine, is reduced to the level of an unfeeling automaton. The dread this vision inspires pervades the literature of expressionism and a play such as *The Bedbug* shares the apprehension. Even considering the absurd and grotesque satire typical of NEP comedy and the play's topical aspect—the dehumanization of society brought on not only by technological advance but also by the rapid growth of a monstrous and impersonal Soviet bureaucracy—Mayakovsky's comedy can be related to such representative Expressionist dramas as the Czech Karel Čapek's once very popular *R.U.R.* (*Rossum's Universal Robots*, 1921), which gave the world the term *robot*, and the German Georg Kaiser's no less famous "Gas" trilogy: *Die Koralle* (*The Coral*), *Gas I*, and *Gas II* (1916–19).

The evolution of Mayakovsky's outlook is interesting to consider at this point. In his early poetry and in his first major dramatic work, *Mystery-Bouffe,* he shared the ideas as well as the stylistic techniques of European futurism. The Futurists welcomed the advances of technology. They measured human progress in technical terms and saw the machine, about which they rhapsodized, as man's liberator and savior. The celebration of the machine with which *Mystery-Bouffe* comes to a joyous conclusion is a typical Futurist response.

But the Mayakovsky of a decade later had different ideas and these found expression in both *The Bedbug* and *The Bathhouse*. So dehumanized does man become in consequence of the advance of the machine and the machinelike bureaucracy that by contrast even a coarse vulgarian like Prisypkin seems attractive. This is the point Mayakovsky makes with the strange events that follow Prisypkin's "resurrection." Prisypkin's zest for life becomes infectious and is regarded as a dangerous malady. Worse than anything, however, is the gradual reawakening of love, long thought totally eradicated in the new society, brought on by the plaintive songs out of the past that Prisypkin sings to his own guitar accompaniment. A reporter describes the effect this has had on one girl:

> The poor thing! She lives next door to that demented mammal [Prisypkin]. At night, while the city slept, she would hear through the wall the twanging of his guitar, followed by long, heart-rending sighs

A scene from the original production of Vladimir Mayakovsky's The Bedbug
by Meyerhold's Theater, Moscow, in 1929.

and a kind of sing-song sobbing. What was it they used to call such things—"love laments," wasn't it? The more she heard, the worse things got, and the poor girl began to lose her mind. Her parents were terribly upset. They called in some medical experts for a consultation. The professors said it was an acute attack of "love"—the name given to a disease of ancient times when sexual energy, which should be rationally distributed over one's entire lifetime, is suddenly concentrated into one inflammation lasting a week, leading to absurd and incredible behavior. *(p. 181)*

The bedbug motif from which the play derives its title operates in a twofold way. The ultrahygienic society of the future, of course, is insect-free, so when a bedbug appears "resurrected" along with Prisypkin it has to be kept in a special glass exhibition cage in a zoo. On one hand, it cannot be allowed to wander about freely lest it spread contagion, while on the other, as a curious natural relic of the past it is worth preserving for public exhibit. The director of the zoo seizes on the idea of advertising for a human being willing to be caged with the bedbug so that it can feed on him and remain alive. Since Prisypkin's presence in the new society is becoming less tolerable with every passing day, the director's hope is that he will come forward and agree to be caged with the bedbug. This is precisely what happens. Prisypkin is not at all unhappy about the situation because in the exhibition cage he is at least able to drink as he pleases and to sing and play the guitar to his heart's content. By remaining in the cage, even though the bedbug feeds on him and his movements are restricted, he has some awareness of himself as a human being. And perhaps even the bedbug crawling on him is not wholly unpleasant, for this too remains a link with a more human past.

By having Prisypkin *prefer* to live in the zoo with the bedbug rather than remain abroad in the new society, Mayakovsky carries his indictment of his projected anti-utopian world to its logical extreme. In terms of his "human-ness," Prisypkin's decision in favor of cohabitation with a bedbug in a cage in preference to the dehumanized conditions he finds all around him in the new world of tomorrow is natural. But as Mayakovsky extends the bedbug motif it becomes apparent that the automated society of the future is not the only target of his satire. However attractive Prisypkin becomes by contrast with the society of the future into which he is resurrected, he remains the same vulgarian, the same travesty of a NEP social climber he was before, and once the satire of the "new world" is unequivocally established Mayakovsky returns to the satire of everything formerly represented by Prisypkin. This intention is clear enough in the long monologue of the zoo director near the end of the play:

> There are two parasites, differing in size but the same in essence: the famous *Bedbugus normalis*—and the *Philistinius vulgaris*. Both have their habitat in the moldy mattresses of time. *Bedbugus normalis*, when it has guzzled and gorged on the body of a single human being, falls under the bed. *Philistinius vulgaris*, when it has guzzled and gorged on the body of all mankind, falls on top of the bed. That's the only difference!
>
> When the toiling humanity of the Revolution was writhing and scratching itself, scraping away the filth, these parasites built their nest and homes in that same filth, beat their wives, swore by false gods, and took their blissful ease in the shady tents of their own riding breeches. But of the two types, *Philistinius vulgaris* is the more fright-

ful. He lured his victims with monstrous mimetic powers, sometimes in the guise of a chirruping rhymester, sometimes as crooning song-bird. In those days even their clothes were mimetic: in their wing ties, swallow-tailed coats, and starched white breasts, they looked just like birds. These birds built nests in box seats at the theaters; perched on oaks at the opera; rubbed their legs together in the ballet to the strains of the "Internationale"; hung head down from the twigs of their verses; made Tolstoy look like Marx; complained and shrieked in disgustingly large flocks; and—please forgive the expression, but this lecture is scientific—excreted in quantities which could not be considered mere small bird droppings. (*pp. 1931–94*)

The mingling of satire, absurd and grotesque humor, and fantasy reappears in *The Bathhouse*, which we examined earlier in terms of theatricalism. But compared to *The Bedbug, The Bathhouse* is less ambivalent in its satire. The target here is the new Soviet bureaucracy. It is embodied, above all, in the figures of Comrade Pobedonosikov, the head of the government Bureau of Coordination, and his administrative secretary Comrade Optimistenko (Optimistic). With Pobedonosikov and Optimistenko bureaucracy has become so much a thing unto itself that its original reason for being is not even a dim memory. The demonstration of this comes in the confrontation between these representatives of the grotesquely self-serving and self-glorifying bureaucracy and the inventor Chudakov. Satirical intent and the reflection of contemporary scientific interest merge in the invention for which Chudakov tries desperately to get government support. It is a time machine which enables a person to go forward or backward in time and to make any segment of time as long or as short as he desires.

The universal interest in Einstein and the theory of relativity is mirrored in many works of European literature in Mayakovsky's time—either in thematic material or in structural experimentation—and *The Bathhouse* is one Soviet example of this interest. Relativity and Einstein are both mentioned, in fact, in *The Bathhouse,* as is H. G. Wells whose writings (for example, *The Time Machine*) were also popular at the time and familiar to Mayakovsky.

Chudakov shares the secret of his invention with his friend Velosipedkin, who immediately sees the wonderful use to which it can be put:

This means that . . . well, let's suppose there's an All-Union Congress on the Problem of How to Hush Up All Problems Raised. And, furthermore, that the welcoming speech on behalf of the National Academy of Scientific Arts is to be given, naturally, by National

Comrade Kogan. As soon as he begins with: "Comrades, through the tentacles of world imperialism there runs, like a red thread, a wave of . . ." I'll switch him off from the presidium and cut in time at a speed of a hundred and fifty minutes per quarter-hour. He'll go sweating and welcoming, welcoming and sweating, for an hour and a half. But with the audience it'll be different. One minute they'll see the academician just opening his mouth, and the next they'll hear deafening applause. Then they'll heave a sigh of relief, hoist their fresh, unwearied behinds up from their seats, and get back to work—right? (*p. 201*)

The ambivalence of the satire in *The Bedbug* and the difficulty of reading into the work a clear chastisement of any specific aspect of the Soviet regime spared Mayakovsky the stern rebuke of censors. Prisypkin, after all, is satirized as much if not more than the projected future society. Moreover, the characterization of this society, of the new world of 1978, is very general. Therefore, critics and Party literary overseers could interpret the play any way they saw fit or simply dismiss interpretation as gratuitous on the grounds that the comedy was just an absurd fantasy, a bit of dramatic buffoonery and not much more. With *The Bathhouse*, the casual dismissal of topical relevance was much harder and Mayakovsky quickly found himself in trouble over the work. What further harassment he might have been made to endure had he continued in the same satirical vein we can only guess, however; his suicide not long after the completion of *The Bathhouse* makes the matter one of conjecture. The satirical topicality of passages like the above-quoted monologue of Velosipedkin raises no doubts as to intent or direction. The more so since it is also what the Russians call *na litso*, directed against a specific person. The Kogan referred to was the president of the Soviet National Academy of Artistic Sciences, and a man with whom Mayakovsky had crossed swords.

Together with his friend Velosipedkin, Chudakov tries desperately to get official government approval of and support for his time machine. But Pobedonosikov and Optimistenko are so wrapped up in themselves, so busy being bureaucrats, that they have no time for the very people whose interests they are supposed to be serving. Chudakov gets nowhere and Mayakovsky again makes Velosipedkin his instrument for a withering assault on just such (presumably) too typical officials as Pobedonosikov and Optimistenko:

Don't worry, I'll take care of everything. I'll gnaw through people's throats and swallow their Adam's apples! I won't just break eggs—I'll break heads! I've been trying to convince that character Optimistenko. I've roared at him. He's as smooth and polished as a ball bearing. His shiny surface reflects nothing but the boss—and upside down, at that. As for that bookkeeper, Nochkin, I've just about got him debureaucratized. But what can we possibly do with that bastard Pobedonosikov? He simply flattens all opposition with his seniority and his distinguished service record. Do you know his personal history? On the questionnaires, in the place where they ask: "What did you do before 1917?" he always puts: "I was in the Party." But nobody knows *which* party. Nobody knows whether it was the Bolsheviks or the Mensheviks, or maybe neither one nor the other. And there's something else. He escaped from prison by throwing tobacco in the guard's eyes. But today, twenty-five years later, time itself has filled his own eyes with the loose tobacco of petty details and minutes, and they are watering with smugness and joviality. With eyes like that, what can he possibly see? Socialism? Not at all! Only his inkwell and his paperweight. (*p. 208*)

Mayakovsky's gift for absurd and grotesque satire shines no less brilliantly in dialogue than in situation, as we could observe earlier in the discussion of *The Bedbug*. The following exchanges between Velosipedkin and Optimistenko handsomely exemplify the material out of which Mayakovsky's comic dialogue is woven. Citing the uses to which Chudakov's time machine can be put, Velosipedkin declares:

For that matter, it can even be coordinated with the Commissariat of Transportation. For example, you get into your seat at three o'clock in the morning, and by five o'clock you're already in Leningrad. (*pp. 216–17*)

Unconvinced, Optimistenko replies:

See? What did I tell you? Proposal rejected—it's not practical. What's the use of being in Leningrad at five in the morning? There's not a single government agency open at that hour. (*p. 217*)

The second exchange, which occurs not much later, is between Pobedonosikov and the artist Belvedonsky, who is doing his portrait:

POBEDONOSIKOV: But . . . if the portrait is necessary for completeness of the historical record, and if it won't interrupt my work, I'll be glad to oblige. I'll sit right here behind my desk. But I want you to paint me retrospectively, as if I were on horseback.

BELVEDONSKY: I've already sketched your horse at my studio, from memory, taking my inspiration from the race tracks. Also, believe it or not, to get certain details right I looked at myself in the mirror. All I have to do now is put you and the horse together. . . . Ah, what modesty in a man who has performed such distinguished services. Now if you'll just straighten out the line of your heroic leg a little . . . How that polished boot does shine! Yes, only in the work of Michelangelo does one find such a clean line! Do you know Michelangelo?

POBEDONOSIKOV: Angelov? An Armenian?

BELVEDONSKY: No, Italian.

POBEDONSIKOV: A Fascist?

BELVEDONSKY: Really, now!

POBEDONSIKOV: I don't know him.

BELVEDONSKY: You don't?

POBEDONSIKOV: Does he know me?

BELVEDONSKY: I don't know . . . He's an artist, too.

POBEDONOSIKOV: Ah! Well, he probably knows me. After all, there's lots of artists, but only one Fedburoco [the government bureau Pobedonosikov heads]. (*pp. 219–20*)

Future time, which Mayakovsky makes the springboard of fantasy in *The Bedbug*, recurs prominently in *The Bathhouse* as well; but not exactly in the same way. In *The Bedbug*, roughly the second half of the play is set in Mayakovsky's future society. In *The Bathhouse*, a visitor from the future (the Phosphorescent Woman) appears by means of Chudakov's time machine. She states her intention of taking into the year 2030 some of the best specimens of the new Soviet society for which she has such high regard. Pobedonosikov and Optimistenko, of course, rush to take their places at the head of those journeying into the future. The rest of the passengers are selected and they all file toward the time machine singing a typically Mayakovskyian Red march. Just before take-off Pobedonosikov is in his glory. Taking credit for his "patronage" of Chudakov's intention, he delivers a farewell speech that demonstrates Mayakovsky's gift for the absurd at its best:

And so, comrades, we are living through an age when, in my administrative apparatus, an apparatus of time has been invented. This apparatus of liberated time was invented in my apparatus, and nowhere else, because in my apparatus there was as much free time as you could want. The present, current moment is characterized by the fact that it is a stationary moment. And since, in a stationary moment, we do no know where the beginning ends and where the end begins, at the beginning I shall say a few concluding words, and then a few beginning ones.

A fine apparatus,
One I'm glad to see!
We're so glad—both me
And my apparatus!

We are glad because, once we go on vacation once a year, and don't
let the year move ahead, we can go on vacation two years out of every
year. And, on the other hand, whereas now we get paid once a
month, once we make a month go by in one day we can get paid every
day of the month. And so, comrades— (*p. 261*)

But before he can continue, Chudakov uses the time machine to make
him inaudible; the same happens to Optimistenko. When the machine
finally begins its trip into the future with a great explosion, Pobedonosikov, Optimistenko, and others are sent sprawling to the ground. The
message is clear: in the millennial socialist society of the far distant future there is no place for the Pobedonosikovs, Optimistenkos, and their
like. Even Pobedonosikov has a glimmering that perhaps this is the case
and asks, his words bringing the comedy to an end: "What have you
been trying to say here? That people like me aren't of any use to communism?" (p. 264).

══════ Melodrama ══════

The antics of a striking variety of rogues, swindlers, and new Soviet
bourgeois social climbers during NEP gave rise to a vibrant comic drama
dominated by elements of the absurd and grotesque. To such playwrights as Romashov, Bulgakov, Erdman, Mayakovsky, Popovsky, and
Shkvarkin the phenomena represented by the Raks, Ametistovs, and
Prisypkins of NEP society were more ludicrous than dangerous and
hence more effectively realized in the theater by means of satirical comedy and the perspectives of the absurd and grotesque. But concern
about the rise of as yet "unassimilated" social elements of a far more
sinister sort than the grotesque types of the NEP comedy of the period
prompted the preference among some playwrights for yet another kind
of drama in the 1920s—the mystery melodrama. The character of the
"internal émigré," the person who opposes the Soviet regime *passively*
(by nonparticipation in the life around him or by the pursuit of individual interests out of disdain for and/or at the expense of those of the collective) or *actively* (as the "wrecker" so familiar from other genres of Soviet literature), was to become a commonplace of Soviet drama in the
1930s as the Party moved to consolidate its power with the implementa-

tion of the first Five-Year Plan. But the drama of the 1920s anticipates the appearance of the type as well as the use of melodrama, a genre in much general favor at the time, as the appropriate vehicle by which to illuminate his machinations.

The role of situation in NEP comedy should not be minimized, but with comic dramatists (Erdman, Romashov, Mayakovsky) depiction of character outweighs the plotting of a suspense-laden intrigue. Among the new artisans of melodrama in postrevolutionary Russian drama, however, the pattern is reversed. Dramatizing the activities of "anti-State" elements virtually obliged plots rich in suspense and surprise and closely paralleling the techniques of detective fiction. These tendencies are all very much in evidence in one of the more representative and, despite obvious contrivances, effective mystery melodramas of the 1920s, the play *Chelovek s portfelem* (*The Man with a Briefcase*, 1929) by the once popular dramatist Aleksei Faiko (1893–   ). Prior to *The Man with a Briefcase*, Faiko's principal efforts in the drama were *Ozero Lyul* (*Lake Lyul*, 1922), a "romantic" melodrama about revolutionary conspiracy set "somewhere in the far West or, perhaps, the extreme East," and *Bubus the Teacher* (1924), a flimsy political farce inspired by the German revolutions of the late 'teens and early 'twenties. Both plays have no great literary or theatrical value save for their curious blend of melodrama, buffonade, and German-influenced expressionism. As early Soviet examples of Expressionist drama, however, they are less interesting than Tretyakov's previously mentioned *Are You Listening, Moscow?* (1923).

The "briefcase" of the title of Faiko's major work has a symbolic significance. It refers, in a political sense, to the shallow and superficial commitment of many outwardly zealous people to the immense task of national regeneration under Soviet leadership. Among such people, Faiko suggests, their contribution to the new society is no greater than the empty briefcase deposited on the speaker's stand at the end of *The Man with a Briefcase*. The other symbolic meaning of the briefcase touches only the personal career of the central character, Dmitri Granatov. Very early in the play the briefcase, given Granatov by affectionate students as he is about to leave Leningrad for Moscow, symbolizes the brilliant future forecast for him by his mother, who travels with him. As the final curtain falls and Granatov lies dead by his own hand, the briefcase, empty and forgotten on the speaker's stand from which Granatov has given his last lecture, assumes a quite different meaning: the shattering of Granatov's dreams, the collapse of his world. What happens between

A scene from the original production of Aleksei Faiko's Bubus the Teacher
by Meyerhold's Theater, Moscow, in 1926.
*One of Meyerhold's most intriguing concepts, the production made extensive
use of dance and jazz rhythms and synchronized the actors' movements with
musical accompaniment. Much of the music was provided by a pianist who
played mostly Chopin and Liszt and was perched high above the stage in full
view of the audience. The striking setting by Ilya Shlepyanov featured a semicir-
cle of suspended bamboo rods and a back wall of flashing neon signs. The production also served as a vehicle for Meyerhold's theory of "pre-acting."*

Granatov's receipt of the briefcase at the beginning of the play and his
abandonment of it on the speaker's stand at the end constitutes the action of a well-constructed, taut melodrama.

The intrigue is set in motion by old acquaintances whom Granatov
meets on the train bearing him to Moscow. The first is a shadowy figure
named Likhomsky whose unctuous manner soon hints at a greater and
more devious familiarity. The second is an old family employee, Redutkin, whom Faiko uses as a narrative device to acquaint the audience
with Granatov's upper-class tsarist general's family background.

Likhomsky and Redutkin have a common interest in Granatov; they want something from him on the basis of past acquaintance. With Likhomsky, with whom Granatov has shared certain unsavory experiences about which Faiko gives little information in order not to dissipate the aura of suspense he has begun building, it is proximity. Likhomsky fears that the past may catch up with him and he sees a physical closeness to Granatov as his best security. To assure himself of Granatov's "protective wing," he discloses the existence of papers incriminating to Granatov. Redutkin, on the other hand, has come upon hard times since the Revolution and asks Granatov to help him with a job. With the insensitivity and cold toughness he displays throughout the play, Granatov bluntly rejects Redutkin's appeal. The matter of Likhomsky's blackmail is more serious and, as the two men leave the dining car of the train on the way back to their compartments, Granatov takes advantage of Likhomsky's partial inebriation by beating him senseless and then throwing his body from the fast-moving train.

Once installed as a prominent member of the State Institute of Culture and Revolution in Moscow, Granatov's success seems assured. He enjoys the friendship and respect of Professor Androsov, the senior scholar of the institute, and romantically pursues the sister of the institute's administrative head.

Faiko's portrait of Granatov emphasizes the character's ruthlessness and egocentricity. Granatov will stop at nothing to get ahead—even murder—and his actions are calculated strategies to realize that goal. It is in this light that his ardent embrace of the new regime must also be interpreted. Whatever the skeletons in his closet Granatov has staked his future on the Soviets and plays his role of enthusiastic champion of socialism and the Party to the hilt. But what Faiko is intent on exposing in the almost hyperbolic characterization of Granatov is the essential hypocrisy and cynicism. Motivating Granatov is no real love or admiration for the Soviet regime—the more understandable in view of his social origins—but a desire to make his place in the new postrevolutionary society as secure and comfortable as possible. This will to self-aggrandizement, of course, has to be attributed to the individualism with which the prerevolutionary past has indelibly stamped Granatov.

The complications of plot in the central parts of *The Man with a Briefcase* serve several purposes. Besides elaborating the façade of melodramatic intrigue they also bring Granatov's ruthlessness into bolder relief. Again, two characters, principally, are utilized toward this end: Professor Androsov and Granatov's wife, Ksenia. The director of the institute,

Ivan Bashkirov, is going abroad at the head of a Soviet delegation; Androsov is favored as his temporary replacement. Granatov covets the position and at the decisive moment, when votes are being taken, viciously repudiates the older professor by exposing Androsov as incapable of effective direction of the institute because of ambivalent political attitudes. His evidence is a manuscript of personal reflections about Russia of a nationalist-mystic character which Androsov had previously given Granatov as a token of his affection. Androsov is so overcome by Granatov's treachery and by a desire to vindicate himself before the members of the institute that he suffers a stroke and falls dead at Granatov's feet. In a sense, it is Granatov's second murder. The third, also committed indirectly, involves Granatov's wife Ksenia. Also of a prerevolutionary upperclass background, she left Russia at the end of the Civil War to join her father in exile in Paris, taking her son Goga with her. When she returns to Russia a few months after her father's death, Granatov is embarrassed by her presence, regarding her now as an obstacle to him, the more so since he is avidly wooing Zina, the sister of the head of the institute. Realizing finally that there is absolutely no hope of a reconciliation with Granatov (he has his mother inform her that he never wishes to see her again) and that he has no feeling even toward their thirteen-year-old son, Ksenia commits suicide by poison.

Granatov's cruelly blunt revelation of Ksenia's death to Goga is preceded by probably the strongest scene of the entire play. Sensing the imminent collapse of his own private world, Granatov pours all the venom of his despair and wrath into a speech to his son on how he will raise him to live successfully in Soviet Russia. The speech amounts, in effect, to a projection of Granatov's own code of behavior:

> You were born in Russia, and you'll be living in Russia. You'll be struggling to exist in this filthy, absurd, cruel, this damned country. . . . I'll bring you up perfectly. I'll kill the seeds of all ideals in you. I'll strip your soul naked and cover it with a coarse, rough skin. You'll be living among beasts and you should strive to become the best beast of them all. Goals? The good . . . ? Future society? The principles of communism? Oh, you'll play with these trinkets so as to beguile your enemy with them, and when the necessary moment comes you'll be able to throw him to the ground and gnaw through his throat . . .[5]

Granatov's downfall is brought about in two ways, both prepared in advance. Urged on by his predatory wife, Redutkin reenters Granatov's life—as a *deus ex machina*—to demand blackmail as the price of silence about the murder of Likhomsky which, it appears, he witnessed during the fateful train ride earlier in the play. Granatov pays him off, but Redutkin's greed gets the best of him and he demands a large sum by a certain deadline.

When it appears that Granatov will not meet it, Redutkin stumbles into an important meeting of the institute during an address by Granatov. The game is up and Granatov will soon end his life by his own hand. Just before Redutkin's appearance at the meeting, Granatov suffers another blow. His self-revealing speech to his son and a frantic scene with his mother about the money pressures on him are overheard by Zina who hides behind a bookcase when a member of the institute comes, after Androsov's death, to recommend that Granatov best leave the institute for a provincial post in the Caucasus. When Zina at last reveals herself Granatov makes an effort to assuage her, but she refuses to hear him out; when he attempts to restrain her physically from leaving his apartment she fires at him (but misses) with a revolver she took from him earlier and with which he had once talked of committing suicide. Perceiving the hopelessness now of his situation Granatov uses the occasion of his lecture (on "The Revolution and the Intelligentsia") to bare his soul to the entire assembly of the institute. To a shocked audience he confesses the murder of Likhomsky and the collusion with him, some years before, in a clandestine anti-Soviet organization. When a member of the institute goes to phone the police Granatov retires to a side room, presumably to write a confession, and commits suicide with the revolver he took back from Zina.

With Granatov, Faiko clearly sought to draw a political example. In doing so, he made use of what may be termed the "genetic" approach to the concept of evil in Soviet society. Despite considerable talent in his field and his desire to find a place for himself in postrevolutionary Russian society, Granatov, as depicted by Faiko, is doomed by *birth*. His egocentricity and ruthlessness are the collective legacy of his past, a poison running through his system that ultimately destroys him. Through Granatov's less than perfectly convincing final speech, Faiko voices the warning that contemporary Soviet society and the contemporary Soviet intelligentsia, above all, harbor many Granatovs, people whose social origins make them suspect irrespective of any superficial accommodation to the new Soviet regime.

It is not, however, for its ideological substance that *The Man with a Briefcase* merits attention. Until Granatov's final lecture, which while obviously useful to Faiko ideologically yet plausible as a component of the plot, the play is a competently structured and suspenseful melodrama. Faiko knows the idiom of the genre and operates with it fluently in *The Man with a Briefcase*. The shadowy figure of mystery appears (Likhomsky), a past criminal deed about which much suspense is built is introduced early, an act of murder is committed and witnessed by someone who exposes his knowledge of the crime only later, revealing scenes (Granatov with his son and then with his mother) are overheard by someone hidden from view, two emotionally distraught people die, one by a stroke (Androsov) the other by poison (Ksenia), gun play with a revolver occurs (shades of Chekhov!) when Zina fires at Granatov when he blocks her exit from his apartment, a criminal commits suicide rather than be taken into custody (Granatov), and so on. The four acts of the play are so plotted as to end either on a note of suspense or when some peak in the action is reached. A sense of mystery and anticipation is built up and maintained and the dialogue often has a sharp edge to it, particularly the early scenes on the train between Granatov and Likhomsky.

In its melodramatic aspect Faiko's *The Man With a Briefcase* recalls, in some respects, Sukhovo-Kobylin's *Trilogy*. The plays that make up the *Trilogy—The Wedding of Krechinsky* (1854), *Delo* (*The Case*, 1861), and *Tarelkin's Death* (1869)—form a distinct unity of action and point of view, if not of dramatic mode. A shrewd gambler of aristocratic origin (Krechinsky) is about to make a financially beneficial marriage to the daughter of a wealthy landowner (Muromsky). When his gambling debts mount Krechinsky, in order to get money to pay them, pulls off a swindle involving a diamond pin belonging to his fiancée. The swindle is discovered and the marriage plans fall through. However, the girl is believed by the authorities to have assisted Krechinsky in the swindle and an investigation is begun (*The Case*). When it drags on for several years Muromsky tries to bribe his way out of it for his family's sake. He is cheated by unscrupulous government officials and the emotional strain results in his death. The government officials responsible for the harrassment of Muromsky and his daughter squabble among themselves over the bribe money stolen from Muromsky (*Tarelkin's Death*). The most corrupt of them, though, through intimidation and torture, triumphs in the end and keeps all the ill-gotten gain.

The *Trilogy* was remarkable, in its time, for its devastating satire of the tsarist bureaucracy and police and the use made in the last play, particularly, of absurd, grotesque, and buffoon elements. In his revival of *Tarelkin's Death* in 1922, Meyerhold emphasized these qualities by stag-

ing the work in the spirit of circus clown routines and the buffonade. It
was this production, more than anything else, that brought about a renewed interest in Sukhovo-Kobylin's *Trilogy* and led to the emergence
of the work as an influence on the drama of the 1920s.

Faiko's apparent indebtedness to Sukhovo-Kobylin in *The Man with a
Briefcase* involves five items. 1) Although unlike in most respects, Granatov does resemble Krechinsky in his cunning and ruthlessness, his
desire to succeed at any cost. 2) Money also proves the key to Granatov's undoing, as it was Krechinsky's. The intense pressure brought on
Granatov by Redutkin and his wife for a large sum of money and their
unwillingness to consider payment beyond the time specified parallels
the pressure brought to bear on Krechinsky by his creditors. 3) In each
case a scheme to get cash quickly is hatched. In *The Wedding of Krechinsky*, the scheme involves the swindle of a pawnbroker and a sleight-
of-hand exchange of a precious stone and its cheap imitation. In *The
Man with a Briefcase*, Granatov urges his mother to sell or pawn a valuable pair of earrings to raise the cash he needs. Jewelry figures in both
cases, though the two schemes are not really comparable. 4) Also, and
more important, the scheme involving jewelry in both plays leads to the
undoing of the principal character. Krechinsky's swindle is detected and
his game is up at the end of Sukhovo-Kobylin's first play. The failure of
Granatov's mother to sell her earrings results in an irate Redutkin's invasion of the lecture hall where Granatov is speaking, apparently to expose him if he is not paid off at once. This appearance of Redutkin must
be seen as the immediate stimulus to Granatov's confession of the
murder of Likhomsky. 5) The death of Professor Androsov in Faiko's
play also has its analogue in Sukhovo-Kobylin's second play, *The Case*.
Androsov's death is directly related to the injustice of Granatov's attack.
Unjust bureaucratic harassment and dishonesty lead to the death, also
by stroke, of the landowner Muromsky.

The points of contact between the Sukhovo-Kobylin and Faiko plays
are small, touching details and not essentials. Sukhovo-Kobylin's *Trilogy*
is a bitter satire directed against official corruption and inhumanity; the
absurd and grotesque are the most potent weapons in the dramatist's ar-
sensal. Faiko's *The Man with a Briefcase* "exposes" a type still prevalent, in the author's view, in the Soviet society of his own time. But his
exposé is far less mordant than Sukhovo-Kobylin's satire; there is also no
comparable use of the absurd and grotesque nor does the Faiko play
have any of the philosophical ramifications of Sukhovo-Kobylin's.

The similarities with the *Trilogy* may be superficial, but Sukhovo-

Kobylin was highly regarded not only for the modernity of his use of the absurd and grotesque but also as a Russian master of the swift-moving and suspenseful play of intrigue, a type of drama of which the Russians had few native specimens prior to Sukhovo-Kobylin and which they tended to regard primarily as a borrowing from the French. Faiko was certainly aware that no better school in Russian drama for this type of playwriting could be found.

SIX

Out of the Mainstream: Serapions and Oberiuty

ANY DISCUSSION of the remarkable variegation of dramatic writing in Russia in the 1920s would be woefully incomplete without consideration of plays and playwrights who for ideological and/or artistic reasons are given little or no place in Soviet accounts of twentieth-century Russian drama. We have already taken note of the repression of Bulgakov because of his treatment of the White milieu in *Days of the Turbins* and his total concentration on émigrés in *Flight*, though these two plays are surely among the better Russian drama of the 'twenties. The overly exuberant satire of some aspects of Soviet society during NEP in the comedies of Bulgakov, Erdman, Mayakovsky, and others resulted in the virtual ostracism from the Soviet theater of such entertaining plays as *Zoya's Apartment*, *The Warrant*, and *The Suicide*. The comic deflation of the new Soviet bureaucracy in Mayakovsky's rollicking *The Bathhouse* guaranteed the play's banishment from the boards.

But if some of the plays of Bulgakov, Erdman, and Mayakovsky were long—or are still—kept from production in Soviet theaters, information about the authors and in some cases the texts of the plays themselves are available. Mayakovsky may have been taken to task for the satire in *The Bathhouse* but he still remains *the* poet of the Russian Revolution and *The Bathhouse*, like the rest of his writings, is readily acquired in the USSR. And although plays of Bulgakov and Erdman are still unprinted in the Soviet Union, both writers have undergone at least a partial "rehabilitation" since the early 1960s.

Less fortunate are writers belonging to two of the more noteworthy Russian literary groups of the 1920s: the Serapion Brotherhood and the Oberiuty. The contributions of both groups to the drama must be recognized as some of the most interesting of the period; but today, half a century later, the plays are impossible to obtain in the USSR, where almost all of them have never been printed and where the authors are all but passed over in silence in Soviet literary and theatrical studies. The reasons for such disregard lie well within our grasp.

In the case of the Serapions (among whose members were the novelist Konstantin Fedin, Vsevolod Ivanov, the Formalist critic Viktor Shklovsky, Yevgeni Zamyatin, and the satirist Mikhail Zoshchenko), it was the group's championhip of the independence of art and their stubborn resistance to demands that literature assume an ideological commitment.[1] As the '20s progressed, the Serapions found themselves increasingly at odds with the Soviet authorities. This expressed itself, on the group's part, in the critical depiction (largely by indirection: allegory, science fantasy, historical parallelism) of the processes of social and cultural regimentation in Soviet Russia, and, on the Party's part, in the repression and ostracism of the Serapions and their writings.

In the case of the Oberiuty, the disregard had far less to do with ideology than with aesthetics. If they did not tag themselves with the labels of Dada and surrealism, the Oberiuty nevertheless were outspoken enthusiasts of nonrepresentational art. Their obvious links with the contemporary European avant-garde and the absence in their works of any perceptible ideological content made them easy targets for official repudiation on the grounds of "formalism."

My discussion of these two vital but little-known episodes in Russian literature and drama of the 1920s begins first with the Serapions and specifically with the dramatic writing of the most talented playwright of the group, Lev Lunts.

Utopias and Anti-Utopias: the Serapion Lev Lunts

Although cloaked in absurdity and grotesqueness, Mayakovsky's last plays reveal an unmistakable undercurrent of disillusionment with the course of Soviet society. The vision of Soviet life in the future, as set forth in *The Bedbug*, is decidedly anti-utopian; it is a totally regimented and automated society in which there is no place for the emotions or for love. The new Soviet bureaucracy, one of the instruments of regimentation, is portrayed in a ridiculous light in *The Bathhouse;* self-serving officials, like Pobedonosikov, must suffer the ultimate punishment of being prohibited from riding a time machine into a far distant future because there their kind can no longer be tolerated.

Actually, Mayakovsky's use of utopian and anti-utopian motifs in drama goes back to his first version of *Mystery-Bouffe* in 1918. Coming almost at the same time as the Bolshevik Revolution, that curious mixture of mystery play, buffonade, theatricalist manifesto, and futurism hailed the anticipated, imminent paradise on earth of the Soviet state. It envisioned a utopia in which man emerges from the night of capitalist exploitation and degradation and enters into a day of socialist egalitarianism and humanism. By the end of the NEP period, however, Mayakovsky's utopian vision had soured into anti-utopian disenchantment. And this despair was bluntly expressed in his plays of 1928 and 1929 and even more eloquently by his suicide in 1930.

The vision of an Orwellian nightmare of an automated and dehumanized future society had already appeared in Russian literature during the 1920s. To Russians hostile to the new regime, within the Soviet Union as well as abroad, the reality of the Bolshevik state was no more than a fulfillment of their direst forebodings. To those who had welcomed the Revolution, the nightmare came as a disheartening disfigurement of their dream. Taken collectively, Mayakovsky's *Mystery-Bouffe, The Bedbug,* and *The Bathhouse* chart the course of this disfigurement in dramatic terms. Elsewhere in Russian literature of the 1920s, the most powerful and most celebrated expression of anti-utopian anxiety was Zamyatin's widely translated novel *My (We,* 1920).

In Russian drama, probably the most unequivocally anti-utopian play of the 1920s appeared not in the Soviet Union but in a Russian émigré milieu in Germany (like Zamyatin's novel, which was never published in Russia). I refer to the little-known *Gorod pravdy (The City of Truth)* by a talented writer named Lev Lunts, who was born in 1901 and who died prematurely of an illness related to a nervous disorder in 1924. Despite his tragically short life, Lunts showed great promise of achieving a brilliant literary career. He wrote short stories, plays which Gorky held in high esteem, and several provocative literary essays, the latter as the chief theorist of the Serapion Brotherhood, which was founded in 1921.

Lunts left the Soviet Union not as a political émigré (although his parents had already resettled in Germany) but as a university graduate in Romance literatures who was on his way to Spain with a stipend to study Spanish literature. Already frail and ill when he set out on his trip West in June 1923, he decided to look into his condition when he reached Hamburg and checked into a sanitorium. He remained hospitalized there nearly a year and finally died on May 9, 1924.[2]

Lunts was long interested in drama and theater but his talent as a playwright was first revealed in his philosophical tragedy *Vne zakona (Outside the Law),* which he began in 1919 and finished in 1920. Although Lunts, like his fellow Serapions, has been relegated to the margins of Soviet literary history, the play demonstrates the extent to which his dramatic writing developed within the context of attempts to create a new Soviet drama along romantic and tragic lines before the epic drama of the Revolution and the Civil War crystallized in the second half of the 1920s.

Like such costume dramas as Lunacharsky's postrevolutionary *Oliver Cromwell* (1920) and the first two parts of the unfinished *Foma Campanella* trilogy (1920), as well as those of Zamyatin—*Ogni sv. Dominika* (*The Fires of St. Dominick*, 1920) and *Attila* (1928)—Lunts' *Outside the Law* retains a non-Russian Western setting, this time Spain.[3] But unlike Inquisitional Spain, which Zamyatin used for obvious analogical purposes in *The Fires of St. Dominick*, Lunts' Spain has no specific time. Thus relieved of historical associations, the audience is free to concentrate on the play's ideas, which are more complex than those developed either in the verbose and static "thesis" plays of Lunacharsky or in the dramas of Zamyatin. The theme of *Outside the Law* is the ultimate necessity for law in society (no man or men can stand higher than the law) and the impossibility of achieving total social equality. What makes the play exceptional for its time and place is not only the irony and subtlety with which Lunts develops his thought but its bristling excitement and movement attesting to an admirable sense of theater.

This same feeling for the theatrical informs his second play, the five-act *Bertran de Born* (1922), which at first glance resembles a Neo-Romantic neo-tragedy with a medieval French (here Provence) setting such as Blok's *The Rose and the Cross*. Extending the theme of *Outside the Law*, Lunts stresses in *Bertran de Born* that not only must a society be based on law to which all men are subject, but that an individual must either move with time or be destroyed by it. The knight-troubadour Bertran sets himself beyond the law and struggles against the new order for the sake of an unretrievable past as much as Olesha's Ivan Babichev, but with no greater success.

Lunts' next play was *Obezyany idut!* (*The Apes Are Coming!*, published 1923), an engrossing mixture of the realistic and fantastic in which the play-within-a-play device is used to explore anomalies of the Revolution. It was followed by the work generally acknowledged as his major contribution to the drama, *The City of Truth*, which, like *Outside the Law*, appeared first (in 1924) in the Russian émigré journal *Beseda* (*Talk*) which Gorky published in Berlin between 1923 and 1925.

In Zamyatin's *We* and in the second half of Mayakovsky's *The Bedbug* the future is depicted in unflinchingly anti-utopian terms. The City in Lunts' play is also a work-dominated, emotionless society, sharing many of the features of Zamyatin's and Mayakovsky's visions of the future. But Lunts' purpose extends beyond just a negative description of the utopia. His main attack strikes out against the very reasoning that underlies the desire and search for a utopia, for a kind of paradise on earth such as Mayakovsky celebrated in *Mystery-Bouffe*; in fact, it may be to *Mystery-Bouffe* that Lunts seeks to reply in *The City of Truth*.

The characters in *The City of Truth*, which has an indeterminate time and setting, are divided into two camps, the soldiers who include the two major figures of the Commissar and the Doctor, and the inhabitants of the City of Equality. As the play opens, the soldiers, whom we can assume are Russians, are being led by the Commissar back to Russia from some locality in the East (we are told that China and the Gobi desert lie behind them). Considering the fact that the soldiers are supposed to be Russians on a return journey, it can be argued that *The City of Truth* was conceived at least partially as a play dealing with the postrevolutionary Russian emigration, somewhat like Bulgakov's *Flight*, though there are considerable differences in dramatic style between the two plays. Lunts' work, however, has broader significance and to think of it only in relation to the emigration would be to read the author's intentions too narrowly.

In exhorting his people to follow him back to Russia, the Commissar ecstatically describes the new land as a place of perfect equality, a true utopia that is free of judges, jails, taxes, and soldiers. Many of the soldiers are reluctant to follow the Commissar, not wanting to leave their jobs and families. The Commissar succeeds, nevertheless, in quieting their doubts, except for the Doctor who remains skeptical and who tries to foment opposition. In fact, the utopian vision of a land of perfect equality is abhorrent to the Doctor; and in the third scene of Act I, he questions:

> Paradise on earth, and all as one? Truth, justice, happiness? And if it is so, if all he says is true, then I surely do not want your paradise! I don't want you to reach there. Perish, I along with you, but I won't let you go there, no, no! I hate your paradise and don't want it! Back! While it's still not too late, back![4]

The Doctor's words fail to stay the soldiers, however, and eventually they reach the City of Truth and Equality (Gorod Pravdy i Ravenstva). But their joyful entry is marred by the Commissar's murder of one of their number, a man who had opposed him all along the way; the Doctor's opposition, by contrast, had been more subtle, for he avoided any direct public confrontation, trying instead to win over converts while the Commissar was asleep. The murder perpetrated by the Commissar is soon followed by another revealed in a theatrically moving dumb scene at the beginning of the second act. The Commissar's young assistant, Vanya, comes across a boy and a girl making love on a sun-drenched hilltop and, out of jealousy and frustration, he slays both of them with a spear. Later, a soldier beats up one of the boys of the City whom he found taking one of his two belts, not realizing that the concept of theft does not exist in the City. Such incidents as these quickly sow seeds of discord among the residents of the City as well as among the newcomers.

Adding to the tension between the two groups is also a conflict in life styles. In the City, all are equal and live only to work, suffering no poverty, misery, or evil, but knowing no emotions or love. As in much anti-utopian literature, complete egalitarianism is realized by a total commitment to work, subservience to the machine, and elimination from life of all passions. Love in the City is reduced to a casual, indiscriminate physical act, devoid of any deeper meaning or any proprietary attitudes.

The newcomers soon chafe under the strict regimen of work, unrelieved by love and play, and quickly become restless. The Commissar himself complains to the Doctor that he does not want such "happiness" or equality. What he wants, he says, is life. And in one of the play's key ideological passages, the Doctor replies that with life injustices and inequalities always coexist. The Commissar cannot be dissuaded, however, from his dream of finding a true utopia of equality and law, and also of life. But before he and his group set out on their renewed journey, they wage a bloody battle with the inhabitants of the City. Led by the young among them who have learned how to fight from the newcomers, the townspeople turn against the outsiders who have brought murder and violence into their midst. Almost all of the townspeople are killed in the battle and so are a number of the Commissar's soldiers. The mind of the Commissar still cannot be dissuaded, however, although the Doctor makes one final plea:

> What is truth? Boredom. What is equality? Boredom. Everything honest and pure is dead. In non-truth there is life; in killing there is life. Life is struggle! What will you do now, Commissar? Again travel farther, deceiving them and yourself; again look for what you've already found . . . and thrown away? Commissar! Leave them. Let's

you and I run away together, and together we'll look for bloody, unjust, happy life! Commissar! (The Commissar dozes.) He's asleep. Listen anyway, Commissar! I also looked for goodness, for the communal way of life, for equality, the same as you. Fool! I gambled my whole life on that, left my home, abandoned my mother. Because of it I'll die a beggar. But then the time came and I saw it was all boredom, boredom, boredom! I no longer believe in anything. I hate those who believe.

The conflict between the Commissar and the Doctor soon surfaces again when the Commissar exhorts his soldiers to follow him to Russia where he promises them that they will find all people equal before the law yet not the same, and happiness but not the peace of the dead. Revealing that the Doctor's words have not been without some influence on him, the Commissar declares that when they finally reach the Promised Land there will not be peace there because peace is only for the dead. Instead, they will find eternal struggle and blood, since there can be no life without them.

Now openly contemptuous of the Commissar who demands complete subservience, the Doctor becomes an obstacle that must be removed. In an ironic twist, the Commissar chooses as his instrument a young boy of the City, the lad who learned to fight from the beating he received from the soldier whose belt he took. With a newly found lust for combat as well as for his safety, the boy begs the Commissar that he be allowed to journey with him and his men. The Commissar agrees, on the condition that he first kill the Doctor with a knife which he gives him. The boy commits the murder; and as the Doctor lies dying, he continues to warn the Commissar that he will never find a Russia of equality and blood, of order and laughter, and of law and struggle, for which he is searching. When the Commissar vows still to continue his journey until he does, the Doctor, with his last breath, tells him that then this quest will be endless.

As in *Outside the Law*, Lunts' position in *The City of Truth* is that the perfect equalization of man in society is possible only at the loss of individuality and human dignity. We are back in the world, of course, of the Expressionist nightmare, the world of Rice, Kaiser, Toller, Čapek, and Witkiewicz. Despite a certain ambivalence, Lunts' views can be read in large part as a criticism of the new Soviet society like Zamyatin's *The Fires of St. Dominick* and Mayakovsky's *The Bedbug*. To anyone familiar with his well-known essay of 1923 "On Literature, Revolution, Entropy, and Other Matters," the influence of Zamyatin on Lunts' thinking is unmistakable.[5] This comes out most clearly in the character of the Doctor who expresses a vitalistic philosophy of life as struggle, inequality, and injustice. The attitude embodied in the Doctor was one Lunts shared with other members of the Serapion Brotherhood, above all Zamyatin. Rejecting ideology, the Serapions advocated an individualistic concept of art free from all external pressures. In art as in life any attempt to impose uniformity for whatever abstract good could result only in sterility and the death of the spirit.

The Doctor's outlook is also reminiscent of Harlequin's affirmation of life and rejection of otherwordly mysticism in Blok's *The Fairground Booth*. Both Harlequin and the Doctor express a desire for life as it is in preference to some exalting philosophy incapable of being transformed into reality. But the Doctor's realism lacks the joyousness of Harlequin's view. He would like to believe as the Commissar does but he cannot, knowing that the Commissar's quest is futile. By contrast, the Commissar is the idealist in search of a perfect utopian society, while in reality the frustrations of the quest so distort his personality that he must despotically uproot all criticism around him. And it is this idealism turned fanaticism that leaves nothing but destruction for the future, thereby becoming a perversion of itself.

The utopian vision invoked by Lunts in *The City of Truth* has much in common with those conceived by Zamyatin and Mayakovsky. But in his play Lunts extends the assault: he lays bare the dangers inherent in any search for the absolutely perfect social structure. To Lunts, all utopias will inevitably become anti-utopias.

As stimulating as Lunts' plays may be for their ideas, they are no less interesting for their formal properties. In *Outside the Law*, for example, three simultaneous stages are used, each with its own curtain: the central one for the play proper, the two side ones for entr'acte skits which were conceived in a commedia dell'arte style. All three stages are integrally related by the play's action and it is this interrelation of the stages with the plot that makes for Lunts' innovation. Dissatisfied with either prose or traditional verse meters for the dialogue of the "new tragedy," Lunts experimented with what he called "scenic speech" in *Bertran de Born*. This was a special combination of prose and free iambics governed by intonation which Zamyatin, I believe, was to pick up from Lunts and use in his later tragedy *Attila* (1928). In *The City of Truth*, Lunts was able to distinguish between the play's two main groups of characters, the soldiers and the inhabitants of the utopian city, not only by the more obvious means of dress, but also by speech. To suggest the complete uniformity of life in the city the townspeople wear one style of clothing and speak in a monotone; the individuality of the soldiers, on the other hand, is conveyed by their variety of garb and speech. Setting Lunts' plays still further apart from the romantic drama of his contemporaries is their lively tempo. The importance of action and movement in Lunts' conception of the drama can be gleaned from his programmatic Afterword to *Bertran de Born:*

> Nowhere has psychology and realism exerted such a destructive influence on the stage [as in Russia, HBS]. The theater, by its very essence, is foreign to trifling manners and subtle psychology. It is concerned with *action*. But in Russia it is taught that one should aim at a reflection of real everyday feelings, of "real" people. And so, instead of Shakespeare, Racine and Hugo, our theater is ruled by the most subtle, by the most tedious rumination of Chekhov. It is "true," it is "fair," and it—and none other!—has brought the theater to ruin. Everyone laments the crisis of dramaturgy—and everyone presents wise dramas without the slightest action, constipated with manners and mood. . . .
>
> And so in approaching a play in a country which does not know and does not want to know the theater, I have consciously set out in the other extreme. Instead of a theater of moods, bare milieu, bare stunts, I have tried to present a theater of pure action. Perhaps only bare action was obtained. This is no great misfortune. The *melodrama* will save the theater. Literarily false, it is *scenically* immortal! And for me, the scenic is of primary importance.[6]

The irony posed by Lunts' plays and theoretical pronouncements on the drama, such as the Afterword to *Bertran de Born*, is excruciating. In all the efforts—by Gorky, Lunacharsky, and others—to create a new Soviet drama in the first few years after the Revolution by means of some alchemist's blending of the romantic, tragic, and melodramatic, the most exciting interplay of idea and form was achieved in the plays of a writer like Lunts whose refusal to wear the strait-jacket of official ideology set him beyond the pale and left him without influence on the later course of Russian drama.

═══ The Oberiuty: Swan Song of NEP ═══

Between the time Mayakovsky began writing *The Bedbug* and his suicide in 1930, one of the more curious albeit short-lived developments in late NEP Soviet literature occurred. This was the formation of the avant-garde literary group known as the Oberiu (the name is derived

from the initials of the group's full name: Obedinenie Realnogo Is-
kusstva, The Society for Real Art; its members called themselves
Oberiuty). The emergence of such a group with links to Dada and surrealism in the late 1920s could not have come at a worse time. The end of
NEP was approaching and with it the end as well of all the creative innovation of Russian art of the 1920s. The first Five-Year Plan and Socialist Realism were around the corner and neither was willing to recognize
the rights of citizenship of an avant-garde nonrepresentational art. As it
was, the Oberiu managed to survive until 1930 and then the boom was
lowered. Its members were subjected to vicious attacks in the press and
greater restrictions on their publication. Two outstanding members of
the group, Aleksandr Vvedensky (born 1904) and Daniil Kharms (born
1905; real name, Yuvachev), were actually arrested in 1941 and were
never heard from again. Kharms presumably died in prison on February
4, 1942, and Vvedensky somewhere in the Ukraine in the early days of
World War II.

The literary activity from the time of the publication of their Manifesto in 1928 to 1930, when it became virtually impossible for them to
publish anything but children's literature, the Oberiuty were a forgotten
chapter in the history of twentieth-century Russian art until the 1960s.
Some of the work of Kharms and Vvedensky began circulating in typescript among small groups of readers in Leningrad, some things were
translated in Poland and Czechoslovakia where avant-garde art has been
less repressed than in the Soviet Union, Kharm's play *Elizaveta Bam*
(*Elizabeth Bam*) was performed in Warsaw and published in the Polish
theater magazine *Dialog*, and in 1967 two articles on Kharms and Vvedensky were read at a student conference on literature at the University
of Tartu in Estonia. The most extensive work on Kharms and Vvedensky
to date, however, has been done by the American Slavist George Gibian, whose book of translations with an introduction of Kharms, Vvedensky, and the Oberiu was published by Cornell University Press in
1971 under the title *Russia's Lost Literature of the Absurd*.[7]

The literary activity of the Oberiuty included poetry, short stories,
and drama, but with the exception of some poetry was known only
through the circulation of manuscripts, readings, or cabaretlike performances featuring a mixed bag of literary and dramatic entertainment. An
independent Oberiu theater to be known as the Radix was a project of
Kharms as early as 1926, but nothing much came of it. Nevertheless, the
interest of the Oberiuty in theater, drama, and film remained high. This
is reflected in the importance of the theater and film sections of the

Oberiu Manifesto of 1928 as well as in the playwriting of Kharms and
Vvedensky. Acknowledging their indebtedness to the native Russian
fair-booth-show tradition, the *balagan* (which Aleksandr Blok drew on
for his *The Fairground Booth* of over a decade earlier), the Oberiuty
make clear in their Manifesto that their concept of theater is modernist
and antirepresentational:

> Until now, all these elements [of theater] have been subordi-
> nated to the dramatic plot—to the play. A play has been a story, told
> through characters, about some kind of event. On the stage, all
> have worked to explain the meaning and course of that event more
> clearly, more intelligibly, and to relate it more closely to life.
>
> That is not at all what the theater is. If an actor who represents a
> minister begins to move around on the stage on all fours and howls
> like a wolf, or an actor who represents a Russian peasant suddenly
> delivers a long speech in Latin—that will be theater, that will inter-
> est the spectator, even if it takes place without any relation to dra-
> matic plot. Such an action will be a separate item; a series of such
> items organized by the director will make up a theatrical perfor-
> mance, which will have its plot line and its scenic meaning.
>
> This will be a plot which only the theater can give. The plots of
> theatrical performances are theatrical, just as the plots of musical
> works are musical. All represent one thing—a world of appear-
> ances—but depending on the material, they render it differently,
> after their own fashion.
>
> When you come to us, forget everything that you have been ac-
> customed to seeing in all theaters. Maybe a great deal will seem ri-
> diculous. We take a dramatic plot. We develop it slowly at first;
> then suddenly it is interrupted by seemingly extraneous and clearly
> ridiculous elements. You are surprised. You want to find that cus-
> tomary logical sequence of connections which, it seems to you, you
> see in life. But it is not there. Why not? Because an object and a
> phenomenon transported from life to the stage lose their lifelike
> sequence of connections and acquire another—a theatrical one. We
> are not going to explain it. In order to understand the sequence of
> connections of any theatrical performance one must see it. We can
> only say that our task is to render the world of concrete objects on
> the stage in their interrelationships and collisions. (Gibian, *pp*.
> *200–1*)

While stressing their repudiation of representationalism, the Oberiuty
also wanted it understood that unlike some of the earlier twentieth-century avant-garde groups such as the more extreme Futurists and the
Surrealists their goal was not to divorce art from life but only to reflect
the life around them in a different nonrepresentational way by jarring
the perception with unusual, unexpected, and disjointed configurations

of the separate components of the given work. The two extant plays of
Kharms and Vvedensky splendidly illustrate the principles on which the
Manifesto was based.

Distantly reminiscent of Maeterlinck's evocation of an atmosphere of
impending doom in his early plays, Kharms' *Elizabeth Bam* immediately plunges the audience into the heroine's dread of someone coming
any minute and dragging her away to a certain death for a crime of
which she herself is unaware. But hardly does Elizabeth express her fear
when her pursuers begin pounding on her door. Who Elizabeth Bam is,
who her pursuers are, what she has done, if anything—remain unans-
wered questions throughout the play. A logical sequence of events and
causality are no concern of Kharms as he strives instead to convey both a
Maeterlinckian and Kafkaesque sense of encroaching, inescapable doom.

As the short play unfolds, one unexpected twist follows another and
the realm of the absurd is soon entered. When Elizabeth accuses one of
her pursuers of having no conscience and of being a crook, it triggers an
argument between the pursuers (Ivan and Pyotr) as to whether or not
the charges against Ivan are true. The grotesque is added to the absurdity of the situation when Elizabeth coaxes Ivan into demonstrating his
ability to hiccup at will as a signal to a colleague standing on guard at
another door. So delighted is Elizabeth with Ivan's performance, that
she calls her mother and father to witness the demonstration. Of course,
the reason the pursuers are in Elizabeth's quarters rapidly diminishes in
significance. This is indicated by Ivan's confusion of Elizabeth's pa-
tronymic (in the same monologue he refers to her as Elizabeth Cockroa-
chovna, Elizabeth Eduardovna, and Elizabeth Mikhailovna) and his
wish that he be permitted to go home because his wife and children are
waiting for him.

The vaguely Maeterlinckian-Kafkaesque aura with which *Elizabeth
Bam* begins gives way at this point to a Gogolian absurdity in which irrelevance is piled on irrelevance; the original issue is soon all but forgotten until something triggers an abrupt return to it.

Shortly after Elizabeth and her mother leave to go for a walk, Ivan
and Pyotr remember that they have come to take Elizabeth away in
order to kill her and they resume their pursuit. No sooner do they find
her on a little bench when a beggar enters and the dialogue moves on to
a surreal level. Ivan tears roots out of something or other (unspecified)
and Pyotr urges the beggar to crawl in. Elizabeth then speaks of her
husband's not coming while Pyotr assumes that he will as he runs
around the stage bawling "Boohoo!" In another abrupt shift Ivan accuses

Elizabeth of killing Pyotr and the ensuing dialogue demonstrates the surreal character of the play from this point on:

E.B.: Hurrah, I did not kill anybody.
IVAN: To take a human being and knife him. That is so perfidious. Hurrah, you did it. Why did you?
E.B. (*walks to the side*): Whoooooooooooooo.
IVAN: She-wolf!
E.B (*trembles*): Whooooooo—black prunes.
IVAN: Great-grandmother.
E.B.: Jubilation!
IVAN: She is destroyed forever.
E.B.: Black horse, and on the horse a soldier.
IVAN (*lights a match*): Dear, darling Elizabeth.
E.B.: My shoulders are like the rising sun. (*She climbs onto a chair*).
IVAN (*squats down*): My legs are like cucumbers. (*Lies down on the floor*). No, no, nothing.
E.B. (*raises her arms*): Ku-ni-na-ga ni-li-va-ni-ba-oo-oo.
IVAN (*lying on the floor*): Fowl, fowl.

    Murka the cat
    Lapped up the milk
    Jumped on the pillow
    Jumped on the stove
    Jump, jump,
    Leap, leap.

E.B. (*shouts*): Two gates, shirt, twine.
IVAN (*raising himself halfway up*): Two carpenters have come and ask, "What is the matter?"
E.B.: Cutlets, Barbara Semyonova. (*pp. 127–28*)

The structure becomes still more incredible when the characters shift to verse and a Chorus, Violin, Drum, and Siren are introduced with speaking parts. The sinister mood of the play's earlier scenes returns when Pyotr, Ivan, and Elizabeth's father quarrel (in verse) over the planned killing of Elizabeth. The scene is reminiscent of the fairy-tale conflicts of knights in puppet plays. When Elizabeth reappears following the clash of knights, Kharms shifts abruptly to the contemporary and mundane. Elizabeth tells her father that she has just returned from the co-op where she bought candy and looked for a cake for tea. The father tells her that he got tired chopping wood. Elizabeth then orders Ivan to run down to the grocery store to get a bottle of beer and some peas. But Ivan's reply immediately restores the absurd and surreal atmosphere:

IVAN: Oh, get some peas and run to the beer and bring the store.

E.B.: Not bring the store, but bring a bottle of beer, and go to some peas.

IVAN: Right away; I'll hide my hat in the store and will wear the beer on my head. (*p. 138*)

The play finally ends when Elizabeth's mother reappears and at once accuses Elizabeth of having killed her son. The last scene almost perfectly repeats the opening scene of the play with Elizabeth trying to barricade herself from her pursuers. This time, however, they accuse her of having murdered Pyotr. Elizabeth protests her innocence and the voice of one pursuer tells her that the court will decide her innocence or guilt. Elizabeth then submits saying, "I am in your power." As Ivan lights a match, she is arrested and led offstage.

A more entertaining exercise in the absurd than *Elizabeth Bam*, Vvedensky's *Yolka u Ivanovykh* (*Christmas at the Ivanovs*) is an "anti-Christmas anti-play" (to borrow George Gibian's characterization) which freely uses absurd, grotesque, and surreal techniques to spoof not only the conventions of Christmas celebrations but the conventions also of traditional representational drama.

The play opens with the seven Ivanov children being given a bath by nurses on Christmas eve. The children all have different names and range in age from one to eighty-two years. While they are in the tub, off to the right cooks are slaughtering chickens and suckling pigs. In the art-as-shock style of Dada and Surrealist drama, violence and/or sex frequently come together. As two of the sisters, Dunya and Sonya, quarrel over the latter's boasts about the size of her breasts and buttocks, a nurse menaces Sonya with an ax because of her bad language. But Sonya is incorrigible and continues to scandalize the rest with frank talk about masturbation and how she intends to expose herself to guests during the Christmas celebration. The nurse finally chops off her head in disgust. After the police remove her, the scene shifts to a forest where woodcutters are felling trees for Christmas. One of them is the nurse's fiancé Fyodor, who boasts of his love for her. When the woodcutters ride out on a sled, animals appear and talk among themselves. The patent surrealism of the first scene is reinforced in the animal scene in which the dialogue takes place between a giraffe, a wolf, a beaverlike animal, a lion, and a "porky" suckling pig. The surreal and absurd merge in the following scene as the dead Sonya's mother and father return home, find their daughter in a coffin with her decapitated head lying on a cushion nearby, and then proceed to have intercourse in the same room. Within the context of the surreal, everything, of course, is possible. And so we find absurd stage directions such as the following in which Vvedensky is obviously having fun with his *readers:*

> *Sonya (formerly a 32-year-old girl) lies like a railway post that has been knocked over. Can she hear what her mother is saying? How can she? She is quite dead. She has been killed. The door opens. Father enters, followed by Fyodor, followed by woodcutters. They carry in a Christmas tree. They see the coffin, and all take off their caps. Except for the tree, which has no cap and which understands nothing about it all. (p. 171)*

Moreover, at the very end of the scene Sonya's head and body engage in conversation:

THE HEAD: Body, you heard everything.
THE BODY: I heard nothing. I have no ears. But I felt it all. (p. 172)

In the realm of the surreal, not only is everything possible but inversion is commonplace. When the murderess-nurse is brought to an insane asylum for examination, it appears that the one who is really insane is the examining doctor. Believing himself to be persecuted he fires a pistol at a mirror which he takes to be one of his enemies. When an attendant enters and asks who fired the gun, the doctor says that it was the mirror. Before the scene ends, Vvedensky manages to slip in another surreal stage direction, this one calling for the doctor's patients to sail away out of the room in a boat, pushing themselves along the floor with oars. They are off to pick berries and mushrooms.

With the third act virtually all pretense of a plot vanishes. The opening stage direction reads:

> *Table. A coffin on the table. In the coffin, Sonya Ostrova. Inside Sonya Ostrova, a heart. In the heart, coagulating blood. In the blood, red and white corpuscles. Also of course gangrene poison. (p. 181)*

The first speaker is the dog Vera, who recites a poem. The one-year-old boy Petya comes in and he and the dog converse. At one point the dog asks him if he is surprised that she is talking and not barking. Petya's answer? "What can surprise me, at my age? Calm down." At the end of the scene, brother and sister Misha Pestrov and Dunya Shustrova enter. Misha wishes her a Happy Christmas, then declares: "Soon there will be a Christmas pee." Dunya replies, "Not pee but bee. No bee but tree. Best wishes. Is Sonya sleeping?" The dog Vera answers the question, saying, "No. She is peeing."

The scene shifts next to a courtroom where no sooner does the judge appear when he declares that he is dying and is quickly replaced with another judge. But the second judge also dies and has to be replaced. The court protocol read by the Secretary consists of nothing more than a series of nonsense quatrains. Finally the nurse who killed Sonya is sentenced to be executed by hanging.

The fourth act opens with another typical Vvedensky stage direction:

The ninth scene, like all the preceding ones, represents events which took place six years before my birth, or forty years ago. That is the least of it. So why should we grieve and weep that somebody was killed? We didn't know any of them, and anyway they have all died. (p. 185)

The children are at last permitted to view the Christmas tree. The mother plays the piano and sings, but the mood becomes somber when the mother recalls Sonya's death and begins to weep. At this point, the twenty-five-year-old son Volodya shoots himself in the temple and then tells his mother not to cry but to laugh for he too has shot himself. The mother replies by singing that she will not spoil their good time. But the topic of death again intrudes when the one-year-old son Petya says that life will pass quickly and soon they will all die. Thereafter the characters onstage die (after announcing that they are about to die), leaving just the father and mother. Before they too die, they exchange the following dialogue:

FATHER P.: They've died too. They say the woodcutter Fyodor has finished his studies and become a teacher of Latin. What has happened to me? A stabbing in the heart. I see nothing. I'm dying.

MOTHER P.: What are you saying? You see there is a man of the common people, and he's worked his way up. God, what an unhappy Christmas we're having. (*She falls down and dies.*) (p. 189)

In their shocking, often puzzling yet often delightful blending of the absurd, grotesque, and nonsensical the plays of Kharms and Vvedensky represent an extreme form, perhaps the most extreme, of Russian avant-garde drama of the first two decades of the twentieth century. But in order to view them in the proper perspective, they should be regarded, I think, as the end of a tradition rather than as an isolated episode in the history of twentieth-century Russian drama or as the beginning of anything new. The absurd and grotesque permeate the most original Russian plays of the NEP era, but the plays of Kharms and Vvedensky are anything but typical NEP satires. Apart from the names of the characters there is nothing Russian about the plays nor do they bristle with the topical satire of the comedies of Erdman, Romashov, Bulgakov, and Mayakovsky. They also lack the philosophical dimension and social implications of the plays of such later absurdists as Ionesco, Beckett, Pinter, and the Poles Sławomir Mrożek and Tadeusz Rózewicz. *Christmas at the Ivanovs* is a spoof on the ritual of Christmas celebration but it cannot be seen as directed against a *Russian* celebration of Christmas. For all its nonsense, *Elizabeth Bam* does evoke a sense of dread but what further or more specific meaning does the play have?

Because of their apparent absence of meaning, their experimental nature, their sexual frankness, and their mocking irreverence, the plays of Kharms and Vvedensky lay beyond any possible redemption once Socialist Realism became the aesthetic law of the land. Their suppression and the fate suffered by their authors meant that a watershed in postrevolutionary Russian literature had been reached; NEP was definitely at an end, not only as an economic policy but, more grievous, as an artistic ambience.

SEVEN

The 1930s:
Socialist Construction and
Socialist Realism

WITH THE end of the NEP and the beginning of the first Five-Year
Plan (1928–32), Russian dramatists turned from their previous preoccupation with the Revolution and the Civil War and with the contradictions of NEP society to a concern with three major issues:

1. The conflicts of individual adjustment to the demands and challenges of the new post-NEP program of "socialist construction."
2. The implementation of the vast program of industrialization insti-
tuted by the first Five-Year Plan.
3. The consolidation of Soviet authority and its universal acceptance
throughout Russia, perceived mainly in terms of the elaboration of a Soviet political mythology.

1. Plays devoted to problems of personal adjustment in the late 1920s
and 1930s are many; my intention is to discuss only a few of the most
representative and the most frequently staged. Although they differ in
several essential respects these plays relate to and, in a sense, continue
an earlier type of drama: the play about the Civil War depicting the
conflicts within White families torn asunder by the Revolution and the
subsequent war with the Reds. In the late- and immediate post-NEP
period, however, the matter of adjustment assumes a purely "internal"
character. By that I mean the individual or individuals concerned no
longer represent political or military hostility to Soviet authority. They
are neither Whites nor émigré activists but people who have already accepted the transfer of political power in Russia to the Bolsheviks. Yet,
for a variety of reasons, they experience difficulty in "locating" themselves comfortably in the new society and hence have not become
wholly assimilated by it.

Probably the most interesting plays on the theme of psychological and emotional adjustment are those in which the principal characters are artists and intellectuals. Considering the manifold importance of such people to the new regime, the prominence of this drama is understandable. Olesha's *A List of Assets,* which has already been examined in a somewhat different context, is a good example of the type. Apart from its partly foreign setting and heavy dosage of melodrama, the essential conflict of the drama springs from the ambivalent attitude toward the Bolshevik regime and its proclaimed egalitarianism on the part of a talented, proud, and vain actress. The resolution of Goncharova's personal dilemma bares no surprises: it is pat and contrived. The actress' experiences in the West make her at last appreciate and long for her Soviet homeland to which she can never return, dying a Red martyr in the streets of Paris. But it is not the resolution that arrests attention so much as the ambivalence of the actress herself and her quest for inner peace. In her artist's pride and vanity, of which Olesha had a keen personal perception, Goncharova becomes an interesting psychological study little marred by the frame of melodrama and the anticipated political resolution in which she must be viewed.

Olesha's *A List of Assets* stands among the earliest serious manifestations of an interest in the disaffected or rootless artist and intellectual in Russian drama of the late 1920s and 1930s. A less exotic and less melodramatic treatment of the theme characterizes the highly regarded play *Strakh* (*Fear*), written the same year as Olesha's work (1931) by one of the major Russian dramatists of the 1930s, Aleksandr Afinogenov (1904–41). Following within a few years were such equally representative dramas as *Tanya* (1938) and *Kremlyovskie kuranty* (*The Kremlin Chimes,* 1940, 1956), by Aleksei Arbuzov and Nikolai Pogodin (pen name of N. F. Stukalov), respectively, two other prominent playwrights of the '30s, who also continued to contribute importantly to Soviet drama after World War II.

Although he started writing plays as early as 1923 (the first was *Robert Tim,* about a revolt of weavers in nineteenth-century England), Afinogenov came to be regarded as a promising, serious dramatist only with the success of the Second Moscow Art Theater's production of his play *Chudak* (*The Eccentric*) in November 1929. Written and staged two years later, *Fear* left no doubt as to the rightness of the earlier assessment.

Long an established classic of Soviet Russian drama, *Fear,* traces the development of social consciousness in the person of a prominent scientist, the sixty-year-old Professor Ivan Borodin, the Scientific Director of the Institute of Physiological Stimuli.

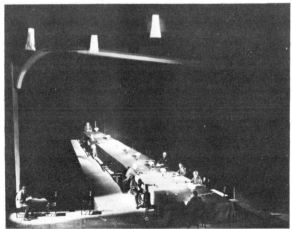

Scenes from the production of Aleksandr Afinogenov's Fear *by the State
Academic Theater of Drama, Leningrad, in 1931.*
(H. W. L. DANA COLLECTION OF THE HARVARD THEATRE COLLECTION)

Borodin's professional association is not irrelevant, for Afinogenov's
consideration of the interrelationship of politics and science (psychology
in particular) in the new Soviet state contributes significantly to the construction of the plot and the ideological foundation of the play. His values and habits shaped in tsarist times, Borodin has not fully adjusted to
the Soviet regime. He recognizes that the institute he heads came into
existence in the Soviet era and that he has been permitted to continue
his scholarly research with no apparent harassment, but he resents the

Soviet policy of pushing the rapid advancement in science of people of little culture and of recent literacy. Representatives of such people are Yelena Makarova, his research assistant at the institute and an ardent Communist, and a backward Kazakh graduate student named Hussain Kimbaev whose thirst for knowledge and intellectual zeal skirt the edge of the ludicrous.

To establish Professor Borodin's social and cultural affinities, Afinogenov surrounds him with a small coterie of like-minded people. Whatever their individuating features, they represent—in varying degrees—familiar negative types in Soviet drama. There is the ambitious opportunist, Nikolai Tsekhovoy, who falsifies his class origins and pretends that his mother is dead in order to advance his career as a "proletarian" scientist; Semyon Vargasov, the Executive Secretary of the institute, a devious, scheming man involved in anti-State activity; Borodin's coeval, Professor Zakharov, his daughter Valentina, and his favorite graduate student Kastalsky—all of whom manifest tastes and cultivate interests which from the early 1920s in Soviet drama have been invested with the significance virtually of symbols of the culture of the *ancien régime*. In the case of Zakharov, it is the refuge from reality represented by Eastern religions and the occult; Valentina sculpts, but cannot overcome an impressionistic manner to achieve the simplicity characterized for her as the highest goal of art by a solid old lady Bolshevik, Klara (Spasova), who belongs to her father's generation; Kastalsky sings, and his taste for romantic songs reminds one of the "decadent" poetic preferences of Bersenev's daughter, Ksenia, in Lavrenyov's *Breakup,* or of the poetic cousin Lariosik in Bulgakov's *Days of the Turbins.*

Kastalsky's opening song in the first scene does more than establish Professor Borodin's milieu; when he comments on the song, Borodin's words immediately reveal the source of the play's conflict. Love—the subject of Kastalsky's song—is, to Borodin's way of thinking (reflecting, of course, his pre-Soviet mentality), one of four eternal unconditioned stimuli: love, fear, rage, and hunger. From these stimuli, argues Borodin, arises all human behavior. From the viewpoint of his opponents, chiefly Yelena Makarova, Borodin's thesis can be faulted on two grounds: first, the professor's researches have been based on laboratory experimentation with animals (thus opening the professor to the accusation that his observations about life and man are drawn not from the study of *life* and *man* but from animals in laboratory situations), and second, that the *human* animal is too complex to be reduced to a system of stimulus-response behavior. Yelena Makarova champions the cause of an Institute of *Human* Behavior to supplant Borodin's institute (the proper study of man, after all, is man) and demands that Borodin and his followers consider the impact of political change on behavioral patterns. As she tells Klara early in the second scene: "Our politics is to transform people. Feelings that were considered innate are now dying out. Envy, jealousy, anger, fear are disappearing. Collectivity, enthusiasm, the joy of life are growing. And we will help these new stimuli to grow."[1]

Submitting not to the pressure of his opponents but rather to his disgust with what he regards as the aggressiveness of social and cultural inferiors, Borodin agrees to establish a laboratory for the study of social behavior. But his true purpose, shared with Kastalsky, is to use all the evidence of scientific research to prove definitively that Russia is being permitted to go down the drain because deficiently prepared workers and peasants are being thrust rapidly up the ladder of scientific advancement thus undermining the authority of established scholars whose superior knowledge and skill they inwardly fear.

The secrecy with which Borodin goes about his new work and the suspicion on the part of Yelena Makarova that he is up to no good result in a vicious tug of war for control of the institute between Borodin's supporters and his opponents. After the clumsiness of the first act with its antiquated pattern of fortuitous arrivals, the play settles into a neater and more plausible course; despite the superfluousness of the simplistically drawn and wholly ideological characters of the Kazakh Kimbaev and Tsekhovoy's daughter by his first marriage, Natasha, the lines of the complicated political infighting are tautly held and easily visible. The high point of the play is reached in the seventh scene of the third act (of four) when Professor Borodin delivers the much anticipated lecture based on the researches of his new laboratory before the staff and students of the entire institute. The act is also the ideological zenith of *Fear* as a whole. Afinogenov dramatizes only the last but ideologically weightiest part of Borodin's lecture. When the professor finishes stating his case the old Bolshevik Klara gets up to rebut it, which she does eloquently and effectively, her rebuttal bringing the act—and its drama of conflicting ideologies—to a close.

Although composed almost exclusively of the lengthy speeches by Borodin and Klara and hence dramatic only in terms of the intellectual, ideological confrontation that occurs, the third act of *Fear* is of more than fleeting interest. It is, properly, the culmination of all the previous maneuvering and infighting among members of the institute. The professor's lecture at last relieves the mystery and suspense aroused by the activities of his new laboratory. What follows the lecture is predictable: Klara, who has been wise in counsel and a voice of moderation throughout the play, rises to deliver the kind of rebuttal capable of turning the tide against Borodin. With the professor's position publicly revealed and ably rebutted, he loses the backing of the Presidium of the institute and is dismissed from his position. Renounced by all his former collaborators and supporters, including Kastalsky, who seek to secure their own political footing by dissociating themselves from and renouncing Borodin, the professor eventually sees the error of his thinking, recants, and is welcomed back to the institute (now headed by Yelena Makarova) by his former opponents, who let him know that they still value his intellect and look forward to a productive relationship with him in the future.

Borodin's lecture itself—or the part of it dramatized in the third act— makes one major point, that the common stimulus of the behavior of eighty percent of the people investigated by the staff of his laboratory is *fear*. The title of the play is at last realized. Borodin's research-supported aprioristic reasoning posits fear as the behavioral stimulus in a majority of Soviet citizens. The source of this fear, the root of the stimulus—and this is what Borodin set out to prove *scientifically*—is the nature of Soviet society itself:

> The milk-woman is afraid that her cow will be confiscated; the peasant is afraid of compulsory collectivization; the Soviet worker is afraid that he will be accused of deviations; the scientific worker is afraid that he will be accused of idealism; the technical worker is afraid that he will be accused of sabotage. . . . Fear compels talented intellectuals to renounce their mothers, to fake their social origin, to wangle their way into high positions. . . . But fear stalks everyone. Man becomes suspicious—shut in—dishonest—careless—and unprincipled. Fear gives rise to absences from work, to the lateness of trains, to breakdowns in industry, to general poverty and hunger. No one attempts anything without an outcry, without having his name inscribed on a blackboard, without the threat of arrest or exile. (*pp. 450–51*)

The twenty percent of the populace with nothing to fear, in Borodin's judgment, is made up of the *vydvizhentsy*, the workers and peasants who have been pushed, with minimal preparation in most cases, into all sorts of positions of responsibility in order to hasten the "proletarianization" of Russian culture. Borodin closes his lecture with an emotional exhortation to the institute to: "Destroy fear—destroy everything that occasions fear—and you will see with what a rich creative life our country will blossom forth!" (*p. 451*)

In her rebuttal Klara sets her concept of fear in the context of the class struggle and declares that fear has lived on earth for "many hundreds and thousands of years" and is not peculiar to the new Soviet society:

Ever since the earth has known a world of slavery and oppression, fear has existed as a mighty weapon for the suppression of man by man. To frighten, to paralyze the wills to break the opposition of those who are oppressed, to transform people into obedient rabbits—this is what the boa constrictors of all time and all peoples have striven for. To frighten! (p. 452)

But fear, continues Klara in the climax of her address, has given birth to fearlessness:

. . . the fearlessness of the oppressed who have nothing to lose, the fearlessness of proletarians—of revolutionists—of Bolsheviks. . . . When we break the resistance of the last oppressor on earth, then our children will look for the explanation of the word "fear" in a dictionary. (p. 453)

Exposed for residual class hostilities and the use of scholarship to protect certain vested interests, Professor Borodin eventually comes around, accepts Yelena's invitation to rejoin the staff of the institute, and in the end renounces his earlier attitude in these words:

I will tell how I joyously greeted every manifestation of fear and how I failed to notice fearlessness. I welcomed the madness of Kimbaev, and I overlooked the growth of his reason . . . I lived a phantom life. I created it in my home and in my study. I did not understand real life. And life penalizes those who shun it—with loneliness . . . This is really a frightful vegeance! (pp. 468–69)

The remarkable thing about the third act of *Fear* is the dramatically plausible way Afinogenov has succeeded in doing justice to two conflicting ideological positions. The predictable conclusion of the play and the defeat of Borodin's concept of fear notwithstanding, *Fear* does give voice to the legitimate apprehension of many intellectuals in Soviet society in the 1930s concerning the encroachment on science and scholarship by politics and the dangers inherent in a hasty proletarianization of culture. That Afinogenov was able to bring this considerable measure of objectivity to his play in its most ideologically substantive passages without foreclosing on its stage future must be attributed to his able delineation of the most important personage, Professor Borodin. The climactic lecture in the third act, both in terms of its structural functions in the play and its contents, proceeds integrally from the characterization of the professor as previously elaborated. The lecture, in all its ideological ramifications, exists and succeeds because, above all, it is artistically valid. A fair comparison can be made with Olesha's handling of the ambivalence toward the proletarian egalitarianism of the new regime and the artist's sense of pride in the characterization of Lyolya in *A List of Assets*.

Before considering the treatment of the maladjusted or "unassimilated" artist or intellectual in the Arbuzov and Pogodin plays, I want to interpolate at this point a brief review of a four-act play by Bill-Belotserkovsky—*Zhizn zovyot (Life Is Calling)*,[2] written in 1933, two years after Afinogenov's *Fear*. Although devoted in broad terms to the theme of alienation and rootlessness, the play introduces a problem figure who is neither an artist nor an intellectual and thus would seem to call for scrutiny under a different rubric. Yet there are some interesting parallels with Afinogenov's *Fear* in Bill-Belotserkovsky's play, and for that reason *Life Is Calling* is being examined in the present context.

A less interesting and complex dramatic work than *Fear* in all respects, including the ideological, *Life Is Calling* deals with the apparently hopeless inability of Fyodor Nikitin to adjust to the new Soviet society. Bemoaning the fact that the Revolution, the Civil War, and the tumultuous years immediately following the Bolshevik seizure of power cost him the best years of his life, Nikitin recognizes that he cannot make a viable place for himself in Soviet society and advance in a career without knowledge. But knowledge requires study and Nikitin, at the age of forty, finds study a formidable challenge. Unable to meet the challenge adequately he despairs and turns to drink for solace. When his "weakness" becomes known, he is dismissed from the Communist Party and his plight worsens. The situation is one that will become formulaic in Soviet drama.

No less formulaic is the play's romantic triangle. Nikitin is married to Galina, the daughter of a distinguished professor named Chadov. Early in the play her social consciousness is not as well developed as her father's and personal concerns take precedence. But she is presented as a person of growth (unlike Nikitin) and by the final curtain she has come to realize the need for the supremacy of the collective. In social terms, Nikitin is unworthy of his wife; he cannot equal her capacity for growth and he becomes in fact an impediment to her own progress. Following a familiar pattern of Soviet drama, Bill-Belotserkovsky complicates Nikitin's domestic situation by introducing the requisite contrasting figure with whom Galina must inevitably become united. This is Pavel Kashirin, the director of a chemical trust and a model Communist. He and Galina try to help Nikitin find himself, but their efforts prove vain. When Nikitin recognizes that they love each other and that in his "positiveness" Pavel is a more appropriate partner in life for Galina, he thinks of committing suicide. Eventually, however, he simply goes away with the vague hope of finding himself, thus leaving Galina and Pavel free to unite.

The banal family drama of Nikitin merits slight attention. But the figure of Professor Chadov is another matter. Like Afinogenov's Professor Borodin, Chadov is a distinguished old scientist. In his social awareness and desire to serve the collective, however, he is not only unlike Borodin but seems to have been conceived as an antithesis to Borodin, that is, as a scholar, a man of science, formed in pre-Soviet Russia, but fully assimilated into the new society and devoted utterly to its betterment. So great in fact is Professor Chadov's sense of social commitment that it becomes the pivot on which the play turns. In Afinogenov's *Fear* it is the civic zeal of younger students and colleagues and the ideological assault on him of his coeval Klara that finally accomplish the transformation of Borodin's views. In *Life Is Calling* no such transformation is required. Professor Chadov's enthusiasm for a scientific plan to convert the eastern regions of Siberia into a rich "new world" is so great that he puts aside all consideration of his advanced age and poor health in order to press the campaign for his plan's acceptance. Fearing for his health and thus placing personal concern (her love for her father) above the civic, Galina seeks to curb Chadov's zeal by keeping him from delivering an important address about his project before the government body which must decide the issue of its acceptance. This address of Chadov thus takes on an importance in the drama similar to that of Borodin's in Afinogenov's *Fear*.

In both plays the lecture (delivered, in part, onstage in *Fear;* a reported offstage action in *Life Is Calling*) represents a culmination, but there the similarity ends. For Borodin, it is the culmination of a vast program of research initiated to give scientific objectivity and credence to his festering animosity toward Soviet rule; for Chadov, conversely, it is the fulfillment of a dream to enrich the Soviet state by making possible the cultivation and habitation of vast areas of Siberia. If Borodin represents a perversion of science and intellect from the Soviet point of view, Chadov demonstrates the beneficence to be reaped from their proper application. To the "obscurantism" of Borodin, Bill-Belotserkovsky opposes the "enlightenment" of Chadov, and where the dedication and zeal of others must bring about the transformation of Professor Borodin, it is Chadov whose dedication and zeal not only point up the failure of Nikitin but eventually work the necessary maturation of his daughter Galina's social consciousness. That Afinogenov's *Fear* was the point of departure for Bill-Belotserkovsky's *Life Is Calling* is more than likely. Although *Fear* closes on the bright note of Borodin's conversion, the portrayal of the central character throughout is in essentially negative albeit compassionate terms. Placing his own professor figure at the center of the plot, Bill-Belotserkovsky drew a contrasting image in *Life Is Calling:* the man of science whose talents are in the vanguard of Soviet progress, who is an inspiration to others. From a largely negative characterization, the shift is to a wholly positive and exemplary parallel character. In a classicist sense, goodness (as conceived in Soviet terms) reaps its just rewards. After his conversion, Professor Borodin regains "life," so to speak, by being accepted back into the institute as a working scientist. The "return to life" in Bill-Belotserkovsky's play has a totally physical aspect. After the delivery of his address, which is enthusiastically received and results in the acceptance of his Siberian project, Professor Chadov seems well on the way to a splendid recovery from his previous illness, a recovery heralded by the sounds and colors of spring flooding his room at the end of the play.

Although they have little in common, Bill-Belotserkovsky's *Life Is Calling*, with its centrality of the issue of the personal versus the collective and its romantic intrigue, is more closely related to Arbuzov's *Tanya* (1938) than to Afinogenov's *Fear*. Now recognized as one of the better Russian plays of the 1930s—its reputation doubtless enhanced, in part, by its author's post-World War II popularity—*Tanya* takes up the theme of social adjustment again in terms of an artist or intellectual. But the central figure is no luminary of the world of art like Olesha's Goncharova or of the world of science like Afinogenov's Professor Borodin. It is, instead, an attractive, vivacious young woman named Tanya who, before marrying a promising geological engineer (Gherman Galashov), has decided on a career in medicine and attends a medical college.

Arbuzov's choice of a main protagonist is not without interest, for it points up an ever more noticeable tendency of twentieth-century post-revolutionary Russian drama to favor heroine over hero. Among plays of the 1920s dealing with the events of the Revolution and the Civil War the outstanding example of this was Trenyov's *Lyubov Yarovaya*. Anatoli Glebov's *Inga* (1928), which we have yet to discuss, was the first Russian play to deal exclusively with the problem of women in the new Soviet society. But with the 1930s what had been only fitful previously took on the semblance of a major current. The central character of Olesha's *A List of Assets* is the actress Lyolya Goncharova. In Afinogenov's *Fear* the ideological lever of the play is the old Bolshevik Klara, who more effectively than anyone else brings about Borodin's transformation. Professor Chadov's Siberian project and Nikitin's inability to find himself command much of the interest in Bill-Belotserkovsky's *Life Is Calling*, yet of greater significance ultimately and the ideological pivot on which the play turns is the evolution of Chadov's daughter Galina's civic consciousness. Vishnevsky, in his romantic-revolutionary drama *An Optimistic Tragedy*, also dating from 1933, gives greatest prominence to a lady commissar who succeeds in welding a group of anarchic sailors into a tough and effective fighting unit. In his play about the life of a former tsarist general's family during the NEP period, *Maria* (written 1933, first published 1935), Isaak Babel never introduces the titular character onstage. Yet she is a strongly felt presence throughout the drama and is invested with an ideologically symbolic significance. *Tanya*, with its outstanding portrait of a young woman, appeared in 1938. Two years later it was followed by another major Soviet play about a young woman, Afinogenov's *Mashenka*.

Tanya is a two-part drama evenly subdivided into eight scenes. The division follows chronological lines. The play as a whole covers the period from November 14, 1934, to November 15, 1938; each scene marks a different time segment with a two-year gap (1936–38) and a major change of place separating parts one and two.

The plot of *Tanya* can be summarized briefly. Out of love for her husband and in order to devote herself completely to him and his career, Tanya drops out of medical school. So utterly is her life bound up with and devoted to her husband's that she cultivates no interests and even appears disinterested in children. The latter point is established indirectly when she learns in an unobtrusive foreshadowing scene in Part One that a neighbor's child dies. Exhibiting no emotion, Tanya simply inquires if the child was a boy or a girl and then lets the matter go at that. Her superficially happy marriage with Gherman is shattered, however, when a prominent woman geologist, Maria Shamanova, enters their lives. Gherman and Maria share common interests; Maria heads the Siberian mine where a new dredge designed by Gherman will be tried out. Dissatisfied with Tanya's lack of interest in anything or anyone other than himself, and strongly attracted to Maria both because of their shared interests and Maria's productive career, Gherman quickly finds himself in love. Here we have a minor variation of a common structural configuration in Soviet drama, one we have already met in Bill-Belotserkovsky's *Life Is Calling*. The basic pattern is that of the romantic triangle. Soviet drama often introduces an ideological dimension simply by positioning a positive (or potentially positive) heroine between two contrasting male characters: one (often the husband) who is maladjusted, "rootless," has found no real place for himself in Soviet society and hence is negative, and another who is a productive contributor to the betterment of the Soviet state, a "positive hero" who comes close to being, or is, an idealization. Since, in Soviet drama, likes must eventually attract one another—and unite—the "negative" character must either experience a positive transformation (which rarely happens) or in some way remove himself or be removed as an obstacle impeding the union of the two positive heroes.

What Arbuzov has done in *Tanya* with this classic Soviet configuration is to reverse the male-female relationship. Now, instead of a woman posed between two contrasting male types, it is a positive hero (Gherman) who is posed between two contrasting female types: the positive heroine Maria Shamanova, and Gherman's wife Tanya, who is presented as negative, however charming, because of her utter subordination both of any sense of the collective and of her own individual personality to an all-consuming devotion to her husband. Faithful to the ideological ground rules of Soviet drama, Arbuzov must link Gherman and Maria romantically. The attraction they feel for each other becomes then wholly natural, but following another ground rule of Soviet drama, this time moral, the positive hero or heroine who completes the romantic triangle must not willingly assume the role of a homebreaker. He or she must suppress personal desire, overcome love, and offer to step aside in order to spare the shaky relationship or marriage. This is the noble gesture made, for example, by Pavel Kashirin in Bill-Belotserkovsky's *Life Is Calling*, when there is no doubt anymore that he and Galina love each other and that her marriage to Nikitin is in jeopardy. But the spiritual nobility of the positive hero or heroine in Soviet drama is paralleled by a similar nobility on the part of the negative hero or heroine. Since a traditional Soviet play without a happy and ideologically correct ending is virtually unimaginable, the negative hero or heroine, once convinced of the love between the positive characters, must redeem himself or herself, at least partially, by demonstrating a capacity for the nobility required to recognize the inevitable and withdraw of his or her own volition.

And so Tanya, too, must choose withdrawal. Not content merely to accept formulae without modification and aiming usually for psychological verisimilitude, Arbuzov brings about Tanya's retreat in this way: he has her overhear a conversation between Gherman and Maria that leaves no doubt as to their feeling for each other and, at the same time, their agreement to part so as to spare the marriage of Gherman and Tanya. Seeing her whole world crumble before her, Tanya withdraws without letting Gherman know where she is going. To enrich and, at the same time, sentimentalize his plot, Arbuzov complicates the intrigue by having Tanya discover that she is pregnant and linking in time her planned announcement of the happy news to Gherman and her discovery of his infatuation for Maria. The plot becomes still more sentimental when Tanya is made to "pay" for her indifference to others by the loss of her baby son through diphtheria. The foreshadowing of the earlier scene with her friend Dusya in which she learns of the death of a neighbor's boy at last materializes.

Part One of *Tanya* establishes the nature of the heroine's personality, her relationship with Gherman, the rapid growth of his love for Maria Shamanova, and the collapse of Tanya's private world of domestic felicity. Part One, in effect, traces the "fall" Tanya must experience as the consequence of the imbalance in her life. But since she is the central character of the play, Tanya must "rise" after her "fall" and it is to her rise, to her "rebirth" that the second part of Arbuzov's play is devoted.

In the two-year period intervening between parts one and two, Tanya returns to medical school and completes her studies, aspiring to "atone" for her previous selfishness through self-sacrifice in service to others. When Part Two opens, she appears as a respected and admired doctor, serving the common people in a provincial community somewhere in the Siberian taiga. The transformation Tanya has undergone can be appreciated by comparing two fragments of dialogue from parts one and two. When Gherman asks her very early in the play if she regrets leaving medical school with only a year left to finish, she replies: "There you go, again! You should never say that to me. . . . I love you, after all, and to love—means to forget yourself, to forget for the sake of the person you love . . ."[3]

But in conversation with Aleksei Ignatov, the head of state gold-mining operations in the Siberian district where she has taken up service, Tanya declares in scene five (the first of Part Two): "Only work can bring a person real happiness. Everything else is nothing but a lie!" When Ignatov asks her if she truly means everything, friendship included, she tells him that sincere friendship demands time, and she has no time for it where she is. Falling into a pensive frame of mind Ignatov observes: "You no doubt believe that solitude makes a person strong. Beware of the idea, because it can lead you to egotism." (p. 79)

Without knowing Tanya's background Ignatov's observation is a perceptive assessment of her new state. Where earlier Tanya's life was imbalanced because of her willingness to sacrifice all other interests in the name of love, she has now swung to the other extreme: a willingness to sacrifice everything—including friendship and love—in the name of work. The result is still imbalance. Moreover, in going from one extreme of self-dedication to another, Tanya exchanges one form of self-gratification for another, without being aware of it. Before the play ends, she must discover this for herself and then move to restore to her life the missing balance.

When *Tanya* first appeared on the stage in 1939, drama critics complained about the second part of the play, objecting mainly to Arbuzov's apparent shift from a concern with character in Part One to an excessive concern with incident in Part Two. Although there is an obvious sentimentalization of Tanya's predicament in the first part of the play, it is Tanya herself, Tanya as a character study, who dominates the first half of the drama.

In Part Two, however, Tanya tends to recede somewhat into the background as the audience's attention is diverted by incident. This has come about as a result of Arbuzov's desire to achieve a high degree of symmetry. Not hearing from Tanya after her sudden disappearance, Gherman naturally assumes that she has walked out on him. He feels free, therefore, to pursue his love for Maria Shamanova and eventually they marry. To strike a balance in his character relationships, Arbuzov felt obliged to introduce a positive male parallel to Gherman with whom Tanya will unite in time once she works out her personal problems. That is Aleksei Ignatov, who is more mature than Gherman was in Part One of the play and wisely counsels Tanya by helping her realize that a life without love is as extreme as a life that consists only of love. All this is plausible and a fair degree of symmetry obtains. But Arbuzov's too fastidious sense of dramatic neatness led him to fall back on contrivance and weave a richer tapestry of incident in Part Two than in Part One.

Not only do Gherman and Maria marry but they settle in Siberia. Arbuzov prepared for this in Part One by establishing the fact that Gherman's father was from Siberia and that Maria was working there on a project in which Gherman was to become personally involved. What strains credulity is the coincidence that Tanya is serving as a doctor in precisely the same Siberian district in which Gherman and Maria live and work. Still more fortuitously, Ignatov, whom Tanya meets in a winter wayside lodge just by chance, is in charge of all gold-mining operations throughout the entire district and is a personal friend of Gherman. Circumstances are thus ripe for a meeting between Gherman, Maria, and Tanya in a setting reminiscent of Chekhov's early one-act play *On the Highway* (1885).

Arbuzov brings it about in a manner that subjects plausibility to its worst assault. In order to carry symmetry still further, Arbuzov gives Gherman and Maria an infant son of their own. When the audience learns of this in Part Two, it is reminded not only of Tanya's son, who died of diphtheria, but of her neighbor's son, whose death Dusya told her about in Part One.

Gherman's son is the immediate device Arbuzov uses to bring Gherman, Maria, and Tanya together once again. Before too much time elapses in Part Two we learn that the boy is critically ill (recall, again, the illness culminating in the death not only of her neighbor's son, but of Tanya's own). On his way into town for a doctor, Gherman stops at the wayside lodge in which Tanya and Ignatov have accidentally met at the beginning of Part Two. Gherman meets Ignatov and the latter tells him that he does not have to go into the city for a doctor since there is a doctor (Tanya) also stopping at the lodge.

Here Arbuzov mounts a little suspense and teases his audience. Ignatov and Gherman go to fetch Tanya and the audience expects the chance reunion to occur at any moment now. But no sooner do they exit when Tanya reappears together with the woman in charge of the lodge, whose sick daughter Tanya has come to visit on a house call. A moment later Ignatov returns, without Gherman. He and Tanya talk briefly and then she goes on her way; Ignatov has said nothing about Gherman and his son. When Gherman reappears moments after Tanya's exit he asks about the doctor and Ignatov berates himself for having forgotten to say anything to Tanya. Here Arbuzov's flirtation with suspense gets him into trouble. For Ignatov to forget to say anything about his friend Gherman's need of a doctor, in view of the context of the first scene of Part Two of the play and the very short space of time in which the actions described occur, seems so unlikely as to border on the improbable. Nevertheless, Arbuzov extracts his measure of suspense and delays the reunion by a few scenes.

When it is finally permitted to occur, it is delivered piecemeal. The condition of Gherman's scn worsens and Tanya agrees to go to the mine of which Maria is the director, since the district doctor who services that area is himself ill (to add to the impressive number of chance happenings). Overcoming her fear of traveling a distance of thirty kilometers at night on snowshoes, Tanya sets out. When she arrives at the mine she quickly encounters Maria (Gherman happens to be away in Moscow at the time) and learns that the sick child is hers and Gherman's. This occurs in the seventh scene.

Only in the eighth and last scene of the play do Tanya and Gherman finally meet, and then not until the scene is half over and Tanya has had the chance to tell Maria everything that had happened to her, except the birth and death of her own son. Using contrivance again to round out the play's structural symmetry, Arbuzov brings Tanya and Gherman together at last on the fifteenth of November, 1938, the fifth anniversary of their first meeting in 1933 and a day they had drunk to in the first scene of the play as the anniversary of their own private Five-Year Plan. The reunion with Gherman is low-key except for an emotionally charged moment when Tanya appears on the verge of telling him about their own son who died. But she checks herself in time, realizing that to tell him now would serve no purpose.

The long-awaited reunion between Tanya and Gherman works a double therapy. Gherman's son is put back on the road to recovery (again balance of a sort: having "lost" Gherman one son, Tanya "returns" him the life of another). Then, after her meeting with him, Tanya realizes that she no longer feels toward Gherman as she once did and that she is no longer afraid, of life, of love. She explains her feelings to Ignatov at the end of the play:

> How strange, as though I had to see him again in order to understand that I'm now an entirely different person! And what a wonderful sense of freedom I feel, as if I hadn't yet lived through a single day of life and only youth were ending! Dear, funny youth . . . (p. 107)

No longer carrying the burden of the past, Tanya is at last free to become a whole person, to fulfill herself as a social being by placing her skills at the service of the collective, and yet at the same time to be capable of loving and being loved, thereby fulfilling herself as a woman. When this realization impresses itself upon her, Ignatov is at her side and the favorable resolution of their relationship is beyond any doubt. Arbuzov has the good stage sense not to handle this overtly but by implication, bringing his play to a more subtle end.

Although more recent Soviet studies of the drama of the 1930s[4] tend to treat the structural deficiencies of Arbuzov's *Tanya* less severely than earlier critics, there is no denying that contrivance and incident are not held in proper restraint in the second part of the play. Chance intrudes too often and the resulting implausibility weakens the effectiveness of the work. Yet there are positive aspects of *Tanya* which should not be overlooked. However correct the ideological posture of the play, ideology is not blatantly proclaimed as it is, for example, in Afinogenov's *Fear* or Bill-Belotserkovsky's *Life Is Calling*. It exists, to be sure, but it is kept in the background with greater emphasis placed on the psychology of character and the role of love in life, generally, and in the new society of Soviet Russia in particular. The social negativism of Tanya is rooted not in any hostility toward the regime, as in Afinogenov's *Fear*, or in ambivalence toward certain aspects of Soviet culture, as it is with Lyolya Goncharova in Olesha's *A List of Assets*, or in a fundamental inability to discipline oneself intellectually in order to meet the challenge necessary to make a meaningful place for oneself in society, as it is with Nikitin in Bill-Belotserkovsky's *Life Is Calling*. Tanya renders herself useless to society by denying it the skills she has studied to acquire in the name of the primacy of the emotions. Arbuzov is saying that a full life requires moderation and a balance between obligations to oneself and obligations to society. Excess either way becomes destructive.

The novelty of *Tanya* when it appeared was fourfold: a) Arbuzov's deemphasis of overt ideological didacticism; b) his highlighting of unheroic, ordinary human emotions; c) his use of time to trace psychological development; and d) the subtlety and even delicacy with which the relations of people, things, events, and nature are not infrequently informed. Flawed though it may be, *Tanya* offered Soviet audiences enough that was new when it appeared to establish it as one of the foremost Russian plays of the 1930s.

Still another treatment of the theme of adjustment distinguishes Nikolai Pogodin's best-known dramatic work, *Kremlyovskie kuranty* (*The Kremlin Chimes*, 1939–40; revised 1955), the second and most highly regarded part of his Lenin Prize-winning trilogy, which includes also *Chelovek s ruzhyom* (*The Man with a Gun*, 1937) and *Tretya, pateticheskaya* (*Third, Pathetique*, 1958). The play is set in the early 1920s, a time when Lenin was preoccupied with a grand scheme for the electrification of Russia as the first step toward the industrial transformation of the country. The plot is far simpler than that of Afinogenov's *Fear* or Arbuzov's *Tanya*. An engineer named Zabelin is hostile to the new So-

Scenes from the 1942 production of Nikolai Pogodin's The Kremlin Chimes
by the Moscow Art Theater.

viet regime and prefers to eke out a living hawking matches in the vicinity of Moscow's Iberian Gates rather than serve the Soviets as an engineer. Eventually he has the opportunity to meet Lenin, who shares with him his vision of the electrification of Russia. Shrewdly avoiding political debate and appealing instead to Zabelin's sense of patriotism and professional pride, Lenin succeeds in convincing him that his skills are needed and wanted. Won over, Zabelin at play's end agrees to work again as an engineer. The foundation for his reconciliation with the Soviet regime is thus established.

Openly hostile to the Soviets, unlike Afinogenov's Professor Borodin, for example, Zabelin denies the new regime his professional training for political reasons, which makes his social alienation entirely different from that of Arbuzov's Tanya. Finding a figure so overtly ill-disposed toward Soviet authority in a play of the late 1930s may seem strange at first but we have to bear in mind that Pogodin's play is set in the early 1920s. The Civil War was a recent memory; Russia was economically enfeebled, Soviet authority was not yet confidently consolidated, and out of dire necessity the retrogressive New Economic Policy was launched in 1921. In such circumstances the complete suppression of malcontents such as Zabelin was not yet feasible (even though Zabelin expects to be arrested at any moment) and, in the light of the urgent national need of his professional competence, was highly undesirable.

While certainly an "ideological" play in the sense that its purpose is a glorification of the wisdom of Lenin, *The Kremlin Chimes* cautiously avoids the grotesque panegyrics of later Soviet plays about national heroes. Although there is a fair measure of didacticism and occasionally gratuitous scenes interpolated primarily to satisfy a didactic purpose, such as Lenin's interview with an English journalist (Act IV, scene 2), Pogodin strives, and with some success, to keep his characters plausible, the political didacticism as integral and unobtrusive as possible, and to portray the figure of Lenin above all in human terms. The last is evidenced not only in the way in which Lenin eventually succeeds in overcoming Zabelin's resistance but in the easy, even folksy behavior he exhibits in the home of the peasant Chudnov in two largely superfluous scenes in the first act and in his nocturnal encounter near the Kremlin embankment with the lovesick sailor Rybakov, also in the first act. Pogodin seems particularly intent on emphasizing Lenin's continuity with Russian tradition, as if thereby to soften the image of a revolutionary leader dedicated to the complete overthrow of all vestiges of the national past. With the immediate postrevolutionary "free love" mania doubtless in mind, Lenin tells Rybakov: "Since you *have* fallen in love, just go right on loving. Only let me give you a piece of advice. Don't go in for newfangled ways. Keep to the old way, Comrade Rybakov." [5]

Although flecked with the gold dust of idealized portraiture, Lenin's characterization impresses nevertheless by the extent to which Pogodin was able to invest it with life. This, despite scenes which begin to appear as obligatory in such mythmaking plays of the 1930s as *The Kremlin Chimes* in which the universality of Lenin's appeal is established. The formula behind such scenes is simple: by means of a series of short episodes (a legacy of the episodic construction of earlier Soviet drama), the better of which are reasonably well integrated into the plot, Lenin (or Stalin, as the case becomes later) encounters a variety of common people—peasants, workers, soldiers, and sailors (and in *The Kremlin Chimes*, an intellectual such as Zabelin)—with whom he usually establishes immediate rapport and communicates easily and who, in turn, respond to him positively and actively contribute to the legend of omniscience and omnipotence.

In *The Kremlin Chimes* one of these "common people," the sailor Rybakov, serves both a structural and an ideological function. The subplot of the play turns on the love affair between Rybakov and Zabelin's daughter Masha. Because of his hostility toward everything Soviet, Zabelin hotly opposes Masha's relationship with so ardent a Communist as Rybakov. The bias is social as well as political. But Rybakov is on close terms with Lenin (Pogodin, alas, never bothers to explain how this came about), and when Zabelin agrees to work on the electrification project and is given an office, Rybakov is assigned to him as an assistant. Lenin explains the reason for this when Zabelin suggests that a Marxist theoretician would probably have been more in order:

LENIN: Now, I ask you, what do you want with a theoretician?
ZABELIN: You sound as if you're joking.
LENIN: I'm not joking. What do you want a theoretician for?
ZABELIN: Well, I'm what's called a bourgeois specialist. Don't I have to be schooled?
LENIN: But it was not because we expected you to take a course in Marxism that we approached you. We want you to work and to work good and hard. That will be the best Marxism—both for you and for us. Sasha Rybakov isn't much of a theoretician but he's a brilliant organizer. I sent him to you to carry out the dictatorship of the proletariat with you. For without the dictatorship of the proletariat we'll never achieve electrification and all your work will be wasted. (p. 87)

Through his professional association with Rybakov and Rybakov's relationship with Masha, Zabelin's "adjustment" to the new society is thus made easier and given more depth. Rybakov is also a link with the symbolism from which the play's title derives. The mechanism controlling the operation of the Kremlin's chimes on the Spasskaya Tower has ceased functioning and Lenin is anxious to have it repaired. From very early in the play the return of the chimes to normal functioning becomes equated with the return of Russia itself to normality after the disruption of the Revolution and the Civil War, a disruption for which the Bolsheviks are held responsible. Rybakov is entrusted with the task of finding a clockmaker capable of fixing the chimes and finally produces one of the play's more colorful minor characters—an old man who once repaired Count Leo Tolstoy's watch, who quotes Hamlet, and who was dismissed from a cooperative workshop for quoting a fable of Aesop when he was accused of wasting an inordinate amount of time on the repair of an antique English clock. The clockmaker accepts the assignment and sets to work. His efforts are crowned with success and in a symbolic finale the chimes begin to play again, heralding not only their return to normal functioning, with the broader implications of this for the nation as a whole, but the end of the play and, in the "enlightenment" of engineer Zabelin, his integration into the new society. Just as Zabelin is about to take his leave of Lenin, after all outstanding issues between them have been resolved, Lenin detains the engineer, almost prophetically sensing that the chimes are about to start playing again. At precisely this moment Lenin's secretary, Dzerzhinsky (the head of the CHEKA), Rybakov, and the clockmaker enter to announce that the chimes' mechanism is about to be started:

> SECRETARY: Comrade Lenin, you wanted to see the clockmaker at the exact moment the Kremlin chimes . . .
>
> CLOCKMAKER: Sh . . . please!
>
> DZERZHINSKY: Excuse us for this sudden invasion, Vladimir Ilyich, but . . it's quite an event, you know . . . the clock . . .
>
> CLOCKMAKER (*to* DZERZHINSKY): Please . . . there's only a second left.
>
> LENIN: The clock's working, Sasha?
>
> RYBAKOV: I think so. Wait . . . wait . . .
>
> (*The clock begins to strike the hour.*)
>
> ZABELIN: What's that? The Kremlin clock? Why, so it is.
>
> DZERZHINSKY: I bet you used to rail at us. . . . Those Bolsheviks! Why under them even the Kremlin clock stopped!
>
> ZABELIN: I plead guilty.
>
> DZERZHINSKY: Did you use good strong words?
>
> ZABELIN: Sometimes.
>
> LENIN: Do you hear? The chimes. . . . This is a great thing. When it all comes true—all that we're only dreaming about now, and arguing about and worrying about— Then the Kremlin clock will chime a new day, and that day will witness new electrification plans, new dreams, new daring quests. (*pp. 87–88*)

2. The merging of the themes of assimilation and industrialization in Pogodin's *The Kremlin Chimes* also characterizes several of the foremost postrevolutionary Russian plays dealing with the first Five-Year Plan and "socialist construction." The subject of a great deal of fiction of varying quality, "socialist construction" produced a bumper crop of dramatic works as well, a few of the most important of which we shall consider now.

One of the earliest—and one of the more interesting—was the four-act *Inga* (written 1928, produced March 1929 in the Theater of the Revolution in Moscow) by Anatoli Glebov (pseudonym for Kotelnikov; 1899–1964), a prolific dramatist in his time and a man very active in the organizational area of "proletarian" theatrical culture. He was the first secretary of the Theater Section of RAPP and one of the heads of the Proletarian Theater society between 1928 and 1931. Although a collection of six of his plays was published in Moscow in 1967, Glebov is best remembered today for two plays, *Zagmuk* (first produced 1925) and *Inga*. *Zagmuk*, about a popular uprising in ancient Babylonia, has always been considered a play better read than staged and had a very brief stage career; *Inga*, on the other hand, is rightly regarded as Glebov's best work and has fared well in the theater. Significantly, it was the only play of his to attract attention abroad; an English translation is included in *Six Soviet Plays*, edited by Eugene Lyons and published in 1934, and a German version of the play was staged at Piscator's theater in Berlin under the title *Frau in Front*.

Inga first impresses an audience as a feminist play, that is, a play about women's rights, in which the major roles are played by women. Set in an unspecified large industrial town in the period of the first Five-Year Plan, the play focuses on the professional and emotional problems of the titular character (Inga Rizer), the thirty-year-old manager of a clothing factory. Working under her are several rough-hewn lesser factory officials, who are offended by the thought of taking orders from a woman. The most outspoken are Ignat Ryzhov, the assistant manager of the factory whose incompetence results in Inga's disciplining him, and Sofron Boltikov, the foreman of the women's apparel shop and a wife-beater. The tenor of the conservative resentment against Inga and everything she represents is conveyed in no uncertain terms in a tirade of Boltikov directed at his much abused wife Nastya:

> You vermin have been given freedom! (*Spits violently.*) Tfui! The whole factory is full of your kind! All sorts of women's departments! For forty years I have been working quietly without trouble. But *they* won't let a fellow be! They've started shock-brigades, socialist competition . . . (*Spits again*) Tfui! I, an experienced master operator, have to compete! Think of it! Has anybody ever heard the like! And *who* is the brigade-leader. A wo-man. Who is the manger? A wo-man! A manager with a skirt on. Eh? And what kind of a skirt, eh? (*Indicates above the knees.*) Up to there! Eh? What do you call that? What have we come to? . . . Shaming me at the conferences. Threatening a trial! (*Spits.*) Tfui! A nightmare. What *is* this? When will this rule by women be overthrown? They've bound me hand and foot, damn them.[6]

The Soviet program of equal opportunity for women and the full utilization of women in the program of socialist construction upsets the obscurantists who not only rebel at the very thought of women superiors but find it difficult to adjust to new ideas in general. The problem of ad-

justment posed in *Inga* is twofold: a) the need for overcoming the unyielding, unbending conservatism of just such old-line Bolsheviks as
Ryzhov and Boltikov who while nominally active supporters of the new
regime become, in fact, obstacles in the way of progress; and b) the personal sacrifices demanded by the great program of construction.

Conflict springs from two sources: the tug of war between Inga and
her opponents, and the emotional drama involving Inga, the weak and
indecisive Factory Committee chairman, Dmitri Grechannikov, and his
wife Glafira. The romantic triangle contains familiar elements already
encountered in Arbuzov's *Tanya*. Glafira, like Tanya in the first half of
the Arbuzov play, devotes herself fully to her husband and their one
child. But Dmitri falls prey to a sense of nagging insufficiency in much
the same way that Tanya's husband Gherman does and like Gherman he
soon finds himself strongly attracted to a dynamic woman of professional
accomplishment. For Gherman, it was Maria Shamanova; for Dmitri, it
is Inga. But Dmitri is drawn less sympathetically than Gherman. Profes-
sing love for Inga, which she returns, he cannot bring himself to break
definitively with Glafira because of their child and suggests a liaison instead of marriage. Although urged to accept this arrangement by a rabid
exponent of women's rights, the seven-times married radical intellectual
Mera Gurvich (one of the more felicitous characters in the play), Inga
refuses and demands that Dmitri choose either to give up his wife and
family or forget her. When Glafira confronts Dmitri with evidence of
private meetings with Inga, a nasty scene follows in which Dmitri announces his intention of leaving Glafira. After he walks out on her,
Glafira attempts suicide by poison (Act II, scene 7).

Much of what follows in *Inga* recalls the pattern of the second part of
Arbuzov's *Tanya*. Having resolved to "transform" herself, Glafira throws
herself energetically into work at the factory. She becomes a new
woman, more sure of herself, more attractive and admired. But unlike
Tanya the romantic triangle in *Inga* is not enlarged to a quadrangle (as it
is in Arbuzov's play with the addition of Ignatov). Dmitri, whose relationship with Inga is anything but smooth largely because of Inga's insistence on her own independence, is overcome by the change in Glafira
and still cannot bring himself to break off with her formally. Instead, he
proposes that all three of them—he, Glafira, and Inga—live together as
the best method of resolving his dilemma. Both women refuse and Dmitri finally decides in favor of Inga. As time goes on, however, relations
between the two of them deteriorate. Inga cannot be dominated and refuses to retreat from her professional career for the sake of her domestic

life. Her attitude is manifest in the question she puts to Dmitri at a tense moment near the end of the play:

> INGA: What do you expect me to do—sacrifice my duty as I under-
> stand it, my work? . . .
> DMITRI: What does this mean, then? The end?
> INGA: If you put it that way, I can do only one thing: go. I cannot
> choose between my work and you. (*p. 384*)

Not long after, Inga restates her position in still more positive terms in conversation with the *raisonneur* of the play, the old Communist Somov:

> Everything which stands in the way of reconstruction . . . everything
> external, internal, personal, general, has to be swept away . . . Sen-
> timents are mobilized, too! Oh, you know that this is not easy! But
> however it may be, the personal life of Inga Rizer will give you no
> more trouble! (*p. 387*)

Realizing the impossibility of dedicating herself fully to her work and at the same time gratifying Dmitri's emotional needs, Inga bars any compromise and dooms the romance. Despite Mera Gurvich's chiding that the triangular love relationship could have been resolved in a more satisfying way, the play ends with Inga stoutly defending her attitude and the final settlement of the relationship between Dmitri and Glafira left ambiguous.

Glebov's play is usually characterized as an examination of conflicting attitudes toward the role of woman and the family in the new Soviet society during the era of the first Five-Year Plan. The Plan itself and the whole program of socialist construction represent a panoramic background against which the socially relevant drama of Inga, Dmitri, and Glafira is played out. Yet granted this, it would be an oversimplification to insist that *Inga* is not really a play about the Plan and reconstruction.

The campaign to overcome lingering obscurantist hostility to the extension of full partnership in the construction of the new society to women and even the several allusions to Freud in *Inga* relate, and not at all marginally, to the overriding matter of the transformation of prevailing social attitudes called for in order to make a success of the program of socialist construction.

To make his points Glebov operates with an interesting variety of contrasting characters representative of specific contemporary attitudes. Ryzhov and Baltikov are obscurantists clinging to outmoded ideas; Somov is the familiar wise old Communist; and Dmitri, the romantic male lead whose weakness and indecisiveness prevent him from perceiving the calamitous effect which the intrusion of the personal can have on the work of construction. Among his women, Glebov places Glafira, who easily emerges as the most important figure of the play (as the bearer of a new Soviet ideal of marital relations and family life), between several extremes: Nastya, Boltikov's wife, a throwback to the "old order" whose religious devotion borders on fanaticism and who accepts the beating of her husband as the natural order of things; Mera Gurvich, whose flamboyant sexual radicalism is viewed as ultimately socially destructive; and Inga herself, whose uncompromising sense of utter commitment to her work diminishes a womanishness Glebov ardently defends in his play through implication, if not directly. Moreover, while certainly harboring some admiration for Inga, Glebov takes pains to establish the fact that the character is *exceptional*. The extent to which Inga is finally capable of holding her emotions in check and efficiently excluding them from her professesional activities is certainly not within every woman's grasp. And were that the case, Glebov implies, what would become of family life? From this point of view the more womanly, more rounded Glafira is a character of richer promise than Inga, for Glafira, once liberated, no longer enslaved by a husband and domestic routine, will in time be able to achieve the reconciliation of the demands of the personal life and the collective life which Glebov implies is ultimately desirable for the establishment of a Soviet concept of a family life composed of true equals. Arbuzov had already made such a concept the basis of his play *Tanya*.

How exceptional Inga truly is Glebov reaffirms by assigning his character an obviously foreign (German) name, by indicating that Inga was reared abroad, and by pointing out quite unequivocally that Inga cannot bear children. The words of Somov, in Act III, scene 10, shed the most light on Glebov's true intentions regarding the character of Inga. Attacking the sexually permissive philosophy of Mera, Somov says:

> To me such a union, when both are equal, friendly, free, is the ideal . . . One can chatter about anything. But just you try to abolish all law, give freedom to such types as this . . . (*points to Ryzhov*) . . . Ask yourself, what would happen then? You don't know? Well, I'll tell you. There will be abortions, there will be infanticides, another hundred thousand homeless children! And as a result, such specimens—(*points again to Ryzhov*)—and we have plenty of them—will push woman back along the entire line. This is what will happen! One has to be realistic . . . I admire Inga. I like her decisiveness, her firmness. She lives audaciously, strongly. But, after all, she is—how

shall I put it?—a laboratory product . . . But the millions? The millions are praying to God . . . The millions are suffocating in kitchen stench, and carrying bruises from their beatings! You won't find many like Inga. That's what you have to understand. The millions have other problems. They need the family. (*p. 360*)

This, then, is Glebov's main argument in *Inga*. In order for a viable socialist Russia to be constructed not only are dedication and a great capacity for work demanded but indeed new social attitudes which will finally raise woman to full partnership with man, with the eventual strengthening of the family which Glebov sees as the backbone of the new society. As admirable as Inga may be in some respects she is, as Glebov carefully shows, an exception and, the title of the play notwithstanding, it is Glafira who must truly become an exemplar to Soviet womanhood.

If Glebov's play now seems dated, even in Soviet terms, and its characters seldom more than types, *Inga*'s psychological orientation and its often vivid dramatization of specific social concerns of the tumultous 'twenties in Russia (sexual permissiveness, the new concept of woman and the family, Freud) establish it as one of the more unusual plays on the theme of the first Five-Year Plan.

Nikolai Pogodin's first play, *Temp* (*Tempo*, 1929; first produced in 1930 in the Vakhtangov Theater in Moscow), is his best-known work after *The Kremlin Chimes* and a classic of Soviet drama. Compared to Glebov's *Inga*, *Tempo* addresses itself much more directly to the monumental task of transforming the dream of the first Five-Year Plan into reality. The play came about originally as a newspaper assignment. A member of the editorial staff of the Moscow *Pravda* at the time, Pogodin was sent to Stalingrad to write about the tractor plant then under construction along American lines (something the dramatist alludes to in Act II, scene 4, of *Tempo* when the engineer Goncharov says at one point that, "A fool in *Pravda* has been writing about our tempos and the progress we've made"—p. 186). Pogodin was stunned by the pace of the construction (compared to pre-Revolution days) and the way peasant workers were incorporated into the project. Out of his impressions came not only the article he was commissioned to write but his first play, *Tempo*.

Pogodin's enthusiasm for his subject is amply evident throughout the play, the ideological sense of which is summed up in the closing words of Boldyrev, the director of the entire construction project: "On one sixth of the globe, in pain and joy, a socialist world is being born" (p. 224). But Pogodin's enthusiasm—and the "classic" status of *Tempo* in the annals of Soviet dramaturgy—are not enough to compensate for the play's serious weaknesses. Timing, we know, often has much to do with the success or failure of a literary work. In the case of *Tempo* Pogodin was fortunate in that timing worked to his advantage. On its merits, *Tempo* is of slight value as drama. It has neither the sociological interest nor the psychological dimension of Glebov's *Inga*. But it was an early attempt to dramatize the frenzy of construction of the first Five-Year Plan (which is *not*, as we have seen, Glebov's primary interest in *Inga*) and apppeared at precisely the right moment to assure its historical importance. Moreover, Pogodin balances his dramatized account of a particular feat of construction with considerable humor, and it is this humor more than any other component of the play that can beguile an audience into taking little notice of its defects.

The plot as such is so thin as to require little comment. The workers on the construction project directed by Boldyrev are determined to score a triumph for socialism by even exceeding what they understand to be standard American work tempos. "Tempo" and "American" are integrally related in the play, for assisting in the construction is a taciturn American engineer named Carter (modeled on an American engineer who did, in fact, participate in the construction of the Stalingrad tractor plant). Carter acquaints the Russians with American work tempos, which the Russians in turn not only accept as their own norms but which they strive to surpass. Lurking among the staff of construction engineers, however, is the familiar "wrecker," in this case an engineer of prerevolutionary stamp named Goncharov, who harbors deep-seated grievances against the new regime. Goncharov tries his best to sabotage the construction project but is discovered when he tries to frame a happy-go-lucky fellow engineer, Kastorkin. When he realizes the game is up and Kastorkin confronts him with the truth, Goncharov kills himself. With the "wrecker" out of the way and the threat of further sabotage removed, the construction is continued at a splendid pace and completed well ahead of schedule.

In dramatic terms, there seems hardly enough to such a plot to make *Tempo* theatrically viable. The introduction of an earnest and nonpolitical American engineer is a curiosity that attracts some attention for a while, and the sabotage, discovery, and suicide of Goncharov supply a dash of melodrama. Perhaps to add more flesh to the bare bones of his plot Pogodin introduced other items of little perceptible relevance, such as the entire fifth scene of Act II, in which Boldyrev thinks his younger sister Valka, a medical student, has died, and the drunkard in Act IV, scene 8, who sings a song, alludes to such literary figures as Balmont and Mayakovsky, rhapsodizes about the great transformation of Russia that he sees taking place before his very eyes and, apart perhaps from ideology, serves no purpose in the play.

Yet, with its faults, *Tempo* did score a success with audiences and attracted enough attention to be translated. The one clearly discernible reason for this, as I have already indicated, is the healthy dose of humor in the play. Basically, the humor springs from a single source. The actual construction workers—as distinguished from engineers—whom Pogodin brings onstage are *peasants*. Their antics, their colorful, earthy peasant speech, their superstitions and fears, the confusion and misunderstanding resulting from their feeble literacy make up a considerable part of the playing time of *Tempo* and virtually guarantee its success with Russian audiences. A keen observer, particularly of the so-called common people, Pogodin shrewdly got as much mileage as he possibly could out of the participation of barely literate peasants in a great construction project. Without the peasant workers *Tempo* would have been stillborn as a drama about the Five-Year Plan. But with them, with their splendidly comic behavior and speech, Pogodin's essentially inconsequential and schematic play acquires an engaging liveliness and good humor that rescue it from oblivion.

Pogodin's common touch served him well again in the play generally conceded to be his best on a Five-Year Plan theme—*Aristokraty* (*Aristocrats*, 1935). A better-structured and more interesting drama than *Tempo*, *Aristocrats* deals with the use of the inmates of a prison camp somewhere in the Baltic region to assist in the construction of the Baltic-White Sea Canal. As in *Tempo*, plot and conflict in any conventional sense barely exist. Representing a wide variety of contemporary offenders, both political and criminal, the inmates at first oppose any cooperation with the prison authorities (most of whom are rehabilitated former criminals themselves) and, in broader terms, with the Soviet regime.

Three figures soon emerge as the most prominent among the inmates: the engineers Botkin and Sadovsky, political offenders imprisoned for "anti-State wrecking activities," and the captain, Kostya Dorokhov, a former thief. The prison camp is administered by a CHEKA official (Gromov) who fulfills a function analogous to that of Boldyrev in *Tempo* and is presented as being as much interested in reforming and rehabilitating the prisoners as in building the canal.

The resistance of the inmates weakens as they are apprised of the fact that participation in the construction of the canal will bring an improvement in their situation and a reduction of their prison sentences. Among the political prisoners the first to cooperate is the aristocratic engineer Botkin, followed not long after by Sadovsky. In both cases the motivation is very much like that of engineer Zabelin in Pogodin's somewhat later play *The Kremlin Chimes:* the desire to put their professional skills to use once again, the understandable human desire to resist stagnation and vegetation. At the end of the play both men are pardoned and even decorated by the Soviet government (or, in other words, virtue again is rewarded).

Among the criminals there is no dramatic metamorphosis, no sudden reversal of positions. By participating in the construction of the canal they realize that they can make life easier for themselves and get out of the camp earlier. In its plausibility their motivation compares favorably with that of Botkin and Sadovsky, although it is of an entirely different order. The captain, Kostya, emerges as the leader of the criminal faction and when he shifts from outright rejection to a sort of begrudging willingness to cooperate, the others follow his lead. As they get deeper into the occasionally dangerous work, they begin to respond to the challenge and experience a sense of rebirth. The shrewd but gentle treatment of Gromov, his willingness to entrust the criminals with a variety of responsibilities in time encourages feelings of commitment and even pride among them. Were Pogodin a more subtle artist he might have curbed the ideological zeal that led him to carry the regeneration of his criminals to the point where they even indulge in a form of "socialist competition" among themselves. But granted this deficiency, Pogodin did take pains to make the conversion of his criminals psychologically plausible and, in large measure, he succeeded.

Since conflict in *Aristocrats* takes the form only of the initial resistance of the inmates to cooperation in the canal project and is in no way powerfully dramatized, Pogodin attempted to relieve the general blandness of the "postconversion" part of the plot by introducing a "lapse" or "deviation" toward the end of the play. When Kostya is crudely denied some glue to repair a broken accordion and is called a thief (after he considers himself already reformed) for no particular reason, it appears for a while that he attempts to escape from the camp bearing with him a typewriter pilfered from the office of the secretary who denied him the glue. But the suspense is of short duration (any greater complication of plot would surely have taxed Pogodin's talent for dramatic construction). Kostya soon reappears, explains the reason for

A camp scene from the production of Nikolai Pogodin's Aristocrats *by the Moscow Realistic Theater under the direction of N. P. Okhlopkov in 1935.*
(H. W. L. DANA COLLECTION OF THE HARVARD THEATRE COLLECTION)

his actions, and returns the typewriter; the incident is promptly forgotten and the callous secretary herself is disciplined.

At the conclusion of *Aristocrats* (the title is ironic and refers to the camp inmates), when the canal is opened and the first steamer is prepared to sail through it, a meeting is held at which the prisoners are asked to explain how their lives have been changed by participation in the building of the canal. The most important address is that of Kostya who suggests that the chance to work on the canal restored life to him by enabling him, perhaps for the first time, to experience a feeling of purpose and even dignity as a man. That his words, enriched with musical allusions and punctuated by tears, are meant to express the collective attitude of the former inmates is not to be doubted.

The meager plot of *Aristocrats* transfers the main interest to a specific set of characters (the inmates), just as in *Tempo* in the case of the peasants. Not since Gorky's *The Lower Depths,* which Pogodin must surely have had in mind (along with, undoubtedly, the works of several Russian prose writers of the 1920s—Babel and Leonov, for example—which display a wide variety of contemporary criminal types), had a Russian dramatist taken up the challenge of bringing another motley crew of criminals and social outcasts on the stage.

The analogy with Gorky's play is entirely reasonable. Much like Gorky Pogodin strives to compensate for the lack of any extensively elaborated intrigue by enriching the fabric of his play with the coarse but engrossing language and mannerisms of unusual characters. But Gorky's focus is exclusively on a naturalistically conceived and portrayed basement milieu peopled by the dregs of contemporary society. In Pogodin's play, the appearance of representatives of the intelligentsia (Botkin, Sadovsky) and government officialdom (Gromov) introduces another, different dimension. Moreover, no external possibility of self-reform and regeneration exists for the inhabitants of Gorky's sordid underground world.

In *Aristocrats*, participation in the Baltic-White Sea Canal project affords the prisoners the opportunity to engage in some socially useful activity, to regain or acquire a sense of social identity and purpose. Initially, to be sure, they are motivated only by the desire to improve their lot in the camp (Pogodin is careful to establish this, though the point is sometimes overlooked in criticism), but as time goes on their active role in a great undertaking works on their consciousness and the way toward their regeneration is prepared. At least, that is what Pogodin would have us believe.

Given its "plotlessness," *Aristocrats* must sustain interest in the only way it really can: through its characters and the degree of skill with which Pogodin makes their transformation psychologically reasonable. If the camp official Gromov bears a trace of idealization in his compassionate understanding and Botkin and Sadovsky are familiar stereotypes, the criminals, male and female, are sufficiently diversified and colorful (like the peasants in *Tempo*) to attract—and hold—attention. Again, knowing where his strength lies, Pogodin makes them the dominant element in the play.

The nightmarish vision of Soviet prison life unfolded by Aleksandr Solzhenitsyn in his short novel *Odin den Ivana Denisovicha* (*One Day in the Life of Ivan Denisovich*, 1962) and in his play *Olen i shalashovka* (*The Love-Girl and the Innocent*, 1954) may be only faintly (and not purposefully) foreshadowed in Pogodin's *Aristocrats*, but the world of the camp inmate was still enough of a rarity in the Russian drama of Pogodin's time to virtually guarantee strong initial audience interest. The realism with which Pogodin's prisoners are invested, the fair degree of psychological plausibility, and the shrewd deflection of the forced labor aspect of the subject (which Solzhenitsyn sheds much light on in his *The Gulag Archipelago*) contributed to the sustenance rather than diminution of this interest, making *Aristocrats* not the outright ideological exhortation it might easily have been, but an occasionally diverting and stageworthy play and one of the more curious on the theme of the Five-Year Plan and socialist construction.

3. To the nonspecialist first becoming acquainted with twentieth-century Russian drama and with postrevolutionary Russian literature in general it might seem that with the gradual consolidation of Soviet power and its more confident control over the arts, literature could be organized completely to serve the needs of Party and State and, in the instance of something as nationally important as the first Five-Year Plan, a tailor-made panegyric exalting goals and accomplishments could quickly be delivered on order. The expectation then would be that with relatively minor variations in plot and character, such a literature would be characterized by a dreary sameness.

The imposition by the Party of controls on all the arts and literature in particular in Russia is a fact beyond dispute. But the institution of controls was not an accomplished fact until the mid-1930s. Before that time far more freedom of individual expression and experimentation existed than is commonly appreciated. The campaign to organize literature in support of the first Five-Year Plan indeed yoked the talents of many writers to the chariot of socialist construction; yet the ideological orthodoxy with which literary works on the theme of the Plan are informed did not inhibit the search for variety in both subject matter and technique. If socialist construction in its manifold aspects had to be uniformly presented as a glorious enterprise capable of transforming Russia in no less far-reaching a way than the transformation wrought in the early eighteenth century by the reforms of Peter the Great, writers still enjoyed some latitude as to focus. The sameness I spoke of before undeniably exists but within well-defined limits: the undertaking (the Five-Year Plan) is glorious and hence must be glorified, Communists must be shown as the principal agents under whose guidance the miracle of industrial transformation will be accomplished, all opposition to the program (and the new regime), whatever the source, must eventually be overcome, and virtue in the form of the successful fulfillment of whatever aspect of the Plan being dealt with must be rewarded by the conclusion of the work. The expectation of an almost unavoidable schematism is high. But surprisingly, even granted the obvious limitations, artistic ingenuity found ways of achieving a fair range of originality. To be sure, schematism and predictability plague the drama devoted to the glories of the Five-Year Plan no less than the prose fiction of the late 1920s and early 1930s. A vast quantity of paper was expended on potboilers. But works of originality, quality, and interest still managed to appear from time to time to remind readers—and theatergoers—that genuine talent invariably finds ways of circumventing externally imposed limitations of whatever character. Consider the plays that we have surveyed so far on the theme of industrialization. If Pogodin, for example, is more schematic and ideologically obvious on the whole than such contemporaries in the drama as Bulgakov, Mayakovsky, Glebov, and Kirshon (about whom more shortly), we still have to appreciate the dramatist's desire to strike an original chord by focusing in such industrialization plays as *Tempo* and *Aristocrats* on the participation of *peasants* and *camp inmates*. More attentive to character psychology and plot than Pogodin, Glebov sought an original dimension for *Inga* by viewing industrialization primarily in terms of the position of *women* in contemporary Russian society.

A wholly different aspect of the Five-Year Plan and socialist construction comes to the fore in one of the most exceptional plays of the period, *Khleb* (*Bread*, 1930) by Vladimir Kirshon (1902–38), whose promising career was cut short by execution in the wake of the purge trials of the late 'thirties. Kirshon was condemned on a charge of "Trotskyism" and was put before a firing squad on July 28, 1938. Although a name now virtually unknown outside of Russia, Kirshon's first play *Konstantin Terekhin* (also known by the title *Rzhavchina, Rust*, 1926), written in collaboration with his friend Andrei Uspensky, was another Soviet play of the 1920s to find its way, under the title *Red Rust*, into the repertoire of the New York Theatre Guild. Its first production, by the Guild Studio, was at the Martin Beck Theater on December 17, 1929, with Lee Strasberg, Luther Adler, and Franchot Tone among the members of the cast. The American acting version of the play by Virginia and Frank Vernon, a rather free adaptation, was published by Brentano's (New York) in 1930.

Kirshon followed *Konstantin Terekhin* with a still-admired industrialization play, *Relsy gudyat* (*The Rails Are Humming*), in 1927. *Gorod vetrov* (*City of the Winds*), about the Revolution, came in 1929. *Bread*, dealing with the impact of the first Five-Year Plan on rural Russia, and

A scene from the 1929 Theatre Guild production of Vladimir Kirshon's Red Rust *at the Martin Beck Theater, New York. Directed by Herbert J. Biberman. The cast included such well-known actors as Luther Adler, Gale Sondergaard, Lee Strasberg, George Tobias, and Franchot Tone.*

Kirshon's most important dramatic work, was written in 1930. Within the next six years Kirshon brought three more plays to the stage: *Sud* (*The Court*, 1932), notable for its Western setting, *Chudesny splav* (*The Miraculous Alloy*, 1934), his most popular work, a contemporary social comedy against the background of the search for a certain alloy for airplane construction, and in 1936—two years before his execution—*Bolshoy den* (*A Great Day*), a drama about pilots and life in the Soviet armed forces of the time.

A masterpiece of construction in comparison to the plays of Glebov and Pogodin previously discussed, *Bread* deals with two issues of considerable contemporary relevance: 1) the obstacles posed by the kulaks—

A scene from the original production of Vlaldimir Kirshon's The Rails Are
Humming *by the MGSPS (Moscow District of Soviet Trade Unions) Theater,*
Moscow, in 1928.
(H. W. L. DANA COLLECTION OF THE HARVARD THEATRE COLLECTION)

well-to-do peasants whom the Soviets annihilated as a class—to the
implementation of the agricultural goals of the first Five-Year Plan, and
2) the procedures Communists should follow in bringing their economic,
political, and social ideas to fruition. In a grain-producing region of the
Soviet Union in the autumn of 1929 a rural community is asked to
supply the state with a certain quantity of grain. In the 'twenties in Russia the matter was one of national urgency. The kulak element in the
community, organized and led by the sixty-year-old Kvasov, an outstanding dramatic portrait, opposes further grain requisitions and fo-
ments an armed revolt in protest. The revolt is crushed with the aid of
local Communists and pro-regime peasants and the kulaks are taken into

custody. Credit for the defeat of the kulak "conspiracy" belongs to the Communist hero of *Bread*, Dmitri Mikhailov, the Secretary of the Regional Committee of the Communist Party.

Through a variation of the familiar romantic triangle Kirshon introduces the second major issue of *Bread* and at the same time integrates the sociopolitical and psychological "dramas" of his play. An old wartime friend of Mikhailov, Pavel Raevsky, returns from a sojourn in the West and is assigned as a delegate to the Regional Committee headed by Mikhailov. Not long after Raevsky is brought onstage the nature of the imminent conflict involving Mikhailov and Raevsky—political and personal—becomes apparent. The fervor and excitement of revolutionary and Civil War years now just memories, Mikhailov devotes himself fully to the efficient execution of his official duties. Kirshon depicts him as hardworking, methodical, reasoned, and unemotional. Raevsky, however, is a contrasting figure. Surrounded by an aura of romantic glamour he views present conflicts in the light of the combat and derring-do of past years and is contemptuous of what he considers Mikhailov's stodginess and lack of passion. Raevsky's dash and cosmopolitanism (he has travelled in the West and paints a glowing picture of much of what he saw there) greatly impress Mikhailov's wife, Olga, who is dissatisfied with life in the provinces and regards her husband as no more than a Party automaton whose affection "is lavished only on resolutions, decrees, regulations!" (p. 245).

The latent conflict between Mikhailov and Raevsky comes to the fore and assumes a political dimension when Raevsky is entrusted with the requisitioning of the grain. Romantically drawn to him, Olga chooses to leave with Raevsky as he sets forth to expedite matters. Once among the peasants Raevsky bungles his commission. He is easily duped by the shrewd kulaks and when an error in judgment triggers the incident that culminates in armed revolt, the unreasoned romantic gesture and heroism which characterize his personal style prove counterproductive. At the crucial moment Mikhailov steps in and saves the day, demonstrating thereby the superiority of his own unromantic but effective approach.

The problem posed by the character of Raevsky, which crops up in one form or another in a number of Russian plays of the late 1920s and 1930s, is really common to all revolutionary societies and hardly unique in a Soviet context—the frequent inability of former revolutionary activists to recognize that in a postwar era of reconstruction revolutionary tactics and revolutionary ardor, romanticism and heroism, are often woefully inadequate to insure the implementation of the revolution's goals and the efficient operation of the new social mechanism. In Glebov's *Inga* the problem characters, though less prominent than in Kirshon's play, are tough old Bolsheviks who are willing to shed their blood for the Red cause yet stubbornly cling to outmoded social attitudes and bitterly oppose the full equality of women guaranteed by the new regime. Nikitin's weakness in Bill-Belotserkovsky's *Life Is Calling* derives from essentially the same source; a zealous fighter in the Civil War he proves nevertheless incapable of making a place for himself in postrevolutionary society and turns to drink for solace.

The mutually incompatible positions of Mikhailov and Raevsky are established at the very beginning of the play during Raevsky's account of his foreign adventures. Describing the plight of the proletariat in Germany, Raevsky declares: "There blood is spilled when the proletariat takes the street." The following dialogue ensues:

MIKHAILOV: Are you referring to the large demonstrations?

RAEVSKY: All demonstrations are dispersed, large or small. I went to the Reichstag with a crowd of unemployed. The police beat us with rubber clubs and with the butts of their revolvers. One of my arms was broken, and I barely managed to avoid the Schüz-polizei.

MIKHAILOV: What a wasted gesture! You shouldn't have gone.

RAEVSKY: You think I should have stepped aside and watched from the sidelines how the workers were being clubbed?

MIKHAILOV: If you had been caught by the Schütz-polizei, the German police could have framed some fable about Russian spies who organize workers' demonstrations. [A point made also, but with reference to France, by Olesha in *A List of Assets.*—HBS] Believe me, that would have been more harmful than your standing aside.

RAEVSKY: You have a very level head. But there are times, if you know what I mean, when reasoned behavior borders on the criminal.

OLGA: Dmitri [Mikhailov], I am sure, would not have gone to the Reichstag.

MIKHAILOV: You're right. Unreasoned behavior, it seems to me, is always criminal.

RAEVSKY: Then I'm a criminal. But if the same situation were to be repeated tomorrow, I should again throw myself in front of the Schütz-polizei's clubs together with the Germans workers. I'd let you do the watching while we were being beaten.

MIKHAILOV: Spoken like a hero. From my point of view, however, purposeless heroism is but the reverse side of cowardice. (*pp.* 236–37)

The compatibility of Mikhailov's attitude and that of Kirshon himself is beyond any doubt. Besides attacking the stubborn resistance of the kulaks, *Bread* also exposes the limitations—and dangers—of the simplistic belief, current in some quarters of Soviet society at the time, that hardly a problem exists which is incapable of solution once revolutionary zeal and revolutionary tactics are brought into play. In broader terms, what Kirshon is striking out at in *Bread,* in the area of domestic political policy, is the incapacity of a continued revolutionary romanticism and individualism to cope with the many and varied problems of national regeneration. That is why the dispassionate, reasoned, and disciplined pragmatism of Mikhailov is ideologically so important in the play and why a contrasting character like Raevsky is introduced. If the struggle with the kulaks is at the center of the plot, the conflict between Mikhailov and Raevsky as representatives of two opposing and mutually incompatible modes of political behavior is not only the ideological core of *Bread* but indeed its very foundation. That is because as the drama unfolds it becomes increasingly obvious that the struggle with the kulaks is permitted to take on the proportions of an armed rising in order to provide a crisis situation in which to test the validity of the respective approaches of Mikhailov and Raevsky. Needless to say, Raevsky makes a mess of things and it is only the intervention of Mikhailov that prevents a complete breakdown.

The analysis of *Bread* so far may create the impression that the play is primarily ideological. This is anything but the case. Once Raevsky is introduced, the first difference of opinion with Mikhailov occurs, Mikhailov's wife Olga becomes romantically interested in her husband's old friend, and Raevsky is assigned the job of requisitioning the grain from the village, an element of predictability certainly enters. But Kirshon has done such a skillful job of constructing *Bread* that this predictability works only in the most general way. Raevsky's adventures among the villagers and kulaks, and the kulak uprising and its suppression are beyond the range of audience predictability. As the intrigue gathers momentum the play becomes suspenseful and even exciting.

With a good sense of detail and timing Kirshon orchestrates for a gradual buildup of tension and suspense. The high point comes in the fifth and last act when the kulak conspiracy bursts on the village and is finally quelled. To get the rhythm of fast-moving events Kirshon structures the act differently from the preceding four. Like Acts I and IV (Acts II and III are made up of a single scene each), Act V is divided into two scenes (8 and 9). This division was necessitated by Kirshon's desire to catch the action from different points of view (those opposed to the kulaks and the kulaks themselves). But then a further subdivision is made: the last scene (9) is broken up into three episodes involving the use of a revolving stage, song, and music in order to achieve a brisk pace corresponding to the events and to create a general sense of excitement.

Kirshon's skillful play construction is equaled by his characterization. His major characters, whatever they represent ideologically, come to life vividly on the stage. Mikhailov and Olga are well drawn and plausible and, in a departure from the usual practice of Soviet drama in Kirshon's time, the resolution of their domestic conflict is left hanging in the air for greater psychological verisimilitude. Olga reproaches Mikhailov for ordering the recall of Raevsky after his mishandling of the grain assignment:

> OLGA: He went to certain death to save you, all alone he went. Just for you he attacked the whole mob . . . and you, is that all you have to say to him? (*p. 309*)

In a deft stroke, Kirshon has Mikhailov address Raevsky first, not Olga, and when he turns to his wife he dismisses her in a few words:

> MIKHAILOV: Thank you, Pavel! But you'll have to stand trial. (*Sharply*). I'm sorry, Olga, I haven't time to talk to you now. (*p. 310*)

Raevsky and the kulak Kvasov are clearly the most memorable characterizations of the play. Although ultimately negative, Raevsky is nonetheless sympathetically portrayed as attractive and personable. His quixotic romanticism, while clearly rejected by Kirshon as anachronistic, is made human and even appealing both in order to increase its psychological plausibility and to sharpen the imminent clash with Mikhailov. When Olga succumbs to Raevsky's charm, there is nothing artificial or inadequate in the motivation. Kirshon convincingly establishes Olga's restlessness and dissatisfaction with Mikhailov's way of life; when Raevsky appears she is psychologically ready to respond to his appeal. Kirshon's effort to avoid making Raevsky a romantic fool and hence only ludicrous and to strike a balance between his romantic individualism and his Party loyalty is apparent from a lengthy passage in Act I, scene 2.

Talking about the Communist Party with Olga, Raevsky describes it as "a ring . . . an iron thong which holds people together" (p. 242). When Olga protests that Raevsky is too much of an individual to allow himself to be completely molded to conform to Party standards, he disagrees with her and qualifies his own sense of individualism in a lengthy monologue in which the character assumes a richer psychological dimension:

> It's all very complex, Olga. I haven't had to explain before. Picture a crowd. A crowd composed of identical people, a crowd composed of standardized people. They are all wearing neckties of the same color. They are all walking in the same direction. They all speak the same measured words. I don't want to be one of this crowd. There are times when I'm horrified at the thought that each day I put on the same kind of necktie everyone else is wearing. But I know a feeling which is even more terrifying. Picture, Olga, this crowd going by without you. And that you are left alone, all alone with your thoughts, with your doubts, while the columns keep passing by. They pass by forever without you. They reiterate their words. They sing their songs. Not a single one of them turns his gaze in your direction. Their measured steps are merciless. And precisely because I myself am filled with thoughts which are not attuned to those of the others, with emotions which do not correspond to those of my companions, I cannot step out of the ranks. I dare not leave. I must feel another shoulder next to mine. I need someone to give me orders, someone to discipline me. I can't get along without those iron fetters which weld together the diverse sides of my "I." (pp. 242–43)

Kvasov, the kulak, is introduced in Act II. Shrewd, ingratiating, forceful, unscrupulous, despotic, superstitious, religious, he gradually emerges as a sinister yet powerful character and, by all means, the most compelling in *Bread*. Despite the inadequacy of the translation, something of Kvasov's tough shrewdness, the earthy style of his peasant language, and the seething kulak resentment against collectivization can still be felt in this typical exerpt from Act IV when he and another kulak, Kotikhin, begin to formulate a plan of action to prevent the grain collection:

> KOTIKHIN: Couldn't we run a blade through them? Have you given that a thought?
> KVASOV: We can't take the time to sharpen the blades. We need an ax now. You always want to play the fox, Vasili Afanasevich, when we must play the bear.
> KOTIKHIN: The bear has too broad a chest—too good a target for a gun.

KVASOV: Hide behind the logs. Throw oak trees at the hunter. Arouse the beasts in the forest so that even the squirrel begins to throw cones. The forest is large—the hunters small in number.

KOTIKHIN: If only there were amity among the beasts in the forest. But the hare won't associate with the wolf.

KVASOV: Force the hare to associate with the wolf, scare him into joining the other beasts. (*Addressing everybody.*) We have gathered here, dear guests, in secret. In our own home village we must hide our heads from everybody. We must behave as if we were in the house of a stranger where we didn't belong. Yet who are we? We are the foundation. The belly of Mother Russia is filled with our bread. It is we who clothe Moscow, we who provide shoes for her, we who feed her. But who orders us about? Ragged tramps, beggars, drunkards. And those who live in Moscow? Little have they to worry about. All of Russia is but a field for their experiments. They want to raise a special brand of European herb on it. On that field we are the poisonous weeds—the broom-rape, the wild grass. They've begun to weed us out. By the roots they are weeding us out. They're mowing us down with a scythe. The time has come when we must either lie down under the scythe or shout so that all Russia should hear us: "You're wrong, you Moscow agronomists! We're not weeds—we're oaks!" (*Pounds the table with his fist. Pause. More quietly.*) We will break your scythes. Trusty people have said—the straw around the village is dry—strike but one match and it will be devoured by flames. With God's help, we will start the conflagration. (*pp. 290–91*)

Kirshon's dynamic and knowledgeable portrait of a kulak—certainly one of the most vivid in Soviet literature—carries a hint of the fate of the entire class at the end of *Bread*. As he is about to be taken into custody, Kvasov tells Mikhailov: "Aren't you celebrating too early? It's all one—either you or we must disappear from the face of the earth. There isn't room enough for both of us in this world." "I'm afraid it will be you," replies Mikhailov—and in truth it was.

If *The Miraculous Alloy* proved to be Kirshon's most successful play as measured by popular acclaim, there is no doubt that *Bread* was his most important and most discussed work. Kirshon's skill at dramatic construction, the smooth integration of the various component parts of *Bread*, the play's intellectual substance, and the vivid character portraits won high praise. On ideological grounds, however, the play was faulted for what some Communist critics regarded as serious deficiencies. The portrayal of the various social forces in contemporary village life was held to be inadequate, Mikhailov's final victory tactic was criticized for its indi-

A scene from the original production of Vladimir Kirshon's Bread *by the Moscow Art Theater in 1930.*
(H. W. L. DANA COLLECTION OF THE HARVARD THEATRE COLLECTION)

vidualistic aspect, the rationale behind agricultural collectivization was insufficiently propagandized, and so on. But the greatest amount of flak was drawn by the portraits of Mikhailov and Raevsky, particularly the latter. By comparison with the obviously more colorful figure of Raevsky, Mikhailov was thought to be too bland, except for the last act; Kirshon's emphasis seemed to direct more attention to a "negative" character, Raevsky, rather than to the "positive" one, Mikhailov. Raevsky's portrayal also raises psychological and philosophical questions concerning political romanticism and the individual versus the collective which some critics saw as detracting from its sociopolitical significance. Much of the debate over *Bread* took place in a discussion devoted to the play at a meeting of the Communist Academy in 1931.[7] Among Kirshon's more ardent supporters were Lunacharsky and Afinogenov who, while acknowledging some ideological "lapses," stressed the essential validity of Kirshon's emphases and praised the artistic merits of *Bread*. It is those artistic merits for which the play has won a prominent place in the history of postrevolutionary Russian drama despite the carping of critics distressed by Kirshon's failure to propagandize collectivization in shrill ideological terms.

EIGHT

The Fantasy World of Yevgeni Shvarts

SHINING BRIGHTLY amidst the grimness of the 1930s and early 1940s—with their massive construction projects, assaults on human dignity in the name of ideological purity, and finally the convulsion of war—were the fairy-tale plays for adults of the extremely popular writer Yevgeni Shvarts (1897–1958).

Most of Shvarts' literary career revolved around the world of the child. He was a close collaborator of Samuil Marshak at the State Children's Publishing House (DETGIZ) in Leningrad, a long-time associate of the Leningrad Children's Theater as well as of Nikolai Akimov's Comedy Theater, and editor of the children's magazine *Yozh* (*The Hedgehog*). Shvarts also took an early interest in the drama and wrote nearly a dozen plays between 1925 and 1958. Of these, the most noteworthy are the satirical fantasies *Goly korol* (*The Naked King*, 1934), *Tyen* (*The Shadow*, 1940), and *Drakon* (*The Dragon*, 1943).[1]

Shvarts' experience with all forms of children's literature, including plays, created a natural preference for fantasy drama. The political climate also tended to reenforce the preference. Conditions in the Soviet Union between the writing of *The Naked King* and *The Dragon* hardly favored the kind of freewheeling satirical comedy of manners typical of the NEP period. Stalinist repression intensified and culminated in the notorious purge trials of 1936 to 1938; in literature, a rigid adherence to the principles of Socialist Realism came to be demanded.

Whether or not Shvarts was at all interested in a NEP-style comedy of manners we can only speculate. The evidence, in any case, of a definite satiric bent is incontrovertible. But the focus of Shvarts' satire was far less local and topical then that of the Russian comedy writers of the 1920s. If the dramatists of a decade earlier found their subjects principally in the ludicrous aspects of life during NEP, Shvarts' attention was drawn to the rise of totalitarianism and militarism in Europe, a source of profound anxiety in Russia in the '30s. This led inevitably to a consideration of the nature of authoritarian rule in general and to the related issue of individual-state relations. Translated into dramatic form, Shvarts' observations assume a universal character of no less relevance for the Stalinist regime of his own country than for any contemporary totalitarianism in the capitalist world.

Shvarts could not have been unaware of the dangerous terrain he was entering and to spare himself an endless tug of war with the censors— and possibly worse—he had recourse to the "Aesopian language" long used by writers whenever stringent literary controls have made it extremely difficult, if not impossible, to deal with "sensitive" topics. In an East European and Russian context Aesopian writing has meant, above all, historical fiction and fantasy. In view of Shvarts' long involvement with children's fiction the latter alternative was the most natural. So it is, then, that Shvarts' most political and philosophical plays are at the same time his most Aesopian.

The Naked King, The Shadow, and *The Dragon* all share a common fairy-tale character. The first two plays, in fact, are woven out of motifs borrowed from several tales by Hans Christian Andersen while the third is based on the familiar legend of Sir Lancelot and the Dragon.[2] In keeping with the conventions of the fairy tale each play is set in an unspecified faraway kingdom where time has long stood still, where good and bad characters are pitted against each other, and where young lovers eventually find bliss after overcoming a host of trials and tribulations. Enlivening the commonplaces of the genre, however, are Shvarts' allegorical satire and a splendid comic gift which add the absurd, grotesque, and farcical to the whimsy, fancy, and naïveté of the fairy tale.

The satire with which all three plays are permeated is developed organically with relation to character and situation and never strikes a discordant departure from the overall tone of the individual play. Generally speaking, the satire is concentrated against two targets: authoritarian political rule and those areas of the human psyche which either quest for power or readily submit to tyranny. The evils for which authoritarianism is chastised are manifold: corruption, reaching up to the highest levels of government, militarism, indifference to the needs and aspirations of the populace, and the vanity of rulers. All receive a due measure of rebuke in *The Naked King,* the closest in time of any of Shvarts' plays to the rise of totalitarianism in the West and undoubtedly a response to it.

Not long after the play begins, the audience is apprised of the core situation. A princess is being wed against her will to the ruler of a neighboring kingdom. In order to thwart the marriage, Heinrich the swineherd, who loves and is loved by the princess, and his friend Christian concoct a scheme to so embarrass the king that the princess' father will be obliged to call off the wedding. Their plan involves flattering the king's boundless vanity. Pretending to be weavers they convince the king that they have woven a magnificent wedding costume for him that will be invisible to fools. So great is the king's vanity that he cannot admit he sees nothing when the "weavers" bring him his new robes. When the king steps out of his carriage to show himself before the public during the wedding celebrations he is, of course, completely naked. This results not only in the collapse of his marriage plans but in the deposition of the king himself. With the hasty retreat as well of the princess' father who as a king also fears for his own safety, Heinrich and the princess are at last free to marry.

The satirical point of the king's "special" wedding costume is obvious. When a ruler is stripped of his robes and thus "bared" as the ordinary man that he is, the mystique of authority evaporates and the road to popular upheaval is opened. No sovereign, implies Shvarts, can risk such exposure and what traps "the naked king" is the extreme vanity and self-concern common to all rulers.

Satire of this type is certainly universal and strikes out in more than one direction. More topical are the play's obvious allusions to book burning, anti-Semitism, and Nazi Aryan theory. Because of these, a case can be made for the play's overriding anti-Nazi character and the universal aspect of the satire of the king's robes can be minimized. One would imagine, therefore, that there would have been little or no opposition to the stage production of *The Naked King*. But, surprisingly, this was not the case. Seven years had to pass after Stalin's death before *The Naked King*—which was written in 1934—could be staged, by the Sovremennik (Contemporary) Theater of Moscow, in 1960.

Clearly the most mirthful of Shvarts' major plays with the love motif in much greater prominence than in *The Shadow* or *The Dragon*, the social ideology of the romance between the princess and the swineherd also should have enhanced the play's "acceptability." After all, king, court, and aristocracy are made to look silly by commoners (Heinrich and Christian)—representatives of the people—and class barriers are eliminated as princess and swineherd unite at play's end. Moreover, the union of the princess and Heinrich occurs in conjunction with the apparent destruction of the old order and the collapse of the monarchy. Even the world of the fairy tale has not been permitted to remain privileged sanctuary from the class struggle!

Whatever pleasure a Soviet audience might take in this, it would be sure to derive still greater pleasure from the way the romance of the princess and her swineherd is developed dramatically. The characters are anything but the pale cardboard lovers of much traditional comedy, no more than a mechanism to set a plot in motion. Heinrich has an endearing craftiness and audacity and the princess is a purely Shvartsian invention: fun-loving, saucy, outspoken, with a mind of her own. The interaction of the two together and each with other characters gives *The Naked King* a delightful piquancy, rendered still more engaging by liberal doses of the absurd and grotesque. When the First Court Lady protests at one point, for example, that the princess is permitting Heinrich to embrace her about the waist, the princess' reply is: "What's disgraceful about it? If he were embracing me by the . . ." Before she can finish, however, the First Court Lady cuts her off with words of meaning for Shvarts' satirical fairy-tale drama as a whole: "I beg you, keep quiet. You're so innocent that you can say absolutely terrible things!"[3] The same pattern of naïve sauciness is repeated a little later on when Heinrich asks the princess to kiss him ten times. The following dialogue ensues:

PRINCESS: Ten?

HEINRICH: Because I love you very much. Why do you look at me so strangely? Well, then, not ten; five.

PRINCESS: Five? No!

HEINRICH: If only you knew how happy I would be, you wouldn't argue . . . Well, then kiss me just three times . . .

PRINCESS: Three? No! I refuse.

FIRST COURT LADY: You are behaving absolutely correctly, Your Highness.

PRINCESS: Ten, five, three. To whom are you suggesting this? You forget that I am the king's daughter! Eighty, that's what!

LADIES OF THE COURT: Ah!

HEINRICH: Eighty what?

PRINCESS: Kiss me eighty times! I'm the princess!

LADIES OF THE COURT: Ah!

FIRST COURT LADY: Your Highness, what are you doing? He's going to kiss you on the lips! That's disgraceful!

PRINCESS: What's disgraceful about it? After all, it's on the lips and not . . . (*p. 148*)

When the princess realizes that the king can see her from the windows she is not in the least deterred and issues the following command to the women of the court: "Come stand around me! You hear me! Stand around! Shield us with your kerchiefs. Hurry up! It's unheard of—interfering with people about to kiss each other! Come here, Heinrich!" (p. 148).

The same kind of mirth touches even the passages of unmistakable anti-Nazi satire, enabling Shvarts to loose his barbs without altering the tone or mood of the play. Iron military discipline, for example, is turned into a laugh-provoking puppet routine in the spirit of Alfred Jarry's grotesque French farce *Ubu Roi* (1896) or the clownish puppet routines in Sukhovo-Kobylin's *Tarelkin's Death*. In Shvarts' comedy a platoon of soldiers enters the royal reception room and the sergeant commands them in this way:

> Ten-tion! (*the soldiers stand still.*) (*Commands.*) Upon entering the royal reception room give a sigh of de-vo-tion! (*The soldiers all together give a loud groaning sigh.*) Thinking of his power and might, tremble with awe and ven-er-a-tion! (*Their arms spread wide, the soldiers tremble.*) Hey, you there, spaghetti-legs, what kind of trembling is that? Tremble precisely, the whole forefront! Fingers! Your fingers! So! I don't see any trembling in the belly! All right. 'Ten-tion! Listen to my order! Thinking of the good fortune of being one of the king's soldiers start dancing from an excess of joyous e-mo-tion! (*The soldiers dance in time to the drum, all together as one man, without breaking ranks.*) (*p. 168*)

The princess' displeasure with regimentation, expressed later in the play, bears the same stamp of absurdity:

> It's very difficult and wearisome, living in somebody else's country. Everything here is . . . oh, what's the word . . . mili . . . militarized. . . . Everything is done to the drum. The trees in the garden are lined up in platoons. The birds fly in battalions. And besides that, there are these awful, centuries-old, sacred traditions which make it completely impossible to live. At dinner you get served chops, and then orange jelly, and then soup. It's been done like that since the ninth century. They powder the flowers in the garden, and they shave the cats, leaving only sideburns and a little brush on the end of the tail. And you can't change it or go against it at all, or else the whole state will perish. (*p. 189*)

Anti-Semitism is handled in like manner. When, in Act II, the king queries a scholar about his fiancee's, the princess', family tree, the scholar begins by mentioning Adam. Upon hearing the name Adam the king interrupts and declares:

> How awful! The princess is a Jewess?
> SCHOLAR: What do you mean, Your Majesty!
> KING: Well, after all, Adam was a Jew.
> SCHOLAR: That's a moot question, Your Majesty. I have evidence that he was a Karaite.[4]
> KING: Well, there you are! For me the chief thing is that the princess is pure-blooded. That's very fashionable now, and I'm a man of fashion. (*p. 177*)

A deeper play philosophically than *The Naked King, The Shadow*—which was pulled off the boards of Akimov's Comic Theater in Leningrad almost as soon as it opened in 1940, to be revived only in the 1960–61 season of the same theater—is also less mirthful. The central character is a young scholar who wants to make the whole world happy and comes to study the history of a "southern country" where, he is informed, "Everything that's told as happening in fairy tales, everything that in other nations seems made up—actually occurs here every day."[5]

Before long, the scholar also is made privy to the secret of the late king's testament, namely that his daughter, the princess, should marry not a prince but someone good, honest, and intelligent—even a commoner—who might be able to rule the kingdom well and wisely. As he ponders this and muses aloud about his own desire to bring happiness to the world, the scholar finds himself overheard by a girl on the opposite balcony. From her conversation, the scholar believes that she is the princess in disguise. When she returns to her room, the scholar addresses his shadow on the floor and jestingly suggests that it get up and follow the girl and declare his—the scholar's—love for her. This is precisely what the shadow does. Discovering this, Pietro, the keeper of the hotel where the scholar has a room, and a newspaperman named Caesar Borgia hatch a plot to win the shadow over to their side and then destroy the scholar. What they fear in the scholar is honesty and goodness which, if the princess makes him her choice for a husband, threaten to overturn the whole corrupt order of their society. This anxiety is shared by officials of the government as soon as the story of the scholar is spread throughout the kingdom. Through the offices of Pietro and Caesar Borgia the shadow is brought to their attention and eventually agrees to work in collusion with them against the scholar.

By this point, the twofold nature of the satire in *The Shadow* has become clear. Corruption in the social order parallels and reflects corruption in the governmental order and both fear anything or anyone that threatens reform, for implicit in reform is the end of privilege. Where such societal and governmental corruption is prevalent, suggests Shvarts, the mere hint of reform is enough to galvanize the perpetuators of corruption into a massive campaign not just to block reform but to eliminate it at its source. As a doctor brought in to examine the shadowless scholar tells the hotel-keeper's daughter, Annunziata, with whom the scholar eventually falls in love, the only way one can survive in a corrupt society is to "learn how to look at the world through his fingers, wave his hand in disgust at everything, and possess the art of shrugging his shoulders" (p. 418). The point is made still more insistently to the scholar himself by the doctor somewhat later in the play: "But you want to live in order to make as many people as possible happy? The officials will certainly take care of you! And the people themselves can't stand it. Wave your hand in disgust at them. Look through your fingers at this mad, unhappy world" (p. 434). The predicament in which the scholar finds himself is not, of course, perfectly analogous to that of Christ in the "Legend of the Grand Inquisitor" in Dostoevsky's *The Brothers Karamazov*, but the similarity in essential meaning is enough to warrant considering the novel a possible source of Shvarts' play.

While on the subject of sources, the separation of the shadow from the scholar and its subsequent autonomous behavior recall the vast European literature of the double or *Doppelgänger*, to use the German term often met in this context. The double crops up in a number of Russian literary works of the nineteenth century, notably Gogol's story "The Nose" and Dostoevsky's short novel *The Double*. Neither, of course, had to have functioned as a source for the separated shadow motif in the Shvarts play, but they ought to be taken into consideration in any analysis of *The Shadow*, especially in view of the importance of authors such as Gogol and Dostoevsky for Shvarts' literary and intellectual development. Echoes of the "Legend of the Grand Inquisitor" are audible in *The Shadow* and this leads to the temptation to posit a Dostoevskian source also for the shadow motif. But the catalyst for the separation and autonomous behavior of the shadow is the scholar's half-jesting suggestion that the shadow assume the burden of the amorous pursuit of the girl on the balcony (in reality, the princess). The sexually projected "liberation" of the shadow as double, which is essentially what happens in Shvarts' play, does bring to mind not so much *The Double* of Dostoevsky as "The Nose" of Gogol and it is this work rather than the former that weighs more as a possible influence.

The importance of the shadow motif is philosophical as well as literary. The shadow is a part of, an extension of, the scholar—as it discovers to its chagrin when it realizes that its separation from the scholar cannot be total or absolute. With this in mind it becomes plausible to see a deeper purpose in Shvarts' introduction of the shadow, namely that as an ultimately inseparable part of the scholar it represents another, darker aspect of the scholar, another dimension of his psyche. What Shvarts seems to be saying, in effect, is that the human soul is a duality; within each man there is a capacity for good and evil. Unless properly restrained, the darker, irrational, malevolent nature of man will surface ultimately to destroy man. Hence, each man's responsibility to society as a whole is the suppression of this capacity for evil within him. Only in this way can society be healthy, be prosperous, and survive.

The shadow's plan to woo the princess, marry her, and become king nearly succeeds. The scholar has become discredited, even in the eyes of the princess, because of the shadow's duplicity and its support by officials of the government. Even when the scholar proves that the shadow is only that—his own shadow—they refuse to withdraw their support and become more adamant about ridding themselves of the scholar. Beheading is decreed but when the shadow loses his head the moment the scholar's is chopped off, the officials decide that to preserve the shadow they will have to resurrect the scholar by means of a miraculous spring water effective only with good people. The resurrection of the scholar also restores the shadow's head. Realizing that he cannot live without the scholar, the shadow begs him to stay in the kingdom and offers him the prime ministership and even the opportunity to "make a certain number of people happy." By now cognizant of the futility of any fundamental reform, the scholar refuses and prepares to leave together with Annunziata. Recognizing, at last, that the scholar was the good man whom she had long sought the princess also entreats him to remain, at the same time banishing the shadow. Her courtiers, catching in the princess' behavior a shift in the political wind and anxious to be on the winner's side, join in imploring the scholar not to go. But his mind made up, the scholar calls for Annunziata to join him and the play ends with their departure.

Whimsy, an engaging naïveté, and absurdity still characterize Shvarts' comic style in The Shadow, but the farce and vaudeville elements blended in to invigorate The Naked King are a greatly diminished presence. So, too, is the saucy spirit of the earlier play. With The

Shadow, the allegory moves on to a more universal and at the same time a more philosophically substantive level. Because of this, Shvarts may have regarded the style of *The Naked King* inappropriate to *The Shadow*—or, for that matter, to *The Dragon* as well—and hence assigned farce either a much smaller role in the cumulative impact of the plays or eliminated it altogether.

In *The Shadow*, Shvarts' central themes are the unyielding resistance of corruption to reform and the willingness of people (represented by both the princess and her courtiers) to worship "shadow" despots, the shadows, as it were, of real men. To preserve such "shadows" in power there is even no reluctance to sacrifice good and honest men who are capable of effecting change for the better.

The ideas developed in *The Dragon*, which followed *The Shadow* by three years, are closely related. The despot of the previous plays is here replaced by a ferocious, awe-inspiring dragon who can assume human form and has held sway over the town in which the play is set for some four hundred years. Each year the dragon exacts tribute from the town in the form of a girl whom he takes to his cave and devours.

The story of the town and the dragon is told to Lancelot, a knight errant and "distant relative" of *the* Lancelot, by a talking cat that he meets upon his arrival. The cat also tells Lancelot that the new girl to be taken in tribute is Elsa, the daughter of Charlemagne, the town's Keeper of Public Records. When Lancelot meets Elsa and Charlemagne, he is startled to discover that the townspeople have lived so long with the tyranny of the dragon and the apparent impossibility of ending his tyranny that their attitude toward him is one of utter docility and submissiveness. Not only that, but they can even find some *good* things to say about him. In an allusion requiring no explanation they point out that one of his good deeds was to get rid of the town's Gypsies. As Charlemagne explains to Lancelot:

> They're vagrants by nature and by blood. They have no sense of law and order, otherwise they'd settle down somewhere and not wander about all over the place. Their songs are decadent and their ideas are disruptive. They steal children. They get in everywhere. We're completely rid of them now. But only a hundred years back anybody with dark hair had to prove he had no Gypsy blood.[6]

Charlemagne admits that he has never seen a Gypsy and when Lancelot asks him where he got his information about them, he replies: "Our dragon told us. The Gypsies actually had the nerve to oppose him in the first years of his rule" (p. 149).

In another obvious allusion particularly to Western fascism, Shvarts establishes that the presence of the dragon has the additional benefit, as Charlemagne tells Lancelot, of insuring that the town will not be disturbed by *other* dragons.

Hardly does Lancelot determine to fight the dragon and destroy him once and for all when the dragon appears to him in human form and attempts to dissuade him. When this fails, he and Lancelot settle on the conditions of their battle. Soon the entire town hears of the impending contest, but to Lancelot's dismay the townspeople are unhappy about his challenge and prefer that he abandon the idea and go away.

Equipped by dissidents among the townspeople with a flying carpet, a hat that makes him invisible, and other "special" equipment, Lancelot succeeds in besting the dragon by severing all three of his heads. The fickleness of the crowd, the easy and rapid shifting of positions in order to be on the winning side, which Shvarts had satirized in *The Shadow*, reappear in *The Dragon*. As the three severed heads of the dragon lie on the ground and call out for help before expiring, the populace, headed by the mayor and his son Henry, pay no heed and rejoice in their new-found "liberation." Lancelot, however, has been so weakened by the battle that he is more dead than alive and is removed by friends to nearby mountains for a long period of convalescence. During his absence, a new despot has assumed control of the town—the mayor. Venerated according to the new mythology as the real killer of the dragon, not Lancelot, the mayor has replaced the old tyranny of the dragon with his own. Using the technique of what has become known as "the big lie," the official version of the slaying of the dragon is articulated by the mayor's son, Henry:

> A year ago a conceited upstart challenged that bane of our lives, the dragon, to a duel. A special committee, set up by the city council, established the following: all the wretch, who is now dead, had succeeded in doing was to inflict a slight wound on the monster, which merely enraged him. Then, our mayor, now President of our Free City, heroically flung himself at the dragon and killed him once and for all, performing in the process various extraordinary feats of bravery. (p. 209)

Again, the fickleness, shallow loyalty, and docility of the populace, which now supports the mayor as once it did the dragon, are targeted for the barbs of Shvarts' satire. On the first anniversary of the dragon's death a delegation of townspeople come to congratulate the mayor in the name of the whole town. After their "hurrahs," the mayor addresses them:

Quite so, quite so. Slavery is a thing of the past and we are reborn. Do you remember what I was like under that wretched dragon? I was sick, I was out of my mind. And now? Right as rain. To say nothing of you. You're always so joyful and happy, like my little birdies. Well, fly home now. Look sharp! Henry, see them off. (*p. 196*)

No sooner do the townspeople leave than the mayor turns to Henry and asks him how all the people whom he put in prison since his take-over are faring. Such well-timed thrusts of irony are among Shvarts' most effective satirical weapons.

The culmination of the mayor's anniversary celebration will be his marriage to Elsa. But on the wedding day Lancelot, now restored to health and strength, reappears. He and Elsa confirm their love for each other and thwart the mayor's plans. Dismayed, however, by the easy acceptance of a new tyranny on the part of the populace, Lancelot determines not to leave the town with Elsa but to remain in it in order to kill the dragon in each and every one of its inhabitants. The play closes on the joyous note of the wedding of Elsa and Lancelot.

When *The Dragon* first appeared in the war year of 1943, it was praised as an antifascist and antiwar "pamphlet."[7] Yet the play was withdrawn after a single performance each in Leningrad and Moscow in 1944. It was revived only in 1962, when Shvarts' plays enjoyed a new popularity, but despite a positive response from critics and public alike it was again taken out of production and has not appeared since.

The possible reasons for official uneasiness over *The Dragon* are several. The satire, as elsewhere in Shvarts, cuts two ways at once. The theme of the replacement of one tyranny by another has as much meaning for twentieth-century Russia as it does for the emergence of fascism and militarism in pre-World War II Italy, Germany, and Japan. Furthermore, as in *The Shadow*, there is virtually none of the topical satire of *The Naked King* to offset the universal (with the exception of the remarks about Gypsies—an allusion, doubtless, to the Jews in Germany in the 1930s). Since *The Dragon* admits, therefore, of different interpretations—despite the official one attributed to it in 1943—it was bound to arouse suspicion.

Shvarts' treatment of the townspeople in *The Dragon* also met with disfavor in official circles. As depicted in the play the people are sheep-like and docile. One cause of their submissiveness in the face of tyranny is that they have lived under it so long they cannot easily imagine a different system and so quickly adapt to any new tyranny that happens to supplant the old. The point is driven home when near the end of the play Lancelot queries the dissidents who helped him against the dragon and receives no satisfactory explanations as to why even they were so reluctant to oppose the mayor when he assumed power.

Recalling "The Legend of the Grand Inquisitor" still more vividly than *The Shadow*, *The Dragon* seems to be asserting Shvarts' belief— hinted at in other works—that people cannot cope with the responsibilities of freedom and willingly accept a yoke of tyranny so as to be spared the burden of decision-making. Because, in Shvarts' view, people cannot exist without a dragon over them they actually desire the rule of a dragon and will create one, if necessary, to fill a void—as is the case with the mayor after the slaying of the dragon by Lancelot. Given this underlying meaning of *The Dragon* the logic of Lancelot's decision to remain in the town in order to combat the dragon in each and every one of the townsfolk is eminently reasonable. Without individual reform there can be no social reform.

Whatever the light tone, gaiety, and positive conclusion of *The Dragon*, the play's pessimistic political philosophy and commentary on human behavior are not easily dismissed or easily reconciled with the tenets of Socialist Realism. No wonder then that the play, for all its brilliance, received the treatment it did.

There are, to be sure, many fine comic moments in *The Shadow*, but with *The Dragon*—its fundamental pessimism notwithstanding—Shvarts was able to activate the more dynamic humor of *The Naked King*. Elements of farce are still minimally significant but irony and absurdity are permitted freer rein, with the result that the play creates the impression of greater mirth than *The Shadow*. Much of the humor revolves around the dragon, who is endowed with many human qualities, and the townspeople's reactions to him. On the occasion of their first meeting, for example, the dragon tries to frighten Lancelot off, and when he boasts that his aim is deadly, shoots flame from his forefinger. Unabashed, Lancelot uses the flame to light his pipe and then thanks the dragon for his courtesy. The play abounds in such delightful comic touches. When the mayor, at one point, refuses to believe Henry's opinion that the dragon is worried about the upcoming duel with Lancelot, Henry attempts to bolster his argument with the following additional information:

No, really. The old boy's been out all night, working his wings off, flying around God knows where. He only got back at dawn. He had that awful fishy smell he always gets when he's worried. You know? . . . I don't know what sort of low-down places he's been to, in the Himalayas, on Ararat, in Scotland, or in the Caucasus, but anyway he's

found out that Lancelot is a professional hero. I just despise people of
that sort. But old Drag, bless his little heart, as a professional villain,
evidently attaches some importance to them. He's really been carrying on, what with swearing and cursing, and moaning and groaning.
Then the old boy felt like a drink of beer. He guzzled a barrel full of
his favorite brew, and without a word he spread his wings again and
he's still cruising around up there like a blooming skylark. (*pp.
162–63*)

Despite the awe in which they hold the dragon the townspeople are also
so used to him that their talk about him among themselves takes on a
quality of amusing hominess exemplified by Henry's above remarks to
the mayor.

Much of the absurd comedy of *The Dragon* is assigned to the mayor.
When guests are being seated for the wedding ceremony and banquet in
the third act, the mayor announces:

Please take your places, ladies and gentlemen. We'll soon be over
with the ceremony—we don't hold with pomp and circumstance—and
then we'll get down to the banquet. I've got you a fish specially made
to be eaten. It laughs when it's being cooked, and tells the cook when
it's ready. And here's a turkey stuffed with its own chicks. Such a
touching family scene, don't you think? And here are some suckling
pigs which were not only fed but specially bred for us to eat. They can
still sit up and beg with their trotters even though they've already
been roasted. Don't howl, boy, there's nothing to be frightened of, it's
great fun. And this wine here is so old it's in its second childhood, and
that's why it's bubbling away like a baby. And here's vodka that's so
pure that it looks as if there's nothing in the bottle. My God, it really
is empty. (*p. 208*)

In one of the key moments of the play (in Act II) the dragon explains
to Lancelot the true cause of the mayor's madness and the ultimate
reason for the submissive behavior of all the people of the town:

You wouldn't die for cripples like these. I made them cripples, my
dear fellow. I crippled them properly. The human spirit is very hardy.
Cut a man's body in half and he pegs out. But break his spirit and
he'll eat out of your hand. No, you won't find any others like these
anywhere. Only in my town. Spirits without arms, without legs, deaf
and dumb spirits, spirits in chains, sneaking spirits, damned spirits.
Why do you suppose the Mayor has to pretend to be mad? It's to hide
the fact that he has no spirit at all. Threadbare spirits, venal spirits,

gutted spirits, dead spirits. Ha! What a pity the spirits are invisible so you can't see them. (*p. 173*)

Here, amidst the romance, whimsy, naïveté, and absurd humor of his fairy-tale world, Shvarts has laid bare, again, the fundamental truth of despotic rule. The long road back to a desire for freedom and the willingness to bear the responsibilities of freedom begins with the resurrection of the spirit. And Shvarts suggests that the miraculous agency through which this will be accomplished is love; this is the balancing optimism in his parables. Hence the prominence of the love theme in his plays and the joyful words of Lancelot at the conclusion of *The Dragon,* his most pessimistic play:

My friends, I love you all. Why should I take so much trouble over you, otherwise? And if I love you, everything will be wonderful. And after all our trials and tribulations we're going to be happy, very happy at last! (*p. 218*)

NINE

The Gathering Clouds: On the Eve of War

INTERNATIONAL EVENTS in the 1930s were followed with intense interest in the Soviet Union. The triumph of fascism in Italy and Germany and the Japanese invasion of China were viewed as ominous developments of profound potential danger to the Soviet state. The defeat of the Loyalist cause in Spain and the gradual clarification of German and Japanese political goals in Eastern Europe and Asia, respectively, made the threat of war no longer merely a possibility but a virtual certainty. The necessary preparations began to be undertaken in the late 'thirties; this meant above all the raising of the military to a level of preparedness but also the psychological conditioning of the people to the hardships and sacrifices that lay ahead.

This preparedness for war became the focus of much literature of the period. Of the plays devoted to the subject, only a few succeeded in rising above the level of outright propaganda. The best of these were: *Polovchanskie sady* (*The Orchards of Polovchansk*, 1938), by the major Soviet novelist Leonid Leonov (1899–   ); *Feldmarshal Kutuzov* (*Field Marshal Kutuzov*, 1939), by Vladimir Solovyov (1907–   ), one of the more able writers of historical drama in the USSR; and Aleksandr Afinogenov's *Nakanune* (*On the Eve*, 1941).

Apart from dramatizations of his novels *Barsuki* (*The Badgers*, 1927) and *Skutarevsky* (1934), Leonov has a number of original plays to his credit: *Untilovsk* (1928), about life in an out-of-the-way community in Siberia; *Provintsialnaya istoriya* (*A Provincial Story*, 1928), a somber picture of rural life; *Usmirenie Badadoshkina* (*The Taming of Badadoshkin*, 1930), about a NEP profiteer; *The Orchards of Polovchansk* (1938); *Volk* (*The Wolf*, 1939), also about preparedness for war and the efforts to quash enemies within the Soviet state; *Metel* (*The Snowstorm*, 1939, 1962), the (better) original version of which develops a novel contrast between two brothers, a corrupt Soviet official and a sympathetically conceived émigré, and was suppressed during rehearsals at the Maly

Theater; *Obyknovenny chelovek* (*An Ordinary Person*, 1940–41), Leonov's only designated "comedy," about false values in life represented by the ultimately unsuccessful materialistic ambitions of a mother for her daughter; *Nashestvie* (*Invasion*, 1942) and *Lyonushka* (1943), both about Russian heroism during the war; and *Zolotaya kareta* (*The Golden Coach*, 1946–55), the original version of which was another casualty of Party suppression, dealing with the psychological and emotional complexities of readjustment to peace among the residents of a devastated provincial town immediately after the war.

The Orchards of Polovchansk is Leonov's best-known and, at the same time, most problematic play. It can also serve as something of a paradigm of the acrobatics—and compromises—of revision in which Leonov has had to engage, especially in the 1930s and '40s, in order to overcome objections that his stylistic individualism and psychological complexity obscure ideological purpose.

Reminded of Chekhov by the summertime country setting, the orchard motif, the family milieu, and the play's largely static quality, critics have long imputed a Chekhovian character to *The Orchards of Polovchansk*. At some level, Chekhov clearly figured in the conception of the work, but in its conceptualization aspects of Chekhovian dramatic technique barely extend beyond the external. *The Orchards of Polovchansk* dramatizes the intrusion of hostile, alien elements into a tranquil and happy family atmosphere. The family is that of the Makkaveevs, headed by the family patriarch, the earthy, life-loving, and hardy Adrian Makkaveev, a character more familiar to readers of Gorky than of Chekhov. Makkaveev's accomplishments are a testament to his productive capacity. On the former estate of a nobleman he has cultivated a magnificent fruit orchard in which he can justifiably take pride. This is the most obvious Chekhovian element in the play. Makkaveev's orchard is meant to recall that of *The Cherry Orchard* and his successful working of the land is intended as an example of what could be accomplished in Soviet times. The orchard that symbolizes a way of life coming to an end in Chekhov's play now becomes a symbol of a reborn Russia. Because of his rough-hewn and dynamic character the temptation also exists to view Makkaveev as an extension of Chekhov's Lopakhin. There are similarities, certainly, but Makkaveev's gilt-edged revolutionary background (he underwent campaigns of the Civil War) and immense love for the land set him far apart from Lopakhin. Given his origins, his shrewd business sense, and his drive, Lopakhin could more easily have become a NEP speculator than a Makkaveev.

Makkaveev's productive capacity is emphasized by the family stitua-tion as well: seven children by two wives (the second much younger than himself), six of them boys. With the exception of his youngest son, a cripple, the men of the family are all successful in their careers, all pa-triotic and heroic—true sons of their father. The exception of the youngest son is explained by a moral code of Russian drama which we noticed operating earlier in the case of Gorky's *Vassa Zheleznova*, namely that the offspring of an illicit union is stigmatized by some physi-cal defect. With Makkaveev's youngest son the suspicion is firmly im-planted that his birth resulted from a wartime affair between Makka-veev's second wife, Aleksandra, and a shadowy character named Pylyaev.

The surprise reappearance of Pylyaev after an absence of eighteen years offsets the mood of joyful family reunion occasioned by the return home for a brief stay of Makkaveev's oldest sons and his daughter, Masha, and injects into the play its major element of intrigue.

The return of Makkaveev's children sets the stage for a Chekhovian drama of family relationships explored against the background of a pro-vincial estate in summer. But the anticipation of the Chekhovian mood is unfulfilled. The arrival of the children is unobtrusive and undramatic, and the children themselves are paragons of virtue in their respective ways. Hence, the placid family setting remains essentially unchanged in dramatic terms. There is a great deal of the usual sort of family small talk and the incidents that go together to make up a family reunion, but none of the subtle character interaction of a Chekhovian drama material-izes.

Leonov attempts to create interest by injecting a note of suspense regarding the delay of one son, Vasili, who is in the navy and has been away on a secret and dangerous submarine assignment, presumably in the Baltic. Late in the play, the Makkaveevs learn that Vasili was killed in an accident while on the assignment, but since he is then invested with the aura of a national hero no scene or scenes of visible remorse occur and the suspense evoked by the anticipation over his arrival and failure to appear really leads nowhere. To compensate, as it were, for the loss of Vasili, Leonov introduces the character of a young officer (Otshelnikov) who was a friend of Vasili, who is the bearer of the sad tid-ings of his death and with whom Makkaveev's daughter will become romantically linked.

Whatever dramatic interest *The Orchards of Polovchansk* generates stems from the play's negative forces—Pylyaev and the gathering clouds of war. Neither of these, to be sure, has anything to do with Chekhovian drama. Pylyaev emerges instead out of the ample Soviet tradition of the "wrecker," who filled the Soviet stage to overflow in the paranoid 1930s. In an earlier version of the play, Leonov's conception of the character was considerably different. Related more to the common figure of the unassimilable malcontent of Soviet literature of the '30s, Pylyaev (named Usov in the earlier version) was originally an unsuccessful, bitterly frustrated, Salieri-like man envious of his friend Makkaveev's accomplishments and determined to ruin his domestic happiness.[1] Bowing to criticism principally from theatrical administrative quarters that the play lacked political content, Leonov reworked Usov into the sinister anti-Soviet schemer Pylyaev, thereby transforming the drama itself from a psychological study of Ibsenian resonance into a sociopolitical play in which themes of patriotism, heroism, obscure political intrigue, and impending conflict contend awkwardly for balance with ingredients of Chekhovian style. The problems raised by the transformation of the character of Usov-Pylyaev eluded a satisfactory solution; once the integrity of the original conception was compromised, neither the dramatic characterization nor the play itself fully recovered. The Moscow Art Theater rehearsed the play for fifteen months before its première in 1939, delayed largely by the difficulties the actor N. N. Sosnin experienced in trying to infuse life into the role of Pylyaev. After nearly three years work on the play, and the exceptionally long rehearsal period, *The Orchards of Polovchansk* had a run of just thirty-six performances and to generally poor reviews.

Playing on ironic contrast, Leonov times the reappearance of Pylyaev to coincide with the scheduled arrival of Makkaveev's children. Although he is very sparing of details concerning the reasons behind Pylyaev's return visit after so long an absence, he leaves little doubt: a) that Makkaveev's youngest son is really the illegitimate offspring of Pylyaev and Aleksandra and that Pylyaev wants to see him again; and b) that Pylyaev who, it is established, has spent time in prison, has been up to further wrongdoing and is a fugitive from the law. From the instant he appears Pylyaev is wholly unappealing: insinuating, presumptuous, conniving. But at the same time he is presented as so shadowy, that the characterization never truly coheres. The result is that the Pylyaev-Aleksandra-Makkaveev relationship arouses some interest but not enough to sustain the play as a whole. At the end of the work, moved no doubt by what he considered a sense of dramatic symmetry, Leonov has Pylyaev arrested by the same Otshelnikov who brings the news of Vasili's death and with whom Masha falls in love.

More convincing an aspect of *The Orchards of Polovchansk* is the ominous aura of imminent war. Significantly, Makkaveev's oldest sons are in the armed forces: Vasili, who was killed, and another son on military maneuvers in the very vicinity of Polovchansk. The sounds of tanks, artillery, and rockets reverberate throughout the play underscoring in a sense the fragility of the calm reigning at Polovchansk. It is also made clear against whom the military precautions are being taken. The Germans and Japanese are mentioned directly on a few occasions and as if to emphasize the point Makkaveev frequently recalls his fighting against the Germans (possibly in World War I and certainly in the "intervention" during the Civil War).

Leonov's efforts to re-create the atmosphere of Chekhovian drama and to enrich the intrigue of his play by introducing an evil and mysterious figure such as Pylyaev fail. But where *The Orchards of Polovchansk* does succeed is in capturing the sense of evil encroaching on a calm, orderly way of life. The sounds of war games are distant at first, but they continue to draw nearer with a portentous insistence. In trying to strengthen the underlying meaning of his play it is possible that Leonov was operating symbolically both with the death of Vasili and the ironically juxtaposed arrival of Pylyaev. If Vasili's untimely death foreshadows the death of many heroic young men in the war to come, then Pylyaev's reappearance seems to suggest the impossibility of ever fully eradicating evil from life.

To Vladimir Solovyov, an old associate of Meyerhold whose reputation in Soviet drama rests principally on such historical plays as *Veliky gosudar* (*The Great Sovereign*, 1943–55), about Ivan the Terrible; *Feldmarshal Kutuzov* (*Field Marshal Kutuzov*, 1938–39); *Denis Davydov* (1953–55), about the Romantic hussar poet and partisan fighter; and *Pobediteley sudyat* (*The Victors Are Judged*, 1953), set in the time of the Franco-Prussian War of 1871, the gathering clouds of war awakened associative recollections of past threats to Russian sovereignty posed by the armies of foreign invaders. The historical parallel of richest dramatic potential was that of the Napoleonic invasion of 1812, and Solovyov used the event as the basis for his most highly regarded historical drama, the verse play *Field Marshal Kutuzov*. Produced at the Vakhtangov Theater in 1939 and later awarded a Stalin Prize, the play proved immensely popular and continued to be performed in a number of Soviet theaters throughout the war years.

The popularity of *Field Marshal Kutuzov* rests mainly on its unabashed patriotism and on the titular character who is meant to appear as a repository of traditional Russian wisdom. No matter how great the pressures on him Kutuzov cannot be swayed from his decision, once taken, to retreat as far into Russia as necessary without giving the French battle until the possibility of victory is greatest. The troops under him and several of his highest ranking officers thirst for the chance to cease any further retreat and fight the French. To them, the honor of the Russian army and indeed of Russia itself is at stake. But Kutuzov will not be deterred; his strategy has been formulated and he must see it through to the end. So admired and respected is he by his men that even where doubts exist there is no active opposition to his plan. When it ultimately succeeds, Kutuzov's innate wisdom—the wisdom of a Russian patriot and leader whose thoughts for the well-being of his country are not predicated on the glory of a single battlefield success—is vindicated.

Apart from structural changes effected by some rearrangement of scenes, it was principally in the delineation of the character of Kutuzov that Solovyov introduced the most significant revisions in the first version of his play.[2] In the earlier version Solovyov emphasized both the doubts of others (above all the tsar, Alexander I) concerning the elevation of Kutuzov to the head of the Russian armies over General Barclay de Tolly and the reluctance of Kutuzov to assume the responsibility in view of his own uncertainty about the best course to pursue against Napoleon. In the revised version, however, the heroic stature of Kutuzov is magnified by the total elimination or reduction of those scenes devoted to the politics behind Kutuzov's appointment and the old soldier's doubts surrounding the formulation of his strategy. Moreover, in the later version, Solovyov sharpens the ideological conflict engendered by Kutuzov's strategy. Tsar Alexander's appointment of Kutuzov—in the earlier version of the play—comes as a reluctant submission to the will of the Russian people for whom Kutuzov is the only Russian military leader capable of freeing Russia from the French. Alexander's personal choice—one aggressively supported by Sir Robert Wilson, the English military attaché to the Russian army—is General Bennigsen, the commander of the Russian cavalry. In the revised version, Solovyov draws the lines more sharply between the conflicting interests represented by Bennigsen and Kutuzov. Bennigsen's German name compromises his ultimate loyalty to Russia in both versions of the play. But when Solovyov made his revisions, Bennigsen became unequivocally a tool by which Wilson hoped to put the Russian military to the best service of *English* interests. Wilson desires an immediate battlefield encounter between the French and Russians. Kutuzov opposes this on the grounds that the

Russians should not meet the French in battle until a reasonable chance for victory exists; that can come only when French supply lines are lengthened and bad weather and partisan raids have begun to take their toll.

In the same spirit, Kutuzov firmly opposes Wilson's urgent insistence that the Russians continue the war against Napoleon in the West, once the French are defeated in Russia and in retreat. The issue of the possible Russian pursuit of the French across Europe assumes such significance in Solovyov's play that the closing words are those of a dying Kutuzov again admonishing Tsar Alexander to hold Russia's interests paramount and avoid the temptation to extend the war beyond the Russian frontier.

The opposition of conflicting ideologies in the later version on the play turns on the now elevated issue of loyalty and patriotism. As a *native* Russian, a true son of mother Russia, Kutuzov must place the well-being of his country and its people above all other considerations. But in the case of Bennigsen, other factors intrude. Because of his German origin Bennigsen is presented as more susceptible to the influence of the English military attaché and hence capable of taking strategic positions ultimately deleterious to the Russian cause. The danger of this influence is spelled out in no uncertain terms in the later version of the play. In Act I, scene 7, Solovyov has Kutuzov declare at one point to Prince Bagration, the commander of the Second Russian Army, that Wilson is a spy. Earlier, Solovyov had been content merely to imply that Wilson's advice to the Russians was guided by English self-interest. Tsar Alexander's confidence in Wilson and his support of Bennigsen are likewise contrasted with the confidence in and support of Kutuzov by the Russian people and the masses of the Russian armed forces. This implication, present in the first version of the play, that Alexander's enthusiasm for Bennigsen is motivated in large part by a desire to see the popular Kutuzov humbled by the failure which Alexander sees as inescapable, is also less veiled in the later version. Shortly after declaring flatly that Wilson is a spy Kutuzov adds that Wilson's spying serves not one but two courts, with the strong suggestion that the second court is the Russian one of Tsar Alexander whose motives in advancing Kutuzov to the command of the armies are tied to interests incompatible with those of the Russian people. Hence in the later version of the play dramatic conflict takes on another dimension, ideological in origin. Kutuzov and the Russian people, whose support propels him to the command of the armies over the objections of many, assume the collective role of de-

fender of the country, its institutions and traditions, against enemies
from without and within. The external enemy is Napoleon, plainly visible, portrayed, at times convincingly, as clever and cynical; less obvious,
though hardly less pernicious, is the internal enemy represented in the
later version by Wilson, the emissary of an ally who seeks to promote
only the interests of England, and Tsar Alexander himself, whose jealousy and lust for vengeance on Kutuzov cast him in the role of an enemy
of the Russian people of whose collective will Kutuzov appears a manifestation.

The sharper lines of ideology and shifted emphases of the later version
of *Field Marshal Kutuzov* assume a significance extending beyond Solovyov's play. The more imminent war appeared to the Soviet Union in
the late 1930s the more intensified became the spirit of Russian nationalism (as opposed to an official "Party line"). Symptomatic of this are two
aspects of the play in particular. The first is the exaltation of "Russianness"; this is conveyed by the towering figure of Kutuzov himself and by
the heroic Russian peasant-partisans welded into an effective fighting
force by the hussar poet Denis Davydov (whom Solovyov made the subject of his next historical drama after *Field Marshal Kutuzov*). By weight-
ing the role of the partisans (their harassment of the French is presented
as a major contributing factor to the success of Kutuzov's strategy),
Solovyov not only gestures in the direction of Communist ideology (the
heroic people, the *narod*, are the backbone of the campaign against the
enemy), but he also completes the equation of conflicting forces within
the Russian camp: Kutuzov emerges as the extension of the will of the
people and eventually triumphs because he has the support of the people; the smug plan of Alexander and Wilson to humble Kutuzov fails
because it runs counter to the interests of the Russian people. The second aspect of the play reflective of a Russian nationalism is the shadow
cast over the loyalty of non-Russians or people of non-Russian origin living within the borders of the state, especially Germans; because he is of
German descent Bennigsen *must* be made to oppose Kutuzov as the
symbol of the popular Russian will and to champion the policies of Wilson. What we have here is a Russian xenophobia rooted in centuries-old
historical antecedents and suspicious of the motives even of potential
allies.

Like Solovyov's other historical dramas (for example, *The Great Sov-
ereign*), *Field Marshal Kutuzov* is written in verse. But even though
Solovyov subtitled his work a "historical chronicle," which brings
Shakespeare to mind, he made no attempt really to revive the neo-

Shakespeareanism of, let's say, Pushkin's *Boris Godunov*. The basic meter of *Field Marshal Kutuzov* is not the iambic pentameter "blank verse" of *Boris Godunov* but the iambic version of the twelve-syllable alexandrine used for most tragedy in Russia down to the middle of the nineteenth century. However, to avoid the monotony of a completely regular metric pattern, Solovyov achieved some variety by introducing lines of shorter length and imperfect rhymes in different rhyming arrangements. The play also has frequent (though less abrupt) changes of scene, in the manner of *Boris Godonov*, as well as substantial monologues and soliloquies placed at key junctures. But Solovyov's language, though in verse, is functional and essentially unpoetic; moreover, the principal neo-Shakespearean components of Pushkin's drama—the mixture of poetry and prose, the juxtaposition of the serious and ludicrous, the interpolation of musical and choreographical elements, and the dramatic use of light—remain unrepresented. The sense of the historical past is reinforced by Solovyov's use of verse, an older metric pattern, and certain devices of the antique historical chronicle-drama tradition such as soliloquies, a large number of dramatis personae, and many changes of scene. The end result, however, is an occasionally interesting historical drama in verse, but not poetic drama.

The aptness of historical analogy and ideological emphasis in Solovyov's *Field Marshal Kutuzov* was reaffirmed in other plays of the time. An example is Afinogenov's *Nakanune (On the Eve)*, written actually after the Nazi invasion in June 1941—the playwright himself was killed in an air raid on November 5, 1941—but set in the June days immediately preceding the outbreak of hostilities and in the first month of war.

The three-act play is definitely not one of Afinogenov's best and ought to be regarded as little more than an exercise in devotional drama. Its aim, at the outset of the war, was to inspire courage and heroism and a belief in ultimate victory. The first scene of Act I introduces the principals, particularly Andrei Zavalov, an agronomist in his middle thirties, and his Turkmen wife Yeren. The gathering clouds of imminent war cast a long shadow over the party being held in the country house of Andrei's father, the old smelter Timofei Zavalov, on the outskirts of Moscow to celebrate the arrival of Andrei's older brother, Ivan, a major-general in the Red Army. The late June evening, the sounds of music, and the effort of the guests to savor fully the remaining days of peace establish an unmistakable lyrical aura. But the drone of planes, the rumble of tanks, and war news bulletins over the radio at the beginning of the second scene of Act I shatter the mood. The Zavalovs and their friends now caught up in the conflict quickly adapt to the new circumstances of their life with its demands and sacrifices. The culminating point of their personal drama is the painful decision to put to the torch the huge wheat field near the Zavalov home around which so much of their lives has revolved. When the German advance is beyond halting, the decision is made to burn the field rather than permit the wheat to fall into the hands of the invaders. The action costs Yeren her life. At the end of the play, when she is being carried in near death, her last words are: "The wheat is burning. We'll live, Andrusha, I know. We're on the eve . . ."[3] The silence that follows is gradually filled with the deafening sound of bombers flying overhead. Ivan and the others assembled onstage close the play with a vow to avenge Yeren's death, and as all exclaim "We swear!," the drone of the bombers changes into a mighty symphony of battle.

The scorched-earth policy symbolized by the torch put to the wheat field reiterates the Russian tactics of Napoleonic times; the burning wheat conjures up the collective recollection of the firing of Moscow. In *Field Marshal Kutuzov*, Solovyov had emphasized Russianness and the transformation of civilians, especially simple people, into guerrillas. These emphases reappear in *On The Eve*. Once they are involved in the war, men and women alike, the Zavalovs and their friends swiftly transform themselves into heroic guerrilla fighters. The Russianness emphasized by Solovyov, above all through the figure of Kutuzov, expresses itself in Afinogenov's play by means of an insistent cultural continuity. To celebrate Ivan's homecoming one of the characters is asked to recite poems by Mayakovsky and Bagritsky, but the greater preference is more classical: Lermontov's very Romantic poem with a Georgian setting, *Mtsyri*. Classical Russian literature again appears as a link with the past in Act II, scene 2, when the actress Garaeva reads selections from Tolstoy's Napoleonic epic *War and Peace* to the men of an anti-aircraft battery now located on land adjacent to the Zavalov home. When Ivan, the Red Army general, continues the reading he chooses significantly a passage from the novel in which Kutuzov expounds the rationale behind his strategy of allowing the invader to advance as far as necessary until, like a ripe fruit, he is ready for the picking.

TEN

The War Years

T̲HE YEARS 1941 to 1945 produced, expectedly, a rich harvest of plays about the war. Most were schematic exercises in the propaganda of heroism and nationalism. There were a few, however, that stood above the ordinary, such as *Dym otechestva* (*Smoke of the Fatherland*, 1942), a joint effort by the Brothers Tur (the collective pseudonym of Leonid Tubelsky, 1905–61, and Pyotr Ryzhey, 1908–   ) and Lev Sheynin (1905–   ); *Russkie lyudi* (*The Russian People*, 1942), by the best-known Russian writer of the war period, Konstantin Simonov (1915–   ); *Nashestvie* (*Invasion*, 1942), by Leonid Leonov; and *Front* (1942), by the popular Ukrainian playwright Aleksandr Korneychuk (1905–72).

The Brothers Tur, as a team or in collaboration with other dramatists, began their career in the late 'twenties and early 'thirties. Together with Yakov Gorev and Aleksandr Shteyn, Pyotr "Tur" wrote *Neft* (*Oil*, 1929), about workers in the Baku oil fields, *Utopia* (1930), about the construction and launching of a vessel named Utopia and used here to symbolize the Soviet Union, and *Sem voln* (*Seven Waves*, 1935), about imprisoned criminals. With the minor playwright Iosif Prut, who specialized in military subjects, the Brothers Tur wrote *Vostochny batalyon* (*The Eastern Battalion*, 1935), which deals with a foreign legion composed of various nationalities. The collaboration with Lev Sheynin, a coroner who had won some literary renown with his detective fiction, proved the most productive. Several plays of a distinctly melodramatic character about the adventures of spies in Russia and of Soviet diplomats abroad were written by the Tur-Sheynin team in the late 1930s. The best of these was *Ochnaya stavka* (*The Confrontation*, 1938). Their collaboration continued throughout the war years and resulted in three plays: *Smoke of the Fatherland*, *Chrezvychayny zakon* (*The Extraordinary Law*, 1943), and *Poyedinok* (*The Duel*, 1944).

More substantial as a war play than Afinogenov's *On the Eve*, *Smoke of the Fatherland* is striking, above all, for its heavy dosage of melo-

A scene from the play Oil *by the writing team of Yakov Gorev, Aleksandr Shteyn, and Pyotr "Tur" in the 1930 production by the State Academic Theater of Drama in Leningrad. The production was notable for its divided masking curtain composed of factory symbols that revealed various scenes as sections of it were raised or lowered.*

drama attributable doubtless to the Sheynin collaboration. The audience is again plunged into the grim days of the invasion of 1941, but before much time elapses it discovers a novel element in the by now familiar setting: the figure of a "White" Russian, a landowner's son who returns to his father's estate in the village of Vyazovka with the invading Germans, reclaims the family property, and promptly sets about restoring the old order. His own cruelty and that of the Germans in relation to whom he is a mere puppet ultimately bring him and his fantastic vision of a resurrected prerevolutionary Russia to ruin. But before his just deserts as the villain of the piece are meted out with all the inexorable logic of traditional melodrama, he remains the central focus of interest through much of the play. The brave partisans led by Kasatkin and even the stereotyped betrayer figure—the character Lissovsky—are little more than devices of contrast and conflict until melodrama completely dictates the tempo of the last two scenes (the play is divided into seven) and suspense and action impel the interest away from character to incident.

The Brothers Tur and Sheynin strive for a high degree of excitement early in the play and use classical melodramatic techniques to achieve their goal: scene endings coinciding with peaks in the action or invested with suspense, withheld information, and onstage physical confrontations and violence. Because of its pervasive melodramatic rhythm, *Smoke of the Fatherland* is really a very theatrical play and not without interest despite its many familiar ingredients (brutal Germans, heroic Russian partisans, the brash prank-loving but colorful and endearing guerrilla hero, Petya Zabudko, the traitor Lissovsky who stays behind to throw in his lot with the Germans, the eventual Soviet victory, and so on). As the returned White, Zhikharev rivets attention although far more because of what the figure represents and his relative novelty as a character in the drama of the period than for his intrinsic worth as a dramatic portrait. Again, for its novelty and unexpectedness, some interest also attaches to the figure of the Jewish doctor Shapiro, who gives blood to save a wounded German officer and is later shot to death by the same man. At the melodramatic peak of the drama, when a clash between disguised Soviet partisans and the Germans looms imminent, one episode is particularly noteworthy for its stageworthiness. It comes about midway in the last scene of the play, scene 7. The peasants of Vyazovka are being positioned for the filming of a German propaganda documentary. They will appear at the bottom of a staircase ready to present the traditional Russian "bread and salt" greeting to their returned master Zhikharev who will emerge at the top of the staircase wearing a black suit laid out for him by the servant Yefim. At the crucial moment, when everyone's gaze is directed to the top of the staircase, illuminated now with Klieg lights, and the cameras have begun whirring, a German military orchestra playing stirring music all the while in the background, it is not Zhikharev who appears but Yefim. Moving slowly down the staircase with a swaying motion he announces to the incredulous onlookers that he has just snuffed out the life of Zhikharev.

The kind of theatrics manifest in such a scene were by no means extraordinary in Soviet drama of the 1930s, but their reappearance in the usually conservative Soviet war plays is less expected and hence the more curious. Even when writing about the German invasion, the Brothers Tur and Sheynin could not divest themselves completely of their older melodramatic habits. The result was that their plays about the war, while generally schematic, nonetheless exert an undeniable theatrical appeal.

Beyond doubt, the most internationally acclaimed play to come out of wartime Russia was Konstantin Simonov's *The Russian People* (1942). So well known was it in the United States that no less distinguished a figure in the contemporary American theater than Clifford Odets prepared an "American acting version" of it for the Theatre Guild of New York.

Simonov's playwriting began in 1938 when he wrote his first dramatic work, *Obyknovennaya istoriya* (*A Familiar Story*), about an Arctic explorer. It was revised and produced two years later in Moscow under the new title *Istoriya odnoy lyubvi* (*A Story About One Love*). If this play fared badly with the critics, Simonov more than made up for it not long after with his eminently successful *Paren iz nashego goroda* (*A Fellow from Our Town*, 1940–41), about a tank driver, for which he was awarded a Stalin prize of 100,000 rubles. Certain of the play's characters (Safonov, Lukonin), who had virtually become household names in the Soviet Union, were reintroduced in *The Russian People*. Simonov's other wartime plays were *Zhdi menya* (*Wait for Me*, 1942) and *Tak i budet* (*So Will It Be*, 1944). The first, about the heroic escape from behind German lines of a downed Russian pilot driven, above all, by the desire to return to the wife he left behind, was a dramatization of an immensely popular poem "Zhdi menya i ya vernus" (*Wait for Me and I'll Return*) from a collection of poems written by Simonov to his wife and titled *S toboy i bez tebya* (*With You and without You*).

The lines of a fairly predictable Soviet war drama are traceable in Simonov's *The Russian People*. The time is the initial war period (autumn 1941); the place—a German-occupied town; the exploits of heroic Russians, men and women alike, the touch-and-go struggle with the Germans, the daring and danger of secret missions behind enemy lines, and chance encounters once again churn up the froth of melodrama; the romantic love of hero and heroine, the death of a noble comrade, and the heroic transformation of ordinary people make for the inevitable lyricism and poignancy. For dramatic interest and the illusion of verismilitude, the Russian ranks include cowards, defectors, and traitors as well as heroes; for historical continuity, some vestige of prerevolutionary Russia is introduced; overt Party propaganda gives way to patriotism and nationalism and, finally, the drama concludes with a Russian triumph. The familiar ingredients indeed exist in Simonov's play but the recognition of them hardly defines the appeal of the work and the sure sense of theater behind it.

Leon Ames (left) and Luther Adler (right) in the 1942 production of Konstantin Simonov's The Russian People *by the Theatre Guild, New York.*
Directed by Harold Clurman.

Although similar in some respects to *Smoke of the Fatherland* of the Brothers Tur and Sheynin, *The Russian People* is better constructed and broader in its appeal. In the former play, dramatic interest is divided between Zhikharev, on the one hand, and Kasatkin's partisans, on the

other. In *The Russian People* the dramatic interest is more concentrated. A young partisan girl, Valya, slips back and forth on secret assign-
ments between the German-held town and Russian forces in free territory on the other side of a river. Her dangerous exploits and the
constant threat of seizure maintain a high degree of suspense and serve
not only as a link between the two camps but, more importantly from a
dramatic point of view, as a useful means of relating principals on both
sides of the river to the central action. In the occupied town Valya is
sheltered by the wife of the German-appointed mayor who in effect col-
laborates with the invaders by meekly doing their bidding. The cruel
death of his soldier son, his wife's vengeance on their tormentors, and
her calculated involvement of her husband in her own noble death—all
occurring at a fast tempo in Act II, scene 1—justifiably rank among the
most powerful moments in Russian World War II drama and are as theatrically gripping as the staircase scene in *Smoke of the Fatherland*.

The Russian army people across the river, including Valya's dedicated
romantic partner, Ivan Safonov, are so much a gallery of familiar Soviet
wartime dramatic types as to need no special commentary. But one figure in particular stands out: Vasin, a former tsarist officer in his early sixties. He and Zhikharev from *Smoke of the Fatherland* both represent a
common type in Soviet war drama: the character with prerevolutionary
associations. In the Brothers Tur–Sheynin play, Zhikharev is the former
White who returns to Russia with the German army in the hope of restoring the old order. Stretching the imagination slightly, he becomes a
sequel, as it were, to a figure like Colonel Talberg in Bulgakov's *Days of
the Turbins*. From the White who flees revolutionary Russia with the
Germans we now have in Zhikharev the White who returns to Soviet
Russia with Germans some twenty years later driven again by the dream
of a Red-free Russia. Vasin is the other side of the coin and a throwback
to another prominent character-type in earlier Soviet drama: the tsarist
officer (like Captain Bersenev in Lavrenyov's *Breakup*) who makes common cause with the Soviets.

The catalyst to the action of choice in Simonov's play is provided by
the figure of Kozlovsky (alias Vasilenko), a defector type (like Lissovsky
in *Smoke of the Fatherland*). Kozlovsky is a pivotal character in the play.
A German spy, he infiltrates the Russian camp by taking Valya's route
across the river. His mission is to collect intelligence and to lay a trap for
Valya. The trap and the response of the Russians to Valya's eventual capture and imprisonment trigger much of the melodramatic intensity of
the play. And it is also Kozlovsky who is used to define the ideological

significance of Vasin. In his one major reliance on contrivance in the
play, Simonov establishes a family bond between Kozlovsky and Vasin
by making Kozlovsky Vasin's nephew whom the older man has not seen
in a long time. After revealing his identity to Vasin, Kozlovsky discloses
his true loyalties and attempts to enlist Vasin's support. Not only does
Vasin not assist Kozlovsky in his mission he turns him over to Safonov,
thereby setting in motion the ultimately successful plan to rescue Valya.
The favorable treatment of an old tsarist officer such as Vasin who sides
with the Soviets, even to the point of sending his own nephew to certain
death, has a lineage in Russian postrevolutionary drama going back to
the 1920s as I indicated above with reference to Lavrenyov's *Breakup*.
The ideological significance of Vasin is sufficiently clear. Common cause
against a traditional enemy (the Germans) outweighs partisan antagonisms rooted in the Civil War. In the face of a *German* invasion, there
are *only* Russians, not Reds or Whites, and the defense of the native
country far overshadows the defense of a political system.

A familiar setting (a small Russian town in the initial period of the
war), familiar characters (an anti-Red former Russian émigré, Mosalsky;
a heroic Communist, Kolesnikov; compromising Russians anxious to preserve their skins at any cost, Fayunin and Kokoryshkin; "good" Russians, Dr. Talanov and his family; hard-as-rock Germans, Wiebel,
Spurre, and Kuntz), and a familiar "happy ending" (the final-curtain liberation of the occupied town by Soviet parachutists) reappear in
Leonov's best-known and most frequently performed war play, *Invasion*. But as the world of the drama is entered, the terrain seems distinctly less recognizable than a first glance indicates. If partisan resistance and heroics dominate the action of such plays as *Smoke of the
Fatherland* and *The Russian People*, the thrust of *Invasion* moves in a
very different direction. War is the inescapable fact of Leonov's play; it
is the background against which everything in the drama has to be
viewed and against which everything, indeed, has to be measured. Yet
within this context the dramatist's concern shifts from the epic to the
lyric, from the drama of the group to the drama of the individual. This
shift enabled Leonov to write a play which has flaws (the *deus ex machina* triumphant ending is trite and weak) but which deserves to be
considered one of the most interesting of the war period and one reflecting a sincere effort on the part of the dramatist to work the familiar stuff
of war into an intellectually and psychologically more provocative experience than the rousing patriotism of most of his contemporaries' plays.

Psychology is the key word here, the indisputable focus of *Invasion*.

At the core of the drama is an inquiry into the psychologically transformative power of war's suffering, a power sufficient to metamorphose an arrogant, self-centered, young ne'er-do-well into a man possessing the spiritual courage to sacrifice himself so that a better man (in a civic sense) might live. The subject of this metamorphosis is the erring son, Fyodor, of the town doctor, Talanov. In the first draft of the play the cause of Fyodor's rupture with his family is his (innocent) involvement in a political crime. In the final version, it is because of a sordid love affair about which, perhaps wisely—from a dramatic point of view—Leonov is very sparing of details. Apparently incapable of killing himself (rather than the woman he is involved with), Fyodor breaks with her—temporarily—and returns to his father's home after an absence of three years. Shortly thereafter, the town is occupied by the invading Germans. The residents begin to adjust to the drastically changed pattern of their lives and it is the process of adjustment that Leonov chooses to dramatize rather than the more conventional heroics of resistance. The restlessness and recalcitrance of Fyodor seem impervious to change, however, until the pivotal episode of the play occurs: the brutal assault by Germans on the teen-age Aniska, the granddaughter of the Talanovs' servant, Demidevna. Typical of Leonov's low-keyed approach throughout the play, the assault on Aniska (like all other brutalities in *Invasion*) is relegated to an offstage action, only the effects of which are shown onstage. Aniska's assault becomes the turning point in Fyodor's life. The horrible violation of innocence succeeds in cracking the wall of arrogance and self-interest narcissistically nurtured over several years. An inner compulsion to atone, to reestablish contact with the collective is born and requires only the proper catalyst to realize itself. This comes when a local Communist official, Kolesnikov, now presumably a partisan fighter (again, this is implied by Leonov but not spelled out in the dramatic action) is given shelter in the Talanov home after he is brought there, wounded, by Fyodor's sister, Olga, a schoolteacher. Fyodor's earlier relationship with Kolesnikov (in Act I) was marked by a kind of resentful acrimoniousness. But now the wounded (and hunted—there is a price on his head) Kolesnikov crystallizes as the instrument of Fyodor's self-transformation and regeneration.

When it becomes apparent that the Germans have traced Kolesnikov to Dr. Talanov's house and will arrest him the moment he leaves it, Fyodor takes Kolesnikov's place. Since neither Fyodor nor Kolesnikov are familiar faces to the Germans, the ruse goes undetected. The possibility of revelation arises in the third act of the play during the interrogation of Fyodor at which his own parents are present. But at the crucial moment, when they perceive what is happening, the Talanovs resist the naturally human impulse to divulge their son's true identity and thus save his life, aware perhaps intuitively of Fyodor's spiritual need. The final act of Fyodor's personal drama, when his self-fulfillment at last is attained, comes in the fourth and last act. In a prison cell awaiting execution Fyodor is not at once automatically accepted by his fellow Russians as Kolesnikov's surrogate, worthy of being executed *as* Kolesnikov. The inmates debate the matter and finally accept Fyodor in recognition of his undeniable heroism. He and two other prisoners die before the others are rescued in a daring surprise raid by Soviet parachutists.

The ending, and the few genuflective references to Stalin's military leadership preceding it, produce the only really discordant notes in an otherwise subdued psychological drama almost wholly devoid of heroics, strident patriotism, and overt political propaganda. The subdued quality of *Invasion*, which sets it apart from most Russian plays about the war, is carefully developed from the beginning of the action with the lack of hysteria among the townspeople in the face of the German occupation to the very moment when Fyodor quietly confronts his death. As I pointed out earlier, virtually all brutalities and heroics are kept offstage and introduced only in so far as they have any bearing on the activities and relationships of characters onstage. The actual occupation of the town by the Germans is not dramatized as the focus shifts entirely to the process of adjustment by the townspeople and their efforts to preserve a semblance of a normal routine of life within the framework of occupation. Aniska's brutalization occurs offstage and produces no emotional excesses onstage. The murder of German occupation officers by Kolesnikov and his guerrillas is never seen by the audience. The seizure of Fyodor is also kept offstage as well as his death and the appearance at play's end of the parachutists who appear out of nowhere in the sky.

If there is less overt action in a physical sense in Leonov's play than in other Russian war dramas, it is also true that significant character interrelations and transformations proceed from action rather than from words or from the confrontation of opposing personalities. Leonov's technique in this respect is nowhere better observed than in Fyodor's metamorphosis and the emotion-charged (if emotion-less) interrogation scene in Act IV where his parents are faced with the agonizing decision whether or not to reveal to the German authorities that their son is not Kolesnikov. In the first instance, the virtual absence of any "soul-searching" on Fyodor's part articulated in the form of a soliloquy or in

dialogue with other characters may create the impression that his metamorphosis is inadequately or imporperly motivated. But this is not the
case. The transformation is not arrived at suddenly; it is not overt or theatricalized. It springs from the circumstances of Fyodor's private life and
his psychological state at the moment he beholds the battered body of
Aniska before him. In keeping with the low-keyed mood of the entire
play the transformation of Fyodor is not, therefore, thrust suddenly
upon the audience but disclosed piecemeal, unobtrusively, and only
through action.

On the formal level one further aspect of *Invasion* invites comment—
Leonov's extensive use throughout the play of long, detailed stage directions. These not only fulfill the primary function of providing precise information on attire, gesture, and props but at times are so literary and
narrative as to seem aimed principally at a reader. Certainly, to the
director and actors their imagery, humor, and irony are of no particular
value. Reflected here is not just a concern for the manner in which the
dramatist wishes his work brought to the stage, but the dissatisfaction
with the limitations of the dramatic form on the part of a writer ultimately more at ease with the expansiveness of the novel. Some of the best
examples of such stage directions occur in the dramatically effective
third act in which Fyodor, impersonating Kolesnikov, is interrogated in
the presence of his parents, and at the very beginning of Act IV. Looking
more closely at the directions especially in Act III, one has the distinct
impression, moreover, that Lenonov was striving for something even
beyond narration. The room in which the interrogations are conducted
is filled with a variety of characters, Russian and German alike. When
the Germans are first introduced into the scene, the stage direction calls
for their moving in a rigid, wooden manner reminiscent of pasteboard
figures or puppets: "Now guests of a secondary significance are visible.
They are pasteboard, with the restricted movements of mannequins. At
the non-Russsian speech of the new arrivals, Kokoryshkin peeped out
and then seemed even to shrink in size."[1]

In the light of other directions in the same act it is apparent that
Leonov sought not only to convey the impression of something non-
human about the Germans through their physical movements, but also
to introduce an element of the grotesque into the scene. Consider, for
example, the directions governing the movements of the German officer
Spurre and the Russian flunkey Kokoryshkin. Spurre has just come into
the room and Kokoryshkin begins to greet him. But before he finishes
Spurre obviously mistakes him for the prisoner Kolesnikov. Kokoryshkin

barely perceives what is happening when the German grabs him by the collar and rushes him out of the room. The first part of the stage direction reads as follows: "Like a little feather he turns Kokoryshkin around with his back to the door and leads him with his extended arm. They exit rhythmically, as though dancing, leg to leg and face to face. Kokoryshkin offers no resistance and is just very afraid of stepping on Spurre's toes . . ." (p. 58). For stage directions such as these employed, above all, to reinforce through physical movement and gesture language the already grotesque character of the entire act one has to go back to the comic art of a Gogol or Sukhovo-Kobylin whose inspiration at least for the act should not be discounted.

The enthusiasm and popular acclaim with which such plays as Simonov's *The Russian People* and Leonov's *Invasion* were greeted were paralleled by the controversy touched off by the play *Front*, also dating from 1942, by the prolific and highly regarded Ukrainian dramatist, Aleksandr Korneychuk. The esteem in which Koreneychuk has long been held in the Soviet Union is reflected in the inclusion of his name in virtually all studies and discussions of Soviet *Russian* drama, despite his use of Ukrainian. Although several of his plays such as *Pravda* (*The Truth*, 1937), *Bogdan Khmelnitsky* (1939), and a few war dramas are set in the Ukraine and feature Ukrainian characters, his most successful works deal with issues of supraregional significance and operate with more or less generalized Soviet (hence Russian) types rather than with characters of pronounced regional coloration. The best examples of this, prior to *Front*, are his first important play *Gibel eskadry* (*The Sinking of the Squadron*, 1933), about heroic Red seamen during the Revolution in the same line as Vishnevsky's *Optimistic Tragedy*, and *Platon Krechet* (1934; revised 1963), a popular work in its day featuring a self-effacing surgeon who performs an important operation while under a cloud of suspicion of professional malpractice. So widely have Korneychuk's plays been published and staged in Russian, that he exists, to all intents and purposes, as a *Russian* dramatist in the consciousness of the Soviet threatergoing public and is usually treated as such by Soviet theater historians. In devoting space to him in the present book, I am following the usual practice of Soviet writers on drama and theater.

Returning now to *Front*, there is little doubt that the play owed a considerable part of its fame to the nature of the conflict portrayed. As a war drama it is as capably crafted as most of Korneychuk's works but less gripping than Simonov's *The Russian People* or Leonov's *Invasion*. There are no noteworthy structural features, no innovations in technique, no memorable moments, no characters developed beyond types. But it is bold in an ideological sense and it was this boldness that attracted so much attention to the play when it first appeared on the pages of *Pravda* in the fall of 1942.

In Russian drama of the 1930s especially, conflict often turned on the figure of a person who, in one way or another, becomes an obstruction in the path of Soviet progress. In Korneychuk's *Front* the anti-State theme has simply been updated and adapted to the circumstances of World War II. The *antiobshchestvennik* or "wrecker" is now a stubborn, inflexible old general of Civil War fame who occupies a position of immense importance as a front-line commander against the Germans. General Gorlov's "wrecking" consists of a total inability to assimilate the methods of modern warfare. He believes that his way is best, but his faulty strategic planning results in a series of blunders which eventually contribute to the death of his son Sergei, who serves in his command. Through Gorlov and the sycophantic flunkies who surround him and flatter his ego, Korneychuk attacks the ineptitude and outmoded thinking of older officers whose military experience was acquired in the Civil War and who obstinately refuse to recognize that any changes in the concept and technique of warfare have taken place since then. Although he exhibits at times a genuine feeling for the heroism and sacrifice of men serving under him, Gorlov adds to his old school complacency an unpardonable vanity and a contempt for younger officers whose skills far surpass his. Having distinguished himself in the Civil War Gorlov assumes that there is nothing more for him to learn about warfare, especially from younger men who did not share his Civil War experiences.

Predictably, the negative portrait of Gorlov is balanced by the positive figure of a brilliant younger officer, Ognev (or Ognyov). Ognev chafes under Gorlov's obstinacy and stupidity and in a decisive campaign countermands Gorlov's orders and turns a potential disaster into victory. Gorlov is wrathful over the challenge to his authority posed by Ognev and the other officers who support him and he attempts to break the younger man. By this time, however, higher military authorities and presumably Stalin himself as Commander-in-Chief have become apprised of Gorlov's blunders and Ognev's brilliance and remove the older man, replacing him as commander with Ognev. Opposed to Gorlov is also the general's own brother Miron, the director of an airplane factory. The conflict between Gorlov and Ognev is of sufficient plausibility and substance to sustain the play without the addition of Miron Gorlov, whose role is gratuitous. When a military assignment brings Miron to his brother's theater of operations, he soon learns of the "crisis of command" and himself urges General Gorlov to step down. In so adding a family dimension to the conflict of his play, Korneychuk was merely following an old path in Soviet drama. Husband and wife belonged to opposing camps in Trenyov's *Lyubov Yarovaya* and sisters on opposite sides of the political fence were similarly contrasted in Lavrenyov's *Breakup* and in Babel's *Maria*. Korneychuk invests Miron with the function of a *raisonneur* through whom he voices his own (and the Party's) attitude concerning obstructionist figures out of the past like General Gorlov; apart from this function, the character has little significance in the drama.

Front may be of small value as dramatic literature but there is no denying its importance in 1942 as a vehicle for thinly veiled criticism of older members of the military establishment such as the Civil War heroes Budyonny and Voroshilov. The despair over early Russian defeats in the second year of the war and the agonizing search for causes created a climate in which the appearance of a play such as *Front* would have aroused no small amount of discussion and controversy. Obviously, much of what Korneychuk portrays in *Front* struck a sympathetic chord and opinion swung in favor of the play. But Korneychuk's "daring" was also tempered by good judgment; while exposing the anachronistic outlook of a General Gorlov, *Front* is careful to indicate the possibility of an Ognev circumventing orders he considers ill-conceived and the speed with which a Gorlov is removed from a position of command when higher governmental authorities become aware of the true situation. In the end, in the manner of all didactic drama, evil is punished and good rewarded. General Gorlov is made to pay for his vanity, intransigence, and blundering with the loss of his son and the loss of his command. Through the vindication of Ognev and his elevation to Gorlov's commandership, virtue once again receives its just rewards. Bearing Korneychuk's high Party connections in mind, *Front* can be read as a calculated endeavor to prepare public opinion for the deposition of outmoded but popular military leaders of Civil War vintage and their replacement by younger, better-trained, more up-to-date generals like Konev and Zhukov whom Ognev undoubtedly represents in the play.

ELEVEN

The "Freeze" of 1946 to 1952

Oᴜᴛ ᴏꜰ necessity, certain "relaxations" had to be permitted by the Soviet authorities during the war years. Whatever the previous condemnation of the capitalist West, England and America were allies of the Soviet Union and no longer could be dealt with vituperatively in official publications, the press, or imaginative literature. Such matters as the extent of American aid, the motivation behind some of the Allied military campaigns, and the alleged anti-Soviet political machinations of Winston Churchill were still capable of producing calculated distortions of one sort or another but, in general, the wartime treatment of the West was far milder than ever before, especially when compared with that of the purge-ridden, Fascist-menaced 1930s.

Domestically, victory was considered impossible without the full support of the war effort by the entire population. To mobilize this support, wounds legacied by the past first had to be healed. Hence, the appeal to a nationalistically conceived patriotism (the emphasis on "Russian" and corresponding deemphasis of "Bolshevik" and "Communist"), the greater permissiveness regarding various forms of religious practice, and a more sympathetic treatment toward past opponents of the regime. In consequence of the latter, as we have seen, wartime dramatists were able to portray former Whites in a positive way as opponents of the Bolsheviks who had joined in the struggle against the Nazis out of patriotic considerations. Not since Bulgakov's controversial *Days of the Turbins* was the favorable depiction of a former White possible, whatever the rationale.

With the end of the war in 1945 and the beginning of a new program of postwar reconstruction, the small liberties permitted by the realities of the military and political situation were abruptly canceled. From the Soviet point of view, their continuation and possible augmentation posed grave dangers to internal stability. Doors were partly opened that might be very difficult to close again if left open or opened further.

In retrospect, it is apparent that whatever lessening ot tensions was granted between 1941 and 1945 both with regard to contacts with the West and in domestic life, this was not the result of any evolutionary process pointing toward a greater democratization of Soviet life, but merely a war-necessitated expediency. Stalin really had no desire to maintain any of the relaxations of the war years, to say nothing of increasing them, and when the war ended he moved to reestablish the kind of firm control that had characterized Soviet internal policy before the outbreak of hostilities in 1941.

The postwar political situation also seemed to make such a move the more urgent. The war had expanded contacts with the West and Stalinist politics recognized in these a potential source of trouble if allowed to go unchecked. More importantly, crystallizing Western reaction to the political ramifications of the postwar disposition of the Soviet armed forces, the free elections in Eastern Europe agreed to by Stalin with no thought of implementation, the thorny problem of Berlin, and the profound danger represented at the time by the American nuclear monopoly contributed immeasurably to a new state of international tension and a jeopardized Soviet sense of security. Following a by now discernible pattern in the domestic response to shifts in Soviet-Western relations, the predictable result was a marked tightening up of Soviet internal policy. Contacts with Westerners both in and outside the Soviet Union were made all but impossible, except on an official level. Indeed, any other way was practically out of the question since travel to the Soviet Union by Westerners or to the West by Soviet citizens was severely restricted. Suspicious of the motives of its former allies, above all the Americans, and at the same time anxious to exploit to the fullest the political advantages of the Red Army advance, the Soviets unleashed a campaign of vilification against the West harsher by far than prewar propaganda and matching in intensity the postwar anti-Communist hysteria emanating from some quarters in the West. The era aptly known as the "cold war" was initiated.

Vilification of the West and rigidly limited minimal exposure to the West were paralleled by a new campaign to buttress any of the supports of Communist ideological orthodoxy possibly weakened during the war years. The process of rehabilitation of former antagonists of the Soviet state was brought to a halt and the simplistic black-white polarities of the 1930s were restored. New pressures were brought to bear on the Church and religion again became a target of official assault as all sectors of contemporary cultural life were subjected anew to a close scrutiny in order to determine (or redetermine) ideological purity.

The consequences of this policy for literature and the drama were immensely harmful. The primacy of Socialist Realism in the arts was reaffirmed with still greater insistence, obliging a new search for deviations pursued with true missionary zeal. The search held no respect for the past. Earlier departures from the path of literary virtue—as conceived by the Party—were as culpable as those by contemporary writers. The harassment of a Pasternak, Sinyavsky, or Solzhenitsyn is closer to us in time and hence more familiar, but the cases of these writers can be regarded as only the most recent and noteworthy examples of a long and tragic history of Soviet attempts to suppress manifestations of artistic individualism. One of the bleakest chapters in this history was written in 1946 when the ideology of the cold war was reaching its definitive expression. On February 9 of that year Stalin delivered a speech in which he warned that constant preparedness had to be the Soviet way of life since the continued existence of capitalism spelled the inevitability of conflict. Here was the rationale for new exhortations to increased industrial output and, at the same time, for the reimposition of strict internal controls "loosened" temporarily during the war. Literature soon felt the full weight of this policy. Spurred on by Andrei Zhdanov (1896–1948), a prominent political figure close to Stalin and the Party's self-appointed spokesman on literary matters, the Party's Central Committee published an edict on August 14, 1946, condemning two literary magazines, *Zvezda* (*Star*) and *Leningrad*, for having published works of the satirist Mikhail Zoshchenko and the poet Anna Akhmatova now considered incompatible with Socialist Realism. The writers, whose literary reputations were made in prewar years, were summarily expelled from the powerful Union of Soviet Writers and the editors of *Zvezda* and *Leningrad* were replaced with politically more reliable men. The Central Committee's edict, the expulsions, and Zhdanov's ferocious attacks in articles and speeches served the collective purpose of putting literature on notice that henceforth only works exhibiting unquestioned fidelity to the theory and method of Socialist Realism would be judged fit for publication. No deviations were to be tolerated. Literature responded accordingly and settled into a dull conformity, relieved only in 1951 and 1952 when questions again began to be raised concerning the quality of Soviet literary output.

The situation with respect to dramatic writing was all but hopeless. Responding to the new pressures on artistic expression, dramatists became circumspect about the themes and subjects of their plays. Because war was a fresh, almost too vivid memory, plays about the war in the immediate postwar period had to be anticipated and indeed many were written. But their quality fell far below that of such wartime plays as Leonov's *Invasion*, Simonov's *The Russian People*, and Korneychuk's *Front*. The partial rehabilitation of former Whites noted in several of the wartime plays was no longer possible and so a potentially productive source of psychological inquiry and character development was cut off. The kind of questioning of higher authority that we find in Korneychuk's *Front* was now not only unthinkable but politically dangerous. Collectively, the postwar plays about the war shared the common goal of glorification; the realities of postwar Soviet life until the death of Stalin left no room for the depiction of any significant weaknesses or failures. In a dreary, largely schematic uniformity, the Russian people became wholly heroic and capable of superhuman endurance and self-sacrifice. Their leadership during the war bordered on the inspired; the victories of the Red Army and the final defeat of Nazi Germany were attributed to immensely capable generals and other officers who were entrusted with the responsibility of carrying out the brilliant strategies of the supreme commander, Stalin, who directed every facet of the war effort and whose genius was a virtual guarantee of ultimate triumph. In drama, as elsewhere in Soviet literature at the time, the demands of the "cult of personality" were oppressive.

Closely related to the postwar plays about World War II but ideologically more interesting for what they reveal about the sources of Cold War international tensions were the plays with (usually) a near-the-end-of-the-war setting projecting the Soviet view of the geopolitical realities of immediate postwar Europe. The cessation of hostilities in 1945 found the Red Army as far West as Berlin and firmly entrenched throughout Eastern Europe. As part of its overall postwar European strategy, the Russians sought the dismemberment of Germany and the establishment of pro-Soviet regimes in the neighboring East European countries. Toward the realization of the first goal, the Soviets effected the installation of a Communist government in their part of occupied Germany and the creation of a separate German Communist state—the *Deutsche Demokratische Republik* (German Democratic Republic; DDR). With no thought of implementing the wartime guarantees of free elections in Eastern Europe to determine by popular referendum the postwar political structure of the states concerned, the Russians greatly extended their authority by using the presence of the occupying Red Army to assure the successful acquisition of power by pro-Soviet leftist factions whose ranks in many cases were dominated by Communists trained and long

resident in the USSR and who returned to their native countries with
the advancing Red Army. Accompanying the Communist assumption of
political leadership in East Germany and Eastern Europe was a relentless Soviet propaganda barrage aimed at legitimizing the takeovers either by portraying them as manifestations of the popular will or as democratic bulwarks against the return of revanchist Nazism in West
Germany or semifeudal military dictatorships in Eastern Europe. Drama
proved a useful tool in this propaganda campaign and between 1945 and
1952 many plays were produced purporting to show the struggle in
Eastern Europe particularly between the forces of democracy and reaction in the last days of the war and the beginning of the postwar period.
Needless to say, in plays of this sort the Russians appear as the principal
architects of a new postwar political and social order, the indefatigable
pursuers of the remnants of reaction and the admired allies and de-
fenders of "people's democracy."

A typical specimen of this kind of postwar Soviet playwriting designed
to promote some aspect of the official foreign policy was Konstantin
Simonov's *Pod kashtanami Pragi* (*Under the Chestnut Trees of Prague,*
1945). Highly acclaimed for his great wartime success *The Russian People,* Simonov, like other Russian writers of comparable stature in the
harshly repressive years from 1945 to Stalin's death in 1953, was not
above keeping himself alive as a writer by turning out insipid propaganda thinly disguised as imaginative literature.

In *Under the Chestnut Trees of Prague* Simonov zeroes in on conservative elements in Czech society opposed to the establishment of a
postwar pro-Soviet government. Set in Prague toward the end of the
war, in May 1945, the play develops its conflicts primarily within a family context. Dr. Prochazka is a well-intentioned but conservative Czech
gentleman who distrusts the Soviet Union. His views are not shared,
however, by his son Stefan and his daughter Bozhena. In each case,
Simonov makes the point that contact with the USSR and Russians is a
prime factor in the liberal pro-Soviet attitudes of the Prochazka children. This is a common theme running through much of the Soviet
drama of the period: the progressive political education of (above all,
younger) Czechs, Poles, Hungarians, Rumanians, and so on develops
under *direct* Soviet influence. Or to put it somewhat differently, Soviet
tutelage (requiring, of course, proximity of one sort or another) is indis-
pensable to the properly "democratic" political evolution of Eastern
Europe. In the case of Stefan, his enthusiasm for Russians and the Soviet Union stems from his military service in the USSR. After Czecho-

slovakia fell to the Germans, he fled East and fought with the Russians throughout the war until the liberation of his own country. Bozhena's pro-Russian sentiments are also provided a rational basis. After her arrest by the Germans, Bozhena shares quarters with a captured Russian girl, Masha, with whom she becomes close friends. Although somewhat more sympathetic, at least initially, toward the "old" Czechoslovakia, Bozhena eventually comes to share her brother Stefan's pro-Soviet enthusiasms. Responsible for her political "enlightenment" is not only Masha (who never loses a chance to speak of the wonderful aspects of Soviet life) but also the romanticized figure of the Russian parachute officer and Spanish Civil War veteran, Petrov, with whom Bozhena falls in love.

Politics and romance are closely linked in Simonov's play; both are used to enrich the plot and to achieve the sort of symmetry characteristic of Simonov's dramatic style. Just as Bozhena falls in love with Petrov, who together with Masha completes her political maturation, Stefan falls in love with Masha. Both romances suffer setbacks, however, because of Simonov's fidelity to something of an unwritten code of Soviet literature of the time according to which Soviet heroes and heroines, models always of devotion to country as well as of high moral principles, are not permitted to fall in love with foreigners, marry them, and then take up residence outside the Soviet Union. Thus, while Stefan and Masha love each other she must return to the Soviet Union. In order to marry her, Stefan vows to rejoin her soon in *her* country where perhaps he will continue his studies. As a romantic and somewhat mysterious figure, clearly a career officer, Petrov is even less likely a candidate for a home and hearth in Czechoslovakia than Masha. In this period of Soviet drama any conflict between duty and passion involving an exemplary Soviet figure is resolved in favor of duty. Hence, Petrov, though responsive to Bozhena's love for him, must heed the call of duty and leave her. Out of deference to her ideological conversion, however, Bozhena cannot be left with the sorrow of unrequited love. She is pursued for a time by another representative of the "old" conservative Czech bourgeoisie, Grubek, but he is eventually exposed as a former German collaborator who commits suicide when faced with arrest for the murder of Dr. Prochazka's other son, Ludvik. When the patriotic and antifascist Czech poet Tihy enters her life, their predictable union not only restores the play's romantic balance but acquires a symbolic political significance as meaningful as the Stefan-Masha relationship.

No less noteworthy than the character relations in Simonov's play are certain aspects of its political orientation. The character of a blind pro-Soviet Montenegran (Dzhokich) who exposes Grubek as a former German collaborator also takes on a distinct ideological meaning as a symbol of the pan-Slavic sentiment the Russians sought to exploit in the consolidation of their post-World War II political position in Poland, Czechoslovakia, Bulgaria, and Yugoslavia. This pan-Slavic motif crops up in a number of Russian literary works dating from the hotter Cold War period.

Despite the indirect appeal to pan-Slavism in *Under the Chestnut Trees of Prague*, however, Simonov permits his characters to make a number of uncharitable remarks on the matter of Czech patriotism and heroism. These follow a line heard often in some quarters in Eastern Europe after the war that the Czechs were cowardly and offered virtually no resistance to the Nazis. In Simonov's play this putative Czech cowardice and negligible patriotism are the faults, above all, of the "old order," the prewar Czech bourgeois who thereby forfeit their right to determine the future of the Czech nation to political progressives of the younger generation such as Stefan, Bozhena, and Tihy who actively oppose the aggressor. Whatever the ideological rationale, Simonov's faulting of Czech courage and patriotism still skirts the offensive. And to make matters worse, the Czechs are frequently compared unfavorably in the play to the Russians. Early in the work, the point is made that the reason the Russians fought so much harder against the Nazis than the Czechs was their greater love for liberty. Nothing is said about the relative size of the two countries or the viability of their respective defense postures before the Nazi onslaught or the political betrayal of Czechoslovakia at Munich. The issue was simple, at least from the point of view of Soviet audiences at the time: the Russians succeeded in driving out the invader because their greater love for liberty enabled them to fight harder; conversely, the Czechs were incapable of serious resistance because their "unenlightened" bourgeois culture made them weak in courage and patriotism; it was also for this same reason that they produced a number of collaborators (like Grubek in the play); and finally, since the prewar Czech society had to assume the responsibility for the collapse of the country it was to be denied a role in building its future. This role was now to be assumed by progressive elements in Czech society favorable to the Russians—fellow Slavs—whose superior political and social system had made it possible for the Red Army to liberate Czechoslovakia. Given this line of reasoning and the whole ideological tenor of Simonov's *Under the Chestnut Trees of Prague*, it is fair to assume that the play was intended only for internal consumption. That it would have helped the Soviet cause in Czechoslovakia at the time seems doubtful.

Another obvious target of this highly charged Soviet propaganda drama of the immediate postwar period was the United States. As the Cold War intensified, a number of plays were written attacking postwar American imperialism and its anti-Soviet machinations. In the heat of the ideological struggle, the massive American contribution to the Russian defense effort and the overall American role in the eventual defeat of Germany and Japan were either greatly minimized or passed over in silence. However, following a long-established (and still applicable) tradition in Soviet anti-American propaganda, a distinction is usually drawn between the American people and the American "ruling circles." Recruited and supported by the "military-industrial complex," the latter is characteristically presented as seeking the destruction of the USSR which it fears as the greatest threat to its self-interest. To accomplish this goal, it dupes the American people into an almost irrational hatred of socialism, communism, and the USSR. In every way misrepresenting the Soviet system and Soviet foreign policy objectives, it methodically prepares the "holy war" it regards as absolutely essential to the preservation of American capitalism and America's postwar international political and military hegemony. Opposed to this policy of the "ruling circles" in Washington are certain progressive elements in American society friendly toward the Soviet Union. These may be found in any walk of life, but journalists and scholars predominate. Their struggle is often portrayed as futile in the immediate present but destined ultimately to triumph as the American people slowly but surely become enlightened as to the true nature of their political leadership.

There is not much to be gained from any extensive analysis of Russian anti-American plays of the post-World War II era; a rapid glance at a few representative works should provide sufficient acquaintance with the genre. The majority are made-to-order propaganda pieces of little weight as dramatic literature. Produced in large measure by the tensions of the cold war and reflecting those tensions, they offer dreary testimony once again of the stifling impact on artistic creativity of politically guided repressive policies in the cultural sphere. Available evidence suggests that the plays were never particularly popular in their day—the international political situation notwithstanding—and virtually all have disappeared from the boards, permanently one hopes.

Throughout his substantial career as a writer, Konstantin Simonov has shown a splendid (if no doubt convenient) ability to move with the changing political climate in the USSR; in this respect he has hardly been unique among Russian writers in the Soviet era. When the Soviets launched their propaganda campaign in fact before the actual end of the war in 1945 in order to lay a smoke screen for their true political intentions in Eastern Europe, Simonov lost little time in coming up with an appropriate dramatic vehicle, *Under the Chestnut Trees of Prague* (1945). As the cold war with the United States began to crystallize, Simonov responded accordingly and in 1946 wrote one of the best-known and most often performed Russian anti-American plays of the period, *Russky vopros* (*The Russian Question*). A few years later, as we shall soon see, Simonov demonstrated still greater agility by including himself in the front rank of writers calling for a liberalization of Soviet cultural policy!

Simonov's *The Russian Question* is as good an introduction to the Soviet anti-American drama of the period 1945 to 1952 as any. Set in the New York City area in the winter and summer of 1946, the play focuses on the efforts of corrupt American publishers to feed the fires of anti-Soviet hatred by commissioning books "proving" the USSR's desire for imperialist expansion at the risk of a new war. The hero of this all too obvious and predictable play is an honest American reporter named Harry Smith, the author of a wartime book favorable to the Soviet Union. Because of his credibility as an objective journalist, Smith is approached with a commission for a new, *anti-Soviet* book by the publishers Macpherson and Gould. Out of financial need, he accepts the contract and goes to the USSR for research. What he finally writes is an honest book full of praise for the Soviet Union's desire for and attempts to achieve peace. Macpherson and Gould are furious, refuse to publish the book, and block every effort by Smith to have it printed, even as a series of articles in the left-oriented press. In the course of his campaign for honest and free journalism Smith loses whatever money he has, his home, and his wife. Crushed but refusing to compromise, he vows to go on living as best he can.

The message of *The Russian Question* is plain. In the United States decent people who respect the truth and refuse to betray their own ethical and moral principles are intimidated and victimized by Capital (Wall Street). The situation is critical because Capital controls the media of communication and dupes the unsuspecting American people into believing that the Soviet Union is pursuing policies leading to a new war. Because it seeks an ultimate showdown in order to destroy communism and the USSR, Capital uses the media to foment anti-Soviet sentiment and war hysteria in the United States. There are good Americans, like Harry Smith, who know better and fight for the truth, but they are powerless before the might of Capital and are crushed. Hope for the future, however, lies with such people who may yet somehow make the truth known to their fellow Americans.

Most of the time these cold war anti-Western and, specifically, anti-American plays err so much on the side of excess, whatever their other shortcomings, that they become more ludicrous than offensive. Simonov's *The Russian Question* is no exception. In the typical style of the genre, the play assumes the character of a kind of Soviet morality play. Heaven and Hell, Good and Evil are sharply distinguished and easily identified. Characterization is simple and almost allegorical. The only difference is that at play's end virtue goes unrewarded. Evil triumphs, but there is that hint anyway in Harry's will to live and fight that the triumph will not long endure. To paint his picture of evil (read Capital) as black as possible for the maximum emotional impact, Simonov carries matters too far and falls into his own trap of near absurdity by including in his play the sad story of Harry's best friend, a fellow journalist named Murphy, who gets killed in a stunt to promote what proves to be an unsafe plane manufactured by a new company. Desperate for funds, Murphy accepts the dangerous and humiliating assignment, only to lose his life. Capital claims another victim.

Russian concern at the time over the American nuclear monopoly is reflected in several of the anti-American plays. Lev Sheynin's *V seredine veka* (*At Mid-Century*, 1950) is a good example. The setting, as in Simonov's *Under the Chestnut Trees of Prague* and *The Russian Question*, is non-Russian, this time Norway and America. Reminiscent of prewar Soviet melodramas, the play is rich in intrigue at the expense of characterization; only now the villains are not shady NEP types or dissident elements within Soviet society, but anti-Soviet lackeys of Capital or, to be more precise, American government officials (including representatives of the FBI).

During World War II, American agents smuggle the distinguished physicist Berg out of Norway under the very noses of the Germans. The Norwegian setting of the first part of the play gives Sheynin a chance to introduce the figure of the well-known Norwegian writer Knut Hamsun, who is taken to task for his pro-fascist and racist views. It is for the latter, in fact, that Berg drops his friendship with Hamsun, pointing up the role that race will come to play in *At Mid-Century*.

Once in the United States, Berg is put to work on the atomic bomb project. A black man is his closest associate, but after a while he is phased out of the project because, as Berg learns (and this marks the beginning of his disenchantment with the United States), government officials believe that scientific secrets should not be entrusted to blacks. The atomic destruction of Hiroshima and Nagasaki intensifies Berg's disenchantment, for he feels that his talents have been exploited by the American government for purposes of which he was not informed. Berg's black associate shares his feelings and becomes increasingly more vocal in his repudiation of American policies. To silence him, government officials decide to put him out of the way and stage an automobile accident in which he is killed. Berg, too, becomes a more active dissident and the decision is made to deport him. Exploiting Berg's long friendship with a Russian woman scientist, a plot is hatched involving Berg's son-in-law, a former collaborator with the Germans and Quisling, whereby Berg is falsely accused of passing secrets to Soviet agents. After his conviction, he is taken in handcuffs to an ocean liner and returned to his native Norway. The American efforts to discredit Berg and through him the international peace movement in which he has become deeply involved prove to no avail. At the end of the play, a still-respected and admired Berg appears at a great International Peace Congress to deliver an impassioned plea for peace and a condemnation of those who would unleash a new war.

Sheynin's play, like Simonov's or like another well-known exercise in anti-American propaganda *The Mad Haberdasher* (1949), an attack on President Truman by the Stalin Prize-winner Anatoli Surov (1910–   ), attempts to portray the Americans as anti-Soviet and the true instigators of the Cold War. The possibility of American nuclear blackmail is also suggested and the implied condemnation of the atomic bombing of Hiroshima and Nagasaki is best read in this light. Several other motifs not remarked in the Simonov play became commonplaces of Soviet anti-American drama between 1946 (when *The Russian Question* appeared) and 1950 (the date of Sheynin's *At Mid-Century*): the injection of the race element treated hyperbolically by Sheynin (the killing of Berg's black associate because of his oppsoition to American domestic and foreign policy); the association of West Germany with the postwar American anti-Soviet crusade, suggested in *At Mid-Century* by the German scientist Meier, a former Nazi supporter, who is brought to the United States to assist in the anti-Soviet war campaign; the introduction of a positive Soviet character whose principal purpose is to spout the official

Soviet position (the scientist Prokhorova, in Sheynin's play); and the vig-
orous promotion of the international peace movement.

Representative anti-American propaganda plays such as Simonov's
and Sheynin's rarely exhibit any outstanding features of style or structure. With the greater emphasis on ideology than art, the style is generally flat and functional. Characterization, with only rare exceptions, is
one-dimensional and structure relies heavily on contrivance to create a
shallow melodramatic suspense without which the plays would be able
to hold the interest perhaps only of the most fanatically partisan. Gross
exaggeration and implausibility abound everywhere, producing an often
unexpected source of comic relief. In Sheynin's play, for example,
frequent references to and citations from the works of Marx and Lenin
occur. When the speakers are Russians or those sympathetic to the Soviet cause, the effect is not particularly striking or ludicrous as such,
though the frequency of such occurrences only serves to add weight to
the play's already burdensome didacticism. What does become ludicrous, however, is the excellent knowledge of Marx and Lenin exhibited
by a rabid anti-Soviet American character who believes that to fight the
devil one has to know the devil and becomes so conversant with
Marxism-Leninism that he can quote chapter and verse.

Certainly an important contributing factor to the poor state of Russian
drama in the first half dozen years after World War II was the currency
enjoyed at that time by the "no conflict" theory of drama. As simply
stated as possible, the idea was that communism in Russia had eliminated the familiar conflicts—economic, social, racial, sexual, and so
on—of the capitalist world. Conflict, therefore, could have no place in
Soviet Russian drama since as a reflection of the society in which it is
created drama must reflect the "conflictlessness" of Soviet society. Now
we appreciate the fact that to all intents and purposes drama cannot exist
without conflict of some kind and the question is legitimately posed,
how can a "conflictless" drama be written? The answer is that it cannot.
If only positive, exemplary characters make up the cast of a play, it is
difficult to imagine ways in which the play can be made to hold an audience's interest. To be sure, the problem of "conflictlessness" is not limited solely to the drama in Soviet Russian literature since the doctrine of
Socialist Realism, in force in Soviet literary culture since the 1930s,
operates generally with idealized constructs. The *true* Socialist Realist
literary work features idealized Soviet people and an idealized Soviet society as existing realities. If the prescribed method of Socialist Realism is

realistic, there is no doubt that its conception of Soviet society owes much to romanticism.

Rare indeed, of course, is the theory of art rigidly adhered to and Socialist Realism is hardly an exception. Were it not, Russian literature since the 1930s would present a far bleaker picture. Soviet society is anything but a millennial ideal; conflicts abound in it just as they do under capitalism if not always of the same kind or to the same degree, and these have been and are reflected in Soviet literature. Moreover, absolute fidelity to the tenets of Socialist Realism has not been demanded always with the same degree of insistence since the 1930s. What obtains elsewhere in Soviet literature, therefore, with regard to conformity with Socialist Realism has been similarly true of the drama. Soviet plays devoid of any conflict in the strict sense have been few and far between. But between 1947 and 1952 particularly, during that "dark age" of post-World War II Soviet literature, dramatists, responding to the pressures on the literary community represented by the phenomenon of Zhdanovism, did attempt to "play it safe" from the point of view of contemporary literary politics by writing plays featuring a relative "conflictlessness." The anti-Western, anticosmopolitan, anti-American drama of the time presented no problem since the plays sought to depict the heroic struggle of progressive freedom-loving peoples everywhere under Soviet leadership against the warmongering imperialists of the capitalist West. The conflict, in a dramatic sense, was ready-made.

But the problem of conflict in the drama was most acute, for obvious reasons, in plays dealing with contemporary Soviet life. Some dramatists sought to avoid the problem altogether by joining the anti-Western, anticosmopolitan, anti-American propaganda campaign where approved sources of conflict were readily available. Others turned to the writing of historical drama as a means of evading the issue. Still others concentrated on plays about the recent war with the Germans as their principal source of antagonists. But those who attempted to deal in their plays with postwar Soviet life soon found it virtually impossible to write drama wholly free of conflict and conjured up a kind of pseudo-conflict in which the good and the better are opposed. The results were uninspiring, to put it mildly, and provoked a crisis in Soviet dramaturgy that came to a head in 1952.

Although the theory of "no conflict" drama never achieved the status of a postulate of Soviet literary method, the repression and extreme conservatism characteristic of the domestic political situation in the USSR in the first half dozen years after the war produced an almost numbing caution among writers. Never quite sure from one moment to the next what they could write about and how possible confrontations with the Party's literary overseers could best be avoided, most writers understandably followed the more obvious paths of least resistance. If, with respect to drama, it was felt that it was decidedly more politic in a difficult time to deal only with varying degrees of good, in a Soviet sense, rather than to follow the more dangerous route of probing indeterminate areas of genuine dramatic conflict, it is small wonder that a "no conflict" concept of drama came to have a certain respectability—until its patent uselessness as a method of dramatic writing and, in fact, its positively harmful effects on dramatic creativity became impossible to evade.

The inevitable reaction against the *Zhdanovshchina*, as the period of extreme literary repression dominated by the unyielding figure of Andrei Zhdanov is often called in Russian, set in in 1951 and 1952. In his general survey, *Russian Literature Since the Revolution*, Edward J. Brown offers this succinct summation of the incipient reaction against reaction:

> In 1951 and 1952 a reaction set in, and the Party press for those years revealed that floundering efforts were being made to correct a disastrous situation. Editorials and critical articles called for the injection of "new life" into literature, spoke of the need to portray "living men," demanded that writers show life "as it is," featuring the "bad" as well as the "good," and deplored the "varnishing of reality."[1]

An attack on the "no conflict" theory of drama had been made as early as 1948 by the dramatist Aleksandr Kron (1909–)[2] in his essay entitled "A Dramatist's Reply" in the ninth issue for that year of the leading Soviet theater journal *Teatr* (*Theater*). But Kron's attack at the time was a voice in the wilderness. A victim himself of the anticosmopolitan campaign of 1948–49, denounced as "antipatriotic" along with other dramatists and theater critics at the Twelfth Plenum of the Union of Soviet Writers in December 1948 and again at a special meeting of Communist Party members of the Union on February 9 and 10, 1949, presided over by the Stalinist and Stalin Prize-winning dramatist Anatoli Sofronov (1911–), his views were not likely to have attracted many adherents.

By 1952, however, the situation had changed considerably. Calls for the opening of a new era in Soviet literature and lamentations over the plight of Soviet dramaturgy had risen in frequency. Recognizing, finally, the pernicious influence of the "no conflict" theory of drama, *Pravda* appeared on April 7, 1952, with an editorial denouncing the theory and declaring it a literary aberration. A scapegoat had to be found, of course, and the burden came to rest squarely on the shoulders of the dramatist Nikolai Virta (1906–76) who had been among the most ardent champions of "conflictlessness."

Four years after the *Pravda* attack, during the great Soviet literary thaw of 1956, a number of striking works of protest and dissidence appeared in the memorable collection of poetry, fiction, and criticism known as *Literaturnaya Moskva* (*Literary Moscow*), II. Prominent among the critical pieces was a vitriolic commentary on Soviet drama and theater by the previously mentioned dramatist Aleksandr Kron and the literary critic Mark Shcheglov. Their remarks on the damage wrought by the foolishness of the "no conflict" theory are well worth recounting:

> The notorious theory of the "struggle between the good and the still better" proved to be just as unfounded, and it served as a theoretical prop for those who sought to falsify and prettify reality. It becomes clear who needed these theories and for what purpose if we recall that they arose during the years when even such an exact science as statistics was used by the hallelujah singers for creating all sorts of falsifications. If this was true of statistics, it is all the more true of the theater.
>
> Not nearly all these bureaucratic delusions became an accepted part of our theory. That does not make them any less tenacious of life. The conviction has become deeply rooted that the subject matter of an artistic work is not the invention of the author, and that therefore "themes" can be planned from above as easily as industrial output. That the plot of a play is like a Gospel parable, necessarily embodying a moral lesson. That the spectator's most immediate need is to imitate and that he only awaits an opportunity to copy in life the outline he has seen on the stage. That whenever a negative character attempts to justify his base actions, the author is yielding the rostrum to the enemy. That every work in which evil remains unpunished is a sign of pessimism. That the second or connotative level of meaning—the hidden, unspoken undertones and overtones which determine to a great extent the ideological and emotional effect of a play and a performance—is a crafty subterfuge, hard to evaluate and control; and that therefore characters should express their thoughts unambiguously and distinctly. Lastly, thoroughly distorted conceptions prevail concerning the relation between the individual and the "type."[3]

TWELVE

The "Thaw" of 1953 and 1954

THE "no conflict" theory was finally—and definitively—consigned to oblivion in the early 1950s. But the attempts to apply the theory to playwriting and the intense propagandizing to which Russian drama was subjected from the end of World War II to 1953 had taken their toll. Drama was in the doldrums. Few of the postwar plays possessed real literary merit and even in the darkest days of Cold War anxieties and pressures few attracted audiences. Theatergoing declined, and to win back the public many theaters began relying heavily on the production of nineteenth- and early twentieth-century classics as well as on the revival of several of the more outstanding plays of the 1920s and early 1930s. But even the revolutionary heroics of some of the latter seemed strangely out of place in the Russia of the later 1940s and early 1950s, and aroused little public response.

Although voices of discontent about the plight of the drama and Soviet literature in general began to be heard more often and more loudly in 1951 and 1952, it was only with the death of Stalin in 1953 that any fresh winds were permitted to blow through the corridors of Soviet art. In the "thaw" that followed the dictator's demise, Soviet artists showed less reluctance to make their true feelings known and started pressing not only for a liberalization of the Party's policy toward the arts but also for an "opening up" of the arts themselves. They sought, above all, greater freedom for the individual artist, the right of the artist to create independently of Party control or interference. Reacting against the burdensome and artistically stifling Party-enforced obligations that the arts depict Soviet life in positive, even idealized terms, they pleaded for the right of the artist to portray the life around him as he saw it, realistically, as mindful of its deficiencies as of its strengths. So long harnessed to the chariot of industrialization, collectivization, and the supremacy of the collective over the individual, the Soviet artist yearned to tear free of his yoke and wander wherever his own thoughts and feelings led him. Oppressed by the seemingly never-ending celebration of the great goals of socialist construction, the artist begged to be permitted to direct his attention to the myriad small pleasures and sorrows that go to make up man's everyday existence. Not wishing to denigrate the rights of the collective, the artist now asked for the right to devote equal time to the individual. And in a society in which the emotional life has always been collective, the artist asked also for the right to make this emotional life a legitimate object of investigation free of other considerations. As Edward J. Brown puts it so aptly, "One reflects that in the Soviet Union the rediscovery of alphabets is a regular occurrence."[1]

The various manifestations of this first post-World War II "thaw" in Soviet Russian literature have been discussed in many publications in English and need no further elaboration in a book on the drama. The nonspecialist reader would be well advised to consult a good general survey such as Brown's *Russian Literature Since the Revolution* for an overview of the articles, novels, and stories whose appearance in 1953 and 1954 gave ample evidence of a new spirit in Russian writing.

How the drama responded to this new spirit can be determined by considering such representative "thaw" plays—all dating from 1954—as *Gosti (The Guests)* by Leonid Zorin (1924–), *Personalnoe delo (A Personal Matter)* by Aleksandr Shteyn (1906–), *V dobry chas! (Good Luck!)* by Viktor Rozov (1913–), and *Gody stranstviy (Years of Wandering)* by Aleksei Arbuzov.

A common theme of much of the "thaw" literature of 1953 and 1954, and one hardly capable of having been dealt with at all meaningfully by writers before the death of Stalin, was corruption in high places. This, of course, in the name of the new realism, honesty, and objectivity. Communist Party and government officialdom was not, to be sure, made up exclusively of do-gooders, of wise, dynamic, self-sacrificing idealists, despite the assiduous efforts of earlier Soviet literature to portray them as such. Hence the desire of the "thaw" literature to shatter the myth of Party and State infallibility by showing that even the Party and State hierarchies are not free of the weaknesses and evils afflicting the rest of human society the world over. In a Soviet context this was, needless to say, daring stuff no matter what strategies writers used to soften the blow. That the wrath of the Party would be incurred and an anti-"thaw" reaction initiated was almost a foregone conclusion. But before taking up the matter of the reaction, let us have a closer look at the stimulus that produced it.

Misuse of authority, the quest for privilege, and unabashed bourgeois materialism on the part of Party officials are at the center of interest in

Zorin's *The Guests* and Shteyn's *A Personal Matter*. Like many Soviet plays of the mid-1950s, neither work is outstanding as dramatic literature. But their frankness in dealing with highly sensitive issues of contemporary Soviet society lifts them out of the ordinary. This is especially true of Zorin's play, which is by far the bolder of the two.

In some Soviet drama of the late '30s and the war years conflict was developed out of a clash of attitudes among representatives of different generations, often within a single family. Generally, though to be sure not always, the older generation came off second best in these clashes, condemned for inflexible, anachronistic, and simplistic views born of the Revolution and Civil War era but no longer applicable in the changing circumstances of the rapidly evolving Soviet Union.

The motif of the conflict of generations is used again by Zorin in *The Guests,* but in a significant departure from the earlier pattern it is now a sympathetically drawn old revolutionary whose idealism and integrity become newly attractive when contrasted with the elitist arrogance and bourgeois materialism of his son, a high-ranking official in the Ministry of Justice. More than a dramatic character, the son is intended by Zorin as a collective portrait of the middle-generation Stalinist bureaucracy. To the son, the old revolutionary ardor and idealism of his father are little more than distant echoes of a romantic past to which he, the son, feels only the bonds of history. In a position of importance, the son relishes the taste of power but his use of it is not for the common good but for self-improvement in a material sense. Contemptuous of ordinary citizens, the son is even willing to go so far as to conceal a miscarriage of justice rather than run the risk of humiliation and loss of power and privilege which would be the result of exposure. This abuse of official responsibility is compounded by the son's relentless acquisition of material goods and comforts: a luxurious apartment, an attractive summer house, and a chauffeur-driven automobile. To the father, the son's attitude toward power and his values are a perversion of the ideals of the Revolution and a tragic betrayal of the blood and toil expended in the cause of the consolidation of Soviet power. Not only the old revolutionary but other characters including the minister's own son perceive the irony of the *embourgeoisement* of the minister and other self-serving bureaucrats like him for whom the ideals of the Revolution are now empty slogans solely of historical interest.

The death of Stalin and the relaxation of some of the old tensions of Soviet society brought the partial exposure—and punishment—of wrongdoing in high places. This culminated in the now-famous denunci-

ation of Stalin by Khrushchev at the momentous Twentieth Congress of
the Communist Party of the USSR in February 1956. In the background
of Zorin's play was the public exposure of crimes in the Soviet Ministry
of Justice after the execution of the notorious hatchetman Lavrenti
Beria. For that reason I think it fair to assume that the Ministry of Justice affiliation of the central character of *The Guests* was anything but a
whim on Zorin's part.

Perhaps because of the revelations of crimes by officials of the Ministry of Justice Zorin felt reasonably secure in making a corrupt official of
this ministry the leading figure of his play. The Ministry of Culture
thought otherwise and not without reason. The minister is so depicted
as to leave little doubt, as I suggested earlier, that he is anything but an
isolated instance of corruption. Alert to the broader implications of
Zorin's study of a "lapsed" official, the Ministry of Culture lost little time
in condemning the play as compounded of falsehoods and distortions
and in calling for its suppression.

The Guests extends the conflict of generations by introducing the
character of the minister's son. And here Zorin no doubt sought a somewhat more positive ending for his somber play, an ending capable also of
placating officials who might otherwise take umbrage against it. Through
the minister's son, who rebels against his father near the end of the play
and repudiates him and everything he stands for in much the same spirit
as the minister's father, Zorin suggests that once the self-serving Stalinist bureaucracy of the middle generation is exposed and removed from
power the younger generation will be able to return the country to its
proper course, to restore to it the temporarily abandoned ideals of such
old revolutionaries as the minister's father. The mild note of optimism
about the future struck at the end of *The Guests* left little impact on the
play's stern critics at the Ministry of Culture. And indeed the son's outburst against his father does little to offset the bitterness informing what
must be regarded certainly as one of the most powerful and unequivocal
indictments of the Stalinist bureaucracy ever recorded in Soviet literature.

Shteyn's *A Personal Matter* is much like Zorin's *The Guests* in subject,
but weaker in two important respects. The central figure of a corrupt
Party official is developed less powerfully and the play has a conventional happy ending; evil is exposed and punished and virtue is rewarded. In *The Guests* Zorin concentrated as much on the bourgeois
materialism of his minister as on his abuse of power. Shteyn's target is
the lack of democracy in the Party and the use of Party position to set-

tle personal scores. The plot revolves around the attempt on the part of a jealous Party official to oust a talented and valued engineer from the Party and to make it impossible for him to receive an important professional position. The official's strategy rests on the use of circumstantial evidence of impropriety on the part of the engineer, but by the end of the play the engineer is vindicated and receives the promotion due him; the corrupt official, on the other hand, comes before his peers for judgment.

Only slightly less reprehensible to Shteyn than the corrupt official is the individual who becomes a tacit participant in injustice by refusing to speak out against it when he can in order to avoid jeopardizing his own security. When a crucial vote on the engineer's Party status is taken, several of his colleagues boldly speak in his behalf, to the obvious displeasure of his antagonist, the Party official, Poludin. But a family friend, Kolokolnikov, abstains under pressure from his wife and out of his own desire to avoid trouble. Counterposed to Kolokolnikov's timidity is the enthusiastic support of the engineer's cause by another Party official, Dergacheva, whose own marriage was ruined because she lacked sufficient faith in her husband, a teacher, when he was wrongly accused of the uncredited use of his students' work in the preparation of a book. The social contagion represented by a Poludin is spread all the more, suggests Shteyn, by people like Kolokolnikov, who refuse to be counted when justice and common decency hang in the balance and hence must share the guilt of the Poludins. The subplot involving Kolokolnikov and the introduction of the character of Dergacheva are motivated by the author's desire to excoriate the tacit complicity in injustice as much as injustice itself and to demonstrate that this complicity can tear at the fabric not only of family life but of society itself.

Unlike the plays of Zorin and Shteyn, those of Rozov and Arbuzov concentrate on personal relationships and are markedly free of political concern. The new "realism" of the first "thaw" is immediately manifest in them and amounts to a conscious effort on the part of the dramatists to avoid the sugarcoating of less attractive aspects of contemporary Soviet society. Striking especially in view of the idealizing tendencies of much Soviet drama is the willingness to highlight the ordinary, the unexceptional, to stress the need in Soviet life for self-awareness and honest self-appraisal.

Consider Rozov's *Good Luck!*, for example. The underlying theme of the play is that not every person can be a hero, can accomplish great things in life, can realize youthful dreams of grandeur. Such dreams,

Rozov argues, are not bad; they are natural and give one the incentive to strive. But failure to realize the dreams must not lead to despair but instead to a self-awakening capable of bringing the maturity of compromise and eventually an inner peace. The theme is exemplified in many situations in the play. The young actor, Arkadi, can never connect with big parts though he demonstrates ability in small ones and must learn to content himself with such parts knowing that in all probability he will never become a famous actor. His girl friend, Masha, once had the ambition to become a concert pianist but could not make the grade and eventually found contentment, self-expression, and self-fulfillment as a photographer. When some of the younger people in the play talk among themselves of the futures they plan, the issue comes up of big dreams, of ambitions, and the too prevalent tendency, especially of the young, to scorn those of little or no outstanding accomplishments. One character, the country lad Aleksei, says at one point: "And I think it's bad when, for example, a writer starts telling himself: 'I'll be another Leo Tolstoy!'" His city cousin, Vadim, whom he has come to visit, answers him: "But a writer can and must dream about becoming another Leo Tolstoy!" Aleksei's simple answer, "To himself only," conveys much of the wisdom of the play.

Aleksei's arrival in the city and his contact with Vadim and other members of his family—the core situation of *Good Luck!*—serves as Rozov's mechanism to make a number of critically telling observations about contemporary Soviet life. Vadim's mother (Aleksei's aunt) is visibly upset at the prospect of making room in her house for her young relative who has come to the city to continue his education and anticipates living with his relatives. The aunt's selfishness is presented by Rozov as essentially un-Soviet in spirit and symptomatic of the unattractive bourgeois attitudes and manners so widespread in Soviet society. The bourgeois ambitiousness for their children of parents willing even to employ unethical means to achieve their goals is also exposed through the character of the aunt. To insure her son Vadim's acceptance into a prominent technical institute, entrance into which is highly competitive, the aunt pressures her husband, a well-known biologist, into using his influence to pave their son's way. When Aleksei learns of this he berates Vadim for his high-sounding talk about ambition and goals while all along scheming to use family influence to gain unfair advantage over others in the advancement of his career. Vadim dismisses Aleksei's complaints as mere jealousy, but the latter insists that he surrender his Komsomol pin since he is no longer worthy of being a member of the

Communist Youth Organization. Eventually, the pressures mount on Vadim against using influence to get into the institute, and when he fails the entrance examinations the matter is definitively laid to rest.

Vadim's failure conforms to the principles of Soviet morality according to which punishment of one sort or another ultimately awaits a citizen guilty of "antisocial" activities or proclivities. Because he cannot measure up to the standards of a good Communist, Vadim must fail. Rozov is wholly traditional and conservative in this respect. But the play's most positive character among the major figures, Aleksei, also fails. He fails, literally, on the entrance examinations of the school he hoped to enter. Here, however, the failure of a positive character relates to the play's dominant theme, that not everyone can become a great success and that after reconciling oneself to failure a person must attempt to seek his level and place in society, as unglamorous and unromantic as it may turn out to be. Aleksei's failure, therefore, exemplifies the plays's thesis. Instead of grieving or unduly berating himself, Aleksei calmly makes up his mind to return to his native Siberia, to work to build its future as well as his own. When he leaves, he does not go alone but with Vadim's younger brother, Andrei, who is disenchanted with his family and the bourgeois life around him and who believes that in Siberia, under the guidance of Aleksei, he will find his true self.

Aleksei's and Andrei's return to Siberia reveals another facet of the theme of Rozov's *Good Luck!* and by no means a minor one if viewed in the context of the literature of the "thaw" as a whole. That is the somewhat neo-sentimentalist contrast of town and country, to the decided disadvantage of the former. In eighteenth-century sentimentalism the city was viewed more often than not as the repository of most social maladies, ranging from venereal disease to the use of cosmetics by women. In the city, removed from nature, people lived lives of artifice, shallowness, and pettiness. It was only in the country and among the simple folk of the country that one could know oneself and become truly human again. Very much the same outlook pervades Rozov's play. Throughout the work the vices of selfishness, pettiness, duplicity, and arrogance are almost consistently associated with city people, above all Aleksei's aunt and his cousin Vadim, who have become contaminated like so many other Soviet citizens by the disease of bourgeois culture infesting Soviet urban life, in Rozov's view. By contrast, it is the Siberian-reared Aleksei and a few of the friends who have come with him to the city who represent an admirable wholesomeness and naturalness. When Aleksei leaves the city at the end of the play, it is as much a flight from the bourgeois pettiness of the city as from his lack of success in it and when Andrei chooses to share his return to Siberia, the symbolism of the gesture is easily grasped by the audience.

In *Years of Wandering* Arbuzov touches on some of the same issues raised by Rozov, but in a play of broader sweep and richer texture. Interested always in character growth and change, Arbuzov again uses the format of the chronicle play. Over the period from 1937 to 1945 (hence from prewar to immediate postwar Russia), political, economic, and cultural changes are traced within the context of the growth and maturation of the young people whom Arbuzov makes the focus of interest. As the play opens, a hot August day in 1937 is drawing to an end. The young people assembled onstage are in a lighthearted mood—war is still a few years away—and they exchange banter about the professional training (medicine) they are about to begin. Arbuzov often has a hard time restraining himself from obvious symbolism and *Years of Wandering* is no exception. The waning of summer connotes the waning of the youth of the principal characters and lest the point be lost on any member of the audience, Arbuzov has one of the cast ask, almost rhetorically: "And perhaps we are all taking leave of our youth today?"

Although Arbuzov develops the relationships of parallel sets of characters—a technique used in earlier plays—attention rapidly centers on the obviously talented but egoistic Vedernikov. In his self-centeredness, self-confidence, and ambition Vedernikov is something of an older version of Rozov's Vadim. His first setback is the loss of a senior assistantship at the Experimental Institute, a prestigious position Vedernikov fully anticipated receiving. The job goes instead to Vedernikov's friend, Lavrukhin, whom Arbuzov contrasts with Vedernikov. Lavrukhin is modest and unassuming and even capable of turning down the position to spend a year and a half in a remote area practicing medicine, being of use to the community, and developing independence and self-reliance before tackling anything involving greater responsibility. When war comes, Vedernikov and Lavrukhin, the women in their lives, and other friends are all taken up with wartime medical service. Greatly matured by the war, Vedernikov regrets the time he wasted in the past. Struggling to overcome the egoism that obstructed his manhood, he at last perceives that in wanting to do everything himself he was the architect of his own failure. In a throwback to a motif used in an earlier play, *Tanya* (1938), Arbuzov visits Vedernikov not only with professional loss (the position that went to Lavrukhin) but personal loss as well: as in *Tanya*, Vedernikov's selfishness and egoism are punished by the loss of a child through illness (in Vedernikov's case, his little girl). Vedernikov's maturation moves through two more stages before it is completed: important medical research began by Vedernikov is finished by Lavrukhin, now a distinguished man of medicine, and rather than resenting Lavrukhin, as earlier, Vedernikov asks that he be permitted to work as his assistant; and Vedernikov finally chooses to remain with his wife despite his romance with Lavrukhin's former sweetheart.

Compared to an earlier play like *Tanya*, *Years of Wandering* reveals little advance in Arbuzov's dramatic technique. The basic plot, the sets of characters, the use of time and symbol, the lyricism, the happy ending are all familiar items. Perhaps at first glance *Years of Wandering* may seem little more than an updated *Tanya*—the gradual development, through adversity, of a sense of the collective on the part of a self-centered individual. In both plays, moreover, the central character finds fulfillment in medicine. What makes *Years of Wandering* different, however, and a product of the concerns of the literature of the first "thaw" as much as Rozov's social drama is the fundamental difference between Tanya and Vedernikov as personalities. Until events effect her self-awakening, Tanya's weak sense of the collective stems from her lack of personal ambition and her belief that all that life expected of her was that she devote herself completely to her husband. In the case of Vedernikov, the obverse obtains, namely a weak sense of the collective attributable to considerable ambition and an egoism which the Soviets like to regard as fundamentally bourgeois and un-Soviet. In the final analysis, Tanya and Verdernikov reach the same truth by the same road of adversity and maturity, but they start from different points. And it is the difference of the point of departure that sets *Years of Wandering* apart from *Tanya*, despite the obvious similarities between them, and that enables us to relate the more recent play to problems in Soviet society pertinently raised in the "thaw" literature of 1953 and 1954.

THIRTEEN

From the Twentieth Party Congress to 1959 : The "Year of Protest" and Its Aftermath

FEARFUL THAT matters might be getting out of hand, that the new-found individualism of artists might prove difficult to restrain if permitted too free rein, Party and literary conservatives began a counteroffensive against the "thaw" before it was even a year old. More liberal writers were attacked on a variety of charges, real or imagined, and several were expelled from the Union of Soviet Writers. A special meeting of the collegium of the Ministry of Culture was convened with the express purpose of condemning Zorin's *The Guests* and Aleksandr Tvardovsky, a poet and the respected editor of the literary journal *Novy mir* (*New World*). Much of the literature of the "thaw" had first appeared in *Novy mir;* because of this Tvardovsky was relieved of his responsibilities and the editorial board of the journal itself was officially censured.

The Party's "hard line" on literature was restated unequivocally at the Second Congress of Soviet Writers, held in December 1954, by the poet and playwright Aleksei Surkov, who urged a return to the principles of literary Zhdanovism. Surkov's argument was no isolated phenomenon. There were a number of conservatives among the assembled writers who were similarly troubled by the new directions Soviet literature seemed to be following and shared his views. But the conservatives, for all their vehemence and official support, did not carry off a clear victory. Many writers defended the new trends with equal vigor and even the ever politically trustworthy Simonov, now Tvardovsky's replacement as editor of *New World*, advocated a less doctrinaire interpretation of Socialist Realism. Simonov, moreover, spoke of the merits of republishing some of the long-banned satirists of the 1920s.

As if anticipating the startling revelations and anti-Stalinist posture of the Twentieth Party Congress of February 1956, the Second Congress of Soviet Writers closed inconclusively and in this very inconclusiveness the liberals scored a certain triumph. The top Party echelon refrained from direct intervention in the proceedings of the Congress, and if writers were chided and urged to return to more conservative attitudes, there were no mass expulsions and, on the other hand, no significant chest-beating public recantations on the part of the dissidents.

The Twentieth Party Congress gave the liberals a still greater sense of security and confidence. The assault by Khrushchev on the cult of Stalin promised an end to despotism and the dawning of a new era. And in the two speeches on literature delivered at the Congress, the unflagging, unyielding conservatism of Surkov was again opposed by the far more liberal position of another respected, politically reliable, and influential member of the Soviet literary community, the novelist Mikhail Sholokhov of *Quiet Flows the Don* fame. What made Sholokhov's relatively liberal repudiation of doctrinaire Socialist Realism more telling than Simonov's at the Second Congress of Soviet Writers was the disavowal of old-style Soviet literary politics, of the Party management of literary and indeed of all cultural matters, of the pernicious and crippling Soviet system of literary overlords.

Profoundly encouraged by the results of the Twentieth Party Congress, liberal Soviet writers sought to seize the moment and to extend the frontiers of the first "thaw." The miscellany *Literary Moscow* and the journal *New World* were again in the vanguard and again a pivotal work that seemed to set much of the tone of the new writing appeared. In 1954 it was Ilya Ehrenburg's novelette *The Thaw* (which gave its name, in fact, to the major developments in Russian literature after the death of Stalin) and in 1956 Vladimir Dudintsev's symptomatic but weak novel *Not By Bread Alone*. The high point of the "year of protest," as 1956 has been aptly dubbed by Hugh McLean and Walter Vickery, the editors of a valuable anthology of translations of Soviet writings of that year, was undoubtedly the Pasternak affair. Feeling that the time was ripe for the publication of the now-famous novel on which he had long been working, *Doctor Zhivago*, Boris Pasternak submitted it to the editorial board of *New World*. It was rejected, but in a far gentler way than surely would have been the case in the past. It then went on surreptitiously to foreign publication and international acclaim, culminating in the award of a Nobel Prize for literature to Pasternak and his refusal to accept it under immense political pressure. The international *cause célèbre* that grew out of Pasternak's *Doctor Zhivago* left no doubts concerning the extent to which the limits of Soviet literary liberalism and individualism could be pushed.

The Soviet suppression of the Hungarian revolt in October 1956 dispelled any lingering illusions as to the capacity of the Soviet political system for dynamic, sweeping change. But the events of 1953 and 1954, and again of 1956, demonstrated no less clearly that any return to the darker days of Stalinist dictatorship was also no longer truly possible. Protest, dissent, and the restless struggle of the artist for the freedom of self-expression had by now become incontrovertible realities of Soviet life. They could be kept within certain limits, as the Pasternak and, later, the Solzhenitsyn episodes showed but total extirpation was henceforth out of the question.

Despite the brevity of the interval, the literary harvest of the "year of protest" was impressive in all genres. In the drama especially notable was the continued involvement of playwrights in the major themes of the earlier "thaw." Romantic love now came to assume an even greater prominence; more striking, writers were willing to depart in their approach to form from the accepted, traditional patterns of Soviet dramaturgy of the previous twenty years.

As is usually the case, formal innovation lagged behind new thematic lines. We can see this, for example, in two sensations of the 1956 theatrical season, Nikolai Pogodin's *Sonet Petrarki* (*A Petrarchan Sonnet*) and Samuil Alyoshin's *Odna* (*Alone*). In both plays a conventional "realistic" dramatic structure serves as the frame in which bold and far-reaching questions about contemporary Soviet society are posed.

Pogodin's is clearly the more provocative of the two and the controversy it gave rise to is not hard to understand. So simple is the plot that it can almost be dismissed as little more than a pretext for a forceful attack on the petty bourgeois values of the new Soviet middle class and an appeal at the same time for privacy and the rights of man's emotional needs.

An unhappily married middle-aged engineer (to whom much of the aura of the traditional positive hero of Soviet literature still clings) falls in love with a girl half his age whom he barely knows. Malicious friends and the engineer's shrewish wife misconstrue the nature of the relationship and try to cause him trouble with the Party because of his "immoral" behavior. The relationship, pursued almost wholly through correspondence, is highly romantic, idealistic, and pristine, much in the spirit of Petrarch and the Laura of the sonnets, to which the engineer's letters to the girl are compared. But others cannot accept it for what it is and reduce it to a tawdry extramarital affair. Their efforts to harm the engineer come to no avail and in the open-ended conclusion to the play, favored by many post-Stalinist Russian dramatists as more truly realistic than the often mechanical "happy endings" of Socialist Realist drama, the engineer and the girl part, perhaps forever, perhaps not, each transformed by the "pure love" that touched—and ennobled—both their lives.

The right of the individual, in Soviet society as indeed anywhere else, to the privacy of his own emotions is Pogodin's most ardently pursued argument in A Petrachan Sonnet. The implied indictment of the nature of Soviet society in the Stalin era is unmistakable.

The invasion of the privacy of the engineer and the girl, involving mainly the dissemination of their correspondence, is undertaken by friends and colleagues, who believe that their betrayal of a confidence ultimately serves the best interests of the Party. The origin of such behavior is twofold, suggests Pogodin: a warped sense of the goals of communism according to which Party loyalty and a person's right to a private emotional life are incompatible, and the pettiness and moral hypocrisy of bourgeois mores which have reasserted themselves in an ever more materialistic Soviet society.

A devoted Party member, the engineer, Sukhodolov, pleads his own case for his right to privacy when he tells the head of the Party regional committee:

> Understand, again, that there are things which you can't tell the Party. If it were something political, why then you could have my head. . . . But what's political about it? I pledge my heart and soul to the Party; I'd lay down my life for it. . . . But still a man can have a private side to his life, a side which he'll let no one else into. He simply doesn't have to, and there's no law which says he does.[1]

The "rehabilitation" of Russian literary figures of the past under a cloud for one reason or another in the Stalinist era, which was to become a noteworthy feature of post-Stalinist Russian literature in general, is also hinted at in Sukhodolov's plea when he prefaces his above remarks with a paraphrase from Dostoevsky to the effect that "A great Russian writer once said that even a father couldn't talk about his relations with a woman to his son—never mind you and me—and even if those relations were the purest. Why can't we follow the laws established by the highest morality?" (p. 110).

Castigated by Pogodin no less than the denial of privacy is the simplis-

tic attitude of Soviet conservatives that one is either right, from a rigidly
and narrowly conceived Party point of view, or wrong, as the liberally
inclined head of the Regional Committee declares at one point:

> According to that logic of yours, the world consists of two antagonistic
> colors, black and white. All the rest is simply double-dealing, be-
> trayal, and what have you. . . . You can't understand or even imagine
> any other position? . . . But there is a third . . . and a fifth, and a
> tenth. . . . There's a whole mass of positions which, to put it bluntly,
> refute our old petrified dogmas. According to dogma, Sukhodolov is a
> dishonorable man, but according to real life, he's fully reliable, holy.
> . . . (p. 122)

Behind the simplistic Soviet morality censured above often lay the
fear of individual responsibility. Hence the need for "guidelines" imposed from above; the simpler the guidelines, the easier to enforce
them. The point is made unequivocally in the following scene between
the head of the Regional Committee, Pavel, and Klara, who betrays her
girl-friend's confidence:

> KLARA: I don't understand. Here you're reproaching me, but you
> can't give me any directives.
> PAVEL: No, I can't. It's not something you can give orders about.
> Here we are, two Party members, but in this case our views are dif-
> ferent. We're working out a new communist morality, and it's a
> long, drawn-out, harrowing, even tragic business.
> KLARA: Haven't we worked it out already? This is the first I've heard
> about that. I thought everything about all this was clear.
> PAVEL: I don't know about you, but it isn't for me.
> KLARA: A person can't help being confused. . . . What am I supposed
> to do? How should I behave?
> PAVEL: Alas, I can't give instructions on that. . . .
> KLARA: And the result? Honestly, I really don't know what I ought to
> think now.
> PAVEL: Thinking is one thing, but living off other people's thoughts is
> another. Try to think for yourself. You see, our Party's program
> allows great scope for independent thinking . . . and how much
> Lenin offers. . . .
> KLARA: No, you may think so, but I disagree. That causes complete
> confusion. To think individually on each issue, individually to come
> to a decision—you would go mad, first of all. You can't live without
> guidelines.
> PAVEL: You need guidelines for emotions, too?
> KLARA: Why not? Of course. Emotions, too, belong within definite
> frames. (p. 114)

As a progressive, enlightened Party dignitary, Pavel fulfills a particularly important role in the play as an "official" exponent of the new liberal post-Stalinist ideology. Or perhaps, implies Pogodin, this ideology is not so new, after all, in the history of the Soviet regime. On a few occasions Pavel warmly recalls the name of Sergei Kirov, who was second only to Stalin in the Party after Lenin's death until his assassination in 1934. There is the suggestion here, I believe, that Kirov represented a more liberal point of view in the Party, which was opposed by Stalin and his supporters. With the death of Stalin, the "spirit" of Kirov could be restored and the Party set on a new path.

Partly because Sukhodolov reminds him of Kirov, Pavel supports the engineer and ultimately wins a dismissal of the charges against him. Moreover, Pavel is placed in contact with such representatives of the "old" ways and views as Klara and Sukhodolov's colleague, Dononov, in order to expose their narrowness, rigidity, and hypocrisy. In Pavel's humanistic vision of Soviet society, there is a place for the feeling and beauty capable of uplifting the spirit of Soviet man. As he tells Dononov in Act III:

> What is most terrible, Afanasi Kuzmich, is that you have no idea of how to ennoble life. Probably you often say that life is beautiful. But what does "beautiful" mean? As I understand it, the most beautiful thing in life is man . . . and not every man. . . . He can be disgusting and even unfit to live with others . . . but when I meet a man, a contemporary Soviet man in our country, endowed with great spiritual beauty, I feel even more delighted to be alive. For a man, free from capitalism, new, purposeful, and endowed with spiritual beauty, is for me a sort of perfection, a delight. In him I see the future of the world, communism. But communism isn't in stones; it's in people. (p. 124)

Much of the ire of Pogodin's A Petrarchan Sonnet is reserved for the re-emergence in Soviet society of bourgeois materialism and philistinism, frequent targets of the new realism of post-Stalinist Russian drama. To Sukhodolov, the chief cause for the failure of his marriage is his inability to reconcile himself to his wife's "middle-classness, her loud manners, her petty mind, the fact that she seems to be a stone statue" (p. 98). Reflecting on the growing curiosity and suspicion concerning Sukhodolov's relations with his wife and the young girl, even the conservative Dononov recognizes that "there's a pinch of philistine inquisitiveness in that, too. We all like to peek through the crack into the neighbors' apartment. There's that about it, of course there is. Have to check these leftover, bourgeois habits" (p. 106). The final word on the subject is left, not unexpectedly, to Pavel who tells Sukhodolov: "A new world is only born in pain and struggle. I reiterate that simple truth to emphasize that it's being born. These petty middle-class people have to be fought. Why, they even want to see communism turned into a middle-class paradise. Comfort, satiety, and empty-mindedness" (p. 126).

With regard to its formal properties, Pogodin's A Petrarchan Sonnet warrants no great attention. The style of the play is conventional and the subject of an unhappily married middle-aged man belatedly finding "pure" love with a young woman half his age—despite plausible characterizations—is familiar to the point of being trite.

But it is not because of its form or subject that A Petrarchan Sonnet became a theatrical sensation. In its unvarnished indictment of the simplistic morality, suspicion, and oppression of Stalinist Russia, its repudiation of the new philistinism of contemporary Soviet society and its plea for a Soviet humanism respectful of the dignity of man and the right of the individual to the privacy of his own thoughts and feelings, the play was one of the boldest events in Russian dramatic literature of the "year of protest" of 1956. And in that light it can still be read with interest.

Alyoshin's Alone also deals with marital conflict and extramarital relationships. But the breakup of a marriage in this play is not merely the platform from which an author filled with a humanistic reformist enthusiasm lashes out at what he regards as major weaknesses in contemporary Soviet society. The marital conflict in Alone is more complex and has a greater dramatic integrity than in Pogodin's A Petrarchan Sonnet. Through it, in the name of greater realism in Soviet drama, Alyoshin strives to demonstrate the ability of the individual to overcome adversity, especially emotional adversity, and the need for the Soviet public to face a true image of its problems on the stage. The plot of the play concerns the stubborn but honorably motivated refusal by a talented engineer, Platonov, to agree to the release of a new motor design until it has been perfected to his satisfaction. The pressures on him are considerable. A female colleague, with whom he beomes romantically involved, Varvara (Varya) Nefedova, is convinced that the motor cannot be improved and urges him to release it. A superior, concerned only about meeting the deadline for the submission of the design to a government ministry, presses him relentlessly. To assuage an official of the ministry, a friend of Platonov, Kolya Krasnushkin, even lies about the outcome of tests on the machine. But so important is the principle to Platonov that not only does he refuse to give in to the pressures on him, but even goes so far as to risk incurring official displeasure on a high level by calling the ministry and telling the truth about the unsatisfactory performance of the motor after he discovers Kolya's lie.

Now this is all routine material to anyone even passingly familiar with Soviet Socialist Realist drama. Platonov is another in a long line of Soviet positive heroes, a man of talent and high principles who is unwilling to compromise with mediocrity. The outcome, of course, is predictable. Platonov succeeds in improving the motor brilliantly and so vindicates himself. The positive hero is once again triumphant.

But the episode of the motor design is not much more than a springboard for a matter of greater relevance to the "new thematics" of 1956. Although married and a father, Platonov falls in love with Varya and she with him. Alyoshin treats the relationship sensitively. Platonov and Varya are shown as mature, considerate adults who worry lest they hurt others. In this spirit, Platonov resolves the struggle within himself by determining not to leave his wife and daughter. In the pre-"thaw" Soviet drama, such a play—if love had been permitted to figure in it at all prominently—might have ended at this point.

But not so *Alone*. Platonov tries to pick up the threads of his former life but soon discovers that his love for Varya is too strong to permit him to be more than a husband in name only to his wife. He becomes restless, dissatisfied, irritable, and then finally recognizes that he can be true to himself only if he leaves his wife and goes off with Varya, which he does. Again, he refuses to compromise his ideals for the sake of convenience, and the relationship with Varya parallels his stand on the motor. The pressures on him to renounce his love and return to his family are as great as those urging the premature release of the motor, but in love as in his profession the pressures only strengthen his resolve. In order to drive home the type of stigma faced by Platonov should he finally abandon his family for "the other woman," Alyoshin interpolates the episode of a fellow worker named Ignatyuk, whose extramarital affair results in the loss of his Party membership.

The meaning of the title of Alyoshin's play is elusive until well into the drama and the emergence of Platonov's wife, Maria, as a more significant element in the author's plan than at first apparent. *Odna* in Russian is the nominative singular feminine form of the word for "one" or "alone" and hence can mean a woman who is alone. In Alyoshin's play that woman is Maria and it is with *her* "aloneness" that the play ends. When Platonov finally leaves her and their daughter, Maria becomes an exemplary figure of strength by refusing to give in either to remorse or to recrimination. Alone if necessary, she determines not to allow anyone else to spoil her life and will face the future resolutely. In a symbolic gesture reminiscent of Chekhov, at the very end of the play, she indicates that henceforth *she* will wind the clock that formerly only Platonov wound.

Considering the importance Maria comes to assume in *Alone*, at least symbolically, the character is not developed in sufficient depth to become a commanding stage presence. This is perhaps the major deficiency of Alyoshin's play. Attention for too long is riveted on Platonov whose conduct is consistent throughout, even if it does not fully accord with the general image of the positive hero of Soviet literature. With Platonov, Alyoshin attempted to establish the equal rights of citizenship of the emotions and largely succeeded. Whatever the cost, Platonov must be true to himself and follow the path of genuine love. In keeping with the new spirit of the "thaw" literature, or perhaps better said, the spirit of the new realism as distinct from the artificial conventions of the idealizing Socialist Realism, Alyoshin shuns the pat solution. Platonov does, in the end, leave his wife and daughter to go off with the other woman. No moral judgment is passed by the author. And then, perhaps to compensate partially for the absence of a moral position and a conventional happy ending. Alyoshin gratifies the audience's sympathy for Maria's plight by depicting her in the last moments of the play as unbroken, courageous, and obviously willing and able to fend for herself. But apart from this compensatory element in the play's conclusion, Alyoshin is demonstrating through Maria that however much the breakup of a marriage and a family may hurt it is not the end of life. By avoiding either a neat ending with all knots tied or a happy ending, in the old style, Alyoshin takes his stand firmly on the side of those anxious to make Soviet literature a truer reflection of human relationships as they are—individual, unique, no two precisely alike—and not as they may be imagined to be in idealistic constructs. Very probably the key line of *Alone* is spoken by Varya's father Vasili, who addresses himself at one point in a soliloquy: "Don't generalize, Vasili Fyodorovich, don't generalize. Medicine teaches us that in life and in man everything is individual."[2]

A similar concern with individualism and individual reaction to adversity is expressed in another popular play of the year 1956, Viktor Rozov's *Vechno zhivye! (Alive Forever!)*. Based on an earlier play from 1943, *Alive Forever!* itself served as the basis for a movie which attracted much favorable notice abroad, *Zhuravli letyat (The Cranes Are Flying)*.

The 1943 origin of *Alive Forever!* is evident in its World War II setting. Boris and Veronica, the play's romantic leads, are separated when Boris is called to active duty. Eventually Veronica receives notice that he is missing in action and she marries his cousin, Mark, to whom she had given herself once out of loneliness and despair during Boris' absence. Marriage to Mark, however, brings Veronica no peace. She soon discovers that he is not only keeping company with other women among friends of questionable character, but that he connived to have himself deferred from military service. Not long after her break with Mark, a young man (Volodya) tells Veronica that Boris died at the battle of Smolensk while trying to save the young man's life. In the last scene of the play, the war now over, Veronica has come to the western outskirts of Smolensk to search for Boris' grave. She cannot find it, but cranes flying overhead remind her of a poem Boris used to recite to her. Recalling past times together she addresses her dead lover for the last time, telling him that he is hers forever, forever alive, and that she is taking his life with her.

The "new" realism—and lyricism—of so representative a post-Stalinist play as Rozov's can best be appreciated by comparing it to the vast majority of pre-1952 plays set also in World War II. We notice very soon in the work, for example, that the familiar heroism of the average Soviet war play has all but disappeared. Boris, it is true, is anxious to volunteer for the army in order to defend his country. In this respect he is like so many young men in other wars in other times and places. But his loved ones do not share his enthusiasm and prevail upon him to wait until he is drafted. His cousin, Mark, even conspires to keep himself out of army service. The cowardice of Mark looms as large in the drama as the heroism of Boris. And perhaps more so in view of the fact that the understatement characteristic of Rozov's playwriting is particularly noteworthy in the treatment of Boris' heroism. Little is made of Boris' entry into military service; it takes place unobtrusively and the greater concern is for its impact on the lives of others. The same is true of the news that Boris is missing in action. We learn of it in a very low-key scene, almost in passing, in the second act. It is the occasion neither for rhetoric nor for emotion. The fact of the war itself is inescapable, to be sure, but no war scenes appear in the drama. The sole exception perhaps is Volodya's account of Boris' death in Act III. But the rescue of Volodya and the death of Boris are not dramatized; they are reported by Volodya long after the events. Hence, military action, instead of dominating the stage as it often does in romantic-heroic plays about the Civil War of the 1920s and early 1930s and in World War II plays, intrudes indirectly via narration and then not for the purpose of heroics but to enable Veronica to learn, finally, what became of the man she loves.

Not only does Rozov conspicuously avoid heroics, he shares with other post-Stalinist Russian playwrights a marked anti-heroic bias. But this "anti-heroicism" proceeds not from a moral objection to war so much as from a desire to break away from the exaggerated heroics of Soviet Civil War and World War II drama and from the larger-than-life proportions of the positive heroes and heroines of Socialist Realist drama. The central characters of Rozov's play are drawn instead to human scale and his theme is love, not war, the latter hardly more than a background against which the dramatist traces the impact of adversity on the individual spirit and the transformation of a young girl into a woman.

This demythologizing of the heroic and romantic, which clearly is one of Rozov's principal aims in *Alive Forever!*, asserts itself at the very outset in the seemingly trivial activity in which Boris and Veronica are engaged when the curtain rises. They are hanging a blanket over a window to darken a room as an air raid precautionary measure. The reason for their hanging the blanket is not immediately established. The audience quickly surmises what is happening, but notable in Rozov's handling of the opening is his almost complete deemphasis of the war context in favor of a casual scene of mundane activity. The lighheartedness of the mood is soon bolstered by Veronica's recitation of a stanza of a lyric poem about cranes flying overhead. The verses became something of a leitmotif of the play; they recur several times and especially in the more poignant scene at the end.

Symbolic touches vaguely reminiscent of Chekhov also contribute to the play's mood. Boris' nickname for Veronica is Squirrel and before going off to the army he arranges to have his grandmother present Veronica with a big toy squirrel on her birthday. Ultimately, the squirrel is all that remains to Veronica of Boris, besides memories. Because of this, the toy assumes a very special significance in the play, an object associated with Boris' love for Veronica, and a symbol of the happiness and future promise of their relationship before his departure for war. Conversely, Mark's cynical use of the toy (he pretends that it is a present he bought specially and gives it to a girl he is having an affair with) is used to show his moral baseness and insensitivity from yet another perspective. The confrontation between Veronica and Mark in Act II over the toy and Boris' letter to Veronica stuffed inside it and discovered acciden-

tally by Mark's girl friend, Antonina, provides one of the play's dramatically stronger moments.

Rozov's use of music, too, reminds one of Chekhov. At the end of *The
Three Sisters* the stirring martial music of the military band accompanying the soldiers leaving the provincial town contrasts with the melancholic mood of the sisters. The departure of the soldiers operates as a
symbol for the departure of whatever hopes remain to the sisters of their
leaving their provincial world and returning to Moscow. The greater the
distance of the soldiers from the town, the greater the distance between
the sisters' dreams of going to Moscow and the realization of their
dreams. The point is made superbly, in a theatrical sense, by the fading
away of the band's music as the departing soldiers disappear from sight.

Rozov's use of music and the sounds of marching soldiers in Act I of
Alive Forever! is less subtle. Boris is already in uniform and about to
leave for the front. Hoping to relieve Veronica's sadness Mark tells her
that "the chief thing in wartime is to keep the rhythm of normal human
life. Not to give up your joys, your cherished wishes even to war."[3] He
then plays on the piano to show Veronica what he means. Rozov says
nothing about Mark's choice of music, but we can assume that since he
is trying to cheer Veronica the music must be gay. Not long after he
starts to play, the sound of marching feet is heard, loud enough, as
Rozov indicates in a stage direction, to break through the music. It is
the Moscow men marching off to war. Mark interrupts his playing as he,
Veronica, and Boris' grandmother go up to the window to watch the soldiers. Mark comments, "There's something triumphant in it . . . and
terrifying." Her thoughts only on Boris, Veronica addresses him softly
out the window with the words, "Come back alive!"—and at this point
the act ends.

In *The Three Sisters*, the music is played by a military band making its
way out of the provincial town together with the rest of the soldiers. The
contrast with which the final scene is stamped derives from the nature of
the band's music and the mood of the sisters. Dramatically, the most important element in the sharpening of the contrast is the fading away of
the music, with the symbolic significance for the sisters mentioned
above. In *Alive Forever!*, contrast is still the key to the scene, but it
functions differently. By playing the piano Mark hopes to dispel Veronica's sadness, to divert her attention from the thought (and, soon, the
sound) of Boris' departure for war. The contrast is most distinct when
the sound of marching feet is first heard, when Mark is still at the piano.
But Rozov wants to stress the urgency of the moment for Veronica.

Hence, the sound of the marching feet is permitted to break through that of the music and, in fact, to cause it to stop. The reality and presence of war are not to be denied, a point made unequivocally by Mark's cessation of playing and his joining Veronica and Boris' grandmother at the window.

Music again appears suggestively near the end of *Alive Forever!* when the strains of a symphony are used to set the mood for the lyrical finale of the play. The preceding scene closes with a radio march in celebration of the Russian recapture of Smolensk. As the march fades, the stage goes dark, marking the end of the scene. Symphonic music is heard and the transition to it from the march connotes the transition from war to peace. When the curtain is raised on the last scene, the audience beholds a field of grain; the anticipated transition from war to peace heralded by the shift in musical accompaniment is thus realized.

A striking aspect of post-Stalinist Soviet drama, evident in Rozov's *Alive Forever!,* is a reasserted Russianness, an almost self-conscious determination to oppose the intense ideologization of Russian life in the Soviet period by the rediscovery of permanent values in the Russian cultural tradition. This Russianness is usually conveyed by the introduction of traditional Russian social customs and by allusions to the great literary figures of the nineteenth century. At times it even includes elements of Russian Orthodox belief and practice.

In *Alive Forever!* when Boris is about to depart for war, his sister Trina gives him a small volume of Lermontov's poetry and his grandmother tells him that before (that is, in pre-Soviet Russia), she would have hung a little cross on him, but now she does not know what to give him as a good luck charm. Deciding finally on a button from her dress, she gives it to him and then blesses him with the sign of the cross. If at least two concessions are made to the official Soviet position on religion—Boris is *not* given a cross and the expression of traditional religious belief and practice is relegated to an older woman and is presented in a wartime context—the fact remains that Rozov does have Boris' grandmother *mention* the cross she *would* have hung on his neck in another time and the sign of the cross *is* made over him. A traditional religious practice is thus introduced in a perfectly natural way and unaccompanied by anything mocking or derisive.

More overt is the introduction of the Orthodox priest in Alyoshin's play *Vsyo ostayotsya lyudyam* (*Everything Is Left to People,* published in 1958). Just as in *Alone,* work on an important new engine design functions as a device to set in motion a plot in which psychological and social attitudes are the author's main concerns. In *Everything Is Left to People* the professional antagonism and jealousy of Fomin nearly bring a halt to the dying academician Dronov's greatest project; the unwillingness, moreover, to accept responsibility for possible failure on the part of a coworker and friend, Morozov, ultimately results in the breakup of the personal relationship between two of Dronov's most able younger assistants, Rumyantseva and Vyazmin, and the latter's death, a possible suicide. The engine eventually proves successful, however, as in *Alone*, and the hero is vindicated. Given only a year to live, Dronov at last sees his project crowned with success. In the play's concluding monologue Dronov has the final word in a discussion with a priest about the question of man's life after death. Man's life, declares Dronov, is what he accomplishes while alive and then leaves to other people when he dies; beyond that there is no other life. Dronov's own death soon after he is told of the successful tests of the new engine leaves no doubt as to the final impression Alyoshin wanted his play to convey.

The main debate between Dronov and the priest occurs in Act III and is the most interesting part of the play, not only because of the appearance of a priest, which is quite rare in Soviet drama, but because of what the priest is permitted to say in defense of man's need for religion and about the immortality of the soul. The debate between the two men is intelligent and the figure of the priest is neither unsympathetic nor implausible. Although Alyoshin gives the antireligious Dronov the last word, the debate in which the priest is able to state the case of religion must have been important to the dramatist in the conception of the play for the priest, as a character, is otherwise extraneous. He is presented as a relative of Dronov's wife, who comes to visit the scientist when he is confined to his bed because of illness.

Adversity as the crucible of character appears as a common theme in plays of Arbuzov, Alyoshin, Rozov, and indeed other Soviet dramatists. Frequently, the main protagonist of such plays is a younger woman. This is the major link between such otherwise disparate works as Arbuzov's pre-World War II *Tanya*, Alyoshin's *Alone*, and Rozov's *Alive Forever!*

Young women again come to the forefront in two plays of the later 1950s by Aleksandr Volodin (real name: Lifshyts, born 1919): *Fabrichnaya devchonka* (*The Factory Girl*, 1956) and *Pyat vecherov* (*Five Evenings*, 1959). But distinguishing Volodin's plays from those, let's say, of Alyoshin and Rozov among major post-Stalinist dramatists is the degree of formal innovation attempted by the playwright. New form, or the effort at least to revitalize dramatic structure, and the new content of post-Stalinist drama merge more convincingly in *Five Evenings* than in *Factory Girl*.

In the earlier play, Volodin's first, the theme is the often hypocritical disparity in Soviet society between reality and the façade erected over reality by the processes of official iconography. Volodin's protest in behalf of the "new realism" is embodied in the individualistic and self-assertive Komsomol factory worker, Zhenka Shulzhenko. Natural, straightforward, full of life, and fun-loving, Zhenka comes into conflict with the system when she opposes the sham and pretense around her.

The visit of a film crew to photograph the "best" Komsomol group, of which she is a member, triggers her opposition. Taking due note of the artificality attendant on such ceremonies, the prettying up that goes into the preparation for such self-congratulatory official outings, Zhenka declares that "Life is one thing, the cinema another." Nowhere is her indictment of artificiality and hypocrisy more overt than in the fifth scene (of the play's seven), when she tells a visiting official that in preparation for his coming an entire week was spent in cleaning the machines in the factory. Because of this, the machines were taken out of production and the output of the plant slowed down. Moreover, once the official completes his tour of inspection and leaves, the machines will no longer be cleaned—except on the occasion of another official visit.

Zhenka's outspoken manner and her undisguised impatience with the rhetoric and rigamarole of Komsomol meetings earn her official disfavor. She also suffers the humiliation of an article about her in the Komsomol paper, *Komsomolskaya Pravda* (Komsomol Truth), in which she is held up as an example of indifference, irresponsibility, and frivolity. Her sternest critic is the local Komsomol secretary, Bibichev, a negative portrait of a Soviet bureaucrat—colorless, humorless, interested only in appearances.

The Factory Girl closes in a partially open-ended manner. After leaving the factory and her "group," Zhenka eventually returns; when she discovers that the other girls not only accept her willingly but in the interim have come to appreciate her view of the life around them, she determines to seek her old position. She is still opposed by Bibichev, but the ending of the play hints that Bibichev's voice will no longer command the authority that it did previously and that Zhenka's vindication will be complete.

Cinema, which Volodin uses early in the play to expose the artificiality of official image-making, also contributes to the composition of the play. *Factory Girl* is divided into four acts and seven scenes. Within this structure scene changes are sometimes effected in a cinematographic style. This is particularly evident in the dancing scene in the first act. Bibichev, who has asked Lyolya to write the denunciatory article for *Komsomolskaya Pravda,* advises her to keep a close watch on Zhenka. The curtain falls, signaling a change of scene. But the curtain does not rise. Instead, as the curtain is lowered dance music is heard and when the curtain is down, pairs of girls and boys appear from the wings dancing along the length of it. When the dance scene is over, the dancers disappear into the wings and the curtain rises on a new scene. Following the lap-dissolve technique of the film, Volodin superimposes the dance scene on the previous scene between Irina (another member of Zhenka's Komsomol group), Lyolya, and Bibichev; simultaneously with the lowering of the curtain, the music of the dance band is heard and the new scene introduced during the fade-out of the preceding. A similar use of the lap-dissolve technique occurs on several other occasions in the play, establishing a definite cinematographic pattern throughout.

Basically the same pattern recurs in Volodin's *Five Evenings,* a modest play of no discernible ideological thrust about young people discovering love and middle-aged people rediscovering it. Offsetting the simplicity of situation and dialogue is the theatricalist frame in which the play is set.

As the title indicates, the work is divided into five scenes or evenings, somewhat reminiscent of the division of Bulgakov's much earlier *Flight* into eight dreams. Light figures importantly in both plays. In *Flight,* each dream opens in darkness or dim light and closes in darkness. Bulgakov, as we saw, was attempting to reconstruct the pattern of dream experience. In *Five Evenings,* Volodin's use of light is far less provocative. Although the specific indications are lacking, the stage directions suggest that a split stage is called for on several occasions with change of setting effected simply by the shifting of light from one part of the stage to another. By Western production standards of the period this would hardly have been anything sensational. But against the background of the far more conservative Soviet drama and theater in the Stalinist and immediate post-Stalinist periods, Volodin's use of light to change setting on a split stage must be viewed as an attempt to extend the structural innovations introduced in *The Factory Girl.*

This is more patently obvious in Volodin's familiar theatricalist introduction of an author-narrator. Each scene (or "evening") is in-

troduced by a walk-on appearance of the author-narrator, whose principal task is to describe the setting and set the mood. Here, for example,
is the author's introduction to the first evening:

> It all happened in Leningrad, in a street in Leningrad, in a house
> there. It started way back, long before the five evenings. And it will
> go on for quite a while. Imagine it's winter. It snows in the evenings.
> And the snow brings disturbing memories—of school holidays, of
> meetings in the front hall, of winters past . . .
> The first evening.[4]

The mild humor which informs a number of situations in *Five Evenings* occasionally colors the author-narrator's prefaces, as in the opening of the second scene: "So ended the first evening. The second evening. We'll go on with the second evening immediately because nothing
important happened during the day" (p. 35).

Music, used liberally in *The Factory Girl*, is still more in evidence in
Five Evenings. Characters listen to music on records (including the then
popular French song *C'est si bon*), or sing, or play the guitar.

Thematically, *Five Evenings* adheres to the main emphases of most
post-Stalinist Russian drama. Ideology is reduced to a minimum or
spurned entirely; personal emotions, above all those associated with
romantic love, come to the fore. Young people predominate among the
dramatis personae and idealization is supplanted by what is intended to
be the unvarnished presentation of ordinary people in ordinary situations. The deemphasis of the heroic in *Five Evenings* takes the form
principally of the revelation that the adult male romantic lead, Ilyin, is
not the chief engineer of a great chemical combine that he pretends to
be early in the play to impress an old sweetheart, Tamara, but a truck
driver. When the truth comes out, Ilyin assumes a more positive stance.
In having him take a belated pride in his work, Volodin, in effect, is
using his character to make a plea for what perhaps can be termed the
dignity and even heroism of the ordinary:

> Unless I'm mistaken, you've got it into your head that I'm a failure, in
> a manner of speaking. . . . I consider myself a useful member of soci-
> ety. And incidentally more useful than the lot of you put together.
> Just you try driving a Studebaker through the taiga. There you are
> behind the wheel with all the elements against you. And supposing
> you have a hundred lads like this one under you? Not counting the
> porters, of whom there's a shortage, or the maintenance men, whom
> we don't get at all. It's one of two things: either they worship you or

tie you up in knots and after a month send you to the mainland for a rest cure. It may seem strange, but I like it. So do realize, friends, that I don't intend to make myself out better than I am just to please you. A man must always be himself. (*pp. 98–99*)

FOURTEEN

The New Theatricalism

IN VOLODIN'S *Factory Girl* and *Five Evenings* the de-romanticization of content is counterbalanced by an accompanying romanticization of form. In the first play, the technical innovations can be traced to the cinema, while in *Five Evenings* the author-narrator device is remembered as one of the favorite techniques used by the theatricalists of the earlier years of this century.

Apart from the fact that a creative artist ever seeks out new forms of expression, there seems to be another reason behind the kind of theatricalization we find in Volodin and in a number of Russian plays from the late 1950s on. As Volodin's *Factory Girl* argues, the gap between the reality of Soviet life and the depiction of that reality in Soviet literature has been too great. With the initial exposure phase of the "thaw" period passed, Mayakovsky's plea in *The Bathhouse* (1929) for topical satire as a proper concern for Soviet drama had taken root. But the scope of drama had to be enlarged if audiences were to be enticed to the theaters to watch plays with contemporary settings.

This enlargement of scope was accomplished in three ways. First, the emphasis in the plays was shifted from an attempt to expose self-serving, cynical, and malevolent officials to a concern with unglamorous people in ordinary situations. How ordinary people do ordinary things can in its own way be heroic and romantic; by focusing on this, playwrights were able to achieve a certain romanticism of the everyday. We can clearly see this change of subject emphasis by comparing Zorin's *The Guests* (1954) and Volodin's *Factory Girl* (1956).

Second, a new lyrical drama appeared in which ideology was made subordinate to the trials and tribulations (romantic, above all) of the young. Arbuzov and Rozov are the dramatists most often associated with this type of Soviet drama. Rozov's *Alive Forever!* (1956), Arbuzov's *Irkutskaya istoriya* (*It Happened in Irkutsk*, 1959) and *Moy bedny Marat* (*My Poor Marat*, 1964), and Zorin's *Varshavskaya melodiya* (*A Warsaw Melody*, 1967) are excellent examples of the genre.

Third, this drama of young and/or ordinary people was romanticized stylistically by the use of various cinematic and theatricalist devices, such as the flashback and the flashforward, a rapid shifting from scene to scene, the superimposition of one scene upon another often accompanied by changes of lighting and split stages, choruses and narrators, prologues and epilogues, and direct addresses to the audience. Quite often since the late 1950s these three currents have merged in drama. In *Factory Girl*, for example, Volodin employs numerous songs, dances, and cinematic devices to romanticize the problems of a young female factory worker. The heroine is young and ordinary, but her story is lifted beyond the everyday by Volodin's techniques in the play.

Beyond any doubt, the most enthusiastic practitioner of this new lyricism and theatricalism in the drama is Aleksei Arbuzov. Before considering such representative plays of the late 1950s and '60s as *It Happened in Irkutsk*, *My Poor Marat*, and *Schastlivye dni neschastlivogo cheloveka* (*The Happy Days of an Unhappy Man*, 1967), it might be instructive to consider briefly a relatively insignificant play by an important orthodox dramatist to demonstrate how this new theatricalism found its way even into the more conventional drama of Socialist Realism. The play, *Tretya, pateticheskaya* (*Third, Pathetique*, 1958), is the concluding part of Nikolai Pogodin's prize-winning Lenin trilogy, and is by far the weakest and least enthralling of the three works.

Set in the period 1922–24, during the early years of the New Economic Policy, its subject is Lenin's busy routine shortly before his death. The play deals almost totally with trivia and its monotony is relieved only by the antics of the speculators and "new capitalists" whom Pogodin introduces into the NEP setting. The end of the play warrants a closer look, however, because this is where the theatricalist elements are clustered. The closing scenes deal with recollections of Lenin experienced by one of the major characters, a Party official named Dyatlov. Even after his death, Lenin remains to Dyatlov a living, shining memory. But what is most striking about his recollections is that they are given dramatic form, that is, they are acted out. In the first recollection, the play's opening scene of Lenin and his sister visiting a steel plant is repeated. This is followed by a dramatized recollection of a scene from Dyatlov's past in which he remembers the lights burning in the Smolny Institute, where Lenin often worked late into the night. There the great leader urged Dyatlov, above all, to remain loyal to the Party. This crystallizes the main ideological thrust of Pogodin's last Lenin play. The admonition, that Party members must overcome all doubts and vacillations and must remain steadfast in their commitment to the Party, was not an insignificant one, considering the circumstances of Soviet political life when the play was published. For the non-Soviet observer, the interesting thing here is the theatricalist packaging in which the message is presented.

In Arbuzov's *It Happened in Irkutsk* theatricalism combines with the lyricism of young love and the quiet heroism of the everyday to produce the ingredients of one of the most popular plays of the Soviet repertoire of the late 1950s. Set in Siberia near the construction site of a hydroelectric station, the plot includes familiar elements of Arbuzov's dramaturgy: young characters, a romantic triangle, loss and compensation in life, and personal growth realized through suffering. The romantic triangle involves two construction workers, Viktor and Sergei, and a gay, frolicsome girl (reminiscent of Volodin's Zhenka in *Factory Girl*) named Valya. Valya works in a nearby shop and has a reputation for easy virtue. Viktor goes on dates with Valya but while he likes her, he considers marriage out of the question because of her reputation. On one occasion, when Viktor cannot keep a date with Valya, he sends Sergei, his friend, who immediately falls in love with her. Unlike Viktor, Sergei has no qualms about marrying the girl and soon proposes to her. Although drawn more romantically to Viktor, Valya accepts Sergei's offer and the two are wed. As time passes, Valya gives birth to a set of twins and the family appears quite happy. However, Viktor is remorseful and envious of Sergei, and shuns the couple as much as possible. Then tragedy strikes. While trying to rescue children from an overturned river raft, Sergei drowns. Valya is beside herself with grief and loses interest in everything but her children. Now overwhelmingly in love with her, Viktor suggests at a meeting of the construction team that they stop giving Valya the equivalent of Sergei's salary as charity and that instead they offer her work on an excavator. She would then become a part of the team, replacing Sergei and, it was hoped, develop a more positive outlook on life. Valya finally accepts the proposal and, in her return to work, gradually does come to find happiness in life again. As the play closes, Arbuzov hints that in time she and Viktor will find love together and eventually marry.

As we can see, there is nothing really novel in the plot. The characters and situations are new neither to Arbuzov nor to Soviet drama. But through the use of theatricalist techniques, Arbuzov infuses the play with a distinctly romantic aura.

Most noteworthy is his use of the Chorus. It is the Chorus that appears first and in a narrative role introduces the story and principal characters. Thereafter, the Chorus appears at key junctures throughout the play, not only to provide comment for the benefit of the audience but also to engage in dialogue with the characters, sometimes functioning as the characters' alter egos. For example, toward the end of the play, as Valya ponders alone whether or not to accept the offer to join the construction team, Sergei's voice emerges from the Chorus to urge her to accept. And at the very end of the play, after Arbuzov has hinted that Valya and Viktor might eventually be reunited, the Chorus wishes Viktor good luck. The Chorus also conjures up voices from the past, as in the scenes with the middle-aged boss of the construction team, Serdyuk. As romance again enters Serdyuk's life, his past loves are invoked by the Chorus and are then permitted to speak for themselves, shedding light on Serdyuk's attitudes toward women and love.

The addresses directed to the audience by the Chorus are paralleled by others delivered by the characters. At the beginning of the play Valya, Viktor, and Sergei follow the lead of the Chorus and step forward to introduce themselves directly to the audience. Such direct speaking between the characters and the audience continues throughout the play, as well as the dialogue between the characters and the Chorus.

In Pogodin's *Third, Pathetique*, which antedates *It Happened in Irkutsk* by a year, we noticed that at the very end of the play Dyatlov's first dramatized recollection of Lenin repeats the play's opening scene. The same device, though in reverse order, is used by Arbuzov in *It Happened in Irkutsk*. After the introductions of the Chorus and the principal dramatis personae, the first scene of the play occurs, which will then be repeated as the last scene of the play. Hence, the story of the triangular relationship of Valya, Viktor, and Sergei becomes a flashback framed between the play's opening and concluding scenes, which are identical.

Mime, another familiar theatricalist device, also appears in *It Happened in Irkutsk*, once at the wedding of Valya and Sergei and again at the hospital where their friends come to visit Valya after the birth of her twins. The first mime scene is the more important of the two. The stage directions call for the wedding procession to march gaily through the town, accompanied by music and avoiding the rain by carrying umbrellas and sidestepping the puddles. The wedding celebration, with its Russian folk dancing calculated to appeal to the audience, is also left to the improvising, mime skills of the actors.

In spite of its thin plot, sketchy characterization, and a certain naïveté, *It Happened in Irkutsk* has some charm. When the play appeared in 1959 it did mark a departure in postwar Soviet dramaturgy and it owed no small part of its success to the relative novelty of its style. Not since the romantic-heroic drama of the 1920s and 1930s had theatricalist techniques been employed so lavishly in a Soviet play. Indeed, were it not for these techniques, *It Happened in Irkutsk* would hardly merit a second glance. But compared to the plays of the 1920s and 1930s, what seemed striking in Arbuzov's work was that the romantic-revolutionary style had now been applied to a subject and to characters of an undistinguished and ordinary nature.

The popular success of *It Happened in Irkutsk* did not carry over into its critical reception. While some critics were enthusiastic about the play, others expressed reservations about the naïveté of the characters, especially Sergei, and about the gratuitousness of the play's theatricalism, particularly with regard to the Chorus. Arbuzov gave some indication of his reaction to this negative criticism in his next play, *Poteryanny syn* (*The Lost Son*, published in 1961), subtitled a "melodrama in three acts."

Set in 1955, the play concerns a writer, Anton Okhotnikov, who achieves a literary reputation through a book he has written on his war experiences. He is, then, a writer in the romantic-heroic tradition. Accompanied by his literary colleague and steady companion, Irina, who is eight years his senior, he leaves Moscow for the provinces, to return to the family he has not seen in ten years.

As the play unfolds, we discover that Anton is not a particularly noble character. When he first left his family, he promised his adopted brother, Pyotr, that he would return in a year to work with him in the new hospital where Pyotr is the director. (Before the war, Anton had been trained as a physician.) But the promise was never kept. Furthermore, Anton and his brother's wife, Natasha, used to be sweethearts. Pyotr is resentful both because Anton failed to join him at the hospital and because he suspects that Natasha is still in love with Anton. Relations with his wife worsen on the eve of Anton's arrival, and Natasha and Pyotr resolve to separate. After Anton's return, the former sweethearts become inseparable, to the chagrin of both Irina and Pyotr.

Soon, however, the visit home becomes a spiritual and moral awakening for Anton. He realizes that his literary fame has run its course and that he may never write another book. Furthermore, he loses both Irina, who returns to Moscow once she believes that Anton and Natasha are truly in love, and Natasha, who eventually returns to Pyotr. At the end of the play, as if to atone for his broken promise made ten years earlier, Anton decides to remain at home and to join his brother's hospital as a doctor.

The family drama of *The Lost Son* is melodramatically intertwined with a professional drama involving Pyotr. Because he antagonized a local official in the past, Pyotr has become the object of a vendetta aimed at depriving him of his post on the grounds of malpractice and misuse of state funds. A negative report is submitted by a government medical inspector named Shvarts, a lonely, cynical man of sixty-five. Shvarts is clearly the most interesting character in the play, in a role Arbuzov created expressly for the actor R. N. Simonov. In a manner recalling the rediscovered parent or child motif of especially eighteenth-century European comedy, Shvarts accidentally discovers that Pyotr is his own son, whom he abandoned with his wife many years earlier. Although Pyotr's problem is left open-ended, there is a strong suggestion at the end of the play that he will win his fight to remain as director of the hospital. Because of Pyotr's hatred for the father whom he never knew, Shvarts resolves not to reveal his identity. After doing his best to help his son out of the trouble which he himself has been responsible for creating, Shvarts bids his son farewell in an emotionally tense scene, promising never to return.

The play's title, *The Lost Son*, has a twofold symbolic significance. Anton is lost in the sense that he has been separated from his family for ten years. However, after finding himself spiritually, he decides at the end of the play to remain and so becomes the prodigal son returned. Also, more concretely, Pyotr is Shvarts' lost son whom Shvarts discovers near the end of the drama. The system of moral justice to which Soviet literature subscribes demands, of course, that both Anton and Shvarts be punished for their egoism and an indifference to the needs and feelings of others. In meting out this justice, Arbuzov again introduces an ironic double evolvement of loss. After rediscovering his real love for Natasha, Anton loses her a second time when she decides to return for good to Pyotr; also, he loses his best friend, Irina. After discovering his lost son, Shvarts again loses him when he realizes that Pyotr's hatred for his lost father makes any reconciliation impossible, and so he departs without disclosing their true relationship.

Interpolated into the drama of *The Lost Son* is a meaningful polemic on drama between Anton's friend, Irina, who is also a writer, and a local librarian, Cheremushkina. Although Cheremushkina invites Anton to address a gathering of his admirers, he refuses because he realizes that he can no longer live with the fame of his one book. Irina defends his book before Cheremushkina as the clearly romantic-heroic novel it is. She tells Cheremushkina that the heroic theme cannot endure the competition of all sorts of "playlets" on domestic themes (*semeynye temy*). Young dramatists, she argues, now like to burrow into the lives of ordinary people, whereas the "chief task of the theater is to rise above reality." Cheremushkina answers her in this way:

> You said, "rise above reality." This sounds nice, but does it have anything to do with truth? (*Confusedly.*) Readers come to me, and there are those among them who don't have it easy, whose lives are hard . . . They believe that they will live better, but the war brought so much grief, brought it and left it, do you understand? People have hard destinies, loneliness—but that's life, after all, and you can't get away from it. Tell people how to overcome their problems, how to get rid of them. How to endure the solitude, how to find the road to people again . . . I don't need any fairy tales or consolations; only the truth is beautiful.[1]

The polemic breaks off at this point as Irina protests that Cheremushkina does not understand what she has said.

The introduction of the polemic is artistically plausible in view of the fact that both Irina and Anton are writers who, having lived a number of years in the capital, are presumably more worldly and sophisticated in their literary tastes than Cheremushkina with her provincial outlook. Moreover, Irina—as Anton's closest friend and admirer—would naturally be disposed to defend his major professional achievement. That the polemic reflects a response of sorts by Arbuzov to the negative criticism which was directed against *It Happened in Irkutsk* seems certain. But the playwright's precise point of view is difficult to establish because the polemic is left insufficiently developed. Through Irina, a caustic jibe is thrown at the spate of plays about "little people" that began appearing in Russian drama in the mid-1950s. In the light of Arbuzov's own approach to ordinary people in *It Happened in Irkutsk*, a certain sympathy for Irina's position has to be credited to him. On the other hand, the plea by Cheremushkina for an instructive drama of reality (a drama essentially of Socialist Realism) is made so emotionally and forcefully by a woman "of the people" that it is hard not to believe that through it Arbuzov was attempting to placate his critics. This belief is reinforced by the fact that in *The Lost Son*, Anton, a fashionable writer, regains a sense of purpose and personal dignity by returning to the people, symbolized by his family and his townspeople. The return is presented as a form of spiritual therapy. Opposed as he appears to be in *The Lost Son* to the romantic-heroic drama, Arbuzov did not hesitate even after this play to enhance his plays about ordinary people with techniques borrowed from the romantic-heroic tradition. Notice that in the polemic between Irina and Cheremushkina nothing is said about form, only about theme. With respect to theme, Arbuzov would clearly side with Cheremushkina; but regarding form, Irina's position would be bound to be the more sympathetic one.

Arbuzov's *The Lost Son* appeared in 1961. Seven years later, in 1968, his highly theatricalized *The Happy Days of an Unhappy Man* was published in the fourth quarterly issue of *Teatr*. Between the two, the playwright published two plays of a formally conservative nature indicating perhaps a desire to conform more with the Cheremushkina position he appears to take in *The Lost Son*. The plays were *Moy bedny Marat* (*My Poor Marat*, retitled in English *The Promise*, completed in 1964 and published in 1965) and *Nochnaya ispoved* (*Nocturnal Confession*, written in 1966 and published the following year). As if taking their cue from Cheremushkina's words in *The Lost Son*, both plays operate, for the most part, with World War II settings. *Nocturnal Confession*, the later of the two plays, is a conventional war drama about captors and captives in a German-occupied town in Russia on the eve of a Wehrmacht evacuation of the area. Several Russians have been arrested on suspicion of aiding a German army deserter and are awaiting possible execution the next morning. During a long night of interrogation and confinement, concealed truths emerge in the form of "nocturnal confessions." A German commandant of the occupied town, a former actor who still enjoys playing roles, must decide finally which three of the prisoners will be executed, which adds to the play's dramatic suspense. Although Arbuzov strives to make the German commandant a compelling psychological portrait, to solidify the tension by concentrating the action in a single night, and to create dramatic interest by keeping the final choice of victims to be executed unrevealed until near the end of the play, *Nocturnal Confession* is too much like many other Russian World War II plays to command any real serious attention.

Such is not the case, however, with *My Poor Marat*. Not only has the play proven immensely successful in the Soviet Union, but it has also done well abroad; it has been staged in Holland, Belgium, Yugoslavia, France, Brazil, Argentina, Israel, Pakistan, India, Australia, and Japan. In London, a production was staged in 1966 at the Fortune Theatre under the title of *The Promise*. It is also one of the very few Soviet plays to have been given a run on Broadway, where it opened, also under the title of *The Promise*, in 1967 at the Henry Miller Theater. It was revived in New York in 1978 by the Roundabout Theater.

Drawing heavily on formulae long associated with his dramatic technique—the "chronicle" play, the triangular love affair, young people, sentiment, unobtrusive ideology, and a more or less optimistic ending—Arbuzov has succeeded in *My Poor Marat* in creating a play of distinct appeal. Divided into three acts, the drama ranges in time from 1942 to 1960, including the blockade of Leningrad in 1942, the postwar reconstruction year of 1946, the post-Stalinist and "thaw" periods of the 1950s, and the eve of the New Year, 1960, the date of the last scene of the play. This eighteen-year period of history includes momentous events in Soviet life, but since *My Poor Marat* is primarily a play about the interrelationships of three young people, first thrown together by chance and then interacting with one another as they pass from their teens into their twenties and thirties, the external historical events are important only to the extent that they influence and mold these relationships.

It may be suspected at first that the lengthy time covered by the play would result in a crowded dramatic story, yet this is not the case. Arbuzov is considerably more spare here than in most of his other plays and the economy is advantageous. Only a single setting is used throughout the play, the interior of a Leningrad flat, and only three characters appear, Lika, the girl, and Marat and Leonidik, the boys.

Buffeted by the war and confined by the blockade of Leningrad, Lika, a homeless fifteen-year-old, takes refuge in a bare flat in a semiderelict house on the Fontanka River. She is soon joined by the eighteen-year-old Marat whose family, now lost in the war, used to live in the apartment. After initial awkwardness, the two young people evolve a kind of brother–sister relationship and struggle to make the best of their situation. The nucleus of a future romantic triangle is formed when a third teen-ager, Leonidik, enters the apartment, also seeking shelter.

Having established the background of war and having brought his characters together, Arbuzov then concentrates wholly on the human drama, on the interplay of three different personalities. The first act is the best of the three and is generally the most appealing to audiences. The war and the blockade have infected the characters' lives with anxiety and insecurity, though these are never depicted directly on the stage. Instead, interest is focused on the now sad, now lighthearted personality adjustments of the two boys and one girl.

While frightened by the sounds of war around her and grateful for Marat's comforting and providing efforts (before Leonidik appears on the scene), Lika is the most stable of the three. A fondness on her part for Turgenev also reveals a romantic facet in her nature. Leonidik becomes an immediate contrast to Marat. Whereas the latter dreams of becoming a great builder of bridges, Leonidik wants only to write poetry. In a long recollection of his unhappy childhood, Leonidik reveals a jealousy and hatred toward his stepfather, who he feels took his mother's love away from him. Although recognizing that his stepfather and mother truly loved each other, Leonidik's recollection of his past establishes his emotional vulnerability and dependence. Perhaps as a sign of an identity problem on the character's part, Arbuzov has Leonidik frequently refer to himself throughout the play in the third person.

Although survival is the chief concern of the young occupants of the Leningrad flat, the mood of the first act is far from somber, even when the noise of bomb explosions shatters the outside silence. In an easy, skillful way, Arbuzov explores the adjustments of his characters to one another, especially the early awkwardness between Lika and Marat and their hesitancy and uncertainty about establishing emotional bonds. To the pressures of their unsettled environment are added the pressures of adolescence. Their speech reflects their sense of awkwardness and tension, of insecurity, and of fear. The dialogue between them is often short, choppy, and separated by pauses. Shifts of tone and gesture accompany the uneven posturing of adjusting personalities. Awkwardness and tenderness alternate. Near the end of the second scene, when Marat strokes Lika's hair to comfort her, distraught and in tears, she pulls away, fearful of surrendering herself completely to Marat.

The third scene closes on a similar note. While Lika and Marat are dancing, Marat kisses her; but again, before emotion can gain the upper hand, they are interrupted by the sudden appearance of Leonidik. With the coming of the second boy into the apartment, a subtle competition for Lika's affection begins. Marat pursues Lika through a show of bravado and exaggerated masculinity, even going so far as to fabricate a story of his capturing a German parachutist. Leonidik, on the other hand, aware of Marat's prior claim on Lika's feelings and envious of it, tries to reach out to her by projecting his deep need for tenderness and affection. The first act ends with the boys going off to war; characteristically, Marat is the first to volunteer.

The second act reunites the trio in the first postwar year of 1946. Lika remained behind in the flat when Marat and Leonidik went off to fight. Leonidik is the first to return, and he has lost an arm in battle. His emotional dependence, exposed in the first act, now has an added dimension. The delayed return of Marat enables Arbuzov to develop a closer bond between Lika and Leonidik, but the girl's persistent anxiety about Marat's failure to appear leaves little doubt that her feelings for Marat run deeper than those for Leonidik. Marat finally appears, unharmed. However, after the initial celebrating and reminiscing have passed, it becomes clear that the basic problems remain. As the conversation turns to love, Leonidik openly admits his love for Lika. Marat, however, is afraid to surrender to his true feelings. He fears that by giving himself to love prematurely he will be unable to realize his life dream of becoming a bridge-builder, thus compromising his own self-fulfillment. Aware, moreover, of Leonidik's great need for Lika, he appears willing to make a "sacrifice" of the girl as an honorable way of resolving their personal dilemma. And so, because neither Marat nor Lika can articulate their real feelings for each other, Marat is the one who decides to go.

The third and last act takes place thirteen years later, in December 1959. The time gap between the second and third acts serves to extend the action of the play beyond the death of Stalin and the post-Stalinist "thaw" to the threshold of the optimistic 1960s, and then to allow a sufficient passage of time for the marriage between Lika and Leonidik to settle into an obvious pattern of failure and hence to make plausible, as well as morally and emotionally acceptable, the play's final resolution.

The predictability so evident in several of Arbuzov's other plays mars the third act, making it the weakest of the three. By the end of the second act it becomes mandatory for Arbuzov to temporarily withdraw one of the two males competing for Lika's affection. After Marat's departure, Lika and Leonidik marry; but while there is tenderness and affection between them, the union is a failure. Lika has gone on to complete medical training and to find professional employment. Two books of Leonidik's poems have been published and a third is due to appear soon. But because his poetry is so intensely personal, it has very little popular appeal, is printed in small editions, and sells badly. Together with his wife's professional success and his increasing dependence on her, this rejection produces such a profound frustration in Leonidik that he is driven to seek an escape in drink. So dependent on Lika has Leonidik become, in fact, that he is quite willing to allow her to argue with his publishers for a larger printing of his newest book of poetry.

From earlier Soviet plays featuring a romantic triangle, we are familiar with the character who is a professional and social failure and who, married to a positive woman, turns to drink to drown his frustration.

These recurrent conflictive tensions are usually resolved in a quite specific way, namely, the husband is withdrawn by one cause or another,
making way for the reunion of the positive woman (the wife) with her
earlier romantic partner, who has himself also gone on to achieve a positive self-realization. After Arbuzov has established the impossibility of
any fundamental change in the situation between Lika and Leonidik, his
next step is to return the missing member of the romantic triangle and
then eliminate the impediment to the reunion of the positive characters.
The return of Marat, now a successful builder of bridges, is first prepared by a symbolic playing at the end of Act III, scene 1, of the waltz
played at the end of Act I, scene 3, when on her sixteenth birthday Lika
and Marat kissed for the first time. The repetition of this waltz, after the
failure of Lika's marriage to Leonidik has been shown, conveys Lika's
continuing attachment to the memory of Marat. The way is now open for
Marat's return, which occurs in the second scene of Act III. As the three
friends are brought together again, there is naturally a great deal of
reminiscing about the past, about their youthful ideals and promises,
and about the lack of responsibility of youth. Questions then arise about
the success which each of them has found in his or her goals. It soon
becomes obvious that Lika has long remained on Marat's mind and that
he feels unfulfilled without her. Unable to restrain himself, Marat asks
Lika and Leonidik if they are happy. When they evade the question,
Marat confesses to Lika that in losing her he feels that he has lost everything in life. Frustrated, Marat storms out of the apartment, bringing
the scene to an explosive end.

Although the outcome of the third act is more or less obvious to anyone familiar with Soviet drama, the reunion of Lika, Leonidik, and
Marat in the penultimate scene is not without interest. It is, in fact, one
of the key ideological moments of the play. Apart from the importance of
the scene to the overall structure of the plot, Arbuzov uses the scene to
argue, in the spirit of post-"thaw" Russia, that emotional dilemmas and
conflicts, very much like existential problems themselves, are not, in
most cases, resolved merely by the passage of time nor by changes in
the external environment. Individual human dilemmas can be resolved
only individually. This is the lesson that the three characters of *My Poor
Marat*, primarily Marat himself, learn in the course of the play's action.
Not without a certain poignancy, Marat at last perceives the naïve idealism of the belief that he, Lika, and Leonidik held earlier that once the
war ended people would be happy. Even such great events as the end of
the war, the passing of Stalin, and the major changes in Soviet society

that followed in the wake of the dictator's death could not guarantee happiness any more than they could resolve personal dilemmas. The individual having left the shelters of childhood must eventually face up to the demands of maturity and to the needs of assuming responsibility for individual decisions. Arbuzov suggests that in order to cope the first step in self-awareness is to recognize one's own strengths, weaknesses, and fears. This call for honesty and realism in self-appraisal as well as in the solving of individual dilemmas relates unmistakably to the appeal for honesty and realism in post-"thaw" literature. Marat's revelation of a recurrent dream to Lika and Leonidik in the last scene of the play functions as a recapitulation of the drama's central issue. In his dream, Marat sees himself standing on an unfinished bridge which he must complete. A strong wind is blowing. On one shore he sees the world after the war, the new life. But try as he might, Marat is unable to unite the two shores, to bridge the gap between childhood with its stability, cheerfulness, and shelteredness, and maturity where the individual must face his conflicts and responsibilities alone.

Leonidik adds to Marat's words, saying that without love, self-realization and self-fulfillment are very difficult to achieve. Not only self-awareness but love is necessary to bridge the gap between childhood and maturity. The moment for Leonidik's self-awareness is at hand. Moved by a new understanding and by his love for Marat and Lika, who he now realizes are better suited to each other for their mutual self-fulfillment, he resolves to leave. The New Year's Eve setting of this last reunion and the friends' farewell toasts to each other as well as to their childhood and to romanticism have almost excessive sentimentality, but one which nevertheless appeals to Soviet as well as to foreign audiences. With Leonidik disappearing into the wintry night, presumably still in quest of himself, and with Lika and Marat at last reunited in love, the play closes on a note of subdued optimism with the beginning of a new year, a new decade, and a new promise of happier days ahead.

After *My Poor Marat*, Arbuzov in 1965 began another excursion into theatricalized drama, *Schastlivye dni neschastlivogo cheloveka* (*The Happy Days of an Unhappy Man*), but interrupted work on it in order to write *Nocturnal Confession*. With this latter play out of the way, he returned to *Happy Days* and completed it in 1967. It opened at the Bolshoy in Leningrad in September 1968, and was published in *Teatr* the same year.

Subtitled a "Fable [*pritcha*] "in Two Parts," *Happy Days* marks a serious departure from most of Arbuzov's previous writing for the theater. Although the effort falls short of success, one can see in *Happy Days* that the dramatist was aiming for greater psychological complexity and sophistication. Whatever the appeal of *It Happened in Irkutsk* and *My Poor Marat*, these plays remain basically happy ending dramas. While they are superior in style, they are similar in theme to many other Soviet plays based on romantic triangles and using pathos to achieve a degree of sentimentality calculated to win over the audience. However, the familiar Arbuzov sentimentality all but disappears in *Happy Days*, and the play's ending is happy only in the ironic and ambiguous sense that the concept is developed in the play.

The outward structure of *Happy Days* is simpler than anything Arbuzov wrote before. The curtain opens on a dimly lit stage, empty but for a bed standing in the middle of it. Seated on a chair near a door whose outline also is only barely visible is a woman garbed in dark clothes. Three spotlights are turned on to illuminate the faces of the male members of the Chorus who appear throughout the play and who assume the role of narrator. The Chorus identifies the figure in the bed as a scholar named Krestovnikov, who is soon to die. After the opening banter of the Chorus, Arbuzov introduces the scholar's most devoted student, who has come to pay his respects to the dying man. In his conversation with the student, Krestovnikov, in surveying the whole panorama of his life, recalls that he was happy only twice. The rest of the play becomes a dramatization of those two occasions, hence the two part division of *Happy Days*.

If the outer frame of *Happy Days* is uncluttered, the same cannot be said for the two middle plot segments. Using only two days out of the past in order to reconstruct Professor Krestovnikov's philosophy of happiness, Arbuzov has ended by cramming so much into each of the two segments that a jarring imbalance has resulted between the simplicity of the play's initial and concluding frame scenes and the complexity of the rest of it.

In the first episode or day, Krestovnikov is twenty-four years old and at a turning point in his career. He faces an excellent chance of being taken on an important medical-scientific expedition to the Far East, headed by Professor Berg under whom he is studying and in whose nineteen-year-old daughter, Arisha, he is romantically interested. Arbuzov seeks in the first episode to acquaint the audience with Krestovnikov's family situation and to show how the failure to join Berg's expedition and the loss of Arisha can be psychologically construed (or misconstrued) as success for Krestovnikov, in the light of his concept of happiness that emerges. With each of the major elements in the seg-ment—family, career, and romance—Arbuzov, however, has failed to exercise restraint.

In terms of dramatic structure, each of the key elements making up the play's two major segments operates with its own conflict. Thus, in the first part of *Happy Days* the conflict in Krestovnikov's family situa-tion originates with his father's desertion of the young Krestovnikov and his mother. This desertion has led to a greater emotional claim, and dependence, on his mother. Because of this, Krestovnikov bitterly op-poses her impending marriage to her present suitor, Boris Nikolaevich. However, when it seems to him that all his efforts are in vain, he decides to leave rather than to face a situation in which he is sure he will be deserted once more by his mother, whose feelings for him he imag-ines will be transferred to Boris.

Arbuzov has tried to link the components of each episode into a struc-tural and narrative whole. In the first part, Boris Nikolaevich happens to be the father of Krestovnikov's best friend, Volodya Kostenetsky. The network of relationships is further complicated by the fact that Kres-tovnikov and Kostenetsky are both students of Professor Berg as well as rivals for the position of Berg's assistant on the Eastern expedition. Ar-buzov resolves the conflict relating to the career element by revealing another flaw in Krestovnikov's character. Sacrificing friendship for ambi-tion, Krestovnikov tells Berg that certain malicious epigrams about him were written by none other than Volodya Kostenetsky. Krestovnikov's purpose is to discredit Kostenetsky, who is known to be the Professor's favorite, and so gain for himself the expedition assistantship. But Kres-tovnikov's plans are again thwarted. Berg drops Kostenetsky from the expedition, but then berates Krestovnikov for his meanness in betraying a friend. This chastisement, coupled with Berg's prediction that his mother and Boris Nikolaevich will definitely get married, so unsettles Krestovnikov that he chooses to take a position in Kazan that was offered to him earlier. His departure disrupts his growing relationship with Berg's daughter, Arisha. Possibly fearing another disappointment here, Krestovnikov prefers to head it off by suggesting to Arisha after his last meeting with Berg that his unhappiness is caused by her inability to love him. Thus, by making Arisha the focus of Krestovnikov's romantic inter-est and by closely linking in time Berg's scolding of Krestovnikov and his prediction of his mother's marriage, on the one hand, and Kres-tovnikov's break with Arisha, on the other, Arbuzov seeks to tie together the family, career, and romantic components of Krestovnikov's first happy day. Irony is then added toward the end of the episode when Berg receives permission to take both Kostenetsky and Krestovnikov along with him on the expedition. Of course, this happens after Krestovnikov has already left for Kazan.

Krestovnikov's second happy day, comprising the second part of the play, occurs in his forty-second year, in 1956. Arbuzov now introduces a new setting, the Baltic coast, and an entirely new group of supporting characters: a retired circus clown, Michel Filippov; his thirty-year-old daughter, Nastya; Krestovnikov's steady romantic interest, Nina Zimina, one year younger than himself; and Zimina's son, Alyosha.

The relationship between Krestovnikov and Zimina is curious. Although they are deeply attached to each other, they have neither married nor do they live together. Zimina's explanation for this is that she feels she should respect Krestovnikov's need to feel free and so should never impose any restraints upon him. Their bond is a common professional interest in medicine, though as a measure of her devotion to Krestovnikov Zimina never becomes the doctor she studied to be but works instead as a medical journalist, thus subordinating her own career to Krestovnikov's. Her son Alyosha deeply admires Krestovnikov and never opposes his mother's relationship with him.

Since the relationship delineated in the second episode between Krestovnikov, Zimina, and Alyosha is so workable, it presents no conflicts such as the family situation in the first part of the play. Therefore, to create both dramatic interest and a balance of tension with the first day, Arbuzov introduces another woman, Michel Filippov's daughter. Her straightforwardness, optimism, and somewhat skeptical outlook on life parallel qualities in Krestovnikov himself and attract him to Nastya. He begins to spend more and more time with her and the attraction becomes mutual, although Nastya already has a suitor, a circus performer who is closer to her own age and whom her father prefers. But Krestovnikov again finds himself beyond the grasp of love. In a visionary scene, paralleling the one in the first episode in which his father reappears to him, he and Kostenetsky meet again. The scene serves two purposes: first, to trace briefly the later career of Kostenetsky, material which can be considered extraneous, and, second, to turn the dialogue to love and implicitly to Krestovnikov's feelings for Nastya; the second purpose is accomplished by the recalling of Arisha who it appears really did love Krestovnikov. Thus in a way the vision becomes an extension of Krestovnikov's ambivalence toward Nastya.

The second episode of the play ends as the first, with a flight. The motivation remains partly the same, although the issues are slightly more complicated in Part One. There, Krestovnikov flees, fearing a triple rejection, by Berg in favor of Kostenetsky, by his mother in favor of Boris Nikolaevich, and by Arisha in favor of Kostenetsky. In Part Two, the mature Krestovnikov's flight is twofold—from his institute because of the belief that his students want only to exploit his talents, and from Nastya, whose love he is incapable of returning. Both factors shed light on Zimina's role. Whatever the precise nature of their feelings for each other, Krestovnikov's attachment to Zimina is more firmly rooted in a psychological and emotional dependence than he understands. Zimina grasps this, allowing Krestovnikov his independence and even encouraging his feelings of persecution and grievance toward his students at the institute. Arbuzov never really defines Krestovnikov's difficulties with his students. Although this is an untidy element in the design of the play, one can reason from the situation that Krestovnikov's general sense of hurt and lack of trust contribute to a problem of communication that touches virtually every aspect of his life.

By the time the second episode ends, Arbuzov's point of view and the irony of the play's title are manifest. Although real happiness requires a capacity for love, faith, and self-sacrifice, Krestovnikov equates happiness with independence. His understanding of independence, however, is perverse for it is rooted in a distrust and fear of emotional involvement. The first happy day of his life came with the supposed rejection by Berg that caused him to break with his previous life and to strike out on his own. But no less important in Krestovnikov's retreat to independence was his unwillingness to allow his mother to find her own happiness and to work out his emotionally strained relationship with Arisha. The happiness of the second day was achieved when Krestovnikov rejected the love offered by Nastya.

Throughout Arbuzov's dramatic writing happiness is conceived of as a self-fulfillment achieved through self-sacrifice and an acceptance of the responsibilities of emotional involvement. It is ironic in *Happy Days* that the two days in his life when Krestovnikov felt he had found true happiness were the two days when he turned his back on love. The irony becomes almost gratuitously and anticlimactically bitter in the play's closing scene when the student who visits Krestovnikov on his deathbed opens the notebook containing Krestovnikov's unfinished research. The notebook becomes a kind of legacy between Krestovnikov and the only student with whom he was apparently able to establish a rapport. "You are very dear to me," he tells the student. "Why? I don't know. You never contradicted me, and I poured into you everything I knew . . ." (p. 665). Like Zimina, the student wins Krestovnikov's approval by subordinating his own ideas and desires to those of Krestovnikov, and by flattering and thus appeasing the latter's emotional insecurity. Illuminated by a single beam of light on the darkened stage and surrounded only by the Chorus, the student opens Krestovnikov's notebook and begins to leaf through the pages. Struck by what he reads, he is speechless for several moments, then says: "My God! What childish nonsense! Antiquated . . . (*Turns pages.*) Antiquated . . . hopelessly antiquated! (*One by one the pages slowly slip out of his hands.*)" (p. 666).

At the end of the play, Arbuzov stresses the total deceit of Krestovnikov's life. A false concept of independence has resulted in isolation. Emotionally, Krestovnikov never experiences real love. But in his professional life, as well, his inability to establish productive relationships with colleagues and students alike results in research carried on in a vacuum and hence unnourished and unchecked by the fertile ideas of others.

The Happy Days of an Unhappy Man is no less striking for its theatricalism than *It Happened in Irkutsk*, although its devices are much the same as those used in the earlier work. Both plays begin and end at the same point in time and place. In both there are movements back in time. Each play employs a Chorus with narrative and commentative roles. In each, the Chorus is distinct from the other characters; consisting of several figures in both *It Happened in Irkutsk* and *Happy Days*, the Chorus represents a separate dramatic persona. To achieve greater interest and a certain humor, the Chorus in *Happy Days* is more varied than in *It Happened in Irkutsk*. Besides their collective narrative function, each of the three Chorus figures comments on Krestovnikov's life from a different point of view. The first member of the Chorus generally takes a favorable position toward Krestovnikov's deeds, viewing them in a positive light. The second member is inclined to be negative and skeptical, while the third usually draws attention to the play's ironies and what little humor there is. When the Chorus introduces Krestovnikov's mother in the first flashback episode, the first Chorus member says, "The woman whom he loves is our hero's mother. It's not quite two years that her husband left her." The second adds, "I wouldn't call their marriage happy . . . ," to which the third replies excitedly, "But he loved his son" (p. 592). Or again, in the same episode when Arisha is introduced, the first Chorus member says, "The girl there, the one standing by the fence, is his [Berg's] daughter. And she's full of anticipation of something wonderful. (Smiles.) She's all of nineteen . . ." The second comments, "Too fickle and saucy," while the third notes, "But I've always had a weakness for girls like that."

The visionary scenes at the end of each part of *Happy Days*, the first introducing Krestovnikov's father and the second, Volodya Kostenetsky, also recall a theatricalist device used previously by Arbuzov in *It Happened in Irkutsk*. In the earlier play, visionary scenes are used to introduce voices out of the past in order to throw light on Serdyuk's attitudes toward women and love, as romance again enters his life.

The last noteworthy theatricalist element in *Happy Days* is related to a volleyball match which can be heard at various moments during the development of the play's action and is finally brought onstage as a kind of dumb scene following the death of Krestovnikov. In the two major parts of *Happy Days*, Arbuzov has tried to capture the rhythm of a Chekhovian play, based on the unobtrusive unfolding of the drama out of the interaction of the characters rather than through external events. To Chekhovian inspiration I think we must also ascribe Arbuzov's use of sound and sound symbolism. Musical sound is used in a particularly effective way in the first episode of *Happy Days* when Krestovnikov's father appears to him in a flashback-within-a-flashback. To prepare the audience for a further movement back in time, Arbuzov uses the ticking of clocks and, more interestingly, gramophone recordings of familiar songs by well-known older singers. This structural use of recorded sound is, of course, a standard technique of theatricalist drama.

The volleyball match and the sounds coming from it are also important in *Happy Days*. The noise of the ball being hit back and forth echoes the striking of a clock and hence suggests both the passage and the continuum of time. Note that the last sounds heard onstage are those related to the volleyball match. The nature of the game, involving the tightening and releasing of tensions and the give and take between players, becomes symbolic of the full, interacting life which Krestovnikov never found.

Arbuzov had used mime before, in *It Happened in Irkutsk*, but not at the very end of the play. The inclusion of the volleyball match in the closing scene of *Happy Days* faintly recalls the lonely figure of Firs and the distant sounds of the chopping of wood in *The Cherry Orchard*. Of course, the spirit of Arbuzov's ending is very different from that of Chekhov's play. As *The Cherry Orchard* ends, the mood is melancholic; the old servant Firs has been left behind and the audience is aware of a

way of life passing into oblivion. At the end of *Happy Days,* the mood is
not melancholic even though the final monologue of the student is
meant to crown the play with a mixed bitterness and mockery. When
the stage lights dim, marking the departure of the student, and come on
again to illuminate the closing volleyball match, the aggressive shouts
and cries of the players are gradually drowned out by the beating of
drums until nothing can be heard. As the curtain falls, the insistent
pounding of the drums becomes a pulsating symbol of the elemental life
force itself, the life force beyond which Krestovnikov sought to set himself and without success.

FIFTEEN

The Dissidents:
Ivanov, Amalrik, Solzhenitsyn

THE WIDESPREAD expectation of liberalization engendered by the death of Stalin and Khrushchev's revelations in 1956 also counted among its various manifestations the dynamic dissident movement of the late 1950s, the '60s, and '70s. In view of the prominence of writers in the movement, particularly Andrei Sinyavsky (pseudonym Abram Tertz) and Aleksandr Solzhenitsyn, whose cases attracted worldwide attention, the role of literature in the evolution of the campaign of protest has been understandably great. While associated mainly with poetry and prose fiction, the dissidents also contributed an interesting body of plays which tend to be less well known and which this chapter will examine.

The principal dissident dramatists were Andrei Remezov (1925– ; pseudonym I. Ivanov), Andrei Amalrik (1938–), and the most famous of the three, Aleksandr Solzhenitsyn (1918–). Because political factors negated any possibility of the publication and production of their works in the Soviet Union, the dissidents' plays were published abroad and in most cases have already been widely translated. Strikingly different on the whole from the plays of such an "Establishment" dramatist as Arbuzov, the dissident drama was no less a response to the post-Stalin "thaw" mentality than other departures from the stringent norms of Socialist Realism already considered and should be viewed ultimately as another dimension of the same phenomenon.

A sometime research assistant in the Moscow Library of Foreign Literatures, Andrei Remezov's reputation as a dissident writer rests on two works, the play *Yest-li zhizn na Marse?* (*Is There Life on Mars?*, published in 1961) and an essay "American Pangs of the Russian Conscience" published in English in *Encounter* magazine in 1964. A political allegory, *Is There Life on Mars?* was written in 1958 and 1959 and hence was spawned by the same climate of liberal reaction following the Twentieth Party Congress as such monuments of dissident literature as Abram Tertz's *The Trial Begins* and *Fantastic Tales*. Remezov, as a matter of fact, was involved in the famous trial of Sinyavsky (and another dissident writer, Nikolai Arzhak, pseudonym of Yuli Daniel) in February 1966. He turned State's evidence and testified against the defendants, naming Sinyavsky as the person who helped him smuggle his works out of the USSR for publication abroad.[1]

One aspect of Stalin's reign on which the dissidents fixed particular attention is anti-Semitism. Apart from any universal humanitarian repudiation of bias, the dissident concern seems to have been a response specifically to the anti-Jewish hysteria surrounding the infamous "Doctors' Plot" of December 1952, just a few months before Stalin's death in March 1953. Solzhenitsyn's documentary *The Gulag Archipelago* (1973) reveals perhaps for the first time the full implications of the campaign against Jews in the last months of Stalin's reign. Earlier revelations were sufficient, however, to have influenced the liberal Soviet literary conscience to the extent that the dissident fiction reflects. Allusions to the "plot" appear in Tertz's *The Trial Begins*, while Remezov's *Is There Life on Mars?* springs wholly from it.

The three-act play, set in Moscow in 1956, opens with a Prologue in which a large number of people have come together to witness a great achievement of Soviet science: the telescopic observation of life on Mars. The rest of the play, excepting the Epilogue, is a dramatization of what the spectators observe through the telescope.

Viewed up close, Mars, not surprisingly, bears a striking resemblance to the Soviet Union in the time of Stalin. Life is strictly regimented and deviations from the proscribed order of behavior and thought are not tolerated. The punishment for deviation is death, which in Remezov's play is visited upon the erring in the manner of divine retribution by the all-seeing all-knowing Minister of Thunder and Lightning, the Right Hand (*Pravaya Ruka*) of the great Father and Teacher. Hardly is a sinner found out by a magnificent system of electronic surveillance than he is struck dead by a bolt of lightning.

What we have so far is a variation on familiar motifs of allegorical satire. The Mars of Remezov's play is a totalitarian nightmare genetically related to the anti-utopian visions conjured up in Zamyatin's novel *We* and in Mayakovsky's *The Bedbug* and *The Bathhouse*. However, instead of locating his anti-utopian world in future time or on a remote island somewhere in the style of the literary utopias of the seventeenth and eighteenth centuries, Remezov places it on another planet within the earth's solar system.

Now the most serious internal political problem of Remezov's Mars involves the largest ethnic minority on the planet, the Lunatics (*Luna-tiki*), former inhabitants of the planet Luna (Moon). Although discrimination is officially outlawed on Mars, the Lunatics are, nevertheless, second-class citizens; they are, for example, denied admission to Martian institutions of higher learning. This, despite the fact that the originator of *marsianstvo*, the guiding ideology of Mars, was Karl Mars who was himself a Lunatic.

In order to counter growing skepticism especially among students over the disparity between official Martian minority policy and the situation of the Lunatics, the Minister of Thunder and Lightning plans a propaganda campaign around two Lunatics in the philosopher Materialist Dialektikov's study group, the Lovely Esther, a veterinarian, and her musician husband, Solomon Solomonovich. By now it should be obvious whom the Martian Lunatics represent; the profession of the Lovely Esther also has to be seen as an oblique allusion to the "Doctors' Plot."

Much of Remezov's play is taken up with incidents depicting various facets of Martian tyranny and the maniacal absolutism of its supreme ruler. These include such things as the diversion of funds from Academician Zachumelov's spaceship to a dacha for the supreme ruler's favorite actress, Vera Vasilevna ("a talented representative of Martian realism"), the liquidation of a citizen for the telling of a joke about the great Father and Teacher, and the torture of an artist who attempts to secure the reversal of an espionage charge against his father, who has been imprisoned in a well for twenty years. Well imprisonment is a favorite Martian punishment. Yet a definite plot does come into focus involving the Minister of Thunder and Lightning's efforts to win the affection of the Lovely Esther. After all, according to the Martian Central Bureau of Statistics he has already loved 3,278 of the most beautiful Martian women. Although the Minister's aide, the Colonel, ascertains that Esther does not love her husband, she does have principles which do not allow her to give herself to the Minister. At the mention of principles, the Minister is confused. The word is strange to him and he has to look it up in a dictionary. This recalls the elimination of love and the emotions from the future society into which Mayakovsky's Prisypkin is resurrected in *The Bedbug* and the relegation of such concepts to dictionaries, where they are classed as archaisms.

Despite his insistence, the Minister's efforts fail to move the Lovely Esther. He wants to speak only of love while she queries him as to the reasons for Martian anti-Lunaticism. When the Minister starts to force his attentions, she hits him in the face. Angry and frustrated, the Minister conceives a plan to intimidate Esther by having her favorite cow, Buryona, poisoned and the rumor spread about that the Lunatics are poisoning cattle everywhere in a plot to weaken Mars through hunger preparatory to an invasion from Luna. This will be followed by mass arrests of the Lunatics on Mars and finally a campaign against Luna into which all other planets will be dragged. What began as a sinister plot to bring Esther to submission now becomes a grandiose scheme aimed at nothing less than interplanetary conquest.

The official newspaper *Istina* (*Truth*) carries word about the Lunatic plot to poison cattle, all Lunatics are rounded up, and the production of Academician Zachumelov's spaceship is given top priority. The Minister's latest scheme calls for one structural change in the plane's design— it must be outfitted with a three-million seating capacity so that all the Lunatics on Mars can be placed on board and then dumped out when the spaceship is over Earth. Because of his still tender feelings toward her the Minister decides to spare Esther and to replace her on board the *Chum-115*, as the spaceship is now designated, with a Martian student who resembles her.

The time for the takeoff arrives in a scene reminiscent of the time-machine departure in Mayakovsky's *The Bathhouse*, a crowd is assembled, and rousing speeches are delivered. But when the attempt to start the engines is made, nothing happens. It appears that the motor has been stolen by none other than the inventor, Academician Zachumelov, who now refuses to see his invention used for destructive purposes. Before the matter can be resolved, however, the Colonel rushes in with the news that the great Father and Teacher, who in the meantime has taken over the direct operation of the complex machinery of surveillance and destruction of the Ministry of Thunder and Lightning, fouled up the mechanism and was himself struck dead by lightning. As all stand dumbstruck, recalling the mute scene at the end of Gogol's *Inspector-General*, the light gradually goes out and Mars disappears from the telescope's field of view.

In the Epilogue, confusion reigns as a result of the events witnessed on Mars. In another obvious allusion to the "Doctors' Plot" of 1952, mention is made of the death by heart seizure of one of the scientists who designed the telescope, Academician Aron Moiseevich Zilberstein, who was badly shaken by what he observed on Mars and already had a weak heart because of his first attack in 1953.

In the play's concluding irony, the Russian observers of life on Mars express their gratitude that they are citizens of the Soviet Union, where under the leadership of the wise Communist Party the nationality question has been settled for all time and where it would be unthinkable that Russians could act toward a small nation, like the Gypsies, the way the Martians do toward their Lunatics. The play closes with the drinking of toasts to good people everywhere such as Academician Zachumelov. The celebration is soon broken off, however, by the Party Organizer (Partorg) who declares that due to the imperfections of the telescope, on which much work remains to be done, nothing was seen, there was no observation of the life on Mars. Moreover, he orders two plainclothesmen to take into custody the scientists who worked on the telescope. His parting words, addressed to the characters remaining onstage, need no elaboration: "That's the way it is, Comrades. No matter how sad it may be, we must honestly and openly tell the people the whole truth: We saw nothing. We heard nothing. We know nothing. Understood?"[2]

Owing much as a play to Mayakovsky's satirical fantasies and also to Yevgeni Shvarts' dramatic fairy tales of the 1930s and 1940s, Remezov's work lacks the delightful comic portraits of both Mayakovsky and Shvarts and their sustained farcical humor. *Is There Life on Mars?* is rather obvious allegory with occasionally clever dialogue and a few good comic situations. Despite its weaknesses, the play is competently structured and can be easily staged. The motif of telescopic observation integrally relates the Prologue and the Epilogue to the main body of the drama and the Minister's surveillance and punishment machinery makes possible some fine sound effects.

As the best specimens of absurdist drama in Russia since the plays of the Oberiuty of the late 1920s, the works of Andrei Amalrik are far more amusing and provocative than Remezov's. A maverick and nonconformist since the late 1950s at least Amalrik, like Solzhenitsyn, has a firsthand familiarity with the Soviet penal system.[3] His troubles with the authorities began while he was a student at the Historical Faculty of Moscow University, which he attended in 1959 and again from 1962 to 1963 and from which he was finally expelled in 1963 for his unorthodox views and for his attempt to send to Denmark via the Danish Embassy in Moscow a controversial essay on *The Norsemen and Kievan Russia*. It was in the period of his expulsion from the university and during the following year, 1964, that Amalrik wrote the five short plays that resulted in his being sentenced in 1965 to a two-and-a-half-year penal exile on a Siberian collective farm near Tomsk.

While under detention in 1965 for his "parasitism" (meaning, in So-

viet parlance, no regular employment) and suspicious contact with foreigners, Amalrik's apartment was searched by the police. The search
brought to light not only the avant-garde paintings and drawings by
Anatoli Zverev, Dmitri Plavinsky, and others, which were the immediate concern of the police, but also five short plays. The pictures and
plays were confiscated. An investigation ensued and Amalrik soon found
himself accused of producing, harboring, and disseminating pornographic works (with reference to Zverev's paintings, Amalrik's plays,
and Zverev's illustrations for the plays). He was given a psychiatric test
after a week's detention, but the day after the test the case was dropped.
Zverev's pictures were judged not pornographic by the Moscow branch
of the Union of Artists, but were dismissed as the work of a madman. A
drama specialist, Tatyana Sytin, the literary consultant of the Lenin
Komsomol Theater, had been asked meanwhile to examine Amalrik's
plays as to their pornographic content. Because of her uncertainty concerning a precise definition of pornography, she declined to pronounce
judgment on them. This decision led to the dropping of the pornography
charge against Amalrik. A trial was still held, however, to take up the
matter of Amalrik's "parasitism." The outcome was the imposition of a
sentence of exile of two and a half years with release possible after half
the term had passed.

In July 1966, while Amalrik was serving his time in Siberia, the Russian Supreme Court reversed his sentence, clearing the way for his
return to Moscow later on that month. Amalrik's experiences in exile
and the events that led up to it, especially his trial, served as the material for his first major literary work, *Involuntary Journey to Siberia*.[4]
While working as a journalist specializing in theater and the arts,
Amalrik's nonconformist dissident behavior continued. The results were
not surprising. At the end of 1968 he was dismissed from his job with
the Novosti Press Agency. His activities in 1969 embroiled him in still
more difficulties with the authorities. In his "Open Letter to Anatoli
Kuznetsov" (November 1, 1969) he attacked Soviet intellectuals for their
abandonment of what Amalrik speaks of as their "inner freedom." Far
worse, however, was the publication in the West in the autumn of 1969
of Amalrik's literary bombshell, *Will the Soviet Union Survive Until
1984?*,[5] a theoretical study which predicts, among other things, a decisive war between the Chinese and Russians and the collapse of the Soviet empire.

Amalrik was arrested again in May 1970. This time the charge was
more serious: circulating "literature containing slanderous fabrications

defaming the Soviet political and social system" (Articles 190–191 of the Russian Criminal Code). The trial was held in Sverdlovsk rather than in Moscow in order to diminish attention to it, especially from outside the USSR. Publicity was inescapable, however, and appeals were made. But the State was adamant on meting out some form of punishment for the publication in the West of works like *Involuntary Journey to Siberia* and *Will the Soviet Union Survive Until 1984?* and for Amalrik's too frank interviews with foreign correspondents. Amalrik refused to participate in the trial, denying the charge of slander and the anti-Soviet content of his writings. Nevertheless, the trial was held on November 10–11, 1970, and he was sentenced to a three-year term in the Kolyma forced labor camp some six thousand miles from Moscow. Following his release, Amalrik eventually succeeded in emigrating and now resides in the United States.

To date, Amalrik has written six plays, none of which has been staged. The Russian originals were published in one volume in Amsterdam in 1970 by the Alexander Herzen Foundation. The English translation of the volume, by Daniel Weissbort, was published in 1970 by Harcourt Brace Jovanovich. The most recent of the plays is a dramatization of Gogol's short story "The Nose," completed in 1968. Four of the other plays are one-acters: *Moya tyotya zhivyot v Volokolamske* (*My Aunt Is Living in Volokolamsk*, 1963, 1964, 1966), *Chetyrnadtsat lyubovnikov nekrasivoy Meri-Enn* (*The Fourteen Lovers of Ugly Mary-Ann*, 1964), *Skazka pro belogo bychka* (literally, *The Story of the Little White Bull*, meaning, a cock-and-bull story, 1964), and *Konformist li dyadya Dzhek?* (*Is Uncle Jack a Conformist?*, 1964). *Vostok-Zapad: Dialog, vedushchiysya v Suzdale* (*East-West: A Dialogue in Suzdal*, 1963), has three short acts and was Amalrik's longest play before the Gogol adaptation.

Amalrik's interest in the theater began, as he tells us in his essay "On Himself as a Writer of Plays" (1967),[6] at the age of thirteen when he set up his own little puppet theater and staged plays in it with the help of two friends. He may have been unaware of it at the time but his career in the theater began in much the same way as that of another literary maverick, Alfred Jarry. The Frenchman's scandalous *Ubu Roi*, with which the modern tradition of the absurd really begins in 1896, originated as a puppet play staged by Jarry in his Rennes apartment.

Amalrik's early interest in theater was abandoned, however, when as a form of protest against what he considered the pseudo-art propagated in it he stopped going to the theater almost entirely from about the age of fourteen. The interest was resumed seriously again only after he returned from exile and began working as a theater and arts journalist, which necessitated visits to theaters and meetings with theater people. It was as a result of these visits, he writes, that he realized that much in the theater had changed for the better.

The actual stimulus to Amalrik's own playwriting seems to have been his reading in 1962 of a very short play of four-and-a-half pages called *Gospozha Lenin* (*Mrs. Lenin*, 1913) by Velimir Khlebnikov (1885–1922), the founder of Russian futurism.[7] The characters in the play are in fact articulate senses of the dying Mrs. Lenin which record the coming and going of a doctor and finally the removal of the deceased. In its static quality, the figure of an old person, and an evocation of an atmosphere of mystery, doom, and approaching death through silence, on the one hand, and the sounds of footsteps, creaking doors and fences, and keys turning in locks, on the other, the playlet recalls the early exemplary Symbolist dramatic pieces of Maurice Maeterlinck more than it does the plays of the Futurists.

Despite the inspiration of Khlebnikov, Amalrik made slight progress until he happened upon a crude translation of Ionesco's *The Bald Soprano*. Overwhelmed by it, Amalrik started writing anew and in three days finished a three-act play which was, as he characterizes it, "a curious mixture of classical Russian drama and unassimilated absurdist elements." After writing several other pieces and understanding better what he was after in the drama, he returned to the earlier work, revised it extensively, and shortened it to one act. The interest in Ionesco, in the meantime, proved short-lived and was replaced by Beckett, Amalrik's "second major revelation in contemporary drama."[8] Among his favorite Russian dramatists, Amalrik mentions Gogol, Sukhovo-Kobylin, and Kharms. Underlying Amalrik's enthusiasm for Ionesco and Beckett and his preference among Russian playwrights for Gogol, Sukhovo-Kobylin, Khlebnikov, and Kharms is an obvious predilection for the absurd.

All of Amalrik's plays are in the vein of absurdist theater. If we acknowledge a native Russian tradition of absurd and grotesque drama beginning with Gogol in the first half of the nineteenth century and continuing through Sukhovo-Kobylin and the early Chekhov to NEP comedy (Erdman, Romashov, Mayakovsky) and the plays of Kharms and Vvedensky, then it is by no means an exaggeration to see Amalrik not only as the most recent expression in Russia of that type of drama but also the most important to appear since the early 1930s. When plays of Ionesco and Beckett came to Amalrik's attention, his enthusiastic reception of them was already prepared by a predisposition to this kind of literature.

The absurdism of Amalrik's own playwriting is immediately apparent. Customary logical sequence is of minimal significance. Characters appear out of nowhere and disappear as strangely as they appear. Puppetlike, they have no past, do not advance in time, and in no sense have a future. Sometimes connections between characters are rationally perceptible; other times they are not. Often, characters change identity. Almost all characters have generic names (Wife, Professor, Neurasthenic, Motorist, and so on), in the pattern of much absurdist drama. What is true of character applies also to situation. Plot in any conventional sense does not exist. Some incidents relate to each other sequentially; often they do not and seem to stand alone. With the exception of the Gogol adaptation, all the plays (including the three-act *East-West: A Dialogue in Suzdal*, which is less than fifty pages long) are short and exhibit a marked economy of means. Characters are few in number and settings of virtually no consequence. Only *My Aunt Is Living in Volokolamsk*, *East-West: A Dialogue in Suzdal*, and *Is Uncle Jack a Conformist?* contain allusions to anything specifically Russian. Dialogue is very simple and colloquial, again like that of a great deal of avant-garde and absurdist drama, and where long monologues occur such as those involving Indian and Chinese philosophy, literature, and folklore between the student and the maid in *East-West: A Dialogue in Suzdal* their disparate length and contents in the given situation invest them with absurdity. Often, dialogue consists of nothing more than free association or the repetition of slogans, popular aphorisms, or clichés.

Taken as a whole, Amalrik's plays share with much absurdist drama a pessimistic view of the world which becomes the bleaker because of the contrasting surface nonsense. One facet of this pessimism is the importance in the plays of the inability of individuals to develop lasting and rewarding relationships. This is often conveyed by the inconsequentiality of family and especially marital relations. In *My Aunt Is Living in Volokolamsk*, a professor's wife and one of his students, who had not known each other before, on the occasion of their first meeting in the professor's apartment immediately become intimate, exchange confessions about their sexual experiences, and then start to make love. The professor, on the other hand, is accused by a maid of robbing her daughter's innocence. In *East-West: A Dialogue in Suzdal*, a student and his older mistress no sooner check into a hotel when they are informed that they must share the room with a third party, a political instructor named

Ivanov. As soon as Ivanov and the mistress meet, Ivanov declares his love for her and the two scheme to go off together. Ivanov is exposed, however, as a Chinese agent assigned to Suzdal and is killed by the Overseer. When the mistress is apprised of the situation by the Overseer, he declares his love for her and she accepts. The student, meanwhile, meets a maid in the hotel, a former assistant to a Greek-American CIA agent, and like the professor's wife and student in *My Aunt Is Living in Volokolamsk* they soon exchange erotic confessions and profess their love for each other. In *The Fourteen Lovers of Ugly Mary-Ann* as the Storyteller hurriedly dresses after a sexual encounter with Mary-Ann he reveals his fear of his wife's reaction to his possible late return and virtually in the same breath launches into a bizarre narration of the punishments he inflicts on her. In *The Story of the Little White Bull*, the character Niki comes into a toyshop to buy a doll as a birthday present for his five-year-old sister. Within moments he declares his love for the salesgirl and just as quickly begins quarreling with her about the different things love means for a man and a woman. A woman and her daughter enter the shop and soon want to buy the same doll Niki wanted and begin a conversation with him. With the cooling of his ardor for the salesgirl, Niki switches his interest to the rather precocious daughter. His friend Koki then tells him that the girl's mother seduced him when he was fourteen but that she turned out to be a lesbian. Moreover, he declares that the woman is really Niki's sister in disguise and that she wants to destroy him because their parents love him more. At the end of the play, after much talk of Freud, dreams, and the subconscious, Niki and Koki go off dancing, the mother and the salesgirl exit together, and the daughter is left alone to play mother to the inanimate object, the doll.

The prominence of eroticism in the plays, which was the basis of the charge of pornography leveled against them, has two probable sources. One is the desire to shock, which Amalrik shares with other practitioners of the absurd. In *The Story of the Little White Bull*, for example, when Koki confesses his affair with the woman they meet in the toyshop Niki asks him: "But even so, you were attracted to her? How did you usually do it?"

> KOKI: Usually she stood at the window, leaning on the sill and keeping a lookout for her husband, and I was behind her, half hidden by the curtains.
> NIKI (*his curiosity aroused*): A complicated position.
> KOKI: She taught me it, and no doubt her husband, as a classical ex-

pert, taught her. (*Remembers.*) We practiced other positions, too! The filthy things she taught me! It came in very useful later on. (*p. 143*)

In the West, the absurdist writer often flouts bourgeois conventions with gusto. In the case of Amalrik, shock is achieved not by slapping the bourgeois in the face but by introducing in his plays the taboos which Soviet literature diligently avoids, above all explicit sex, homosexuality, and Freudian psychoanalysis. This shock-motivated eroticism has its antecedents in earlier twentieth-century Russian avant-garde drama with which Amalrik doubtless was acquainted. Although he does not mention Vvedensky, it seems likely that he must have been familiar with some of his work given his interest in Kharms and the evident influence on his own playwriting of Oberiu drama. Vvedensky's major play, *Christmas at the Ivanovs,* includes several explicit sexual scenes, as we saw earlier in the discussion of the Oberiuty. Amalrik is never as bizarre as Vvedensky and where sex is unrelated to an attitude toward life it is used to heighten a general sense of absurdity. In *East-West: A Dialogue in Suzdal,* for example, the student tells the hotel maid about his first love affair with a plump teacher:

STUDENT: . . . She had a black mustache, shifty little dark eyes, and pimples on her chin and forehead. Her favorite writer was Heinrich Böll. However, I spent only one night with her.

GIRL: Very romantic, I must say.

STUDENT: Yes. And you don't know the most romantic part of it: when we kissed in the street.

GIRL: Who kissed whom?

STUDENT: She kissed me. (*Pause.*) I bit her playfully on the breast and she decided she couldn't allow her pupils such liberties. That was how our story ended. (*p. 75*)

The other likely source of Amalrik's eroticism is his pessimistic attitude toward life and human relations. Although characters profess love for one another in the plays and yearn for love, love is reduced to sex or, to put it differently, sex is the only way by which love can be expressed. But even here gratification is elusive. In *My Aunt Is Living in Volokolamsk,* the neurasthenic student who starts to make love to the professor's wife confesses that because of his neurasthenia he can have sex only occasionally. The absurd humor of the dialogue at this point, as is often the case in Amalrik and absurdist drama generally, temporarily shifts attention from the underlying pathos. When pressed about the frequency of his sexual activity, the student replies:

> Only very occasionally. Usually the first Tuesday of each month.
> WIFE (*amazed*): Really?
> NEURASTHENIC: Yes. Why are you so surprised?
> WIFE (*solemnly*): The first Tuesday of each month is when the store where I work is inspected. (*p. 21*)

The student and his mistress in *East-West: A Dialogue in Suzdal* check into a shabby hotel and discover shortly thereafter, to their annoyance and frustration, that they must share the room with a third person. Marring whatever pleasure he experiences with Mary-Ann in *The Fourteen Lovers of Ugly Mary-Ann* is the Storyteller's fear of returning home late and his obsession with the punishment he metes out to his wife. His infidelity with Mary-Ann in fact is nothing more than a form of punishment of the Storyteller's wife.

The emphasis on sex in Amalrik's plays is paralleled by the emphasis on violence and the two are related. The neurasthenic student in *My Aunt Is Living in Volokolamsk,* who becomes intimate with the professor's wife, is accused later in the play of having an unwholesome ideological influence on the professor. This follows immediately upon the accusation leveled against the student that it was he and not the professor who seduced the maid's daughter. Calls for the killing of the student are heard from characters in the play designated as Professor's Caution, Professor's Ambition, Professor's Good Nature. But the murder becomes unnecessary. The pressures on the student prove too much and he falls dead near the end of the play.

In *East-West: A Dialogue in Suzdal,* the political instructor Ivanov with whom the student and his mistress must share their hotel room is revealed to be a Chinese spy named Tsu Syao. Before the mistress and the spy can run away together, however, he is shot to death by the Overseer who exposes him as an anti-Soviet dogmatist engaged in espionage in, of all places, Suzdal.

The play the guests are assembled to witness in *Is Uncle Jack a Conformist?* intertwines sex and violence in its plot. The title of the work is *Tsirlin and Tsipelzon; or, the Apotheosis of Good* and the first three or four acts are taken up with the title's characters alternately raping each other.

The most violent of Amalrik's plays is *The Fourteen Lovers of Ugly*

Mary-Ann. Much of the dialogue of the first part of the play between Mary-Ann and the Storyteller concerns the latter's account of the physical abuse to which he subjects his wife. The cataloguelike narration of violence distantly brings to mind the grotesque and absurd violence of King Ubu in Jarry's *Ubu Roi:*

> STORYTELLER: . . . I even beat her sometimes.
> MARY-ANN (*surprised*): You do?
> STORYTELLER: Yes. But not often.
> MARY-ANN (*still surprised*): You get hold of her and beat her?
> STORYTELLER: Yes. It's all pretty run-of-the-mill stuff. First I slap her face.
> MARY-ANN: Oh!
> STORYTELLER: You should hear her yell! Then I slap her on the jaw and punch her in the belly. The whole thing is not to waste any time.
> MARY-ANN (*curious*): Really?
> STORYTELLER: Yes. You should see her doubling up at that! Anyway, I don't give her a chance to come around—I throw her down and really start laying it on.
> MARY-ANN: Oh . . .
> STORYTELLER (*with gusto*): I trample on her, smash a bottle over her head, and drive the glass splinters into her ribs with all my might. Then I tear out her hair and sink my teeth into her cheeks, her breast, and her belly, till the blood flows.
> MARY-ANN (*moaning*): Oh . . .
> STORYTELLER: Then I force open her mouth, plunge my arms right down her throat—you can see what slender aristocratic arms I've got—and start tearing out her insides. (*pp. 93–94*)

And so the list of horrors continues with the Storyteller telling Mary-Ann that he sometimes carves patterns in his wife's body with a razor blade or penknife and occasionally sets fire to her pubic hair which then "crackles like a log fire" (p. 94).

Later in the play there is a repetition of the Storyteller's inventory as the Motorist, who accuses him of stealing the cherished letter of Mary-Ann's first lover, threatens him with the same tortures which the Storyteller had committed against his wife. Toward the end of the play, the Motorist demands that the other characters recite such slogans as "Long live chemical engineering!" and "Long live the technical intelligentsia!" in memory of Mary-Ann's first lover, who was a chemical engineering student. When Mary-Ann's latest admirer, a young foreign prince, refuses to do so, the Motorist orders the other characters to throw him out a window. The execution is carried out, but when Mary-Ann expresses pity she is thrown out, too, on the Motorist's command. Finally, when the Storyteller's voice cracks while reciting the slogans, the Motorist, who in a delightful absurdist touch was temporarily incapacitated earlier by a stroke and a fall downstairs, threatens to throw him out the window also—as soon as he is back on his feet.

The violence in Amalrik's plays often has a political dimension. In *The Fourteen Lovers of Ugly Mary-Ann*, the Motorist's demand that the other characters recite certain slogans and his punishment of those who refuse or falter establish an unmistakable political reality. Whatever the absurdity of the situation, the thrust of Amalrik's intention is clear. Near the end of the play, the Motorist who is, ironically, nearly completely incapacitated as the result of his accident, asserts himself as the strongest of the characters. This assertion of strength is then followed by an insistence on the submission of the others to his will and the conformity of behavior represented by the demand that all recite the Motorist's slogans. Backing up the imposition of conformity is the threat of violence. Any deviation is punishable by death. We may have exchanged Remezov's Mars for the absurd world of Amalrik, but the essential threat to human dignity remains unaltered. What makes the situation absurd in Amalrik, of course, is the physical weakness of the self-appointed dictator, the Motorist.

The issue of conformity comes even more to the fore in the riotous *Is Uncle Jack a Conformist?*, which ends with the collapse of the stage scenery in a way reminiscent of the ending of Blok's *The Fairground Booth*. Here, Uncle Jack's play about the mutual ravishment of Tsirlin and Tsipelzon triggers a debate about meaning which Amalrik uses to satirize the pretentiousness of Soviet literary society. After the critic summarizes Uncle Jack's play, the following dialogue takes place:

> HOSTESS: It's most daring. Nothing direct, yet it manages to hit the nail on the head. I think it's superb.
> LADY: Yes, from a social point of view the play can't be faulted. The only thing is, it's pointless using expressions like "ass." In the 'twenties, it might have seemed very new and daring, but nowadays it just looks like obscenity for its own sake.
> SON: In my opinion, "ass" is very much to the point here and carries considerable semantic weight. But as regards the social aspect, don't you feel that at the end of the play the author is compromising with what he starts off by attacking and is trying to get around the

authorities by tacking on a happy ending—this move to a new apartment—so that they'll let the rest pass?

CRITIC: I totally disagree with you. You've completely missed the irony of it. As it happens, that's the best part of the play.

DAUGHTER: What's so good about it! He's simply being obsequious and trying to show that people are well off in our country, since they get new apartments.

LADY: But you've got it all wrong! On the contrary, what he's trying to say is that the new apartments are in no way better than the old ones, but even worse.

SON: All the same, the author is showing a tendency to conformism.

CRITIC: Not in the least! He's a regular nonconformist.

SON (*aggressively to the critic*): I assure you he's a conformist.

CRITIC (*aggressively to the son*): And I'm telling you he's a nonconformist.

SON: A conformist, a conformist!

CRITIC: A nonconformist, a nonconformist!

SON (*furiously*): A conformist!

CRITIC (*furiously*): A nonconformist! (*pp. 160–61*)

From meaning, the argument passes next to the play's style on which, again, total disagreement reigns:

SON: I'm not saying the play hasn't got its points, but from a purely literary point of view it's very old-fashioned. At first glance it seems to be in the tradition of the absurd, almost like Ionesco, but on closer examination, it's just Ostrovsky updated a little.

CRITIC: That's simply ridiculous. There's not a trace of Ostrovsky there. Now Gogol—that's another matter.

LADY: I'd say Sukhovo-Kobylin.

DAUGHTER: And I'd say Saltykov-Shchedrin. (*pp. 161–62*)

The "oneupmanship" of the salon, Soviet style, soon shifts to the apparently inescapable issue of anti-Semitism. In Uncle Jack's play which, in another splendid absurdity, none of its argumentative discussants has yet seen, it so happens that Tsirlin and Tsipelzon are Jews. Because each one violates the other, Jews are violated and hence the play must be anti-Semitic. It was on the same grounds, incidentally, that the dissident writer Tertz-Sinyavsky was accused of anti-Semitism with reference to the character of Dr. Rabinovich in *The Trial Begins*. The ensuing dialogue is in the best tradition of absurdist drama but the underlying issue brings us back to Remezov's Mars, the grim reality of the "Doctors' Plot," and the injection of the anti-Semitic issue into the Sinyavsky-Daniel trial of 1966:

CRITIC: I beg your pardon, but that's nonsense. Just the fact that the author depicts Jews being violated doesn't mean he's an anti-Semite! On the contrary, he's defending the Jews.

SON: But in the play a Jew rapes a Jew.

CRITIC: Surely you noticed that the Jew who raped the Jew was himself raped afterward. And anyway, how can the author be an anti-Semite—he's a Jew himself. (p. 163)

The theme of anti-Semitism also appears in *My Aunt Is Living in Volokolamsk*. The character called the Professor's Good Nature tells a Jewish joke at one point and when he is through reflects a moment and asks, "I wonder who makes up all those Jewish stories?" What follows is a kind of catalogue—with appropriate absurdist touches—of familiar clichés about Jews:

AMBITION (*confidently*): The Jews themselves.

NEURASTHENIC: Yes, the Jews are a very talented people.

POET: Especially in the field of literature.

NEURASTHENIC: Yet I've heard that they're not very welcome in publishing jobs these days.

AMBITION: You know, I'm not anti-Semitic at all, but I'm bound to say that if a Jew fails to get a job somewhere it's only because all the positions are occupied by other Jews.

PROFESSOR (*circuitously*): Do you know that the famous ukase on the Pale of Settlement was introduced by Catherine II as early as the eighteenth century . . .

NEURASTHENIC (*interrupting*): And the first Jewish pogrom, so poetically described in the chronicles, took place in Kiev as early as the twelfth century . . .

POET (*interrupting*): And have you noticed that all the prominent people of the twentieth century are Jews: Einstein, Freud, Kafka . . .

AMBITION (*in the same tone*): Mussolini, Hitler, Stalin . . .

GOOD NATURE: Bolivar, Napoleon, Cromwell . . .

CAUTION: Pizarro, Borgia, Savonarola . . .

PROFESSOR: Tamerlane, Genghis Khan, Attila . . .

POET: Sukarno, Castro, Mao Tse-tung . . .

NEURASTHENIC: Makhno, Petlyura, Stenka Razin . . .

WIFE (*surprised*): Was Stenka Razin a Jew?

NEURASTHENIC: Yes, he was. His real name was Rabin, not Razin.

CAUTION: Are you a Jew too?

NEURASTHENIC: No, I'm not a Jew.

CAUTION: But there's a certain Jewish slyness and cunning about you.

AMBITION: A Jewish coldness and heartlessness.

GOOD NATURE: A Jewish presumptuousness and insolence.

PROFESSOR: A Jewish cowardliness.
WIFE: A Jewish shrewdness.
POET: A Jewish . . . (*at a loss of words.*). (*pp. 26–27*)

We might dwell for a moment at this point on Amalrik's links with earlier Russian absurdist drama. For the absurdity of the sudden irrelevance, which he uses often, Amalrik had no finer source than Gogol. In Sukhovo-Kobylin's theatrically fascinating *Tarelkin's Death*, absurd and grotesque characters and situations combine to create a nightmarish vision of corruption and inhumanity aimed specifically at the tsarist bureaucracy and police of the time. Amalrik uses similar techniques and in one instance in *East-West: A Dialogue in Suzdal* even repeats a minor episode that occurs in Sukhovo-Kobylin's work. In the earlier play the now much-harrassed petty bureaucrat Tarelkin who is accused of vampirism and of being the mastermind of a plot against all Russia is asked during a brutal interrogation to reveal his accomplices. He replies that they are all Petersburg and all Moscow. In Amalrik's play, it is the Chinese agent who is being "grilled" by the Overseer. When the Overseer asks him to name the agents he's been recruiting, Tsu Syao eagerly replies: "Two hundred and twenty-five million Soviet people."

Compared to his nineteenth-century Russian predecessors in the tradition of the absurd, Amalrik operates with a much more compressed dramatic format, derived not only from Khlebnikov and the Oberiuty, but also from Blok whose *The Fairground Booth* he admired. Although a few of his plays deal with specific aspects of Soviet life and can be regarded as topical in their own way as Sukhovo-Kobylin's *Trilogy*, the majority encompass universal human behavior. This universality, however, has a social and political orientation reminiscent of Ionesco and so eminent an exponent of the absurd in Eastern Europe as the Polish writer Sławomir Mrożek. In contrast to Beckett, fundamental ontological questions are not raised.

Despite Amalrik's obvious links with a prior Russian tradition of the absurd and grotesque and his indebtedness to Ionesco and Beckett, the complexity of his plays sets him apart. Strange configurations of character and incident often make interpretation a matter of intuition or impression. In this respect, Amalrik resembles, though distantly, Beckett and Pinter more than Ionesco or Mrożek. This special kind of obscurity derives, I believe, from the work of the Oberiu dramatists Kharms and Vvedensky. In *Elizabeth Bam*, Kharms creates so complex a work involving a number of seemingly unrelated and disparate elements that the only sense one can extract is a kind of Kafkaesque doom. Vvedensky's anti-Christmas play, *Christimas at the Ivanovs*, is composed in a similarly fragmented and puzzling way. Behind this technique is the aesthetics of surrealism and it is the merging of both the surreal and the absurd that gives the little plays of Amalrik their special flavor.

When we turn to the more conventional plays of Solzhenitsyn, we have to bear in mind that his dramatic writing represents a small part of his total literary output to date. The situation was different with the other dissidents whose plays we have examined. Remezov's one major work so far is *Is There Life on Mars?* and while Amalrik attracted considerable attention with *Will the Soviet Union Survive Until 1984?* his plays are no less important and may prove more durable than the pamphlet, especially after 1984. With Solzhenitsyn, the obverse is true. His reputation rests on his novels *One Day in the Life of Ivan Denisovich*, *The Cancer Ward*, *The First Circle*, *August 1914*, and his account of the Soviet secret police and penal system, *The Gulag Archipelago*. If his plays attract any attention, it is primarily because of the fame of the other works and, of course, the worldwide interest in his summary expulsion from the USSR in mid-February 1974.

Solzhenitsyn has so far written three plays: *Olen i shalashovka* (*The Love-Girl and the Innocent*), *Pir pobediteley* (*The Feast of Conquerors*), and *Svecha na vetru* (*Candle in the Wind*). Only two of these have been published: *The Love-Girl and the Innocent* and *Candle in the Wind*. *The Feast of Conquerors*, an unflattering picture of aspects of the Soviet army during and after World War II, was composed in verse while Solzhenitsyn was in a labor camp and later transcribed from memory. Solzhenitsyn contends that he destroyed all copies of the play except one which was removed from his archives by the secret police and distributed by them in order to damage him.

The first play, *The Love-Girl and the Innocent*, is the most stageworthy of the two that have been published. It was written in 1954 and was rehearsed by the Sovremennik in Moscow in 1963. However, it never received official approval for production and was dropped from the theater's schedule. Both it and the weaker *Candle in the Wind* appeared in print for the first time in the Russian émigré journal *Grani* and thereafter in the fifth volume of a collected edition of Solzhenitsyn's works published in Frankfurt, Germany, in 1967. Both are available in English: *The Love-Girl and the Innocent* in a translation by Nicholas Bethel and David Burg was published in London in 1969; *Candle in the Wind* was translated by Keith Armes and Arthur Hudgins and published in Minneapolis in 1973.

The Love-Girl and the Innocent is set in a Soviet prison labor camp in

1945 and thus operates with much the same kind of material as Solzhenitsyn's now famous novel *One Day in the Life of Ivan Denisovich*. In fact,
the play can be viewed as an extension of the novel, although it is not
simply a dramatization of it. As in most of his other writings, Solzhenitsyn's plays consider fundamental questions of human life and morality.
The Love-Girl and the Innocent deals with the place of morality in the
harsh circumstances of a Soviet labor camp. Interest centers on the adjustment of a former army officer, Nemov, to camp life and on his relationship with another recently arrived inmate, Lyuba, the love-girl of
the play. The plot itself is thin. Nemov, an intellectual with a strong
sense of honesty and decency, is given the job of camp production chief.
But his approach is at variance with the inefficiency, waste, greed, and
corruption all around him at the camp, from the commander on down.
Instead of accommodating himself to the prevailing conditions, Nemov
tries to proceed as he would in a normal situation. The results are predictable and disastrous. He is squeezed out of the position to make way
for someone more pragmatic, and therefore Nemov becomes just another working prisoner.

Like much of Solzhenitsyn's writing, *The Love-Girl and the Innocent*
seethes with irony. Although relieved of the moral burden of a camp job
which demanded a corruption that Nemov could not propagate, he is
perversely rewarded by his return to the ranks of ordinary workers. In
an accident at the camp foundry whose unsafe production methods
Nemov tries to improve for the sake of other prisoners, he nearly loses
his life.

The greatest challenge to Nemov's code of personal morality and the
most bitter irony of the play involves his relationship with Lyuba.
Coarse, cynical, and morally flexible, the girl provides an interesting
contrast to Nemov. And possibly because of their differences, they are
attracted to each other. Nemov soon falls in love with Lyuba, despite
hints from other inmates that she is a love-girl, that is, a female prisoner
who is willing to trade her body to improve her material lot in camp.
Again, the inevitable occurs. Lyuba catches the eye of the camp doctor,
who proposes to her that she become his "wife" in return for his protec-
tion, meaning a light work load and a steady food supply. Lyuba accepts,
but because of her feelings for Nemov she suggests that if they are
discreet they might continue to see each other from time to time. The
dilemma for Nemov is painful. His love for Lyuba is too great to be denied or limited by rare, secret meetings, yet he cannot bear the thought
of sharing her with the doctor. In the end, his sense of moral right

triumphs and he rejects her proposal. Shortly afterward he is nearly killed in the foundry accident. In the final scene of the play, while Nemov is recovering from his accident, Lyuba enters the doctor's quarters, removing her scarf, thus symbolically signaling the end of her relationship with Nemov and the start of her new life with the doctor.

The relationship between Nemov, Lyuba, and the camp doctor distantly echoes that of He, Consuella, and the Baron in Andreev's *He Who Gets Slapped*. Like He, Nemov is an upright, honorable man whose decency brings him only suffering. His need to love and to find beauty amidst wretchedness, hypocrisy, and deceit leads him, like Andreev's character, to invest his emotions in a woman unworthy of him, and to whose banality he is blind because of his idealism. With Lyuba, as with Consuella, this romantic attachment is subverted by the woman's susceptibility to material blandishments. In both cases, moreoever, idealism and nobility are rewarded only with suffering and deprivation, although far less drastically in Solzhenitsyn's play than in Andreev's.

Despite fundamental differences between the Solzhenitsyn and Andreev works, a certain similarity of outlook exists. In *He Who Gets Slapped*, Andreev almost perversely traces the subversion of the main character's belief in idealism and nobility and his faith in the power of beauty to elevate man. Here banality and hypocrisy triumph as surely as they do in Chekhov. In Solzhenitsyn, the problem is formulated more precisely in moral terms, but the philosophical posture is much the same. In a world of evil and injustice, a man can survive only by compromising his moral principles and by retreating from his nobility. If he chooses instead to remain true to them, he risks bringing down his own destruction, as is the case specifically with Nemov. Even love is no more than an illusionary good since it becomes a deeper source of moral anguish. The sufferings of both He and Nemov are intensified because of their unwillingness to make the moral compromise that love demands. Rather than surrender Consuella to the materialism that the Baron represents to He, he chooses to destroy both the girl and himself. Solzhenitsyn's Nemov refuses to share Lyuba with the camp doctor because of his own moral sense of right; as a result, he loses irrevocably the only happiness he has known in the camp, the only joy that has made his imprisonment bearable.

The love motif in *The Love-Girl and the Innocent* is important for two reasons. First, its use reflects, I believe, Solzhenitsyn's awareness of the emergence of romantic love as a dominant theme in Russian literature of the "thaw" period of the 1950s; remember that *The Love-Girl and the Innocent* was written at least as early as 1954. In this respect, it can be related to this major development in post-Stalinist Russian literature. Second, the love motif is inextricably bound up with the play's central issue of morality and conscience. It becomes, as it were, the supreme test of Nemov's moral courage and strength.

Whatever its importance in the overall intellectual fabric of *The Love-Girl and the Innocent*, love never loses its identity as a component related to the play's setting. That is, it is part of the life of a labor camp, and it is this life that Solzhenitsyn has set out to portray above all else in his play. The detailed, novelistic stage directions and the variety of characters, accents, and events all serve to bring vividly to life onstage the experience of a labor camp.

So concerned is Solzhenitsyn with setting and with the creation of the atmosphere of the camp that he not only makes use of lengthy stage directions but he introduces as well techniques characteristic of the new theatricalism of Russian drama of the late 1950s and the 1960s. This is best seen in the lengthy prefatory note on what the audience will see as it enters the theater:

> The audience will walk from a brightly-lit foyer into the darkened auditorium. In here the only light comes from a number of tinplate hooded lanterns which are placed, almost like crows, on a semicircle of posts right along the edge of the orchestra pit. The posts are quite low, so as not to interfere with the audience's view of the stage. They are wrapped with barbed wire which vanishes down into the orchestra pit. The center post carries an indicator to mark the dividing point in the field of observation from the two nearest watch-towers.
>
> There are two camp watch-towers standing to the right and to the left of the arch of the stage. Throughout the play the towers are manned by sentries.
>
> The curtain rises. It is an ordinary theater curtain, but is not used again until the end of the play. Behind it there is a second curtain—a length of fabric crudely painted with a poster-like industrial landscape, depicting cheerful, apple-cheeked, muscular men and women working away quite effortlessly. In one corner of the curtain a joyful procession is in progress complete with flowers, children and a portrait of Stalin.
>
> To start the show a loudspeaker plays a lively melody from a concertina. It is the march from the film *The Jolly Fellows*.
>
> As the curtain is raised the melody is taken up by an actual concertina-player, sitting quite far back in the stage by the camp gates.
>
> Behind the curtain one can hear the harsh sound of a crowbar banged against a metal rail.

The camp zone lanterns go out. They are not re-lit until the last
scene of the play.[9]

When the painted curtain falls at the end of the first act and before it
rises on the second, a brief interval occurs during which Solzhenitsyn
uses one of the most common theatrical devices by having the actors
move into the audience. The stage direction indicates quite clearly that
the purpose is to continue to involve the audience in the camp atmosphere:

> During the interval, though not immediately after the end of the
> act, there is a change of sentries on the towers at the side of the
> stage. Having relieved one sentry, the guard party marches down
> into the stalls and across the auditorium in front of the first row. If
> members of the audience are in their way, the officer shouts at
> them rudely, "Get back from the wire! Stop crowding!" Then they
> relieve the other sentry. (p. 54)

The same activity is repeated in precisely the same way at the end of
the second and third acts. The play itself ends with the dumb scene of
Lyuba entering the camp doctor's cabin. As the door opens to let her in,
one can see her shadow in the windows as she removes her scarf. Then
the painted curtain falls, concluding the play. The auditorium of the theater remains dark, however. The only light comes from the lanterns on
the barbed wire around the orchestra pit. This time the sentries on the
watchtowers do not move. The loudspeaker introduced at the beginning
of the play starts up a tune. Throughout the departure of the audience,
the overhead lights in the theater remain off and the regular stage curtain is not lowered. Nothing is done to dissipate the atmosphere of the
play as the audience leaves the auditorium.

The significance of the arrangement of the curtains at the end of the
play should also be noted. Throughout, Solzhenitsyn operates with two
curtains, the ordinary stage curtain and the second, inner curtain,
painted as described in the prefatory note with the all too familiar Socialist Realist scene. As we have seen, much of Russian drama since the
death of Stalin strives to expose the gap that exists between the official
representation of Soviet life and the reality of that life in its unvarnished
state; it is in this light that Solzhenitsyn uses the painted inner curtain to
contrast the reality of labor-camp existence with the idealized portrayal
of the workers' paradise. The continued suspension of the ordinary curtain at the end of the play, leaving only the inner curtain in view, can be
seen as the crown that caps the overall irony of the play.

Related to the use of the inner curtain as a device of ironic contrast but more obviously theatricalist in character is the play-within-a-play of Act III, scene 3, "The Concert." The stage setting is arranged to include a small crude stage on which two performances are to be presented by several of the camp inmates. The first is a farcical Soviet sketch with a World War II setting. The other is the play *Volki i ovtsy* (*Wolves and Sheep*) by the nineteenth-century Russian dramatist Aleksandr Ostrovsky. Through the character Gontoir, a Belgian intellectual who came to Russia after the Revolution only to end up imprisoned in the labor camp, Solzhenitsyn is able to contrast the false art of Socialist Realism represented by the war sketch with the promise that was held of a great free Russian art which would be liberated by the creative energies of the Revolution. Commenting on the sketch, Gontoir asks, "Is this the kind of art we used to dream about? We were so enthusiastic back in 1919. We came to young Russia to create the neo-theater, the first in the history of mankind . . ." (p. 104).

Earlier, Gontoir had attempted to entertain his fellow inmates by reading a passage from Tolstoy's *War and Peace*, but the reading fell mostly on deaf ears as few in the audience paid any attention or could appreciate it at all. Gontoir refuses to be discouraged, however. "Insist on believing," he says, "that beauty elevates human beings. I keep wanting to cheer them up, to tell them that there is more to life than work parades, searches, and prison soup."

Solzhenitsyn's irony has a twofold aspect at this juncture. He clearly sympathizes with Gontoir's idealistic conception of art and his repugnance at the banality of much of Socialist Realism. Yet at the same time the "Concert" episode demonstrates his belief that where survival is of paramount concern, art cannot be a substitute for food. When one inmate reports that an extra supper of one jam roll and two spoonfuls of boiled rice per person will be given to the players for their performances, the talk turns immediately to food, and art is forgotten. In conditions of repression and deprivation, the idealistic and noble concept of art for art's sake becomes as false and unreal as the grotesque distortions of the idealism of Socialist Realism.

Solzhenitsyn's second play, *Candle in the Wind*, has the subtitle "The Light That Is Within You," a biblical allusion reminiscent of some of Tolstoy's later works. This play has much less theatrical potential than *The Love-Girl and the Innocent*. With a non-Russian setting, a simple division into six untitled scenes (unlike the more classical act and scene division of the first play), an absence of a descriptive list of characters, and far fewer and less-detailed stage directions, *Candle in the Wind* is a static work consisting primarily of dialogues on morality and science.

The play opens as the protagonist, Alex, has come to visit his uncle, Maurice, after a fifteen-year exile. Nine of the fifteen years were spent in prison together with a friend for a murder which they did not commit and for which they were eventually pardoned. Alex then spent a number of years teaching school in a town near the prison, where life was so primitive that he says it resembled a "stone age." Maurice regards these years as lost, but Alex views them as beneficial in teaching him to differentiate between the necessities and luxuries of life.

The more Alex talks, the more his views on life resemble those of Dostoevsky and Tolstoy. With Dostoevsky he shares a belief in the spiritual value of suffering and with Tolstoy he shares an esteem for the simple and essential elements of life. By contrast, Uncle Maurice is egocentric and hedonistic. Now seventy years old and a famous musician, Maurice has been married three times, each time to a girl of eighteen. He has lost contact with his daughter, Alda, an emotionally fragile and vulnerable person, whom Maurice veered away from a musical career toward a comfortable, secure, and traditional family life. However, besides abandoning her career in music, she has failed as a wife; in fact, she has been married twice and divorced twice.

Alex and Maurice are soon joined by Philip Radagais, a neighbor of Maurice and, it appears, the friend of Alex who had been wrongly sentenced with him. Solzhenitsyn draws another contrast now, between Alex and Philip. The latter is ashamed of his prison experience, despite the fact that he was innocent and was subsequently pardoned, and he seeks to conceal the stigma of his past beneath a successful career as the head of a biocybernetics laboratory. Alex, on the other hand, values the spiritual benefits of his imprisonment and later life in the primitive penal community and he has since come to suspect the values of materialism and science. Philip defends science for its contribution to the material betterment of man; it is, for him, the soul of the twentieth century. Arguing that material benefits do not really improve man, Alex rejects science as being soulless. At the end of the first scene, the limitations of science are poginantly demonstrated by the information that Philip's wife is wasting away from an incurable disease. Despite his misgivings about science, however, Alex agrees to join Philip's laboratory.

The personal relationships and inner workings of the laboratory extend the debate concerning science and its place in man's life, initially introduced by Alex and Philip. Two camps emerge. Philip and his scientific friends contend that every truth is concrete and that every ethic is relative. However, the antagonists, who oppose the hegemony of science, doubt the ability of science to reshape the character of man and to assume the decision-making role of human conscience. Holding the latter view are Alex, the African student Kabimba, to whom science means a loss of national identity, and Alda, who has undergone a treatment of cybernetic neurostabilization in Philip's laboratory to enable her to overcome her hypersensitivity and nervous disorders.

The disagreement reaches its peak at the party given in honor of a visiting general from whom Philip seeks to obtain funds to support his laboratory. Toward the end of the party, Maurice's wife, Tilly, arrives and informs Alda that her father is dying. On his deathbed, Maurice voices regret over the materialism and petty self-concern of his life. Alda plays a Schubert melody while her father dies, and Aunt Christina, an old eccentric with whom Alda lives, comes in with a candle to recite biblical verses from St. Luke, from which the play's subtitle is derived.

The symbolism of the candle is clarified when Alex confesses to Alda, after Maurice's death, that he now feels that it is his mission "to carry the wavering candle of the soul to the twenty-first century." Although this suggests an irreconcilable break with science, Alex leaves Philip's laboratory in order to join a rival institute headed by the social cyberneticist Terbolm whose conception of science does not negate the conscience and who in fact aims to make science relevant not only for the mind, but for the soul as well. At the root of Terbolm's system is the desire to discover certain laws in human society by which algorithms can be constructed and progress charted on an electronic machine, thereby eliminating the time-consuming and natural process of social trial and error. In the meantime, Alex has received a tape recording from Terbolm in which Terbolm seeks to remove Alex's remaining doubts about the possible reconciliation of science and conscience. Part of the tape is a recording of the voice of Philip's wife, Nika, who is dying in a hospital and pleads with him to visit her.

The playing of the tape is followed by a mute scene which ends the play just as the wordless scene is used at the end of *The Love-Girl and the Innocent*. The scenes in both plays have a certain resemblance. In the first play, Lyuba's entry into the doctor's cabin and her removal of her scarf mark the definitive end of her affair with Nemov and the full acceptance of her new role as a love-girl. In *Candle in the Wind*, Alex remains standing in a mood of depression after listening to Terbolm's tape. He is saddened by Philip's callous treatment of Nika, which only confirms his feelings about the kind of science promoted by Philip and his associates, and he is frustrated by his failure to persuade Alda, whom he loves, not to resume the stabilization treatment interrupted by Maurice's death. As Alex lingers over the tape, the Schubert melody from Maurice's deathbed scene can be heard faintly from somewhere. Unseen by him, the doleful figure of Alda, draped in mourning garb, comes up and looks at him sadly for a few moments through a window before slowly moving away with lowered head. As in *The Love-Girl and the Innocent*, the unspoken scene at the play's end marks the triumph, at least for the time being, of the false gods. When Lyuba enters the camp doctor's cabin, it is her weakness of spirit and her need for material security that have guided her steps. This, to Solzhenitsyn, damns her and destroys the love between her and Nemov. Alda, too, seems to vacillate briefly before turning her back on Alex and returning to the false world of Philip and his laboratory. Here the weakness is the need not for material but rather emotional security. Despite Alex's urging that she not resume the stabilization treatment, she so fears a life still capable of touching her that she returns to her therapy. So, like Lyuba, she spurns the proffered hand of spiritual independence and, in walking away from Alex, separates herself from love as well.

As dramatic art, *Candle in the Wind* leaves much to be desired and compares badly with *The Love-Girl and the Innocent*. It is a very long play concerned with ideas and lacking any kind of propulsion. Dynamic plotting is also negligible in *The Love-Girl and the Innocent*, but by way of compensation the play offers an intimate glimpse of a dreadful milieu, a variety of sometimes striking characters, and an idiom unusual in Russian drama. The non-Russian, vaguely Anglo-Saxon setting of *Candle in the Wind* contributes nothing to the play other than to reflect Solzhenitsyn's desire to project his moral philosophy onto a more universal plane. Apart from the scientific character of much of the dialogue, there is nothing in the diction of the play to warrant any special attention. With the exception of Alex, characters are important only as vehicles for ideas or as symbols of a particular life style, as is the case with Maurice and Tilly. Even so potentially effective a character as Alda is not fully developed nor is her relationship with Alex given the degree of depth necessary to make of it more than a device of structure. Scenes are not as well balanced as in *The Love-Girl and the Innocent*, which affects the play's rhythm; and the death scene of Maurice is discordant and too melodramatic. Music (the Schubert melody, for example) is used occasionally to create a mood in *Candle in the Wind*, but without the ironic bite that makes it more effective in *The Love-Girl and the Innocent*. Like most "thesis" plays, whatever appeal *Candle in the Wind* exerts is intellectual rather than artistic. Just as *The Love-Girl and the Innocent* developed out of the experiences and ideas explored more fully in *One Day in the Life of Ivan Denisovich,* so *Candle in the Wind* reflects the concern over science, morality, and man's happiness manifest in Solzhenitsyn's major novels.

In *The Love-Girl and the Innocent,* conscience and suffering are inextricably interwoven but together they become the crucible in which the true life of the spirit is forged. In *Candle in the Wind* it is shown that a science which refuses to take cognizance of that spirit is false and hence has no place in man's world. By recognizing the need for conscience and thus an innate moral law and by seeking to combine a belief in conscience with the enlightened social cybernetics of Terbolm, a type of science evolves which Solzhenitsyn can approve. To eliminate science from life is neither desirable nor possible, as *Candle in the Wind* makes abundantly clear. But a science that dehumanizes man by refusing to accept the spiritual dimension of his being must be exposed as the enemy of man. In repudiating Philip's biocybernetics, Alex tells him that as a scientific system it utlimately must fail because it is an "intrusion into the most perfect thing that is on earth—man." Terbolm's science, on the other hand, "dares to bring reason where only chaos and injustice have reigned eternally, to intervene in the most imperfect of all human constructs—human society" (p. 202). When it seeks to reshape man's environment, that is, human society, science can be as necessary to man as his conscience, for it holds forth the promise of eradicating from life the chaos and injustice that inhibit the growth of the spirit. But when science seeks instead to reshape man himself, it denies him the control of spirit and so becomes the desecrator of his immortal dignity.

SIXTEEN

From Dissent to Divertissement: The 1960s and 1970s

WITH Solzhenitsyn's expulsion from the Soviet Union in 1974, the subsequent emigration of several literary malcontents including Amalrik, and the increasingly effective efforts of the authorities to curb and undermine the protest movement in the country, the once dynamic dissident writing of the 1960s and early '70s seems to have run its course, at least for the time being. What the future may hold obviously cannot be predicted; in the meantime, the few years that have gone by since the resettlement in the West of Solzhenitsyn, Amalrik, and others permit a more balanced appraisal of the dissidents' literary achievements.

In the drama, by far the most interesting development was Amalrik's conscious linkage of his own absurdist style with the earlier Russian tradition of absurd and grotesque satire from Gogol to the NEP playwrights of the 1920s, on the one hand, and with the surrealism of the short-lived Oberiuty group of the late '20s and early '30s, on the other.

Despite the official discouragement of all manifestations of avant-garde art, Amalrik's revival of a domestic tradition of the absurd and grotesque was paralleled in the second half of the 1960s and early 1970s in the work of younger dramatists unaffiliated with the protest movement in the USSR, as exemplified by the careers of two of the most original Russian writers of the past decade and a half, Vasili Aksyonov (1932–) and Aleksandr Vampilov (1937–72).

A medical doctor by training, Aksyonov began his literary career in the late 1950s as one of several younger Soviet writers who rose to prominence after the death of Stalin and became identified with the new "Young Prose" movement in Soviet literature and the journal *Yunost* (*Youth*), founded by Valentin Kataev in 1955.[1]

Aksyonov's reputation rests primarily on such novellas about adolescence and growing up in the Soviet Union as *Colleagues* (1960), *A Ticket to the Stars* (1961), *Oranges from Morocco* (1962), and *It's Time, My Love, It's Time* (1963). In his later writing he has tended to move away from social problems and the everyday idiom of contemporary Soviet youth toward the grotesque and fantastic with far ranging stylistic experimentation. This departure in literary technique has also been accompanied—perhaps even inspired—by a conscious reassimilation of the Russian avant-garde literary heritage of the 1920s—a phenomenon previously observed in the case of Amalrik.

These newer literary concerns of Aksyonov found a felicitous creative outlet in dramatic writing before they became manifest, in fact, in his prose fiction. To date, Aksyonov has two plays to his credit—*Vsegda v prodazhe* (*Always on Sale*) and *Vash ubiytsa* (*Your Murderer*).

Although neither play has yet been published, they have become known through production in one case and translation in the other. *Always on Sale* attracted considerable attention when it was staged at the Sovremennik Theater in Moscow in 1965 under the direction of Oleg Yefremov; *Your Murderer* was published in English translation in New York in the Spring 1977 issue of *Performing Arts Journal*.

Employing a variety of theatricalist and avant-garde techniques, many derived from popular culture (songs, dances, masks, film, TV, and so on), both plays are satires rooted in a darkening vision of an increasingly conformist society. While a realistic setting and particularized Russian social types situate a play like *Always on Sale* within the grotesque tradition of Mayakovsky and NEP, the theatrically more striking *Your Murderer* assumes a greater universality through its parable form reminiscent in some ways of Faiko and Shvarts in Russia and of the later Brecht and Ionesco in the West.

Subtitled "An Antialcoholic Comedy in Eight Scenes with a Prologue and Epilogue," *Your Murderer* has a tropical, vaguely Spanish-American setting and characters. The play's central figure is the writer Alexandro, who stubbornly resists the efforts of the powerful octopuslike Masculinus whisky company to dominate society by getting everyone to drink their product. When his opposition—which we can see as the attempt by a creative artist to maintain integrity and independence in the face of conformist pressures—serves only to isolate him, Alexandro despairs and tries to commit suicide by throwing himself beneath the luxurious foreign car being driven by friends who have left him to join forces with Masculinus. Interpreting his survival as a sign that he has been spared in order to make common cause with Masculinus, Alexandro follows his friends' example. His principal contribution is the creation of a popular idol, a folk hero, who will promote the universal drinking of Masculinus whisky. A brilliant television campaign featuring the ingratiating man-of-the-street humor of Alexandro's concoction, Pork Sausage, scores great gains for Masculinus. But when Alexandro sees the lawlessness and even the killing Pork Sausage inspires, he decides to do away with his own creation by not writing any more speeches for him.

The attempt to destroy Pork Sausage fails, however, and the monstrosity reappears in a variety of guises from that of a delivery man to the Director of Public Harmony. Finally, it is Alexandro who is killed by electrocution, but in the surreal fantasy style of Oberiu drama. When his body is dumped on the stage's proscenium at the end of the play, his girl friend Maria asks him if he is dead and he replies that it seems so. It depends on the fictional characters he had created for the novel he has been writing; if they are dead, so is he. When he cannot think up a happy ending for his fictional work, his characters disappear.

The play's Epilogue is set on the same tropical island of the Prologue. The island represents an alternative society to the besotted one dominated by the Masculinus Company and Alexandro and his friends have come to it seeking refuge. As they cluster around the Freedom Tree, which is to inspire them to create the True and the Beautiful, Alexandro shakes it for the coconuts on which they sustain themselves. Out of the tree comes tumbling the head of Pork Sausage, which declares that it is an intrusion by life, by ordinary capitalist reality. Alexandro and the others play soccer with it until they finally kick it offstage. Shaking the tree again, Alexandro brings down a hail of multicolored parachutes laden with all kinds of food as well as two lovely bathing beauties. The last parachute to descend bears a huge dark bottle with its neck wrapped in silver foil. Greeting it with a "hurrah," Alexandro announces that it is a bottle of Soviet champagne—and on this note of patent mockery the fantasy parable ends.

Aksyonov's indebtedness especially to NEP literary traditions in *Your Murderer* comes through audibly in the echoes of Olesha's novel *Envy* (1927). With its similar theme of the tragically futile attempt of the individual to preserve his identity in the rapidly collectivizing and depersonalizing society of the new socialist state, and its surrealistic-expressionistic style, *Envy* was a natural source of inspiration.

The symbol of the conquering collectivist principle in *Envy* is the grotesque figure of Andrei Babichev, the Director of the Food Industry Trust, who revolutionizes the industry and resolves the food supply problem by inventing a special kind of salami that is nourishing, clean, and cheap. As the narrator of *Envy*, Ivan Kavalerov, says of Babichev at one point: "He is a statesman, a Communist. He is building a new world. And the glory in this new world flares up when a new salami is delivered by a salami man."[2] Pork Sausage's role in the Masculinus-dominated society of Aksyonov's fantasy is fundamentally analagous to that of Andrei Babichev's super salami in *Envy* and it would be hard to imagine that the concept did not derive from the latter work.

Aksyonov doubtless knew *Envy* but seems likely to have also known Olesha's dramatization of the novel under the title *The Conspiracy of Feelings* at a time when his own literary interests were strongly directed toward the drama.[3] The play version of the novel, notable above all for its intensified expressionistic character, was first staged in a stunning production at the Vakhtangov Theater in Moscow on March 13, 1929. The work proved immensely controversial and was soon denounced for its "decadence" and expressionism. Although it has not been staged in the Soviet Union since 1929 it was published there for the first time in 1968, that is during the period of Aksyonov's preoccupation with dramatic writing. Cognizant of Olesha's courageous defense of the rights of the individual and the creative autonomy of the artist in Soviet society, Aksyonov could easily have been attracted to both the form and the subject of *The Conspiracy of Feelings* when it appeared in print in 1968 and been stimulated by it to devise his own play along similar lines, *Your Murderer*, in the form of a fantasy.

About the same time that Aksyonov began writing plays in the fantastic and grotesque style which was to characterize his later prose fiction as well, another writer of the same generation, the Siberian Aleksandr Vampilov, made his own debut in the drama. Until his untimely death by drowning in 1972, Vampilov seemed clearly destined to become the outstanding dramatist of the contemporary Russian stage.[4]

A graduate of Irkutsk University, Vampilov worked as a journalist on local newspapers gaining valuable literary experience in this way as well as from extensive traveling. After the publication of a collection of humorous stories (*A Concatenation of Circumstances*) with which his career as a writer of fiction began, he soon turned to the drama and in 1962 wrote a one-act comedy called *Dvadtsat minut s angelom* (*Twenty Minutes with an Angel*); the play was not published until 1970—in the literary almanac *Angara*. It was followed in 1964 by the one-act comedy *Dom s oknami v pole* (*The House with a View of the Fields*), the two-act comedy *Proshchane v yune* (*Farewell in June*; written in 1965, published

Scenes from the original production of Yuri Olesha's A Conspiracy of Feelings *by the Vakhtangov Theater, Moscow, in 1929.*
(H. W. L. DANA COLLECTION OF THE HARVARD THEATRE COLLECTION)

in 1966), the two-act comedy *Starshy syn* (*The Elder Son;* written in 1967, published under the original title of *Predmeste* [*The Suburb*], in *Angara* in 1968 and under its present title as a separate edition in 1970), the three-act drama *Utinaya okhota* (*Duck Hunting*, written 1967, published 1970), the one-act play *Istoriya s metranpazhem* (*An Incident with a Typesetter;* written 1970, published 1971), the incomplete two-act vaudeville *Nesravnenny Nakonechnikov* (*The Incomparable Nakonechnikov*, the first scene of which was published in the Irkutsk paper *Sovetskaya molodyozh* [*Soviet Youth*], on September 23, 1972), and the two-act comedy *Poslednym letom v Chulimske* (*Last Summer in Chulimsk*, published in 1972).

A sketch of Vampilov's literary career suggests certain superficial parallels with Chekhov's: his debut as the author of humorous short stories, the progression to comic one-act plays, his writing of full-length plays incorporating techniques of the stories and shorter plays. The Chekhovian parallels become more substantive when the plays are more closely viewed. Inspired, like Aksyonov, by prior Russian literary traditions, Vampilov inclined not to the fantastic-grotesque satirical tradition of Gogol, Sukhovo-Kobylin, Mayakovsky, and others, but rather to the tradition of Russian farce and vaudeville going back certainly to Gogol's *Zhenitba* (*Marriage*) but deriving more immediately from the dramatic "jests" (*shutki*) of Chekhov.

This orientation is apparent in the first play of Vampilov to be staged—*Provintsialnye anekdoty* (*Provincial Anecdotes*)—and in *The House with a View of the Fields*. *Provincial Anecdotes* is the title now given to the combination of the one-act comedies *Twenty Minutes with an Angel* and *An Incident with a Typesetter*. The two small plays were brought together, with revisions, and mounted as a single production for the first time on March 30, 1972, at the Leningrad Bolshoy Theater under the direction of G. Tovstonogov. The production was then called *Dva anekdota* (*Two Anecdotes*). It was staged under the same title in Moscow in May 1974 by the Sovremennik Theater and acquired its present title for the collected edition of Vampilov's plays in 1975. *The House with a View of the Fields* was first staged in 1974.

As the more amusing of the two *Provincial Anecdotes*, *An Incident with a Typesetter* provides a good point of departure for a consideration of Vampilov's farcical style.

The privacy of a female guest (Viktoria) in a provincial hotel is disturbed when a male guest asks if he can borrow the radio in her room in order to listen to a soccer match since his is out of order. She agrees, but he soon returns declaring that the radio does not play in his room so he must listen in hers. Almost immediately thereafter the hotel manager appears and orders the male guest to leave on the grounds that by being in the woman's room he is violating a hotel code. Besides, he suspects that the relationship is anything but innocent. With Viktoria's complicity, however, the male guest, Potapov, sneaks back but again is prevented from hearing his game in peace by the reappearance of the manager, Kaloshin, before the door to the room can be locked.

Potapov's movement back and forth from his room to the young woman's, the central absurdity of the radio that will play only in her room, and the transition of the quarrel with Kaloshin from verbal to physical (Kaloshin finally succeeds in throwing him out) quickly evoke the tempo and humor of farce and vaudeville.

Potapov's abrupt departure from the hotel sets the stage for the dramatic jest proper and the intensification of the farce style. In about the only reflection of an aspect of Soviet society in the play, hardly does Potapov leave the hotel when Kaloshin worries that perhaps he threw out an important person. From the hotel register he learns that Potapov is a "metranpazh," but he has no idea what the word means; nor does anyone else he asks. With Viktoria's help he decides that Potapov must be employed by some big newspaper from the capital or may perhaps even be an official from some ministry.

When efforts to locate Potapov fail, Kaloshin loses his wits and takes to the bed in Viktoria's room, where he happens to be at the moment. His wife's discovery of him there, followed by a shrieking bout between her and Viktoria and various strategies to rouse Kaloshin from the bed produce the play's wildest scene. Eventually, Kaloshin learns that a "metranpazh" (from the French *mettre en page*) is a printshop compositor or typesetter, regains his sanity, and reconciles with his wife. As the comedy ends—in a parting farcical touch—Potapov reappears to announce that his favorite soccer team won the match, while Kaloshin swears that he will get out of the hotel business.

Although propelled along an essentially similar if less madcap track, *The House with a View of the Fields* introduces lyrical, romantic elements and a pervasive bittersweet mood which extend virtually throughout the rest of Vampilov's dramatic writing. When we reach Vampilov's last—and best—work, *Last Summer in Chulimsk*, we shall see how close he was able to approach the style of Chekhovian drama without sacrificing or seriously compromising his own individuality as a creative artist.

Outwardly spare in the manner of Chekhov, *The House with a View of the Fields* derives its title from the house of a young woman director of a rural dairy farm which happens to be the last on the way out of town with a fine view of nearby fields. The little play is about the departure from the town of a teacher of geography who has put in a three-year tour of duty teaching in the provinces. Baggage in hand he makes the rounds of the townspeople and finally comes to the last house, that of the dairy farm director. Attracted to the woman, the teacher lingers longer in his farewell to her until the appearance of a chorus of singers under her window makes his departure out of the question. The young woman feels that if the singers see the teacher leaving at a late hour her marital prospects will be impaired. When the people in the chorus finally disperse, and the coast is clear, the teacher decides he really doesn't want to leave, not that day anyway, and so informs the bus driver who comes looking for him.

The comedy's situation is humorous and vaguely recalls Chekhov's *The Bear*. But unlike Chekhov, in the farces anyway, Vampilov mutes the furious bustle and farfetchedness of farce in order to accommodate a lyricism generally unmarked in Chekhov's dramatic writing until the major full-length plays. Although not thought of as a writer in the newer Soviet Russian rural tradition of Belov, Shukshin, or Soloukhin, Vampilov nevertheless has a very real, even profound affection for nature, its beauties and harmonies, if not primarily for rural life as such. In *The House with a View of the Fields*, for example, the leave-taking between the young woman and the teacher approaches the character of a dialectic over city life as opposed to rural life. Touching an emotional substratum of which the teacher himself has been largely unaware, the young woman accuses him of having slept away his three years in the town in the sense that for all the time he was there he remained peculiarly unresponsive to the nature around him. In contrast to cities in which people are proud and vain and unaware of what others are thinking, everything in the country is open, clear, and known in the sense of eternal verities. As elsewhere in Vampilov, reflecting a key aspect of Chekhovian technique, space plays an important role. In the woman's house from which he sees only fields—thus nature—and nothing of the greater world beyond, the teacher seems to perceive the meaning of the young woman's words and at last dares to confront his own emotional nature and the hithertofore ambiguous feelings toward the woman that barred a relationship between them.

Frivolity and awakening self-realization again interact in Vampilov's first full-length play, *Farewell in June*, which underwent several revisions before its production by Tovstonogov at the Moscow Dramatic Theater in the Name of Stanislavsky in 1972.

At the outset, the play again appears slight. A young man (Kolesov) tries to pick up a girl (Tanya) at a bus stop and take her to a friend's wedding party. She refuses and Kolesov goes off alone. The wedding party itself becomes a boisterous affair with a guest's boorish behavior prompting the bride to call the whole thing off. Kolesov's eventual appearance adds another dimension of lighthearted boisterousness: he is arrested for having disrupted a well-known singer's performance in a wild attempt to get her to go to the wedding party with him. Although the singer appears to intercede in his behalf, Kolesov is expelled from the university by the rector who, it turns out, is Tanya's father. Regarding Kolesov as a prankster and hooligan, the rector makes a deal with him, agreeing to permit him to reenter the university on the promise that he will leave his daughter alone. Kolesov agrees, finishes his exams, and receives his diploma. When a graduate student appointment is dangled before him on the further condition that he promise to leave Tanya, whom he now knows he loves, alone forever, Kolesov agrees once more. But during a second celebration of the bridal couple who have since reunited, Kolesov publicly tears up his diploma thereby repudiating his pact with Tanya's father. The union of the young lovers now seems at hand, but Vampilov chooses to end the play ambiguously. Kolesov and Tanya meet again as at the beginning of the play and he asks her to go with him. Again she refuses and as the curtain descends they remain standing a few steps away from each other, perhaps to come together finally or, more likely, to part forever. Kolesov and Tanya both experience an awakening but the play's ambiguous ending suggests that self-awareness is often achieved at a price; aware now of who they are and the choices open to them, they can only glide past each other.

A similar transition from levity to seriousness in the context of an emotional coming-of-age occurs in Vampilov's next full-length play, *The Elder Son*. The play had its première in November 1969 at the Irkutsk Dramatic Theater under the direction of another major Soviet directorial talent, N. P. Okhlopkov, and a Moscow production in 1972.

For the first of its two parts, *The Elder Son*'s antic humor and improbabilities keep it well within the pale of Vampilov's—and Chekhov's—dramatic "jests." Two young men (Busygin and Silva) accompany girls they met the same day to their homes in the sticks. When they dally too long to catch the last public transportation back to the city, the boys plead with the girls to put them up overnight. The girls refuse and the boys then go asking—in vain—for a night's lodging of several people in the neighborhood. When they spot a local musician (Sarafanov) leaving his own house to pay a call on the older woman with whom his son Vasenka is infatuated, they seize on the idea of taking shelter in his house for at least as long as he is away. On a ruse they gain entry to the house and then raise their prank several powers higher when they declare to Vasenka that Busygin is his brother from an earlier relationship between Sarafanov and Busygin's mother toward the end of World War II. The "news" hits Sarafanov himself like a bolt out of the blue, but when he overcomes initial incredulity he recognizes the possibility and even probability of the story. Romantic subplots involving Sarafanov's real children, Vasenka and Nina, and dissension between Busygin and Silva, who remains ever the glib prankster, flesh out the play and provide much hustle and bustle. But Sarafanov's eventual acceptance of Busygin and Busygin's awakened compassion for Sarafanov as a human being lift the play from a sprightly comedy of situation into a good example of modern tragicomedy.

Out of love for his "sister" Nina and a mixture of sympathy and compassion for Sarafanov—who is on the verge of losing his children—Busygin confesses the truth, first to Nina, and when Silva in anger unmasks him to Sarafanov, to his "father" as well. But the interaction of play and life has created a new reality with the result that Sarafanov truly accepts Busygin as a son and wants him to live with him. Busygin declines, promising to visit the day after and every day after that, but as the play ends there seems little doubt that Busygin has found a new home and Sarafanov a new son. In a symbolic gesture, Sarafanov gives Busygin the silver snuff box that always went to the eldest son in the family.

Following a pattern of his earlier dramatic writing, Vampilov finds the intertwining of farcical frivolity (here the initial prank of the fun-loving, carefree Silva and Busygin) and poignancy (the sadness and isolation of Sarafanov) the appropriate dramatic context in which to portray (in Busygin) yet another illumination of self-awareness that permits a transcendence of self and an identification with the needs of others.

Vampilov's next play, *Duck Hunting*, was written in 1967, published in 1970, long unstaged in the USSR, but produced to good reviews at the Arena Stage in Washington, D.C., in May 1978. Despite its favorable reception in this country, *Duck Hunting* falls below the level of Vampilov's previous works. At times witty, clever, and ironic, the play is also uneven, overworked, and in places clumsy. The central character,

Stanley Anderson in the lead role of Zilov in the 1978 production of Aleksandr Vampilov's Duck Hunting *by the Arena Stage, Washington, D.C. Directed by Zelda Fichandler.*
(ARENA STAGE)

Zilov, was doubtless intended as another study of egocentricity and selfishness, but the overcrowding of incident and the technical fussiness of multiple phone calls and flashbacks detract from rather than enhance the play's effectiveness. All of Zilov's practical joking, selfishness, and callousness concentrate on a single point—his determination not to let anything stand in the way of his going on a duck hunting trip during his upcoming vacation. His obsessive selfishness and cynicism eventually cost him the affection of his friends and the love of his wife. Once again, an illumination of self-awareness occurs: cognizant of his frightening isolation Zilov contemplates killing himself with the same gun he planned to use on ducks. But the urge for self-destruction dissolves into a paroxysm of hysterical crying and laughing, and when the rays of the sun at last break through the clouds and rain which impose a mood of gloom on the play to this point, Zilov regains his composure and decides to go duck hunting after all. The ending of the play is weak and an audience can only speculate as to whether Vampilov intended to suggest—as his other plays might lead one to believe—that Zilov has been "reborn" by the trauma of his near suicide or that after the duck hunt he will resume his old pattern of relationships. Only fitfully convincing, *Duck Hunting* lacks the simple earnestness of Vampilov's better efforts and probably for this reason has been the least staged of his major plays.

Before his death in 1972 Vampilov managed to complete the play that is justifiably regarded as his best work, as well as one of the best Russian plays of the contemporary period, *Last Summer in Chulimsk*, and an attempt at a full-length vaudeville, *The Incomparable Nakonechnikov*, which remains incomplete.

Last Summer in Chulimsk, which has proven a great stage success since its première in 1974 at the Bolshoy under Tovstonogov's direction, makes us more keenly aware of the significance of Vampilov's loss for contemporary Russian drama and the Soviet stage. It is Vampilov's wisest and warmest play and the one in which in some ways he comes closest to fulfilling the Chekhovian expectations of him.

Set in and around a tavern in the kind of small Siberian town Vampilov knew well from personal experience, the lives of several people follow a seemingly random, uneventful path until gradually and unobtrusively the disconnected segments interlock and a pattern of Chekhovian tension surfaces. One web of emotional intrigue involves the managers of the tavern, the quarrelsome husband and wife team of Afanasi and Anna and her illegitimate son, the resentful, possessive, violence-prone Pasha whom she bore to another man while already engaged to Afanasi. Reminiscent more of the dark family secrets of Ibsen and Gorky than Chekhov, the relationship between these three characters seethes with an anger threatening to explode from beneath the surface at any moment. Another relationship focuses on the uncertain romance between Zina, a young divorcée of lighter virtue who lives in the tavern, and a troubled (and married) court investigator named Vladimir Shamanov. Like Afanasi's Anna, Shamanov also bears a burden from the past in the form of a sense of personal failure at his inability to bring in a conviction against the son of a prominent official who killed someone in an automobile accident. As if an outlet for his frustration or a menacing foreboding of self-destruction, Shamanov carries around a revolver which he prominently displays to Zina, who hates the sight of it. Guns appear elsewhere in Vampilov's plays and seem to be an "inside joke" alluding to the prominent melodramatic motif of the gun in Chekhov. Shamanov's gun takes on a more immediately sinister role later in the play, but although no one is ever in fact shot, the firearm enables Vampilov to use it as a signal for Chekhovian association and yet as an irony pointing to the differences between his own dramatic style and that of Chekhov.

As the play of apparently unrelated private dramas progresses, it becomes obvious that the catalyst for the meshing of the separate narrative currents will be the waitress Valentina. Young, attractive, shy, and tentative in her relations with others, she is frequently observed in a Chekhovian defining action of mending a fence gate that is forever getting unhinged by people's laziness at trying to pass around it rather than opening and closing it properly. In a potentially unstable environment Valentina's constant attention to the gate indicates a desire to impose order, stability, perhaps even a moral structure on her surroundings and in so doing she becomes the play's one wholly positive character.

Dramatic conflict arises when Zina and Pasha observe a scene between Valentina and Shamanov that leaves little doubt as to a romantic feeling between them. Much like Chekhov, the relationship between Valentina and Shamanov or, more precisely, Valentina's feelings for the man, are handled by Vampilov with indirection, sublety, and the use of the dialogue more to mask than reveal the emotional undercurrents of the speakers.

Soon the mechanism of evil is set in motion by the passion of jealousy. Covetous of Valentina himself, Pasha has a nasty confrontation with Shamanov, who at one point gives Pasha his gun and exhorts him to pull the trigger. When he does, enraged, the hammer clicks but the gun does not fire and Pasha staggers off like a drunk.

Attention shifts next to Zina's intrigue to disrupt the budding romance between Valentina and Shamanov. Here distant echoes of Turgenev's A Month in the Country commingle with those of Chekhov's plays. Recalling Yelena's attempts, in Turgenev's play, to palm her ward Vera off on a well-to-do merchant because she is jealous of the younger woman's relationship with the tutor with whom Yelena herself is infatuated, Zina plots to encourage a marriage between Valentina (who is eighteen) and a fortyish, heavy, bald, altogether ludicrous member of a local Trade

Union Committee named Mechetkin, who speaks in a natural falsetto voice which he cannot hide. Playing cleverly with his vanity after laughing off as absurd his proposal of marriage to her, Zina steers Mechetkin in Valentina's direction. When Mechetkin woos and wins support for his suit from Valentina's taciturn, somber father, Pomigalov, the web of conspiracy around the young girl tightens.

As in Chekhov, a minor incident moves the play toward its final resolution of anticipated but thwarted violence. To placate Pasha, Valentina agrees to go with him to a dance in a nearby town. Shortly after they leave, Mechetkin comes in looking for her followed by a hopeful Shamanov who had sent her a note earlier that day proposing a nighttime rendezvous; Zina, however, intercepted the note and made sure that Valentina knew nothing of its existence. Upon learning from a distraught Anna that Valentina went with Pasha to a dance, Shamanov hastens off in pursuit of them. The pace of the play now matches the buildup of melodramatic suspense—the more intense for the concentration of the action within a classical twenty-four hour period.

Stirred up by Mechetkin, Pomigalov hops on his motorcycle and races off to find Valentina, whom he believes to be with Shamanov. Moments later, the reentry of Valentina and Pasha leaves little doubt that Pasha either had attacked her or made love to her against her will, which he confesses to Anna, who pleads with him to go away. As Valentina, too, urges him to go, Zina comes in and belatedly delivers Shamanov's note. Then Shamanov returns and a tender scene with Valentina ensues. The moment of greatest tension in the drama—after the gun play between Pasha and Shamanov in the first part—occurs when Pomigalov rides in on his motorcycle and demands to know where and with whom Valentina has been. Both Shamanov and Pasha step forward each to declare that Valentina was with him. Knowing the violence her father is capable of and fearing the worst, Valentina becomes a captivating study of submissiveness and courage as she declares that she was with neither Shamanov nor Pasha, but with Mechetkin (whom, as we know, Pomigalov approves of as a marital prospect). The tense atmosphere of expectant violence dissipated, with no further ado Valentina says nothing else and goes home with her father.

The following morning is typical Chekhovian anticlimax, marked also by a familiar Chekhovian pattern of departure. Pasha is about to leave; so, too, is the colorful old Siberian indigene Ilya, who refuses to press a law suit against her daughter who abandoned him, preferring instead to find solace in the woods he knows so well; and finally Shamanov, chastened by his experience, having passed through another Vampilovian crisis of self-knowledge, now anxious to return to the city to testify in the upcoming trial of the man he lacked the fortitude to convict earlier. The dialogue in the last scene is all Chekhov: fragmentary, trivial, real feelings kept suppressed beneath the weight of words. Silence, again in the manner of Chekhov, breaks off the dialogue when Valentina enters. All eyes fix on her. Hardly uttering a word, she makes her way to the gate of the fence, which is again out of place, and in a symbolic act admirers of Chekhov would have no trouble recognizing, hangs it back on its hinges with the help of old Ilya.

By their originality and provocativeness, Aksyonov and Vampilov stand in the forefront of Russian dramatists of the generation that came to prominence after the death of Stalin. Their revival of styles of Russian drama going back to Chekhov as well as to nineteenth- and early twentieth-century vaudeville, farce, and absurd or grotesque satire delineates distinct patterns of Soviet Russian dramatic development. But to appreciate the fact that these are neither the only—nor even the predominant—patterns of dramatic writing in the Soviet Union at present we have but to consider the work of a popular writer of the same generation as Aksyonov and Vampilov, such as Mikhail Roshchin (1933–   ), as well as the more recent plays by older dramatists such as Viktor Rozov and Aleksei Arbuzov, who are still commanding presences in the Soviet theater.

Roshchin's greatest success to date has been his play *Valentin i Valentina* (*Valentin and Valentina*, 1971). With its subject young love amidst generational conflict, its use of a split stage for simultaneous action, and characters acting as narrators and/or commentators for scenes in which they themselves have no parts, *Valentin and Valentina* easily relates to the tradition of the new dramatic lyricism and theatricalism of the late 1950s and '60s. That this type of drama still holds its own as well as it does on the Soviet stage attests to the continuing enthusiasm for a literature largely free of the ideological and heroic and devoted mainly to honestly depicted contemporary social problems, above all the attitudes of the young toward their parents and toward society in general, and relations between the sexes—again mainly of the young and younger adults but occasionally of older people as well (as we shall see later with Arbuzov).

Roshchin's *Valentin and Valentina*, which premiered at the Moscow Art Theater in 1971 in a production directed by Vladimir Kuzenkov, can be regarded as paradigmatic of the "youth theme" in contemporary Soviet fiction. Valentin and Valentina are both eighteen years old and very much in love. They even want to marry. (Young couples in the USSR have little opportunity to live together outside of marriage, and even when married have a hard enough time getting housing.) But there are obstacles. Their friends make fun of them because they want to marry at such a young age and their parents are even more inhospitable to the idea. If literature and the drama are any reasonably faithful reflection of present-day Soviet society, then the efforts of parents to dissuade their children from early marriage are rooted in their own failures and disappointments. When Soviet writers turned away from heroic and mythic subjects and undertook, especially after the death of Stalin, to portray contemporary society more candidly than ever before, they exposed what can only be regarded as a crisis of married life manifest in a progressively higher rate of divorce and the frequency of separation. The literary evidence is certainly overwhelming. Consider Roshchin's *Valentin and Valentina*, for example (and there will be further examples to consider in the plays of Rozov and Arbuzov).

Valentin's mother sounds the frequent Soviet parental complaint about long hair, jeans, the amount of money spent on pop records, and so forth and so on, and tries to dissuade her son from a premature assumption of the heavy responsibility of marriage. Since we never see Valentin's father we can assume that his mother is a woman alone. Nothing has to be assumed in the case of Valentina's mother. Much of her extreme antagonism to her daughter's romantic relationship with Valentin has to be attributed to bitterness caused by her husband's abandonment of her and their two daughters. As if the mother's experience might not be enough, Roshchin introduces the figure of Valentina's older sister Zhenya, who has already been married and divorced and is now involved with a married man. With the example of Zhenya before them and fearing the worst with Valentin and Valentina it is hardly to be wondered that Valentina's mother and grandmother fret as they do about young people's morality. From their point of view, the fault lies, in part, with the fascination of Soviet youth with foreign ways and values. Displaying his own fascination with the modish cosmopolitanism of literary allusion and quotation of contemporary Soviet drama, Roshchin has one of his characters quote Pushkin on the fact that what is good for London is too early for Moscow. Literary citations balance each other out in *Valentin and Valentina*, however, and just as Pushkin is enlisted in the campaign to curb the enthusiasm of Soviet youth for things foreign, so Freud, Saint-Exupéry, and Aleksandr Blok are quoted in defense of love and fidelity to one's emotions.

A scene from the production of Mikhail Roshchin's Echelon *by the Alley Theatre of Houston, Texas, in 1978. The production was directed by the visiting Soviet director, Galina Volchok, of the Sovremennik Theater of Moscow.*
(ALLEY THEATRE)

The trials and tribulations of Valentin and Valentina come to a head when the girl leaves home and is taken in by Valentin and his mother. When Valentina's mother and sister arrive to claim her, an ugly confrontation erupts, with the mother going so far as to concoct the story that the girl's grandmother is dying. Predictably, however, true love conquers all. Drawing on her own experiences, Zhenya urges her younger sister to heed their mother's words no longer and to go to the man she loves—which is exactly what she does. At the end of the play, with music in the background and poetry by Blok on the magic of love quoted by a Passerby to set the stage for their union, Valentin and Valentina meet on a bench, exchange light banter, and bring down the curtain with a burst of wholesome youthful laughter.

Roshchin's success in his own country with a "slick" youth play like *Valentin and Valentina*, which combines by now commonplace pseudo-modernist Soviet theatrical techniques with an equally commonplace but popular subject of self-assertive youth and the power of love, has been paralleled by the interest in him abroad. In the United States, for example, there have already been productions of *Valentin and Valentina* and Roshchin's newer play *Echelon*. *Valentin and Valentina* was staged by the American Conservatory Theater (ACT) of San Francisco in 1977. Although the work was directed by an American, on hand to lend their support at the time were Roshchin himself and Oleg Yefremov, now the head of the Moscow Art Theater, who directed one of the Moscow productions of the play.

The American stage debut of *Echelon* is still more interesting. On her visit to the Soviet Union in May 1977, Nina Vance, the founder and head of the Alley Theatre in Houston, Texas, saw and was favorably impressed by Roshchin's play and the production of it at the Sovremennik Theater by Galina Volchok. On invitation from Vance, Volchok came to Houston and spent six weeks preparing the Alley's company in what amounts to a reproduction of the Moscow production. As T. E. Kalem pointed out in his *Time* magazine review of February 6, 1978, "this is the first time that an American audience has had an opportunity to see a Russian play in English as it appears before audiences in the Soviet Union."[5]

Roshchin's skill at using stage effects to lend a facade of greater substance to characters who rarely develop beyond types and to familiar subjects chosen for their appeal to audience emotion is also evident in *Echelon*. The play is about the Soviet use of special trains to evacuate women and children to the East during the German advance in World War II and is based on experiences shared by Roshchin and his mother, to whom the work is dedicated. Although the action of the play is static, confined to the interior of a boxcar, the stage effects—whether those written into the text by Roshchin or achieved by Volchok in her production—create an undeniable sense of movement and the endless tedium of an interminable boxcar ride over vast stretches of territory in wartime. Moreover, the boxcar setting itself, with one side open to the audience, creates a pervasive sense of near claustrophobic cattle-car confinement that intensifies the emotional and psychological reactions of the women aboard.

Like the bulk of Soviet literature about World War II, *Echelon* has a definable ideological foundation lacking in *Valentin and Valentina*. If the latter play is a commentary on the relations between youth and adults in contemporary Soviet society, then *Echelon* revives the patriotic mythico-heroic traditions of Soviet revolutionary and war drama. The underlying purpose of the play is to show both the suffering of the Soviet civilian population during the war and its heroic ability to endure. Clever stage effects informed with a patriotic hymnlike tone would hardly be enough to explain the play's popularity. What they provide is an appealing frame for Roshchin's tapestry of varied female types (again *types* rather then three-dimensional characters) and their individual reactions to the oppressiveness of their circumstances.

On the "serious" or "heavy" side are a dying woman, a woman who has been driven mad by the absence of her husband, a pregnant woman who gives birth, a hysterical nursing mother, a woman factory worker who has experienced worse misery in the first world war and tirelessly strives to bolster others' flagging spirits, and the car commander herself, who has her own problems but makes a conscientious effort to keep her group from dissolving into complete despair and hysteria. For the sake of a little "lightness" in the otherwise somber situation and mood, Roshchin rounds off his cast of characters with a Moscow "playgirl" (as she calls herself) with a fondness for the bottle and a lusty appetite for sex, and her opposite number, a prim and prissy spinster whose self-assured singleness crumbles in one revealing outburst of desperate loneliness.

Between its stage devices and the novelty of its emphasis on women enduring the hardships of war somewhere in a no-man's land between the front lines and the home front, in movement through time and space yet as if in the static, confining wretchedness of a camp, *Echelon* provides moments of affective theater. It attempts a more original treatment of the war theme, but its commonplaces and tonality deprive it of real dramatic distinction.

Experimentation with techniques of farce and vaudeville, a revival of absurd and grotesque satire, neo-Chekhovian drama, and provocative stage effects have considerably extended the range of Russian dramatic writing in the 1960s and 1970s. Yet the majority of plays conform to established patterns of social (as opposed to Socialist) realism in content and style. There is a marked lessening of ideology, often no discernible ideological purpose at all, an attempt to portray social conflicts and problems earnestly, and a continued commitment to the rights of individual feelings.

These tendencies are all very much in evidence in the works not only of younger Russian playwrights just coming to public attention, but also in the plays of older established dramatists such as Viktor Rozov and Aleksei Arbuzov, who continue to be as prolific as they are popular.

Looking at some of Rozov's more recent plays we find much the same interest in moral strength and courage, in the portrayal of men and especially women discovering (usually in moments of crises) and summoning previously unrecognized and untapped reservoirs of inner strength and purpose. Again, the locus of conflict is the family with environment in a physical as well as psychic sense as important in illuminating character as in Rozov's earlier dramatic writing.

Two of Rozov's plays (contained in the collection *Moi shestidesyatye, My Sixties*, Moscow, 1969)—*V den svadby* (*The Day of the Wedding*) and *Zateynik* (*The Social Director*)—feature portraits of strong women who succeed in finding the inner resolve to spurn temporary happiness for the sake of moral integrity as well as love.

In *The Day of the Wedding* the return after a long absence of a woman whom her fiancé once loved convinces the bride, Nyura Salovaya, that her bridegroom, Mikhail, is still in love with her. Despite the embarrassment that the refusal to go through with the wedding will surely cause her in the small Volga city in which the play is set, Nyura chooses honesty and integrity in preference to marriage to a man who wants to marry her but who obviously remains in love with another woman. The flight from marriage on the day of the wedding makes for a tense drama of personal conflict, a tension exacerbated—as in the nineteenth-century Russian dramatist Aleksandr Ostrovsky's major work, *Groza* (*The Storm*, 1860)—by the provincial milieu in which the events take place.

To a great extent, *The Social Director* is a variation on the same theme, except now the female protagonist is already married. As the drama unfolds, we learn that once upon a time Galina and Sergei were in love but that Galina was pressured into marrying another suitor, Valentin, by his father, a public prosecutor. Some years later at a Black Sea resort Valentin comes across Sergei working there as its social director. Sergei harbors no ill will toward either Galina or Valentin and the encounter is friendly. But when Valentin asks Sergei for a key to his room so that he can spend some time in private with a woman he met at the resort, Valentin's moral shabbiness is established. This premonition of marital strain is confirmed upon Valentin's return. Wanting Galina to love him Valentin is ever trying to embrace her, but is always repulsed. As if to bury a haunting and divisive memory, Valentin tells Galina that while at the Black Sea resort he did hear from someone who knew

Sergei that he had died. When she becomes visibly upset, he reveals the truth but then at once lies again by telling her that Sergei is alive but unsuccessful, shabby, old-looking, and reclusive. The malice is compounded with additional lies—first, that Sergei is married, then that he is having an affair with the woman Valentin, in fact, kept company with. Seeing through his lies, realizing the lie of her marriage to Valentin, and at last summoning the courage to act decisively for love, Galina determines to go to Sergei at the expense of the comfort and security she has in her present life. Repentantly, Valentin's father seconds her decision.

The play's subplot is structured on a contrastive device previously encountered in Russian drama of the post-Stalin period. Valentin's cousin Edward, who is twenty years old, marries his girl friend, Tamara, against his mother's wishes. The situation repeats that of *Valentin and Valentina*. But the Edward-Tamara relationship as subplot has a didactic role in relation to the play's action. As usually the case in the Soviet "youth" literature of the 1960s and '70s, the young people have minds of their own, are unafraid of responsibility, and ask only that adults have faith in them. By standing up to opposition and finally overcoming it for what he believes in—love, in this instance—Edward does what Galina failed to do years before. The young people in the play, as elsewhere in Rozov, avoid the mistakes of their elders and in turn become models for them. That Galina understands this herself is indicated clearly when she asks Edward how he would react if someone threatened to arrest him if he did not give up Tamara.

For a dramatist who is as concerned with the details of his characters' physical environment as Rozov is, it is quite natural that objects often acquire symbolic meanings or functions. In *The Social Director* it is the malfunctioning toy train that Valentin's father plays with. Throughout the play Edward offers to repair it but is spurned by the old man, who has no trust in the youth's ability. He changes his mind, however, after supporting Galina's decision to rejoin Sergei. As if compensating, in part, for his earlier mistreatment of Galina, the old man now offers Edward and Tamara all the help he can. In a symbolism in need of no explanation, Galina's departure at the end of the play coincides with Edward's skillful repair of the old man's train.

Another play from the *My Sixties* collection, *Traditsiony sbor* (*The Reunion*), deals with material similar to that of *The Day of the Wedding* and *The Social Director*, but from a somewhat different angle and in a theatrically more interesting structure. A woman is again the center of focus—Agnia Shabina, an up-and-coming literary critic and successful doctoral candidate who is as ruthless as she is clever. Materially, she has everything she needs for happiness—a good career and a comfortable marriage—but she is not happy. Why? Because her thirst for success led her to dissolve a previous marriage to a man she obviously still loves.

Success or failure in a career, in a material sense, occupies Rozov's attention in this play as in others. For a social dramatist as concerned with moral values as Rozov, the preoccupation is natural. But Rozov is not only a keen observer. He has a definite point of view which his plays propagate as if a corrective to the prevailing bourgeois strivings of contemporary Soviet society, and that is that success, interpreted materially, is seldom achieved without the moral compromises Rozov is personally unwilling to accept. That is why "successful" people in his plays are usually unscrupulous and morally bankrupt and, conversely, why his sympathies with people judged failures by the materialistic standards of contemporary society—Sergei in *The Social Director*, Shabina's first husband, Sergei, in *The Reunion*, and Kim in the later *From Night till Noon*—are never difficult to discern.

The event referred to in the title of the play *The Reunion* is a jubilee school reunion in Moscow, which Rozov uses to bring together a heterogeneous group of people who have only one thing in common—the secondary school they attended—and who have not seen one another for a long time.

When the reunion finally occurs, the inevitable contrasting of present realities and past expectations endows the play with a certain dramatic interest supported by the spatial aspect of the school setting and its associations with youth. But the reunion's principal importance is its usefulness to Rozov as a device to bring together Shabina and her first husband, Sergei, whose easygoing nature and inability to satisfy her craving for success compelled her to end their marriage. The reunion with Sergei in a setting calculated to engender thoughts of the past, of the early days of their marriage and their love, leaves little doubt that Agnia's feelings are fundamentally unchanged. The point is made in the play's most emotional scene, near the end, when the singing of old school songs to the accompaniment of Sergei's guitar playing succeeds in bringing tears to her eyes. When her present husband remarks enthusiastically that it is the only time he has ever seen her cry, he is in effect commenting on her life—a life so dedicated to success defined as professional stature that it leaves little room for the kind of sentiment evoked by Sergei's songs.

Loath, as ever, to end a play on a downbeat, Rozov brings onstage just before the final curtain a young boy and girl who arrive to clean up after the jubilee guests have left to resume again their separate ways of life. As she waters the flowers on the window sills, the girl notices that a new bud has appeared on a crocus and excitedly runs to tell the boy of her discovery. As the curtain descends, the young pair—representing the youth which is forever the source of Rozov's optimism—remains silently contemplating the blossoming flower, itself a frequent symbol in Rozov's plays of the poetry without which a life, like Shabina's, can never be whole.

Agnia Shabina is Rozov's obvious center of interest in *The Reunion,* but one of the play's subsidiary characters deserves separate mention. That is the gas station attendant Maxim Petrov, who also attends the reunion. In his early forties, Petrov is a decorated World War II hero who became an incurable drunk when postwar reality caught up with him and he discovered that his decorations were not enough to secure the future for him. When we meet Petrov in the play, not only does he comment cynically on aspects of Soviet life but, more boldly, draws unfavorable comparisons between Soviet and American ways of doing things. When a customer tells him that cars are much better serviced at gas stations in the United States than in the Soviet Union, Petrov replies that it is not hard to understand why: first of all, the station attendants are afraid that if they don't provide good service they can lose their jobs in the batting of an eye, and then that money is worth something in America.

What Rozov intended with Petrov is hard to say. In the spirit of the "unvarnished" treatment of society in post-Stalinist Soviet literature, negative aspects of contemporary life are often brought to light in direct and indirect ways. The emphasis on professional and material success in Soviet society is portrayed in an unfavorable light by the character of Agnia Shabina in *The Reunion.* It is what Shabina represents as a contemporary social phenomenon rather than what she says specifically that implies a negative commentary on prevalent Soviet social values. With Petrov, however, the criticism is direct and blunt, yet hedged in a sense by the fact that the critic is a self-confessed disgruntled drunk; in other words, Petrov has an ax to grind and need not be taken seriously. Furthermore, he has many antecedents in Soviet literature, especially in the 1930s, when the individual who for one reason or another could not make a place for himself in post-NEP society turned to drink and periodically relieved his frustrations by sounding off on Soviet inadequacies. Petrov can easily be dismissed as just such another personal failure who has become a malcontent, but his indictment of some Soviet attitudes and institutions, especially in the context in which they are articulated in the play, is not so easily dismissed and doubtless was intended not to be.

The consistency of Rozov's moral concerns and conventional techniques as a dramatist is brought home by a play postdating the *My Sixties* collection, *S vechera do poludnya* (*From Night till Noon*), which Oleg Yefremov produced at the Sovremennik in 1970.

The play is again a family drama and again introduces a couple who have come to a parting of the ways over divergent attitudes toward ambition and success. And again, it is the woman whose ambition has prompted a change of mates. In *From Night till Noon* the wife, Alla, leaves her athletic coach husband Kim, whose dreams of becoming a great track star never materialized, to become the wife of a successful diplomat much of whose career is spent outside the USSR. And like Sergei in *The Reunion*, Kim is unequivocal in condemning his former wife, and people like her, for their pursuit of careers and their abandonment of human values.

Just as in *The Reunion*, success and the lack of it are contrasted on more than a single level in *From Night till Noon*. But Rozov always finds ways of differently configuring the same basic material. In *From Night till Noon*, a distinct pattern of family "failure" emerges, bearing on the resolution of the play's conflict. Kim is a failure in the sense that he has never realized his lifelong ambition to become a great runner; his father was launched by circumstances into the literary career his meagre talent is unable to sustain after a first book, hence, he, too, is a failure; and Kim's sister Nina is an invalid who yearned for marriage and motherhood but lost the one man she loved and who cannot persuade him during a visit to let her become pregnant by him so that she can at least have his child; she, too, has to be reckoned a failure.

The play's conflict is triggered by the reappearance after a long absence of Kim's former wife and her desire to take their young son Albert to London for the summer. The boy is the apple of Kim's eye, and he is afraid that he will lose him if he permits him to be lured away by the more interesting experiences his wife's new life can offer. The boy himself is obedient and will do whatever his father wishes, no matter what his personal preferences may be.

True to a pattern already established in Rozov's other plays, characters judged successful by contemporary social standards are usually portrayed as lacking in humanity, while the "failures" generally are sensitive, compassionate, and morally superior. With one major and one minor variation, *From Night till Noon* adheres to this pattern.

The minor variation is Kim's sister Nina's moral lapse when she proposes to her patently opportunistic former boyfriend that he at least leave her with child. Her request, however, is an act of desperation on the part of a physically and emotionally crippled woman who will never know the kind of life she dreams of; her friend's refusal to accommodate her only heightens the poignancy of the scene. Circumstances, therefore, mitigate Nina's moral breech.

The major variation, where it comes as something of a surprise, is Alla who, despite the pursuit of a more interesting and successful life style, is not portrayed as either demonstrably opportunistic or unfeeling.

The acid test of Kim's moral fiber is his decision regarding Albert's trip to London with Alla. At first, he refuses adamantly; but as the play ends he summons the courage to act in accordance with his conscience. He permits the boy to go, knowing that to hold him by intimidation would be to lose him permanently and that the boy must mature into a young man on his own and have the opportunity to expand his consciousness.

From Night till Noon has a seemingly happy ending—Albert is going to London for the summer with his father's blessings and at least a temporary reconciliation has been effected by the previously estranged Kim, Alla, and Albert. But the upbeat ending is a distraction, because the overwhelming condition of frustration in the lives of Kim, Nina, and their father is actually exacerbated at the end of the play when the common source of joy—Albert—leaves them. By having Albert go off with his mother, Rozov may be hinting at a permanent relocation and the boy's definitive break from the pattern of frustration of his father's family. Yet with the final curtain, the muted anguish of Kim, Nina, and their father, all of whom know only loss, is unresolved. In the final analysis, its happy ending notwithstanding, *From Night till Noon* is pervaded by a mood of embittering frustration that is hardly typical of Rozov and may have come about unwittingly by his overstatement of a case argued in more positive terms in his other plays.

Usually linked with Rozov as the most durable major talent of Soviet Russian dramaturgy is Aleksei Arbuzov. His output shows no signs of diminishing even though he is now in his seventies and to his steady popularity at home can be added his reputation abroad as undoubtedly

the Soviet Union's best-known contemporary dramatist. His more recent plays were published in the collection *Vybor* (*Choice;* inaptly
named after the weakest play in the collection) in Moscow in 1976.

A multifaceted if not brilliant dramatist, Arbuzov has always been sensitive to the winds of change and willing to step out in new directions.
Both attributes are much in evidence in his newest collection, although
the plays as a group fall below the standards of his previous works.

Less preoccupied with social and moral issues than Rozov, Arbuzov's
more recent plays concentrate on love. Arbuzov has dealt with the same
subject before in several of his plays; there, however, the emphasis was
on younger people and the changes in relationshps wrought by time.
While the newer plays resist easy categorization, they are notable, in
one respect, for the shift of emphasis from younger people to mature
adults. Moreover, they reflect a widening of Arbuzov's range of characters and a continuing effort to experiment in the area of dramatic genre.
Except for the two-part division now favored by almost all Soviet dramatists, no two plays in the 1976 collection belong to the same genre. The
first play, *Skazki starogo Arbata* (*Tales of the Old Arbat District of Moscow*) is a "comedy"; *Vybor* (*Choice*) is a "drama"; *V etom milom starom
dome* (*In This Pleasant Old House*) is a "vaudeville-melodrama"; *Moyo
zaglyadene* (*My Eye-Catcher*), an "optimistic comedy"; *Vecherny svet*
(*Evening Light*), a "tale for the theater"; and *Staromodnaya komediya*
(*An Old-Fashioned Comedy*), a "presentation."

Trying to isolate an overriding pattern or patterns of structure in Arbuzov is a risky business and the more recent plays only confirm this.
Although he is best known for the long time-span "chronicle" form he
used in *My Poor Marat*, for example, Arbuzov has used too many other
play forms to be readily pigeonholed. If the plays postdating *The Happy
Days of an Unhappy Man* show no distinct architectonic pattern, at least
certain tendencies present themselves for consideration.

One of these tendencies simply continues the earlier pattern of the
"new theatricalism" and "new lyricism" of the late 1950s, and that is the
ample use of musical and choreographical elements to enlarge the visual
and auditory dimensions of the play. To be sure, this vaudevillean am-
plification of the text—which can incorporate pantomime and the recitation of poetry as well as song and dance—is hardly unique with Arbuzov. It represents, as we have seen, certainly an important feature of
Soviet Russian dramatic writing of the 1960s and '70s. Arbuzov, however, was one of the architects of this new dramatic theatricalism

beginning with *It Happened in Irkutsk,* and the fact of his continued use of these techniques in his playwriting of the 1970s is worth noting.

In *In This Pleasant Old House,* which Arbuzov has designated a "vaudeville-melodrama," music and dance pervade the entire atmosphere of the play. The title refers to the pleasant South Russian seaside home of the eccentric Gusyatnikov family, all of whose members, from the oldest to the youngest, are musicians. Constituting their own orchestra, the family lives and breathes music, especially Mozart, passages from whose *Eine kleine Nachtmusik* become a leitmotif of the play. But the Gusyatnikovs are not the only ones in the play with musical associations. Song and dance are also made a part of the life of the actress Julia who is separated from the Gusyatnikovs' son and has now returned to visit their children whom she has not seen in a long time. The warmth of the Gusyatnikov home casts a spell on Julia as surely as the music of Mozart's *Nachtmusik;* she realizes that she still loves her husband and she hopes that he will ask her to stay and become a part of the household once again. But when she learns that he has fallen in love with another woman who has also come to town to meet his children and parents, Julia—as one of Arbuzov's noble female characters who can magnanimously sacrifice her own love for the sake of someone else's—refuses to impede the new relationship and retires from the Gusyatnikov home for good.

Until her final departure, which is accompanied by the fading music of Mozart's *Nachtmusik,* Julia herself is a source of song and dance in the play. When she first appears onstage she hears the music of a nearby restaurant orchestra and sings along with it as she unpacks her bags in a hotel room. The play opens, in fact, much in the manner of a musical comedy and never entirely loses this quality. Later, in the play's second part, at a Gusyatnikov family concert, Julia plays a tape of herself singing, then sings this and other popular songs while dancing or accompanying herself on a guitar. The music she herself brings the Gusyatnikovs is perhaps intended to strike a note of poignancy over her final break with the family and its "pleasant old house," since Julia obviously fits into the atmosphere of the home much more easily than her rival, Nina, who is a dentist. But as we understand Arbuzov's romantic dialectics from other plays, once love has been spurned or abandoned, there is rarely any successful return to the past and an old love has to give way to a new one.

A musical comedy ambience also characterizes the plays *My Eye-*

Catcher and *An Old-Fashioned Comedy*. Subtitled an "optimistic comedy," the first play is the closest Arbuzov has come to outright vaudeville. Composed of pasteboard characters, improbable happenings, absurd situations, farcical humor, and dialogue that alternates between the colloquial and a ridiculously stilted and formal diction, *My Eye-Catcher* recounts the romantic trials and tribulations of a young man named Vasya Listikov and the women in his life all of whom he names Milochka (hence, Milochka-1, Milochka-2, Milochka-3). The opening and closing of the vaudeville-comedy provide enough information as to why Arbuzov calls it "optimistic." The almost too frothy work has a philosophy to convey, you see, and that is that it is good to be alive, after all, and that the game of love (at which one wins and loses) helps make it that way.

This "philosophy" is exemplified presumably by Vasya, who first appears on his way home from work on a bright spring day singing about how happy he is to be alive. In the musical comedy tradition, Vasya sings at other opportune moments as well. When he recalls his mother's hard life and the burdens of womanhood, for instance, he bursts into a touching "Song about Mothers." As the play's first part draws to an end, Vasya recites a "melodeclamation" addressed to the woman he may yet love when he completely falls out of love with his latest Milochka. In the spirit of theatricalism and the music hall, Vasya, now speaking directly to the audience, declares that his new love might even be one of them. Arbuzov's stage directions call for music appropriate to the "mood" of Vasya's songs. Since his "melodeclamation" holds out the promise of romantic hope for the woman Vasya may yet fall in love with, the accompanying music should be "touching." A tongue-in-cheek pseudogloomy quality should inform the music near the end of the play when Vasya announces that for the time being anyway he will not marry Milochka-3 since it is more important for her to go on with her study of classical Greek. The "sad" music intensifies and increases in tempo when Vasya's former wife, Milochka-2, throws out her present lover, Seva, who happens to be Vasya's best friend, and Vasya packs his suitcase in rhythm to it, in a kind of half dance. But the music turns gay and sprightly again as the curtain descends on a song declaring that nice people can still be found on earth and that therefore one should be happy to be alive. True to its origins, the comedy ends as all characters on the stage dance after Vasya on his way out.

A serious play of interlocking social and romantic concerns, *Evening Light*, like the equally serious *Choice* which preceded it, has virtually no musical comedy or vaudeville elements. Where music is totally absent in *Choice*, a play about the moral ramifications of choices made at key junctures in a scholar's life, it does make an appearance toward the end of *Evening Light*. The play is about a potential ecological scandal and the vindication of a fearless newspaper reporter whose writing about it threatens the loss of his job. The resolution of a social problem is followed by a resolution of the play's potential romantic problem when the lovely newspaper archivist Tamara leaves before she can prove a disruptive force in the domestic life of the deputy editor, Palchikov, who supports the reporter. Shortly before the end of the play, as Tamara sails away on a Volga River boat, a band on the pier strikes up a stirring march. As the sound grows louder, everything is bathed in light and the ship slowly passes from sight. In view of the feelings between her and Palchikov, which are never verbalized, Tamara's departure has a melancholic quality to it. Here a recollection of the finale of *The Three Sisters* is inescapable. But the music of the band fades away in the Chekhov play hinting at the fading of the sisters' hopes despite their proclaimed optimism. That the music does not fade away at the end of Arbuzov's *Evening Light* can be explained by the fact that the drama was not intended to close on the sad note of Tamara's departure. The play celebrates a triumph over ecological danger, in the social sphere, and triumph as well over romantic danger in the domestic sphere. Palchikov's wife Inna had left her first husband (Schneider) for Palchikov and resists the love of Kovalyov, the editor who had attempted to suppress the article about the ecological problem, for the sake of the stability of her home. When Kovalyov at one point expresses regret that his love for her is not being reciprocated Inna tells him that "Life comes clearer as the years go by and you see how little everything matters, except work—only that has any value . . ."[6] A similar sense of responsibility motivates Palchikov as well. When he and Schneider—they are friends—go off to console the remorseful Kovalyov after his professional humiliation, they discuss Tamara. Palchikov confesses that although he obviously cares for Tamara he would not leave Inna for her because of the love for Inna of both Schneider and Kovalyov and their loss of her. In other words, apart from any other reasons, Palchikov would not desert Inna out of respect for Schneider's and Kovalyov's feelings and her loyalty to him. The end of *Evening Light* thus hails a twin victory, conveyed by the rousing music of the band on the pier: that of the orchard (another conscious allusion to Chekhov?) and what it represents over the narrow self-interest that wanted to raze it to make room for garages, and that of maturity over romantic emotion. There is irony in

Evening Light, but not the irony of plays like *The Three Sisters* and *The Cherry Orchard.* Here the irony springs from the play's conclusion. In the case of the orchard, nature and beauty prevail over the pragmatic and utilitarian; but in the case of the triangular relationship of Palchikov, Inna, and Tamara, it is reason and sober judgment that prevail over sentiment.

But sentiment cannot be long suppressed in Arbuzov's plays which generally draw much of their sustenance from it. Arbuzov's last play in the 1976 collection, the very popular *An Old-Fashioned Comedy,* abounds in it, as it does in music and dance. Staged on Broadway in January 1978 under the title *Do You Turn Somersaults?* with Mary Martin and Anthony Quale in the lead roles, the "old-fashioned comedy" turns the tables on *Evening Light* by celebrating—more plausibly—the triumph of feeling on the part of two senior citizens who long ago entered the age of reason.

Since the play has only two speaking parts, the poetry, song, and dance which Arbuzov introduces into it put a bright and cheerful aspect on the rediscovery of love by two people in the autumn of their years and also add some flesh to a thin play.

Although little poetry is recited during the performance, it is referred to as a pastime in which the She of the play, Lidia, indulges—along with the singing of songs—at night. Since She is a patient in a Baltic Sea sanatorium, the noctural recitation of poetry helps establish the character's "eccentricity." So, too, do her singing, dancing, and occasional clowning. Like Julia of *In This Pleasant Old House,* She is—or was—an actress who left the stage when war made acting and the theater seem like silly make-believe. Her husband, who eventually left her for a younger woman (what Palchikov could do but does not in *Evening Light*), was a musical clown who brought her into the circus. It was there that she learned the sad-faced clown song-and-dance number she performs in the course of the play, evoking musical comedy as well as circus associations. Song and dance become another high point of the play when He (Rodion, a crusty widower doctor who heads the sanatorium) and She leave a seaside restaurant, where they have celebrated their first night out together. The evening is lovely and they are both happy and tipsy. Finally animated under the spell of the evening and his growing fondness for Lidia, the doctor recalls the dances of his youth and with the music of the restaurant orchestra audible in the background at first clumsily and then more assuredly dances the shimmy.

After his solo performance, both characters move into a valiant Charleston topped off by a romantic waltz that continues to the end of the scene. Unadulterated schmaltz, to be sure, but a great success with audiences fatigued by the conventional fare of Soviet theaters. When the play opened in Washington, D.C., and New York in late August 1977 and January 1978, respectively, American reviewers were quick to note its sentimental sweetness, which sometimes alternates between mawkishness and winsomeness, but had to give Arbuzov his due at bringing such unabashed sentimentality back to the stage in this day and age.

The other outstanding tendency of Arbuzov's recent playwriting, besides its music hall features and its gallery of charming eccentrics, is its use of vaudeville. On the basis of the most vaudevillean of his plays—*In This Pleasant Old House* and *My Eye-Catcher*—we can get an idea of what vaudeville means to Arbuzov as well as to other contemporary Russian dramatists such as Vampilov who have written plays in this vein.

True to its modern origins as a form of romantic situation comedy enlivened by songs and occasional dances, the contemporary Russian vaudeville, like its antecedents in the early nineteenth century, intersperses songs and dances in generally light comedies devoted mainly (but not exclusively) to romantic love. Characters are traditionally one-dimensional, often mere puppets, and devices of plot rather than vehicles for any examination of human psychology. Situations in vaudeville are usually improbable and at times even absurd. The dialogue is mostly colloquial and snappy, though never coarse, since its primary purpose is to enhance the sprightliness of the plot rather than to reveal or probe motivation. Speech is often humorous by virtue of comical misunderstandings or the juxtaposition of incongruous styles. While it is true that the songs in vaudeville traditionally could contain social and political satire, they did not have to and they seldom do in the contemporary Soviet theater. The vaudeville plot customarily turns on one or more romantic misunderstandings which are resolved by the end of the play so that the works conclude happily. Apart from its possible satire, the vaudeville was conceived as a form of popular theatrical entertainment blending together singing, dancing, and romantic fluff with a good dash of hustle and bustle to entertain unsophisticated and sophisticated audiences alike and to spare their minds as little exertion as possible.

Although there are easily discernible elements of vaudeville in *Farewell in June*, *The Elder Son*, and even *Last Summer in Chulimsk—*

including the easily overlooked musical elements in the first two—
Vampilov's one play plainly designated as a vaudeville is the unfinished
The Incomparable Nakonechnikov.

Despite its incomplete state, Vampilov's play establishes some of the
main properties of the genre which we can expect to find later in Arbuzov. The pop singer Eduardov and the barber Nakonechnikov are
pure vaudeville creations, possessing no significance but the comedic.
By making Eduardov a singer whose fame Nakonechnikov hopes to
duplicate, Vampilov accomodates the musical element of vaudeville. Almost as if a mockery of vaudeville itself it is not Eduardov who sings in
the play but Nakonechnikov, who of course lacks all vocal ability. In the
same vein, Nakonechnikov dances, adding a choreographical element to
the musical. The dancing is sheer travesty since the barber can dance no
better than he can sing. Vampilov then extends his mockery by having
Nakonechnikov finally settle on becoming a dramatist. Since he knows
nothing about playwriting, the "instructions" he gets from an only
slightly more enlightened Eduardov are among the play's funnier moments.

Apart from its abundance of musical elements, *In This Pleasant Old-
Fashioned House* assumes a distinct vaudeville character through its romantic complications, its improbability, and its reliance on contrivance.
Hardly does Julia check into a hotel room in the town she has come back
to after a long absence when who should appear to share the room but
Nina, Gusyatnikov's new romantic interest. And to carry the improbability still further, Nina has arrived in town the same day to meet Gusyatnikov's parents and children. With the typical tongue-in-cheek naïveté of vaudeville, both women confide in and encourage one another
without mentioning the name of the man whom they love. For the
vaudeville to be a success, of course, the two women must be kept from
discovering the truth about each other until late in the comedy. To
make the vaudeville more piquant the author has to tease his audience
with suspense by bringing Julia and Nina to the Gusyatnikov house at
the same time on more than one occasion and yet keep them from running into each other. Expectedly, this involves some fast footwork which
Arbuzov handles well up to the last scene of the play, in which Julia has
to hide in a room next door in the hotel to avoid detection at a crucial
moment.

Other common vaudeville techniques appear in the play: mistaken
identity, for example, as when Gusyatnikov initially confuses Julia for
Nina on the latter's first visit to the house; physical humor, as when the

eccentric after-dinner custom of the music-loving Gusyatnikovs of lock-
ing all doors to the house and disconnecting all bells so that they can
enjoy music without outside distraction forces Nina in one scene to
climb through a window to get into and later to exit from the house; and
deadpan naïveté, such as Gusyatnikov's sheer delight that Julia's visit coincides with Nina's since Julia's understanding of love and impressionable nature will enable her to understand what he now feels for
Nina. When Julia speaks of her own desires, her own love, it is apparent
that Gusyatnikov has no real idea what she is talking about; sensing this,
Julia then pretends to be joking.

In This Pleasant Old House, of course, has a serious side to it. That is
Julia's story of a woman who deserted her husband and children for
another man some years previously and now after breaking with her
lover returns to her family ostensibly to visit her children but desperate
to reunite with them and her husband.

Love and the past intertwine in different ways in Rozov and Arbuzov.
In a play such as *The Social Director*, we meet the type of heroine who
can summon the courage at a certain point to rebel against the security
of bourgeois values for the sake of true love spurned in the past. As if in
the nature of a reward, there is a high level of expectation that the
threads of the past can be picked up again. Rozov's *The Day of the Wedding* presents a heroine closer to what we find in Arbuzov, the woman
who is capable of sacrificing her own happiness for the sake of others'
love. When Nyura clearly perceives that her fiancé still loves a woman
out of his past, she prefers to cancel her wedding rather than marry a
man who wants to marry her but still harbors feelings for another
woman.

Arbuzov has given us similar heroines in *Tales of the Old Arbat District* and *In This Pleasant Old House*. In the first play, a young girl accidentally enters the lives of a father and son team of puppeteers. The
father falls in love with the girl and under the spell of this love succeeds
in executing a pair of beautiful puppets of Helen and Paris for an important production of *Helen of Troy*. Unconsciously, the girl has become
the model for Helen and his son, for Paris. The son, who unbeknownst
to his father has become his professional rival, falls in love with the girl
and so becomes a romantic rival as well. When the father erroneously
understands that the girl wants to marry him (instead of his son), he tells
her that it cannot be because of the age difference between them,
among other things. Rather than hurt the father by marrying his son and
thus revealing to the older man that it was the son and not him she con-

templated marrying, the girl chooses to go away on her own. Since she cares for both men, albeit in different ways, she willingly sacrifices her own happiness in order to reconcile father and son. Just before she leaves she pleads with the son not to part with his father. With neither man understanding the other's relationship with the girl, they both agree to work together on the *Helen of Troy* project rather than separately as rivals, and so the girl, by a sacrifice made out of love, has succeeded in bringing father and son together. Although *Tales of the Old Arbat District* has almost nothing of the vaudeville in it, we do notice that a stage direction at the beginning of the play calls for it to be performed in a brisk manner which suggests Arbuzov's desire at least to infuse the play with the gaiety of its conception as a modern fairy tale by means of the tempo of vaudeville.

Julia's sacrifice in *In This Pleasant Old House* is more akin to that of Nyura in Rozov's *The Day of the Wedding*. When she at last grasps her former husband's feelings for Nina and his apparent inability to understand her longing for him and their children, Julia declines to challenge Nina and goes away leaving her rival a clear field. Although Julia still has to be "punished" for her earlier desertion of her husband and children in accordance with the moral principles operative in Soviet literature, her plight at the end of the play does have a touching quality. But poignancy and sentimentality are not Arbuzov's purposes in *In This Pleasant Old House*. By building a vaudeville around the kind of dramatic material out of which he could as well have fashioned a serious play, Arbuzov was doing the expedient thing. But it is precisely the elements of vaudeville—the contrivances and improbabilities, the suspense involving Julia and Nina, the musical motifs in the play, the verbal humor, and the eccentricity of the Gusyatnikov family—that effectively dampen the poignant and in fact divert attention from it.

My Eye-Catcher is pure vaudeville from start to finish and lacks any of the serious undertones of *In This Pleasant Old House* (which may explain the "melodrama" part of the latter play's subtitle). Also advising that the play be performed in a "very animated" manner, Arbuzov loads the work with stock vaudevillean techniques. Vasya and his first wife, Milochka-1, are divorced; she is being "consoled" by Avenir Nikolaevich, an intellectual; Vasya's present wife, Milochka-2, and his friend and coworker, Seva Polonsky, are having an affair in the meantime behind his back; the girl who is soon to be called Milochka-3 has a secret crush on Vasya, whom she has been observing from afar for some time; Vasya falls in love with Milochka-3 and plans to marry her until they decide that she had best finish her Greek studies before getting married. An on-again off-again relationship between an older couple, Auntie Sasha and Valentinov, who are friends of Vasya, adds still more froth as well as an absurdist touch to the comedy.

All this romantic intrigue obviously necessitates a great deal of movement, without which the play would not be the vaudeville it was meant to be. And so, in a manner vaguely reminiscent of Kataev's 1920s farce *Squaring the Circle*, a rearrangement of lovers and living quarters takes place, to last, of course, only until a new configuration emerges. The comings and goings of Vasya, Seva, Avenir Nikolaevich, the two Milochkas, Auntie Sasha, and Valentinov assume an almost kaleidoscopic quality and intensify the improbability factor. Even the standard farcical climbing of walls or crawling through windows is retained, as it was in *In This Pleasant Old House*. At one point, Vasya climbs up a drainpipe to leave a bouquet of flowers on the window sill of Auntie Sasha's apartment. As one might expect, the pipe breaks on the descent and Vasya crashes to the ground.

My Eye-Catcher has some genuinely funny moments in both action and dialogue and through Valentinov and the character of Milochka-3's prominent TV personality father even manages a little mild social satire. But as elsewhere in his dramatic writing, Arbuzov finds it difficult to restrain himself and carries the complications of plot and effects too far. The result, in *My Eye-Catcher*, is a vaudeville so overloaded with romantic intrigues, improbability, and absurdity that it lapses into silliness. And yet, when this silliness—even for a vaudeville—is taken into consideration together with the play's other excesses, the suspicion arises that the whole thing was conceived as a spoof; that Arbuzov's purpose here was not to write a vaudeville so much as to pull out all stops in a parody of the vaudeville form as a contemporary Soviet theatrical craze with which Arbuzov's own sympathies are only partly in line. If this interpretation of Arbuzov's intentions is correct, then the title of the play refers to Arbuzov's *own* enterprise; the eye-catcher is the play.

It may also suggest a link between Arbuzov's "super vaudeville" and the extreme simplicity and sentimentality of his most successful new play to date, *An Old-Fashioned Comedy*. Sentiment is nothing new to Arbuzov's playwriting, but his return to it in so demonstrative a way after the madcap exuberance of *My Eye-Catcher* may have been meant as a calculated exercise in timing signaling that the vaudeville mania was—or should be—coming to an end and that the moment was ripe perhaps for good old-fashioned sentiment. Read in this light, a parallel can be drawn between Arbuzov's *An Old-Fashioned Comedy* and the public response to Erich Segal's *Love Story* in this country. That the "novelty" of sentiment was appreciated when *An Old-Fashioned Comedy* opened in the United States is evident from the opening remarks of Frank Trippett's *Time* magazine review of September 5, 1977: "In this jaded day, it takes nerve to present the shockaholic public with a romance unmitigated by violence, treachery, despair, psychosis or death, not even an ugly disease. A similar risk would be to serve Kool-Aid to cocaine sufferers. Surely the hazard is doubled when the offering is built on the doings of two gerontic specimens who do not even talk dirty or expose any personal equipage more intimate than the inside of an umbrella."[7]

For all the sentimentality of *An Old-Fashioned Comedy*, vaudeville effects, as we have already seen in part, are not entirely dispensed with. The play is sprinkled with song and dance, but they relate far more to the play's sentimental underpinnings than they do to vaudeville. In the case of Lidia, it is true that the character becomes more theatrically interesting because of her circus background. But her poetry recitation, singing, dancing, and clown routines are not just informed with the nostalgia of a happier past. They also serve as weapons in the armor of light-heartedness and eccentricity with which Lidia wages her struggle with loneliness. Thus, the vaudeville elements illuminate both character and situation and as they entertain in their own right they also induce a mood of poignancy.

Much the same is true in the case of Rodion. For most of the play his posture is that of a distant, detached professionalism which arose also in the wake of loss (his wife during the war, his daughter through marriage and a new life elsewhere). No less lonely than Lidia, he hids his loneliness beneath a cloak of fixed routine. When he breaks his routine, breaks through the wall behind which he has immured feeling, and takes Lidia out for dinner he succumbs to the enchantment of the evening and expresses himself in dance. However awkwardly executed, his dancing is at once a return to a happier youth, like Lidia's circus routine, and at the same time a symbolic act of emotional liberation.

The theme of *An Old-Fashioned Comedy*—that of older people overcoming defenses to feeling and discovering or rediscovering in themslves a capacity for love—is again nothing new in contemporary Russian drama. Volodin's use of it in *Five Evenings* and Arbuzov's in *It Happened in Irkutsk* in the late 1950s heralded the advent of the "new lyricism" which has been a major presence in the Soviet theater to the present. The writer Anatoli Sofronov, who has a number of largely mediocre plays to his credit, made it the basis of a more traditional vaudeville in his comedy *Stranny doktor* (*A Strange Doctor*) in 1972. The noteworthy thing about *An Old-Fashioned Comedy* in comparison to these other works is that Arbuzov has taken the theme of older people finding love again—without the intermediary of youth for a change—and used it as the basis for a very simple play of unconcealed sentimentality at a time in Russian drama when such sentimentality within a spare structure would appear anachronistic. This seems all the more striking in view of the continued vitality of farce and vaudeville on the Soviet stage in the 1970s. When we consider Aksyonov's and Vampilov's plays from the 1960s and early '70s and the attempts by long established dramatists such as Sofronov (*A Strange Doctor*; *Starym kazachim sposobem* [*In the Old Cossack Manner*], 1974), Arbuzov himself (*In This Pleasant Old House, My Eye-Catcher*), and even Rozov (*Chetyre kapli* [*Four Drops*], 1974, consisting of four separate "tragicomic" sketches with authorial digressions) to write vaudeville and/or farce, we have a sense of the prominence of these popular comedic forms in contemporary Russian drama.

Conjecture concerning possible reasons for Arbuzov's writing two such radically different plays as *My Eye-Catcher* and *An Old-Fashioned Comedy* within a few years of each other and in such an order must remain only that. Sentiment has always had an appeal to Russian audiences and can be expected to be well represented in Russian drama. Thus, whether Arbuzov really intended *An Old-Fashioned Comedy* as a kind of corrective to the new fascination with vaudeville has to remain a moot point. But just as Russian drama will continue to find a place for sentiment, so too will forms of farce, vaudeville, and musical hall fare continue to be cultivated and for equally good reasons. As audiences have tired of doctrinaire Socialist Realism, romantic heroism, and overt ideological didacticism—and the political climate has begrudgingly permitted an expansion of both content and form—Soviet dramatists have responded accordingly. Reflecting the general situation in contemporary Russian art, traditional Socialist Realism in the drama has give way to critical realism, romantic heroism to romantic as well as un-romantic ordinariness, ideology to sensibility.

From the late 1950s on, the stage has been dominated not by Party activists, idealized workers, and other stalwart figures from the Soviet portrait gallery of positive heroes and heroines, but by a host of ordinary citizens from every walk of life, the successful and the unsuccessful, the fulfilled and frustrated, and above all by young people—indifferent or hostile to ideology, unconcerned about the collective, unmoved by the vaunted ideals of the Revolution, skeptical of the values of their parents, restless, anxious to create a life style of their own, to determine their own futures even at the risk of failure. In the light of these social developments, and—to stress the obvious once again—an appropriate political environment, there should be nothing at all surprising in the emergence of a drama largely free of ideology and addressed to the emotional and even spiritual needs of the individual. Not only has such a drama indeed emerged in the USSR since the death of Stalin, it has been handsomely served by new theaters, such as the Sovremennik, which have come into existence since the 1950s as manifestations of the same ferment.

By the same token, as Soviet audiences have been permited the enjoyment of a drama able to explore the realm of human emotion with greater freedom, domestic conditions have also lent new immediacy to the concept of the theater as sheer entertainment. And in response to this craving for dramatic fare of no demonstrable social purpose, a resurgence of farce and vaudeville has occurred in Russian drama.

Determining the nature of their interaction would be difficult, but it would seem more than a coincidence that the reappearance of farce, vaudeville, and music hall-cabaret fare in contemporary Russian drama and theater came at a time when modern minstrels were also appearing in the Soviet Union. Uusually accompanying themselves on guitars, poets singing songs of their own composition in a way reminiscent of Wedekind and Brecht in the days of the early twentieth-century German cabaret started to become a part of the Soviet entertainment landscape especially in the late '50s and the '60s. Before long, the romantic, melancholic, pacifistic songs of Bulat Okudzhava (born 1924; expelled from the Communist Party in 1962), the humorous songs of Vladimir Vysotsky, a popular actor in the Taganka Theater, and the often topically sharp satirical and political ballads (for which he was expelled from the Soviet Union in 1974) of Aleksandr Galich (1918–77)[8] became enormously popular. Since the subjects of many of the balladeers' songs made publication out of the question, they were recorded privately on tape and circulated by means of *magnitizdat* (an "underground" dissemination of magnetic tapes akin to the privately printed literature known as *samizdat*). The intensely intimate poetry of the foremost young woman poet of post-Stalin Russia, Bella Akhmadulina (born 1937), shared much the same preoccupation with individual emotions, ordinary people, the young, and life's smaller lyrical joys, and fused with the troubadour current. Arbuzov's use of a song by Akhmadulina in *An Old-Fashioned Comedy* underlines not only the celebration of sentiment in the play but also, it seems, the impact of the new minstrel phenomenon on the form as well as the content of drama.

No less persistent in the post-Stalinist typology of Russian drama is the heroic play, but with the important qualification that the contemporary depiction of heroism lacks the romantic and mythopoeic aspects of the revolutionary heroic plays of the 1920s and '30s. Instead, the newer heroic play finds its material either in World War II, which can be expected to generate imaginative literature in the USSR for some time to come, or in the activities and attitudes of ordinary unheroic and unromantic people who are more apt nowadays to manifest their heroism in defying the bureaucracy or championing some ecological cause.

In its all female cast and its clever stage effects, Roshchin's *Echelon* is a good example of the contemporary play on a war theme that preserves ideological correctness yet strives to avoid stereotypicality of character and subject. Ecology may not yet be the popular public cause in the USSR that it is in the United States, but it is making headway and offers material for new types of positive heroes and heroines in an ideologically acceptable drama of critical realism. The conflict of Arbuzov's *Evening Light* turns on an ecological motif, as we have seen, and so, too, does the popular play *Maria* (1970) by the dramatist Afanasi Salynsky (1920–   ).[9] Here a young woman engineer named Maria Odintsova risks death and suffers serious physical injury in a successful effort to block the detonation of a mountain at a Siberian construction site when arguments about the local economic value of the mountain's marble fall on deaf ears. Replete with theatricalist stage techniques, songs, quotes from a poem by Apollinaire, and pleas for the rights of the individual, *Maria*, like Roshchin's *Echelon*, typifies the ongoing effort by Russian dramatists to innovate within the boundaries of conventional dramatic structures and subjects.

The expansion of content in Russian drama has also been accompanied by corresponding changes in form. The transition from socialist to critical realism has ended the hegemony of the "happy ending" play and resulted in many "open-ended" works in which the dramatists not only spurn happy endings but either proffer no solutions to conflicts raised in the plays or close with deliberate ambiguity. In real life, after all, not all endings can be happy or all conflicts resolved.

Three particularly interesting examples of the newer "open-ended" critical realist play are the internationally known *Voskhozhdenie na Fud-ziyamu* (*The Ascent of Mount Fuji*) by the Kirghiz writers Chingiz Ait-matov and Kaltai Mukhamedzhanov, which had its première at the Sovremennik Theater in the winter of 1973 and an American production at the Arena Stage in Washington, D.C., in June 1975; *I prosnulis po utru* (*And in the Morning They Woke Up*, 1975), another Sovremennik production by the talented writer and former actor Vasili Shukshin, who died prematurely in 1975; and Aleksandr Gelman's *Protokol odnogo zasedaniya* (*Minutes of a Meeting*, 1976).

The Ascent of Mount Fuji is a deceptively simple play on the theme of moral integrity and responsibility constructed around the same device as Rozov's *The Reunion*. Set in the Kirghiz homeland of its authors, the play similarly brings together past and present as a group of four former schoolmates and the wives of all but one of them hold an informal re-union, to which they have invited their old teacher, on a mountain dur-ing summer. According to Japanese belief, once on Mount Fuji a person is supposed to open the innermost secrets of his soul. The mountain on which the characters of the Soviet play convene for an overnight cam-ping-out becomes a local Mount Fuji where they meet again after many years apart in an atmosphere of openness and honesty among them-selves and before God.

The Fuji legend and the mountain setting weave their spell over the characters and their reunion rapidly assumes the aspect of a group ther-apy session. The play is divided into the familiar two acts and by the end of the first mutual antagonisms, personal failures, fragile marriages, and career opportunism are all bared. But the greatest secret that emerges and still plagues the consciences of the men after a quarter of a century concerns one of their number who is not at their reunion, the poet Sabur (perhaps modeled on Bulat Okudzhava) who served with them during the war but, because of a long poem of a pacifist nature written near the end of the war, was taken into custody, exiled, and eventually released. Although his privileges of citizenship were restored after his exile, Sabur is a broken man: his wife has left him, his daughter refused to have him at her wedding, he has turned to drink and avoids the com-pany of people.

As *The Ascent of Mount Fuji* unfolds it becomes apparent that at least one, if not more, of the men present, was responsible for Sabur's arrest by informing his military superiors of the poem. They all, however, share a sense of collective guilt.

After the departure of the old teacher the men, later joined by their

A scene from Chingiz Aitmatov's and Kaltai Mukhamedzhanov's The Ascent of
Mount Fuji *in the 1975 production by the Arena Stage, Washington, D.C.
Directed by Zelda Fichandler.*
(ARENA STAGE)

wives, drink, sing, behave boisterously, and hurl rocks down the moun-
tainside for amusement. As they prepare to break camp the following
morning a forest ranger appears to tell them to remain where they are
until police come to interrogate them. The reason is that an old woman,
the wife of a local shepherd, was killed during the night by the stones
the campers threw down the mountain. As it draws to its ambiguous
conclusion, the play concentrates on the individual reactions of the characters to their part in the accidental homicide. The successful, pompous,
obviously careerist scientist and the vain self-centered journalist of mediocre literary talent are the first to leave before the police arrive on the
excuse that they will clear the matter up in town and want to be spared

the embarrassment of a police investigation. That they have no intention of implicating themselves is patently obvious. The local agronomist who arranged for the reunion follows soon after. Left behind are the outspoken, somewhat envious and embittered local history teacher and the wife of the agronomist, who are suspected of having an affair. To her, the fact that the history teacher remains means that he could not have been the one who betrayed Sabur, though circumstantial evidence makes him the likeliest candidate. At the end of the play, the agronomist appears to be returning, a fact which his wife interprets as an indication of his innocence too in the betrayal of Sabur.

Although it concludes on a note of provocative ambiguity—we never know who really betrayed Sabur and what the outcome of the peasant woman's death will be—*The Ascent of Mount Fuji* makes a strong unequivocal statement in a style as simple as that of a parable about human pettiness, moral cynicism, the failure of the collective conscience to pass the test of concrete challenge, and the inability to learn from the past. Instead of forthrightly accepting joint responsibility for the killing of the old woman in the light above all of their professed remorse over the Sabur incident, the group dissolves into an individual scramble for safety. *The Ascent of Mount Fuji* brings a brief confrontation with an ugly truth and changes nothing.

Nothing changes either at the end of Shukshin's *And in the Morning They Woke Up*. Although the author died before he could devise an appropriate conclusion to the play, given its subject of alcoholism—the most persistent social problem in the Soviet Union—the ending must necessarily be "open."

Its title derived from a popular Russian drinking song, Shukshin's play splendidly exemplifies the type of unflinching dramatic fare for which the Sovremennik Theater enjoys its justifiable reknown. The problem of alcoholism has cropped up from time to time in Soviet drama, but for the most part obliquely, in terms, that is, of an individual (like Rozov's Maxim Petrov in *The Reunion*) who has turned to drink out of frustration at not being able to adjust to Soviet society. In virtually all cases where such characters figure, the plays leave little doubt that the failure is that of the individual, not society.

Alcoholism comes more obviously to the fore in Aksyonov's satirical fantasy *Your Murderer* in which the mass consumption of spirits is presented as the insiduous means by which social conformity is pressed. But Aksyonov's immediate targets are conformity and authoritarianism, not alcoholism as such, and no analytical examination of the social phenomenon of heavy drinking is undertaken in the play.

The striking feature of Shukshin's work is that the subject of the play itself is drunkenness and the author's principal concern an attempt to come to grips with the cause of its prevalence. Shukshin does this in a manner similar to that of Roshchin's *Echelon* and Aitmatov's *The Ascent of Mount Fuji*. Using only a single stage setting, that of a police sobering-up station, and a short time span, he introduces eight inmates who first appear motionless lying on hospital cots (the stage is otherwise bare) and the figure of a sociologist who visits the station to learn how the inmates got there. Overcoming their initial antagonism to the sociologist, the inmates gradually loosen up and begin to talk about themselves. What follows is a succession of individual sketches, now dramatic, now humorous, animated by a racy colloquial language which itself constitutes a highlight of the play.

For Shukshin to infer, as Aksyonov might well have intended through the medium of fantasy, that alcoholic abuse in the Soviet Union attests to a failure of the Soviet social system—if indeed he held such a view at all—would certainly have made production of the play out of the question. As the inmates reveal themselves in the vignettes, the reasons for their alcoholism are common and predictable: romantic jealousy, petty misunderstandings, brawls, and so on. In one instance only is there a suggestion that the Soviet way of life—with its perennial shortages, cues, discomforts, and opportunism—is at least partially a contributing factor. This is the episode involving an older man who is cheated by a butcher after standing in a cue to buy meat. When the man protests, the butcher is defended by another customer who hopes that by so winning the butcher's favor he will get a better cut of meat for himself.

When the interviews are over, the sociologist closes his notebook and leaves, still in a quandry as to the root causes of heavy drinking in the country and what remedies may be possible. A policeman appears next and orders the inmates to collect their belongings; the cots have to be used by a fresh batch of drunks in need of enforced drying-out. Underscoring its "open-ended" conclusion is a recorded epilogue by the prominent actor Mikhail Ulyanov acknowledging the delicacy of the subject as well as Shukshin's inability to complete the play any more conclusively. In closing remarks to the audience, Ulyanov informs them that Shukshin regarded drunkenness as a disaster and that it is up to them, the audience, to imagine an ending to the play and to regret that the urgency of the problem makes imagining any ending so hard.

Aleksandr Gelman's *Minutes of a Meeting* lacks the taut spare quality of *The Ascent of Mount Fuji* and the stark grim honesty of *And in the Morning They Woke Up*, but it makes similar use of a confrontation with inescapable reality to disclose harsh truths. In doing so, it typifies a new breed of Russian plays dealing with industrial themes from more complex social and psychological perspectives than Soviet drama has ventured since Glebov's *Inga* of 1928.

The head of a construction brigade (Potapov) refuses to accept a prize for the overfulfillment of an industrial plan on the grounds that since pertinent figures for the plan were deliberately falsified to conceal shortages and mismanagement the prize was undeserved. An extraordinary meeting of the local Party committee to hear Potapov and deal with the highly unusual matter is convened. The entire play is devoted to the meeting and the clash of the moral integrity of Potapov, on the one hand, and the hypocrisy and dishonesty of members of the committee, on the other.

When the truth about mismanagement and falsification becomes impossible to evade and efforts alternately to placate and intimidate Potapov fail, a vote is taken on whether or not to accept the declined prize money and reestablish the original construction plan which, with the proper cooperation, Potapov is convinced his brigade can fulfill honestly. The vote results in a tie which is broken by the committee chairman, Batartsev. What finally convinces Batartsev to support Potapov by casting the crucial vote in his favor is the fortuitous revelation of yet another construction scandal. The timing of the revelation is an obvious contrivance but one that detracts only slightly from the tension generated by the play's psychological conflict. The spare single set, the temporal concentration of the action, and the almost complete elimination of physical movement achieve a considerable intensification of the confrontation of opposing social and moral positions. Although Gelman's play ends with the victory of Potapov, the conclusion is still "open-ended" in that questions must remain in the minds of the audience about the political ramifications of the reinstitution of the original construction plan, the consequences of the revelation of mismanagement for the members of the Party trust responsible for the original decisions, the eventual success or failure of Potapov in fulfilling the first plan, and the social impact of Potapov's "rebellion."

Taking the overview of Russian drama from Stalin's death to the present permits us a cautiously optimistic estimation of the progress of playwriting in the Soviet Union. Earlier narrow strictures against stylistic and structural departures from the method of Socialist Realism have quietly been laid aside with the results that theatricalist, vaudeville, and music hall techniques have been able to widen the horizons of the contemporary drama. Sometimes, as we have seen, these techniques have been employed mainly for theatrical novelty or to enliven plays of almost schematic simplicity about ordinary people and events. This is especially true with regard to the many plays devoted to individual emotions, love, and young people that have crowded the Soviet stage since the late 1950s. In plays of this type, such as several by Arbuzov, Sofronov, and Volodin, song, dance, mime, and poetry reenforce the plays' essential lyricism. In some instances, as with Vampilov in particular, vaudeville techniques fuse with a conventionally realistic style or with a Chekhovian ambience to create a play in which the comic and the serious are two sides of the same coin.

Closely akin to vaudeville, farce has also enjoyed a revival on the Soviet stage. Again, a deemphasis of ideology has permitted the cultivation of a form of drama whose principal reason for being is entertainment. The success of Vampilov's *Provincial Anecdotes* leaves no doubt as to the popularity of a drama of divertissement.

The ability of dramatists now to deal far more frankly than ever before with contemporary society has also influenced dramatic form. Boldness of subject—collective moral responsibility in *The Ascent of Mount Fuji*, the problem of drunkenness in *And in the Morning They Woke Up*, gross industrial mismanagement in *Minutes of a Meeting*, to mention three more prominent recent examples—often has a structural correlate in the form of the "open" (as opposed to "closed") or ambiguous ending. This structural principle also accords with the critical realism with which much Russian drama has been informed since Stalin's death. Some social problems admit no facile solution and one, that of alcoholic abuse, is so presented in the Shukshin play. The moral and social issues raised in *The Ascent of Mount Fuji* and *Minutes of a Meeting* are still part of Soviet society, hence the ambiguity and "openness" with which these plays conclude.

Another striking property of a number of the plays representative of the new lyricism and critical realism—plays like Volodin's *Five Evenings*, Arbuzov's *An Old-Fashioned Comedy*, *The Ascent of Mount Fuji*, *And in the Morning They Woke Up*, and *Minutes of a Meeting*, among others—is their simplicity of form and style. External conflict is pared down to a minimum or completely dispensed with; single, sparsely furnished sets, a small number of actors, "unity" of time as well as of place and action are common features; diction is colloquial and natural to the characters portrayed. What emerges is a trim play in which nothing extraneous detracts from an extreme concentration on the human psyche, a play similar in some formal aspects to Western and East European absurdist reductivism.

The greater latitude the Soviet dramatist now has in dealing critically with contemporary society—if not with the premises on which that society is based—has also witnessed the fitful reemergence of the absurd, grotesque, and fantastic. That the Soviet authorities are less hospitable to drama of this type is evident from the difficulties involved in arranging productions for such plays, their usually short runs or abrupt closures as well as the long delays in the publication of play texts or the absence of any publication. Not insignificantly, comedy in this vein remains the most outstanding aspect of the dissident drama of the 1960s. But the appearance of absurd, grotesque, and fantastic elements in the works of writers unassociated with the dissident movement attests to a definite vitality of the genre.

There are, it would seem, sound reasons why this should be so. As dramatists level their critical sights at contemporary social mores and institutions, their attention is often riveted on what are judged to be negative aspects of the Soviet state stubbornly tenacious after sixty years of Bolshevik indoctrination: an unwieldy and inefficient bureaucracy which breeds an unwillingness to assume responsibility, conformist pressures, and the materialistic bourgeois values we collectively identify as philistinism. As it so happens, these were among the most frequent targets of the comic drama spawned in the era of the New Economic Policy of the 1920s. Then, the internal contradictions of NEP society prepared a fertile field for a satirical comedy of the absurd and grotesque. This comedy reached its apogee in the dramatic writings of Bulgakov, Erdman, Kataev, Mayakovsky, Romashov, and Shkvarkin for whom the nineteenth-century grotesque comedy of Gogol and Sukhovo-Kobylin was an acknowledged precursor tradition. Enhancing the perception of shared affinities with the comedy of Gogol and Sukhovo-Kobylin was the aesthetic interest in the grotesque in the earlier twentieth century and the theatrical revivals of Gogol and Sukhovo-Kobylin by Meyerhold especially in the 1920s.

It would be preposterous, of course, to contend that present-day Soviet society and the NEP era have a great deal in common. Yet in view of the extent to which bureaucratic excesses and philistinism are among the favorite targets of critical realism and satire, some similarities are undeniable. The awareness of these similarities naturally inclines the comic satirist to the rich domestic tradition of absurd and grotesque satirical comedy which when viewed from the vantage point of the second half of the twentieth century consists not only of Gogol and Sukhovo-Kobylin, but also of the entire corpus of NEP comic dramatists mentioned above.

Further enhancing the attractiveness of the absurd and grotesque comedy of the 1920s and early 1930s for contemporary artists is the rehabilitation of several writers of the period—Bulgakov, Erdman, Zoshchenko, among others—whose best works were long impounded by an official ban seriously impeding their accessibility. A good illustration of the interaction of this earlier Soviet tradition of the absurd, grotesque, and fantastic and the contemporary stage is the production in 1977 of a dramatization of Bulgakov's fantastico-satirical novel *The Master and Margarita* at the Taganka Theater, which favors satire and irreverence, under the direction of the fine director Yuri Lyubimov.

The novel, which Bulgakov worked on between 1928 and the late 1930s, was allowed to appear for the first time in magazine installments in 1966 and 1967. The production based on it began its run in repertory on April 6, 1977, and attracted much favorable attention.

Despite (or because of) this response, the production soon came under harsh criticism in *Pravda* on ideological grounds. It was faulted, above all, for unjustified and subjective analogies between present-day Soviet society and the period in which the work arose, the '20s and '30s, analogies which could lead to a distortion of historical perspective. Although the work was originally cleared by the appropriate authorities in the Ministry of Culture, apparently second thoughts about the matter or disagreements within the Party and government resulted in the *Pravda* denunciations and subsequent pressures for the cessation of the production in view of Lyubimov's usual firmness against modifying plays once in performance.

The difficulties encountered by the Taganka production of *The Master and Margarita* exemplify the tenuousness of absurd, grotesque, and fantastic satire in Soviet art. This is not to suggest, certainly, that satire has no place in the Soviet Union. The social and ideological utility of satire as a means of identifying correctable shortcomings within the established social structure has long been recognized and a large body of satirical writing in all genres exists. But the art of the absurd, grotesque, and fantastic has been viewed with suspicion since the 1920s, when it blossomed forth so richly in Russia. In a time of harsh repression, such as the 1930s, it has been ruthlessly suppressed, with authors jailed, or worse. At other times, token, more digestible manifestations of it have been tolerated or it has simply been prevented from seeing the light of day.

Since the death of Stalin and Khrushchev's bombshell at the Twentieth Party Congress, however, greater flexibility in cultural affairs has extended the range of subject matter, lessened the weight of ideology, and permitted some departures from the orthodoxy of literary form. The latter phenomenon began to manifest itself in the 1960s in such prose works as *Sud idyot* (*The Trial Begins*, 1960), *Fantasticheskie povesti* (*Fantastic Tales*, 1961), and *Lyubimov* (best known in English as *The Makepeace Experiment*, 1964) by the gifted dissident writer Andrei Sinyavsky (pseudonym Abram Tertz; born 1925), the *Antimiry* (*Antiworlds*, 1964) poetry of Andrei Voznesensky (born 1933) and a satirical revue of his which ran at the Taganka Theater for two days before being closed down, Kataev's surprising blend of fantasy and satire in his dreamlike book of recollections *Svyatoy kolodets* (*The Holy Well*, 1966), Bulat Okudzhava's Gogolian-grotesque "historical" novel *Bedny Abrosimov* (*Poor Abrosimov*, 1969), Yuri Dombrovsky's three novelettes about Shakespeare and Mary Fitton published under the collective title *Smuglaya ledi* (*The Dark Lady*, 1969), Andrei Amalrik's absurdist plays of the 1960s, and such later fiction by Aksyonov as the stories "Zatvorennaya bochkotara" ("The Shopworn Tare of Barrels," 1968) and "Rendezvous" (1971) as well as his fantastico-satirical play *Your Murderer* (1975).

The same political changes underlying the emergence of the "youth" theme and similar phenomena in literature in the late '50s and the '60s also permitted the partial rehabilitation of several of the outstanding writers and artists of the 1920s and early '30s. Hence, when it became possible for the Russian writer as well as theatrical director to broaden the range of form in addition to that of content much of the avant-garde art of the early twentieth century was available as a model of often brilliantly imaginative creative innovation. What then occurred was a fascinating confluence of contemporary potential and past achievement in the exploratory character of works such as those mentioned above.

The impact this development has had on the stage is of considerable importance. New productions of plays long withheld from public view by Erdman, Mayakovsky, and Bulgakov, together with the rehabilitation of the early twentieth-century theatrical avant-gardists, Meyerhold above all, and the first productions of the plays of Bertolt Brecht ever permitted in the USSR, proved a dynamic stimulus to contemporary directors excited by what appeared to be at last a license to pursue different directions in scenic form. The emergence of smaller and newer

theaters unbound by tradition—such as the Sovremennik and Taganka—
as vehicles for experimentation with content as well as form seemed to
confirm that the new "freedoms" were not just wishful thinking or a fig-
ment of the imagination.

The gains for the drama in all this ferment have been much less
impressive. The director's ability to innovate in techniques of production, to translate into deed nonrepresentational concepts of staging does
not as yet extend to the dramatist's choice and treatment of subject. In
view of the long-standing political recognition of the ideological usefulness of drama, the more conservative official attitude toward drama as
opposed to theater, where orthodoxy can afford to be less stringent, is
entirely understandable.

This official conservatism reasserted itself in the mid-1960s after the
great openness of the late '50s and early '60s and the explosion of dissident literature, *samizdat, magnitizdat,* and related cultural phenomena.
The invasion of Czechoslovakia in 1968, preceded by the arrest in 1965
and the trial a year later of Andrei Sinyavsky and Yuli Daniel (pseudonym Nikolai Arzhak), and followed in the 1970s by the expulsion and
emigration of such writers as Amalrik, the poet Iosip Brodsky, Galich,
the novelists Vladimir Maksimov and Viktor Nekrasov, Sinyavsky, and
Solzhenitsyn, mark the visible signposts of politically mandated cultural
retrenchment.

The loosening of reins precipitated by the euphoria of Stalin's death
and the famous Khrushchev speech gave ample evidence in a relatively
short period of time that the Soviet Union was no less fertile a ground
for artistic experimentation than it had been earlier in the century. The
drama proved as hospitable to the avant-garde as other literary and artistic media and the "phantasmagoric art" Sinyavsky and later Volodin
called for seemed to be within reach. In his remarkable essay "On Socialist Realism" (1960), Sinyavsky defined that art as one

> in which the grotesque will replace realistic descriptions of ordinary
> life. Such an art would correspond best to the spirit of our time.
> May the fantastic imagery of Hoffmann and Dostoevsky, of Goya,
> Chagall, and Mayakovsky (the most socialist realist of all), and many
> other realists and non-realists teach us how to be truthful with the
> aid of the absurd and fantastic.[10]

In an essay included in his volume *Dlya teatra i kino (For Theater and
Film,* 1967), Volodin expressed a similar desire:

> It seems to me that in art a time of interpenetration of strata is at
> hand: for example, the dramatic and comedic—which has already

become commonplace, but also, the real and the fantastic. There has been scientific fantasy (Jules Verne) and social fantasy (Wells). Now the fantastic is becoming emotional, moral, spiritual, whatever you like—that is one of the contemporary ways of artistic conceptualization. (. . .) Only fairy tales, legends, and fables have come down from ancient times to our own. Now it is possible that even then there existed critical and realistic currents in art, but only those works which conveyed a sense of the wonderment of life traversed the centuries.[11]

And so, for a brief time, as if in answer to the appeals of Sinyavsky and Volodin, the absurd, grotesque, and fantastic began to take their place in Soviet Russian drama alongside the patently less problematic works of romantic and mundane heroism, critical realism, satirical and light social comedy, and the newer lyrico-theatricalist drama enlivened by elements of farce and vaudeville.

But the absurd, grotesque, and fantastic have always been precariously situated in Soviet art. Their extreme formal departure from approved methods of artistic expression expose them to charges of the ever suspect and villified "formalist" experimentation and "decadence." Worse still, from the official point of view, their unusual and distorted angles of vision extend far beyond the tolerated foci of satire and insinuate profoundly disturbing questions not just about this or that aspect of society, but about ways of thinking, seeing, and feeling. By opening up new and radical perspectives an art inspired by the absurd, grotesque, and fantastic becomes ultimately subversive. That it is viewed in just such a light on the level of official perception is all too apparent from the stifling of the avant-garde of the 1920s and early 1930s, the gingerly and only partial rehabilitation of the artists of that period during the "thaws" of the 1950s and '60s, the limited toleration of the new avant-garde of the first post-Stalin decade, and the subsequent intensification of pressure on such art in the later 1960s and the '70s. And yet, though temporarily discomforted, silenced, or driven underground, an art expressive of the will to imagine cannot forever remain submerged.

Guide to Pronunciation

As an aid to the reader who knows no Russian, the following lists indicate the stressed syllable of names and terms appearing in the book. Note additionally that while vowels in Russian are usually pronounced much as they are in other European languages, the "e" is pronounced in most cases as if it had a "y" before it. Although it would be awkward to indicate this each time in transliteration, names such as Andréev, Dostigáev, Olésha, Pasternák, and so on are really pronounced Andréyev, Dostigáyev, Olyésha, Pastyernák. Also, genitive case endings in "-ogo" or "-ego" are always pronounced "-ovo" and "-evo," though never so transliterated.

Names of dramatists, directors, actors, others

Afanásev
Afinogénov, Aleksándr
Aitmátov, Chingíz
Akhmadúlina, Bélla
Akhmátova, Ánna
Aksyónov, Vasíli
Alyóshin, Samuíl
Amalrík, Andréi
Andréev, Leoníd
Ánnensky, Innokénti
Arbúzov, Alekséi
Arzhák, Nikolái
Bábel, Isaák
Bagrítsky
Bálmont, Konstantín
Bély, Andréi
Béria, Lavrénti
Bill-Belotserkóvsky
Bryúsov, Valerí
Budyónny, Semyón
Daniél, Yúli (Arzhák, Nikolái)

Dombróvsky, Yúri
Dovzhénko
Dudíntsev, Vladímir
Dzerzhínsky
Éhrenburg, Ílya
Érdman, Nilolái
Faikó, Alekséi
Fédin, Konstantín
Filósov
Gálich, Aleksándr
Gélman, Aleksándr
Gíppius, Zinaída (Híppius)
Glébov, Anatóli
Górev, Yákov
Górky, Maxím (Peshkóv)
Griboédov, Aleksándr
Gumilyóv, Nikolái
Ivánov, Vyachesl003v
Kharms, Daniíl (Yuváchev)
Khlébnikov, Velimír
Khrushchev (Khrushchóv)

Kírov, Sergéi
Kírshon, Vladímir
Komissarzhévskaya, Véra
Komissarzhévsky, Fyódor
Korneychúk, Aleksándr
Kuzenkóv, Vladímir
Kuzmín, Mikhaíl
Kuznetsóv, Anatóli
Lavrenyóv, Borís
Leónov, Leoníd
Lyubímov, Yúri
Máksimov, Vladímir
Mayakóvsky, Vladímir
Merezhkóvsky, Dmítri
Meyerhóld (Meyerkhóld), Vsévolod
Mukhamedzhánov, Kaltáy
Nekrásov, Víktor
Nemiróvich-Dánchenko
Okhlópkov, Nikolái
Okudzháva, Bulát
Olésha, Yúri
Ostróvsky, Aleksándr
Pasternák, Borís
Petlyúra
Pilnyák, Borís
Plavínsky, Dmítri
Pogódin, Nikolái (Stukálov)
Popóvsky, Aleksándr
Pudóvkin
Rádlov, Sergéi
Rémezov, Andréi (Ivánov, I.)
Rémizov, Alekséi
Romashóv, Borís
Rózov, Víktor
Róshchin, Mikhaíl
Rýzhey, Pyótr
Salýnsky, Afanási
Saltykóv-Shchedrín
Shéynin, Lev
Shklóvsky, Víktor
Shólokhov, Mikhaíl
Shukshín, Vasíli

Shkvárkin, Vasíli
Shvarts, Yevgéni
Símonov, Konstantin
Sobolévsky
Sofrónov, Anatóli
Sologúb, Fyódor
Solovyóv, Vladímir
Solzhenítsyn, Aleksándr
Sinyávsky, Andréi (Tertz, Abrám)
Stanislávsky, Konstantín
Sudéykin
Sukhovó-Kobýlin, Aleksandr
Súrkov, Alekséi
Súrov, Anatóli
Sýtin, Tatyána
Taírov
Tovstonógov, Geórgi
Trenyóv, Konstantin
Tsvetáeva, Marína
Tubélsky, Leoníd
Tvardóvsky
Ufimtsev
Ulyánov, Mikhaíl
Uspénsky, Andréi
Vakhtángov
Vampílov, Aleksándr
Vilénkin,
Virtá, Nikolái
Vishnévsky, Vsévolod
Volchók, Galína
Volódin, Aleksándr (Lífshits)
Voroshílov
Vysótsky, Vladímir
Vvedénsky, Aleksándr
Yefrémov, Olég
Yevréinov, Nikolái
Zóshchenko, Mikháil
Zhdánov, Andréi
Zhúkov
Zórin, Leoníd
Zvérev, Anatóli
Zamyátin, Yevgéni

Titles of plays and other literature

Anfisa
Antimíry

Aristokráty
Balagánchik

Bánya
Barsuki
Bédny Abrósimov
Beséda
Bésovskoe déystvo
Blokáda
Bolshóy den
Boris Godunóv
Bronepóezd
Chelovék s portfélem
Chelovék s ruzhyóm
Chetýri kápli
Chetýrnadsat lyubóvnikov nekrasivoy
    Méri-Enn
Chórnye máski
Chrezvycháyny zakón
Chudák
Chudaki
Chudésny splav
Den svádby
Dáchniki
Dar múdrykh pchol
Denis Davýdov
Dityá Allákha
Dni náshey zhizni
Dni Túrbinykh
Dom s óknami v póle
Don Zhuán v Egipte
Drakón
Dva anekdóta
Dva bráta
Dvádsat minút s ángelom
Dvenádsat mólodtsev iz tabakérki
Dym otéchestva
Fabrichnaya devchónka
Fákely
Falshivaya monéta
Famira-Kifared
Fantasticheskie póvesti
Fédra
Féldmarshal Kutúzov
Féniks
Fomá Gordéev
Gibel eskádry
Gódy stranstviy
Golovlyóvy
Góly koról

Góre ot umá
Górod právdy
Górod vetróv
Gospozhá Lénin
Gósti
Grozá
Igrá
I prosnúlis po utrú
Irkútskaya istóriya
Istóriya odnóy lyubvi
Istóriya s metranpázhem
Kabalá svyatósh
Khochú rebyónka
Khristós, ángely i dushá
Komsomólskaya Právda
Kompromiss Naib-Khána
Konstantin Terékhin (Rzhávchina)
Kon v senáte
Konéts Kazanóvy
Konéts Krivorýlska
Konformist-li dyádya Dzhek?
Korábl právednykh
Koról na plóshchadi
Koról, zakón i svobóda
Kremlyóvskie kuránty
Krivóe zérkalo
Krýlya
Kvadratúra krúga
Laodámiya
Lévo rulyá
Lirícheskie drámy
Literatúrnaya Moskvá
Litúrgiya mne
Lyónushka
Lyubimov
Lyubóv k blizhnemu
Lyubóv Yarováya
Mákov tsvet
Mandát
Máshenka
Maskarád
Melanippa-filósof
Mélky bes
Meshcháne
Metél
Milye prizraki
Mir isskústva

Mistériya-Buff
Mládost
Moí shestidesyátye
Moy bédny Marát
Moyá tyótya zhivyót v Volokolámske
Moyó zaglyadéne
Na dné
Nakanúne
Naródnye rússkie skázki
Nashéstvie
Nesravnénny Nakonéchnikov
Nyé ubíy
Neznakómka
Nochnáya ispoved
Nochnýe plyáski
Pésnya sudbý
Nóvy Lef
O Aleksée chelovéke bózhem, íli
Potéryanny i obrashchónny syn
Obezyány idút!
Obyknovénny chelovék
Ochnáya stávka
Odín den Ivána Denisovicha
Odná
Ógni sv. Dominíka
Okeán
Olén i shalashóvka
O Martiniáne
Opásnaya predostorózhnost
Optimistícheskaya tragédiya
Otrávlennaya túnika
O Yevdókii iz Geliópolya, íli
   Obrashchónnaya kurtizánka
Ózero Lyúl
Páren iz náshego góroda
Past nóchi
Personálnoe délo
Pérvaya kónnaya
Pésnya sudbý
Pir pobedíteley
Platón Kréchet
Pobéda smérti
Pobedíteley súdyat
Pod kashtánami Prági
Póle i doróga
Polovchánskie sady
Poslédnye

Poslédnym létom v Chulimske
Potéryanny syn
Poyedínok
Po zvyózdam
Predméste
Prekrásnye Sabinyánki
Priklyuchénie
Prishédshy
Proféssor Storítsyn
Prometéy
Proshcháne v yúne
Protesiláy umérshy
Protivogázy
Protokól odnogó zasedániya
Provintsiálnaya istóriya
Provintsiálnye anekdóty
Pútnik
Pyat vécherov
Rabotyága Slovotyókov
Rámzes
Rélsy gudyát
Rossiya
Róza i krést
Rússkie lyúdi
Rychí, Kitáy!
Sámoe glávnoe
Samsón v okóvakh
Sávva
Schastlívye dni neschastlívogo
   chelovéka
Sévernye tsvetý
Shúler
Skázka pro bélogo bychká
Sházki stárogo Arbáta
Skutarévsky
Slýshish, Moskvá?!
Smert Tarélkina
Smúglaya lédi
Sómov i drugíe
Sonét Petrárki
Sovétskaya Molodyózh
Spísok blagodeyánniy
Starík
Staromódnaya komédiya
Stárym kozáchim sposóbom
Svádba Krechinskogo
S véchera do polúdnya

Svyatáya krov
Svyatóy kolodéts
Tak i búdet
Tantál
Tánya
Teátr
Teátr: Kniga o nóvom teátre
Teátr véchnoy voyný
Tezéy
Tot, kto polucháet poshchóchiny
Továrishch Tsátkin i Ko
Traditsióny sbor
Tragédiya ob Iúde, printse
  Iskariótskom
Trétya, patetícheskaya
Tri rastsvéta
Tri volkhvá
Tsar-Gólod
Tsar Iksión
Uchitel Búbus
Untilóvsk
Uslóvnosti
Usmirénie Badadóshkina
Utínnaya okhóta
Vánka klyúchnik i pazh Zheán
Vash ubiytsa
Vássa Zheléznova
Vdokhnovénie
Vechérny svet
Véchno zhivýe
Velíkaya síla
Velikorússkie naródnye pésni
Velíky gosudár
Venetsiánskie bezúmtsy
Vésy
Vesyólaya smert
V étom milom stárom dóme

V kulísakh dushí
Vne zakóna
V ogné
Voskhozhdénie na Fudziyámu
Vostóchny batalyón
Vostók-západ: Dialóg, vedúshchiysya
  v Súzdale
Vozdúshny piróg
Vragí
Vrédny elemént
Vsegdá v prodázhe
Vsyó otstayótsya lyudyám
Výbor
Výbor nevésty
Yegór Bulychóv i drugie
Yekaterina Ivánovna
Yevgráf, iskátel priklyuchéniy
Yólka u Ivánovykh
Yúnost
Zágovor chúvstv
Zapíski chudaká
Zatéynik
Zatvórennaya bochkotára
Zelyónoe koltsó
Zemlyá
Zhdi menyá
Zhizn chelovéka
Zhizn zovyót
Zhurávli letyát
Znánie
Zolotáya karéta
Zolotóe runó
Zolótoe sérdtse
Zóykina kvartíra
Zvezdá
Zýkovy

Names of characters in plays

Abrám
Afanási Kuzmích
Akímov
Akulína
Ametístov
Anatóli
Andrósov

Andrúshka
Aníska
Antípa
Antonína
Arísha
Artyóm Godúm
Avenír Nikoláevich

Bábichev
Bashkírov
Básov
Bayán, Olég
Belvedónsky
Bersénev
Beryózkina, Zóya
Bessemyónov
Bíbichev
Bóldyrev
Bóltikov, Sofrón
Borís
Bórodin
Bótkin
Bózhena
Bubnóv
Búrdin, Zakhár
Busýgin
Chádov
Charnóta
Cheremúshkina
Cherkún
Chudakóv
Chudnóv
Demídevna
Donónov
Drónov
Dyátlov
Dzhókich
Eduárdov
Faína
Falkóvsky
Filíppov, Michel
Fitílev
Fólgin
Fyódor
Galashóv, Ghérman
Galína
Glafíra
Goloshchápov
Golubkóv
Goncharóv
Goncharóva, Yeléna (Lyólya)
Górlov
Granátov
Grechánnikov
Groznóy

Grúbek (Hrúbek, in Czech)
Gúbin
Gudzónov
Gusyátnikov
Hévern
Ignátov
Ilyín
Irína
Isláev
Kalabúshkin, Aleksándr Petróvich
Kaléria
Kalóshin
Kasátkin
Kashírin, Pável
Kastálsky
Kastórkin
Kavalérov
Khlúdov
Kimbáev
Kízavetter
Kizyakóvsky
Kolésnikov
Kolesóv (Kolyósov)
Kolokólnikov
Kólosov
Kormýslov, Ílya
Kokorýshkin
Korzúkhina, Serafíma
Kóshkin
Kostenétsky, Volódya
Kóstya
Kotíkhin
Kostylyóv
Kozlóvsky (Vasilénko)
Kovalyóv
Krasnúshkin, Kólya
Krássnov
Krechínsky
Krestóvnikov
Krivóy Zob
Ksénia
Kváshnya
Kvásov
Láptev, Yákov
Lavrúkhin
Leonídik
Lévshin

Líka
Líka
Likhómsky
Lípa
Lissóvsky
Lístikov, Vásya
Lóbzin, Nartsiss
Lopákhin
Luká
Lúkin
Lyúba
Lyudmíla
Lyúska
Makárova, Yeléna
Makkavéev, Adrián
María Lvóvna
Mastakóv
Mechétkin
Medvédev
Melánia
Mikhaíl
Mikháilov
Mílochka
Mindál, Yásha
Mishláevsky
Monákhov
Mordáev
Morózov
Morzhínsky
Murátov
Múromsky
Nádya
Nadézhda
Nakonéchnikov
Nefédova, Varvára (Várya)
Némov
Nestráshny
Nezelásov
Nikítin
Nikóla
Nyúra
Obolyáninov
Obrýdlov
Odintsóva
Ógnev (Ognyóv)
Okhótnikov, Antón
Olég Leonídovich

Ólga
Optimístenko
Otshélnikov
Pafnúti
Pálchikov
Panóva, Pávla
Pásha
Pável
Pávla
Pávlin
Peklevánov
Pépel
Perchíkin
Pestróv, Mísha
Petróv, Maxim
Pétya
Plyúkhov, Adám
Podsekálnikov
Polónsky, Séva
Polúdin
Pomigálov
Portupéya
Potápov
Potékhin
Prisýpkin
Próchazka
Prókhov
Pylyáev
Raévsky
Raísa Fillípovna
Rakítin
Ranévskaya
Redútkin
Renaissance, Elzevíra
Rodión
Ryábtsov
Rybakóv
Ryúmin
Rýzhov, Ignát
Sadóvsky
Sarafánov
Semyón
Serdyúk
Shábina, Ágnia
Shamánov
Shamánova, María
Shúra

Shústrova, Dúnya
Shvándya
Sílva
Skróbotov
Slúnsky
Sónya Óstrova
Spásova, Klára
Strumiliyán
Studzínsky
Sukhodólov
Sulzhénko, Zhénka
Sysóev
Súslov
Taísya
Talánov
Tatárov
Téterev
Tíhy
Tíkhy
Tónya
Treplyóv
Tsekhovóy
Tsygánov
Turítsyn
Tyátin
Vadím
Vadímovna, Álla
Valentín
Valentína
Valentínov

Vargásov, Semyón
Varvára
Vasilísa
Vásin
Vassílev
Vásya
Vedérnikov
Velosipédkin
Vershínin
Volódya
Vyázmin
Yákov
Yarovóy
Yefím
Yemilyán
Yerén
Zabélin
Zabúdko, Pétya
Zachumélov
Zakhárov
Zaválov, Timoféi
Zheléznov, Zakhár
Zhénya
Zhíkharev
Zílov
Zímina, Nína
Zína
Zakátov
Zont, Mirón
Zvóntsov

Russian terms, place names, theaters, societies, ships, etc.

agítka
Aleksandrínsky
antiobshchéstvennik
burzhúy
diversánt
Fontánka
Kámerny
magnitizdát
Málaya Brónnaya
marsiánstvo
Obériu

Oberiúty
Právaya Ruká
samizdát
shútki
Sovreménnik
Tagánka
Verkhopóle
Vyázovka
vydvizhéntsy
Zaryá
Známensky

Notes

---

1. IN SEARCH OF THE NEW RUSSIAN: GORKY'S PREREVOLUTIONARY PLAYS

1. *M. Gorky i A. Chekhov: Perepiski, stati i vyskazyvaniya*, p. 55; translation mine. For selections from Chekhov's correspondence with Gorky in English translation and valuable related information, see *Anton Chekhov's Life and Thought: Selected Letters and Commentary.*

2. *M. Gorky i A. Chekhov*, p. 59.

3. *Ibid.*, pp. 62–63, 82, 84.

4. The literature on Gorky is vast, especially in Russian. For good accounts in English of his literary contributions and his place in Russian literature, see Helen Muchnic, *From Gorky to Pasternak*, and Irwin Weill, *Gorky: His Literary Development and Influence on Soviet Intellectual Life.* The popular account of his life by Dan Levin, *Stormy Petrel: The Life and Work of Maxim Gorky*, is readable and makes some interesting observations. Four important Russian studies of Gorky's dramatic writing are B. M. Byalik, *Gorky—dramaturg;* S. Kastorsky, *Dramaturgiya M. Gorkogo;* V. Novikov, *Tvorcheskaya laboratoriya Gorkogo-dramaturga;* and Yu. Yershov, *Maxim Gorky i ego dramaturgiya.*

5. Franklin D. Reeve, ed., *An Anthology of Russian Plays*, 2:111. Italics here and in following quotations mine. Page references are given in text.

6. For another comparison of the Gorky and O'Neill plays, see the essay "Circe's Swine: Plays by Gorky and O'Neill," in Helen Muchnic, *Russian Writers: Notes and Essays*, pp. 233–49.

7. Eugene O'Neill, *The Iceman Cometh* (New York: Vintage, 1946), p. 81.

8. *M. Gorky: Five Plays*, p. 243. Page references hereafter are given in text.

9. *Seven Plays of Maxim Gorky*, p. 117. Page references hereafter are given in text.

10. The play has attracted attention in recent years in the English-speaking world because of the well-received British première production by the Royal Shakespeare Company in London on July 22, 1971. A new translation of *Enemies* was made for the production. See *Enemies*, Kitty Hunter-Blair and Jeremy Brooks, trs.

---

2. GORKY'S LATER PLAYS: THE SOVIET PERIOD

1. Quoted in Nikolai A. Gorchakov, *The Theater in Soviet Russia*, p. 424.

2. Text in E. E. Leytnekker, ed., *Gorky ob isskustve*, pp. 176–77.

3. Gorky's interest in melodrama and, in fact, his sponsorship of a melodrama writing contest in 1919 are discussed by Daniel Gerould in "Gorky, Melodrama, and the Development of Early Soviet Theatre," pp. 33–44.

4. See the articles grouped under the general heading "K voprosu o repertuare" (On the Question of Repertoire) in A. V. Lunacharsky, *Sobranie sochineniy*.

5. On this phase of Gorky's career, see B. Byalik, *M. Gorky—dramaturg*, pp. 373–74.

6. *Ibid.*, pp. 374–75.

7. Gorky, *Sobranie sochineniy*, pp. 150 and 187. Translations mine.

8. On this subject, see Rufus W. Mathewson, Jr., *The Positive Hero in Russian Literature*.

9. S. Kastorsky, *Dramaturgiya M. Gorkogo*, p. 160.

10. N. Gorchakov, *The Theater in Soviet Russia*, p. 110.

11. Very few of the earliest Soviet plays have ever been reprinted. One available collection is that of V. F. Pimenov, ed., *Pervye sovetskie pesy*.

12. For a history of RAPP, see Edward J. Brown, *The Proletarian Episode in Russian Literature*.

13. Vs. Vishnevsky, "O tragedii," *Sovetskie dramaturgi o svoyom tvorchestve. Sbornik statey*, V. Pimenov, ed. (Moscow, 1967), p. 122.

14. *Ibid.*, p. 120.

15. Vs. Vishnevsky, *Stati, dnevniki, pisma*, pp. 37 and 39.

16. *Sovetskie dramaturgi o svoyom tvorchestve*, p. 52.

17. *Ibid.*

18. *Ibid.*, pp. 53–54.

19. Quoted in L. Tamashin, *Vladimir Kirshon: Ocherk tvorchestva*, p. 145.

20. *Sovetskie dramaturgi o svoyom tvorchestve*, pp. 106–7.

3. THE REVOLT AGAINST NATURALISM: SYMBOLISM, NEO-ROMANTICISM, AND THEATRICALISM

1. On Mallarmé and the drama, see Haskell M. Block, *Mallarmé and the Symbolist Drama* (Detroit: Wayne State University Press, 1963). There is a good introduction to French Symbolist drama and theater in the chapter "The Symbolist Theater" in Anna Balakian, *The Symbolist Movement* (New York: Peter Smith, 1967), pp. 123–55.

2. For an English translation of the work, see Villiers de L'Isle Adam, *Axel*. The Afterword by Guicharnaud, pp. 191–98, is helpful. My account of the stage history of *Axel* follows that of Guicharnaud.

3. For a good introduction to Maeterlinck in English, see Bettina Knapp, *Maurice Maeterlinck*.

4. Maurice Maeterlinck, *The Treasure of the Humble*, Alfred Sutro, tr. (New York and London, 1903), pp. 99, 105–6.

5. Konstantin Balmont, another major Russian Symbolist writer, did several Calderón translations.

6. For the texts, with extensive commentary, see Z. N. Gippius, *Pesy,* Temira Pachmuss, ed. (Munich, 1972).

7. Bryusov, *Sobranie sochineniy,* pp. 71–72.

8. Quoted in Konstantin Mochulsky, *Andrei Bely: His Life and Works,* p. 24. There is also a discussion of *He Who Has Come,* pp. 44–45.

9. The play's form and imagery are discussed by Daniel Gerould in his article "Andrei Bely: Russian Symbolist," pp. 25–29.

10. Andrei Bely, *The Jaws of Night,* pp. 35, 36.

11. The Russian texts of all Ivanov's articles on drama and theater as well as of his own plays can be found in the second volume of the excellent two-volume edition of his works, *Sobranie sochineniy.* For a general study of Ivanov and Russian symbolism, see James West, *Russian Symbolism: A Study of Vyacheslav Ivanov and the Russian Symbolist Aesthetic.*

12. "The Theater of One Will," Daniel Gerould, tr., *The Drama Review* (December 1977), 21:88, 88–90, 98, 99. See also Gerould's introductory essay on Sologub in the same issue, pp. 79–84.

13. My principal sources for Meyerhold are K. Rudnitsky, *Rezhisser Meyerkhold,* the best Russian study to date; and *Meyerhold on Theatre,* an excellent survey of Meyerhold's career with translations of many of his most important essays on theater.

14. Bryusov, *Sobranie sochineniy,* p. 11. Translations mine.

15. *Tri rastsveta* was published in *Severnye tsvety* in 1905.

16. V. Vsevolod-Gerngross, *Istoriya russkogo teatra* (Leningrad and Moscow, 1929), 2:248.

17. See especially: the Kuzmin poems, in the original Russian and English translation, in *Modern Russian Poetry: An Anthology with Verse Translations,* Vladimir Markov and Merrill Sparks, eds. (Indianapolis: Bobbs-Merrill, 1967), pp. 206–33, and the remarks on Kuzmin on pp. lx–lxi of the Introduction; the translation of his play *The Venetian Madcaps* by Michael Green in *Russian Literature Triquarterly,* pp. 118–51, as well as Michael Green's article, "Mikhail Kuzmin and the Theater," in the same issue, pp. 243–66; and the volume of Kuzmin translations by Neil Granoien and Michael Green published by Ardis under the title *Wings: Prose and Poetry by Mikhail Kuzmin* (Ann Arbor: University of Michigan Press, 1972). My information on Kuzmin owes most to Michael Green's article "Mikhail Kuzmin and the Theater."

18. A three-volume edition of Kuzmin's works, edited by John E. Malmstad and Vladimir Markov, was published by Wilhelm Fink of Munich in 1978.

19. The most complete information on Kuzmin's dramatic writings appears at the end of Michael Green's article "Mikhail Kuzmin and the Theater."

20. Blok, *Sobranie sochineniy,* p. 166.

21. The most useful introduction to Yevreinov in English is the essay "Nikolai Evreinov as a Playwright" in Christopher Collins, ed. and tr., *Life as Theater: Five Modern Plays by Nikolai Evreinov* (Ann Arbor: University of Michigan Press, 1973), pp. xi–xxviii.

22. George Kalbouss, "From Mystery to Fantasy: An Attempt to Categorize the Plays of the Russian Symbolists," p. 490. This article is a valuable succinct introduction to Russian Symbolist drama.

23. Yevreinov, *Dramaticheskie sochineniya* (St. Petersburg, 1914), p. 52. Translation mine.

24. Blok, *Sobranie sochineniy*, pp. 148–49.

25. Sologub, *Sobranie sochineniy* (St. Petersburg, 1910–14), 8:21. See also the interpretation of the passage in A. V. Fyodorov, *Teatr A. Bloka i dramaturgiya ego vremeni* (Leningrad, 1972), p. 84.

26. There is some further information on the production in Daniel Gerould, "Sologub and the Theatre," p. 82.

27. Sologub, *Sobranie sochineniy*, p. 254.

28. Quoted in Mochulsky, *Andrei Bely: His Life and Works*, p. 86.

29. *Letters of Gorky and Andreev 1899–1912*, Peter Yershov, ed., Lydia Weston, tr. (New York: Columbia University Press, 1958), pp. 91–92.

30. See James B. Woodward, *Leonid Andreev: A Study*, pp. 211–14.

31. *Anathema*, p. 5.

32. Woodward, *Leonid Andreev*, p. 209.

33. *Plays by Leonid Andreev*, pp. 26–27.

34. Quoted in Alexander Kaun, *Leonid Andreyev: A Critical Study*, p. 173.

35. The literature on Blok is sizable. The two best studies of his plays are A. V. Fedorov, *Teatr A. Bloka i dramaturgiya ego vremeni* and T. M. Rodina, *Aleksandr Blok i russky teatr nachala XX veka*.

36. Blok's gnosticism is discussed by Ewa M. Thompson in her article "The Development of Aleksandr Blok as a Dramatist," pp. 341–51.

37. Blok, *Sobranie sochineniy*, pp. 171, 174, 245.

38. Sologub, *Sobranie sochineniy*, 8:210. Translation mine.

39. *Ibid.*, p. 54.

40. *Ibid.*, p. 55.

41. There is some discussion of Annensky's tragedies in Vsevolod Setchkareff, *Studies in the Life and Works of Innokentij Annenskij*.

42. Annensky, *Stikhotvoreniya i tragedii*, p. 450. Translation mine.

43. Simon Karlinsky, *Marina Cvetaeva: Her Life and Art*, pp. 237 and 258.

44. Karlinsky, pp. 259–60.

45. All quotations are from the Biblioteka Poeta edition of Tsvetaeva's works, *Izbrannye proizvedeniya*.

46. N. Gumilyov, *Sobranie sochineniy*, p. xv.

47. *Tsvetaeva*, p. 779.

48. Karlinsky, p. 240.

49. Karlinsky, p. 248.

50. Tsvetaeva, p. 589. Translations mine.

51. James B. Woodward, *Leonid Andreev*, p. 248.

52. Andreev, *Pesy*, pp. 359–60. Translation mine.

53. F. D. Reeve, ed., *An Anthology of Russian Plays*, 2:174.

54. *Five Russian Plays*, C. E. Bechhofer, tr. (New York, 1916), p. 33. Cf. also the translation of the play in Christopher Collins, ed. and tr., *Life as Theater: Five Modern Plays by Nikolai Evreinov*, pp. 1–19.

55. Bechhofer, pp. 14–15. Cf. also Collins, p. 10.

56. It was produced by the Theatre Guild of New York on March 22, 1926. Yevreinov, who was then visiting the United States to sponsor an Operatic Arts

Institute (which went bankrupt by the time he arrived), assisted in the production. Among the players were Lee Strasburg, Harold Clurman, and Edward G. Robinson. The Guild's acting version, based on translations by Herman Bernstein and Leo Randole, was published under the title *The Chief Thing* (Garden City, N.Y., Doubleday, 1926). For an account of Yevreinov's visit to America in 1926, see Anna Kashina-Yevreinova, *N. N. Yevreinov v mirovom teatre XX veka*, pp. 33–46.

57. *The Chief Thing*, Herman Bernstein and Leo Randole, trs., p. 83. Citations are from this translation, with page numbers given in text. Cf. also the translation under the title *The Main Thing* in Collins, *Life as Theater*, pp. 32–118.

58. Michael Green, "Mikhail Kuzmin and the Theater," p. 263.

59. Kuzmin, *The Venetian Madcaps*, p. 150.

60. For an excellent study of Mayakovsky, especially of his poetry, see Edward J. Brown, *Mayakovsky: A Poet in the Revolution*.

61. Mayakovsky's essays on theater and film as well as the texts of all his dramatic works and film scenarios can be found in V. V. Mayakovsky, *Teatr i kino*. The introduction by B. Rostotsky (pp. 5–112) gives a fair overview of Mayakovsky's contributions to drama and film.

62. *The Complete Plays of Vladimir Mayakovsky*, Guy Daniels, tr. (New York: Simon & Schuster, 1968), p. 38. Page references to this translation hereafter given in text.

63. This and the following quotes are from *The Complete Plays of Vladimir Mayakovsky*, pp. 46–47.

64. The name is probably modeled on that of Konstantin Pobedonostsev (1827–1907), Procurator of the Holy Synod from 1880 to 1905, and an extreme reactionary.

65 Chudakov and Velosipedkin are "telling names": *chudak* in Russian means "an eccentric," while *velosiped* is the Russian word for "bicycle."

4. THE 1920s AND EARLY 1930s:
THE REVOLUTION AND THE CIVIL WAR
IN RUSSIAN DRAMA

1. The best sources on Tretyakov are the following: V. Pertsov's introduction (pp. 3–22) in Sergei Tretyakov, *Den Shi-Hua. Lyudi odnogo kostra. Strana-perekryostok;* the essays by A. Fevralsky (pp. 186–206) and B. Rostotsky (pp. 207–40) in Sergei Tretyakov, *Slyshish, Moskva?! Protivogazy. Rychi, Kitay!* and Vasil Choma, *Od futurizmu k literatúre faktu*, pp. 161–210.

2. There are some interesting observations of the "literature of fact" in Choma, *Od futurizmu k literatúre faktu*, pp. 196–210.

3. For a translation of the entire *Trilogy*, with an analysis of the plays, see my *The Trilogy of Alexander Sukhovo-Kobylin* (New York: Dutton, 1969).

4. *The Early Plays of Mikhail Bulgakov*, p. 216. Page references in text are to this edition.

5. B. Lavrenyov, *Razlom*, p. 60. Translation mine.

6. For a good introduction to Olesha's works, see Elizabeth K. Beaujour, *The Invisible Land: A Study of the Artistic Imagination of Iurii Olesha.* Olesha's plays are discussed on pp. 102–14.

7. Yuri Olesha, *Envy and Other Works.* Page references to this edition are hereafter given in the text.

5. THE 1920s AND EARLY 1930s:
SOCIAL COMEDY, ABSURD AND GROTESQUE NEP SATIRE, MELODRAMA

1. B. Romashov, *Pesy*, p. 68. The translations from *The Sweet Soufflé* here and in the following quotation are mine.

2. *The Early Plays of Mikhail Bulgakov*, p. 158.

3. *The Suicide* has never been printed in the USSR. My translations are based on a Xerox copy of a typescript of the play kindly furnished me by Professor Daniel Gerould of the City University of New York.

4. *The Complete Plays of Vladimir Mayakovsky*, Guy Daniels, tr. (New York: Simon & Schuster, 1968), pp. 160–61. Hereafter page references are given parenthetically in the text.

5. Faiko, *Chelovek s portfelem* (Moscow and Leningrad, 1929), p. 61. Text also in Faiko, *Pesy. Vospominaniya.* Translation mine.

6. OUT OF THE MAINSTREAM: SERAPIONS AND OBERIUTY

1. For a good introduction in English to the Serapions and their writings, see Kern and Collins, *The Serapion Brothers: A Critical Anthology.*

2. My biographical information on Lunts comes chiefly from the best study of the writer to date: Gary Kern, "Lev Lunc, Serapion Brother."

3. There is some discussion of Zamyatin's plays in the monograph by Alex M. Shane, *The Life and Works of Evgenij Zamjatin*, pp. 43, 64, 78, 137–39.

4. My translations from Lunts' *The City of Truth* are based on a Xerox copy of the play kindly given me by Mr. Edward Kline of the Chekhov Publishing Corporation of New York.

5. For a translation of the essay, see *A Soviet Heretic: Essays by Yevgeny Zamyatin*, Mirra Ginsburg, ed. and tr. (Chicago: University of Chicago Press, 1970), pp. 107–12.

6. The full texts of the Afterword and *Bertran de Born*, Gary Kern, tr., appear in *Drama and Theater*, pp. 51–65. Lunts expressed similar thoughts on the drama and theater in *Na zapad!* (Go West!), a speech delivered at a meeting of the Serapions on December 2, 1922, and later published in *Beseda*. For a text of the speech in English, see Kern and Collins, *The Serapion Brothers: A Critical Anthology*, pp. 147–57.

7. My account of the careers of Kharms and Vvedensky is much indebted to Gibian's Introduction to *Russia's Lost Literature of the Absurd*, pp. 3–38; information on the partial rediscovery of Kharms and Vvedensky appears on pp. 4–5. Page references hereafter given parenthetically in the text are to this volume.

7. THE 1930s: SOCIALIST CONSTRUCTION AND SOCIALIST REALISM

1. Eugene Lyons, ed., *Six Soviet Plays*, p. 408. Page references hereafter appear parenthetically in text.

2. A translation, by Anthony Wixley, was published in London in 1938.

3. Aleksei Arbuzov, *Dramy*, p. 36. Translations here and in the following quotations mine.

4. For example, A. O. Boguslavsky and V. A. Diev, *Russkaya sovetskaya dramaturgiya: Osnovnye problemy razvitiya. 1936–1945*, pp. 120 ff.

5. *Three Soviet Plays*, Asya Shoett, tr. (Moscow, n.d.), p. 35. Future page references to this edition are given in text.

6. Eugene Lyons, ed., *Six Soviet Plays*, p. 344. Future page references to this edition are given in the text.

7. The discussion is taken up at some length in L. Tamashin's *Vladimir Kirshon: Ocherk tvorchestva*, pp. 120 ff.

8. THE FANTASY WORLD OF YEVGENI SHVARTS

1. The first Russian collection of Shvarts' plays appeared posthumously in 1960, marking the beginning of a new wave of interest in Shvarts. Another manifestation of the Shvarts "revival" was the first full-length monograph on him by Sergei Tsimbal, *Yevgeni Shvarts: Kritiko-biografichesky ocherk*.

2. On Shvarts' sources, particularly Hans Christian Andersen and Charles Perrault, see Irina H. Corten, "Evgenii Shvarts as an Adapter of Hans Christian Andersen and Charles Perrault," pp. 51–67.

3. F. D. Reeve, ed., *Contemporary Russian Drama*, pp. 145 and 146. Page references to this translation of *The Naked King* are given parenthetically in the text.

4. A heretical Jewish sect now small with what remain of its followers living mainly in southern Russia.

5. F. D. Reeve, ed., *An Anthology of Russian Plays*, 2:389. Page references to this translation of *The Shadow* are given parenthetically in text.

6. Glenny, ed., *Three Soviet Plays*, p. 148. Page references to the Glenny edition are given in the text.

7. This is still, essentially, the Soviet characterization of the work. See, for example, S. Tsimbal's remarks in his introduction to the 1962 Moscow-Leningrad edition of Shvarts' plays, pp. 30–31. Tsimbal even goes on to say (p. 31) that in the light of new manifestations of fascism and militarism in the West since the end of World War II, Shvarts' play has lost none of its relevance.

9. THE GATHERING CLOUDS: ON THE EVE OF WAR

1. The original version of the play and its theatrical history are discussed in L. Fink, *Uroki Leonida Leonova*, pp. 123–32. See also Janina Sałajczyk, *Teatr Leonida Leonowa* (Warsaw, 1967), pp. 33–37.

2. The English translation by J. J. Robbins in *Seven Soviet Plays* is based on the revised version.

3. H. Dana, ed., *Seven Soviet Plays*, p. 229.

10. THE WAR YEARS

1. Leonid Leonov, *Teatr* (Moscow, 1960), 2:64. The Leonov translations are mine.

11. THE "FREEZE" OF 1946 TO 1952

1. Edward J. Brown, *Russian Literature since the Revolution*, p. 230.

2. Kron is best remembered as a dramatist for his play *Kandidat Partii* (*The Party Candidate*), which was severely criticized in 1950 when it was scheduled for production by the Moscow Art Theater, extensively altered, and staged finally by the Vakhtangov Theater in 1953.

3. Quoted from Hugh McLean and Walter N. Vickery, eds., *The Year of Protest 1956*, pp. 167–68.

12. THE "THAW" OF 1953 AND 1954

1. Edward J. Brown, *Russian Literature since the Revolution*, p. 240.

13. FROM THE TWENTIETH PARTY CONGRESS TO 1959: THE "YEAR OF PROTEST" AND ITS AFTERMATH

1. F. D. Reeve, ed., *Contemporary Russian Drama*, p. 110. Page references to the Reeve translation hereafter given in the text.

2. Hugh McLean and Walter N. Vickery, eds., *The Year of Protest 1956*, p. 79.

3. Reeve, ed., *Contemporary Russian Drama*, p. 37.

4. Volodin, *Five Evenings*, p. 13. Page references in text are to this edition.

14. THE NEW THEATRICALISM

1. Aleksei Arbuzov, *Dramy*, pp. 383–84. The translations from Arbuzov in this chapter are mine.

15. THE DISSIDENTS: IVANOV, AMALRIK, SOLZHENITSYN

1. For an account of the trial in English, see *On Trial: The Soviet State versus "Abram Tertz" and "Nikolai Arzhak,"* Max Hayward, ed. and tr. (rev. and enl. ed.; New York: Harper, 1967).

2. *Yest-li zhizn na Marse?* (Paris, 1961). Translation mine.

3. My account of Amalrik's career follows that of Daniel Weissbort in the introduction to his volume of translations of Amalrik's plays, *Nose! Nose? No-se! and Other Plays*, pp. ix–xix.

4. An English translation by Manya Harari and Max Hayward was published by Harcourt Brace Jovanovich (New York, 1970).

5. An English translation was published in 1970 (rev. ed., 1971) by Harper and Row. The publication also includes a translation of the "Open Letter to Anatoli Kuznetsov."

6. Included in Daniel Weissbort's volume of translations.

7. A translation of the play, under the title *Mrs. Lenine*, appears in Velimir Khlebnikov, *Snake Train: Poetry and Prose*, pp. 132–36.

8. *Nose! Nose? No-se!*, p. xxii. Page references to this edition hereafter given parenthetically in the text.

9. Solzhenitsyn, *The Love-Girl and the Innocent*. Parenthetic page references are to this edition.

16. FROM DISSENT TO DIVERTISSEMENT: THE 1960S AND 1970S

1. For additional information on Aksyonov, see Priscilla Meyer, "Aksenov and Soviet Literature of the 1960s," pp. 447–60, and also the same author's "Interview with Vasily Pavlovich Aksenov," pp. 569–74; Daniel Gerould, "Vasili Aksenov: Contemporary Russian Playwright," pp. 108–10; and *Soviet Literature in the Sixties: An International Symposium*.

2. *Envy and Other Works*, p. 28.

3. For discussions of the play, see William Harkins, "Jurij Oleša's Drama *Zagovor čuvstv*," pp. 129–35, and Bernard F. Dukore and Daniel C. Gerould, eds. *Avant-Garde Drama: A Casebook 1918–1939* (New York: Crowell, 1976), pp. 202–6.

4. The best discussion of Vampilov's dramatic writing is A. Demidov's afterword "O tvorchestve A. Vampilova," in Aleksandr Vampilov, *Izbrannoe* (Moscow, 1975), pp. 461–92.

5. *Time* (February 6, 1978), p. 65.

6. V. Komissarzhevsky, *Nine Modern Soviet Plays*, p. 599.

7. *Time*, September 5, 1977, p. 53.

8. Galich's difficulties with the authorities especially over the ban imposed on his play about Jews before and during World War II, *Matrosskaya tishina* (*Sailors' Rest*, begun 1945, completed in the late 1950s), are described in his book *Generalnaya repetitsiya*.

9. The play is discussed at some length in Yakov Feldman, *Dramaturgiya Afanasiya Salynskogo*, pp. 195–243.

10. Sinyavsky, *On Socialist Realism*, pp. 94–95. On Sinyavsky's ideas and writings, see additionally Richard Lourie, *Letters to the Future: An Approach to Sinyavsky-Tertz*, and Rufus W. Mathewson, Jr., *The Positive Hero in Russian Literature*, pp. 341–55.

11. Volodin, *Dlya teatra i kino*, pp. 307–08. Translation mine.

Bibliography

Afinogenov, A. N. *Stati. Dnevniki. Pisma. Vospominaniya.* Moscow, 1957.

Alpers, B. *Teatralnye ocherki.* 2 vols. Moscow, 1977.

Alyoshin, S. *Pesy.* Moscow, 1972.

Anastasev, A. *Viktor Rozov. Ocherk tvorchestva.* Moscow, 1966.

Andreev, Leonid. *Pesy.* Moscow, 1959.

Annensky, Innokenti. *Stikhotvoreniya i tragedii.* Leningrad, 1959.

Anton Chekhov's Life and Thought: Selected Letters and Commentary. Simon Karlinsky and Michael Heim, trs. Berkeley and Los Angeles: University of California Press, 1975.

Arbuzov, Aleksei. *Dramy.* Moscow, 1969.

—— *Vybor.* Moscow, 1976.

Babel, I. *Izbrannoe.* Moscow, 1957.

Bakshy, Alexander. *The Path of the Modern Russian Stage and Other Essays.* London, 1916.

—— *The Theatre Unbound.* London, 1923.

Beaujour, Elizabeth K. *The Invisible Land: A Study of the Artistic Imagination of Iurii Olesha.* New York: Columbia University Press, 1970.

Bill-Belotserkovsky, V. *Pesy.* Moscow and Leningrad, 1950.

Blok, Aleksandr. *Sobranie sochineniy.* Vol. 4. Moscow and Leningrad, 1961.

—— *Sobranie sochineniy.* Vol. 5. Moscow, 1971.

Boguslavsky, A. O. and V. A. Diev. *Russkaya sovetskaya dramaturgiya: Osnovnye problemy razvitiya, 1918–1935.* Moscow, 1963.

—— *Russkaya sovetskaya dramaturgiya: Osnovnye problemy razvitiya, 1936–1945.* Moscow, 1965.

—— *Russkaya sovetskaya dramaturgiya: Osnovnye problemy razvitiya, 1946–1966.* Moscow, 1968.

Boguslavsky, A. O., V. A. Diev, and A. S. Karpov. *Kratkaya istoriya russkoy sovetskoy dramaturgii.* Moscow, 1966.

Brown, Edward J. *Mayakovsky: A Poet in the Revolution.* Princeton, N.J.: Princeton University Press, 1973.

Brown, Edward J. *The Proletarian Episode in Russian Literature.* New York: Columbia University Press, 1953.

—— *Russian Literature since the Revolution.* New York: Collier, 1963; rev. ed., New York: Macmillan, 1969.

Bryusov, Valeri. *Sobranie sochineniy.* Vol. 6. Moscow, 1975.

Bulgakov, Mikhail. *Black Snow: A Theatrical Novel.* Michael Glenny, tr. New York: Simon & Schuster, 1967.

—— *Dni Turbinykh. Poslednye dni (A. S. Pushkin).* Moscow, 1955.

—— *Dni Turbinykh.* Letchworth, Herts. England, 1970.

—— *Don Kikhot.* Letchworth, Herts. England, 1971.

—— *Kabala svyatosh.* Letchworth, Herts. England, 1971.

—— *Pesy.* Paris, 1971.

—— *Poslednye dni.* Letchworth, Herts. England, 1970.

Burlakov, N. S. *Valeri Bryusov.* Moscow, 1975.

Byalik, B. M. *Dramaturgiya M. Gorkogo sovetskoy epokhi.* Moscow, 1952.

—— *Gorky—dramaturg.* Moscow, 1962.

—— *Gorky v borbe s teatralnoy reaktsiey.* Leningrad and Moscow, 1938.

Choma, Vasil. *Od futurizmu k literatúre faktu.* Bratislava, 1972.

Corten, Irina H. "Evgenii Shvarts as an Adapter of Hans Christian Andersen and Charles Perrault," *Russian Review* (1978), 37:51–67.

Crowell's Handbook of Contemporary Drama. Michael Anderson et al., eds. New York: Crowell, 1971.

Danilov, S. S. *Ocherki po istorii russkogo dramaticheskogo teatra.* Moscow and Leningrad, 1948.

Diev, Vladimir. *Trilogiya N. Pogodina o Lenine.* Moscow, 1965.

Faiko, Aleksei. *Pesy. Vospominaniya.* Moscow, 1971.

—— *Teatr.* Moscow, 1971.

Falen, James E. *Isaac Babel: Russian Master of the Short Story.* Knoxville: University of Tennessee Press, 1974.

Fedorov, A. V. *Teatr A. Bloka i dramaturgiya ego vremeni.* Leningrad, 1972.

Feldman, Yakov. *Dramaturgiya Afanasiya Salynskogo.* Moscow, 1976.

Fevralsky, A. *Mayakovsky—dramaturg.* Moscow and Leningrad, 1940.

Fink, L. *Uroki Leonida Leonova.* Moscow, 1973.

Frolov, V. *O sovetskoy dramaturgii.* Moscow, 1957.

—— *Zhanry sovetskoy dramaturgii.* Moscow, 1957.

Galich, Aleksandr. *Generalnaya repetitsiya.* Frankfurt/Main, 1974.

Gassner, John. *Form and Idea in Modern Theatre.* New York: Dryden, 1956.

Gassner, John and Edward Quinn, eds. *The Reader's Encyclopedia of World Drama.* New York: Crowell, 1969.

Gerould, Daniel. "Andrei Bely: Russian Symbolist," *Performing Arts Journal* (Fall 1978), 3:25–29.

—— "Gorky, Melodrama, and the Development of Early Soviet Theatre," *Yale/Theatre* (Winter 1976), 7:33–44.

—— "Sologub and the Theatre," *Drama Review* (December 1977), 21:79–84.

—— "Valerii Briusov: Russian Symbolist," *Performing Arts Journal* (Winter 1979), 3:85–91.

—— "Vasilii Aksyonov: Contemporary Russian Playwright," *Performing Arts Journal* (Spring 1977), 2:108–10.

Gibian, George, ed. and tr. *Russia's Lost Literature of the Absurd*. Ithaca, N.Y.: Cornell University Press, 1971.

Ginsburg, Mirra, ed. and tr. *A Soviet Heretic: Essays by Yevgeny Zamyatin*. Chicago: University of Chicago Press, 1970.

Glebov, Anatoli. *Inga: Sbornik pes*. Moscow, 1967.

Goldberg, Isaac. *The Drama of Transition*. Cincinatti: Appleton, 1922.

Golovashenko, Yu. *Geroika grazhdanskoy voyny v sovetskoy dramaturgii*. Leningrad, 1957.

Gorchakov, Nikolai A. *The Theater in Soviet Russia*. Edgar Lehrman, tr. New York: Columbia University Press, 1957.

Gorky, Maxim. *Pesy*. V. Fridlyand, ed. Moscow, 1964.

—— *Pesy*. B. A. Byalik, ed. Moscow, 1966.

—— *Sobranie sochineniy*. Vol. 18. Moscow, 1952.

Green, Michael, "Mikhail Kuzmin and the Theater," *Russian Literature Triquarterly* (Fall 1973), 7:243–66.

Gumilyov, N. *Sobranie sochineniy*. Vol. 3. G. P. Struve and B. A. Filippov, eds.; intro. by V. M. Setchkareff. Washington, D.C., 1966.

Harkins, William. "Jurij Oleša's Drama Zagovor čuvstv," *Symbolae Honorem Georgii Y. Shevelov*. Munich, 1971.

Ivanov, I. *Yest-li zhizn na Marse?* Paris, 1961.

Ivanov, Vsevolod. *Pesy*. Moscow, 1964.

Ivanov, Vyacheslav. *Po zvyozdam*. St. Petersburg, 1909.

—— *Sobranie sochineniy*. Vol. 2. Brussels, 1974.

Kalbouss, George. "From Mystery to Fantasy: An Attempt to Categorize the Plays of the Russian Symbolists," *Canadian-American Slavic Studies* (Winter 1974), 8:488–500.

Karlinsky, Simon. *Marina Cvetaeva: Her Life and Art*. Berkeley and Los Angeles: University of California Press, 1966.

Kashina-Yevreinova, Anna. *N. N. Yevreinov v mirovom teatre XX veka*. Paris, 1964.

Kastorsky, S. *Dramaturgiya M. Gorkogo*. Moscow and Leningrad, 1963.

Kaun, Alexander. *Leonid Andreyev: A Critical Study*. New York: Viking, 1924.

Kern, Gary. "Lev Lunc, Serapion Brother." Ph.D. dissertation, Princeton University, September 1969.

Kern, Gary and Christopher Collins, eds. *The Serapion Brothers: A Critical Anthology.* Ann Arbor, Mich.: Ardis, 1975.

Khlebnikov, Velimir. *Snake Train: Poetry and Prose,* Gary Kern, ed. Ann Arbor, Mich.: Ardis, 1976.

Kirshon, V. and A. Uspensky. *Konstantin Terekhin (Rzhavchina).* Moscow and Leningrad, 1927.

Kirshon, Vladimir. *Izbrannoe.* Moscow, 1958.

—— *Stati i rechi, o dramaturgii, teatre i kino.* Moscow, 1962.

Knapp, Bettina. *Maurice Maeterlinck.* Boston: Twayne, 1975.

Kron, Aleksandr. *Pesy.* Moscow, 1955.

—— *Teatr.* Moscow, 1971.

Kuzmin, M. *Komedii.* St. Petersburg, 1908.

—— *Uslovnosti.* Petrograd, 1923.

Lavrenyov, B. *Pesy.* Moscow, 1961.

—— *Razlom.* Moscow, 1966.

Leonov, Leonid. *Pesy.* Moscow, 1976.

—— *Teatr.* 2 vols. Moscow, 1960.

Levin, Dan. *Stormy Petrel: The Life and Work of Maxim Gorky.* New York: Meredith, 1965.

Leytnekker, E. E., ed. *Gorky ob isskustve.* Moscow and Leningrad, 1940.

Literature and Revolution in Soviet Russia 1917–62. A Symposium. Max Hayward and Leopold Labedz, eds. London: Oxford University Press, 1963; reprinted, Westport, Conn.: Greenwood, 1976.

Lounatcharsky, Anatoli Vassilievitch. *Théâtre et revolution.* Preface and notes by Emile Copferman. Paris, 1971.

Lourie, Richard. *Letters to the Future: An Approach to Sinyavsky-Tertz.* Ithaca, N.Y.: Cornell University Press, and London, 1975.

Lunacharsky, A. V. *Sobranie sochineniy.* Vol. 3. Moscow, 1964.

McClean, Hugh and Walter N. Vickery, eds. and trs. *The Year of Protest 1956.* An Anthology of Soviet Literary Materials. New York: Random House, 1961.

Marshall, Herbert. *The Pictorial History of the Russian Theatre.* New York: Crown, 1977.

Matlaw, Myron. *Modern World Drama: An Encyclopedia.* New York: Dutton, 1972.

Mathewson, Rufus W., Jr. *The Positive Hero in Russian Literature.* New York: Columbia University Press, 1958; 2d ed., Stanford, Calif.: Stanford University Press, 1975.

Mayakovsky, Vladimir. *Pesy.* A. V. Fevralsky, ed. Moscow, 1971.

—— *Teatr i kino.* 2 vols. Moscow, 1954.

Merezhkovsky, Dmitri. *Polnoe sobranie sochineniy.* Vol. 23. Moscow, 1914.

Meyer, Priscilla. "Aksenov and Soviet Literature of the 1960s," *Russian Literature Triquarterly* (Spring 1973), No. 6, pp. 447–60.

—— "Interview with Vasily Pavlovich Aksenov," *Russian Literature Triquarterly* (Spring 1973), No. 6, pp. 569–74.

Meyerhold on Theatre. Edward Braun, ed. and tr. New York: Hill & Wang, 1969.

M. Gorky i A. Chekhov: Perepiski, stati i vyskazyvaniya. Moscow and Leningrad, 1927.

Mikhalkov, Sergei. *Sem komediy.* Moscow, 1961.

Mochulsky, Konstantin. *Andrei Bely: His Life and Works.* Nora Szalavitz, tr. Ann Arbor, Mich.: Ardis, 1977.

Monter, Barbara Heldt. "The Plays of Alexander Solzhenitsyn," *Canadian-American Slavic Studies* (Winter 1974), 8:539–54.

Muchnic, Helen. *From Gorky to Pasternak.* New York: Random House, 1966.

—— *Russian Writers: Notes and Essays.* New York: Random House, 1971.

Newcombe, Josephine M. *Leonid Andreyev.* New York: Ungar, 1973.

Novikov, V. *Tvorcheskaya laboratoriya Gorkogo-dramaturga.* Moscow, 1965; 2d rev. ed., 1976.

Ocherki istorii russkoy sovetskoy dramaturgii. Vol. 1 (1917–34), Leningrad and Moscow, 1963; vol. 2 (1934–45), Leningrad and Moscow, 1966; vol. 3 (1945–1967), Leningrad, 1968.

Olesha, Yuri. *Pesy.* Moscow. 1968.

—— *Povesti i rasskazy.* Moscow, 1965.

Panova, Vera. *Pogovorim o strannostyakh lyubvi . . . Pesy.* Leningrad, 1968.

Pimenov, V. F., ed. *Pervye sovetskie pesy.* Moscow, 1958.

Pogodin, Nikolai. *Chelovek s ruzhyom. Kremlyovskie kuranty. Tretya pateticheskaya.* Moscow, 1969.

Remizov, Aleksei. *Besovskoe deystvie.* In *Fakely* (St. Petersburg, 1908), 3:33–88.

—— *Tragediya ob Iude, printse Iskariotskom.* In *Zolotoe runo* (Moscow, 1909), 10:15–50.

Rice, Martin P. *Valery Briusov and the Rise of Russian Symbolism.* Ann Arbor, Mich.: Ardis, 1975.

Rodina, T. M. *Aleksandr Blok i russky teatr nachala XX veka.* Moscow, 1972.

Romashov, B. *Pesy.* Moscow, 1954.

Rozov, Viktor. *Moi shestidesyatye . . .* Moscow, 1969.

Rudnitsky, K. *Rezhisser Meyerkhold.* Moscow, 1969.

Rudnitsky, K. "O pesakh A. Arbuzova i V. Rozova." *Voprosy teatra* 73. Moscow, 1975.

—— *Portrety dramaturgov*. Moscow, 1961.

Setchkareff, Vsevolod. *Studies in the Life and Works of Innokentij Annenskij*. The Hague: Mouton, 1963.

Severnye tsvety. Vols. 1–4. Munich, 1972.

Shane, Alex M. *The Life and Works of Evgenij Zamjatin*. Berkeley and Los Angeles: University of California Press, 1968.

Sheynin, Lev. *Pesy*. Moscow, 1969.

Shvarts, Yevgeni. *Pesy*. Leningrad, 1972.

Sinyavsky, Andrei [Abram Tertz]. *On Socialist Realism*. George Dennis, tr. New York: Pantheon, 1960.

Slonim, Marc. *Russian Theater from the Empire to the Soviets*. New York: Collier, 1961.

—— *Soviet Russian Literature*. 2d rev. ed. New York: Oxford University Press, 1977.

Sofronov, Anatoli. *Uragan: Pesy poslednykh let*. Moscow, 1975.

Sokolova, A. *Idei i obrazy sovetskoy dramaturgii: Pesy 1946–1952 godov*. Moscow, 1954.

Sologub, Fyodor. *Dramaticheskie proizvedeniya*. Vol. 8. St. Petersburg, 1910–14.

Solovyov, Vladimir. *Istoricheskie dramy*. Moscow, 1960.

Solzhenitsyn, Aleksandr. *Sobranie sochineniy*. Vol. 5. Frankfurt/Main, 1969.

Soviet Literature in the Sixties: An International Symposium. Max Hayward and Edward L. Crowley, eds. New York: Praeger, 1964.

Sovetskie dramaturgi o svoyom tvorchestve. Sbornik statey. V. Pimenov, ed. Moscow, 1967.

Struve, G. P., ed. *Neizdanny Gumilyov*. New York, 1952.

Sukhovo-Kobylin, Alexander. *Trilogy*. Intro. by Harold B. Segel, tr. New York: Dutton, 1969.

Tamashin, L. *Vladimir Kirshon: Ocherk tvorchestva*. Moscow, 1965.

Thomson, Boris. *The Premature Revolution: Russian Literature and Society 1917–1946*. London: Weidenfeld, 1972.

Thompson, Ewa M. "The Development of Aleksandr Blok as a Dramatist," *Slavic and East European Journal* (Fall 1970), 14:341–51.

Trenyov, Konstantin. *Lyubov Yarovaya*. Moscow and Leningrad, 1940.

Tretyakov, Sergei. *Slyshish, Moskva?! Protivogazy. Rychi, Kitay!* Moscow, 1966.

—— *Den Shi-Hua. Lyudi odnogo kostra. Strana-perekryostok*. Moscow, 1962.

Tsimbal, Sergei. *Yevgeni Shvarts: Kritiko-biografichesky ocherk*. Leningrad, 1961.

Tsvetaeva, Marina. *Izbrannye proizvedeniya*, A. Efron and A. Saa-kyants, eds. Moscow and Leningrad, 1965.

Tur, Ariadna and Pyotr Tur. *Pesy*. Moscow, 1975.

Tur, Bratya. *Dramy*. Moscow, 1962.

Villiers de L'Isle Adam, Philippe Auguste. *Axel*. June Guicharnaud, tr. Englewood Cliffs, N.J.: Prentice-Hall, 1970.

Vishnevsky, Vsevolod. *Stati, dnevniki, pisma*. Moscow, 1961.

—— *Izbrannoe*. Moscow, 1966.

Volkenshteyn, V. *Dramaturgiya*. Moscow, 1929.

Volodin, Aleksandr. *Dlya teatra i kino*. Moscow, 1967.

Voprosy sovetskoy dramaturgii. Sbornik statey. Moscow, 1954.

Weil, Irwin. *Gorky: His Literary Development and Influence on Soviet Intellectual Life*. New York: Random House, 1966.

West, James. *Russian Symbolism: A Study of Vyacheslav Ivanov and the Russian Symbolist Aesthetic*. London: Methuen, 1970.

Woodward, James B. *Leonid Andreev: A Study*. Oxford: Oxford University Press, 1969.

Yermilov, V. *Nekotorye voprosy teorii sovetskoy dramaturgii. O gogolevskoy traditsii*. Moscow, 1953.

Yershov, Peter. *Comedy in the Soviet Theater*. New York: Praeger, 1956.

Yershov, Yu. *Maxim Gorky i ego dramaturgiya*. Moscow, 1959.

Zavalishin, Vyacheslav. *Early Soviet Writers*. New York: Praeger, 1958.

Znosko-Borovsky, Yevgeni A. *Russky teatr nachala XX veka*. Prague, 1925.

Zolotnitsky, D. *Zori teatralnogo Oktyabrya*. Leningrad, 1976.

TWENTIETH-CENTURY RUSSIAN DRAMA IN ENGLISH
TRANSLATION *

Afinogenov, Aleksandr

Distant Point. Translated and adapted by Hubert Griffith. London, 1941.

Far Taiga [Distant Point]. In A. Bakshy, ed., Soviet Scene: Six Plays of Russian Life (q.v.).

Fear. In Eugene Lyons, ed., Six Soviet Plays (q.v.).

Listen Professor! [Mashenka]. American acting version by Peggy Phillips. New York: French, 1944.

* This list is not intended as definitive. For a more exhaustive bibliography of twentieth-century Russian drama in English translation from 1900 to 1969, see "Russian Drama after Chekhov: A Guide to English Translations, 1900–1969," Steven P. Hill and John Dunkelberger, *Theatre Documentation* (Fall 1969 and Spring 1970), pp. 85–108.

On the Eve. Eugenia Afinogenova, tr. In Henry Dana, ed., *Seven So-viet Plays* (q.v.). New York: Macmillan, 1946.

Aitmatov, Chingiz and Kaltai Mukhamedzhanov
The Ascent of Mt. Fuji. Nicholas Bethel, tr. New York: Farrar, Straus, and Giroux, 1975.

Aksyonov, Vasili
Your Murderer. Daniel C. Gerould and Jadwiga Kosicka, trs. *Perform-ing Arts Journal* (Spring 1977), 2:111–44.

Alyoshin, Samuil
Alone. In *The Year of Protest 1956*. An Anthology of Soviet Literary Materials. Hugh McLean and Walter N. Vickery, eds. and trs. New York: Random House, 1961.

Amalrik, Andrei
Nose! Nose? No-se! and Other Plays. Daniel Weissbort, ed. and tr. New York: Harcourt, Brace, Jovanovich, 1973.

Andreev, Leonid
Anathema. Herman Bernstein, tr. New York: Macmillan, 1910.
The Black Maskers [Black Masks]. In *Plays by Leonid Andreyeff* (q.v.).
He Who Gets Slapped. In F. D. Reeve, ed., *An Anthology of Russian Plays* (q.v.).
The Life of Man. In *Plays by Leonid Andreyeff* (q.v.).
Plays by Leonid Andreyeff. Clarence L. Meader and Fred Newton Scott, trs. New York: Scribner's, 1918.
Professor Storitsyn. In G. R. Noyes, ed., *Masterpieces of the Russian Drama* (q.v.).
The Sabine Women. In *Plays by Leonid Andreyeff* (q.v.).
The Waltz of the Dogs. Herman Bernstein, tr. New York: Macmillan, 1922.

Arbuzov, Aleksei
Confession at Night. Ariadne Nicolaeff, tr. London, 1971.
Evening Light. Robert Daglish, tr. In V. Komissarzhevsky, ed., *Nine Modern Soviet Plays* (q.v.).
It Happened in Irkutsk. In *Three Soviet Plays*. Rose Prokofieva, tr. Moscow, n.d.
The Promise. Ariadne Nicolaeff, tr. London: Oxford University Press, 1967.

Babel, Isaak
Maria. Denis Caslon, tr. *Russian Literature Triquarterly* (1966), no. 5, pp. 7–36.
Mary. In Michael Glenny, ed., *Three Soviet Plays* (q.v.).

Sunset. Raymond Rosenthal and Mirra Ginsburg, trs. New York: Noonday Press, 1961.

Bakshy, Alexander, ed. *Soviet Scene: Six Plays of Soviet Life*. Alexander Bakshy, tr., in collaboration with Paul S. Nathan. New Haven, Conn.: Yale University Press, 1946.
Afinogenov. *Far Taiga* [*Distant Point*].
Pogodin. *The Chimes of the Kremlin*.
Trenyov. *Lyubov Yarovaya*.

Bely, Andrei
The Jaws of Night. Daniel Gerould, tr. *Performing Arts Journal* (Fall 1978), 3:30–38.

Bill-Belotserkovsky, Vladimir
Life Is Calling. Anthony Wixley, tr. London: International Publishers, 1938.

Blake, Ben, ed. *Four Soviet Plays*. Anthony Wixley, tr. London: International Publishers, 1937.

Gorky. *Yegor Bulychov and Others*.
Pogodin. *Aristocrats*.

Blok, Aleksandr
The Puppet Show [*The Fair Booth Show*]. In F. D. Reeve, ed., *An Anthology of Russian Plays* (q.v.).

Bryusov, Valeri
The Wayfarer. Daniel Gerould, tr. *Performing Arts Journal* (Winter 1979), 3:92–99.

Bulgakov, Mikhail
A Cabal of Hypocrites. In *The Early Plays of Mikhail Bulgakov* (q.v.).
The Crimson Island. In *The Early Plays of Mikhail Bulgakov* (q.v.).
Days of the Turbins. In Eugene Lyons, ed., *Six Soviet Plays* (q.v.).
Days of the Turbins. In F. D. Reeve, ed., *An Anthology of Russian Plays* (q.v.).
The Days of the Turbins. In *The Early Plays of Mikhail Bulgakov* (q.v.).
The Early Plays of Mikhail Bulgakov. Ellendea Proffer, ed.; Carl R. Proffer and Ellendea Proffer, trs. Bloomington: Indiana University Press, 1972.
Flight. Mirra Ginsburg, tr. New York: Grove, 1969.
Flight. In *The Early Plays of Mikhail Bulgakov* (q.v.).
On the Run [*Flight*]. Avril Pyman, tr. London: Pergamon, 1972.
Zoya's Apartment. In *The Early Plays of Mikhail Bulgakov* (q.v.).

Dana, Henry, ed. *Seven Soviet Plays*. New York: Macmillan, 1946.

Afinogenov. *On the Eve.*
Leonov. *The Orchards of Polovchansk.*
Simonov. *The Russian People.*
Solovyov. *Field Marshal Kutuzov.*
Tur Brothers and Sheynin. *Smoke of the Fatherland.*

Dukore, Bernard F. and Daniel C. Gerould, eds. *Avant-Garde Drama: Major Plays and Documents of Post World War I.* New York: Crowell, 1976.

Erdman, Nikolai
    The Mandate. Marjorie Hoover, tr. Introduction by Marjorie Hoover. In *The Mandate and The Suicide.* Ann Arbor, Mich.: Ardis, 1975.
    The Suicide. George Genereaux, Jr., and Jacob Volkov, trs. Introduction by George Genereaux, Jr. *The Mandate and The Suicide.* Ann Arbor, Mich.: Ardis, 1975.

Glebov, Anatoli
    Inga. In Eugene Lyons, ed. *Six Soviet Plays* (q.v.).

Glenny, Michel, ed. *Three Soviet Plays.* Baltimore, Md.: Penguin, 1966.
    Babel. *Mary.*
    Mayakovsky. *The Bedbug.*
    Shvarts. *The Dragon.*

Gorky, Maxim
    Barbarians. In *Seven Plays of Maxim Gorky* (q.v.).
    Dostigaeff and the Others. In *The Last Plays of Maxim Gorki* (q.v.).
    Down and Out [*The Lower Depths*]. In G. P. Noyes, ed., *Masterpieces of the Russian Drama* (q.v.).
    Enemies. In *Seven Plays of Maxim Gorky* (q.v.).
    Enemies. Kitty Hunter-Blair and Jeremy Brooks, trs.; introduction by Edward Braun; preface by Jeremy Brooks. New York: Viking, 1972.
    The Last Plays of Maxim Gorky. Adapted for the English stage by Gibson-Cowan. New York: International Publishers, 1937.
    The Lower Depths. In *M. Gorky: Five Plays* (q.v.).
    The Lower Depths. In *Seven Plays of Maxim Gorky* (q.v.).
    The Lower Depths. In *The Storm and Other Russian Plays.* David Magarshack, tr. New York: Hill & Wang, 1960.
    The Lower Depths. In F. D. Reeve, ed., *An Anthology of Russian Plays* (q.v.).
    The Lower Depths. Kitty Hunter-Blair and Jeremy Brooks, trs.; introduction by Edward Braun; a preface by Jeremy Brooks. New York: Viking, 1973.

M. Gorky: Five Plays. Margaret Wettlin, tr. Moscow, n.d.

Old Man. In *M. Gorky: Five Plays* (q.v.).

The Petty Bourgeois. In *M. Gorky: Five Plays* (q.v.).

Queer People. In *Seven Plays of Maxim Gorky* (q.v.).

Seven Plays of Maxim Gorky. Alexander Bakshy, tr., in collaboration with Paul S. Nathan. New Haven, Conn.: Yale University Press, 1945.

Summer Folk (Scenes). In *M. Gorky: Five Plays* (q.v.).

Vassa Zheleznova (Mother). In *Seven Plays of Maxim Gorky* (q.v.).

Yegor Bulychov and Others. In Ben Blake, ed., *Four Soviet Plays* (q.v.).

Yegor Bulychoff and the Others. In *The Last Plays of Maxim Gorki* (q.v.).

Yegor Bulychov and the Others. In *Seven Plays of Maxim Gorky* (q.v.).

The Zykovs. In *Seven Plays of Maxim Gorky* (q.v.).

Gumilyov, Nikolai

The Poisoned Tunic. In *Selected Works of Nikolai Gumilev.* Burton Raffel and Alla Burago, eds. and trs.; introduction by Sidney Monas. Albany, N.Y., 1972.

Kataev, Valentin

Squaring the Circle. In Eugene Lyons, ed., *Six Soviet Plays* (q.v.).

Kirshon, Vladimir

Bread. In Eugene Lyons, ed., *Six Soviet Plays* (q.v.).

Kirchon [Kirshon], V. and A. Ouspensky

Red Rust. New York, 1930. Translator not given.

Komissarzhevsky, Victor, ed. *Nine Modern Soviet Plays.* Moscow, 1977.

Arbuzov. *Evening Light.*

Roshchin. *Valentin and Valentina.*

Rozov. *From Night till Noon.*

Salynsky. *Maria.*

Shatrov. *The Bolsheviks (30th August).*

Vampilov. *Last Summer in Chulimsk.*

Kuzmin, Mikhail

The Venetian Madcaps. Michael Green, tr. *Russian Literature Triquarterly* (Fall 1973), no. 7, pp. 118–51.

Leonov, Leonid

The Orchards of Polovchansk. J. J. Robbins, tr. In Henry Dana, ed., *Seven Soviet Plays* (q.v.). New York: Macmillan, 1946.

Lunacharsky, Anatoli
  Faust and the City, Vasilisa the Wise, The Magi. In *Three Plays by A. V. Lunacharskii.* L. A. Magnus and K. Walter, trs. New York: Dutton, 1923.

Lunts, Lev
  Bertran de Born, Gary Kern, tr., *Drama and Theatre* (Fall 1970), 9:51–65.

Lyons, Eugene, ed. *Six Soviet Plays.* Boston: Houghton Mifflin, 1934.

  Afinogenev. *Fear.*
  Glebov. *Inga.*
  Kataev. *Squaring the Circle.*
  Kirshon. *Bread.*
  Bulgakov. *The Days of the Turbins.*
  Pogodin. *Tempo.*

Mayakovsky, Vladimir
  The Bathhouse; The Bedbug; Mystery-Bouffe: Vladimir Mayakovsky, A Tragedy. Guy Daniels, tr.; introduction by Robert Payne. New York: Simon & Schuster, 1968.
  The Bedbug. In Michael Glenny, ed., *Three Soviet Plays* (q.v.).
  The Bedbug. In F. D. Reeve, ed., *An Anthology of Russian Plays* (q.v.).
  Mystery-Bouffe. In G. R. Noyes, ed., *Masterpieces of the Russian Drama* (q.v.).

Noyes, George Rapall, ed. *Masterpieces of the Russian Drama.* Vol. 2. Isaiah Minkoff, George Rapall Noyes, and Alexander Kaun, trs. New York: Appleton-Century, 1933, 1960. 1961.

  Andreev. *Professor Storitsyn.*
  Gorky. *Down and Out* [*The Lower Depths*].
  Mayakovsky. *Mystery-Bouffe.*

Olesha, Yuri
  The Conspiracy of Feelings. In Bernard F. Dukore and Daniel C. Gerould, eds., *Avant-Garde Drama: Major Plays and Documents Post World War I.* New York: Crowell, 1976.
  A List of Assets. In *Envy and Other Works.* Andrew R. MacAndrew, tr. Garden City, N.Y.: Doubleday, 1967.

Panova, Vera
  It's Been Ages! In F. D. Reeve, ed., *Contemporary Russian Drama* (q.v.).

Pogodin, Nikolai
  Aristocrats. In Ben Blake, ed., *Four Soviet Plays* (q.v.).

The Chimes of the Kremlin. In A. Bakshy, ed., *Soviet Scene: Six Plays of Russian Life* (q.v.).

Kremlin Chimes. In *Three Soviet Plays.* Asya Shoett, tr. Moscow, n.d.

A Petrarchan Sonnet. In F. D. Reeve, ed., *Contemporary Russian Drama* (q.v.).

Tempo. In Eugene Lyons, ed., *Six Soviet Plays* (q.v.).

Reeve, F. D., ed. and tr. *An Anthology of Russian Plays.* Vol. 2: *1890–1960.* New York: Vintage, 1963.

Andreev. *He Who Gets Slapped.*

Blok. *The Puppet Show* [*The Fairground Booth*].

Bulgakov. *The Days of the Turbins.*

Gorky. *The Lower Depths.*

Mayakovsky. *The Bedbug.*

Shvarts. *The Shadow.*

—— *Contemporary Russian Drama.* New York: Pegasus, 1968.

Panova. *It's Been Ages!*

Pogodin. *A Petrarchian Sonnet.*

Rozov. *Alive Forever.*

Shvarts. *The Naked King.*

Zorin. *A Warsaw Melody.*

Roshchin, Mikhail

    Valentin and Valentina. Alex Miller, tr. In V. Komissarzhevsky, ed., *Nine Modern Soviet Plays* (q.v.).

Rozov, Viktor

    Alive Forever. In F. D. Reeve, ed., *Contemporary Russian Drama* (q.v.).

    From Night till Noon. Robert Daglish, tr. In V. Komissarzhevsky, ed., *Nine Modern Soviet Plays* (q.v.).

    In Search of Happiness. Nina Froud, tr. London: Oxford University Press, 1961.

Salynsky, Afanasi

    Maria. Robert Daglish, tr. In V. Komissarzhevsky, ed., *Nine Modern Soviet Plays* (q.v.).

Shatrov, Mikhail

    The Bolsheviks (30th August). Robert Daglish, tr. In V. Komissarzhevsky, ed. *Nine Modern Soviet Plays* (q.v.).

Shvarts, Yevgeni

    The Dragon. In Michael Glenny, ed., *Three Soviet Plays* (q.v.).

    The Naked King. In F. D. Reeve, ed., *Contemporary Russian Drama* (q.v.).

The Shadow. In F. D. Reeve, ed., *An Anthology of Russian Plays* (q.v.).

Simonov, Konstantin
The Russian People. In Henry Dana, ed., *Seven Soviet Plays* (q.v.). American acting version by Clifford Odets.

Solovyov, Vladimir
Field Marshal Kutuzov. J. J. Robbins, tr. In Henry Dana, ed., *Seven Soviet Plays* (q.v.).

Solzhenitsyn, Aleksandr
Candle in the Wind. Keith Armes and Arthur Hudgins, trs.; introduction by Keith Armes. Minneapolis: University of Minnesota Press, 1973.
The Love-Girl and the Innocent. Bethell and David Burg, trs. New York: Farrar, Straus, and Giroux, 1969.

Trenyov, Konstantin
Lyubov Yarovaya. In *In a Cossack Village and Other Stories.* J. Atkinson, tr. London, 1946.
Lyubov Yarovaya. In A. Bakshy, ed., *Soviet Scene: Six Plays of Russian Life* (q.v.).
Tretyakov, Sergei
Roar China. F. Polianovska and Barbara Nixon, trs. New York, 1931.
Tur Brothers and Lev Sheynin
Smoke of the Fatherland. Abraham Feinberg, tr. In Henry Dana, ed., *Seven Soviet Plays* (q.v.).

Vampilov, Aleksandr
Last Summer in Chulimsk. Margaret Wettlin, tr. In V. Komissarzhevsky, ed., *Nine Modern Soviet Plays* (q.v.).

Volodin, Aleksandr
Five Evenings. Ariadne Nicolaeff, tr. Minneapolis: University of Minnesota Press, 1966.

Yevreinov [Evreinov], Nikolai
The Chief Thing. Herman Bernstein and Leo Randole, trs. New York: Doubleday, 1926.
The Merry Death. In *Five Russian Plays.* C. E. Bechhofer, tr. New York, 1916.
A Merry Death; The Main Thing; The Theater of the Soul; The Ship of the Righteous; The Unmasked Ball. In *Life as Theater: Five Modern*

Plays by Nikolai Evreinov. Christopher Collins, ed. and tr. Ann Arbor, Mich.: Ardis, 1973.

Zorin, Leonid

A Warsaw Melody. In F. D. Reeve, ed., *Contemporary Russian Drama* (q.v.).

Index

Actheon (Gumilyov), 109

Adam de la Halle, 73

Adventure, An (Tsvetaeva), 112, 115-17, 118

Afinogenov, Aleksandr, 46, 240, 280; involved in polemics over drama in the late 1920s and 1930s, 46-48; quoted, 47, 48; *Fear*, 48, 240-46, 247, 248, 249, 255; *Robert Tim*, 240; *The Eccentric*, 240; *Mashenka*, 249

Agitka, 31, 46, 148

Aiglon, L' (Rostand), 105, 113

Aitmatov, Chingiz, *The Ascent of Mount Fuji*, 446, 449

Akhmadulina, Bella, 444, 445

Akhmatova, Anna, 113

Aksyonov, Vasili, 407-8, 421, 443, 449; *Always on Sale*, 408; *Your Murderer*, 408-10, 448, 454; "Rendezvous," 454; "The Shopworn Tare of Barrels," 454

Aleksandrinsky Theater, 43

Alexis, Man of God (Kuzmin), 71-72

Alive Forever! (Rozov), 350-54, 355, 360

Alley Theatre, 424

Alone (Alyoshin), 344, 348-50, 355

Always on Sale (Aksyonov), 408

Amalrik, Andrei, 380, 407, 408, 454; difficulties with authorities, 384-86; *Involuntary Journey to Siberia*, 385, 386; *Will the Soviet Union Survive Until 1984?*, 385, 386, 397; interest in drama and theater, 386-87; *My Aunt Is Living in Volokolamsk*, 386, 388, 389, 390, 391, 395-96; *The Fourteen Lovers of Ugly Mary-Ann*, 386, 389, 391-93; *The Story of the Little White Bull*, 386, 389-90; *Is Uncle Jack a Conformist?*, 386, 388, 391, 393-95; *East-West: A Dialogue in Suzdal*, 386, 388-89, 390, 391, 396; dramatization of Gogol's "The Nose," 386

American Conservatory Theater (ACT), 424

Anathema (Andreev), 80, 84-86, 88

And in the Morning They Woke Up (Shukshin), 446, 448-49, 451

And Pippa Dances (Hauptmann), 56

Andreev, Leonid, xii; *The Life of Man*, 66, 80-84, 85, 86, 88; decline of reputation, 78-79; *He Who Gets Slapped*, 78, 80, 118-23, 399; *Savva*, 78, 79, 80, 118; *The Days of Our Life*, 79; *Gaudeamus*, 79; *Youth*, 79; *Professor Storitsyn*, 79, 119; *Yekaterina Ivanovna*, 79; *Thou Shalt Not Kill*, 79; *To the Stars*, 79, 80; *Love for One's Neighbor*, 80; *The Fair Sabine Women*, 80; *King, Law and Freedom*, 80; *A Horse in the Senate*, 80; *Monument*, 80; *King Hunger*, 80; *Black Masks*, 80, 86-88, 98; *Anathema*, 80, 84-86, 88; *Ocean*, 80; *Samson in Chains*, 80; *Pleasant Phantoms*, 80; Gorky quoted on *The Life of Man*, 81-82

Anfisa (Andreev), 79, 119

Angara, 410, 412

Annensky, Innokenti, 99, 105, 106, 107, 108; *Melanippe the Philosopher*, 100; *King Ixion*, 100; *Laodamia*, 100-3, 104, 105; *Thamyras the Cythara Player*, 100, 103-5, 107, 108

Antiworlds (Voznesensky), 454

Apes Are Coming, The (Lunts), 225

Arbuzov, Aleksei, 32, 426, 431-32, 451; *Tanya*, 240, 248-55, 261, 341, 355; *Years of Wandering*, 334, 340-41; *My Poor Marat*, 360, 361, 367-72, 373, 432; *The Happy Days of an Unhappy Man*, 361, 367, 372-79, 432; *Nocturnal Confession*, 367, 372; *An Old Fashioned Comedy*, 432, 434, 436-37, 441-43, 451; *Choice*, 432, 434-35; *Evening Light*, 432, 434-36, 445; *In This Pleasant Old House*, 432, 433, 436, 437, 438-39, 440; *My Eye-Catcher*, 432,

Arbazov, Aleksei (*Continued*)
433-34, 437, 440-41, 443; *Tales of the Old Arbat District of Moscow*, 432, 439-40
Arena Stage, 416, 446
Are You Listening, Moscow?! (Tretyakov), 147, 149, 214
Aristocrats (Pogodin), 266-71
Armored Train No. 14-69 (Ivanov), 153-56, 157, 159, 163, 175
Arzhak, Nikolai, *see* Daniel, Yuli
Ascent of Mount Fuji, The (Aitmatov and Mukhamedzhanov), 446-48, 449, 451
At Mid-Century (Sheynin), 327-29
Attila (Zamyatin), 225, 229
August 1914 (Solzhenitsyn), 397
Axel (Villiers de L'Isle Adam), 50-51, 59

Badgers, The (Leonov), 295
Bakst, Leon, 77
Bald Soprano, The (Ionesco), 387
Balmont, Konstantin, 58, 266; *Three Blossomings*, 68, 70
Barbarians (Gorky), 17-19, 20, 22
Bathhouse, The (Mayakovsky), 144-46, 149, 204, 206, 209-13, 222, 223, 224, 360, 381, 383
Bear, The (Chekhov), 414
Beardsley, Aubrey, 71
Beckett, Samuel, 238, 387, 396
Bedbug, The (Mayakovsky), 144, 149, 171, 198-99, 204-9, 210, 211, 212, 223, 224, 225, 228, 381, 382
Behind the Curtains of the Soul (Yevreinov), 128
Bely, Andrei, 125; *He Who Has Come*, 61-62, 63, 75, 77, 125; *The Jaws of Night*, 62-63; *Zapiski chudaka* (*Notes of an Eccentric*), 62; quoted on Symbolist mystery drama, 77-78
Bertran de Born (Lunts), 225, 229, 230
Birth of Tragedy, The (Nietzsche), 99
Bill-Belotserkovsky, Vladimir: *Echo*, 148; *Port the Helm*, 148; *Storm*, 163; *Calm*, 187; *Life Is Calling*, 246-48, 255
Black Masks (Andreev), 80, 86-88, 98
Black Snow (Bulgakov), *see Theatrical Novel, A*
Blind Ones, The (Maeterlinck), 52, 53, 54
Blockade (Vsevolod Ivanov), 153
Blok, Aleksandr, xii, 33, 73, 78, 113, 117, 146, 422; and the Petrograd Theater Section, 31-32; *The Fairground Booth*, 59, 66,

70, 75, 76, 89, 90, 92, 123, 124-28, 131, 145, 229, 232, 393, 396; on Maeterlinck in Russia, 75-76; *The King on the Square*, 89, 90, 91; *The Unknown Woman*, 89-90, 114; *Lyrical Dramas*, 89, 90, 91-92, 94, 97; *The Song of Fate*, 89, 90, 91, 94; *Ramzes*, 89; *The Rose and the Cross*, 89, 90, 92-94, 96, 97, 98, 225
Bogdan Khmelnitsky (Korneychuk), 315
Boleslaus the Brave (Wyspiański), 88
Bolshoy Theater (Leningrad), 38, 412, 418
Boris Godunov (Pushkin), 303
Bread (Kirshon), 47, 48, 271-80
Breakup (Lavrenyov), 156-60, 174, 242, 310, 311, 317
Brecht, Bertolt, 165, 408, 454
Brodsky, Josip, 455
Brook, Peter, 57
Brothers Karamazov, The (Dostoevsky), 287, 292
Brothers Tur: *Oil*, 305; *Utopia*, 305; *Seven Waves*, 305; *The Eastern Battalion*, 305; *The Confrontation*, 305; *Smoke of the Fatherland*, 305-8, 309, 310, 311; *The Extraordinary Law*, 305; *The Duel*, 305
Brown, Edward G., 331, 334
Bryusov, Valeri, 65, 83; and Russian symbolism, 58; on limitations of realism and naturalism in the theater ("Nenuzhnaya pravda"), 60-61; *Earth*, 62, 66-67, 68; *The Wayfarer*, 67-68
Bubus the Teacher (Faiko), 147, 214, 215
Bugaev, Boris, *see* Bely, Andrei
Bulgakov, Mikhail, 149, 452; *Days of the Turbins*, 148, 159, 168, 169-70, 171, 174, 195, 222, 242, 310; difficulties with authorities over *The White Guard*, 167-68; *Heart of a Dog*, 167; *The Fatal Eggs*, 167; *The Master and Margarita*, 167, 171; *Flight*, 168, 170-4, 178, 222, 226; *A Cabal of Hypocrites* (*Molière*), 169; *A Theatrical Novel* (*Black Snow*), 169; *Zoya's Apartment*, 195-99, 222; opposition to production of dramatization of *The Master and Margarita*, 453-54

Cabal of Hypocrites, A (Bulgakov), 169
Calderón de la Barca, Pedro, 73; *Life is a Dream*, 59
Calvary (Yeats), 55
Cancer Ward (Solzhenitsyn), 397

Candle in the Wind (Solzhenitsyn), 397, 402-6
Čapek, Karel, 171, 228; *R.U.R.*, 206
Cardsharp, The (Shkvarkin), 204
Casanova de Seingalt, Giacomo, 112, 114, 115, 116, 117
Casanova's End (Tsvetaeva), 112, 114, 115
Case, The (Sukhovo-Kobylin), 219
Cathleen Ni Hoolihan (Yeats), 55
Chekhov, Anton, ix, x, xi, xii, 33, 121, 350; correspondence with Gorky, 1, 2; *The Cherry Orchard*, 3, 4, 36, 169, 296, 378, 436; compared with Gorky, 4, 5, 6, 7, 15, 16, 18, 21; *Platonov*, 4; *Ivanov*, 4; *Uncle Vanya*, 4; *The Three Sisters*, 4, 353, 435, 436; *On the Highway*, 4, 253; *The Seagull*, 10, 14, 15, 16, 75; *The Wedding*, 198, 412; imitated by Leonov, 296, 297; influence on Arbuzov, 378; parallels with Vampilov, 412, 414, 418, 420, 421; *The Bear*, 414
"Chelkash" (Gorky), 4
Cherry Orchard, The (Chekhov), 3, 4, 36, 169, 296, 378, 436
Chief Thing, The (Yevreinov), 128, 129-36, 145
Child of Allah, A (Gumilyov), 109, 110, 118
Choice (Arbuzov), 432, 434-35
Choice of a Bride, The (Kuzmin), 71
Christmas at the Ivanovs (Vvedensky), 235-38, 390, 397
Christ, the Angels, and the Soul (Merezh-kovsky), 73
City of the Winds (Kirshon), 271
City of Truth, The (Lunts), 224, 225-29
Claudel, Paul, *The Tidings Brought to Mary*, 88
Compromise of Naib-Khan, The (Vsevolod Ivanov), 152-53
Comrade Tsatkin and Co. (Popovsky), 204
Confrontation, The (Brothers Tur and Sheynin), 304
Conspiracy of Feelings, The (Olesha), 177, 410
Coral, The (Kaiser), 206
Counterfeit Coin, The (Gorky), 17, 25
Court, The (Kirshon), 272
Craig, Gordon, 57
Crooked Mirror, The (cabaret), 127, 128
Cyrano de Bergerac (Rostand), 113

Dangerous Precaution (Kuzmin), 71
Daniel, Yuli, 381, 455

D'Annunzio, Gabriele, *Francesca da Rimini*, 88, 98
Dark Lady, The (Dombrovsky), 454
Day of the Wedding, The (Rozov), 426, 439, 440
Days of Our Life, The (Andreev), 79
Days of the Turbins (Bulgakov), 148, 159, 168, 169-70, 171, 174, 195, 222, 242, 310
Death of Cuchulain, The (Yeats), 55
Death of Tintagiles, The (Maeterlinck), 53
Deirdre (Yeats), 55
Denis Davydov (Solovyov), 299
Devil Play, The (Remizov), 68-69
Die schönsten Sagen des Klassischen Altertums (Schwab), 105
Difficult Hour, The (Lagerkvist), 52
Dlya teatra i kino (Volodin), 455-56
"Doctors' Plot," 381, 382, 394
Doctor Zhivago (Pasternak), 343
Dombrovsky, Yuri, *The Dark Lady*, 454
Don Juan in Egypt (Gumilyov), 109
Dostigaev and Others (Gorky), 30, 34, 35, 36, 39-41, 42, 49
Dostoevsky, Fyodor, 87, 403; *The Double*, 287; *The Brothers Karamazov*, 287, 292
Double, The (Dostoevsky), 287
Do You Turn Somersaults? (Arbuzov), *see Old-Fashioned Comedy, An*
Dragon, The (Shvarts), 281, 282, 283, 289-94
Dreaming of the Bones, The (Yeats), 56
Duck Hunting (Vampilov), 412, 416-18
Dudintsev, Vladimir, *Not By Bread Alone*, 343
Duel (Brothers Tur and Sheynin), 305
Duncan, Isadora, 77

Earth (Bryusov), 62, 66-67, 68
Eastern Battalion, The (Brothers Tur and Sheynin), 305
East-West: A Dialogue in Suzdal (Amalrik), 386, 388-89, 390, 391, 396
Eccentric, The (Afinogenov), 240
Echelon (Roshchin), 424-25, 445, 449
Echo (Bill-Belotserkovsky), 148
Ehrenburg, Ilya, *The Golden Heart*, 72
Elder Son, The (Vampilov), 412, 415-16, 437
Elizabeth Bam (Kharms), 231, 233-35, 396
Embezzlers, The (Kataev), 182
End of Krivorylsk (Romashov), 195, 198
Enemies (Gorky), 17, 19-21, 24
Envy (Olesha), 177, 409-10

Erdman, Nikolai, 149, 387, 452, 453, 454;
  The Warrant, 198, 200, 222; *The Suicide*,
  199-204, 222
Eudoxia of Heliopolis (Kuzmin), 71, 72
Euripides, 101
Evening Light (Arbuzov), 432, 434-36, 445
Everything Is Left to People (Alyoshin),
  354-55
Evreinov, Nikolai, *see* Yevreinov, Nikolai
Extraordinary Law, The (Brothers Tur and
  Sheynin), 305

Factory Girl (Volodin), 355-57, 358, 360,
  361, 362
Faiko, Aleksei:*Bubus the Teacher*, 147, 214;
  Yevgraf, Seeker of Adventures, 198; *The
  Man with a Briefcase*, 198, 214-21; *Lake
  Lyul*, 214, 408
Fairground Booth, The (Blok), 59, 66, 70, 75,
  76, 89, 90, 92, 123, 124-28, 131, 145, 229,
  232, 393, 396
Fair Sabine Women, The (Andreev), 80
Fakely, 124
Falkovsky, F.N., 79
Familiar Story, A (Simonov), 308
Fantastic Tales (Sinyavsky-Tertz), 380, 454
Farewell in June (Vampilov), 410, 414-15,
  437
Fastnachtsspiele, 142
Fatal Eggs, The (Bulgakov), 167
Fathers and Sons (Turgenev), 5
Fear (Afinogenov), 48, 240-46, 247, 248, 249,
  255
Feast of Conquerors, The (Solzhenitsyn), 397
Fellow from Our Town, A (Simonov), 308
Field and Road (Vsevolod Ivanov), 153
Field Marshal Kutuzov (Solovyov), 295,
  299-303, 304
Fires of St. Dominick (Zamyatin), 225, 228
First Circle, The (Solzhenitsyn), 397
First Horse Army, The (Vishnevsky), 48, 148,
  163-67, 175
Five Evenings (Volodin), 355, 356, 357-59,
  360, 442, 451
Flight (Bulgakov), 168, 170-74, 178, 222, 226
Fokine, Michel, 77
Foma Campanella (Lunacharsky), 225
Foma Gordeev (Gorky), 4, 5
Fortune (Tsvetaeva), 112, 117, 118
Four Drops (Rozov), 443
Fourteen Lovers of Ugly Mary-Ann, The
  (Amalrik), 386, 389, 391-93

Francesca da Rimini (D'Annunzio), 88, 98
Freud, Sigmund, 177, 188, 264, 422
From Night till Noon (Rozov), 428, 430-31
Front (Korneychuk), 305, 315-17, 321

Galich, Aleksandr, 444, 455, 473
Game, The (Gumilyov), 109
Gas I, II (Kaiser), 206
Gas Masks (Tretyakov), 149-50
Gaudeamus (Andreev), 79
Gibian, George, 231, 235
Gift of the Wise Bees, The (Sologub), 100
Gippius, Zinaida, 83, 157; *Sacred Blood*,
  59-60, 61; *The Red Poppy*, 59; *The Green
  Ring*, 59
Glebov, Anatoli:*Inga*, 248, 259-64, 265, 451;
  Zagmuk, 260
Goethe, Johann Wolfgang von, 31
Gogol, Nikolai, 87, 287, 387, 412, 452, 453;
  The Inspector General, 188, 190, 192-93,
  383; "The Nose," 287, 288, 386
  (dramatized by Amalrik); *Marriage*,
  412
Golden Coach, The (Leonov), 296
Golden Heart, The (Ehrenburg), 72
Golden Helmet, The (Yeats), 55
Goldoni, Carlo, 136
Golovlyov Family, The (Saltykov-
  Shchedrin), 23
Gondla (Gumilyov), 109
Gontaut Biron, Armand Louis, duc de
  Lauzun, 112, 114, 118
Good Luck! (Rozov), 334, 337-40
Gorky, Maxim, x, xiii, 42, 43, 48, 49, 91, 168,
  418; relations with Chekhov and Moscow
  Art Theater, 1-2; hiatus in dramatic writ-
  ing, 29-34; on Andreev's *Life of Man*,
  81-83;*The Petty Bourgeois*, 2, 3, 4, 5, 6, 7,
  9, 10, 13, 16; *The Lower Depths*, 3, 4, 6,
  7-9, 10-11, 12, 13, 18, 24, 27, 81, 129, 268;
  Summer Folk, 13-15, 16-17, 22; *Bar-
  barians*, 17-19, 20, 22; *Enemies*, 17, 19-21,
  24; *The Last Ones*, 17, 21; *Queer People*,
  17, 21-22; *Vassa Zheleznova*, 17, 22-24,
  25, 27, 30, 34, 34, 37, 50, 297; *The Zykovs*,
  17, 25-28, 29, 34, 37; *The Counterfeit
  Coin*, 17, 25; *The Old Man*, 17, 25, 29;
  Somov and Others, 29, 30, 34; *Yegor
  Bulychov and Others*, 30, 34, 35-36,
  37-39, 40, 41, 42, 49; *Dostigaev and
  Others*, 30, 34, 35, 36, 39-41, 42, 49; *The*

Normans, 33, 34; *Workhorse Gabalot*, 33-34
Gozzi, Carlo, 70, 136
Grani, 397
Great Day, A (Kirshon), 272
Great Power, The (Romashov), 189
Great Sovereign, The (Solovyov), 299, 302
Green Ring, The (Gippius), 59
Griboedov, Aleksandr, 117; *Woe from Wit*, 117-18
Grotowski, Jerzy, 57
Guests, The (Zorin), 334-36, 342, 360
Gulag Archipelago, The (Solzhenitsyn), 270, 381, 397
Gumilyov, Nikolai: *Don Juan in Egypt*, 109; *Actheon*, 109; *The Game*, 109; *Gondla*, 109; *A Child of Allah*, 109, 110; *The Poisoned Tunic*, 109, 110-12

Hafiz, 110
Hamsun, Knut, 327
Hannele's Trip to Heaven (Hauptmann), 56
Happy Days of an Unhappy Man, The (Arbuzov), 361, 367, 372-79, 432
Harmful Element, A (Shkvarkin), 204
Hauptmann, Gerhart, 55, 56
Heart of a Dog (Bulgakov), 167
Hedda Gabler (Ibsen), 66
He Who Gets Slapped (Andreev), 78, 80, 118-23, 399
He Who Has Come (Bely), 61-62, 63, 75, 77, 125
Hippius Zinaida, *see* Gippius, Zinaida
Hofmannsthal, Hugo von, 55, 56
Holy Well, The (Kataev), 454
Horse in the Senate, A (Andreev), 80
House with a View of the Fields, The (Vampilov), 410, 412, 413-14
Hugo, Victor-Marie, 31, 33

Ibsen, Henrik, 66, 418; *Hedda Gabler*, 66
Iceman Cometh, The (O'Neill), 11, 12, 13
Imr-ul-Qais, 110-12
Incident with a Typesetter, An (Vampilov), 412-13
Incomparable Nakonechnikov, The (Vampilov), 412, 418, 438
Inga (Glebov), 248, 259-64, 265, 451
Inspector-General, The (Gogol), 188, 190, 192-93, 383
Inspiration (Vsevolod Ivanov), 153
In the Fire (Falkovsky), 79

In the Old Cossack Manner (Sofronov), 443
In This Pleasant Old House (Arbuzov), 432, 433, 436, 437, 438-39, 440
Intruder, The (Maeterlinck), 52, 53, 54
Invasion (Leonov), 296, 305, 311-15, 321
Involuntary Journey to Siberia (Amalrik), 385, 386
Ionesco, Eugène, 238, 387, 396, 408; *The Bald Soprano*, 387
Irkutsk Dramatic Theater, 415
Is There Life on Mars? (Remezov-I. Ivanov), 380, 381-84, 397
Is Uncle Jack a Conformist? (Amalrik), 386, 388, 391, 393-95
It Happened in Irkutsk (Arbuzov), 360, 361, 362-64, 366, 373, 377, 378, 433, 442
Ivanov (Chekhov), 4
Ivanov, I., *see* Remezov, Andrei
Ivanov, Vsevolod: *Blockade*, 153; *Field and Road*, 153; *Inspiration*, 153; *The Compromise of Naib-Khan*, 153; *Twelve Young Men from a Snuffbox*, 153; *Armored Train No. 14-69*, 153-56, 157, 159, 163, 175
Ivanov, Vyacheslav, 63, 64, 65, 66, 99, 105, 124; on Greek drama, Nietzsche, and Wagner, 64; *Po zvyozdam*, 64; *Prometheus*, 100; *Tantalus*, 100
I Want a Baby (Tretyakov), 150

Jacopone da Todi, 73
Jarry, Alfred, *Ubu Roi*, 58, 285, 386, 392
Jaws of Night, The (Bely), 62-63
Jeu de Robin et Marion, Le (Adam de la Halle), 73

Kafka, Franz, 171, 233, 396
Kaiser, Georg: *The Coral, Gas I, Gas II*, 206
Kamerny Theater, 43, 44, 176
Karlinsky, Simon, 106, 113, 114
Kastorsky, S., 42
Kataev, Valentin, 407, 452; *Squaring the Circle*, 148, 182-86, 188, 195, 200, 441; *The Embezzlers*, 182; *Time, Forward!*, 182; *The Holy Well*, 454
Kharms, Daniil, 231, 232, 238, 387, 390, 396; *Elizabeth Bam*, 232-35, 396
Khlebnikov, Velimir, 387, 396; *Mrs. Lenin*, 387
King Hunger (Andreev), 80
King Ixion (Annensky), 100
King, Law, and Freedom (Andreev), 80
King Oedipus (Sophocles), 56

King of the Great Clock Tower, The (Yeats), 55

King of the Square, The (Blok), 89, 90, 91

King's Threshold, The (Yeats), 55-56

Kirshon, Vladimir, 46, 47, 48; "Za sotsialno-obosnovanny psikhologizm," 46; "Za sot-sialistichesky realizm v dramaturgii," 47; *Bread*, 47, 48, 271-80; *Konstantin Terekhin*, 271; *City of the Winds*, 271; *The Rails Are Humming*, 271; *A Great Day*, 272; *The Court*, 272; *The Miraculous Alloy*, 272, 279

Komissarzhevskaya, Vera (theater), 66, 70, 72, 76, 124

Konstantin Terekhin (Kirshon), 271

Korneychuk, Aleksandr: *Front*, 305, 315-17, 321; *Bogdan Khmelnitsky*, 315; *Platon Krechet*, 315; *Sinking of the Squadron*, 315

Korsh Theater, 79

Kotik Letaev (Bely), 63

Kremlin Chimes, The (Pogodin), 240, 255-59, 264, 267

Kron, Aleksandr; attack on "no conflict" theory, 331-32

Kuzenkov, Vladimir, 421

Kuzmin, Mikhail, xii, 146; work with Meyerhold, 70-71; *Wings*, 70; *Dangerous Precaution*, 71; *The Choice of a Bride*, 71; *Two Shepherds and a Nymph in a Hut*, 71; *Alexis, Man of God*, 71-72; *Eudoxia of Heliopolis*, 71, 72; *Martinianus*, 71; *Uslovnosti*, 136; *The Venetian Madcaps*, 136-38

Lagerkvist, Pär; *The Difficult Hour*, 52

Lake Lyul (Faiko), 214

Laodamia (Annensky), 100-3, 104, 105

Last Ones, The (Gorky), 17, 21

Last Summer in Chulimsk (Vampilov), 412, 413, 418-21, 437

Lef, 149

Leningrad, 320

Leonov, Leonid: *A Provincial Story*, 295; *Skutarevsky*, 295; *The Orchards of Polov-chansk*, 295-99; *The Snowstorm*, 295; *The Taming of Badadoshkin*, 295; *The Wolf*, 295; *Untilovsk*, 295; *An Ordinary Person*, 296; *Invasion*, 296, 305, 311-15, 321; *Lyonushka*, 296; *The Golden Coach*, 296

Lermontov, Mikhail, 354; *Masquerade*, 118; *Mtsyri*, 304

Life Is a Dream (Calderón), 59

Life Is Calling (Bill-Belotserkovsky), 246-48, 249, 250, 255, 275

Life of Man, The (Andreev), 66, 80-84, 85, 86, 88

List of Assets, A (Olesha), 177-81, 191, 240, 246, 249, 255

Literaturnaya Moskva, II, 332, 343

Liturgy to Myself, A (Sologub), 76

Lorca, Federico García, 171

Lost Son, The (Arbuzov), 364-67

Love for One's Neighbor (Andreev), 80

Love-Girl and the Innocent, The (Solzhenit-syn), 269, 397-402, 404, 405, 406

Love Story (Erich Segal), 442

Lower Depths, The (Gorky), 3, 4, 7-9, 10-11, 12, 13, 18, 24, 27, 81, 129, 268

Lunacharsky, Anatoli, 33, 280; *Foma Campanella*, 225; *Oliver Cromwell*, 225

Lunts, Lev: *Outside the Law*, 224, 228; *The City of Truth*, 224, 225-29; *Bertran de Born*, 225, 229, 230; *The Apes Are Coming!*, 225; compared with Zamyatin, 225-26, 228-29

Lyonushka (Leonov), 296

Lyrical Dramas (Blok), 89, 90, 91-92, 94, 97

Lyubimov, Yuri, xi, 453

Lyubimov (Sinyavsky-Tertz), 454

Lyubov Yarovaya (Trenyov), 158, 160-63, 248, 317

McLean, Hugh, 343

Mad Haberdasher, The (Surov), 328

Maeterlinck, Maurice, 51, 54, 55, 62, 66, 67, 75, 78, 80, 82, 83, 84, 86, 88-89, 96, 124-25, 233, 387; *The Treasure of the Humble*, 51-52; *The Intruder*, 52, 53, 54; *The Blind Ones*, 52, 53, 54; *The Death of Tintagiles*, 53; *Pelléas et Mélisande*, 53, 98; *Sister Beatrice*, 66, 89

Magnitizdat, 455

"Makar Chudra" (Gorky), 4

Makepeace Experiment, The, see *Lyubimov*

Maksimov, Vladimir, 455

Malaya Bronnaya Theater, xii

Mallarmé, Stéphane, 50, 51, 58

Maly Theater, 43

Man and Superman (Shaw), 109

Man with a Briefcase, The (Faiko), 198, 214-21

Man with a Gun, The (Pogodin), 255

Maria (Babel), 249, 317

Maria (Salynsky), 445
Marinetti, Filippo Tommaso, 57
Marriage (Gogol), 412
Marshak, Samuil, 281
Martinianus (Kuzmin), 71
Mashenka (Afinogenov), 249
Masquerade (Lermontov), 118, 136
Master and Margarita, The (Bulgakov), 167, 171, 453
Mayakovsky, Vladimir, 138, 146, 266, 384, 408, 412, 452, 454; *Vladimir Mayakovsky*, 138-41, 204; "Teatr, kinematograf, futurizm," 138; *The Bedbug*, 144, 149, 171, 198-99, 204-9, 210, 211, 212, 223, 224, 225, 228, 381, 382; *The Bathhouse*, 144-46, 149, 204, 206, 209-13, 222, 224, 360, 381, 383
Melanippe the Philosopher (Annensky), 100
Merezhkovsky, Dmitri: *Return to Nature*, 59; *Christ, the Angels, and the Soul*, 73
Merry Death, A (Yevreinov), 128-29
Merry Theater for Grown-up Children, 77
Meyerhold, Vsevolod, ix, 31, 43, 57, 65, 66, 67, 70, 71, 72, 76, 92, 124, 136, 138, 146, 149, 151, 203, 219, 454; "Fellowship of the New Drama," 65, 66, 68, 73
Minutes of a Meeting (Gelman), 446, 449-50, 451
Miracle de Théophile, Le (Rutebeuf), 73, 92
Miraculous Alloy, The (Kirshon), 272, 279
Mir isskustva, 60
Molière, Jean-Baptiste, 31, 67
Molière (Bulgakov), *see Cabal of Hypocrites, A*
Month in the Country, A (Turgenev), 15, 419
Monument (Andreev), 80
Moscow Art Theater, ix, x, 1, 2, 3, 43, 44, 47, 60, 66, 421
Moscow Dramatic Theater, 415
Mother (Gorky), 22
Mrożek, Sławomir, 238, 396
Mrs. Lenin (Khlebnikov), 387
Mtsyri (Lermontov), 304
Mukhamedzhanov, Kaltai, *The Ascent of Mount Fuji*, 446
My Aunt Is Living in Volokolamsk (Amalrik), 386, 388, 389, 390, 391, 395-96
My Eye-Catcher (Arbuzov), 432, 433-34, 437, 440-41, 443
My Poor Marat (Arbuzov), 360, 361, 367-72, 373, 432
My Sixties (Rozov), 426, 427, 430

Mystery-Bouffe (Mayakovsky), 138, 141-44, 204, 206, 223, 224, 226

Naked King, The (Shvarts), 281, 282-86, 288, 289, 291, 292
Narodnye russkie skazki (Afanasev), 94
Nekrasov, Viktor, 455
Nemirovich-Danchenko, Vladimir, 1
"Nenuzhnaya pravda" (Bryusov), 60-61
"Neoromantizm v drame" (Merezhkovsky), 59
Newcombe, Josephine M., 79
Nietzsche, Friedrich, 64; *The Birth of Tragedy*, 99
"No conflict" theory, 329-33
Nocturnal Confession (Arbuzov), 367, 372
Nocturnal Dances (Sologub), 77, 94
Normans, The (Gorky), 33, 34
Nose, The (Gorky), 287, 288; dramatized by Amalrik, 386
Not By Bread Alone (Dudintsev), 343
Novy Lef, 149
Novy mir, 342, 343

Ocean (Andreev), 80
"O drame" (Blok), 72, 75
Oedipus at Colonus (Sophocles), 56
Oil (Gorev, Shteyn, Pyotr "Tur"), 305
Okhlopkov, N.P., xi, 415
Okudzhava, Bulat, 444, 446; *Poor Abrasimov*, 454
Old-Fashioned Comedy, An (Arbuzov), 432, 434, 436-37, 441-43, 451
Old Man, The (Gorky), 17, 25, 29
Olesha, Yuri: *Envy*, 177, 409-10; *The Conspiracy of Feelings*, 177, 410; *A List of Assets*, 177-81, 191, 240, 246, 249, 255; speech at First Congress of Soviet Writers quoted, 181
Oliver Cromwell (Lunacharsky), 225
On Baile's Strand (Yeats), 55
One Day in the Life of Ivan Denisovich (Solzhenitsyn), 269, 397, 398, 406
O'Neill, Eugene, *The Iceman Cometh*, 11, 12, 13
"On Himself as a Writer of Plays" (Amalrik), 386
Only Jealousy of Emer, The (Yeats), 55, 56
On ne badine pas avec l'amour (Musset), 113
"On Socialist Realism" (Sinyavsky), 455
On the Eve (Afinogenov), 295, 303-4, 305
On the Highway (Chekhov), 4, 253

Optimistic Tragedy, An (Vishnevsky), 148, 175-76, 315
Orchards of Polovchansk, The (Leonov), 295-99
Ordinary Person, An (Leonov), 296
Ostrovsky, Aleksandr, 25, 26, 33; *Wolves and Sheep*, 402; *The Storm*, 426
Outside the Law (Lunts), 224, 228
Ovid, 101

Pantaloon (Ward), 119
Pasternak, Boris, 320, 344; *Doctor Zhivago*, 343
Pelléas et Mélisande (Maeterlinck), 53, 98
Personal Matter, A (Shteyn), 334, 335, 336-37
Petrarchan Sonnet, A (Pogodin), 344-48
Petty Bourgeois, The (Gorky), 2, 3, 4, 5, 6, 7, 9, 10, 13, 16
Petty Demon, The (Sologub), 64
Phaedra (Tsveteaeva), 100, 105, 107, 117
Phoenix (Tsvetaeva), 112, 114-15, 118
Pinter, Harold, 238
Pirandello, Luigi, 125, 131; *Six Characters in Search of an Author*, 145; *Tonight We Improvise!*, 145
Piscator, Erwin, 165, 260
Platon Krechet (Korneychuk), 315
Platonov (Chekhov), 4
Player Queen, The (Yeats), 55, 56
Plays for Dancers (Yeats), 55
Pleasant Phantoms (Andreev), 80
Poe, Edgar Allen, 87
Pogodin, Nikolai, 45, 46, 48; *The Kremlin Chimes*, 240, 255-59, 264, 267; *The Man with a Gun*, 255; *Third, Pathetique*, 255, 361-62, 363; *Tempo*, 264-66, 269, 271; *Aristocrats*, 266-71; *A Petrarchan Sonnet*, 344-48
Poisoned Tunic, The (Gumilyov), 109, 110-12, 118
Poor Abrosimov (Okudzhava),454
Popovsky, Aleksandr, *Comrade Tsatkin and Co.*, 204
Port the Helm (Bill-Belotserkovsky), 148
Pot of Broth, The (Yeats), 55
Power of Darkness, The (Tolstoy), 23
Po zvyozdam (Vyacheslav Ivanov), 64
Pravda, 331, 332, 453
Professor Storitsyn (Andreev), 79, 119
Proffer, Ellendea, 198
Prometheus (Ivanov), 100

Promise, The (Arbuzov), *see My Poor Marat*
Protesilaus and Laodamia (Wyspiański), 100
Protesilaus Deceased (Bryusov), 68, 100
Provincial Anecdotes (Vampilov), 412, 451
Provincial Story, A (Leonov), 295
Przybyszewski, Stanisław, 66
Purgatory (Yeats), 55
Pushkin, Aleksandr, xi, 113, 422; *Boris Godunov*, x, 303

Queer People (Gorky), 17, 21-22, 24

Radlov, Sergei, 34
Rails Are Humming, The (Kirshon), 271
Ramzes (Blok), 89
Red Cavalry (Babel), 166-67
Red Poppy, The (Gippius), 59
Red Rust (Kirshon), *see Konstantin Terekhin*
Reinhardt, Max, 3
Remezov, Andrei (I. Ivanov), 380-81, 394; *Is There Life on Mars?*, 380, 381-84, 397
Remizov, Aleksei, xii, 66; "Tovarishchestvo novoy dramy" (The Fellowship of the New Drama) quoted, 65-66; *The Devil Play*, 68-69; *The Tragedy of Judas, Prince of Iscariot*, 68, 69-70
"Rendezvous" (Aksyonov), 454
Resurrection, The (Yeats), 55, 56
Return to Nature (Merezhkovsky), 59
Reunion, The (Rozov), 427-30, 446, 448
Rice, Elmer, 228
Roar, China! (Tretyakov), 148, 149, 150-52, 153, 157, 163
Robert Tim (Afinogenov), 240
Romashov, Boris, 149, 199, 387, 452; *The Sweet Soufflé*, 188-95, 198; *The Great Power*, 189; *The End of Krivorylsk*, 195, 198
Rose and the Cross, The (Blok), 89, 90, 92-94, 96, 97, 98, 225
Roshchin, Mikháil: *Valentin and Valentina*, 421-24, 427; *Echelon*, 423, 424-25, 445, 449
Rostand, Edmond, 33, 117; *L'Aiglon*, 105, 113; *Cyrano de Bergerac*, 113
Royal Shakespeare Company, 13, 465
Różewicz, Tadeusz, 238
Rozov, Viktor, 421, 422; *Alive Forever!*, 350-54, 355, 360; *My Sixties*, 426, 427, 430; *The Day of the Wedding*, 426, 439, 440; *The Social Director*, 426-27, 428, 439; *The Reunion*, 427-30, 446, 448; *From*

Night till Noon, 428, 430-31; *Four Drops*, 443
R.U.R. (Čapek), 206
Russian People, The (Simonov), 305, 308-11, 315, 321, 322
Russian Question, The (Simonov), 326-27, 328
Russkie simvolisti (Bryusov), 58
Rust (Kirshon). See *Konstantin Terekhin*
Rutebeuf, 73, 92
Ryzhey, Pyotr, *see* Brothers Tur

Sacred Blood (Gippius), 59-60, 61
Saint-Exupéry, Antoine de, 422
Salynsky, Afanasi, *Maria*, 445
Samizdat, 455
Samson in Chains (Andreev), 80
Savva (Andreev), 78, 79, 80, 118
Schiller, Friedrich von, 31, 32
Schwab, Gustav, 105, 106
Seagull, The (Chekhov), 10, 14, 15, 16, 75
Segal, Erich, *Love Story*, 442
Seizure of the Winter Palace, The, 31
Seven Waves (Gorev, Shteyn, Pyotr "Tur"), 305
Severnye tsvety, 61
Shadow, The (Shvarts), 281, 282, 283, 286-89, 291, 292
Shakespeare, William, 31, 32, 33
Shcheglov, Mark, 332
Sheynin, Lev (with the Brothers Tur): *The Confrontation*, 305; *Smoke of the Fatherland*, 305-8, 309, 310, 311; *The Extraordinary Law*, 305; *The Duel*, 305
Ship of the Righteous, The (Yevreinov), 131
Shkvarkin, Vasili, 452; *A Harmful Element*, 204; *The Cardsharp*, 204
Sholokhov, Mikhail, 343
"*Shopworn Tare of Barrels, The*" (Aksyonov), 454
Shukshin, Vasili, *And in the Morning They Woke Up*, 446, 448-49, 451
Shvarts, Yevgeni, xii, 384, 408; *The Naked King*, 281, 282-86, 288, 289, 291, 292; *The Shadow*, 281, 282, 283, 286-89, 291, 292; *The Dragon*, 281, 282, 283, 289-94
Silver Dove, The (Bely), 63
Simonov, Konstantin: *The Russian People*, 305, 308-11, 315, 321, 322; *A Familiar Story*, 308; *A Story About One Love*, 308; *A Fellow from Our Town*, 308; *Wait for Me*, 308; *So Will It Be*, 308; *With You and Without You*, 308; *Under the Chestnut Trees of Prague*, 322-24, 326, 327; *The Russian Question*, 326-27, 328
Sinking of the Squadron, The (Korneychuk), 315
Sinyavsky, Andrei (Abram Tertz), 320, 456; *The Trial Begins*, 380, 381, 394, 454; *Fantastic Tales*, 380, 454; *Lyubimov* (*The Makepeace Experiment*), 454
Sister Beatrice (Maeterlinck), 66, 89
Six Characters in Search of an Author (Pirandello), 145
Skutarevsky (Leonov), 295
Smoke of the Fatherland (Brothers Tur and Sheynin), 305-8, 309, 310, 311
Snowstorm, The (Leonov), 295
Snowstorm, The (Tsvetaeva), 112, 113-14, 117
Social Director, The (Rozov), 426-27, 428, 439
Sofronov, Anatoli, 331; *A Strange Doctor*, 443; *In the Old Cossack Manner*, 443
Sologub, Fyodor, xii, 65, 66; "The Theater of One Will" quoted, 64-65; *The Petty Demon*, 64; *The Triumph of Death*, 66, 76, 77, 94, 96-98; *A Liturgy to Myself*, 76; *Nocturnal Dances*, 77, 94; *Vanka the Valet and the Page Jean*, 94-96
Solovyov, Vladimir: *Field Marshal Kutuzov*, 295, 299-303, 304; *The Great Sovereign*, 299; *Denis Davydov*, 299; *The Victors Are Judged*, 299
Solzhenitsyn, Aleksandr, 320, 344, 384, 407; *One Day in the Life of Ivan Denisovich*, 269, 397, 398, 406; *The Love-Girl and the Innocent*, 269, 397-402, 404, 405, 406; *The Gulag Archipelago*, 270, 381, 397; *The Cancer Ward*, 397; *The First Circle*, 397; *August 1914*, 397; *The Feast of Conquerors*, 397; *Candle in the Wind*, 397, 402-6
Somov and Others (Gorky), 29, 30, 34
Song of Fate (Blok), 89, 90, 91, 94
Sophocles, 31
Sovetskaya molodyozh, 412
Sovremennik Theater, 283, 396, 412, 424, 430, 446
So Will It Be (Simonov), 308
Spring's Awakening (Wedekind), 66
Squaring the Circle (Kataev), 148, 182-86, 188, 195, 200, 441

Stanislavsky, Konstantin, ix, xi, 1, 3, 56, 60, 168

Starinny Theater (Theater of Antiquity), 72-75, 127

Stone Guest, The (Pushkin), 109

Storm (Bill-Belotserkovsky), 163

Storm, The (Ostrovsky), 426

Story about One Love, A (Simonov), 308

Story of the Little White Bull, The (Amalrik), 386, 389-90

St. Petersburg (Bely), 63

Strange Doctor, A (Sofronov), 443

Sudeykin, Sergei, 134, 136

Suicide, The (Erdman), 199-204, 222

Sukhovo-Kobylin, Aleksandr, x, 387, 412, 452, 453; Tarelkin's Death, 171, 203, 219, 285, 396; possible influence on Faiko's Man with a Briefcase, 219-21; The Wedding of Krechinsky, 219-20; The Case, 219

Summer Folk (Gorky), 13-15, 16-17, 22

Sun, The (Minsky), 59

Sunken Bell, The (Hauptmann), 56, 60

Surkov, Aleksei, 342

Surov, Anatoli, The Mad Haberdasher, 328

Sweet Soufflé, The (Romashov), 188-95, 198

Taganka Theater, 444, 453, 454

Tairov, Aleksandr, 31, 43

Tales of the Old Arbat District of Moscow (Arbuzov), 432, 439-40

Taming of Badadoshkin, The (Leonov), 295

Tantalus (Vyacheslav Ivanov), 100

Tanya (Arbuzov), 240, 248-55, 261, 341, 355

Tarelkin's Death (Sukhovo-Kobylin), 171, 203, 219, 285, 396

Teatr, 331, 367, 372

Teatr dlya sebya (Yevreinov), 218

"Teatr i sovremennaya drama" (Bely), 77-78

Teatr kak takovoy (Yevreinov), 128

"Teatr, kinematograf, futurizm" (Mayakovsky), 138

Teatr: Kniga o novom teatre, 77

Tempo (Pogodin), 264-66, 269, 271

Tertz, Abram, see Sinyavsky, Andrei

Teternikov, Fyodor, see Sologub, Fyodor

Thamyras the Cythara Player (Annensky), 100, 103-5, 107, 108

Thaw, The (Ehrenburg), 343

Theater of Dionysus, 68

Theater of Eternal War, The (Yevreinov), 131

"Theater of One Will, The" (Sologub), 64-65, 76, 77

Theater of Popular Comedy, 34

Theater of the Soul, The (Yevreinov), see Behind the Curtains of the Soul

Theatrical Novel, A (Bulgakov), 169

Theseus-Ariadne (Tsvetaeva), 100, 105, 106-8

Third, Pathetique (Pogodin), 255, 361-62, 363

Thou Shall Not Kill (Andreev), 79

Three Blossomings (Balmont), 68, 70

Three Magi, The (Yevreinov), 73, 74-75

Three Sisters, The (Chekhov), 3, 4, 353, 435, 436

Tidings Brought to Mary, The (Claudel), 88

Time, Forward! (Kataev), 182

Time Machine, The (Wells), 209

Tolstoy, Lev, 20, 403; The Power of Darkness, 23; War and Peace, 304, 402

Tonight We Improvise! (Pirandello), 145

To the Stars (Andreev), 79, 80

"Tovarishchestvo novoy dramy" (Remizov), 65-66

Tovstonogov, Georgi, xi, 412, 415, 418

Tower, The (Hofmannsthal), 59

Tragedy of Judas, The (Remizov), 68, 69-70

Treasure of the Humble, The (Maeterlinck), 51-52

Trenyov, Konstantin, Lyubov Yarovaya, 160-63

Tretyakov, Sergei: Are You Listening, Moscow?!, 147, 149; Roar, China!, 148, 149, 150-52, 153, 157, 163; Gas Masks, 149, 150; I Want a Baby, 150

Trial Begins, The (Tertz), 380, 381, 394, 454

Trilogy (Sukhovo-Kobylin). See Wedding of Krechinsky, The; Case, The; Tarelkin's Death

Triumph of Death, The (Sologub), 66, 76, 77, 94, 96-98

"Trudny vopros" (Gorky), 33

Tsvetaeva, Marina, 99, 105-6, 109; Theseus-Ariadne, 100, 105, 106-8; Phaedra, 105, 107, 117; The Snowstorm, 112, 113-14, 117; Casanova's End, 112, 114, 115; Phoenix, 112, 114-15, 118; An Adventure, 112, 115-17, 118; Fortune, 112, 117, 118

Tubelsky, Leonid, see Brothers Tur

Tur Brothers, see Brothers Tur

Tvardovsky, Aleksandr, 342

Twelve Young Men from a Snuffbox (Vsevolod Ivanov), 153
Twenty Minutes with an Angel (Vampilov), 410, 412
"Twenty-six Men and a Girl (Gorky), 4
Two Anecdotes (Vampilov), 412
Two Shepherds and a Nymph in a Hut (Kuzmin), 71

Ubu Roi (Jarry), 58, 285, 386, 392
Ulyanov, Mikhail, 449
Uncle Vanya (Chekhov), 4
Under the Chestnut Trees of Prague (Simonov), 322-24, 326, 327
Unknown Woman, The (Blok), 89-90, 114
Untilovsk (Leonov), 295
Uslovnosti (Kuzmin), 136
Utopia (Gorev, Shteyn, Pyotr "Tur"), 305

Vakhtangov, Yevgeni, ix, 31, 43
Vakhtangov Theater, 410
Valentin and Valentina (Roshchin), 421-24, 427
Vampilov, Aleksandr, 407, 410-12, 421, 443; *Twenty Minutes with an Angel*, 410, 412; *The House with a View of the Fields*, 410, 412, 413-14; *Farewell in June*, 410, 414-15, 437; *The Elder Son*, 412, 415-16, 437; *Duck Hunting*, 412, 416-18; *An Incident with a Typesetter*, 412-13; *Provincial Anecdotes*, 412, 451; *The Incomparable Nakonechnikov*, 412, 418, 438; *Last Summer in Chulimsk*, 412, 413, 418-21
Vance, Nina, 424
Vanka the Valet and the Page Jean (Sologub), 94-96
Vassa Zheleznova (Gorky), 17, 22-24, 25, 27, 30, 34, 37, 50, 297
Vaudeville (recent Soviet), 437-39
Vega, Lope de, 31, 73
Velikorusskie narodnye pesni (Sobolevsky), 94
Venetian Madcaps, The (Kuzmin), 136-37
Vesy, 64, 65
Vickery, Walter, 343
Victors Are Judged, The (Solovyov), 299
Villiers de L'Isle Adam, Philippe August, 50-51
Virta, Nikolai, 332
Vishnevsky, Vsevolod: and the polemics over drama in the late 1920s and 1930s, 45-48; *The First Horse Army*, 48, 148,

163-67, 175; *An Optimistic Tragedy*, 148, 175-76, 315
Vladimir Mayakovsky (Mayakovsky), 138-41, 204
Volchok, Galina, xi, 424
Volkenshteyn, V., 148
Volodin, Aleksandr: *Factory Girl*, 355-57, 358, 360, 361, 362; *Five Evenings*, 355, 356, 357-59, 360, 442, 451; *Dlya Teatra i kino* (For Theater and Film), quoted, 455-56
Voznesensky, Andrei, *Antiworlds*, 454
Vvedenia v monodramu (Yevreinov), 128
Vvedensky, Aleksandr, 231, 232, 233, 387, 396; *Christmas at the Ivanovs*, 235-38, 390, 397
Vysotsky, Vladimir, 444

Wagner, Richard, 50, 51, 64
Wait for Me (Simonov), 308
War and Peace (Tolstoy), 304, 402
Ward, Robert, *Pantaloon*, 119
Warrant, The (Erdman), 198, 200, 222
Warsaw Melody, A (Zorin), 360
Wayfarer, The (Bryusov), 67-68
We (Zamyatin), 224, 225, 381
Wedding, The (Chekhov), 198, 412
Wedding of Krechinsky, The (Sukhovo-Kobylin), 190, 219, 220
Wedekind, Frank, *Spring's Awakening*, 66
White Guard, The (Bulgakov), 167-68, 169
Will the Soviet Union Survive Until 1984? (Amalrik), 385, 386, 397
Wilson, Edmund, 51
Wings (Kuzmin), 70
With You and Without You (Simonov), 308
Witkiewicz, Stanisław Ignacy, 228
Woe from Wit (Griboedov), 118
Wolf, The (Leonov), 295
Wolves and Sheep (Ostrovsky), 402
Woodward, James B., 79, 86
Words upon the Windowpane, The (Yeats), 55
Workhorse Gabalot (Gorky), 33-34
Wyspiánski, Stanisław, 55, 56; *Protesilaus and Laodamia*, 100

Years of Wandering (Arbuzov), 334, 340-41
Yeats, William Butler, 55-56
Yefremov, Oleg, xi, 408, 430
Yegor Bulychov and Others (Gorky), 30, 34, 35-36, 37-39, 40, 41, 42, 49

Yekaterina Ivanovna (Andreev), 79

Yevgraf, Seeker of Adventures (Faiko), 198

Yevreinov, Nikolai, xii, 72-73, 77, 138, 146; and the Theater of Antiquity, 73-74; and the Crooked Mirror, 127-28; Prologue to *Three Magi*, 73, 74-75; *Behind the Curtains of the Soul*, 128; *Vvedenie v monodramu*, 128; *Teatr kak takovoy*, 128; *Teatr dlya sebya*, 128; *A Merry Death*, 128-29; *The Chief Thing*, 128, 129-36, 145; *The Ship of the Righteous*, 131; *The Theater of Eternal War*, 131

Your Murderer (Aksyonov), 408-10, 448, 454

Youth (Andreev), 79

Yunost, 407

Yuvachev, *see* Kharms, Daniil

Zagmuk (Glebov), 206

Zapiski chudaka (Bely), 62

"Za sotsialistichesky realizm v dramaturgii" (Kirshon), 47

"Za sotsialno-obosnovanny psikhologizm" (Afinogenov), 46

Zhdanov, Andrei, 320, 330, 331, 343

Znanie, 78, 79

Zolotoe runo, 64

Zorin, Leonid: *The Guests*, 334-37, 360; *A Warsaw Melody*, 360

Zoshchenko, Mikhail, 146, 453

Zoya's Apartment (Bulgakov), 195-99, 222

Zykovs, The (Gorky), 17, 25-28, 29, 34, 37

Zvezda, 320